TEACHER'S EDITION

Progress ™
English Language Arts

D1251136

7

**For additional online resources, go to www.SadlierConnect.com
and enter the Teacher's Access Code:**

State	Access Code	State	Access Code
Alabama	SBPI01AL78	Missouri	SBPI29MO7L
Arizona	SBPI04AZ79	New Jersey	SBPI34NJ7R
Arkansas	SBPI05ARM8	New York	SBPI36NY72
California	SBPI06CA76	North Carolina	SBPI37NC7S
Colorado	SBPI08CO77	Ohio	SBPI39OH7D
Connecticut	SBPI09CT7V	Oklahoma	SBPI40OKB4
Florida	SBPI12FL7N	Pennsylvania	SBPI42PA7C
Georgia	SBPI13GA7L	South Carolina	SBPI45SC7V
Illinois	SBPI17IL7P	Tennessee	SBPI47TN74
Kentucky	SBPI21KY7Y	Texas	SBPI48TX72
Louisiana	SBPI22LA78	Virginia	SBP51VIPK2
Massachusetts	SBPI25MA7N	Wisconsin	SBPI55WI74
Michigan	SBPI26MI70	All Other States	SBPINA2792
Mississippi	SBPI28MS76		

Sadlier School

TEACHER'S EDITION

Progress™
English Language Arts

Cover: *Series Design:* Studio Montage; *Title design:* Quarasan, Inc. **Photo Credits:** Cover: Getty Images/Handout: *top left*. Millard H. Sharp: *top right*. Tim Zurowski: *bottom right*. Used under license from Shutterstock.com/Sharon Day: *bottom left*; nikolarisim: *background*. Interior: Blend Images/Mark Edward Atkinson/Tracey Lee: T17. Corbis/Hero Images: T3; Ocean: T15. Getty Images/Blend Images/Mark Edward Atkinson: T12; Aldo Murillo: T9. age Fotostock/Monkey Business Image: 262; Stuart Pearce: 152. Alamy/AF Archive: 223 *bottom*; AndySmyStock: 172; Asia Images Group Pte Ltd: 275; Caro: 261, 263; Design Pics Inc.: 88; fStop: 284; ITAR-TASS Photo Agency: 192; Janine Wiedel Photolibrary: 62; Frans Lemmens: 283; Moviestore Collection Ltd: 221, 223 *top*, 225; Pictorial Press Ltd: 67; Sunpix Travel: 291; Top Photo Corporation: 276; Vintage Images: 154; Tony Watson: 188; Worldwide Picture Library/Sue Cunningham: 273; ZUMA Press, Inc.: 76. Associated Press: 70. Corbis: 206; Aurora Photos/Stefan Chow: 47, 49; Christopher Beauchamp: 278; Bettmann: 64, 66, 268, 270, 288; Blend Images/KidStock: 78; CNP/The White House: 265; Dex: 10; Hiya Images: 204; David Howells: 82; Hulton-Deutsch Collection: 264; NASA: 73, 83; NASA/Roger Ressmeyer: 81; Science Faction: 80; National Geographic Society/Kolb Brothers: 250; Ocean: 114; Gabe Palmer: 90; Tim Pannell: 100; Reuters/Charles W. Luzier: 72; HO: 74; Xinhua Press/Liu Shun: 89. Dreamstime/Kodym: 286; Rich Leighton: 190; Rastan: 280; Valentyne75: 8 *bottom right*. Fotolia/Eric Isselée: 186; Siripong Jitchum: 187; Holger Schultz: 272. Getty Images/ColorBlind Images: 165, 167; Comstock: 248; Flickr Vision/Patrick Brion: 266; Galerie Bilderwelt: 267; Handout: 8 *center right*; Jupiterimages: 166; Keystone: 156; Bruce Laurance: 48; The Denver Post/Dave Buresh: 290. Glow Images/Corbis/Michael DeYoung: 247, 249; Jose Luis Pelaez, Inc.: 218. Library of Congress: 151, 153. NASA: 61, 63, 65, 68, 91, 176, 194; JPL-Caltech: 86. Newscom/20th Century Fox/Morgan Creek/Frank Connor: 227. NOAA: 178, 179, 208. Used under license from Shutterstock.com/Ammit Jack: 8 *top left*; Arsgera: 50; Camellia: 203, 205; Lim ChewHow: 295 *left*; exopixel: 309 *bottom*; Paul Fleet: 193; FloridaStock: 184; Nicha: 195; nikolarisim: 1, 8 *background*; Mark Oleksiy: 174; Mahesh Patil: 295 *left*; photka: 309 *top*; Shnycel: 8 *top right*; Syda Productions: 99, 101; sydeen: 274; TerryM: 102; urfin: 8 *bottom left*. Brian Versteeg: 84. Wikipedia: 289. **Text Credit:** Common Core State Standards Copyright © 2010. National Governors Association Center for Best Practices and Council of Chief State School Officers. All rights reserved. **Illustration Credits:** David Belmonte: 28, 29, 30, 31, 32, 34. Nina Caniac: 116, 117, 118, 119, 120, 122. Adrian Chesterman: 11. Lisa Fields: 115. George Hamblin: 168, 169, 170. Ted Hammond: 236, 237, 238, 239. Seitu Hayden: 20, 21, 22, 23, 24, 26. Kanako and Yuzuru: 124, 125, 126, 127, 128, 130. Fabio Leone: 228, 229, 230, 231, 232, 234. Wes Lowe: 12, 13, 14, 16, 18. Tom McNeely: 220, 222, 224, 226. Leonardo Meschini: 219. Amy Ning: 36, 37, 38, 39. Peter Bull Art Studio: 140, 141, 142, 143. Rob Schuster: 177, 180, 182, 282, 296. Lois Sprague: 132, 133, 134, 136, 138. **Lexile Trademark and Copyright Statement:** LEXILE®, LEXILE® FRAMEWORK, LEXILE® ANALYZER and the LEXILE® logo are trademarks of MetaMetrics, Inc., and are registered in the United States and abroad. The trademarks and names of other companies and products mentioned herein are the property of their respective owners. Copyright © 2012 MetaMetrics, Inc. All rights reserved.

William H. Sadlier, Inc.
9 Pine Street
New York, NY 10005-4700

Printed in the United States of America.
ISBN: 978-1-4217-3067-7
1 2 3 4 5 6 7 8 9 WEBC 18 17 16 15 14

Contents

Access Your Digital Resources

Get Started

1. Go to www.SadlierConnect.com

2. Log in

Don't have a username and password? Click "Get Started!" in the Teacher Registration section.

3. Select your program to begin accessing content.

With one username and password, you now have access to all your Sadlier Mathematics and English Language Arts content.

Contents

continued next page

Contents

Unit 4 | ## Text Types and Purposes:
Write Informative/Explanatory Texts

Creating an Introduction to Preview the Topic • Organizing Information by Idea • Using Formatting to Show Organization • Using Transitions to Link Ideas • Including Informative Facts and Details • Using Precise Language • Providing Graphics That Make Information Clear • Summing Up Ideas in a Conclusion

---

Unit 5 | ## Reading Literature:
Craft and Structure

continued next page

Contents

Unit 6

Text Types and Purposes:
Write Evidence-Based Essays

    Using Headings to Show Organizational Structure • Including Background Information • Adding Evidence to Support Ideas • Including Definitions of Unfamiliar Words • Showing Cause-and-Effect Relationships • Using Transitions to Connect Ideas • Adding Multimedia Elements • Adopting a Formal Style/Providing a Conclusion That Shows Results

Unit 7

Reading Informational Text:
Craft and Structure

Contents

Contents

Program Overview

Research indicates that high student performance results from alignment of curriculum, instruction, and assessment. *Progress English Language Arts* is a reading/language arts program that puts standards-based instruction into practice by aligning curriculum, instruction, and assessment in every unit, and at each grade level, K–8.

The foundation of *Progress English Language Arts* is the analysis and integration of state and national standards, curriculum guides and/or frameworks, current research on instruction and best classroom practices. Instruction in reading, writing, vocabulary, conventions of standard English, and speaking and listening is prioritized to create an instructional focus for each unit. Each element of the unit—including direct and guided instruction, and independent work—focuses on these critical skills, and provides students the range of encounters, varied practice opportunities, and levels of application necessary to gain the proficiencies required by the standards.

In *Progress English Language Arts*, students will:

- Engage in close reading of high-quality, challenging informational and literary texts through a gradual-release of responsibility, leading to independent and proficient reading.

- Increase knowledge of history/social studies, science, and technical subjects by reading rich, content-area texts.

- Analyze student writing models and engage in constructing both informational and narrative essays with a focus on appropriate language usage.

- Cite evidence from complex texts to respond to text-dependent questions and support critical thinking.

- Acquire and use academic and domain-specific vocabulary accurately.

- Practice analytical and writing skills with rigorous Performance Tasks that reflect the structure of standardized test tasks.

With the support of a comprehensive Teacher's Edition, teachers will be able to:

- Scaffold student learning with easy-to-use, comprehensive lesson plans.

- Use student assessment data, both observational and formal, to inform and redirect instruction.

- Understand the progression of English Langage Arts requirements across grade levels and tailor instruction to grade-level standards.

- Support diverse learners, including English language learners, struggling learners, and those needing extended learning opportunities.

- Access online and professional development resources to enhance their instruction.

Founded on the Standards

Progress English Language Arts draws on a rich research base and aligns with the Standards for the English Language Arts jointly published by the National Council of Teachers of English (NCTE) and the International Reading Association (IRA) in 1996 and reaffirmed in 2012 by the NCTE Executive Committee, supports the Guiding Visions, and recognizes the central role of the learner in the standards and the four dimensions of language learning: **content, purpose, development,** and **context** that lead to the attainment of the standards. These dimensions are integrated throughout the program and are integral to *Progress English Language Arts* and the sound foundation it provides for student success.

NCTE and IRA Guidance and Standards-Focus		How Addressed in *Progress English Language Arts*
Content Addresses what students should know and be able to do in regards to English Language Arts	The development of literacy and the attainment of English Language Arts standards depend on experience with and systematic study of a wide array of texts.	*Progress* units expose students to a collection of rigorous texts, fifty percent of the texts are informational and fifty percent are literary and encompass a wide range of genres and topics. Through *Progress*, students learn a range of processes and strategies for comprehending and producing texts. Program instruction is centered on texts and skills rather than on related activities that draw attention from texts. Repeated readings and analysis of complex, content-area texts expose all students to new information and ideas. Writing instruction builds on student models and supports students in responding to an array of texts and becoming skilled with writing narrative, informational, and opinion essays, as well as research papers. In addition, *Progress* includes study of the systems and structures of language and of language conventions, including grammar, punctuation, and spelling. Students learn how to apply their knowledge of the systems and structures of language depending on the context.
Purpose Addresses why students use language	English Language Arts instruction should focus on four purposes of language use: for obtaining and communicating information, for literary response and expression, for learning and reflection, and for problem solving and application.	*Progress* integrates reading, writing, language and speaking and listening instruction with the goal of developing students who are independent learners, critical thinkers with deep knowledge, effective communicators, skilled problem solvers, and therefore, prepared for success in college and careers. With *Progress*, students' knowledge of history/social studies, science, and technical subjects and their academic and domain-specific vocabulary increase through reading rich, content-area texts.

NCTE and IRA Guidance and Standards-Focus		How Addressed in *Progress English Language Arts*
Purpose (continued)		Relevant and meaningful opportunities for speaking and listening engage students in developing lifelong oral communication skills. Writing units ensure students develop effective written communication skills for a broad range of purposes. Integrated language instruction develops students' knowledge and use of conventions of standard English. Through a variety of carefully planned tasks that increase in their cognitive demand, students apply and extend the acquired knowledge and skills.
Development Addresses how students develop competencies in English Language Arts	Students acquire knowledge and develop language competencies with practice over time. The quality of students' performance improves over time as students learn to use language clearly, strategically, critically, and creatively.	*Progress* is grounded in research-based learning progressions. Skill-based lessons reflect a gradual release of responsibility instructional model in which students assume increasing independence in reading and analyzing text, writing—including in response to text, developing and using vocabulary, employing the conventions of standard English, speaking, and listening. The program's scope and sequence balances instruction and practice so that students grow in their language competencies and effectively integrate all aspects of language development to learn, think and communicate effectively. For example, the readability of texts increases across units. Guided practice and independent practice are scaffolded and allow students to successfully engage with tasks that increase in cognitive demand.
Context Influences all areas of learning and encompasses the three preceding dimensions	Language is by definition social. Reading, writing, speaking, and listening take place in a context which influences the learning process and the resulting knowledge, skills, and communication. Students' interests and motivations are integral to English Language Arts instruction, practice, and application.	*Progress* is designed to engage and motivate the students who use the program. The magazine-like format was developed with today's learners in mind. The diversity of content, characters, and topics represented is inclusive and the selection was intentional. Each passage, each writing text, each speaking and listening activity was developed with the audience in mind and was purposefully selected with relevance to the participants in mind. Similarly, instruction was developed to guide students to think of the purpose and audience when communicating.

Flexible Program Use

Progress English Language Arts serves as a flexible resource for supporting schools in meeting English Language Arts standards. Reading selections incorporate a variety of genres and reflect English Language Arts expectations regarding text complexity. Writing units reflect English Language Arts text types and language expectations.

Progress English Language Arts can be used as:

- An alternative core English Language Arts program that provides standards-based instruction, which can be supplemented with independent reading materials for additional practice.
- Supplemental lessons to fill curriculum gaps in a current core English Language Arts program.
- Targeted preparation materials for state-standardized assessments.

Linking Reading and Writing

Reading and writing units are linked by theme and, where appropriate, by reading genre/writing type. Students are first introduced to key concepts in reading selections based around a theme, usually a social studies or science topic based on grade-level standards. In the related writing unit, they encounter a Student Model, exemplifying excellent grade-level output in the same theme.

Writing types in *Progress English Language Arts* include:

- Fictional narrative text reflecting the sequential narrative structure of text within the related reading unit.
- Informative/explanatory text with the idea-detail structure of related reading selections.
- Nonfictional narrative text that reflects the structure of an historical text in the related reading unit.
- Opinion piece modeled after a reading selection with a structure identifying an opinion and related supporting reasons.
- Research report whose research topic reflects the setting/theme of the selections within the reading unit.

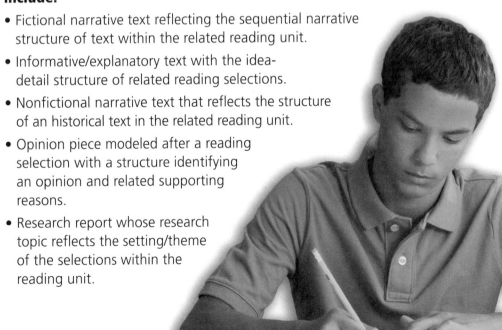

Diverse Grouping Models

The *Progress English Language Arts* program employs diverse grouping and instructional models to help teachers provide effective instruction in key English Language Arts skills/concepts.

Guided Instruction The program uses **whole-class** instruction to provide direct skill instruction and think-aloud modeling while students **read along** with the teacher. Discussion-based comprehension checks provide an opportunity for learners to ground skill instruction in collaborative academic discourse.

Guided Practice Lessons incorporate **partner reading in heterogeneous pairs** for scaffolded practice as the teacher circulates to provide targeted support as needed. Written comprehension checks offer multiple-choice and short-answer questions for pairs to work through together and then share their thinking with the class.

Independent Practice Lessons offer **independent reading application with callout support** as the teacher circulates to ensure that all readers are on task and effectively engaging with text. Written comprehension checks offer multiple-choice and short-answer questions as opportunities to demonstrate standard mastery.

➡ Alternative grouping models are suggested for struggling learners and English language learners, such as **heterogeneous pairing** with more proficient readers or **small group work with the teacher**.

Support for Content-Area Knowledge

Progress English Langauge Arts reinforces content-area instruction in History, Social Studies, Science, and Technical subjects.

- Complex informational texts found in the reading units contain a rich array of informational features to support content-area instruction.

- Both reading and writing units focus on important and interesting history, social studies and science topics, reinforcing student learning in those subjects while addressing vital English Language Arts skills.

Student Worktext

(in print and eBook formats)
Colorful, engaging standards-based instruction including complex, rigorous reading selections and structured writing models. ▶

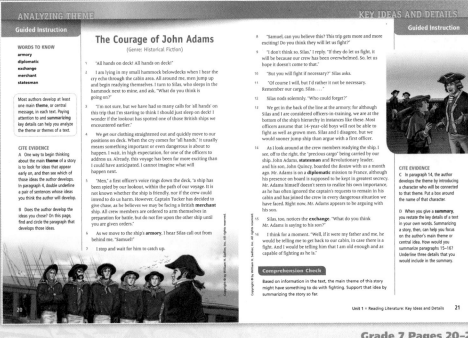

Grade 7 Pages 20–21

◀ Teacher's Edition

(in print and eBook formats)
Teacher-friendly lesson plans with targeted standards instruction and supportive features suitable for both novice and experienced teachers.

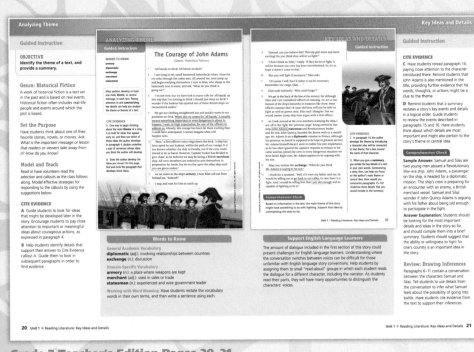

Grade 7 Teacher's Edition Pages 20–21

Progress Monitor* (Optional Purchase)

Four benchmark assessments to identify instructional needs as benchmarked against grade-level English Language Arts skills and concepts.

*Items are mapped to CCSS.

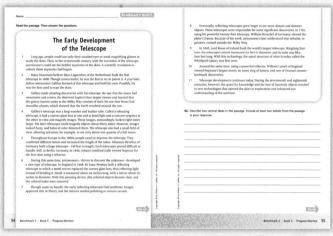

Grade 7 Progress Monitor Pages 54–55

Online Resources

A rich array of online resources at **www.SadlierConnect.com** supports program implementation and extends learning opportunities.

- **Home Connect Activities** support family member involvement.

- **Unit Performance Tasks** provide a wealth of practice opportunities for standardized Performance Tasks related to the content of each unit.

- **Performance Task 1 and 2** enable students to use downloadable unseen text with in-book Performance Tasks and provide teachers with robust evaluation support. These tasks can be used for mid-year and end-of-year assessment purposes.

- **Additional Practice** offers opportunities to augment program practice.

- **Full-Length Reading Selections** provide continuous text passages for fluency practice.

iProgress Monitor* (Optional Purchase)

This dynamic assessment component is available for enhancing grade-level English Language Arts skills and concepts. See page T17 for more information.

*Items are mapped to CCSS.

eBooks (Optional Purchase)

Student Worktext eBook The eBook provides the same quality content as the print Student Worktext. Delivered via Sadlier's one-stop platform at **www.SadlierConnect.com**, the eBook format also provides access to robust tools that allow students to:

- Read Text
- Make notes and highlight important information
- Search for key words
- Zoom in on specific content

Teacher's Edition eBook The eBook provides the same quality content as the print Teacher's Edition. Delivered via Sadlier's one-stop platform at **www.SadlierConnect.com**, in addition the eBook format also provides access to robust tools that allow teachers to:

- Toggle between the Student and Teacher's Edition
- Use Full-screen Mode to project the Student Edition onto a whiteboard to focus on instruction
- Assign lessons to an entire class or a specific group of students to take offline (in PDF format)
- View digital resources at point of use
- Make notes and highlight important information
- Search for key words
- Zoom in on specific content

Progress English Language Arts Grade 6 eBook

Progress English Language Arts contains many formative and summative assessment opportunities to help teachers gather evidence of students' progress toward mastering grade-level skills and concepts and prepare for the new state-standardized assessments.

Integrated, Ongoing Assessment Opportunities

Lesson Observational Diagnostics appear at point-of-use within lessons, reminding teachers to observe student response to instruction and offering a reteaching prescription. ▶

Assess and Respond

If students have trouble answering the questions in the Comprehension Check,

Then have them work with a partner to identify the central ideas of the text first and then go back to answer the questions with the central ideas in mind.

UNIT 3 REVIEW

Read the following explanatory texts that include inferences, central ideas and details, and ideas that are introduced and elaborated upon. Then answer the questions on pages 97 and 98.

A Special Nut

1 Plumpy'Nut is a modern invention that is meant to solve the problem of hunger in developing nations. Malnutrition affects millions of people in poor countries, especially children. Peanuts are high in fat and protein. A French doctor figured out how to make a paste out of peanuts that also had milk, sugar, and oil. It is fortified with vitamins and minerals and packed with calories. Children who eat the sweet paste on a daily basis gain weight quickly.

2 Plumpy'Nut is not the first nutritional supplement meant to help malnourished children. But previous nutritional

supplements were problematic since they had to be mixed with water. Often, water in poor countries contains harmful bacteria. Plumpy'Nut, on the other hand, does not need to be mixed with water and does not need to be refrigerated.

3 The other major advance with Plumpy'Nut is the way it can be administered. It is packaged in such a way that it can be administered at home, rather than in a hospital. This allows many more children to have access to it. About 90 percent of children who ate Plumpy'Nut at home recovered from severe, acute malnutrition in just four to six weeks.

FLAVR SAVR Tomato

1 Producers of agriculture are always looking for ways to keep their products fresher for longer. Keeping produce fresh longer allows it to get to supermarkets across the country when it is ripe.

2 During the 1980s, researchers realized that a fruit enzyme in tomatoes caused a break-down in pectin in the walls of the tomato skin. The breakdown in pectin meant that tomatoes got soft. Researchers figured out a way to introduce a gene that would suppress the production of the enzyme. The process

worked, and tomatoes with this gene did not soften as quickly. This genetically modified tomato, the first food of its kind to be sold commercially in the United States, was called FLAVR SAVR.

3 Instead of being picked before they are ripe and artificially ripened on their way to market, FLAVR SAVR tomatoes could be picked from the vine when ripe. They remained ripe after they were transported to stores. These tomatoes were introduced to the marketplace in 1994.

96 Unit 3 ■ Reading Informational Text: Key Ideas and Details

Grade 6 Page 96

◀ **Unit Reviews** are provided with each unit and offer an opportunity for students to encounter standardized test practice for the skills that have been taught within the unit.

Name _____ Benchmark 1 Book A

Read the passage. Then answer the questions.

The Case of the Mysterious Car Crash

1 "Who would abandon a car after a crash like this?" Derrick wondered as he surveyed the badly damaged vehicle without license plates.

2 "Whoever did it must be injured," Carmen replied. "And look at all of these twenty-dollar bills in the front seat!" Then the detectives noticed something else. The vehicle had no identification number! Had someone intentionally crashed this car? Was someone being set up? She pointed to footprints in the snow and urged, "It's warming up. We have to follow the tracks before the snow melts."

3 The detectives followed the trail, but it soon vanished. Not far away, lights shone from the windows of the town recluse, Mr. McGill.

4 Hours later, the detectives still had no reliable information. The mysterious twenties led them to believe that the collision had been part of a robbery. Suddenly they saw Robbie, a grumpy store clerk, walk by limping as if he had been injured.

5 Derrick commented to Carmen that Robbie's injury was worth investigating. Derrick's eyes widened as he pointed to Robbie's left leg. Robbie denied any wrongdoing and added that he had been laid off.

6 "Hmm, so where were you last night at 10?" asked Carmen.

7 "At my parents' house," Robbie responded, undisturbed. "I hurt my leg falling off a ladder . . . just ask my parents," he explained as he hobbled away.

8 Carmen went to check out Robbie's alibi, while Derrick went to Mr. McGill's house. "McGill could have been robbed last night and not even realize it yet," Derrick surmised. Despite his dilapidated house and unkempt lawn, Mr. McGill owned a multimillion-dollar company that was rumored to be failing. Even so, Mr. McGill could still be a target for theft.

9 Mr. McGill barked a hoarse and unwelcoming sentence that was inaudible from the porch, where Derrick stood knocking. "With his demeanor, no wonder this guy's company is in shambles," Derrick thought as Mr. McGill cracked open the door.

10 "I'm investigating a crash, sir. Did you hear or see anything unusual last night?" Derrick asked.

11 "Nuthin' except your obnoxious sirens that woke me up!" Mr. McGill grumbled and coughed, leaning heavily on his cane. As he peered into the house, Derrick asked Mr. McGill if he had noticed anything missing.

12 "Don't you think I would've called you if something were missing?" griped Mr. McGill and slammed the door in Derrick's face.

Go on

Benchmark 1 • Book A • Progress Monitor 3

Grade 6 Progress Monitor

◀ **Benchmark Assessments*** in Progress Monitor (an optional purchase) provide comprehensive assessments that can be administered periodically throughout the school year to evaluate students' knowledge and skill level relative to grade-level English Language Arts skills and concepts.

*Items are mapped to CCSS.

Unit Performance Tasks provide a wealth of practice opportunities for students to demonstrate their development of critical thinking and analysis skills and the ability to reason in response to text through writing and speaking.

Performance Tasks 1 and 2 ▶ provide tasks that parallel those in standardized assessments. The tasks incorporate both text items and an extended response essay question—which assesses students' ability to think critically about text as well as write using supporting evidence. Performance Tasks 1 and 2 are also available online at **www.SadlierConnect.com**. These Performance Tasks can also be used for mid-year and end-of-year assessment purposes. These Performance Tasks play a vital role in helping you determine if students are able to integrate skills and concepts being taught and apply them in real-life.

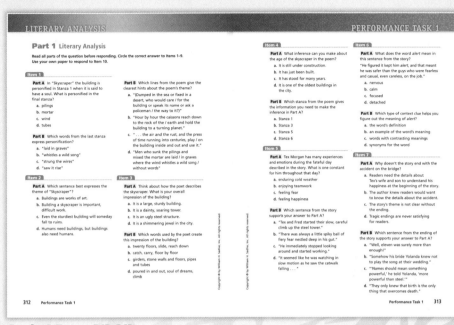

Grade 6 Pages 312–313

iProgress Monitor* (Optional Purchase)

Augment your assesment resources with customized assignments and test-building power!

With the **iProgress Monitor**, teachers can:

- Assign, evaluate, and monitor student progress with preformatted program assessments in an interactive format.

- Build custom assessments with a built-in test generator.

- Track students' progress and guide instruction with real-time data.

*Items are mapped to CCSS.

Student Worktext

With a full-color, magazine-like design, the engaging Student Worktext gives students opportunities to:

- Read both informational and literary texts
- Build knowledge through comprehension of texts
- Encounter increasingly rigorous and complex texts
- Answer text-based questions and engage in academic discussions about text
- Write in a clear and coherent manner using the conventions of standard English
- Build academic vocabulary

Organized by English Language Arts standards, the reading and writing units are linked by theme and, where appropriate, genre. The reading units address a rich variety of genres while the writing units focus on the standards-supported writing types.

A Unit Introduction That Focuses on Standards

Grade 7 Page 61

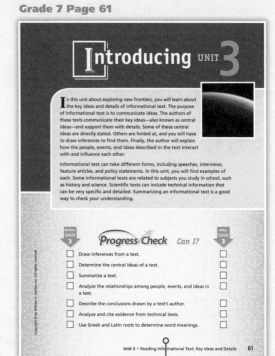

Progress Check at the beginning of each unit allows students to focus on the unit's key skills and concepts, self-assess before learning, and reflect on progress at the end of the unit.

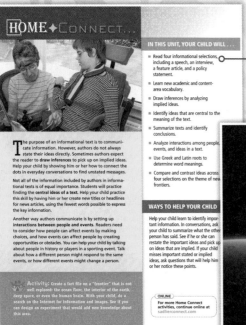

Grade 7 Page 62

Home Connect activities for each unit provide families a window into their child's learning and encourage them to take an active role.

Grade 7 Page 63

An **Essential Question** featured on the Unit Opener serves as a hook into the big idea of the unit and serves as a focal point of rigorous, academic discussion.

Four texts per thematic unit offer ample reading opportunities with complex texts.

T18

Encountering Complex Reading Text: Gradual Release of Responsibility

Each standard is taught using one continuous text following a gradual release of responsibility instructional model. By gradually decreasing the level of support within each text, students are prepared for independent encounters with complex text and can best master complex standards.

Guided Instruction: Direct standard instruction and teacher modeling

DRAWING INFERENCES
Guided Instruction

WORDS TO KNOW
democracy
emerged
reeling
satellite

Sometimes an author's ideas are directly stated in a text, and sometimes they are implied. Use clues in the text to **draw inferences** about implied ideas.

CITE EVIDENCE

A Sometimes an author will state an idea directly, or explicitly. Consider why the United States and the Soviet Union were in competition with each other. Find the stated idea in paragraph 1 and underline it.

B When you are looking for an answer that is not explicitly stated, you must **draw an inference** based on evidence in the text. What was so unusual about using rockets to get into space? This idea isn't stated. Put an asterisk next to each piece of information that tells how rockets had been used previously. How does this information help you make an inference?

A Man on the Moon
(Genre: Explanatory Text with Speech)

1 The Space Race started after World War II. The United States and the Soviet Union had **emerged** from the war as the two most powerful countries in the world. They had different systems of government. The United States was the champion of **democracy**, while the Soviet Union was a defender of communism. Both countries wanted their form of government to succeed in countries around the world. The two countries competed for allies, weapons, and power.

2 Both countries wanted to develop rocket technology for their own power and protection. The United States had an early victory by being the first to develop the nuclear bomb, but space was the next frontier. Although the Germans had been the first to develop modern rocket technology, rocket science had begun long before the war.

A Brief History of Rockets

3 The first rockets were developed in China in the 12th century. The Chinese had already invented gunpowder and fireworks. These rockets were weapons that were an extension of that technology.

4 The technology spread through Asia, and then to Europe, when India used gunpowder rockets against the invading British. Britain then used them against the United States, as the lyrics to "The Star-Spangled Banner" relate: 'And the rockets' red glare/The bombs bursting in air . . .'

a V-2 rocket, used during World War II

64   Unit 3 ■ Reading Informational Text: Key Ideas and Details

Grade 7 Page 64

Academic and **domain-specific vocabulary** is introduced in a text-based context with the appropriate standards-based instruction.

Complex **informational texts** with a rich array of informational features comprise half of each grade's reading selections.

Embedded questions support rigorous, standards-based **conversations about text** in the context of selections.

Guided Practice: Scaffolded standard practice in a partner-reading environment

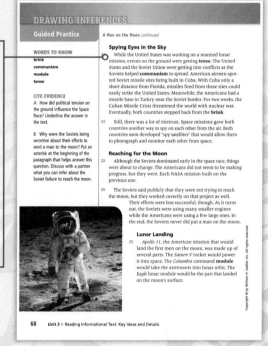

DRAWING INFERENCES
Guided Practice

WORDS TO KNOW
brink
communism
module
tense

CITE EVIDENCE

A How did political tension on the ground influence the Space Race? Underline the answer in the text.

B Why were the Soviets being secretive about their efforts to send a man to the moon? Put an asterisk at the beginning of the paragraph that helps answer this question. Discuss with a partner what you can infer about the Soviet failure to reach the moon.

A Man on the Moon continued

Spying Eyes in the Sky

20 While the United States was working on a manned lunar mission, events on the ground were getting **tense**. The United States and the Soviet Union were getting into conflicts as the Soviets helped **communism** to spread. American airmen spotted Soviet missile sites being built in Cuba. With Cuba only a short distance from Florida, missiles fired from these sites could easily strike the United States. Meanwhile, the Americans had a missile base in Turkey near the Soviet border. For two weeks, the Cuban Missile Crisis threatened the world with nuclear war. Eventually, both countries stepped back from the **brink**.

22 Still, there was a lot of mistrust. Space missions gave both countries another way to spy on each other from the air. Both countries soon developed "spy satellites" that would allow them to photograph and monitor each other from space.

Reaching for the Moon

23 Although the Soviets dominated early in the space race, things were about to change. The Americans did not seem to be making progress, but they were. Each NASA mission built on the previous one.

24 The Soviets said publicly that they were not trying to reach the moon, but they worked covertly on that project as well. Their efforts were less successful, though. As it turns out, the Soviets were using many smaller engines while the Americans were using a few large ones. In the end, the Soviets never did put a man on the moon.

Lunar Landing

25 *Apollo 11*, the American mission that would land the first men on the moon, was made up of several parts. The *Saturn V* rocket would power it into space. The *Columbia* command **module** would take the astronauts into lunar orbit. The *Eagle* lunar module would be the part that landed on the moon's surface.

68   Unit 3 ■ Reading Informational Text: Key Ideas and Details

Grade 7 Page 68

DRAWING INFERENCES
Independent Practice

WORDS TO KNOW
dwindling
joint
meteoroid
stockpiling

CITE EVIDENCE

A Why was docking the two crafts in space hard to do? In paragraph 28, put an asterisk next to the stated reason.

B Why did the astronauts have to leave the *Eagle* behind? Underline the clue that helps you infer the answer. Why was this an important moment in the Space Race?

A Man on the Moon continued

Getting Home from the Moon

27 The *Apollo 11* mission was not complete until the astronauts returned safely home. After studying and taking samples on the moon's surface, Armstrong and Aldrin got back into the *Eagle* and launched it into the lunar sky. Everything would have to function properly, or they would be stranded on the moon with no way home.

28 Meanwhile, Collins had been orbiting in the *Columbia* ever since Armstrong and Aldrin had left in the *Eagle*. The plan was for the *Eagle* and the *Columbia* to dock in space. The measurements and timing had to be exact. Millions of people watched on television and cheered as Armstrong and Aldrin joined Collins. They had done it! The astronauts separated the two crafts and let the *Eagle* drift away into space.

29 The final rocket had just enough thrust to get the *Columbia* out from the moon's orbit. The astronauts splashed down in the Pacific Ocean on July 24. The mission was accomplished, and President Kennedy's challenge had been answered.

Other Apollo Missions

30 In all, six Apollo missions (*Apollo 11, 12,* and *14–17*) sent people safely to the moon, giving humanity a wealth of scientific data and lunar samples. Experiments included the study of soil, **meteoroids**, heat flow, magnetic fields, solar wind, and more.

31 *Apollo 13* captured photographs but did not land on the moon due to a malfunction. An explosion occurred in space. Pilot John L. Swigert, Jr. calmly reported to Mission Control, "Houston, we've had a problem." The whole world held its breath until the astronauts made it back home after overcoming mechanical difficulties and **dwindling** supplies.

From Competition to Cooperation

32 After years of competition, the Soviet Union and America planned a **joint** mission. It was a symbol of hope and goodwill for people at a time when wars were being fought over communism and the superpowers were **stockpiling** nuclear weapons.

70   Unit 3 ■ Reading Informational Text: Key Ideas and Details

Grade 7 Page 70

Text-dependent questions require students to respond with evidence from the text to support their answers.

Each unit contains multiple opportunities to **write to text sources**.

Independent Practice: Extensive independent practice on standards enables students to build mastery.

Close Reading for Critical Comprehension of Text

Close reading—careful, purposeful reading and rereading of text—requires students to integrate the unit's reading standards as they comprehend text and answer questions providing reasons and justifications for their responses. In the Close Reading and the related Unit Review assessment, students build reading stamina, analyze text, grow comfortable with increasing text complexity, and demonstrate an understanding of unit standards. A **language lesson** follows each Close Reading.

Grade 7 Page 88

Close Reading text reflects the unit's content-area theme and related academic vocabulary to **build knowledge through text comprehension**.

Grade 7 Page 92

Two-part questions require students to **apply unit skills and support responses with textual evidence**. Short-answer questions test deeper understanding.

Language page develops **language skills** and academic vocabulary taught in the context of unit texts.

Students engage in **rigorous academic discussion** as they talk about multiple texts and the unit's Essential Question.

Grade 7 Page 94

Grade 7 Page 95

Writing Units with a Standards Focus

Writing units, along with the Writing Handbook, reflect the key writing types in English Language curriculum: opinion, informative/explanatory, narrative (both fictional and nonfictional), and research report. Language and Speaking and Listening pages are integrated to build students' accurate use of academic language in both written and spoken forms.

Each **writing model** is surrounded with support, including an introduction to the related writing standards, explanations of each component of the type of writing, and opportunities for students to analyze, organize, and write a passage of the same text type.

Integrated **Language** pages focus on conventions of English and knowledge of language—grammar, usage, and mechanics—through a gradual release model.

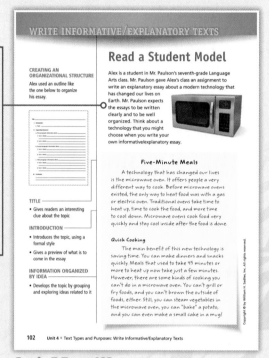

Grade 7 Page 102

Grade 7 Page 106

Grade 7 Page 110

Speaking and Listening lessons support students as they engage in rigorous, academic discourse about the unit's Essential Question about the writing type. A graphic organizer helps to focus students on active participation and employing speaking and listening skills.

Built-In Assessment Practice

Both the reading and writing units conclude with Unit Review assessments that provide practice with items similar to those students will encounter on state-standardized assessments.

Reading Unit Review

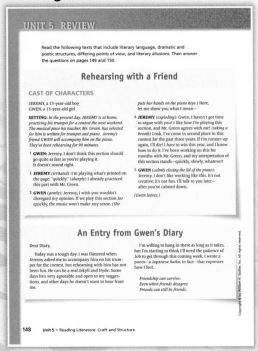

Grade 7 Page 148

Integrated assessment and standardized test practice feature new theme-related texts that reflect a genre introduced in unit selections. **Text-dependent questions** ask students to **write** and cite text evidence. A variety of question formats help teachers assess mastery of unit content, monitor progress, remediate, and prepare students for state assessments.

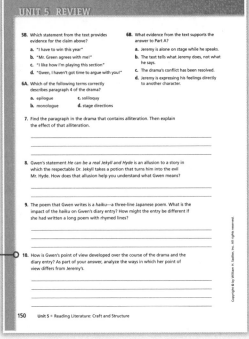

Grade 7 Page 150

Students examine paragraphs from and essay draft and **respond to** questions related to the unit **writing and language skills**.

Students produce writing in the text types commonly found in English Language Arts standards using the writing process. This on-demand writing practice helps to build writing stamina. (Support for teaching the writing process appears in the Writing Handbook at the end of the Student Worktext.)

Writing Unit Review

Grade 7 Page 59

Grade 7 Page 60

Teacher's Edition

Teacher-friendly, easy-to-use lesson plans support teachers in providing systematic instruction, practice, and application of English Language Arts skills and concepts. The Teacher's Edition is also available in eBook format.

- Easy-to-use rubrics at point of use enable busy teachers to assess and modify instruction quickly.

At-a-Glance Unit Introduction Pages

Unit introduction pages, featuring student self-assessment, a home connection, a planner for understanding key concepts at a glance, and learning progressions for comprehension standards, provide a quick reference for busy educators!

Unit Planner

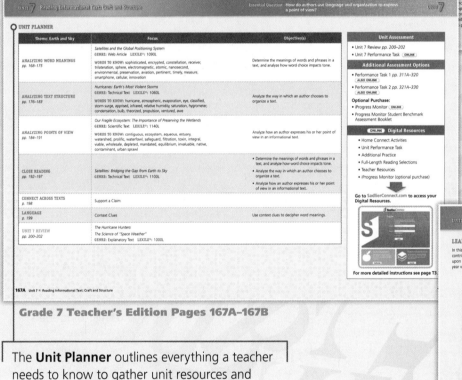

Grade 7 Teacher's Edition Pages 167A–167B

The **Unit Planner** outlines everything a teacher needs to know to gather unit resources and understand unit objectives and selections.

Learning Progressions provide context and background knowledge of the critical skills and skills progression across the years by showing what students learned in the previous grade and connections to what they will learn in the next grade, building coherence within and across the grade levels.

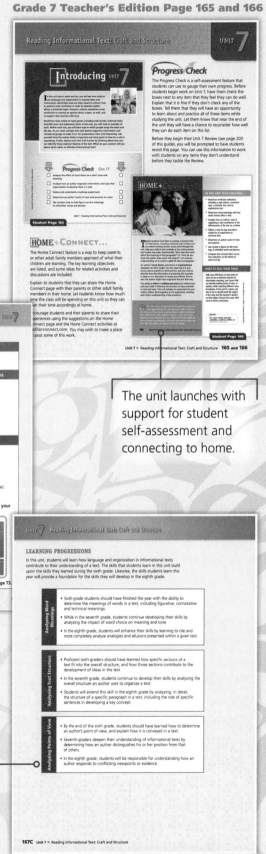

Grade 7 Teacher's Edition Page 165 and 166

The unit launches with support for student self-assessment and connecting to home.

Grade 7 Teacher's Edition Page 167C

On-the-Spot Lesson Support Makes Teachers English Language Arts Experts!

Teacher-friendly Lesson Plans provide targeted standards-based instruction and supportive features suitable for both novice and experienced teachers.

Guided Instruction

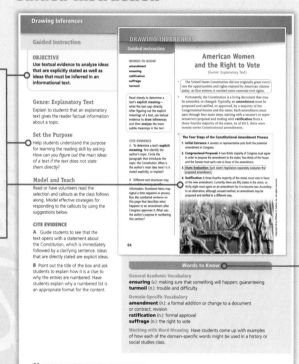

Each lesson segment has **student objectives** clearly noted.

Genre instruction supports close examination of the features of **text types**, which aids text comprehension.

On-page annotations help teachers monitor whether students are identifying text evidence during instruction.

Academic vocabulary is defined, and research-based vocabulary-building activities (e.g., Marzano's six vocabulary acquisition strategies) support acquisition.

Grade 8 Teacher's Edition Page 64

Teacher think-alouds model a good reader's approach to the standard, and an additional prompt **scaffolds skill application** for those who need additional support.

Modifications for English language learners, struggling learners, and students who need additional challenge embrace all learners.

Grade 8 Teacher's Edition Page 65

Successive Increase of Student Responsibility Leads to Success

Answer explanations support the teacher in helping students understand where they may still have gaps in applying the skill or concept effectively.

Guided Practice

Whole-class, partner, and individual instructional settings build scaffolding for all students to be successful with English Language Arts skills and concepts.

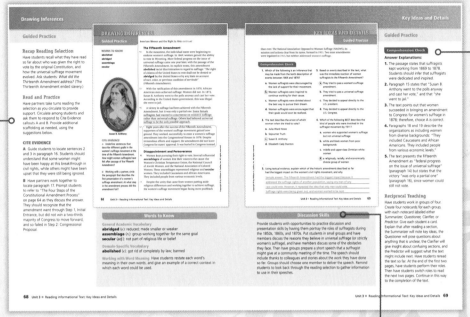

Grade 8 Teacher's Edition Pages 68–69

Discussion Skills, based on key skills and concepts and Resnick's research-based Accountable Talk strategies, integrate speaking and listening instruction into every unit and support **academic discussion** of text.

Digital Connections support students in understanding digital text as a genre in line with the thinking of new standardized assessments.

Grade 8 Teacher's Edition Page 67

Scaffolded Practice Makes Independent Application of Skills Accessible

Progress English Language Arts provides ample opportunity for rigorous independent practice allowing students to develop English Language Arts skills with conceptual understanding.

Independent Practice

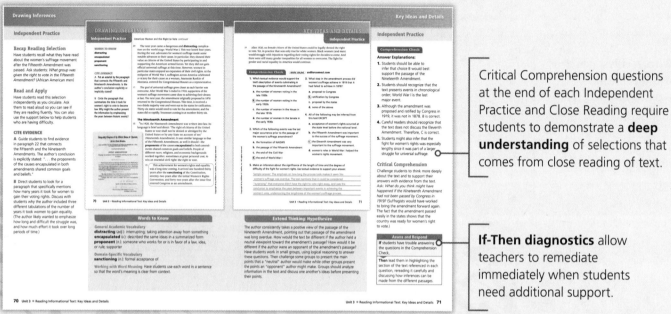

Grade 8 Teacher's Edition Pages 70–71

Critical Comprehension questions at the end of each Independent Practice and Close Reading require students to demonstrate a **deep understanding** of selections that comes from close reading of text.

If-Then diagnostics allow teachers to remediate immediately when students need additional support.

Close Reading

Grade 8 Teacher's Edition Pages 88–89

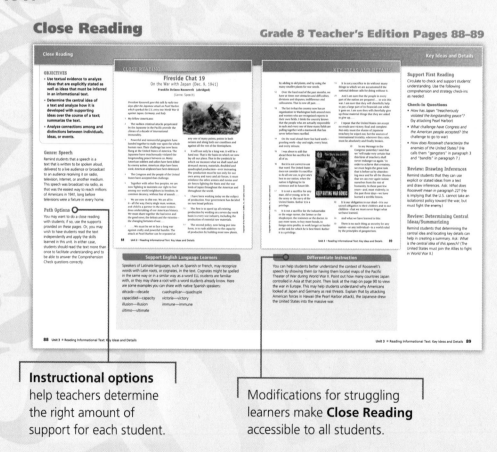

Instructional options help teachers determine the right amount of support for each student.

Modifications for struggling learners make **Close Reading** accessible to all students.

Assessment Tools Make Grading Simple

Progress English Language Arts supports busy teachers by offering easy-to-use rubrics and results charts that outline next steps after grading or assessment.

Grade 8 Teacher's Edition Page 94

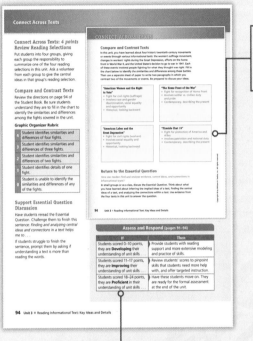

Clear **assignment rubrics** help teachers analyze student work products.

All assessment items are **aligned to an ELA standard** so that teachers can easily determine which standards are mastered.

Assessment rubrics for short-answer questions take the worry out of assigning grades to open-ended questions.

An If-Then chart links grading results to **next steps** after Close Reading activities.

Grade 8 Teacher's Edition Page 98

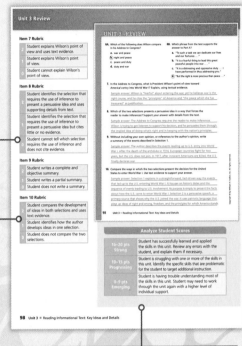

Analyze Student Scores charts detail next steps that teachers should take with students based on assessment results.

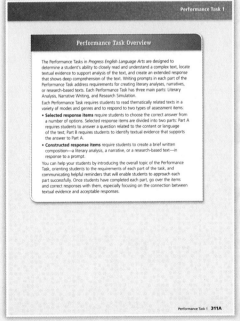

Recommended pacing guides help teachers to implement the Performance Tasks.

Detailed **Performance Task rubrics** provide clear and thorough guidance on how to evaluate written performance tasks.

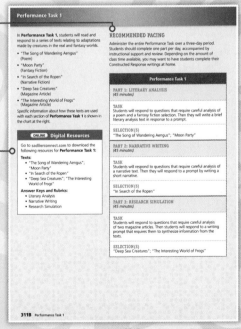

Weeks	Student Worktext	Online Resources to Enrich, Support, and Assess
1–3	Unit 1, pp. 9–46	Unit 1 Performance Task; Additional Practice; Full-Length Reading Selection; Foundational Skills Practice; Teacher Resources Optional purchase: iProgress Monitor
4–5	Unit 2, pp. 47–60	Additional Practice; Teacher Resources Optional purchase: iProgress Monitor
6–8	Unit 3, pp. 61–98	Unit 3 Performance Task; Additional Practice; Full-Length Reading Selection; Foundational Skills Practice; Teacher Resources Optional purchase: iProgress Monitor
9–10	Unit 4, pp. 99–112	Additional Practice; Teacher Resources Optional purchase: iProgress Monitor
11–13	Unit 5, pp. 113–150	Unit 5 Performance Task; Additional Practice; Full-Length Reading Selection; Foundational Skills Practice; Teacher Resources Optional purchase: iProgress Monitor
14–15	Unit 6, pp. 151–164	Additional Practice; Teacher Resources Optional purchase: iProgress Monitor
16	Performance Task 1	Performance Task 1 Selections, Rubrics, and Answer Key
17–19	Unit 7, pp. 165–202	Unit 7 Performance Task; Additional Practice; Full-Length Reading Selection; Foundational Skills Practice; Teacher Resources Optional purchase: iProgress Monitor
20–21	Unit 8, pp. 203–216	Additional Practice; Teacher Resources Optional purchase: iProgress Monitor
22–24	Unit 9, pp. 217–246	Unit 9 Performance Task; Additional Practice; Full-Length Reading Selection; Foundational Skills Practice; Teacher Resources Optional purchase: iProgress Monitor
25–26	Unit 10, pp. 247–260	Additional Practice; Teacher Resources Optional purchase: iProgress Monitor
27–29	Unit 11, pp. 261–298	Unit 11 Performance Task; Additional Practice; Full-Length Reading Selection; Foundational Skills Practice; Teacher Resources Optional purchase: iProgress Monitor
30	Performance Task 2	Performance Task 2 Selections, Rubrics, and Answer Key

Progress Monitor Student Assessments, an optional purchase, contains four comprehensive assessments that you may administer throughout the school year to assess students' mastery of grade-level skills/concepts.

Introducing UNIT **1**

In this unit about courageous actions, you will see how key ideas and details help shape a literary text. Literary texts can be entertaining, but they can also make you think in new ways. Authors communicate a text's central idea, or theme, by providing details that engage the reader. Sometimes the author states the theme directly; at other times, you will use details in the text to draw inferences about the theme. You will also look at how elements of a story combine and interact to communicate the author's ideas.

Literary texts cover many genres, including realistic fiction, historical fiction, drama, and myth. In this unit, you will read an example of each. Within each of these texts, you will meet someone who found the courage to overcome obstacles or explore new worlds. Think about how each story is driven by the main character's reaction to the challenges he or she faces. Ask yourself how the author communicates the key ideas or themes. Finally, pay attention to the important details in the text. How do these key details bring both the story and the theme to life?

Before Unit 1

Progress Check   Can I?

After Unit 1

☐ Find evidence that supports an author's ideas, including inferences drawn from details that the author provides. ☐

☐ Determine the main theme of a text, and analyze how an author develops it. ☐

☐ Summarize a text. ☐

☐ Analyze how setting, characters, and plot interact within a text. ☐

☐ Use affixes to help determine the meanings of unfamiliar words. ☐

Unit 1 ■ Reading Literature: Key Ideas and Details

Student Page 9

Progress Check

The Progress Check is a self-assessment feature that students can use to gauge their own progress. Before students begin work on Unit 1, have them check the boxes next to any item that they feel they can do well. Explain that it is fine if they don't check any of the boxes. Tell them that they will have an opportunity to learn about and practice all of these items while studying the unit. Let them know that near the end of the unit they will have a chance to reconsider how well they can do each item on this list.

Before they begin their Unit 1 Review (see page 44 of this guide), you will be prompted to have students revisit this page. You can use this information to work with students on any items they don't understand before they tackle the Review.

HOME ✦ CONNECT...

The Home Connect feature is a way to keep parents or other adult family members apprised of what their children are learning. The key learning objectives are listed, and some ideas for related activities and discussions are included.

Explain to students that they can share the Home Connect page with their parents or other adult family members in their home. Let students know how much time the class will be spending on this unit so they can plan their time accordingly at home.

Encourage students and their parents to share their experiences using the suggestions on the Home Connect page and the Home Connect activities at **sadlierconnect.com**. You may wish to make a place to post some of this work.

HOME ✦ CONNECT...

When writing a literary text, authors combine the use of explicit ideas, or those that are clearly stated, and **inferred** ideas, or those the reader must discover. As you read the selections in this unit with your child, help him or her discover the meaning beneath the author's words. Questions like, "What does she mean when she says that?" or "Why did he just take that action?" can help your child **draw inferences**.

Authors write with a purpose, which usually centers on a **theme**, or overall message. As you read with your child, encourage him or her to think about the theme.

Analyzing **literary elements**, including **character, plot,** and **setting,** leads to an understanding of the key ideas and details that make a story meaningful. As you read, ask your child to identify key elements of literature. Questions like "Who is your favorite character, and why?" or "Where does the story take place?" will prompt your child to analyze the author's purpose. Help your child summarize the text: Read a section and then ask, "What just happened in the story?"

Activity: Learn about someone who has overcome adversity to accomplish a goal. Help your child research an impressive person, either on the Internet or at a local library. Talk with your child about why this person is a courageous figure and what helped him or her overcome life's obstacles.

IN THIS UNIT, YOUR CHILD WILL...

- Read four literary selections, including realistic fiction, historical fiction, a play, and a myth.
- Identify details that support an author's stated ideas.
- Draw inferences by analyzing implied ideas and use textual evidence to support inferences.
- Analyze a text to determine its theme.
- Summarize the text.
- Analyze the main elements of a drama and how they affect each other.
- Use affixes to figure out the meanings of unfamiliar words.
- Compare and contrast ideas across four selections on the theme of courageous actions.

WAYS TO HELP YOUR CHILD

Help your child identify key details. In regular conversation, ask your child about the events of his or her day. See if your child can identify the most important points about these events. If your child has difficulty leaving out unimportant details, ask questions that will help him or her find the most salient points of a personal story.

ONLINE
For more Home Connect activities, continue online at sadlierconnect.com

10   Unit 1 ■ Reading Literature: Key Ideas and Details

Student Page 10

UNIT PLANNER

Theme: Courageous Actions	Focus
DRAWING INFERENCES *pp. 12–19*	*Courage in the Water* **GENRE:** Realistic Fiction **LEXILE®:** 860L **WORDS TO KNOW:** lurch, tumultuous, feat, diagnosis, affected, endurance, related, onlooker, certification, inspiration, meet, attempt, crewman, tugboat line, elements, encountered, perseveres, jovial
ANALYZING THEME *pp. 20–27*	*The Courage of John Adams* **GENRE:** Historical Fiction **LEXILE®:** 950L **WORDS TO KNOW:** merchant, armory, statesman, diplomatic, exchange, frigate, outfitted, skirmish, routine, vessel, broadside, tailwind, countenance, helm, gallantly, commandeer, authorized, cargo, bemoans, patriot
ANALYZING LITERARY ELEMENTS *pp. 28–35*	*Into the Unknown* **GENRE:** Multi-Act Play **LEXILE®:** NP* **WORDS TO KNOW:** qualifications, chart, passage, manifest, inclement, trade route, duty, dispatched, intact, delirium, climate, torrential, solace, recuperate, relapse, accompany, naïve, incomparable, venture
CLOSE READING *pp. 36–41*	*Theseus and the Minotaur* **GENRE:** Myth **LEXILE®:** 910L
CONNECT ACROSS TEXTS *p. 42*	Analyze Literary Elements
LANGUAGE *p. 43*	Greek and Latin Affixes
UNIT 1 REVIEW *pp. 44–46*	*The Drummer's Courage* *The Story of Hua Mulan* **GENRE:** Realistic Fiction **LEXILE®:** 920L

*Selections comprising more than 50% non-standard or non-conforming prose do not receive a Lexile measure, merely the NP code.

Objective(s)

Use evidence from a text to support an analysis of what the text says explicitly and implicitly.

Identify the theme of a text, and provide a summary.

Analyze how the elements of literature help shape a story or drama.

- Use evidence from a text to support an analysis of what the text says explicitly and implicitly.
- Identify the theme of a text, and provide a summary.
- Analyze how the elements of literature help shape a story or drama.

Use Greek and Latin affixes to decipher word meanings.

Unit Assessment

- Unit 1 Review *pp. 44–46*
- Unit 1 Performance Task (ONLINE)

Additional Assessment Options

- Performance Task 1 *pp. 311A–320*
  (ALSO ONLINE)
- Performance Task 2 *pp. 321A–330*
  (ALSO ONLINE)

Optional Purchase:

- iProgress Monitor (ONLINE)
- Progress Monitor Student Benchmark Assessment Booklet

(ONLINE) Digital Resources

- Home Connect Activities
- Unit Performance Task
- Additional Practice
- Full-Length Reading Selections
- Teacher Resources
- iProgress Monitor (optional purchase)

Go to SadlierConnect.com to access your Digital Resources.

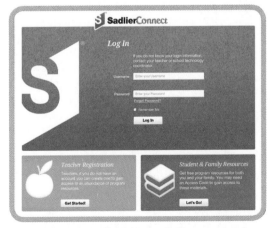

For more detailed instructions see page T3.

LEARNING PROGRESSIONS

In this unit, students will learn how the key ideas and details in literature contribute to their understanding of a text. The skills that students learn in this unit build upon the skills they learned during the sixth grade. Likewise, the skills students learn this year will provide a foundation for the skills they will develop in the eighth grade.

Drawing Inferences

- Sixth-grade students should have finished the year with the ability to cite textual evidence in support of analysis of texts' explicit and implicit meanings.

- While in the seventh grade, students continue developing their skills by citing several pieces of evidence to support their analysis of the explicit and implicit meanings of a text.

- In the eighth grade, students will deepen their skills by learning to cite the textual evidence that most strongly supports their analysis of texts' explicit and implicit meanings.

Analyzing Theme

- Proficient sixth graders should have learned how to use details of a text to determine its theme or central idea, and how to craft an objective summary of a text.

- In the seventh grade, students continue to develop their skills of determining a text's theme and analyzing its development over the course of the text, and objectively summarizing the text.

- Students will extend this skill in the eighth grade by recognizing the relationship of the theme or central idea of a text with the text's characters, setting, and plot, and objectively summarizing the text.

Analyzing Literary Elements

- By the end of the sixth grade, students should have learned how to describe the plot of a story and to determine how specific characters respond to events in the plot.

- Seventh graders deepen their understanding of literary elements by learning how the interaction of plot, setting, and characters shapes a story or drama.

- In the eighth grade, students will be responsible for understanding how plot events and characters' dialogue drive a story or drama's action, reveal information about a character, and affect the plot's climax and resolution.

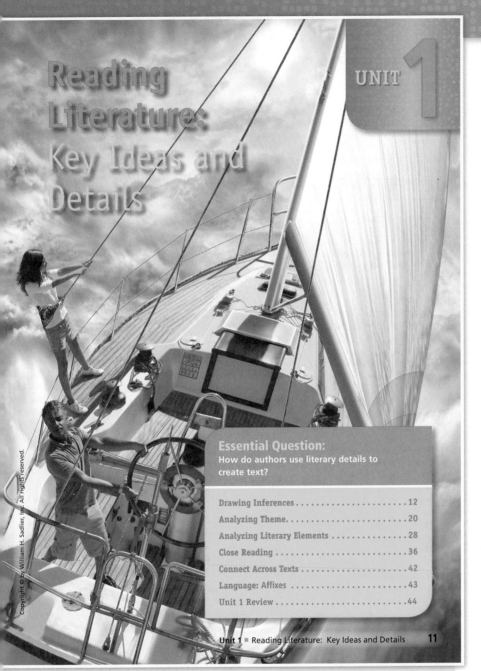

Reading Literature: Key Ideas and Details

Essential Question:
How do authors use literary details to create text?

Essential Question:
How do authors use literary details to create text?

In this unit, students will learn how key ideas and details help contribute to their understanding of a literary text. Specifically, students will learn to draw inferences, determine a theme or central idea, and analyze the literary elements in a text.

Theme: Courageous Actions

Students will read selections that illustrate courageous actions, including realistic fiction about overcoming personal barriers, historical fiction about John Adams's experiences at sea, a multi-act play about Mungo Park's adventures in Africa, and a retelling of the myth of Theseus and the Minotaur.

Curriculum Connection: Social Studies

Several selections in this unit are fictional retellings of historical events. Students will learn about real figures, such as Gertrude Ederle, John Adams, and Mungo Park, whose courageous actions inspired others.

Vocabulary Overview

General Academic Vocabulary

accompany, affected, attempt, authorized, bemoans, certification, climate, countenance, diplomatic, dispatched, duty, encountered, endurance, exchange, feat, gallantly, inclement, incomparable, inspiration, intact, jovial, lurch, naïve, onlooker, outfitted, perseveres, qualifications, related, routine, solace, torrential, tumultuous, venture

Domain-Specific Vocabulary

armory, broadside, cargo, chart, commandeer, crewman, delirium, diagnosis, elements, frigate, helm, manifest, meet, merchant, passage, patriot, recuperate, relapse, skirmish, statesman, tailwind, trade route, tugboat line, vessel

Guided Instruction

OBJECTIVE
Use evidence from a text to support an analysis of what the text says explicitly and implicitly.

Genre: Realistic Fiction

Explain to students that realistic fiction is a literary text that reflects life as it could be lived, although some elements are from the author's imagination.

Set the Purpose

Help students understand the purpose for understanding the reading skill by asking *What details or ideas do you need to understand about a story that the author may not state directly?*

Model and Teach

Read or have volunteers read the selection and callouts as the class follows along. Model effective strategies for responding to the callouts by using the suggestions below.

CITE EVIDENCE

A Help students see how the text directly states that Gertrude Ederle has had an obstacle to overcome. Guide them to see that the narrator mentions "even more difficult odds" and then mentions the specific hardship.

B The information about Gertrude Ederle's struggles and accomplishments, told from Ellie's point of view, helps students infer Ellie's enthusiasm for Ederle.

DRAWING INFERENCES

Guided Instruction

WORDS TO KNOW

affected

diagnosis

feat

lurch

tumultuous

Sometimes an author's ideas are directly stated in a text, and sometimes they are implied, or suggested. Use clues in the text to **draw inferences** about implied ideas.

CITE EVIDENCE

A Sometimes authors state an idea explicitly, or directly, in a text. In this text, the author speaks through a first-person narrator named Ellie. According to Ellie, what is one of the major obstacles in Gertrude Ederle's swimming career? Find the stated idea, and underline it.

B Sometimes authors expect readers to **draw an inference**— that is, make an educated guess— about ideas in a text. You can draw inferences by thinking carefully about details in the text. Put a box around the paragraph whose details help you infer how Ellie feels about Gertrude Ederle.

Courage in the Water
(Genre: Realistic Fiction)

1   The boat **lurches** wildly as I stand looking up at the gray sky. Concerned, I search the water before me, squinting for some glimpse of the swimmer ahead. I know she is out there, but I don't see how anyone can keep going with the seas so rough. We are getting closer to our destination; at least half of the 21-mile journey is already gone. However, the pounding wind and **tumultuous** waves must be taking quite a toll on our swimmer.

2   Suddenly, I feel a tap on my shoulder. I turn to see my father smiling down at me, his expression animated as he gestures ahead. He looks pointedly at me and then slowly says, "There she is—look where I am pointing."

3   I follow the direction of his arm and see a red bathing cap bobbing above the waves. I let out a yell of excitement: "That's it, Trudy, you can do it!" Even though I know she can't hear my words of encouragement, I still can't contain my enthusiasm. It's hard for me to believe I am here, watching Gertrude Ederle attempt to swim the English Channel. Not only is she the first woman to try such a **feat**, she faces even more difficult odds. Like me, Trudy lives with partial deafness. She may not be able to hear everything around her, but she has never let it stand in her way.

12   Unit 1 ▪ Reading Literature: Key Ideas and Details

Words to Know

General Academic Vocabulary

affected (*v.*): had an effect on; impacted

feat (*n.*): extraordinary act; accomplishment

lurch (*v.*): sway or roll suddenly

tumultuous (*adj.*): wild and disordered; turbulent

Domain-Specific Vocabulary

diagnosis (*n.*): a medical decision about what illness or condition is affecting a person

Working with Word Meaning Encourage students to restate the definitions in their own words and then use each word in a sentence.

Guided Instruction

"She may never hear again . . . "

4   Last year, when I was 12, my little brother and I both came home from school feeling poorly. I can still remember walking into my father's grocery store that day in 1925, and feeling as if my head was going to explode.

5   My mother took one look at me, and I could hear the panic in her voice when she said, "Ellie, are you all right?" When I didn't answer, she told my father to run for the doctor and then took my brother and me upstairs to our apartment above the store.

6   The doctor said we had the measles—and that it was one of the worst cases he had seen in years. For a while, my family wasn't even sure if I would pull through. My brother and I are tough, though, and within a few weeks, we had made it through the worst.

7   Unfortunately, it wasn't all good news. At first, I thought maybe I had a cold along with the measles; everything sounded muffled inside my head. The city noises outside my window were quieter, and when people spoke, I had a hard time understanding them. Finally, I told my father about the muffled sounds. He gave me a look of concern and sent for the doctor again.

8   It didn't take the doctor long to give me a **diagnosis**. "The disease has **affected** her hearing," he told my parents. "The loss of hearing will continue, gradually, and it could become complete. In truth, she must face the fact that she may never hear again."

9   After my parents told me what the doctor had said, I panicked. How could I lose my hearing? Would I never hear my parents or my little brother talk to me again? I went back to bed and wouldn't leave my room, telling my parents that I thought the measles had returned.

Comprehension Check

Based on what you have read, will Ellie's feelings about her hearing loss change during the course of the story? Which details from the story help you make this inference?

Guided Instruction

CITE EVIDENCE

C What does the author explicitly state about the cause for Ellie's hearing loss? Put an asterisk by the sentence that gives that information.

D You can infer that Ellie will lose her hearing before the author states it explicitly. Circle the paragraph where you first understand what is going to happen to Ellie's hearing.

E Double underline the sentences that tell you how Ellie's hearing loss made her feel. Which words and phrases help you draw an inference about Ellie's feelings?

Guided Instruction

CITE EVIDENCE

C Guide students to look in paragraph 8 for information the author explicitly states about the cause of Ellie's hearing loss.

D Have students look for clues in paragraph 7 for details that describe a significant change in Ellie's ability to hear.

E Direct students to look in paragraph 9 for descriptive words and phrases, such as *panicked* and *wouldn't leave my room*. Point out how the words and phrases should help students make an inference about Ellie's feelings.

Comprehension Check

Sample Answer: Students should consider Ellie's enthusiastic attitude at the beginning of the story, as she watches Gertrude Ederle swim, to infer that although Ellie initially feels frightened and upset by her hearing loss, she will eventually overcome these feelings.

Answer Explanation: The story begins with the narrator, Ellie, watching Gertrude Ederle attempting to swim across the English Channel despite living with partial deafness. This detail can help students infer that after Ellie initially panics when she discovers her hearing loss, her attitude will change later.

Listening and Viewing Skills

Have students look at the illustration on page 12 while you or a student volunteer reads aloud paragraphs 1–3. Then have students compare the details in the illustration to those in the text. Ask them to identify the details that appear only in the text or in the illustration.

Support English Language Learners

Because of their limited vocabulary, some English language learners may have difficulty identifying key details in a text and using them to make inferences. Suggest that students use the illustrations to preview the text. Have students meet with partners who are proficient in English as they look at the illustrations, describe what they see, and make inferences about the story. Then tell English language learners, as they read the story, to look for details that support or contradict their inferences. Allow time for students to discuss the details and update their inferences with their partners.

Guided Practice

Recap Reading Selection

Have students recall what they have read so far in the selection. Prompt them to review the events in the story, including information about how Ellie became sick and developed hearing loss, but found inspiration in Gertrude Ederle. Let students know that next they will be reading about how Ellie came to be on the boat at the beginning of the story.

Read and Practice

Have partners take turns reading the selection as you circulate to provide support. Circulate among students and ask them to respond to Cite Evidence callouts A and B. Provide additional scaffolding as needed, using the suggestions below.

CITE EVIDENCE

A Have students read paragraph 20 to identify information about Gertrude Ederle's early swimming career. Encourage students to create a time line of her career in their own words, based on details in the text.

B Students should look to paragraph 21 for details about other characters' reactions to Ellie's accomplishments. Students should infer that other people in Ellie's life are aware of her motivation for swimming and winning meets.

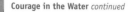

DRAWING INFERENCES

Guided Practice

WORDS TO KNOW

attempt

crewman

meet

tugboat line

CITE EVIDENCE

A The author provides explicit details about Gertrude Ederle's career before the Channel swim. Put a box around the paragraph that gives this information.

B With a partner, draw and discuss an inference about how the effect of Gertrude Ederle's accomplishments on Ellie's life is obvious even to other people. Underline details that help you draw this important inference.

Courage in the Water *continued*

20 Whenever I looked around me at the younger girls in my class, who had already been swimming longer than I, I remembered Trudy. She didn't start swimming with proper form until she was 15, but that never stopped her. At 19, she won a gold medal at the Paris Olympics. A year later, she became the first woman to swim the length of New York Bay, even breaking the men's record!

21 Six months after my first swimming class, I won my first **meet**. You might have thought I was Gertrude Ederle, swimming at the Olympics, the way my parents and brother cheered me on. When I got out of the pool, my coach gave me a big hug. "You did great!" she exclaimed. "You must have had some inspiration out there today!"

22 I looked at my father and grinned. "Well, maybe I just had the right motivation."

The Chance of a Lifetime

23 I have been a swimmer ever since, and I have been following Gertrude Ederle's story every day, reading eagerly as the newspapers tell of her daily training, her decision to hire a new swimming coach, and her struggles to find enough money to **attempt** the swim again. Then, about three weeks ago, my father came home with a big smile on his face. My mother gave him a curious look and asked, "Why are you grinning with such mischief in your eyes?"

24 "I have a surprise," my father replied.

25 My father then explained that he had contacted his cousin in France, who worked as a **crewman** for a **tugboat line**. It seemed this cousin would be working on the tugboat *Alsace*, which was set to follow Trudy Ederle on her second attempt to swim the English Channel.

26 "Oh, Father!" I cried. "Can he take pictures? Will he be able to meet Trudy?"

16

Words to Know

General Academic Vocabulary

attempt (*v.*): to try; to make an effort at

Domain-Specific Vocabulary

crewman (*n.*): a sailor; a worker on a ship

meet (*n.*): a sports competition

tugboat line (*n.*): a business that operates tugboats (small boats that tow or push ships)

Working with Word Meaning Encourage students to draw pictures to illustrate each vocabulary word and to use the vocabulary words in captions that are complete sentences.

27 "Better still," my father said, "for he has invited all of us to France for a vacation. Furthermore, he has permission from his captain for you and me to ride along on the *Alsace*!"

28 I couldn't believe it. This was truly the chance of a lifetime!

Comprehension Check

1. Use your understanding of the story to draw an inference about the characters. Why does Ellie spend her time learning about the life of Gertrude Ederle?

   a. Ellie wants to beat Gertrude Ederle's record.

   b. Ellie relates to Gertrude Ederle's struggles and successes.

   c. Ellie needs something to do while she is recovering from the measles.

   d. Ellie is an avid reader of newspapers.

2. Which of these details does the author state explicitly in the story?

   a. Gertrude Ederle hired a new swimming coach after her first Channel crossing attempt.

   b. It is the goal of Ellie's life to meet Gertrude Ederle in person.

   c. Ellie's father is worried about her feelings after her hearing loss.

   d. Ellie learns to overcome challenges through swimming.

3. Based on text details, you can infer that Ellie's father is taking her to France because

   a. he knows that Ellie has always wanted to visit France.

   b. he hopes that Ellie will become a reporter when she is older.

   c. he wants Ellie to meet his cousin.

   d. he wants Ellie to meet her hero.

4. Draw an inference about Ellie's decision to learn to swim. Based on details from the story, why does Ellie decide to become a swimmer?

   a. She is afraid of being around water and unable to swim.

   b. She thinks that her father wants her to become a swimmer.

   c. She knows that her hearing loss will not stop her from being a swimmer.

   d. She wants to prove that she is as good as Gertrude Ederle.

5. Discuss with a partner how making inferences helps you better understand the story, especially with respect to Ellie's character.

   Sample answer: Ellie does not always state her feelings explicitly, so drawing inferences from what she says and does helps me understand her actions and emotions throughout the story.

Unit 1 ■ Reading Literature: Key Ideas and Details **17**

Comprehension Check

Answer Explanations:

1. Students should recognize that Ellie sees Ederle's situation as similar to her own, so the correct answer is choice B, *Ellie relates to Gertrude Ederle's struggles and successes*.

2. Choice A, *Gertrude Ederle hired a new swimming coach after her first Channel crossing attempt*, is the only detail explicitly stated in the story. Choice B is not stated or implied. Choices C and D are implied.

3. In paragraph 21, students inferred that Ellie's father understands her need for a role model. From that and details in paragraphs 23–28, they should infer that choice D, *he wants Ellie to meet her hero*, is correct.

4. Based on details in the story, students should be able to state a reason for Ellie's decision—choice C: *She knows that her hearing loss will not stop her from being a swimmer.*

5. Students should understand that authors do not always explicitly tell them what a character is feeling or why an event is important, so drawing inferences helps readers to better understand the characters and plot in a story.

Writearound

Have students create a writearound summary of the first two sections of the story. Place students in groups of four, and provide them with a sentence starter: *The lives of Ellie and Gertrude Ederle are similar because* . . . Have one student finish the sentence and then pass the paper to the right. Each student should read the sentence(s) he or she received and then add one of his or her own. Four summaries of the text will emerge.

Discussion Skills

Have students practice discussion skills by having them role-play the roles of Gertrude Ederle and newsreel reporters during 1926, the year Ederle completed her historic swim across the English Channel. Have students work in pairs, with one student playing the role of Ederle and the other playing the reporter. Have students use details from the text as the basis of the questions and answers in their interviews. Ask a pair to volunteer to re-create their interview in front of the class. Then lead a class discussion about how well the interview incorporated details from the text.

Independent Practice

Recap Reading Selection

Have students recall what they have read so far about Ellie's transformation, and her opportunity to watch Gertrude Ederle swim. Ask students why Ellie's father wants to take her to see Gertrude Ederle. Let them know that they will be reading about Ellie's trip in the final section of the story.

Read and Apply

Have students read this selection independently as you circulate. Ask them to read aloud so you can see if they are reading fluently. You can also use the support below to help students who are having difficulty.

CITE EVIDENCE

A Guide students to read paragraph 30 carefully for details that will help them make an inference about Ellie's actions in paragraph 31. Students should infer that Ellie is so excited that she does not want to miss even one moment of Ederle's swim.

B Students should look to the end of the text, particularly paragraph 35, for details about Ellie's feelings about Ederle's success.

DRAWING INFERENCES

Independent Practice

Courage in the Water *continued*

WORDS TO KNOW

elements

encountered

jovial

perseveres

CITE EVIDENCE

A Draw an inference about why, in paragraph 31, Ellie refuses to leave the deck during Gertrude Ederle's swim. Underline a sentence in paragraph 30 that helps you make this inference.

B Circle a detail that explicitly states Ellie's reaction to Gertrude Ederle's success. What can you infer about what her success means to Ellie?

"From France to England . . . "

29   And that's how I came to be standing here, cheering Trudy on in the middle of the English Channel. It hasn't been an easy journey. We left Cape Gris Nez, France, at about 7:00 this morning. The air around us was cold, and my father's cousin said the water would be about 61 degrees. With all of us watching, as well as a boat full of reporters and photographers, Trudy covered herself in all kinds of different greases and oils (to protect against the cold and the jellyfish) and got into the water.

30   The **elements** have not helped, and we have **encountered** some severe storms throughout the trip. My uncle said that some waves were almost 20 feet high! Trudy's coach keeps asking her if she needs to stop, but she **perseveres**. Sometimes, we can hear her singing "Let Me Call You Sweetheart" as she swims, her strokes keeping time with the beat. Sometimes, we join her! The reporters on the boat behind us are a **jovial** group, and they often break into song with "Yes, We Have No Bananas" or "East Side, West Side," trying to keep Trudy's spirits up. <u>Everyone is so thrilled, and although I can't hear everything they say, I can feel the excitement building the closer we get to France.</u>

31   We have been on board the ship for 14 hours, and I have stayed on deck the whole time. My father keeps asking me to come below, just for a time, but I have refused. And so, he has stayed with me, battling the wind and the waves as we watch Trudy move carefully through the water.

32   Finally, my father's cousin leans in to tap us on the shoulder. "We are almost there," he says, waiting until I can see his lips. "She has almost made it."

18

Words to Know

General Academic Vocabulary

encountered (*v.*): came across; met

jovial (*adj.*): happy and cheerful

perseveres (*v.*): keeps trying in spite of obstacles

Domain-Specific Vocabulary

elements (*n.*): weather

Working with Word Meaning Have students come up with examples and non-examples of each word.

33   It's 9:00 at night, and so dark that we can see Trudy only through the tugboat's onboard lights. I lose sight of her for a moment, and then turn to look at him, trying to read his lips. "Has she made it?"

34   "She's made it!" my father says. "From France to England—she's done it!"

35   And, even though I can't hear them, I add my voice to the cheers that I know must be coming from the shore.

Comprehension Check   MORE ONLINE **sadlierconnect.com**

1. What explicit reason does the author give for Gertrude Ederle's covering herself in grease and oil before entering the water?

   a. It protects her against the cold.

   b. It makes her faster in the water.

   c. It wards off sharks.

   d. It keeps the salt water from burning her skin.

2. Which inference can you draw, based on your answer to question 1?

   a. Seawater is less comfortable for swimming than fresh water is.

   b. Cold water presents difficulties for swimmers.

   c. The English Channel is home to dangerous sea creatures.

   d. Long-distance swimming is not an Olympic event.

3. Ederle's coach probably offers her the chance to quit swimming because

   a. Ederle did not complete her first Channel attempt.

   b. there is an increased threat of jellyfish.

   c. daylight is fading and night is falling.

   d. the sea conditions are very rough.

4. Which of these is the most reasonable inference about the historical importance of Gertrude Ederle's accomplishment?

   a. It took Ederle two tries to complete the swim.

   b. Ederle had many reporters following her.

   c. Ederle was the first woman to complete the swim.

   d. Ederle could swim despite being partially deaf.

5. What inference can you draw about the lesson that Ellie learns from this experience? Cite evidence from the text to support your answer.

Sample answer: The lesson is that you can overcome difficulties and achieve

your goals. Although Gertrude Ederle was partially deaf, didn't learn to swim

until she was 15, and failed on her first attempt at swimming the English

Channel, she still became a record-setting swimmer.

Unit 1 ■ Reading Literature: Key Ideas and Details   **19**

Extend Thinking: Compare and Contrast

Have students compare the true events of Gertrude Ederle's life to those of Ellie, the fictional main character in the story. Students should create a compare-and-contrast chart that details how the character's life mirrored Ederle's experiences and how it was different. Then they should present their ideas to each other in small groups of three or four.

Independent Practice

Comprehension Check

Answer Explanations:

1. Students should recall explicit details from paragraph 29 to identify choice A, *It protects her against the cold*, as the answer.

2. The only inference that can be made from the details in question 1 is choice B, *Cold water presents difficulties for swimmers*.

3. The descriptions of the waves in paragraph 30 support the inference stated in choice D, *the sea conditions are very rough*.

4. The only logical inference provided is choice C, *Ederle was the first woman to complete the swim*.

5. Answers will vary. Students should draw a connection between Ellie's and Ederle's abilities to overcome personal obstacles, and cite evidence from the text to support their answers.

Critical Comprehension

Challenge students to think more deeply about the text and to support their answers with evidence from the text.

How do you think Ellie would have reacted if Gertrude Ederle had failed to complete her swim across the Channel? (She would have been disappointed but understood that success comes only with perseverance.)

Assess and Respond
If students have trouble answering Comprehension Check question 5,
Then lead them to highlight details in the text that illustrate the lessons Ellie learns during the course of the story. Have them think about how these lessons would apply to the question.

Unit 1 ■ Reading Literature: Key Ideas and Details   **19**

Guided Instruction

OBJECTIVE
Identify the theme of a text, and provide a summary.

Genre: Historical Fiction

A work of historical fiction is a text set in the past and is based on real events. Historical fiction often includes real-life people and events around which the plot is based.

Set the Purpose

Have students think about one of their favorite stories, novels, or movies. Ask: *What is the important message or lesson that readers or viewers take away from it? How do you know?*

Model and Teach

Read or have volunteers read the selection and callouts as the class follows along. Model effective strategies for responding to the callouts by using the suggestions below.

CITE EVIDENCE

A Guide students to look for ideas that might be developed later in the story. Encourage students to pay close attention to important or meaningful ideas about courageous actions, as expressed in paragraph 4.

B Help students identify details that support their answer to Cite Evidence callout A. Guide them to look in subsequent paragraphs in order to find evidence.

ANALYZING THEME

Guided Instruction

WORDS TO KNOW
armory
diplomatic
exchange
merchant
statesman

Most authors develop at least one main **theme**, or central message, in each text. Paying attention to and **summarizing** key details can help you analyze the theme or themes of a text.

CITE EVIDENCE

A One way to begin thinking about the main **theme** of a story is to look for ideas that appear early on, and then see which of those ideas the author develops. In paragraph 4, double underline a pair of sentences whose ideas you think the author will develop.

B Does the author develop the ideas you chose? On this page, find and circle the paragraph that develops those ideas.

The Courage of John Adams
(Genre: Historical Fiction)

1   "All hands on deck! All hands on deck!"

2   I am lying in my small hammock belowdecks when I hear the cry echo through the cabin area. All around me, men jump up and begin readying themselves. I turn to Silas, who sleeps in the hammock next to mine, and ask, "What do you think is going on?"

3   "I'm not sure, but we have had so many calls for 'all hands' on this trip that I'm starting to think I should just sleep on deck! I wonder if the lookout has spotted one of those British ships we encountered earlier."

4   We get our clothing straightened out and quickly move to our positions on deck. <u>When the cry comes for "all hands," it usually means something important or even dangerous is about to happen. I wait, in high expectation, for one of the officers to address us.</u> Already, this voyage has been far more exciting than I could have anticipated. I cannot imagine what will happen next.

5   "Men," a first officer's voice rings down the deck, "a ship has been spied by our lookout, within the path of our voyage. It is not known whether the ship is friendly, nor if the crew could intend to do us harm. However, Captain Tucker has decided to give chase, as he believes we may be facing a British **merchant** ship. All crew members are ordered to arm themselves in preparation for battle, but do not fire upon the other ship until you are given orders."

6   As we move to the ship's **armory**, I hear Silas call out from behind me, "Samuel!"

7   I stop and wait for him to catch up.

20

Words to Know

General Academic Vocabulary
diplomatic (*adj.*): involving relationships between countries
exchange (*n.*): discussion

Domain-Specific Vocabulary
armory (*n.*): a place where weapons are kept
merchant (*adj.*): used in sales or trade
statesman (*n.*): experienced and wise government leader

Working with Word Meaning Have students restate the vocabulary words in their own terms, and then write a sentence using each.

KEY IDEAS AND DETAILS

Guided Instruction

8   "Samuel, can you believe this? This trip gets more and more exciting! Do you think they will let us fight?"

9   "I don't think so, Silas," I reply. "If they do let us fight, it will be because our crew has been overwhelmed. So, let us hope it doesn't come to that."

10   "But you will fight if necessary?" Silas asks.

11   "Of course I will, but I'd rather it not be necessary. Remember our cargo, Silas. . . ."

12   Silas nods solemnly. "Who could forget?"

13   We get in the back of the line at the armory; for although Silas and I are considered officers-in-training, we are at the bottom of the ship's hierarchy in instances like these. Most officers assume that 14-year-old boys will not be able to fight as well as grown men. Silas and I disagree, but we would sooner jump ship than argue with a first officer.

14   As I look around at the crew members readying the ship, I see, off to the right, the "precious cargo" being carried by our ship. John Adams, **statesman** and Revolutionary leader, and his son, John Quincy, boarded the *Boston* with us a month ago. Mr. Adams is on a **diplomatic** mission to France, although his presence on board is supposed to be kept in greatest secrecy. Mr. Adams himself doesn't seem to realize his own importance, as he has often ignored the captain's requests to remain in his cabin and has joined the crew in every dangerous situation we have faced. Right now, Mr. Adams appears to be arguing with his son.

15   Silas, too, notices the **exchange**. "What do you think Mr. Adams is saying to his son?"

16   I think for a moment. "Well, if it were my father and me, he would be telling me to get back to our cabin, in case there is a fight. And I would be telling him that I am old enough and as capable of fighting as he is."

Comprehension Check

Based on information in the text, the main theme of this story might have something to do with fighting. Support that idea by summarizing the story so far.

CITE EVIDENCE

C In paragraph 14, the author develops the theme by introducing a character who will be connected to that theme. Put a box around the name of that character.

D When you give a **summary**, you restate the key details of a text in your own words. Summarizing a story, then, can help you focus on the author's main theme or central idea. How would you summarize paragraphs 15–16? Underline three details that you would include in the summary.

Support English Language Learners

The amount of dialogue included in the first section of this story could present challenges for English language learners. Understanding where the conversation switches between voices can be difficult for those unfamiliar with English language story conventions. Help students by assigning them to small "read-aloud" groups in which each student reads the dialogue for a different character, including the narrator. As students read their parts, they will have many opportunities to distinguish the characters' voices.

CITE EVIDENCE

C Have students reread paragraph 14, paying close attention to the character introduced there. Remind students that John Adams is also mentioned in the title, providing further evidence that his words, thoughts, or actions might be a clue to the theme.

D Remind students that a summary restates a story's key events and details in a logical order. Guide students to review the events described in paragraphs 15 and 16. Have students think about which details are most important and might also pertain to the story's theme or central idea.

Comprehension Check

Sample Answer: Samuel and Silas are two young men aboard a Revolutionary War-era ship. John Adams, a passenger on the ship, is headed for a diplomatic mission. The ship's crew is preparing for an encounter with an enemy, a British merchant vessel. Samuel and Silas wonder if John Quincy Adams is arguing with his father about being old enough to participate in the fight.

Answer Explanation: Students should be looking for the most important details and ideas in the story so far, and should compile them into a brief summary. Students should suggest that the ability or willingness to fight for one's country is an important idea in the story.

Review: Drawing Inferences

Paragraphs 6–11 contain a conversation between the characters Samuel and Silas. Tell students to use details from the conversation to infer what Samuel feels about the possibility of going into battle. Have students cite evidence from the text to support their inferences.

Guided Instruction

CITE EVIDENCE

A Have students reread paragraphs 21 and 22 to identify key plot details. Have students underline only the most important details in the two paragraphs.

B Guide students to look for a sentence in paragraph 23 that tells why a fight between the two ships might be necessary. Guide students to consider why the Americans might want to take on the British ship and try to weaken the British Army.

ANALYZING THEME

Guided Instruction

The Courage of John Adams *continued*

WORDS TO KNOW
frigate
outfitted
routine
skirmish

CITE EVIDENCE

A When you summarize, remember that not every detail is really important. Underline one detail in paragraph 21 and one detail in paragraph 22 that seem important enough to include in a summary.

B In paragraph 23, put an asterisk by the sentence that explains why a fight might be necessary. How does this explanation develop an important story idea?

17   We watch them for another moment. Finally, the younger Adams turns and walks away, although I notice he does not move as if to return to his cabin.

18   "It appears that he will be allowed to stay," I tell Silas.

19   "Well, we will see how long that lasts," Silas replies. "Mr. Adams is a statesman. He won't be taking up arms once the fighting starts."

20   "We don't even know if there will be any fighting! And I think you're wrong, Silas. When we chased that British **frigate** a few weeks ago, Mr. Adams stood with the first officers—don't you remember?"

21   Our turn in line is up before Silas can answer. <u>We are</u> <u>outfitted with minor weapons</u> and are told that they are for protection purposes only. As we expected, we are instructed not to enter into a **skirmish** unless specifically ordered to do so.

22   A call of "all hands" also means that we are to be at the ready until such time as those of us who are supposed to be off-duty are released. <u>Silas and I take up positions on watch,</u> maintaining our place on the ship's deck, as we move closer to the sails in the distance.

23   When I was assigned to the *Boston*, I was told we would be sailing on a **routine** trip to Europe. In all honesty, there isn't any such thing as a "routine" trip anymore. Every time we set sail, we run the risk of encountering a British ship. And since the Revolution began, neither side can ignore the other. Even when we confront merchant ships, we must engage. Merchant and trade vessels could be carrying supplies to British troops and if we can stop them, we weaken the British army.

22

Words to Know

General Academic Vocabulary

outfitted (*v.*): supplied; equipped
routine (*adj.*): dull; ordinary

Domain-Specific Vocabulary

frigate (*n.*): a fast, heavily armed ship of the 18th century
skirmish (*n.*): a fight between small numbers of opposing troops

Working with Word Meaning Have students draw images of each word, then trade their images with a partner who must guess the vocabulary word illustrated.

Guided Instruction

24   Of course, once Mr. Adams and his son boarded our ship, the trip became anything but "routine." We are responsible for taking one of America's great statesmen safely to Europe. If Mr. Adams can persuade the French to join us as allies against the British, it could help to bring an end to the war.

25   Early on, it was obvious this trip would be different. The weather became rough almost as soon as we left port. Most of the ship's crew, and all of her passengers, were taken ill. The cabin area was full of sick people, and some thought the captain might make us turn back. We continued on, however, and most of us eventually were back up and working.

26   Then we sailed into the midst of three British ships, and we thought we would be overtaken. After a short skirmish with one of the ships, the British vessel turned and disappeared. None of us were sure why she turned, until we were met with the storm that came upon us shortly thereafter.

27   During the storm, the *Boston* was battered and tossed by violent waves and pounded by the wind and rain. The *Boston* was hit by lightning, and one of the crewmen was injured. He later died from his wounds. Taken together, the events of this trip have caused a great amount of apprehension throughout our journey, and having Mr. Adams and his son aboard has increased our concerns significantly.

28   As we continue giving chase to the ship ahead, I start to make out the outline of her sails. Silas, too, is paying close attention to our approach.

Comprehension Check

How does summarizing the story help you understand the author's central idea, or theme?

CITE EVIDENCE

C In paragraph 24, the author uses Samuel's words to explain why John Adams is an important passenger on the *Boston*. Put a box around the sentence that summarizes his importance.

D Reread the final sentence of paragraph 27. Then, in paragraph 26, underline two events to which Samuel refers. Think about how these events also have to do with the theme of fighting in this story.

Guided Instruction

CITE EVIDENCE

C Have students reread paragraph 24 specifically for information about John Adams. Have them identify the sentence that summarizes the reason Adams is aboard the ship.

D Instruct students to reread paragraphs 26 and 27, paying particular attention to the final sentence in paragraph 27. Have students identify, in paragraph 26, the two events that have caused concern aboard the ship.

Comprehension Check

Sample Answer: In order for readers to determine the central idea or theme of a text, they first have to understand the events and characters in the story. Summarizing the text helps readers identify the key details that lead to an understanding of the theme.

Answer Explanation: Students should be able to articulate the idea that key details and events in a story help illustrate the central conflict, the resolution of which leads to understanding the theme. In order to identify key details, students can first summarize the text.

Differentiate Instruction

Help readers who have trouble identifying key details and summarizing by creating a time line for the story. Draw a horizontal line across the board, and call on students to identify key events from the story. Ask students if the event is important enough to go on the time line and, if so, where on the time line it should go. Have students direct you to place the event correctly on the time line. After you have recorded several events, have students work in pairs to verbally summarize the information in the time line. Continue filling out the time line in the successive sections in the story.

Guided Practice

Recap Reading Selection

Ask students to recall important details about the story so far, including why John Adams is on the ship. Tell students they will be learning about Adams's actions aboard the ship.

Read and Practice

Have partners take turns reading the selection as you circulate to provide support. Circulate among students and ask them to respond to Cite Evidence callouts A and B. Provide additional scaffolding as needed, using the suggestions below.

CITE EVIDENCE

A Students should meet with a partner to reread and discuss key details in paragraphs 29–37. Ask them to look specifically for details that pertain to the upcoming battle between the ships and the characters' reactions to it.

B After rereading paragraphs 29–37, students should discuss what the theme of those paragraphs might be. Guide students to look at paragraph 37 for one sentence that expresses an important idea. Point out that the paragraph reveals a key idea about John Adams, a man who, though a diplomat on a mission of peace, is willing and ready to fight for his country.

ANALYZING THEME

Guided Practice

The Courage of John Adams *continued*

29 "Samuel," he asks, "did you notice that the captain is directly bearing down upon that **vessel**? We usually approach other ships with our **broadside** visible. What do you think is going on?"

30 "I think it makes perfect sense. There is no way to hide our approach, but we can hide our guns. If we come at them directly, then they may not realize who we are until it is too late."

31 We make a loop around the deck, keeping watchful eyes open. Suddenly, I spot Mr. Adams talking to the officer on duty at the ship's armory.

32 "Silas," I whisper, "do you see Mr. Adams over at the armory? I wonder what that is all about!"

33 "I'm sure he is getting outfitted for the possible skirmish ahead. After all we have been through, Mr. Adams doesn't strike me as the type to hide in his cabin."

34 We have made good time chasing the unknown vessel ahead. Smooth seas and a good **tailwind** have given us the advantage, and we can distinctly see the ship in front.

35 "At the ready, men!" we hear one of the officers call. Silas and I quickly get into position. My heart is pounding nervously. Even though I am an officer-in-training, my actual combat experience is limited. Despite the fact that we are at war with the British, I have not yet been involved in a real battle.

36 We pull up within fighting distance. Suddenly, there is a wrenching sound in the air, and then I feel the ship shaking around me. Everyone jumps into action, and I hear Silas shout, "They've fired on us!"

WORDS TO KNOW

broadside
countenance
gallantly
helm
tailwind
vessel

CITE EVIDENCE

A With a partner, summarize the events of paragraphs 29–37. Underline five key details that should be included in your summary.

B The theme of paragraphs 29–37 can be found in paragraph 37. Put an asterisk next to the sentence that expresses the theme of this section.

24 Unit 1 ■ Reading Literature: Key Ideas and Details

Words to Know

General Academic Vocabulary
countenance (*n.*): face
gallantly (*adv.*): bravely

Domain-Specific Vocabulary
broadside (*n.*): the side of a ship above the water line
helm (*n.*): place on a ship where the steering controls are located
tailwind (*n.*): wind coming from behind the ship
vessel (*n.*): ship

Working with Word Meaning Have students write the words and their definitions on individual index cards or separate sheets of paper, and then sort the words into categories, such as *People*, *Sailing*, and *Ships*.

KEY IDEAS AND DETAILS

37   For some reason, in the midst of the chaos, I look for Mr. Adams. At first, I can't see his distinctive **countenance** anywhere. And then I see him, standing proudly at the ship's **helm**, weapons drawn.*Statesman or not, right now he is one of us, ready to fight as **gallantly** for his country as anyone else on board. I take heart and feel a surge of pride. I, too, am ready to fight for my freedom.

Comprehension Check

1. On these two pages, the author develops the main theme by

  a. raising questions about what Captain Tucker will do.

  b. creating a conversation between Samuel and Mr. Adams.

  (c.) having the story's characters face an actual battle.

  d. showing the surrender of the British ship.

2. In the story, when the British vessel fires on the *Boston*, John Adams

  a. goes in search of his son.

  (b.) prepares to fight alongside the crew.

  c. urges the captain to hide the ship's guns.

  d. reports to the ship's armory.

3. Which statement best summarizes the story's plot so far?

  a. John Adams teaches his son to fight aboard a ship.

  b. An American ship captures a British vessel during the Revolutionary War.

  (c.) A teenager learns a lesson by watching an American hero.

  d. Two officers-in-training become friends during a battle.

4. Samuel's comments in paragraph 37 suggest which of these central ideas?

  (a.) Brave people will sacrifice safety for the sake of freedom.

  b. Even diplomats can be good soldiers.

  c. It is important to be prepared for any situation.

  d. Few people understand what courage really means.

5. Discuss how the encounter between the *Boston* and the British ship helps illustrate an important story idea. Share story details that support your answer.

  Sample answer: Although he could retreat to his cabin during the encounter, John Adams chooses to stand with the crew of the *Boston*. His actions help develop the idea of the importance of fighting for one's beliefs. This idea also comes across in the final sentence of paragraph 37, in which Samuel talks about being inspired by John Adams.

Unit 1 ■ Reading Literature: Key Ideas and Details   **25**

Comprehension Check

Answer Explanations:

1. Three of the choices are not supported by the text. Choice C, *having the story's characters face an actual battle*, is the only answer that makes sense.

2. Paragraph 37 explicitly states that John Adams prepares for battle, so the best choice is B, *prepares to fight alongside the crew*.

3. The correct answer is choice C, *A teenager learns a lesson by watching an American hero*. Choices A and B do not occur in the story. Choice D is incorrect; Samuel and Silas are already friends.

4. Samuel's thoughts about John Adams and his decision to fight for his freedom suggest that choice A, *Brave people will sacrifice safety for the sake of freedom*, is correct.

5. Students should note that the encounter between the two ships illustrates the willingness of Adams to fight for his freedom alongside the other crewmen. Students should note evidence from paragraph 37, in which Samuel notes Adams's actions.

Turn and Talk

Read aloud Comprehension Check question 5 on page 25. Then have students immediately turn to the person on their right to discuss it. Tell students to work together to come up with an answer. Invite volunteers to share their answer with the class.

Discussion Skills

Place students in groups to discuss the dangers sailors might have encountered on long sea voyages in the late 1700s. Have students think about the kinds of supplies and equipment available during the time, as well as the limitations in technology. Have students divide up roles in the group, including Facilitator, Timekeeper, Recorder, and Presenter. Remind students to ask questions and brainstorm ideas, keeping the discussion going throughout. At the end of the discussion, have students share their ideas with the class.

Independent Practice

Recap Reading Selection

Have students discuss the impact of John Adams's actions on Samuel's ideals in the story so far. Then ask them to summarize the story's events up to this point. Let students know that they will be reading about the outcome of the confrontation between the two ships.

Read and Apply

Have students read this selection independently as you circulate. Ask them to read aloud so you can see if they are reading fluently. You can also use the support below to help students who are having difficulty.

CITE EVIDENCE

A Students should use details from paragraphs 38 and 39 to summarize the story's turn of events.

B Students should look for evidence at the end of paragraph 42 that tells them how Samuel's understanding of patriotism has changed and why. They should explain how the character's change in understanding hints at the theme, or central idea, that freedom is worth fighting for.

ANALYZING THEME

Independent Practice

WORDS TO KNOW

authorized
bemoans
cargo
commandeer
patriot

CITE EVIDENCE

A Summarize how Captain Tucker is able to avoid a naval battle with the British ship *Martha*. Underline details that support your summary.

B Put an asterisk by the sentence in paragraph 42 that emphasizes the result of fighting, rather than the fight itself. How does this sentence develop the main theme of this story?

The Courage of John Adams *continued*

38   However, before I can even draw my weapon, the cry of "Stand down!" roars through the ship. Captain Tucker has turned the *Boston* to her broadside, and we are preparing to return fire on the British vessel.

39   That simple decision changes the course of our encounter. Once the captain of the opposing ship sees our broadside and notes the amount of firepower we can easily access, he immediately surrenders. Our officers board his vessel, **commandeer** all weapons and supplies on board, and take prisoner every member of the crew.

40   As we explore the deck, it becomes apparent that Captain Tucker's decision to give chase was the correct one. The British ship *Martha* is a Letter of Mark, meaning that it is a privately owned ship that the British government has **authorized** to attack and capture enemy vessels—in this case, the *Boston*. On board, we find significant weaponry, as well as a substantial amount of valuable **cargo**. Truly, had we not given chase, the *Martha* would have attacked us, forcing us into a more costly engagement.

41   We bring the ship's crew on board and continue on our journey to Europe. The officers release us from our "all hands" just as I am to begin my watch. Silas, ever the adventurer, **bemoans** the fact that we did not get to fight in a battle with the British. I, on the other hand, am both relieved and, for the first time, ready for the next steps.

42   There will be other battles in which I will be forced to take up arms against my enemies. However, seeing Mr. Adams ready and willing to fight for our country gives me the confidence I need to

26

Words to Know

General Academic Vocabulary

authorized (*v.*): given permission or authority to do something
bemoans (*v.*): complains about

Domain-Specific Vocabulary

cargo (*n.*): items transported on a ship, train, truck, etc.
commandeer (*v.*): take control of for military use
patriot (*n.*): person loyal to a cause or country

Working with Word Meaning Have students work with a partner to create a short, one-paragraph story using these Words to Know.

KEY IDEAS AND DETAILS
Independent Practice

continue. As we sail on toward Europe, I look off into the horizon. I may not know what my future holds, but I know that with dedicated **patriots** like John Adams at our helm, it will be a glorious future, indeed.

Comprehension Check (MORE ONLINE) **sadlierconnect.com**

1. What idea is most clearly expressed by the captain's order for his crew to stand down?

   a. Even when you are weaker than your enemy, you still can win.

   (b.) There is a time to fight, but there also is a time to show restraint.

   c. Defending your country is important.

   d. Even the most important people can fail in a moment of weakness.

2. There can be more than one way to express the theme or central message of a story. Based on the full text of the story, which of these statements best describes this story's theme?

   (a.) Personal principles can overcome fears.

   b. Only soldiers should be allowed to fight.

   c. Statesmen do not make good soldiers.

   d. All of the above.

3. How do Samuel's feelings after a battle is avoided help express the theme?

   a. His fears underscore the theme of keeping young people away from the dangers of war.

   b. Because he is young, he cannot understand the issues behind the war.

   (c.) He is relieved but knows that he will be able to fight in the future if necessary.

   d. None of the above.

4. How does the character of Silas help reinforce a central idea of the story?

   a. His relationship with Samuel shows the importance of friendship.

   b. His words illustrate the dangers of training young people to become officers.

   c. His excitement about the battle supports the idea that only cowards prefer peace.

   (d.) His adventurous (and slightly foolish) spirit helps highlight the change in Samuel's feelings about fighting.

5. In your own words, give a summary of the story, choosing the details that best support the story's theme. At the end, state that theme.

   Sample answer: The frigate *Boston*, carrying John Adams on a diplomatic mission to France, encounters and engages the *Martha*, a British merchant ship. John Adams enters the conflict rather than hide in his quarters. By doing so, Adams teaches Samuel, the story's narrator, about the importance of risking your life to defend the principles you believe in.

Unit 1 ■ Reading Literature: Key Ideas and Details   **27**

Independent Practice

Comprehension Check

Answer Explanations:

1. In paragraph 38, the captain calls for his men to stand down, so choice B is correct: *There is a time to fight, but there also is a time to show restraint.*

2. Only choice A, *Personal principles can overcome fears*, is supported by the events in the story.

3. In paragraph 42, Samuel expresses his feelings about missing a chance to fight. Choice C best restates those feelings.

4. Choice D, *His adventurous (and slightly foolish) spirit helps highlight the change in Samuel's feelings about fighting*, is the only answer supported by details in the story.

5. Answers will vary, but should be supported with evidence from the text.

Critical Comprehension

Challenge students to think more deeply about the text and to support their answers with evidence from the text.

How do you think the outcome of the story would have been different if the captain had fired on the British ship? (Answers will vary, but should include ideas about how the crew and characters would have fared.)

Assess and Respond

If students have trouble answering the questions in the Comprehension Check,

Then lead them to highlight details in the text that can help them summarize it and determine its theme. Have students pay close attention to Samuel's observations about freedom and patriotism.

Extend Thinking: Draw Conclusions

Have students discuss the role of patriotism in the outcome of the Revolutionary War. Have students work in small groups to discuss the challenges faced by American troops and the obstacles they had to overcome in order to win their independence from the British. Allow students to refer to an appropriate Web site for further information.

At the end of the discussion, have each group summarize their conclusions in a short presentation to the rest of the class.

Analyzing Literary Elements

Guided Instruction

OBJECTIVE
Analyze how the elements of literature help shape a story or drama.

Genre: Multi-Act Play

A multi-act play contains more than one act, or set of scenes. Multi-act plays often use different settings and often introduce new characters in each act to illustrate the passage of time and to support a theme.

Set the Purpose

Lead students in a discussion of what makes a play different from other forms of storytelling, such as short stories, novels, movies, and graphic novels. Ask: *How is seeing a performance of a play different from reading a story?*

Model and Teach

Read or have volunteers read the selection and callouts as the class follows along. Model effective strategies for responding to the callouts by using the suggestions below.

CITE EVIDENCE

A Guide students to read the description of the setting at the beginning of the play. Point out that each new act in a play often means a change in the setting, so students can expect to find more of these descriptions as they read the four acts of this play.

B Have students review the cast of characters and then scan the dialogue to see which character speaks first.

ANALYZING LITERARY ELEMENTS

Guided Instruction

WORDS TO KNOW
chart
manifest
passage
qualifications

In fiction, the elements of **setting, plot, and characters interact** to create an engaging story that communicates the author's theme.

CITE EVIDENCE

A In a play, or **drama**, the **setting** (time and place) of the play is typically explained at the beginning of the act or scene. Put a box around the words that describe the setting of Act I, Scene 1.

B In a drama, the dialogue (spoken words) of the **characters** is indicated with the name of the character who is speaking. Circle the name of the first character to speak.

Into the Unknown
(Genre: Multi-Act Play)

CAST OF CHARACTERS
MUNGO PARK, a Scottish explorer
THE BUTLER
DR. JOHN LAIDLEY, an Englishman living in Africa
JOHNSON, Dr. Laidley's African former servant, who will be joining MUNGO PARK as his guide

ACT I, SCENE 1

1 **SETTING:** *The time is 1795. MUNGO PARK, a Scottish explorer, is at home in his study. There are bookshelves lining the walls, filled with old, academic volumes. There is a desk in one corner, and a comfortable couch in the middle of the room. MUNGO PARK paces the floor as he reads a letter.*

MUNGO PARK *(murmuring):* . . . "It has been weeks since we have heard anything from Major Houghton" . . . *(He stops pacing, and looks up.)* As if Major Houghton's situation has anything to do with me! *(He returns to the letter, murmuring and pacing again.)* . . . "However, we are quite satisfied with your **qualifications**" . . . "we wish to recommend you to Dr. John Laidley, currently working in an English factory in Gambia." *(looking up again)* Gambia! That will put me right in line to travel the Niger River. If all goes well, I may be the one to finally **chart** the course of that river, and, with any luck, even discover the exact location of the city of Timbuktu!

(PARK walks purposefully to his desk, picks up a small bell, and rings it. THE BUTLER appears at the door to the library.)

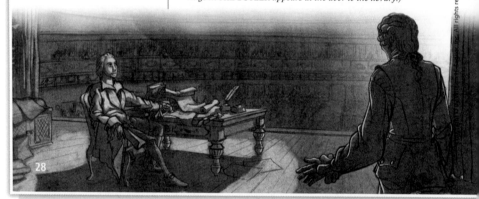

28

Words to Know

General Academic Vocabulary
qualifications (*n.*): skills or experience that fits a person for a job, an office, etc.

Domain-Specific Vocabulary
chart (*v.*): make a map of
manifest (*n.*): list of passengers
passage (*n.*): arrangements to travel as a passenger

Working with Word Meaning Have students work with a partner to use the words in a short skit. Students can use props and gestures to help make the meanings of the words clear.

Guided Instruction

BUTLER: Yes, sir?

5 PARK: The Royal Society has approved my request to travel to Africa and will provide me with the necessary arrangements once I'm there. I should like to begin preparations for the trip immediately, and I will need to book the **passage** for Africa. I trust you can handle the arrangements?

BUTLER: Of course, sir. I will inquire about the passage directly.

(The stage lights come down.)

SCENE 2
(The stage lights come up, revealing PARK, once again in his study. This time, he is sitting at his desk, studying a variety of papers spread out in front of him. A tap is heard at the door.)

PARK: Come in!

10 BUTLER: Sir, the passage has been booked. You sail from Portsmouth on the twenty-second of May, aboard the ship Endeavor.

PARK: Thank you very much for making the arrangements. What type of vessel is the *Endeavor*, and who captains it?

BUTLER: I believe, sir, that the *Endeavor* is a trading vessel. It is primarily known for its trade in beeswax and ivory, and its main point of arrival is in West Africa. According to the ship's **manifest**, the captain is a Mr. Richard Wyatt.

PARK: Thank you for that excellent information. It sounds as though the *Endeavor* will do nicely. Of course, with just a few weeks to go, there is little time to be lost!

(The stage lights come down.)

ACT II

15 SETTING: *PARK is sitting at a small table in Africa, writing in a journal. A gas lamp on the table gives off a soft glow, and a glass of water sits next to the lamp. There is a bed next to the table. PARK is reading aloud as he writes.*

Comprehension Check

The setting changes between Act I and Act II. How does that change help move the plot of the drama forward?

Guided Instruction

CITE EVIDENCE

C The scene between Mungo Park (who was a real-life adventurer) and his butler gives information on the **plot**, or what is going to happen during the play. Underline the dialogue that gives information about when and how Park will travel.

D In Act I, Scene 1, the author (also known as the playwright) tells readers about the setting for the next part of the play. To what location in Africa will Park travel? Put a box around the character dialogue that the author has included to explain this.

CITE EVIDENCE

C Guide students to look at paragraph 10. Have them look at specific sections of the dialogue that help provide key information about Park's voyage.

D Paragraph 12 explicitly states where Park will be travelling. Guide students to identify this information in the dialogue.

Comprehension Check

Sample Answer: Changes in setting help audiences see the passage of time in a play. At the start of Act II, the audience can see that Park has left his home (the setting of Act I) and sailed to Africa. That means several months or more have passed in the play.

Answer Explanation: Students should understand that changes in setting indicate not only a change in place but also in time; as a result, setting changes help the plot move forward without bogging the story down in unnecessary details.

Review: Analyzing Theme

The overall theme for this unit is "courageous actions." After they read the first two scenes of the play, ask students to discuss what the central idea of the play might be and how it connects with the unit's theme. Have students look for details about Park's journey and his goals in order to help them craft a statement of theme.

Support English Language Learners

Because the play is set in eighteenth-century Scotland, English language learners might have difficulty with some of the unusual and specialized words in the stage directions and dialogue. Help students prepare to read by writing on the board such terms as *Mungo Park, Scottish, Gambia, Timbuktu, Royal Society, Portsmouth, Mogadore, wicker*, etc. Make sure students know how to pronounce each word or term, and also give them a working definition of each. As students read the play, they can add more words to the list. After they have read the first section of the play, invite students to revisit the list to categorize the words into place names, nationalities, people's names, and so on.

Guided Instruction

CITE EVIDENCE

A Guide students to look at Park's dialogue in Act II. Have them look for specific place names from his journey to Africa. Have them identify each of those places in the text. If time allows, look online for an eighteenth-century map of Africa to share with students. As a class, look for the place names and trace Park's journey.

B Remind students that the literary element of setting can have a significant impact on the plot of a story or play. Guide students to skim the dialogue on page 30 for clues to how the setting—the River Gambia—affects the events in the play. Help students find relevant information in paragraphs 18 and 20.

ANALYZING LITERARY ELEMENTS

Guided Instruction

Into the Unknown *continued*

WORDS TO KNOW
dispatched
duty
inclement
intact
trade route

CITE EVIDENCE

A In Act II, the author advances the plot through spoken descriptions of various places. Which character speaks these descriptions? Underline each place that this character describes.

B In some dramas, the setting has a strong effect on the characters. Put an asterisk by two sentences that show that the story events are affected by the African setting.

PARK: July 2, 1795. We sailed from Portsmouth on May twenty-second under sunny skies, with little prospect of **inclement** weather. On June 4th, I caught my first glimpse of the mountains of Mogadore, on the coast of Africa. On June 21st, after a fairly pleasant journey with smooth seas, our ship arrived at Jillifree, a small town on the banks of the River Gambia. Jillifree is located in the kingdom of Barra, known for its extensive trade in salt. The king of Barra commands a considerable amount of land and maintains control over the entire salt trade for the region. The **trade route** through Jillifree has been established as a main thoroughfare in the kingdom of Barra. Consequently, the king of Barra collects large trade **duties** on every vessel that docks at Jillifree. The governor of Jillifree handles the collection of these duties, so we did not have the opportunity to see the king himself.

(PARK clears his throat, takes a drink from his glass, and continues writing.)

PARK: We stayed in Jillifree only one day, departing for the town of Vintain, on the northern side of the River Gambia, on the 23rd. Vintain is well known for exporting high-quality beeswax; it is much frequented as a trade destination for European merchants. We stayed two days in Vintain, leaving on the 26th for the town of Jonkakonda.*The trip along the river was not nearly so pleasant as the first portion of the journey. In this area, the river is quite muddy, and the vessel had to be towed through some of the more treacherous areas.

30

Words to Know

General Academic Vocabulary
dispatched (*v.*): sent
duty (*n.*): tax
inclement (*adj.*): stormy; unpleasant
intact (*adj.*): whole; in one piece

Domain-Specific Vocabulary
trade route (*n.*): road or path used for trade between groups

Working with Word Meaning Have students create a graphic organizer for each word. The organizer should include the word, the definition, a restatement of the definition, and a picture representing the word.

KEY IDEAS AND DETAILS

(PARK pauses, smiles to himself, and continues writing.)

20 **PARK:** *Although this part of the journey was tedious, it did present some interesting opportunities for study of the native wildlife. The river is home to a variety of different species of fish, none of which can be found in Europe. Further, the river houses both hippopotami and alligators, making for an interesting—and somewhat dangerous—journey. Our journey from Vintain took us, in total, six days. We are now here in Jonkakonda, where I have recently **dispatched** a letter to Dr. Laidley, informing him of my arrival.*

(PARK closes his journal and gets up from his table. He stretches and yawns.)

PARK: Well, perhaps I will call it a night. I do hope to hear from Dr. Laidley soon—perhaps tomorrow.

(PARK reaches over to the lamp as if to douse it, and the stage lights dim.)

ACT III

SETTING: *At DR. LAIDLEY's house in Pisania, a small village near Jonkakonda, MUNGO PARK sits in a wicker recliner, a blanket covering his body and a scarf around his neck. He is almost asleep but wakes up often to cough. As the scene begins, DR. LAIDLEY walks into the room.*

25 **DR. LAIDLEY** *(cheerfully)*: Good morning! And how's our patient today?

PARK *(hoarsely)*: Feeling much better, thank you. I'm sure I will be up and ready to proceed with our journey soon.

DR. LAIDLEY: I wouldn't count on it, Park. I'm not sure you really understand the extent of your illness. These African fevers can be fatal, and you barely pulled out of yours with your senses **intact**.

PARK: I don't quite understand, Dr. Laidley.

Comprehension Check

How would you describe the way that characters, setting, and plot are working together to help you understand this drama?

Unit 1 ■ Reading Literature: Key Ideas and Details   **31**

Guided Instruction

CITE EVIDENCE

C Toward the end of Act II, the author introduces an important new character. Double underline that character's name.

D It is clear that an important plot event occurs between Act II and Act III. What event is it? Circle the dialogue that explains it.

CITE EVIDENCE

C Have students look in Act II for a new character specifically mentioned in the dialogue. Remind students that they can confirm this new character's name by referring to the Cast of Characters on page 28.

D Reread the beginning of Act III with students. Have them identify what has changed in Park's situation during the time that has elapsed between Acts II and III. Guide them to the last sentence in Laidley's dialogue in paragraph 27.

Comprehension Check

Sample Answer: The characters advance the plot through dialogue. The scene changes show the passage of time and advance the plot.

Answer Explanation: Students should understand that a plot is the series of events (usually in chronological order), and in a drama, those events are often delineated by characters' dialogue and by changes in the setting.

Differentiate Instruction

Creating a graphic organizer will help struggling readers understand how the characters affect the plot of the play. Have students work in small groups to create a chart with the headings *Character*, *Description*, and *Actions*. Students should complete the chart by writing each character's name, personal characteristics, and actions that have contributed to the plot. Bring all the groups together to discuss their completed charts. Ask students for generalizations or observations about how the characters' actions and words shape the events in the play.

Guided Practice

Recap Reading Selection

Remind students that they have read the first three acts of a play about the adventures of Mungo Park. Have them recall the important plot point at the end Act III. Tell them that they will now be reading about the next step in Park's journey.

Read and Practice

Have partners take turns reading the selection as you circulate to provide support. Ask students to respond to Cite Evidence callouts A and B. Provide additional scaffolding as needed, using the suggestions below.

CITE EVIDENCE

A Have students work with partners to read aloud the dialogue between Park and Laidley. Have students identify statements by both Park and Laidley that reveal details about Park's character.

B Have students work with partners to identify words and phrases in Park's dialogue in paragraph 32 that describe the climate of Africa. Important words to note include *torrential*, *oppressive*, and *constant*.

ANALYZING LITERARY ELEMENTS

Guided Practice

Into the Unknown *continued*

WORDS TO KNOW

climate
delirium
recuperate
relapse
solace
torrential

CITE EVIDENCE

A Discuss with a partner how the dialogue between Mungo Park and Dr. Laidley helps readers understand more about Mungo Park's character. Underline evidence to support your ideas.

B In paragraph 32, Mungo Park describes three setting details that reveal his feelings about living in Africa. Put an asterisk next to each.

DR. LAIDLEY: Delirium, man! You've had a very severe fever—tossing and turning, not knowing where you are or to whom you were speaking. If you think you can begin this journey any time soon, you are sorely mistaken.

30 **PARK:** I cannot believe I have been so sick just from spending one night out, observing the eclipse.

DR. LAIDLEY: It's certainly not unheard of. <u>Your body is unaccustomed to the **climate** here</u>, even after a month with us. You are still getting used to living in Africa. I must say, however, that <u>your mastery of the Mandingo language is becoming quite impressive</u>.

PARK: Thank you for your kind words. But truly, I am hoping to try at least a short walk around the village tomorrow, with an eye to increasing my stamina and distance each day. I am feeling so much better, and <u>I am ready to be off</u>. It is only your company that has kept me going.*These **torrential** rains, during the day, followed by*oppressive heat at night, are almost more than a body can bear! And*the constant croaking of those frogs! There must be dozens of species. I don't know how you do it, Laidley.

DR. LAIDLEY: If it is any **solace**, you do become used to it, over time. I believe your fever has prevented you from becoming better accustomed to your surroundings. When one is sick, everything seems that much more difficult to bear.... Well, Park, do as you will, but I can't help but advise against it. <u>Your body still needs to **recuperate**</u>. If you should **relapse**, you won't be able to start until the new year, at the earliest.

32 Unit ■ Reading Literature: Key Ideas and Details

Words to Know

General Academic Vocabulary

climate (*n.*): typical weather conditions of an area
solace (*n.*): something that gives comfort or relief
torrential (*adj.*): falling with great force

Domain-Specific Vocabulary

delirium (*n.*): confusion caused by high fever
recuperate (*v.*): to recover after an illness
relapse (*v.*): to fall back into illness

Working with Word Meaning Have students use several Words to Know to write a news report about a real or imaginary event, and then exchange their work with a partner, who should check it for the correct use of vocabulary.

KEY IDEAS AND DETAILS
Guided Practice

Guided Practice

PARK: I'm sure I'll be fine. In fact, I have no doubt we will be leaving for the next leg of our journey within the month.

35 *(The stage lights dim.)*

Comprehension Check

1. What do Mungo Park's complaints in Act III tell readers about the setting of the drama?

   a. Africa's conditions are very hard on people who are not used to them.

   b. Africa is a dangerous place to live because it makes everyone sick.

   c. Dr. Laidley's house is very uncomfortable.

   d. Park complains only about his illness, not about the setting.

2. The dialogue between Dr. Laidley and Mungo Park advances the plot in Act III because readers learn that

   a. no time has passed between Acts II and III.

   b. Mungo Park has taken some time off from his journey to relax.

   c. Mungo Park has been ill and cannot yet continue his trip.

   d. Dr. Laidley has taken Mungo Park to a hospital.

3. What does Dr. Laidley's dialogue reveal about his character?

   a. He is afraid of the African interior and is content to stay at Pisania.

   b. He is very adventurous and wants to join the expedition.

   c. He is jealous of Mungo Park's determination to keep going.

   d. He is knowledgeable about Africa but also rather cautious.

4. Which statement best describes the relationship between character and plot in Act III?

   a. Mungo Park's unhappiness shows that he should have stayed at home.

   b. Mungo Park's determination indicates that the story of his exploration will continue.

   c. Dr. Laidley's arguments prove that Mungo Park was right to risk coming to Africa.

   d. All of the above.

5. Which element of literature is most important for understanding Act III: plot, character, or setting? Compare answers with a partner, and cite evidence for your answer.

   Sample answer: In Act III, character is the most important element. The act focuses on dialogue between Mungo Park and Dr. Laidley. Through this dialogue, the reader has a better picture of both characters.

Unit 1 ▪ Reading Literature: Key Ideas and Details   **33**

Comprehension Check

Answer Explanations:

1. Since students have already noted the dialogue describing Park as unaccustomed to the climate, the answer choice is A, *Africa's conditions are very hard on people who are not used to them.*

2. Choice C, *Mungo Park has been ill and cannot yet continue his trip*, is correct. The events in the play do not support any of the other choices.

3. Only one choice is supported by Laidley's dialogue—D, *He is knowledgeable about Africa but also rather cautious.*

4. Choice B, *Mungo Park's determination indicates that the story of his exploration will continue*, is the only option supported by the dialogue and the continuing plot.

5. Students should see that in Act III, character development is essential to advancing the plot and understanding the characters. This character development is seen through the dialogue that occurs between Park and Laidley.

Think-Pair-Share

Have students do a Think-Pair-Share to discuss the answer to Comprehension Check question 5. Students should write their own answer to the question, and then share it with a partner. Partners should discuss their answers and then make any changes, based on their partner feedback. Ask volunteers to share their answers with the class.

Discussion Skills

Have students meet in small groups to discuss this question: *Why do you think it is so important to Mungo Park to continue his journey even when he is sick?* Encourage students to quote from the play in support of their answers. Suggest the following sentence stems for students to use in their discussion.

- *Park's decision to _____ supports my idea about _____.*
- *Park tells Laidley that _____, and that means _____.*
- *When Park says _____, he is suggesting that _____.*

Independent Practice

Recap Reading Selection

Remind students that they have been reading about Mungo Park's journeys through Africa. Have students summarize the events of Acts II and III, as they occurred in the last section. Tell students that they will next be reading Act IV, the conclusion of the play.

Read and Apply

Have students read this section independently as you circulate. Ask them to read aloud so you can see if they are reading fluently. You can also use the support below to help students who are having difficulty.

CITE EVIDENCE

A Students should identify the new character introduced in the stage directions at the beginning of Act IV. Students should note that this character is important because he will accompany Park on his journey.

B Students should identify what happened between Acts III and IV, as revealed in Park's dialogue in paragraph 40.

Into the Unknown *continued*

WORDS TO KNOW

accompany

incomparable

naïve

venture

CITE EVIDENCE

A Circle the name of the character the author introduces in Act IV. Why is this character important to the plot?

B Think about the plot events that have occurred between Act III and Act IV, leading to Mungo Park's delay. Then put a box around the dialogue that gives that information.

ACT IV

SETTING: *In DR. LAIDLEY's house, it is now December. MUNGO PARK is standing in the center of the room, dressed in traveling clothes. He is speaking with* JOHNSON, *an African man who will* **accompany** *him on his journey.*

PARK: Well, Johnson, I believe we are set. I must say, I am disappointed to be leaving so late. Who would have anticipated that it would be December before we could begin?

(As JOHNSON nods, DR. LAIDLEY suddenly enters the room.)

DR. LAIDLEY: Why, I would have, of course! I told you it could be the new year before you set off, Park!

40 **PARK:** Well, on that count you were right. The fever had a deeper hold on my body than I realized. Then when the river rose, we couldn't travel.

DR. LAIDLEY: I ask you again, Park, are you sure you want to take on this journey? You know what happened to Major Houghton—

PARK: No one really knows what happened to Major Houghton.

DR. LAIDLEY: Don't be **naïve**. Houghton has disappeared, and I believe he fell victim to one of the wars between the local villages. *(grimly)* And I fear the same may happen to you, Park.

PARK: I will be careful, Doctor. I have a fairly decent grasp of the language, and I understand the respect that must be shown to the chiefs and kings of each village. Besides, I have an excellent guide in Johnson.

45 **DR. LAIDLEY:** He's **incomparable**—none better, no doubt about it. Do you think you can get our man back alive, Johnson?

JOHNSON: Yes, Doctor. I will do my best. The path we travel is difficult and dangerous, but we will be cautious and courageous.

DR. LAIDLEY: Well then, gentlemen, I guess that's all I can ask. But do be careful, Park. I hope you are ready for this **venture**.

PARK: I believe I am, Doctor. Thank you so much for your kind hospitality. And now, Johnson, let us begin our grand adventure!

(Stage lights go dark; house lights come up.)

Words to Know

General Academic Vocabulary

accompany (*v.*): to go with

incomparable (*adj.*): better than the others; beyond comparison

naïve (*adj.*): having a lack of experience or judgment

venture (*n.*): an undertaking involving uncertainty as to the outcome

Working with Word Meaning Have students identify synonyms and antonyms for each word. Next, tell students to scan the text for the boldfaced words, replacing them with the synonyms and antonyms. Have students discuss with a partner how the substitutions change the meaning of the text.

KEY IDEAS AND DETAILS

Comprehension Check

MORE ONLINE sadlierconnect.com

1. The dialogue in Act IV reveals that Major Houghton

   a. had a successful trip through Africa.

   b. left on a similar trip and is now missing.

   c. was able to send a letter to Dr. Laidley.

   d. will be acting as Mungo Park's guide.

2. What do readers learn about the character of Johnson in Act IV?

   a. He is considered an excellent guide.

   b. He once worked for Major Houghton.

   c. He is uncomfortable about guiding Mungo Park.

   d. He has been giving Mungo Park advice on his trip.

3. What are the three main setting locations in this play?

   a. a village in Gambia, Vintain, and Jonkakonda

   b. the Niger River, Timbuktu, and Dr. Laidley's home in Pisania

   c. Mungo Park's home, his lodging in Jonkakonda, and Dr. Laidley's home

   d. the *Endeavor*, Mungo Park's home, and the African interior

4. How does the author indicate plot advancement between the acts of this drama?

   a. by using an outside narrator

   b. by creating dialogue and changes in setting

   c. by introducing new characters

   d. by having characters speak directly to the audience

5. Think again about your answer to the second Cite Evidence question on page 34. How else have plot, character, and setting worked together to keep Mungo Park from pursuing his goal? Be specific.

   Sample answer: Setting has affected both the plot and the characters. The

   setting has kept Mungo Park in place because elements in the environment

   have made him sick and because the river has been too high for travel. Noting

   the setting, the character of Dr. Laidley also has tried to talk Mungo Park out

   of continuing his journey.

Comprehension Check

Answer Explanations:

1. Choice B, *left on a similar trip and is now missing*, is the only answer supported by the text.

2. Dr. Laidley refers to Johnson as an incomparable guide. That means choice A is the correct answer.

3. The settings of the play would be the places where the action and dialogue occur. Therefore, choice C is correct.

4. Students should determine that the author uses character dialogue and setting to advance the plot of the play between acts. Therefore, choice B is the answer.

5. Students should explain that in Act IV, the harsh African setting has affected Mungo Park (by making him sick) and the plot (by stranding him). Students should cite evidence from the text to support their ideas.

Critical Comprehension

Challenge students to think more deeply about the text and to support their answers with evidence from the text.

Why do you think Park was so sensitive to the climate in Africa? (Answers will vary but should be supported with textual evidence. Students may respond that Park is from Scotland and therefore accustomed to a much cooler climate than in Africa.)

Assess and Respond

If students have trouble answering the questions in the Comprehension Check,

Then lead them to identify each of the elements of drama being analyzed (plot, setting, and character) and note how those elements work together to advance the story of Park's adventures.

Speaking and Listening Presentation

Have students prepare a presentation about an historical figure who exhibited courage in the face of adversity. Have students plan by creating a time line with clear goals for completing their presentation. Presenters should include facts and details about the historical figure, using multimedia or visual elements as support; adapt their language for a formal presentation; speak clearly; and maintain eye contact with their listeners. At the end of the presentation, presenters should answer questions and acknowledge listeners' ideas.

Elicit responses from students of different cultural backgrounds.

Close Reading

OBJECTIVES

- Use evidence from a text to support an analysis of what the text says explicitly and implicitly.
- Identify the theme of a text, and provide a summary.
- Analyze how the elements of literature help shape a story or drama.

Genre: Myth

Myths are ancient stories about gods and goddesses that usually tell about supernatural events or heroic journeys. Many myths were originally created to explain some aspect of the natural world and humanity's place in the universe.

Path Options

You may want to do a close reading with students; if so, use the supports provided on these pages. Or, you may wish to have students read the text independently and apply the skills learned in this unit. In either case, students should read the text more than once to facilitate understanding and to be able to answer the Comprehension Questions correctly.

Theseus and the Minotaur
(Genre: Myth)

1   King Minos of Crete was a cruel and harsh ruler. He was also a powerful ruler, and his army incited fear in everyone who encountered it. All of the city-states surrounding the island of Crete lived in fear of King Minos's forces. And King Minos, being a power-hungry and brutal king, took great pleasure in abusing his power and in forcing the rulers of these city-states to do whatever he might ask.

2   King Minos had two possessions of which he was very proud: his labyrinth, and the terrible monster that ruled it—the Minotaur. The Minotaur was a fearsome monster, half-man and half-bull, that lived at the center of the labyrinth. The labyrinth itself was a kind of prison. When King Minos took people captive, he sent them into the labyrinth, knowing that they stood very little chance of finding their way out. The labyrinth had many twists and turns, causing anyone venturing into it to become hopelessly lost and trapped inside.

3   If, by chance, someone did manage to navigate the labyrinth and arrive successfully at its center, the Minotaur would be there, waiting. There, the weary prisoner would be forced to battle the Minotaur, and no one ever survived.

4   The city-state of Athens lay directly across the sea from Crete, and King Minos often turned his cruel eye toward Athens. Every year, King Minos demanded that Athens send seven young men and seven young women as sacrifices to the Minotaur. If Aegeus, the king of Athens, refused Minos's demand, Minos would send his armies to destroy Athens.

5   Theseus was the prince of Athens but also the son of Poseidon, god of the sea. King Aegeus had adopted Theseus as the heir to the throne of Athens, and he loved Theseus dearly. Theseus, however, was angered by the king's willingness to send Athenian citizens to their death.

6   "Father," Theseus argued, "we cannot allow King Minos to take our young men and women as sacrifices to the Minotaur. Minos is not our king, and we owe him nothing."

7   "My son," King Aegeus answered, "Minos is far more powerful than we are. Should we refuse his sacrifice, he will destroy Athens with his powerful army."

8   Theseus knew he must do something to try to stop King Minos. So, when the time came for King Aegeus to send the seven young men and women to Crete, Theseus spoke up.

9   "Father," Theseus exclaimed, "it is time to end our oppression by King Minos of Crete! I, myself, will volunteer as one of the fourteen. I will travel to Crete, enter the labyrinth, and battle the Minotaur!"

Support English Language Learners

Provide English language learners with an introduction to the text by having them first examine the illustrations. Point out that the illustrations show the characters and some of the events in the story of Theseus, a mythical Greek hero who battled a monster called the Minotaur. Have students make inferences about the text based on what they see in the illustrations. Then have students work with a more fluent partner to check their inferences against the actual text later as they read.

KEY IDEAS AND DETAILS

10   King Aegeus was greatly distressed by his son's decision. "But, Theseus, no one can survive a battle with the Minotaur, especially after traveling through the mysteries of the labyrinth. I cannot allow you to do this foolish thing!"

11   "Do not worry, Father," Theseus assured him. "I will return. And after I have defeated the Minotaur, we will finally be free of this terrible threat."

12   King Aegeus saw that he could not dissuade his son from his decision. "Go, then, if you must," he told Theseus. "Defeat Minos's horrible monster, and return to Athens a hero."

13   So Theseus set sail for the island of Crete, along with the six other young men and the seven young women chosen as sacrifices to the Minotaur. When they arrived at the palace, King Minos was eager to send them into the labyrinth.

14   "Ah, another crop of men and women here to feed my Minotaur!" the cruel king exclaimed.

15   Theseus immediately stepped forward. "I am Theseus, son of Poseidon and prince of Athens. I will enter the labyrinth and defeat your miserable monster."

16   King Minos thought for a moment. "If you are the prince of Athens, you must be the son of Aegeus, not the son of Poseidon. Before I will allow you to enter the labyrinth, you must first pass a test."

17   With that, King Minos threw his ring into the sea. "Theseus, son of Poseidon," he roared, "if you are truly who you say you are, dive into the sea and bring back my ring!"

18   Theseus paused only a moment, asking for Poseidon's help in locating the ring, and plunged into the water.

19   As Theseus swam down into the sea, he saw a shadowy figure ahead of him. Through the depths of the ocean, he heard a female voice calling to him.

20   "Theseus, noble son of Poseidon," the voice said, "I am Thetis, nymph of the sea. I am here to assist you on your quest. I come to bring you the ring of Minos."

21   As Theseus swam closer, he saw a beautiful woman floating just below him. Her hair was green, and it floated gently in the current like seaweed. Her eyes were gray, and they reminded Theseus of gray storm clouds building over the ocean. In her hand sat Minos's ring.

22   She held out the ring to Theseus and said, "Take this ring back to Minos, so that you may begin your quest into the labyrinth. But, as a word of advice from your father, remember to trust Princess Ariadne. She understands the workings of the labyrinth, and she will help you on your quest."

23   Theseus thanked the sea nymph and swam quickly back to the surface of the sea. He burst forth from the water and held the ring aloft like a trophy.

24   "Minos," Theseus called, "I bring your ring, and I have passed your test. Now, I will enter the labyrinth and defeat your gruesome monster!"

Support First Reading

Circulate to check and support students' understanding. Use the following comprehension and strategy check-ins as needed.

Check-in Questions

- *What were King Minos's most prized possessions?* (his labyrinth and the Minotaur who lived in it)

- *Why does King Aegeus send young men and women to be sacrificed to the Minotaur?* (He is afraid King Minos will destroy Athens if he does not comply).

- *How does Theseus plan on stopping King Minos's terrible treatment of Athens?* (by offering himself up as a sacrifice for the Minotaur, and then defeating the monster)

- *Who helps Theseus prove to Minos that he is the son of Poseidon?* (Thetis, sea nymph and messenger from Poseidon)

Review: Drawing Inferences

Have students practice drawing inferences about a character. Tell students to work with a partner to scan the text for clues about Theseus's character. After a brief discussion of their findings, ask students to individually write a short statement in which they make inferences about Theseus's character, including his strengths and weaknesses.

Differentiate Instruction

Help struggling readers by having them preview the text before reading. After students look at the illustrations and make predictions about what will happen in the story, have them skim the text to identify any unfamiliar words. Then place students in mixed-ability pairs to look up the words' meanings and identify any synonyms. Have partners take turns explaining how the words are used in the text.

Check-in Questions

- *Why does Ariadne, the daughter of King Minos, wish to help Theseus defeat the Minotaur?* (She admires his willingness to die for his people.)

- *Why does Theseus promise to take Ariadne back to Athens if he is successful in his quest?* (He understands the risk and danger Ariadne has put herself in to help him. He knows he owes her a great deal.)

- *Why does Theseus thank Poseidon before leaving the labyrinth?* (The god Poseidon, Theseus's father, helped Theseus by sending the nymph Thetis to his aid. Poseidon made it possible for Theseus to prove his identity to King Minos and continue his quest.)

Review: Analyzing Theme

Have students practice identifying the theme of a text. First, have students create a short summary of the events on the first two pages of the myth. Then have students use details from the text to develop one sentence that describes a possible theme of the myth. (Possible theme: It takes great courage to stand up for oneself and what one believes in.)

Review: Analyzing Literary Elements

Give students time to think about how the elements of character, setting, and plot interact in the myth. Have them identify and describe the main characters and settings of the myth. Then have students describe the role that each of those elements plays in the plot.

CLOSE READING

Theseus and the Minotaur *continued*

25   "Perhaps," answered King Minos, "and perhaps you will make a tasty meal for my Minotaur. However, it would be poor sport for my Minotaur if I were to serve you up wet and tired from your trip into the sea. Tonight you and your companions will sleep in comfort as guests in my house; then tomorrow, you will enter the labyrinth."

26   That night, as Theseus lay down to sleep, he heard a knock on his door. King Minos's daughter, Princess Ariadne, was waiting outside his room. Impressed by Theseus's noble actions, she had fallen in love with the hero.

27   "Theseus," she whispered, "I am Ariadne, daughter of Minos. I am pleased by your willingness to die for your people, and I wish to help you. I have a gift for you."

28   Ariadne gave Theseus a ball of string. "The trick of my father's labyrinth lies not just in finding the center and beating the Minotaur. The most difficult part of your journey will be finding your way out of the labyrinth, but I have an antidote for your problem, Theseus. You can use this string to mark your path and find your way out."

29   "Thank you so much, Princess," Theseus replied. "Should I defeat the Minotaur, I will certainly owe you my life."

30   Ariadne smiled at Theseus and said, "Should you defeat the Minotaur, and emerge from the labyrinth, you must promise to take me with you back to Athens. My father is a cruel man. If he discovers that I helped you, he will surely have me killed."

31   "I give you my word," Theseus answered.

32   The next morning, Minos and his guards brought Theseus and his companions to the entrance of the labyrinth. Princess Ariadne was there, waiting. She gave Theseus a sympathetic look as the guards opened the gates to the labyrinth and, with a deceptive smile, shoved him inside.

33   The journey through the labyrinth was difficult, as Theseus traveled through dangerous, shifting passages, expecting to encounter the Minotaur at any moment. However, Theseus was prepared, and he held tightly to Ariadne's string, trailing it behind him to mark his path. Finally, Theseus found himself in the center of the labyrinth. There, in a wide room, stood the terrible creature. The Minotaur let out a terrifying bellow and instantly attacked.

34   Theseus felt the Minotaur's massive arms grab his legs and lift him high above the ground. As Theseus looked into the Minotaur's gaping mouth, he saw an opportunity. He swung his arms around and grasped the Minotaur around the neck, holding tightly as the Minotaur struggled against him. After what seemed like hours but was really only moments, the Minotaur collapsed, lifeless, against the ground.

35   During the struggle, Theseus had dropped the end of Ariadne's string, and now he panicked, searching the ground frantically. Finally, he spotted the thread and, with a sigh of relief, began the difficult journey back through the labyrinth.

38   Unit 1 ■ Reading Literature: Key Ideas and Details

Strategic Reading

Encourage students to ask and answer questions as they read a text. After reading a portion of a text, students should ask themselves questions about what they have read and use the answers to make predictions about what may happen next. For example, after reading to paragraph 17 in the selection, a student might think: *I know that Theseus is confident and brave, but how is he going to find that ring? I'll bet that the gods help him out somehow.*

If students employ questioning as a comprehension strategy and are still having trouble understanding the text, encourage them to ask for help from a teacher or classmate.

KEY IDEAS AND DETAILS

36   When Theseus felt the string becoming taut, he knew he was close to the entrance of the labyrinth. He paused to collect his thoughts. He had defeated the Minotaur. His beloved home of Athens would be safe forever from Minos's cruel monster. As he pushed the gate open, Theseus quietly thanked Poseidon. "Lord Poseidon," he whispered, "you have seen me through this far, and I thank you. Now please see me and my companions safely away from Minos's island, so that we may return home in triumph."

Comprehension Check

1A. The character of King Minos can best be described as

  a. merciless and violent.

  b. generous and compassionate.

  c. thoughtful but foolish.

  d. fair and honest.

1B. Which phrase from the text supports the answer to Part A?

  a. "far more powerful than we are"

  b. "sleep in comfort as my guests"

  c. "pleased by your willingness to die for your people"

  d. "took great pleasure in abusing his power"

2A. What can you infer about the way that King Aegeus and King Minos think about each other?

  a. The two kings see each other as equals.

  b. King Aegeus considers his kingdom to be more powerful than that of King Minos.

  c. King Aegeus is afraid of King Minos's power.

  d. King Minos is afraid of King Aegeus's power.

2B. Which sentence from the text best supports the answer to Part A?

  a. "Minos is not our king, and we owe him nothing."

  b. "Defeat Minos's horrible monster, and return to Athens a hero."

  c. "Ah, another crop of men and women here to feed my Minotaur!"

  d. "...he will destroy Athens with his powerful army."

Unit 1 ■ Reading Literature: Key Ideas and Details   **39**

Research to Build Knowledge

Challenge students to identify and research one hero from Greek mythology and compare him or her to someone they admire who is living today. Provide some examples of mythical heroes, such as Perseus, Jason, and Achilles. Students can work together in small, cooperative-learning groups to gather information from multiple sources that are credible and reliable. Remind students to give credit to their sources and use multimedia aids when they present their findings.

Multiple Readings for Critical Comprehension

Have students read and annotate this selection. Then pose questions that focus on critical comprehension.

- *How does the story of Theseus relate to the unit's theme of "courageous actions"?* (Theseus is willing to risk his life in order to save the lives of fellow Athenians.)

- *How would the story have been different had Theseus not accepted Ariadne's help?* (Ariadne provided Theseus with a way to escape the labyrinth. Without her, Theseus might still have defeated the Minotaur. However, he might not have been able to escape the labyrinth.)

Self-Select Text

As preparation for Connect Across Texts, have students choose one selection from this unit and reread it independently. Students can access full .pdf versions of some selections at **sadlierconnect.com**.

Comprehension Check

Begin scoring students' performance of unit skills with this Comprehension Check and continue through Connect Across Texts on page 42. Use students' scores to determine their readiness for the Unit 1 Review on page 44.

Multiple-Choice Questions: *1 point each*

1A. The text supports the description of King Minos as "merciless and violent."

1B. Students should understand that "abusing his power" refers to Minos's cruelty toward his subjects.

Multiple-Choice Questions:
1 point each

2A. King Aegeus allows Minos to kill his subjects every year. Therefore, students can infer that Aegeus is afraid of Minos.

2B. King Aegeus's statement that Minos will destroy Athens supports the idea that Aegeus fears him.

3A. Only choice A is supported by the outcome of the text.

3B. Thetis and Ariadne reward Theseus's courage by helping him complete his task.

4A. Ariadne helps Theseus and in return asks him to take her away from Crete; therefore, choice C is correct.

4B. The fact that Theseus says he will owe Ariadne his life does not have any bearing on her relationship with King Minos.

5A. Because Theseus is brave, not afraid or cruel, only choice A makes sense as an answer.

5B. Theseus's statement that he must stop Minos's reign of cruelty speaks to his desire to fight against injustice.

Short-Answer Questions:
2 points each

Item 6 Rubric

2	Student lists qualities important for a hero and uses text evidence to support the ideas.
1	Student provides a list of qualities for a hero but does not back these ideas up with evidence from the text.
0	Student provides neither a list of qualities for a hero nor evidence about these qualities from the text.

CLOSE READING

3A. Which of the following themes is supported by the text?

  (a.) Courageous actions will be rewarded.

  b. Power is more important than principles.

  c. Always respect your elders.

  d. Never trust strangers.

3B. Which detail from the text supports the answer to Part A?

  a. Princess Ariadne falls in love with Theseus.

  (b.) Both Thetis and Ariadne help Theseus in his mission.

  c. Theseus drops Ariadne's string.

  d. Minos uses the threat of the Minotaur to hold onto his power.

4A. Based on the myth, what can you infer about Princess Ariadne's relationship with her father, King Minos?

  a. She loves and respects her father.

  b. She believes her father is right in his actions toward Athens.

  (c.) She fears her father and does not share his violent tendencies.

  d. She wants to take over the throne from her father.

6. Based on the actions of Theseus, what can you infer are the most important qualities in a hero? Support your answer with evidence from the text.

Sample answer: One quality is a willingness to fight for your principles, as Theseus does with the Minotaur. Others include respect for your parents, as Theseus shows toward Aegeus and Poseidon; bravery in the face of cruelty, as Theseus shows toward Minos; and a desire to help those in need, for which Ariadne and Thetis both help Theseus.

4B. Which detail from the text does NOT support the answer to Part A?

  a. Ariadne begs Theseus to take her away from Crete.

  b. Thetis urges Theseus to trust Ariadne.

  (c.) Theseus says he will owe Ariadne his life.

  d. Ariadne tells Theseus how to return from the labyrinth.

5A. Based on the story, which statement best describes the character of Theseus?

  (a.) He will fight to defeat injustice.

  b. He is afraid of those with power.

  c. He wants to rule like Aegeus.

  d. None of the above.

5B. Which words from the text best support the answer to Part A?

  a. "'Do not worry, Father,' Theseus assured him. 'I will return.'"

  (b.) "'We cannot allow King Minos to take our young men and women.'"

  c. "However, Theseus held tightly to Ariadne's string, trailing it behind him to mark his path."

  d. "His beloved home of Athens would be safe forever."

40   **Unit 1** ▪ Reading Literature: Key Ideas and Details

Extend Thinking: Writing a Modern Myth

Encourage students to write their own myth set in modern times. Have students work individually or in pairs to plan and write a story about a larger-than-life, modern hero. The story should include supernatural elements and display evidence of the qualities necessary for a hero. Have students read their myths aloud to the class. If time allows, tell students to write critical responses to their classmates' myths. Students should evaluate the myths based on how well they included the elements of myth to make for an interesting and compelling heroic story.

7. Based on Theseus's exchange with Thetis, what can you infer about Poseidon?

Sample answer: Even though Poseidon appears to have been absent from his son's

life, he still cares about Theseus and wants to help Theseus succeed.

8. How does King Minos's labyrinth help illustrate the theme of the story?

Sample answer: The labyrinth represents an impossible, deadly obstacle. Theseus shows

a special kind of courage by accepting help from Ariadne, which allows him to beat

the labyrinth.

9. Write a paragraph summarizing this myth. Remember to include only those key details that are most important to the myth's plot and theme. Use a separate piece of paper if you need more space for your answer.

Sample answer: Theseus is angered by King Minos's cruelty toward Athens. Theseus

agrees to enter Minos's labyrinth and battle his Minotaur in order to make Athens free

and safe once more. Theseus receives help from Poseidon, through Thetis, and from

Minos's daughter Ariadne. Theseus defeats the Minotaur and finds his way back out

of the labyrinth.

10. Below are three themes that are represented in the story of Theseus and the Minotaur.

- Bravery and good deeds will be rewarded with success.
- A person must be willing to take a stand against tyranny.
- Difficult tasks can be made easier with help from others.

A. Underline the theme that best represents the author's main message, in your opinion.

B. Write two facts that provide evidence to support the theme that you have chosen.

Sample answer: Each theme has support in the text. Students should cite two pieces

of evidence from the text and show their connection to their choice of theme.

Unit 1 ■ Reading Literature: Key Ideas and Details **41**

Short-Answer Questions: *2 points each*

Item 7 Rubric

2	Student makes an inference about Poseidon and supports the answer with evidence from the text.
1	Student discusses Poseidon but does not provide textual evidence.
0	Student does not discuss Poseidon or support inferences.

Item 8 Rubric

2	Student explains the labyrinth's importance to the theme of the story and includes text evidence.
1	Student discusses the labyrinth without connecting to theme or providing text evidence.
0	Student does not make a connection between the labyrinth and the theme.

Item 9 Rubric

2	Student writes a summary of the text, including three key details.
1	Student summarizes the text, using fewer than three details.
0	Student does not summarize the text.

Item 10 Rubric

2	Student chooses a theme and finds appropriate evidence to support it.
1	Student does not support the chosen theme with textual evidence.
0	Student does not complete the question.

Theme Wrap-Up

Lead a class discussion to answer this question: *What qualities make a person courageous?* (Students should identify some of the qualities of courage depicted in the selections in the unit.)

Differentiate Instruction

Help students recognize the connections between the text and each two-part comprehension question on pages 39–40. As students try to answer each "A" question, remind them to locate evidence in the text that supports it. Then as they answer each "B" question, they can compare the evidence they used to the answer choices. Guide students to notice when the evidence they used to answer question "A" does not match the answer choices in question "B." That might suggest that they have incorrectly answered the "A" question and should review both their answer and their thinking process.

Connect Across Texts: 4 points
Review Reading Selections

Have students work in groups of four to review the unit's reading selections. Each student in the group should analyze one of the selections. Students should be able to identify the selection's literary elements and state its theme. Have each student teach a mini-lesson on his or her selection to the rest of the group.

Analyze Literary Elements

Review the directions on page 42 of the Student Book. Make sure students understand that they are to list information about the main literary elements in each of the four selections they have read.

Graphic Organizer Rubric

4	Student analyzes the literary elements in all four selections.
3	Student analyzes the literary elements in three of the selections.
2	Student analyzes the literary elements in two of the selections.
1	Student analyzes the literary elements in one of the selections.
0	Student is unable to analyze the literary elements of the selections.

Support Essential Question Discussion

Have students reread the Essential Question. Challenge them to finish this sentence: *Understanding how authors use literary details in a text helps me to…*

If a student has difficulty finishing the sentence, prompt him or her by asking how the setting and characters in a text can influence or shape its plot and theme.

CONNECT ACROSS TEXTS

Analyze Literary Elements

In this unit you've read a work of realistic fiction, a work of historical fiction, a drama, and a myth. Think about the elements of literature you have studied: character, setting, plot, and theme. In the chart below, list details that help you understand the author's use of these elements in each selection. Use a separate sheet of paper if you need more room to write. Then choose one element and write a brief essay about how the authors develop that element in the four selections. Refer to what the texts say explicitly and to inferences that you draw from the texts. Be sure to cite evidence for your ideas. Be prepared to discuss your ideas with the class.

Selection 1
- characters: Gertrude Ederle, Ellie, her family, others aboard the boat
- setting: New York and the English Channel
- plot: a girl learns about overcoming obstacles from her hero
- theme: perseverance will help you overcome your obstacles

Selection 3
- characters: Mungo Park, Dr. Laidley
- setting: Great Britain and Africa
- plot: an explorer embarks on a treacherous journey
- theme: courage conquers fear

> Skillful development of character, setting, plot, and theme allows an author to entertain readers and give them something to think about.

Selection 2
- characters: Samuel, Silas
- setting: aboard the *Boston*
- plot: the narrator gains courage from the example of John Adams in the face of battle
- theme: heroes risk their lives to defend their principles

Selection 4
- characters: Theseus, Aegeus, Minos, Thetis, Ariadne
- setting: Crete and Athens; labyrinth
- plot: a hero battles a monster
- theme: true heroes care more about others than about themselves

Return to the Essential Question

How do authors use literary details to create text?

In small groups or as a class, discuss the Essential Question. Think about what you have learned about drawing inferences, determining themes, and analyzing literary elements in a text. Use evidence from the four texts in this unit to answer the question.

42 **Unit 1** ■ Reading Literature: Key Ideas and Details

Assess and Respond (pages 39–42)

If	Then
Students scored 0–10 points, they are **Developing** their understanding of unit skills…	Provide students with reading support and more extensive modeling and practice of skills.
Students scored 11–17 points, they are **Improving** their understanding of unit skills…	Review students' scores to pinpoint skills that students need more help with, and offer targeted instruction.
Students scored 18–24 points, they are **Proficient** in their understanding of unit skills…	Have these students move on. They are ready for the formal assessment at the end of the unit.

LANGUAGE

Greek and Latin Affixes

Guided Instruction Knowing common Greek and Latin affixes, or word parts that can be added onto a word root, can help you determine the meaning of unfamiliar words. You can define a word based on its affix.

Affix	Origin	Meaning
ab-	Latin	away / not
ante-	Latin	before / above
anti-	Greek	opposing
con- / com-	Latin	together / with
intra-	Latin	within
-ive	Latin	with a tendency to
-ize	Greek	to become
-(i)ous	Latin	full of
pre-	Latin	before
pro-	Latin	tending toward
syn- / sym-	Greek	together / with

Examples:

- *antidote* (Greek: dote comes from a root meaning "something given" + anti- = "something given [to be] against something")
  . . . I have an **antidote** for your problem, Theseus.
- *massive* (Latin: mass is "size" or "weight" + -ive = "with a tendency to have weight or size")
  Theseus felt the Minotaur's **massive** arms grab his legs . . .

Guided Practice Find and write the words from paragraphs 32 and 33 of "Theseus and the Minotaur" that match these definitions.

1. full of danger ___dangerous___

2. with a tendency to deceive ___deceptive___

3. people who travel together ___companions___

4. was ready beforehand ___prepared___

Independent Practice Here are other words formed with Greek and Latin affixes. On separate paper, define and write a sentence for each word.

abnormal   antedate   idolize   intramural   prediction

Unit 1 ■ Reading Literature: Key Ideas and Details   **43**

Guided Instruction

Have students review the Guided Instruction on page 43. Help them understand that affixes are word parts that, when added to the beginning or the end of a word root, often change the word's meaning. By familiarizing themselves with Greek and Latin affixes, students can figure out the meaning of unknown words by breaking the words down into individual parts.

Guided Practice

Have students use the information in the chart as well as context clues from "Theseus and the Minotaur" to determine the word that correctly completes each practice sentence.

Independent Practice

Have students work alone or in small groups to craft sentences using words with Greek and Latin affixes. Remind students to refer to the affixes chart, as needed.

Apply to Reading

Have students work in groups to identify additional selection words that contain Greek and Latin affixes. They might identify *abusing* (page 36), *captive* (page 36), and *comfort* (page 38).

Support English Language Learners

Assist English language learners in their understanding of affixes by having them study the words in the affix chart on page 43. Students who speak Latinate languages should be familiar with some of the affixes. However, many English language learners will need additional support with some affix types. Help students find words in everyday writing, such as *protect*, *emphasize*, and *preadolescent*, that will help them better understand how affixes relate to root words. Have students work with partners to define these words and then use them in exemplar sentences.

Unit Summary

In this unit, students have read realistic fiction, historical fiction, a multi-act play, and a myth. They have learned about courageous actions taken by Gertrude Ederle, John Adams, Mungo Park, and Theseus. Students have learned to draw inferences, analyze themes, summarize texts, and analyze the literary elements of setting, plot, and character. They have also practiced working with Greek and Latin affixes to determine word meanings. Students should now be ready to take this unit review.

Introduce the Review

Explain to students that they will read two related passages that continue the theme of "courageous actions." Instruct students to read the passages carefully and return to them as needed while they answer questions 1–10 on pages 45–46.

Answer Explanations (pages 45–46)

Scoring: When scoring students' work, assign one point for each multiple-choice question and two points for each short-answer question, for a total of 20 points.

1A. Students should use evidence from paragraph 1 to infer that the drummer is "anxious about" his impending duties.

1B. Once students identify that the drummer is anxious, they can select the evidence that shows his state of mind.

UNIT 1 REVIEW

Read the following realistic fiction texts that include implied ideas, central themes, and interactions of story elements. Then answer the questions on pages 45 and 46.

The Drummer's Courage

1 Musket fire shatters the day around me as I stand at attention, my drum in position. The cadences I played yesterday, the ones I know perfectly, seem to have disappeared from my mind! I cannot remember even the call forward! Our unit has received notice that the Redcoats are heading this way. The commander has made it very clear that I am to be ready to move at a moment's notice and that I must know the cadences to lead and rally the troops.

2 I look around at the men getting ready for battle. Certainly, we are not so well portioned as the British, as we have neither fancy uniforms nor abundant supplies. Our winters have been hard, and we have struggled against little food and abundant sickness. Nevertheless, we soldier on.

3 Suddenly, a hush sweeps over the chaotic encampment. I look around for the source of the disturbance and see one of our sentinels riding in at breakneck speed. He is waving his arm and frantically shouting, "The Redcoats are on their way! They will arrive within the next quarter-hour!"

4 The encampment is enveloped in a wall of sound, but this time with a purpose. Men gather their muskets and ready their bayonets. I watch the soldiers around me, so willing to die for what they believe is right, and suddenly everything comes back into focus. I pick up my drum, and the rally cadence falls naturally from my fingers. We are going into battle, and I am ready.

The Story of Hua Mulan

1 Hua Mulan was a courageous young woman who, when the time came to fight for her family, answered it without hesitation. Hua Mulan lived in ancient China in a time when each family was expected to provide a son to fight in the Emperor's armies. If the family had no son, then the father, as head of the household, would have to serve.

2 Hua Mulan had no brothers who could serve. When the Emperor's forces demanded a son from Hua Mulan's parents, she knew that her father would have to fight.

3 Hua Mulan's father had trained her in the weapons and skills necessary for battle. So, to protect her father's life and honor, Hua Mulan disguised herself as a man and enlisted in the Emperor's army.

4 Because of her skill in battle, Hua Mulan's true identity was never discovered. For twelve years, she fought for the Emperor. For twelve years, she was promoted and honored for her skill. When her time in the army was over, Hua Mulan chose not to demand accolades or reveal the truth. Instead, she quietly returned home to her family—the silent and courageous hero.

Self-Assessment: Progress Check

Have students return to the Progress Check on page 9 of their book. Have students answer the Progress Check questions again, this time marking the "After Unit 1" boxes. Have students respond to the questions to determine how much progress they have made during the unit.

Then have students meet with partners to discuss what they have learned during the unit. Have students go through each Progress Check question with their partner, offering information about which selections and activities covered the various skills.

UNIT 1 REVIEW

Circle the letter next to the best answer choice.

1A. What can you infer about the drummer's feelings at the beginning of "The Drummer's Courage"?

  a. He feels well prepared for battle.

  b. He is anxious about his duties.

  c. He does not want to be the drummer.

  d. He is excited to march with the troops.

1B. Which comment from "The Drummer's Courage" supports the answer to Part A?

  a. "Nevertheless, we soldier on."

  b. " . . . the ones I know perfectly, seem to have disappeared from my mind!"

  c. " . . . is enveloped in a wall of sound, but this time with a purpose."

  d. "We are going into battle, and I am ready."

2A. Which of these is NOT a theme of "The Story of Hua Mulan"?

  a. Women can fight in battle as well as men can.

  b. You should put your family above yourself.

  c. Those in power are always right.

  d. Some of the greatest heroes are the quietest.

2B. What information from the text supports the answer in Part A?

  a. Hua Mulan violates the Emperor's law to protect her father.

  b. Hua Mulan protests against the Emperor's treatment of women.

  c. Hua Mulan is not a very good soldier.

  d. None of the above.

3A. Which words best describe the character of the drummer in "The Drummer's Courage"?

  a. lazy, but optimistic

  b. loyal and determined

  c. confused and depressed

  d. unwilling to work hard

3B. Which phrase from the text supports the answer to Part A?

  a. "I look around for the source of the disturbance . . . "

  b. "I watch the soldiers around me, so willing to die for what they believe is right."

  c. "I pick up my drum, and the rally cadence falls naturally from my fingers."

  d. "The commander has made it very clear that I am to be ready to move at a moment's notice . . . "

4A. The setting of "The Drummer's Courage" is

  a. a Civil War battlefield.

  b. a World War II battlefield.

  c. a Revolutionary War battlefield.

  d. a World War I battlefield.

4B. What evidence from "The Drummer's Courage" supports the answer to Part A?

  a. The narrator describes the use of muskets and bayonets.

  b. A sentinel is riding a horse to break news.

  c. The narrator refers to "Redcoats" and "the British."

  d. All of the above.

Unit 1 ■ Reading Literature: Key Ideas and Details **45**

Answer Explanations (pages 45–46)

2A. Only choice C is not a theme supported by the events and details in the story.

2B. Hua Mulan's actions in breaking the Emperor's law show her belief that the law was unfair.

3A. Based on the drummer's thoughts and actions, choice B is the correct answer.

3B. Choice C illustrates the drummer's determination to fulfill his duty despite the unnerving circumstances.

4A. The text refers to "Redcoats" and "British," suggesting a battle during the Revolutionary War.

4B. All three examples illustrate the setting of the story; therefore, "All of the above" is correct.

5A. A possible theme of the story is that a young woman is capable of bravery and honor. Choice A states a detail that supports this theme.

5B. Choice C states evidence from the text that supports the theme.

6A. The affix -com- in the word commander means "together" or "with."

6B. Choice B is the definition that suggests the idea of bringing things or people together.

Test-Taking Tips

Explain to students that the two parts of the questions that appear on pages 45–46 and elsewhere in the unit are related. In each case, part A asks a question about a text, and part B asks students to identify text evidence that supports the answer they gave in part A. If students are struggling to answer the paired questions, have them read both questions before answering either. Advise students to work backward, looking for the statement in part A that is supported by the text evidence in part B.

Answer Explanations

Item 7 Rubric

2	Student tells character traits and how they relate to the plot.
1	Student includes information about character traits, not plot.
0	Student does not include information about the character or the plot.

Item 8 Rubric

2	Student includes a brief but thorough summary of the events in the text.
1	Student does not cover all of the key details needed to accurately summarize the text.
0	Student does not provide any summary of the text.

Item 9 Rubric

2	Student draws appropriate inferences about the text and provides supporting text evidence.
1	Student draws appropriate inferences about the text but does not provide supporting evidence.
0	Student does not provide inferences about the text.

Item 10 Rubric

2	Student compares and contrasts the characters with supporting text evidence.
1	Student compares and contrasts characters without giving textual evidence.
0	Student does not compare and contrast characters.

UNIT 1 REVIEW

5A. Which detail helps communicate the theme of "The Story of Hua Mulan"?

- **a.** Hua Mulan takes her father's place. *(selected)*
- **b.** Hua Mulan has no brothers.
- **c.** Hua Mulan refuses all accolades.
- **d.** Hua Mulan has been trained in weapons.

5B. Which statement from the text best supports the main theme, as determined in Part A?

- **a.** "Hua Mulan was a courageous young woman"
- **b.** "For twelve years, she fought for the Emperor."
- **c.** "So, to protect her father's life and honor, Hua Mulan disguised herself as a man" *(selected)*
- **d.** "the father . . . would have to serve."

6A. What is the meaning of the affix in the word *commander* from "The Drummer's Courage"?

- **a.** before / above
- **b.** together / with *(selected)*
- **c.** away / not
- **d.** full of

6B. Based on your answer in Part A, what is the best definition of the word *commander* in the text?

- **a.** someone in charge of an activity
- **b.** one who brings soldiers together *(selected)*
- **c.** the head of the army
- **d.** a high-ranking soldier

7. How does Hua Mulan's character shape the plot of "The Story of Hua Mulan"?

Sample answer: She is a strong character whose main traits include a sense of duty to her family, great skill, and humility. These character traits drive her to take her father's place in the war and succeed while never disclosing her identity.

8. Write a brief paragraph summarizing the "The Story of Hua Mulan."

Sample answer: Hua Mulan's father is ordered to join the Emperor's army because he has no son. He is too old to fight, so she takes his place by dressing as a man. She not only saves her father but also has great military success.

9. What inference can you draw about the treatment of women in ancient China, based on evidence from "The Story of Hua Mulan"?

Sample answer: Women in ancient China were not considered equal to men. Only men were allowed to join the army. Those in power did not believe that women could be successful as soldiers.

10. How are the drummer and Hua Mulan alike? How do they differ?

Sample answer: Hua Mulan and the drummer are both willing to fight for their beliefs. Both are called to battle at a young age. They differ in that the drummer is accepted into the army, but Hua Mulan has to disguise herself as a man to fight.

Analyze Student Scores

16–20 pts Strong	Student has successfully learned and applied the skills in this unit. Review any errors with the student, and explain them if necessary.
10–15 pts Progressing	Student is struggling with one or more of the skills in this unit. Identify the specific skills that are problematic to target additional instruction.
0–9 pts Emerging	Student is having trouble understanding most of the skills in this unit. Student may need to work through the unit again with a higher level of individual support.

Introducing UNIT **2**

In this unit about people who take courageous actions, you will learn how to write a nonfictional narrative. A nonfictional narrative presents a real event or experience in the form of a story. Even though the event or experience actually happened, the text reads like a short story or novel. As a result, the narrative shares some literary elements with fiction, including characters, dialogue, and descriptive details.

As you prepare to write a nonfictional narrative, do some research to make sure that your details are accurate. Then, as you write, create a sequence of events that unfolds naturally. Establish a point of view. Develop the events and engage readers by creating interesting characters and using effective pacing. Include transition words and phrases to connect events or to indicate a change in the story's setting. Use precise words and sensory language to describe events and experiences. Finally, provide a strong conclusion that wraps up the story in an interesting way and leaves readers with a final thought.

Progress Check Can I?

Before Unit 2 / **After Unit 2**

- [ ] Engage readers by introducing interesting characters and establishing a point of view. [ ]
- [ ] Base a narrative on factual evidence that I have researched. [ ]
- [ ] Organize a sequence of plot events. [ ]
- [ ] Use dialogue, pacing, and description to develop a narrative. [ ]
- [ ] Connect details by using transition words or phrases. [ ]
- [ ] Use precise words and phrases and effective sensory language. [ ]
- [ ] Provide a satisfying conclusion to a narrative. [ ]
- [ ] Identify and use various kinds of phrases and clauses. [ ]
- [ ] Use word relationships to learn new words. [ ]

Unit 2 ■ Text Types and Purposes: Write Nonfictional Narratives

Student Page 47

HOME ✦ CONNECT...

The Home Connect feature is a way to keep parents or other adult family members apprised of what their children are learning. The key learning objectives are listed, and some ideas for related activities and discussions are included.

Explain to students that they can share the Home Connect page with their parents or other adult family members in their home. Let students know how much time the class will be spending on this unit so they can plan their time accordingly at home.

Encourage students and their parents to share their experiences using the suggestions on the Home Connect page and the Home Connect activities at **sadlierconnect.com**. You may wish to make a place to post some of this work.

Progress Check

The Progress Check is a self-assessment feature that students can use to gauge their own progress. Before students begin work on Unit 2, have them check the boxes next to any item that they feel they can do well. Explain that it is fine if they don't check any of the boxes. Tell them that they will have an opportunity to learn about and practice all of these items while studying the unit. Let them know that near the end of the unit they will have a chance to reconsider how well they can do each item on this list.

Before they begin their Unit 2 Review (see page 59 of this guide), you will be prompted to have students revisit this page. You can use this information to work with students on any items they don't understand before they tackle the Review.

HOME ✦ CONNECT...

In this unit, your child will learn to **write a nonfictional narrative**. This type of writing presents a real event or experience, but it is written like a fictional story, with **characters, dialogue, description,** and **action**. A nonfictional narrative also includes **precise language** and **sensory language** that make the story come to life for readers. Help your child develop a stronger grasp of this kind of writing by identifying nonfictional narratives in print or online. Discuss the stories the writers tell, including the **research** that the writer probably did, the way the narratives are structured, and the kinds of details that are included.

Do a little research on your own, if needed, and then tell your child a story about a real event from history that will be familiar to him or her. Tell the story with the events in proper **sequence**. Try to include **dialogue** and **description** to make the story come to life. In addition, give your narrative a strong **conclusion** that provides a final thought about the true-life event. Have your child respond by telling you a story about an event that he or she has learned about at school.

 On the Go: As you walk through your neighborhood, talk about courageous actions in everyday life—for example, someone putting out a kitchen fire or confronting a bully. Choose an action that really happened; then work together to research the event (perhaps through an interview). Create a flow chart that shows the step-by-step order of events. Discuss how you could use this chart to write a nonfictional narrative about the courageous action.

48 **Unit 2** ■ Text Types and Purposes: Write Nonfictional Narratives

IN THIS UNIT, YOUR CHILD WILL...

- Learn how to write a narrative about a real event, using descriptive details and a clear sequence.
- Establish a point of view and organize a sequence of events that unfolds naturally.
- Use dialogue, pacing, and description to develop a narrative.
- Use transitions to show a sequence of events or a shift in setting.
- Use precise words and sensory language to describe action and convey experiences.
- Provide a conclusion that wraps up the narrative in a satisfying way.
- Identify and use various kinds of phrases and clauses.
- Analyze and work with synonyms, antonyms, and analogies.

WAYS TO HELP YOUR CHILD

Have your child practice presenting events in a logical sequence. For example, you might ask, "What happened first? Next? After that? At the end?" Help your child record and review the answers, deciding which are most important to include and how to add lively details to them. Encourage your child to write and share a nonfictional narrative about the event.

ONLINE
For more Home Connect activities, continue online at sadlierconnect.com

Student Page 48

UNIT PLANNER

Theme: Courageous Actions	Focus
WRITING MODEL *pp. 50–52*	*To the Top of the World*
WRITING ACTIVITY *p. 53*	**ORGANIZATIONAL STRUCTURE:** Graphic Organizer
LANGUAGE MINI-LESSONS *pp. 54–57*	• Function of Phrases and Clauses • Word Relationships
SPEAKING AND LISTENING *p. 58*	Discuss the Essential Question
UNIT 2 REVIEW *pp. 59–60*	Writing Process Summary

Objective(s)

Write a nonfictional narrative, using appropriate techniques, descriptive details, and logical sequencing of events.

Introduce a nonfictional narrative by establishing a point of view, and develop it with narrative techniques, details, precise language, and transitions that show logical sequencing.

Understand types of phrases and clauses and how they function in sentences.

Use the relationships between words, such as synonyms, antonyms, and analogies, to analyze the meanings of the words in a text.

Engage in a well-informed, collaborative discussion with peers.

Unit Assessment

- Unit 2 Review *pp. 59–60*

Additional Assessment Options

- Performance Task 1 *pp. 311A–320*
  (ALSO ONLINE)
- Performance Task 2 *pp. 321A–330*
  (ALSO ONLINE)

Optional Purchase:

- iProgress Monitor (ONLINE)
- Progress Monitor Student Benchmark Assessment Booklet

(ONLINE) Digital Resources

- Home Connect Activities
- Additional Practice
- Teacher Resources
- iProgress Monitor (optional purchase)

Go to SadlierConnect.com to access your Digital Resources.

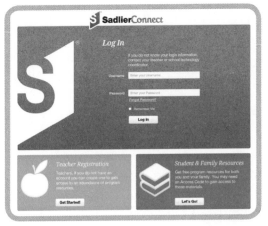

For more detailed instructions see page T3.

LEARNING PROGRESSIONS

In this unit, students will learn how to write a nonfictional narrative on a topic of personal interest. The writing skills that students learn in this unit build upon the skills they learned during the sixth grade. Likewise, the skills students learn this year will provide a foundation for the skills they will develop in the eighth grade.

Establishing a Context

- By the end of the sixth grade, students should be able to establish a context and introduce a narrator in order to create an engaging introduction to a nonfictional narrative.
- During the seventh and the eighth grades, students will learn to craft a nonfictional narrative with an established narrator, context, a point of view, and a logical sequence of events.

Using Narrative Techniques

- In the sixth and the seventh grades, students work to develop nonfictional narratives through the appropriate use of narrative techniques. These include using dialogue, vivid descriptions, and clear sequences of events with appropriate pacing.
- Eighth-grade students will continue to work with these techniques, adding the additional element of personal reflection to help develop settings, characters and events.

Creating a Conclusion

- Sixth graders will have learned to craft a conclusion that follows from the narrated experiences or events.
- As seventh and eighth graders, students will continue to work on creating appropriate conclusions, while further learning to reflect on real-life events, in order to create a final connection with the reader.

Using Language

- By the end of the sixth grade, students should be able to use precise language, descriptive details, and sensory language to convey experiences and events.
- Seventh and eighth graders will learn to use precise language, descriptive details, and sensory language to describe action sequences as well as experiences and events.

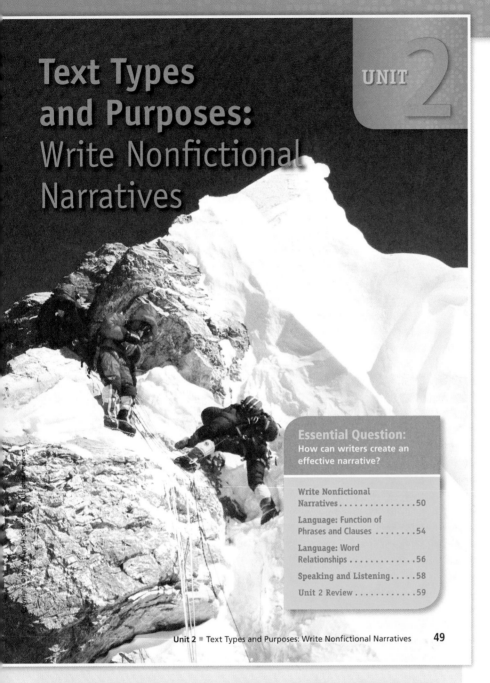

Text Types and Purposes:
Write Nonfictional Narratives

Essential Question:
How can writers create an effective narrative?

Writing Handbook

If students need extra practice with writing nonfictional narratives, refer them to the *Writing Handbook* on pages 299–310 in their Student Books. The *Writing Handbook* gives students detailed instruction on planning, drafting, revising, and editing their writing. They will also find tips on producing, publishing, and presenting their writing.

Essential Question:
How can writers create an effective narrative?

In this unit, students will learn to write a nonfictional narrative text by using appropriate narrative techniques to establish a point of view, develop characters, and sequence events logically. They will also learn to craft an effective conclusion.

Theme: Courageous Actions

Students will continue their exploration of the theme of "courageous actions" by learning about other individuals who ventured to new frontiers, as they read and analyze a nonfictional narrative model.

Curriculum Connection: Social Studies

Students will use what they have already learned about the bold actions of courageous men and women throughout history as they work on their own nonfictional narratives.

Connect Reading to Writing

Remind students that in Unit 1, they explored the lives of courageous historical figures through literature. Review how the authors of *Courage in the Water* (Student Book pages 12–19) and *The Courage of John Adams* (Student Book pages 20–27) created memorable characters, both real and imagined, through their use of dialogue, pacing, and descriptive language.

Write Nonfictional Narratives

OBJECTIVES

- **Write a nonfictional narrative, using appropriate techniques, descriptive details, and logical sequencing of events.**

- **Introduce a nonfictional narrative by establishing a point of view, and develop it with narrative techniques, details, precise language, and transitions that show logical sequencing.**

Introduce: Organizational Structure

Draw attention to the graphic organizer. Ask students to look for the key elements as you read the Student Model together.

Analyze a Student Model

TITLE: Tell students that the title should give information about the topic of the narrative.

CREATING AN ORGANIZATIONAL STRUCTURE

Riley used a graphic organizer like the one below to plan her nonfictional narrative.

> Title _____
> Characters: _____
> Setting: _____
> Sequence of Events: _____
>
> [_____]
>   ▼
> [_____]
>   ▼
> [_____]
>   ▼
> [_____]
>
> Conclusion: _____

TITLE

- Gives readers a clue about the real-life event in the narrative

POINT OF VIEW

- Tells the story from a particular perspective. Riley tells this story from the perspective of someone who is not part of the story. In other words, the story has a third-person point of view.

DESCRIPTIVE DETAILS

- Help readers envision the characters and the setting. For example, Riley writes that Edmund Hillary was "a tall, lanky beekeeper."

Read a Student Model

Riley is a student in Ms. Kim's seventh-grade Language Arts class. Ms. Kim gave Riley's class an assignment to write a nonfictional narrative about a real person who has done something courageous. Ms. Kim expects students to create well-researched, accurate narratives. The narratives should have a clear sequence of events and include descriptive details and sensory language. Think about a courageous person from history to write about in your own nonfictional narrative.

To the Top of the World

Staring at the face of the mountain, Edmund Hillary stood at the base of Mount Everest, about to tackle the greatest challenge of his life: reaching the world's highest peak. One of many slopes along the Himalayas, Everest straddles the border between Nepal and Tibet. At more than 29,000 feet, its summit is "the top of the world." Other people had attempted the climb, but no one had yet made it to the top.

It was the spring of 1953, and a team of mountain climbers was determined to reach the top of Everest. A member of the team, Edmund Hillary was a tall, lanky beekeeper from New Zealand. At 16, he had taken a school trip to a national park, had seen a 9,000-foot volcano, and had become an avid climber. Now, on May 29, he was about to climb the highest mountain of them all.

Genre: Nonfictional Narratives

Inform students that a nonfictional narrative combines elements of informative writing and literary fiction. In nonfictional narratives, writers tell the stories of actual events or people by using the techniques of fictional storytelling. They create engaging characters and use precise language and vivid details to draw the reader into a world of real events.

As students work on their own nonfictional narratives, guide them to look for ways to develop their characters, setting, and events. Have students ask themselves, "Does this read more like a story or a news article?" Help students aim to create a piece of nonfictional writing that is as engaging as a short story.

At 6:30 in the morning, Hillary and teammate Tenzing Norgay made preparations for a final climb. A villager from the valley below, Norgay often scaled very high altitudes. The two men were at a ridge camp near the top; the rest of the team was at base camp or smaller camps down the mountain. Hillary and Norgay gathered ice axes and ropes and added cans of oxygen to their packs. The air was very thin near the top of the mountain, so they needed to make sure they had enough oxygen to breathe. With all their equipment packed, they were ready. Now there was only one way to go: up!

The last 400 feet were very steep, which made the climb tough and grueling. Attached together with ropes, the two climbers took turns cutting steps into the side of the massive mountain. One wrong step and they would both fall. If that happened, a rescue team could never reach them, and they would die on the mountain. A fierce wind howled in their ears and clawed at their faces. The ice axes felt heavy in their hands as they hacked at the snow. Hillary had a lot of experience, so he knew how to find footholds. He was very fit after years of climbing, so he had a lot of energy and endurance. He also had a lot of courage, and he needed every bit of it to make such a difficult, dangerous climb.

Close to the top, Hillary and Norgay came to a smooth rockface. There were no bumps or ridges to use as footholds, and it would be impossible to cut steps into this 40-foot sheet of ice. At first, they were unsure how to continue.

TRANSITIONS

Use transition words and phrases to connect events or show a shift in the setting. In this paragraph, *At 6:30 in the morning* is a transition, shifting the setting to the moment of the climbers' departure.

Circle two transition phrases in the third paragraph on this page.

PACING

Riley uses description to slow down the pace of her narrative and action to speed it up. Varying your pace keeps your reader interested.

Underline the two sentences in the second paragraph where the pace slows down.

SENSORY LANGUAGE

Include details that show what the characters saw, heard, or felt. Here, *A fierce wind howled in their ears* shows what Hillary and Norgay heard as they climbed. Sensory language helps bring the characters' experiences to life for readers.

Box two other examples of sensory language in this paragraph.

Unit 2 ■ Text Types and Purposes: Write Nonfictional Narratives **51**

Analyze a Student Model

POINT OF VIEW: Make sure students understand the difference between first- and third-person points of view. Guide students in a discussion of how the narrative would be different if told from Hillary's or Norgay's point of view, instead of by a third-person narrator.

DESCRIPTIVE DETAILS: Point out how the writer uses descriptive details to make the narrative more vivid. Explain how descriptive details play an important role in making a nonfictional narrative read like a story.

TRANSITIONS: Explain that transitions make connections between ideas clearer, and help connect events and settings in a nonfictional narrative. Guide students to find the transition phrases in the first and last sentences in the final paragraph on page 51.

PACING: Help students visualize the concept of pacing by having them think about their favorite movie. Point out how the most exciting scenes tend to be short and full of action, while the most thoughtful or meaningful scenes tend to be slower. Explain that writers use words to create the same effect in nonfictional narratives. They use short sentences with action words to increase the pace, and long, descriptive sentences to slow the pace. Ask students to think about the pacing in the second paragraph on page 51. Guide them to look for longer, descriptive sentences at the end of the paragraph.

SENSORY LANGUAGE: Remind students that sensory language refers to descriptions that appeal to the five senses. Suggest that students look in the second paragraph on page 51 for descriptions that evoke how things looked, felt, or sounded.

Support English Language Learners

Writing nonfictional narratives can be an excellent way to engage English language learners. Students can select topics that connect with their cultural and historical backgrounds, choosing people and events with which they are already familiar.

As you guide students through the Student Model, have them use a highlighter to identify the examples of the literary techniques the writer uses—point of view, descriptive details, transitions, pacing, and sensory language. Assign each technique a different color, and then have students use that color throughout the model wherever an example appears.

Analyze a Student Model

DIALOGUE: Explain that dialogue is another tool writers use to make a nonfictional narrative read like a story. Dialogue helps the reader better understand what the characters are thinking. If necessary, remind students about how dialogue is formatted.

PRECISE LANGUAGE: Tell students that precise language involves replacing general, vague, or overused words or phrases with language that expresses a particular idea or evokes a specific image. Readers appreciate precise language because it is vivid and clear.

CONCLUSION/RESEARCH: Guide students to find the writer's final thought in the conclusion of the Student Model. Inform students that a conclusion in a nonfictional narrative should be based on facts but should also, as in a good story, express a larger truth about life or the world.

Evaluate a Writer's Work

Have students break into small groups to discuss how the Student Model presents information in a story-like way. Have each group identify one passage that exemplifies an element of nonfictional narratives. Have students share their ideas with the class.

Model: Organizational Structure

Ask students to think about how Riley could have used a graphic organizer to organize her characters, setting, and sequence of events. Post the graphic organizer template that appears on page 53. Point out that well-written nonfictional narratives have a strong organizational structure. Before students fill in the graphic organizer based on the Student Model, remind them to review the notes that appear in the margins of Riley's nonfictional narrative.

WRITE NONFICTIONAL NARRATIVES

DIALOGUE

Include dialogue to make the characters more realistic and to make the narrative read like a fictional story.

Underline the dialogue in paragraph 1 on this page.

PRECISE LANGUAGE

Use precise language that names exact details, such as *At 11:30 in the morning*. Also, use precise verbs to describe actions specifically, such as the verb *embraced*.

Put an asterisk next to three precise verbs in this paragraph.

CONCLUSION/RESEARCH

Riley wraps up her nonfictional narrative with a conclusion. It reflects on the real-life event and leaves readers with a final thought. Here, as throughout the narrative, Riley depends on facts that she has researched to keep her story accurate.

Underline the final thought in this narrative. Where might Riley have done research to find this information?

The two climbers surveyed the mountain, searching for some way to go forward. Then one of them spotted a small space packed with snow off to the right. Could they climb it? Would it hold their weight? "What do you think?" Norgay asked. "That will do," Hillary replied. Norgay drove his ice axe into the space to anchor Hillary, who wedged into the gap then forced himself up, pulling Norgay after him.

At 11:30 in the morning, they reached the peak, and the firm cone of snow was big enough for both climbers to stand on. Filled with joy and relief, they embraced each other. Gazing into the distance, they could see the snow-covered ridges of the Himalayas for a hundred miles in all directions. As Hillary snapped photographs with his trusty camera, Norgay waved flags that represented Britain, Nepal, India, and the United Nations.

However, they could stay for only about 15 minutes because they were low on oxygen. Turning to his teammate, Hillary said, "Let's go," and back down the mountain they went. News of their amazing achievement quickly spread around the world. Both Hillary and Norgay would become world famous as the men who had "conquered Everest." In the years to come, Hillary would make other expeditions to the Himalayas, but never again would he climb to "the top of the world."

Review: Analyzing Literary Elements

Remind students that in Unit 1, they learned to analyze texts to determine how the literary elements of setting, plot, and character interact. Explain to students that this skill also applies to nonfictional narratives, because the writer presents characters, settings, and events, just as he or she would in a story or novel. In order to analyze a nonfictional narrative, students must be able to identify the relationships among characters, events, and settings.

Have students discuss these elements as they appear in the Student Model. They should be able to identify the elements and then analyze how these elements interact in order to make the account read like a story.

Use this graphic organizer to plan a nonfictional narrative for the Unit 2 Review on page 59. Then write your first draft on a separate sheet of paper. Keep your point of view in mind. Remember to use description and dialogue as well as precise words and sensory language. In addition, think about which transition words and phrases might be helpful.

Title: _____

Characters: _____

Setting: _____

Sequence of Events: _____

```
┌─────────────────────────────────────────────┐
│                                             │
└─────────────────────────────────────────────┘
                      ↓
┌─────────────────────────────────────────────┐
│                                             │
└─────────────────────────────────────────────┘
                      ↓
┌─────────────────────────────────────────────┐
│                                             │
└─────────────────────────────────────────────┘
                      ↓
┌─────────────────────────────────────────────┐
│                                             │
└─────────────────────────────────────────────┘
                      ↓
┌─────────────────────────────────────────────┐
│                                             │
└─────────────────────────────────────────────┘
```

Conclusion: _____

_____

Unit 2 ■ Text Types and Purposes: Write Nonfictional Narratives   **53**

Create: Organizational Structure

Brainstorming

Writers write nonfictional narratives about events or people that interest them. As a class, brainstorm topics for a nonfictional narrative about a person who demonstrated great courage. Post the list for students to reference as they decide on a topic.

Planning

Students will use the graphic organizer on page 53 to plan their writing. They should first decide on characters, a setting, and a series of events. Remind students that they should do some research so that the details they include are accurate. They are using story-telling techniques to tell a true story.

Drafting a Nonfictional Narrative

Tell students to consult their graphic organizers as they write the first draft of their narratives on a separate sheet of paper. Be sure that students are presenting a well-researched topic and using literary elements to create a readable narrative.

Introduce the Writing Process

Remind students that good writing happens in stages. After prewriting and drafting, they will revise and edit their essays. For more on the writing process, see the *Writing Handbook* on page 299.

Assess and Respond
If students have difficulty outlining the sequence of events in their narratives,
Then have them create a time line that shows each event in the order it occurs. Tell them to transfer the information from the time line to the graphic organizer.

Extend Thinking: Analyzing Narratives

Help reinforce students' understanding of how the elements of a narrative work together by having them analyze the elements of a literary work. Have partners brainstorm narratives they have read, such as those in Unit 1 of their books. Allow students time to reread the work to identify and analyze the author's use of character, setting, and plot. Afterward, students should be able write a paragraph about the author's use of literary elements. Offer them this paragraph starter: *In the literary work _____, the author uses the literary elements of _____ and _____ to suggest or create _____*. Finally, ask students to give brief presentations of their findings to the rest of the class.

OBJECTIVE
Understand types of phrases and clauses and how they function in sentences.

Guided Instruction

Help students understand the five types of phrases and clauses, as explained on page 54 of the Student Book. Make sure students understand that phrases and clauses are groups of words that can act as a single part of speech in a sentence.

Guide students through each example sentence by explaining how it uses a specific type of phrase or clause. If necessary, review the different parts of speech and how they operate in a sentence.

Clarify the difference between dependent and independent clauses. Write the words *dependent* and *independent* on the board, and ask students to define them by giving real-world examples. Be sure to show students the connection between the words' meanings and how the clauses operate in a sentence.

If time allows, offer additional example sentences that use each type of phrase or clause, and ask students to identify the type of phrase or clause and its function.

LANGUAGE

Function of Phrases and Clauses

Guided Instruction A **phrase** is a group of words that function together as a single part of speech. A **clause** is a group of words that has both a subject and a predicate. Some clauses can also function as a single part of speech.

- A **noun phrase** can do anything a one-word noun can do. It can function as the subject of a sentence or as different kinds of objects.

  The mountain-climbing rope has a grappling hook. (subject, direct object)

  I gave my friend a book about the historic climb. (indirect object, object of a preposition)

- A **prepositional phrase** has a preposition and an object. It can function as an adjective or an adverb.

  We could barely see the stage from our seats in the last row. (adverb [modifies could see], adjective [modifies seats])

- A **verb phrase** can do anything a one-word verb can do. Verb phrases indicate certain times, or tenses, when actions or states of being happen.

  We have been excited about this speaker for some time. (state of being [present perfect])

  She will speak on the challenges of a Mount Everest climb. (action [future])

  Now everyone is watching her great slide presentation. (action [present progressive])

  Keiko would have come, but she is feeling sick today. (action [past conditional], state of being [present progressive])

- An **independent clause** can stand alone. It can be written as a separate sentence.

  Max talked to the speaker later, and he got her autograph.

- A **dependent clause** cannot stand alone. It cannot be written as a separate sentence, but it does have a function: it can function as a noun, an adjective, or an adverb. A dependent clause at the beginning of a sentence should be followed by a comma.

  After we get home, Max will tell us about their conversation. (adverb [modifies will tell])

  We will enjoy hearing whatever he tells us. (noun [direct object])

  Of all of us, he is the one who is most interested in Mount Everest. (adjective [modifies one])

54 Unit 2 ■ Text Types and Purposes: Write Nonfictional Narratives

Support English Language Learners

Help English language learners recognize sentence structure and the function of phrases and clauses by writing several of the example sentences from page 54 on the board. Ask student volunteers to go to the board to identify each sentence's phrases and clauses by underlining and labeling them. For example, for the sentence, *"Max talked to the speaker later, and he got her autograph,"* the student would identify "Max talked" and "he got her autograph" as independent clauses, and "to the speaker later" as a prepositional phrase.

Guided Practice Identify the kind of phrase or clause that is underlined in each sentence. If the phrase or clause functions as a part of speech, explain its function.

1. The soccer players <u>have been practicing</u> for three hours.

   verb phrase

2. During storms, my dog Comet always hides <u>under my bed</u>.

   prepositional phrase, adverb (modifies *hides*)

3. <u>Before Marisol performs</u>, she does several breathing exercises.

   dependent clause, adverb (modifies *does*)

4. Rachel and David played <u>that difficult piano duet</u> beautifully.

   noun phrase, direct object

5. Clouds are gathering, and <u>we probably will see rain soon</u>.

   independent clause

6. A man <u>in a blue plaid shirt</u> just joined the ticket line.

   prepositional phrase, adjective (modifies *man*)

7. <u>What we are having for dinner</u> is anyone's guess.

   dependent clause, noun (subject)

8. Shall we ride our bikes <u>on the city's new bike path</u>?

   prepositional phrase, adverb (modifies *Shall . . . ride*)

Independent Practice Write five original sentences. Three sentences should include a phrase, and the other two should include a dependent clause.
Answers will vary.

1. _____

2. _____

3. _____

4. _____

5. _____

OBJECTIVE
Understand types of phrases and clauses and how they function in sentences.

Guided Practice

Have students work alone or with partners to identify the type of phrase or clause underlined in each practice sentence. Then help students identify its function in the sentence. Remind students to refer back to the example sentences on page 54 if they have trouble identifying a group of words as a phrase or clause or determining its part of speech, or function, in the sentence.

Independent Practice

Once students are able to recognize and name the different types of phrases and clauses and their functions, they should be able to write sentences of their own. Ask students to write five original sentences, each using at least one phrase or clause. Tell students to underline and label the phrases or clauses in at least two of their sentences. Remind them to look at the examples in the practice items if they need models.

Assess and Respond

If students have trouble writing their own sentences using phrases and clauses for Independent Practice,

Then suggest that they write an example sentence from page 54 on their paper and then replace the underlined sections with new words. Challenge students to make the sentences as logical—or as silly—as possible.

Differentiate Instruction

If students are struggling with understanding phrase and clause functions, have them create cue cards for each type. Have students cut a sheet of cardstock in half, or use large-sized note cards. Students should then divide each card into quadrants. In the first quadrant, have the student write the name of the phrase or clause type. In the second quadrant, tell students to write the definition and function of the phrase or clause. In the third quadrant, students should copy one of the example sentences from page 54. In the final quadrant, ask students to write an original example sentence. Allow students to refer to the cards each time they work with phrases or clauses throughout the text.

OBJECTIVE

Use the relationships between words, such as synonyms, antonyms, and analogies, to analyze the meanings of the words in a text.

Guided Instruction

To make sure that students understand the difference between synonyms and antonyms, review the explanation of each type of word relationship on page 56. Also remind students look for cueing words to help determine word relationships. For example:

- Synonyms are often set off by words such as *or*, *like*, and *and*. The use of the word *or* usually signals that a definition or restatement of the word is to follow.

- Antonyms are often signaled by words that suggest contrast, such as *although*, *but*, *not*, *instead*, and *however*.

Tell students that analogies, or word equations, are not used in writing. They are more like word games or puzzles involving the relationships between words. Students are more likely to encounter analogies in test situations than in their regular reading. Their understanding of the relationships between synonyms and antonyms can help them solve some analogies.

LANGUAGE

Word Relationships

Guided Instruction **Synonyms**, **antonyms**, and **analogies** all reveal word relationships. Understanding word relationships can help readers learn new words or better understand familiar words.

- **Synonyms** are words that have the same meaning or a similar meaning. Synonyms must be the same part of speech, such as two nouns or two adjectives.

  After the game, my sneakers were <u>caked</u>, or <u>covered</u>, with dirt.

  As seen from the moon, Earth looks <u>fragile</u> and <u>delicate</u>.

  That <u>gown</u> is an especially formal <u>dress</u>.

- **Antonyms** are words with opposite meanings. Antonyms must be the same part of speech. Words and phrases such as *not*, *but*, and *instead of* sometimes signal that antonyms appear in a sentence.

  We thought the hike would be <u>leisurely</u>, but it was <u>grueling</u>.

  Instead of taking the <u>long</u> route, we went the <u>short</u> way home.

  Although the broken glass seemed like a <u>major</u> clue, it turned out to be <u>unimportant</u>.

- An **analogy** is a kind of word equation based on the relationship between pairs of words. To understand an analogy you first identify the relationship between the first pair of words; then you apply that relationship to the second pair of words. Example:

  PLEASED : DELIGHTED :: hesitant : reticent

  Read this as "*Pleased* is to *delighted* as *hesitant* is to *reticent*." When you identify that the words *pleased* and *delighted* are synonyms, you will know that the words *hesitant* and *reticent* must also be synonyms. You can tell this even if you are not sure what *reticent* means. Here is another example:

  STRONG : WEAK :: calm : boisterous

  Read this as "*Strong* is to *weak* as *calm* is to *boisterous*." When you identify that the words *strong* and *weak* are antonyms, you then know that the words *calm* and *boisterous* must be another pair of antonyms.

  Sometimes you may be presented with an analogy that is missing a part, as in

  TINY : ENORMOUS :: wild : _____

  To solve this analogy you first identify that *tiny* and *enormous* are antonyms. Then look for a word that is the antonym of *wild*, such as *tame*. *Tame* completes the analogy.

Differentiate Instruction

If students are having difficulty understanding how synonyms and antonyms work, have them analyze an example sentence. First, have students write the sentence on a sheet of paper exactly as it appears on the page. Ask students to circle or highlight the first underlined word in the sentence. Then in the margin, students should write at least one synonym and one antonym for the word, using a dictionary or thesaurus as necessary. Next, help students identify the cueing word or words in the sentence to determine the relationship. Finally, have students replace the first underlined word in the sentence with one of their synonyms or antonyms. Students should see that a synonym does not dramatically alter the meaning of the sentence but an antonym does.

Guided Practice Circle the synonyms or antonyms in each sentence. On the line, write whether the words are synonyms or antonyms.

1. The (procession) or (parade) started on Elm Street. _____synonyms_____

2. Shawn exercises in the (evening) but I prefer a (morning) routine. _____antonyms_____

3. Although people call her a (nervous) person, I think she is (easygoing). _____antonyms_____

4. While I (watched) a science program, my brother (viewed) a movie. _____synonyms_____

5. That (green) banana looks even less appetizing than that (unripe) peach.
_____synonyms_____

6. Grandpa always says, "One person's (trash) is another person's (treasure)."
_____antonyms_____

Independent Practice Fill in the blank in each sentence with a synonym or antonym for the underlined word. Answers will vary.

1. In sewing class, Karina made an outfit that looked simple but was actually very _____complicated_____ .

2. The science presentation left Malcolm feeling _____confused_____ and bewildered.

3. That tasty pineapple was very _____delicious_____!

4. The documentary we watched about Russian history was _____exciting_____ —not boring at all!

Solve the analogies below. Then create two analogies of your own. One should include pairs of synonyms, while the other should include pairs of antonyms.

5. ENTHUSIASTIC : EAGER :: kind : _____nice_____

6. GREEDY : GENEROUS :: rude : _____polite_____

7. _____SMART_____ : _____INTELLIGENT_____ :: _____happy_____ : _____joyful_____

8. _____HIGH_____ : _____LOW_____ :: _____easy_____ : _____difficult_____

OBJECTIVE
Use the relationships between words, such as synonyms, antonyms, and analogies, to analyze the meanings of the words in a text.

Guided Practice
Tell students to look for cueing words to help them identify the correct word relationship in each sentence. If necessary, remind students that the synonyms and antonyms are likely to be the same part of speech and that students can "test" to see if words are synonyms by swapping them out. If the sentence has the same meaning with the substituted word, then the words are synonyms.

Independent Practice
For items 1–4, students should look for cueing words to help determine if a synonym or antonym should be used. For items 5–8, remind students to look for the underlying relationship between the first pair of words, and to then apply that relationship to the second pair.

Assess and Respond

If students are having difficulty deciding if a sentence includes a synonym or an antonym,

Then help them create a chart of cueing words that will aid them in determining the correct word relationships.

Numbered Heads Together

Have students work together in teams of three or five to solve analogy "riddles." Tell students to number off, so that each student is assigned a number. Post an analogy that is missing the last part for the class, and then instruct the groups to "solve" the analogy. After a given time limit, call a number, and ask all students with that number to stand and complete the analogy. Recognize correct responses, and engage in a class discussion to help all students better understand the concept.

OBJECTIVE
Engage in a well-informed, collaborative discussion with peers.

Discuss the Essential Question

Copy and distribute the "Did I?" checklist available on **sadlierconnect.com**.

Leading the Class Discussion

1. Remind students to review the sequence of events in Riley's narrative.

2. Students should look at the writer's use of literary elements.

3. Have students scan for transitions.

SPEAKING AND LISTENING

Discuss the Essential Question

How can writers create an effective narrative?

Prepare for a class discussion about the Essential Question by responding to the questions below. Support your point of view with reasons and examples.

1. What is the sequence of events in Riley's nonfictional narrative?

At the ridge camp, Hillary and Norgay prepare to make the final climb. They start climbing, cutting steps into the side of the mountain. At a smooth rock face, they use a small space packed with snow to keep moving. Finally, they reach the top of the mountain and stay for 15 minutes. Then they head back down the mountain.

2. What literary elements did Riley include to bring the story to life?

She includes characters, dialogue, descriptive details, precise language, and sensory language.

3. How did Riley connect ideas and events in her narrative?

She included transition phrases, such as *close to the top*.

Use your notes to discuss the Essential Question in small groups or as a class. Use the rules for being a good speaker and a good listener in the checklist below.

Did I :

☐ Build on ideas expressed by others and express my own ideas clearly?

☐ Come to the discussion prepared and stay on the topic?

☐ Help define individual roles during discussions?

☐ Revise my own views when presented with new evidence or information?

☐ Distinguish claims that are supported by reasons and evidence from claims that are not?

☐ Present relevant claims and other ideas in a logical manner?

☐ Speak in an appropriate volume, pronounce words clearly, and use eye contact?

☐ Use formal English when appropriate?

58 Unit 2 ■ Text Types and Purposes: Write Nonfictional Narratives

---

Discussion Skills

Place students in groups and then assign each a Discuss the Essential Question question from page 58. Students should discuss it and then present their findings to the class. Remind students to follow the rules of collegial discussions and to ask for clarification, rephrasing, and examples from their peers.

Then have students give a brief class presentation based on their discussions. They should recap Riley's nonfictional narrative and use an informal visual aid, such as a chart of literary elements, a time line of events, or a word cloud of the sensory language. Students should use appropriate English in their presentations to the class.

UNIT 2 REVIEW

Read this draft introductory paragraph from a student nonfictional narrative, and answer the questions below.

> (1) The year was 1963, and Valentina Tereshkova was about to do what no woman had ever done before: travel into outer space. (2) She was a cosmonaut in the Soviet Union's space program, which was competing with the U.S. agency NASA in a "space race." (3) After Yuri Gagarin became the first person to travel into space in 1961, she determined, "I would love to do that," so she volunteered. (4) Valentina was not a pilot; she had made more than a hundred parachute jumps.

1. This narrative is told from the point of view of
   a. a Soviet official.
   b. an American official.
   c. an outside narrator.
   d. an American astronaut.

2. Which of the following would be effective sensory language for this paragraph?
   a. It was an historic time for the world.
   b. Her heart pounded with excitement.
   c. People around the world admired her.
   d. Both cosmonauts were very brave.

3. Which is an example of a precise verb from the text?
   a. was
   b. done
   c. became
   d. determined

4. Based on this introduction, which event would best fit in this narrative?
   a. Tereshkova's training
   b. NASA designing its spaceship
   c. the reaction of other astronauts
   d. Gagarin's flight into space

5. Based on this introduction, which detail would NOT fit in this narrative?
   a. a description of a rocket
   b. a description of a parachute
   c. a description of a spacesuit
   d. a description of the NASA offices

6. Which transition word or phrase would best fit in the middle of sentence 4?
   a. meanwhile,
   b. however,
   c. in addition,
   d. for example,

Unit 2 ■ Text Types and Purposes: Write Nonfictional Narratives   59

Introduce the Review

Explain to students that this review will give them an opportunity to apply the language and writing skills they have studied and practiced in this unit.

Language Skills Summary

Inform students that they will use what they have learned about the functions of phrases and clauses, and word relationships to enhance their writing.

- Have students list and describe the five types of phrases and clauses and write an example sentence for each.
- Have students explain what synonyms, antonyms, and analogies are. Ask them to identify a synonym and antonym for *cold*. Have them create an analogy that uses *cold*.

Self-Assessment: Progress Check

Have students revisit the Progress Check on page 47 and compare their answers now to the answers they gave before they started Unit 2.

Answer Explanations

Scoring: 5 points each for items 1–10; 50 points for the final essay.

1. The use of *she* and the objective tone indicate an outside narrator.

2. Students should select the answer choice that appeals to the senses.

3. Students should remember that precise language is specific.

4. Students should base their answer on the sequence of events in the text.

5. Students should base answers on the topic of the text.

6. Students should look for the transition that indicates differing ideas.

Test-Taking Tips

Give students the following reminders and tips to help with taking assessments that include reading passages:

1. Tell students to make sure they read the full text first, before attempting to answer any question.

2. Point out that sentences in the text are numbered. Remind students that these numbers will be often appear in the assessment questions.

3. Tell students that, if they are struggling, they should look closely at each answer choice, and eliminate those that are obviously wrong before narrowing down the other choices.

Answer Explanations

7. Students should choose two words with similar meanings.

8. Students should look for the use of prepositions.

9. Students should change the initial dependent clause into an independent clause.

Item 10 Rubric

2	**5 pts.** Student writes a conclusion that supports details in the text.
1	**2–3 pts.** Student writes a conclusion that is related to the text but does not support details in it.
0	**0 pts.** Student does not write a conclusion that follows from the text or supports its details.

Writing Process Summary

Remind students that planning can help their organization before drafting. Revising and editing improve drafting.

Planning and Drafting

Have students revisit their graphic organizer and draft (page 53). Have them check that the draft includes all items in the graphic organizer.

Nonfictional Narrative Rubric

4	**50 pts.** The text is a narrative with an introduction and point of view. It uses literary elements, precise language, and logical sequence. There are few editing errors.
3	**40 pts.** The text includes the key elements but has minor errors.
2	**30 pts.** The text is missing one or more key elements and contains minor editing errors.
1	**20 pts.** The text is unfinished and shows a lack of understanding of nonfictional narrative style.
0	**0 pts.** The assignment was not attempted.

UNIT 2 REVIEW

Read these next two paragraphs from the student nonfictional narrative, and answer the questions below.

> (1) Two years later, Valentina was ready to make the leap into space. (2) Dressed in an orange spacesuit, she strapped into her seat on board a space capsule or ship called the *Vostok 6*. (3) As the engines fired, roaring in her ears, she bravely declared, "Hey, sky! Take off your hat; I'm coming!" (4) The rocket lifted off and hurled the capsule into space.
>
> (5) Valentina spent three days in space, orbiting Earth. (6) As she circled the planet forty-eight times, she noted the amazing scene beneath her. (7) Finally, gripping the controls tightly to keep the capsule steady, she dropped out of orbit and headed back toward the planet's surface. (8) After reentering the atmosphere, she ejected from the falling capsule and parachuted to the ground. (9) The landing was bumpy and her face was bruised, but she made it back safely.

7. Circle two words in sentence 2 that are synonyms.

8. Write the phrase in sentence 4 that functions as an adverb. <u>into space</u> What kind of phrase is it, and what does it modify? <u>prepositional phrase, the word *hurled*</u>

9. Underline a dependent clause in sentence 6. Rewrite it as an independent clause. <u>She circled the planet forty-eight times.</u>

10. Write a concluding paragraph for this nonfictional narrative. <u>Sample answer: Returning to the Soviet Union after her adventure, Valentina Tereshkova received a huge welcome. More than fifty years after her journey into space, she still remembered what it was like to gaze upon Earth from orbit.</u>

Assignment: On a separate sheet of paper, provide a final draft of the nonfictional narrative you began on page 53. Use what you learned about phrases and clauses and about word relationships in the Language section of this unit. Think about how you and your classmates answered the Essential Question. Check your graphic organizer to make sure you presented events in a logical sequence. Be sure to use precise words, sensory language, and transitions where needed. End with a conclusion that provides readers with a final thought.

Digital Connection: Digital Publishing

Once students have completed their nonfictional narratives, they can use digital tools to publish their work. There are a variety of Web sites that allow students to publish their original works online. Teachers can create class Web pages that allow parents and other students access to the digital publications.

Before attempting any type of digital publishing, all student work should be double-checked to ensure that sources are cited appropriately and that all material not cited is solely the work of the student.

Introducing UNIT 3

In this unit about exploring new frontiers, you will learn about the key ideas and details of informational text. The purpose of informational text is to communicate ideas. The authors of these texts communicate their key ideas—also known as central ideas—and support them with details. Some of these central ideas are directly stated. Others are hinted at, and you will have to draw inferences to find them. Finally, the author will explain how the people, events, and ideas described in the text interact with and influence each other.

Informational text can take different forms, including speeches, interviews, feature articles, and policy statements. In this unit, you will find examples of each. Some informational texts are related to subjects you study in school, such as history and science. Scientific texts can include technical information that can be very specific and detailed. Summarizing an informational text is a good way to check your understanding.

 Progress Check *Can I?*

Before Unit 3 / After Unit 3

- [ ] Draw inferences from a text. [ ]
- [ ] Determine the central ideas of a text. [ ]
- [ ] Summarize a text. [ ]
- [ ] Analyze the relationships among people, events, and ideas in a text. [ ]
- [ ] Describe the conclusions drawn by a text's author. [ ]
- [ ] Analyze and cite evidence from technical texts. [ ]
- [ ] Use Greek and Latin roots to determine word meanings. [ ]

Unit 3 ■ Reading Informational Text: Key Ideas and Details

Student Page 61

Progress Check

The Progress Check is a self-assessment feature that students can use to gauge their own progress. Before students begin work on Unit 3, have them check the boxes next to any item that they feel they can do well. Explain that it is fine if they don't check any of the boxes. Tell them that they will have an opportunity to learn about and practice all of these items while studying the unit. Let them know that near the end of the unit they will have a chance to reconsider how well they can do each item on this list.

Before they begin their Unit 3 Review (see page 96 of this guide), you will be prompted to have students revisit this page. You can use this information to work with students on any items they don't understand before they tackle the Review.

HOME ◆ CONNECT...

The Home Connect feature is a way to keep parents or other adult family members apprised of what their children are learning. The key learning objectives are listed, and some ideas for related activities and discussions are included.

Explain to students that they can share the Home Connect page with their parents or other adult family members in their home. Let students know how much time the class will be spending on this unit so they can plan their time accordingly at home.

Encourage students and their parents to share their experiences using the suggestions on the Home Connect page and the Home Connect activities at **sadlierconnect.com**. You may wish to make a place to post some of this work.

HOME ◆ CONNECT...

The purpose of an informational text is to communicate information. However, authors do not always state their ideas directly. Sometimes authors expect the reader to **draw inferences** to pick up on implied ideas. Help your child by showing him or her how to connect the dots in everyday conversations to find unstated messages.

Not all of the information included by authors in informational texts is of equal importance. Students will practice finding the **central ideas of a text**. Help your child practice this skill by having him or her create new titles or headlines for news articles, using the fewest words possible to express the key information.

Another way authors communicate is by setting up **interactions between people and events**. Readers need to consider how people can affect events by making choices, and how events can affect people by creating opportunities or obstacles. You can help your child by talking about people in history or players in a sporting event. Talk about how a different person might respond to the same events, or how different events might change a person.

Activity: Create a fact file on a "frontier" that is not well explored: the ocean floor, the interior of the earth, deep space, or even the human brain. With your child, do a search on the Internet for information and images. See if you can design an experiment that would add new knowledge about this area.

IN THIS UNIT, YOUR CHILD WILL . . .

- Read four informational selections, including a speech, an interview, a feature article, and a policy statement.
- Learn new academic and content-area vocabulary.
- Draw inferences by analyzing implied ideas.
- Identify ideas that are central to the meaning of the text.
- Summarize texts and identify conclusions.
- Analyze interactions among people, events, and ideas in a text.
- Use Greek and Latin roots to determine word meanings.
- Compare and contrast ideas across four selections on the theme of new frontiers.

WAYS TO HELP YOUR CHILD

Help your child learn to identify important information. In conversations, ask your child to summarize what the other person has said. See if he or she can restate the important ideas and pick up on ideas that are implied. If your child misses important stated or implied ideas, ask questions that will help him or her notice these points.

ONLINE
For more Home Connect activities, continue online at sadlierconnect.com

62   Unit 3 ■ Reading Informational Text: Key Ideas and Details

Student Page 62

UNIT PLANNER

Theme: New Frontiers	Focus
DRAWING INFERENCES *pp. 64–71*	*A Man on the Moon* **GENRE:** Explanatory Text with Speech **LEXILE®:** 1060L **WORDS TO KNOW:** emerged, democracy, satellite, reeling, instrument, orbit, enterprise, exploit, affirmatively, tense, communism, brink, module, meteoroid, dwindling, joint, stockpiling
DETERMINING CENTRAL IDEAS *pp. 72–79*	*Barbara Morgan, Teacher and Astronaut* **GENRE:** Interview **LEXILE®:** 1080L **WORDS TO KNOW:** fateful, assumed, tragedy, solar array, stowage, flight deck, seize, tribulation, documented, long-standing, chemist, decade, singular, perceived, inherent, propelled, telescope, momentary, sustenance
ANALYZING TEXTS *pp. 80–87*	*Destination Mars* **GENRE:** Feature Article **LEXILE®:** 1060L **WORDS TO KNOW:** compound, plummet, dissipate, circumference, mass, isolated, genre, invigorating, marshal, philanthropist, suborbital, cosmic, disorder, impaired, entrepreneur, scout, refined, artifact, transmitted, deposit, sedimentary
CLOSE READING *pp. 88–93*	*Our National Space Policy* **GENRE:** Explanatory Text and Policy Statement **LEXILE®:** 1130L
CONNECT ACROSS TEXTS *p. 94*	Support a Claim
LANGUAGE *p. 95*	Greek and Latin Roots
UNIT 3 REVIEW *pp. 96–98*	*Going Up: Space Elevator* *Going Nowhere: Space Elevator* **GENRE:** Explanatory Text **LEXILE®:** 990L

Essential Question: How can readers find and analyze central ideas in a text?

UNIT 3

Objective(s)

Use textual evidence to support an analysis of both explicit and inferred information from the text.

Identify two or more ideas that are central to the text and analyze how the author develops them. Summarize the text.

Analyze the relationships between ideas, people, and events in a text.

- Use textual evidence to support an analysis of both explicit and inferred information from the text.
- Identify two or more ideas that are central to the text and analyze how the author develops them. Summarize the text.
- Analyze the relationships between ideas, people, and events in a text.

Use Greek and Latin roots to determine word meanings.

Unit Assessment

- Unit 3 Review *pp. 96–98*
- Unit 3 Performance Task (ONLINE)

Additional Assessment Options

- Performance Task 1 *pp. 311A–320*
  (ALSO ONLINE)
- Performance Task 2 *pp. 321A–330*
  (ALSO ONLINE)

Optional Purchase:
- iProgress Monitor (ONLINE)
- Progress Monitor Student Benchmark Assessment Booklet

(ONLINE) Digital Resources

- Home Connect Activities
- Unit Performance Task
- Additional Practice
- Full-Length Reading Selections
- Teacher Resources
- iProgress Monitor (optional purchase)

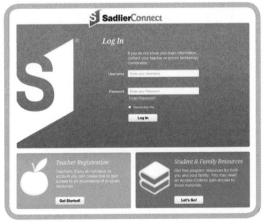

Go to SadlierConnect.com to access your Digital Resources.

For more detailed instructions see page T3.

LEARNING PROGRESSIONS

In this unit, students will learn how the key ideas and details of an informational text contribute to their understanding as they read. The skills that students learn in this unit build upon the skills they learned during the sixth grade. Likewise, the skills students learn this year will provide a foundation for the skills they will develop in the eighth grade.

Drawing Inferences

- Proficient sixth graders will be able to analyze a text to find stated and unstated ideas, and cite textual evidence in support of this analysis.

- In the seventh grade, students will learn to identify and cite multiple pieces of evidence in support of an analysis of stated and inferred ideas.

- In the eighth grade, students will extend this skill by learning to evaluate textual evidence and choose the best support for an analysis of a text's stated or inferred ideas.

Determining Central Ideas

- Sixth-grade students should be able to determine a central idea of a text based on the details provided by the author, and provide an objective summary of the text.

- Seventh graders will learn to determine two or more central ideas, track their development over the course of a text, and provide an objective summary.

- In the eighth grade, students will learn to determine a text's central idea, track its development over the course of a text, and perceive its relationship to supporting ideas. In addition, students should be able to provide an objective summary of the text.

Analyzing Texts

- By the end of the sixth grade, students should be able to analyze how the author of a text introduces and develops key details about individuals, events, and ideas through the use of examples and anecdotes.

- Seventh graders will learn to analyze how individuals, events, and ideas interact in a text.

- Students in the eighth grade will learn to analyze how the author of a text connects or distinguishes individuals, ideas, and events, by making comparisons and analogies or using categorization.

Reading Informational Text: Key Ideas and Details

UNIT 3

Essential Question:
How can readers find and analyze central ideas in a text?

Unit 3 ■ Reading Informational Text: Key Ideas and Details **63**

Vocabulary Overview

General Academic Vocabulary

affirmatively, assumed, brink, decade, disorder, dissipate, documented, dwindling, emerged, enterprise, entrepreneur, exploit, fateful, genre, impaired, inherent, invigorating, isolated, joint, long-standing, marshal, momentary, perceived, philanthropist, plummet, propelled, reeling, refined, scout, seize, singular, stockpiling, sustenance, tense, tragedy, tribulation

Domain-Specific Vocabulary

artifact, chemist, circumference, communism, compound, cosmic, democracy, deposit, flight deck, instrument, mass, meteoroid, module, orbit, satellite, sedimentary, solar array, stowage, suborbital, telescope, transmitted

---

Essential Question:
How can readers find and analyze central ideas in a text?

In this unit, students will learn how to analyze the key ideas and details in an informational text, specifically how to draw inferences from a text, determine its central ideas, and analyze the relationships between its ideas, individuals, and events.

Theme: New Frontiers

Students will read selections related to the topic of space exploration, including an explanatory text about the Space Race between the United States and the Soviet Union in the 1960s, an interview with NASA's "Teacher in Space," an article about preparations for possible exploration of Mars, and an explanatory text about the United States' national space policy.

Curriculum Connection: Social Studies

Students will learn about the history of the space program in the United States, the geopolitical rivalry with the Soviet Union for space dominance, and the factors that affect the United States' current policy on space exploration.

Science

Students will learn about the conditions in space and on Mars, the technology that makes space exploration possible, the effects of space travel on humans, and the requirements of new technology that may one day get humans to Mars and beyond.

Guided Instruction

OBJECTIVE
Use textual evidence to support an analysis of both explicit and inferred information from the text.

Genre: Explanatory Text with Speech

Explain to students that an explanatory text gives the reader information about a topic. A speech is a text written to be delivered orally to an audience.

Set the Purpose

Help students understand the purpose for learning the reading skill by asking: *How can you understand ideas that a text doesn't state directly?*

Model and Teach

Read or have volunteers read the selection and callouts as the class follows along. Model effective strategies for responding to the callouts by using the suggestions below.

CITE EVIDENCE

A Paragraph 1 directly states that the Space Race started after World War II, and gives a reason for the competition.

B Students should use details in paragraphs 3 and 4 to infer that rockets had always been used as weapons; therefore, using them as transportation was a new idea.

DRAWING INFERENCES
Guided Instruction

WORDS TO KNOW
democracy
emerged
reeling
satellite

Sometimes an author's ideas are directly stated in a text, and sometimes they are implied. Use clues in the text to **draw inferences** about implied ideas.

CITE EVIDENCE

A Sometimes an author will state an idea directly, or explicitly. Consider why the United States and the Soviet Union were in competition with each other. Find the stated idea in paragraph 1 and underline it.

B When you are looking for an answer that is not explicitly stated, you must **draw an inference** based on evidence in the text. What was so unusual about using rockets to get into space? This idea isn't stated. Put an asterisk next to each piece of information that tells how rockets had been used previously. How does this information help you make an inference?

A Man on the Moon
(Genre: Explanatory Text with Speech)

1   The Space Race started after World War II. The United States and the Soviet Union had **emerged** from the war as the two most powerful countries in the world. They had different systems of government. The United States was the champion of **democracy**, while the Soviet Union was a defender of communism. Both countries wanted their form of government to succeed in countries around the world. The two countries competed for allies, weapons, and power.

2   Both countries wanted to develop rocket technology for their own power and protection. The United States had an early victory by being the first to develop the nuclear bomb, but space was the next frontier. Although the Germans had been the first to develop modern rocket technology, rocket science had begun long before the war.

A Brief History of Rockets

3   *The first rockets were developed in China in the 12th century. The Chinese had already invented gunpowder and fireworks. These rockets were weapons that were an extension of that technology.

4   *The technology spread through Asia, and then to Europe, when India used gunpowder rockets against the invading British.*Britain then used them against the United States, as the lyrics to "The Star-Spangled Banner" relate: "And the rockets' red glare/The bombs bursting in air . . ."

a V-2 rocket, used during World War II

Words to Know

General Academic Vocabulary
emerged (*v.*): came out of
reeling (*v.*): staggering backward unsteadily, such as after being struck

Domain-Specific Vocabulary
democracy (*n.*): a form of government that recognizes the right of people to rule themselves through elected representatives
satellite (*n.*): an object that travels around a planet

Working with Word Meaning Encourage students to create drawings and diagrams to help them remember the meanings of these words.

KEY IDEAS AND DETAILS

5   In 1898 a Russian schoolteacher, Konstantin Tsiolkovsky, proposed the idea of using rockets to explore space. Although deaf from childhood, Tsiolkovsky was an active inventor, and he developed the math that made modern rocket science possible.

6   The next great advance in rocket science came from an American, Robert H. Goddard. He experimented with liquid fuel for rockets. In 1926 Goddard tested the idea. The flight lasted for only two-and-a-half seconds and landed about half a football field away. Goddard's experiments continued, though, and his work changed how high and fast rockets could fly.

7   Hermann Oberth, another great rocket pioneer, published a book in 1923 about rocket travel into outer space. His writings inspired many small rocket societies around the world. In Germany, members of the Society for Space Travel experimented with rocket designs that eventually led to the development of the V-2 rocket, used by Germany during World War II.

8   After the war, the United States and the Soviet Union captured many unused V-2 rockets. Many German rocket scientists came to the United States. Others went to the Soviet Union.

The Soviet Union Pulls Ahead

9   On October 4, 1957, the Soviet Union launched *Sputnik I,* the world's first artificial **satellite**. It was about the size of a beach ball, weighed about as much as an adult male, and orbited Earth in less time than it takes to watch a movie.

10   The *Sputnik* launch crossed a new frontier for human beings— entering space. Its success captured the world's imagination. It also caught America off guard. Not only had they lost the race to space, but Americans also feared that the Soviets would now be able to launch nuclear missiles from Europe to the United States.

11   While America was still **reeling** from the news, the Soviets chalked up another victory. On November 3, *Sputnik II* carried a dog into space. It was the first animal to orbit Earth.

Comprehension Check

What inferences can you make about the effect of war on the development of space technology?

Guided Instruction

CITE EVIDENCE

C How were the Soviets able to launch *Sputnik I*? Circle the paragraph that gives you some clues.

D Put a box around the word in paragraph 10 that means "an area that forms the edge of settled territory." If you're not sure what word this is, use a dictionary to look up all the unfamiliar words in the paragraph until you find it.

E Double underline a sentence that gives clues about how Americans felt about the Soviet Union at this time. Which words and phrases most helped you to make an inference?

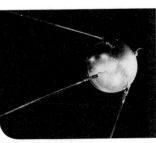

Sputnik I **was the first artificial satellite.**

CITE EVIDENCE

C With students, look for clues in paragraph 8. This paragraph says that many German rockets and rocket scientists ended up in the Soviet Union after World War II. The logical inference is that this influx of knowledge and technology helped the Soviet Union send *Sputnik I* into space.

D Invite students to create a class list of unfamiliar words. Allow students some time to look up words and share definitions with others who marked the same words.

E Direct students to reread paragraph 10. The text states that Americans felt they had lost the space race and feared that the Soviets would use their satellite as a weapon against the United States.

Comprehension Check

Sample Answer: The influx of German scientists and technology to the United States and the Soviet Union after World War II helped both develop space technology.

Answer Explanation: Students should base their inferences on the details in paragraph 8, which suggest that the United States and Soviet Union's advances in space exploration were aided by an influx of German scientists and technology after the war.

Listening and Viewing Skills

Reread paragraph 9 as students listen and look at the photograph on page 65. *What details that you can see in the photograph are not included in the text description?* (*Sputnik I* was made of metal and had antennae.) *What do these details add to your understanding of* Sputnik I? (The antennae are probably for intercepting radio waves.)

Support English Language Learners

English language learners may have a difficult time using a dictionary to determine the meaning of idioms or to choose the appropriate meaning of a multiple-meaning word. Preview with students the meanings of the idioms and words listed below. Have students choose one to use in a sentence they share with a partner.

Idioms: *captured the imagination* (inspired), *caught off guard* (surprised), *chalked up* (scored)

Multiple-meaning words: *champion* (defender), *reeling* (stepping back as if having been hit, used figuratively here), *spread* (traveled)

Drawing Inferences

Guided Instruction

CITE EVIDENCE

A Students should see that the logical place to look for clues is in paragraph 13, under the subhead "To the Moon!" The Russians had one spacecraft crash on the moon and another one in its orbit. Students have already read how the Americans and the Soviets were in competition. Be sure they understand that putting a man safely on the moon was a way for Americans to take the lead in the race to space.

B In paragraph 14, the author explains that America had sent two monkeys into space and recovered them from a splash landing. Lead students to make the connection that this experiment was a necessary precursor to sending humans into space and bringing them safely back.

C Model for the class how to scan the text's subheads to determine where the text shifts to a primary source. Students should be able to see that beginning with paragraph 17, the text becomes a primary source, specifically, a speech given by President John F. Kennedy. Check students' understanding of the concept by asking them to explain why this speech is considered a primary source.

DRAWING INFERENCES

Guided Instruction

WORDS TO KNOW

affirmatively

enterprise

exploit

instrument

orbit

CITE EVIDENCE

A In science, one discovery or accomplishment often leads to another. Underline the sentences that help you infer why Americans started thinking about sending a man to the moon.

B Which American accomplishment would lead to bringing astronauts safely back from space? Double underline this. Explain how you used this information to make your inference.

C A primary source is an original source, a printed or recorded document from the time period being written about. Put an asterisk next to the part of the text that is taken from an actual historical record.

A Man on the Moon continued

America Rallies

12   A few months later, in January 1958, the United States launched *Explorer I*. This satellite carried some scientific **instruments**. The data gathered from this mission led to the discovery of magnetic radiation belts around Earth. Then, in July 1958, Congress passed a law that created the National Aeronautics and Space Administration (NASA). The United States was determined to win the Space Race.

To the Moon!

13   The moon was the next frontier. The Russians again were leading the way. They crash-landed the spacecraft *Luna 2* on the surface of the moon in 1959. Then they sent *Luna 3* in orbit around the moon to photograph its "dark side"—the side that is always turned away from Earth. That was the first time anyone had seen it.

14   Meanwhile, the United States launched two monkeys into space and recovered them from a splash landing in the Atlantic Ocean.

15   The Russians then stunned the world by sending the first human into space. Cosmonaut Yuri Gagarin entered Earth's **orbit** in *Vostok I*. About a month later, the United States launched astronaut Alan Shepard into space on *Freedom 7*.

16   The United States was ready to make a bold move ahead. President John F. Kennedy had a plan, and he shared it in a speech to the United States Congress on May 25, 1961. He asked the nation to pull together to meet the challenge of putting a man on the moon.

*From President John F. Kennedy's Speech to Congress, May 25, 1961

17   Now it is time to take longer strides—time for a great new American **enterprise**—time for this nation to take a clearly leading role in space achievement, which in many ways may hold the key to our future on Earth. . . .

Words to Know

General Academic Vocabulary

affirmatively (*adv.*): positively; in a way that expresses agreement

enterprise (*n.*): a project; an endeavor

exploit (*v.*): to take advantage of

Domain-Specific Vocabulary

instrument (*n.*): a mechanical or electronic measuring device

orbit (*n.*): path one object takes around another object (such as a planet around the sun)

Working with Word Meaning Encourage students to restate these definitions in their own words and to write their own exemplar sentences.

KEY IDEAS AND DETAILS

18   Recognizing the head start obtained by the Soviets with their large rocket engines, which gives them many months of lead-time, and recognizing the likelihood that they will **exploit** this lead for some time to come in still more impressive successes, we nevertheless are required to make new efforts on our own. For while we cannot guarantee that we shall one day be first, we can guarantee that any failure to make this effort will make us last . . . But this is not merely a race. Space is open to us now; and our eagerness to share its meaning is not governed by the efforts of others. We go into space because whatever mankind must undertake, free men must fully share. . . .

19   . . . I believe that this nation should commit itself to achieving the goal, before this decade is out, of landing a man on the moon and returning him safely to the Earth. No single space project in this period will be more impressive to mankind, or more important for the long-range exploration of space; and none will be so difficult or expensive to accomplish . . . But in a very real sense, it will not be one man going to the moon—if we make this judgment **affirmatively**, it will be an entire nation. For all of us must work to put him there. . . .

20   Let it be clear . . . that I am asking the Congress and the country to accept a firm commitment to a new course of action, a course which will last for many years and carry very heavy costs . . . If we are to go only half way, or reduce our sights in the face of difficulty, in my judgment it would be better not to go at all.

Comprehension Check

How does reading the excerpt from President Kennedy's speech help you understand the rest of the selection up to this point?

CITE EVIDENCE

D Why does President Kennedy think America should put a man on the moon? Put a box around his reasons.

E What are some "difficulties" that could come from trying to put a man on the moon? Circle a paragraph whose information helps you answer this question. Why does Kennedy not explicitly state the potential difficulties he hints at here?

JFK asks Congress to support the space program.

Guided Instruction

CITE EVIDENCE

D Point out to students that President Kennedy clearly states his reasons for asking the country to commit to the idea of putting a man on the moon, but they are interwoven through his speech. After students locate the reasons in paragraphs 18 and 19, have students restate them in their own words.

E Students should be able to see that President Kennedy directly states in paragraph 20 that putting a man on the moon will "carry very heavy costs." The costs that he alludes to could include loss of American lives in addition to expenditures of time and money. President Kennedy doesn't spell out these costs because he wants to keep a positive tone in his speech and make the goal seem achievable.

Comprehension Check

Sample Answer: Reading the excerpt from President Kennedy's speech helps me understand what Americans were feeling during the Space Race and why it was important to America to go to the moon.

Answer Explanation: Students should understand that President Kennedy's speech reflects the attitudes and thinking of America's leaders at the time of the Space Race. As such, this primary source document gives more context for understanding the text's earlier descriptions of the Space Race and the Soviet Union's successes.

Digital Connection: Finding Primary Sources Online

Give students the opportunity to do an online search for a video of President Kennedy giving this speech. Students will be more successful with their searches if they include the words: "May 25, 1961 Speech before a Joint Session of Congress." Or locate the video yourself by using the classroom computer, and present excerpts of it during class. Explain that Kennedy's ideas about reaching the moon was part of a longer speech about the state of the country. Ask students to notice which parts of the speech get applause. See if they can make inferences about why those parts get a better reaction.

Guided Practice

Recap Reading Selection

Have students recall what they have learned so far about the Space Race and America's desire to put a man on the moon. Prompt them to tell what they remember about the development of rocket technology, why America had fallen behind the Soviet Union, and what President Kennedy was asking the American people to do. Let students know that they will next be reading about how the Americans got to the moon.

Read and Practice

Have partners take turns reading the selection as you circulate to provide support. Circulate among students and ask them to find stated ideas and to draw inferences using Cite Evidence callouts A and B. Provide additional scaffolding as needed, using the suggestions below.

CITE EVIDENCE

A Have students read in paragraph 21 about political tensions between the United States and other countries. As students read paragraph 22, ask them to think about how spy satellites helped influence the Space Race.

B After reading the page, students should be able to infer that the Soviets' lack of progress in reaching the moon accounted for their secrecy about their efforts.

DRAWING INFERENCES

Guided Practice

WORDS TO KNOW

brink

communism

module

tense

CITE EVIDENCE

A How did political tension on the ground influence the Space Race? Underline the answer in the text.

B Why were the Soviets being secretive about their efforts to send a man to the moon? Put an asterisk at the beginning of the paragraph that helps answer this question. Discuss with a partner what you can infer about the Soviet failure to reach the moon.

A Man on the Moon continued

Spying Eyes in the Sky

21   While the United States was working on a manned lunar mission, events on the ground were getting **tense**. The United States and the Soviet Union were getting into conflicts as the Soviets helped **communism** to spread. American airmen spotted Soviet missile sites being built in Cuba. With Cuba only a short distance from Florida, missiles fired from these sites could easily strike the United States. Meanwhile, the Americans had a missile base in Turkey near the Soviet border. For two weeks, the Cuban Missile Crisis threatened the world with nuclear war. Eventually, both countries stepped back from the **brink**.

22   Still, there was a lot of mistrust. Space missions gave both countries another way to spy on each other from the air. Both countries soon developed "spy satellites" that would allow them to photograph and monitor each other from space.

Reaching for the Moon

23   Although the Soviets dominated early in the space race, things were about to change. The Americans did not seem to be making progress, but they were. Each NASA mission built on the previous one.

24   *The Soviets said publicly that they were not trying to reach the moon, but they worked covertly on that project as well. Their efforts were less successful, though. As it turns out, the Soviets were using many smaller engines while the Americans were using a few large ones. In the end, the Soviets never did put a man on the moon.

Lunar Landing

25   *Apollo 11*, the American mission that would land the first men on the moon, was made up of several parts. The *Saturn V* rocket would power it into space. The *Columbia* command **module** would take the astronauts into lunar orbit. The *Eagle* lunar module would be the part that landed on the moon's surface.

Words to Know

General Academic Vocabulary

brink (*n.*): the edge or critical point after which success or catastrophe occurs

tense (*adj.*): stressed; difficult

Domain-Specific Vocabulary

communism (*n.*): form of government in which the leaders control the economy and many aspects of people's lives

module (*n.*): small section; unit

Working with Word Meaning Have students meet with partners to discuss examples and non-examples of each word.

26   The voyage began on July 16, 1969. Aboard *Apollo 11* were Neil Armstrong, Michael Collins, and Edwin "Buzz" Aldrin, Jr. Everything went as planned. After reaching lunar orbit, Armstrong and Aldrin boarded the *Eagle* and landed it on the moon on July 19, with Armstrong famously reporting, "The *Eagle* has landed." As Armstrong descended the ladder to become the first person to set foot on the moon, he said, "That's one small step for man, one giant leap for mankind."

Comprehension Check

1. America had fallen behind the Soviet Union because

   a. the Soviets put a man in space first.

   b. the Soviets reached the moon with a spacecraft first.

   c. the Soviets launched the first satellite.

   d. all of the above

2. What issue about putting an American on the moon worried President Kennedy?

   a. America could not afford the cost.

   b. The Soviets were too far ahead.

   c. Putting people on the moon was technologically impossible.

   d. Americans would not pull together.

3. Which of the following would be a primary source about the first moon landing?

   a. a textbook chapter about rocket development

   b. a film clip of Armstrong and Aldrin landing on the moon

   c. an encyclopedia entry about the Cuban Missile Crisis

   d. an audio recording explaining NASA's missions in the year 2013

4. What does *covertly* in paragraph 24 mean?

   a. secretly

   b. carefully

   c. quickly

   d. seriously

5. How has drawing inferences helped you understand the text? Specifically, how do you better understand the connection between the Space Race and politics? Confer with a partner and use evidence from the text to support your answer.

   Sample answer: Drawing inferences helps me understand underlying causes

   for events in a text. For instance, the author does not explicitly state that the

   two countries expected the Space Race to decide which country's form of

   government was superior. Yet it is clear that the competition between them

   was in large part based upon their political differences. Both countries tying

   their success in space to their politics is an important idea in this text.

Discussion Skills

Have students practice discussion and presentation skills by having them play the roles of 1960's spokespeople for either the Soviet or the American space program. Put students in small groups of four and assign each group to represent the Soviets or the Americans. Group members should work together to discuss the strengths and history of their country's space program and then prepare a short presentation to tell the rest of the world (the class) why their space program is better.

Remind students to look back through the reading selection to gather information to use in their presentations.

Guided Practice

Comprehension Check

Answer Explanations:

1. Students should be able to recognize from what they have read so far that answers A–C are all Soviet achievements, so the best answer is choice D, *all of the above.*

2. In paragraph 20, President Kennedy strongly and clearly asks the American people to commit to the goal of putting a man on the moon and even warns that the project will be a lengthy and costly one. Therefore, choice D is correct.

3. Students who understand that one type of primary source is a record created at the time of an historical event should recognize that choice B is the correct answer.

4. Students were asked to find the meanings of any unfamiliar words, so they should be able to choose choice A, *secretly*, as the meaning of *covertly.*

5. Students should understand that having satellites in the sky was also about national security. Satellites could monitor the activities of the Soviets, the political enemies of the United States.

Jigsaw

Put students into groups of three, and have them work together as a jigsaw team. That means each member of the team is responsible for one of the three sections of text on pages 68–69 in the Student Book. Have students reread their section and draw one inference from it to share with their group. Have each group choose one inference to share with the whole class.

Independent Practice

Recap Reading Selection

Have students recall what they have read so far about the Space Race and America's first successful lunar landing. Ask students if they can recall the famous statement Neil Armstrong made as he set foot on the moon. Let students know that they will next read about how the astronauts got home from the moon.

Read and Apply

Have students read this selection independently as you circulate. Ask them to read aloud so you can see if they are reading fluently. You can also use the support below to help students who are having difficulty.

CITE EVIDENCE

A Be sure students are looking in paragraph 28 for the stated reason. They should see that "measurements and timing had to be exact."

B Students can read in paragraph 29 that *Columbia's* final rocket had just enough power to propel *Columbia* out of the moon's orbit. They can infer that *Eagle* was left behind because there was not enough rocket power to clear orbit with the combined weight of the two crafts.

DRAWING INFERENCES

Independent Practice

A Man on the Moon *continued*

WORDS TO KNOW
dwindling
joint
meteoroid
stockpiling

CITE EVIDENCE

A Why was docking the two crafts in space hard to do? In paragraph 28, put an asterisk next to the stated reason.

B Why did the astronauts have to leave the *Eagle* behind? Underline the clue that helps you infer the answer. Why was this an important moment in the Space Race?

Getting Home from the Moon

27   The *Apollo 11* mission was not complete until the astronauts returned safely home. After studying and taking samples on the moon's surface, Armstrong and Aldrin got back into the *Eagle* and launched it into the lunar sky. Everything would have to function properly, or they would be stranded on the moon with no way home.

28   Meanwhile, Collins had been orbiting in the *Columbia* ever since Armstrong and Aldrin had left in the *Eagle*. The plan was for the *Eagle* and the *Columbia* to dock in space.* The measurements and timing had to be exact. Millions of people watched on television and cheered as Armstrong and Aldrin joined Collins. They had done it! The astronauts separated the two crafts and let the *Eagle* drift away into space.

29   The final rocket had just enough thrust to get the *Columbia* out from the moon's orbit. The astronauts splashed down in the Pacific Ocean on July 24. The mission was accomplished, and President Kennedy's challenge had been answered.

Other Apollo Missions

30   In all, six Apollo missions (*Apollo 11, 12,* and *14–17*) sent people safely to the moon, giving humanity a wealth of scientific data and lunar samples. Experiments included the study of soil, **meteoroids**, heat flow, magnetic fields, solar wind, and more.

31   *Apollo 13* captured photographs but did not land on the moon due to a malfunction. An explosion occurred in space. Pilot John L. Swigert, Jr. calmly reported to Mission Control, "Houston, we've had a problem." The whole world held its breath until the astronauts made it back home after overcoming mechanical difficulties and **dwindling** supplies.

From Competition to Cooperation

32   After years of competition, the Soviet Union and America planned a **joint** mission. It was a symbol of hope and goodwill for people at a time when wars were being fought over communism and the superpowers were **stockpiling** nuclear weapons.

Words to Know

General Academic Vocabulary
dwindling (*adj.*): becoming smaller or less
joint (*adj.*): united; done by groups working together
stockpiling (*v.*): storing up supplies

Domain-Specific Vocabulary
meteoroid (*n.*): a small space rock traveling through space

Working with Word Meaning Challenge students to use these vocabulary words while practicing with figures of speech, such as simile, metaphor, hyperbole, or personification.

33   On July 17, 1975, the *Apollo* and *Soyuz* crafts docked in space. The hatch opened, and *Apollo* commander Thomas P. Stafford and *Soyuz* commander Alexey A. Leonov shook hands. People back on Earth dared to hope for peace.

Comprehension Check   MORE ONLINE   sadlierconnect.com

1. The word *malfunction* means

  a. machine failure.

  b. pilot error.

  c. carelessness.

  d. natural disaster.

2. Which can you infer from the text?

  a. The Apollo 13 disaster changed the way NASA built rockets.

  b. The joint mission ended conflict between the U.S. and the Soviet Union.

  c. Congress unanimously supported President Kennedy's proposal.

  d. none of the above

3. A recording of the *Apollo 13* astronauts talking to Mission Control in Houston is an example of

  a. scientific data.

  b. a primary source.

  c. a secondary source.

  d. explanatory text.

4. What is the central idea of the text?

  a. America always wins at everything.

  b. The Soviets had better technology.

  c. The United States and the Soviet Union competed in a "Space Race" in the 1960s.

  d. Space exploration is more important than competing for superior technology.

5. Would humans have reached the moon if the United States and the Soviet Union had not been competing? Give reasons for your answer, using both explicit and implicit evidence from the text. Continue writing on another sheet of paper if you need more space for your answer.

Sample answer: Humans would eventually have reached the moon, though it would have taken longer if the United States and the Soviet Union hadn't been competing in the Space Race. As President Kennedy stated, no goal was "more important for the long-range exploration of space." There was too much scientific knowledge to be gained from reaching the moon for the United States not to go there, and any exploration of space has to start with the moon as the closest and most obvious goal.

Extend Thinking: Apply Concepts

Ask students to consider what they think America's next goal in space exploration should be. Since there is no competition between rival countries to push the United States, students should think of other reasons that could inspire the country to commit to this new project. Have students work on a short speech to the class that states a new goal for space exploration and gives some reasons why the country should put money and effort behind this idea.

Independent Practice

Comprehension Check

Answer Explanations:

1. Students should be able to define unfamiliar words and choose A, "machine failure," as the answer.

2. Students should recall details from the text on pages 70–71 to infer that *none of the above* is correct.

3. A recording from the *Apollo 13* mission is a primary source because it is a record from that time period made by people involved in the event.

4. Students should realize that choice C is correct, because choice A is an overgeneralization, choice B is incorrect, and choice D is an opinion not discussed in the text.

5. Answers will vary. Students' opinions must be supported by evidence from the text.

Critical Comprehension

Challenge students to think more deeply about the text and to support their answers with evidence from the text.

What do you think might have happened if the United States had failed in the mission to land safely on the moon? (The Soviets would have had more time to improve their technology and might have ended up being the first to land on the moon. The Soviets would have had a propaganda victory over the United States.)

Assess and Respond
If students have trouble answering the questions in the Comprehension Check,
Then lead them in highlighting the section of the text referenced in the question, finding needed definitions, and discussing inferences and conclusions.

Guided Instruction

OBJECTIVE
Identify two or more ideas that are central to the text and analyze how the author develops them. Summarize the text.

Genre: Interview

An interview is like a formal conversation. The interviewer prepares questions to ask the subject, who answers the questions in conversation.

Set the Purpose

Tell students to think about what ideas they would include if they were telling friends about a party, game or other event that they missed. Ask: *How would you summarize this class today for a friend who was out sick?*

Model and Teach

Read or have volunteers read the selection and callouts as the class follows along. Model effective strategies for responding to the callouts by using the suggestions below.

CITE EVIDENCE

A Have students locate the information in paragraph 5. Help them see that these details about the mission are too specific and relatively insignificant to be a central idea in an article about Morgan.

B Students should recognize the similarities in the words. The central idea—Morgan's enthusiasm for her job—will become more evident throughout the text.

DETERMINING CENTRAL IDEAS
Guided Instruction

WORDS TO KNOW
assumed
fateful
flight deck
solar array
stowage
tragedy

A text's **central ideas** are the most important ideas the author wants you to understand. Look for ideas that are repeated or stressed in the text.

CITE EVIDENCE

A Circle the information in paragraph 5 that tells the purpose of the shuttle mission. Would this information be a **central idea** in an article or encyclopedia entry on Barbara Morgan? Explain.

B How does Barbara Morgan stress her feelings about going to space? Underline the words that she lists. What do these words have in common? How are these words important to the central ideas of the text?

Barbara Morgan, Teacher and Astronaut
(Genre: Interview)

1   Barbara Morgan was selected as a backup candidate for NASA's Teacher in Space Program in 1985 and trained with Christa McAuliffe and the *Challenger* space shuttle crew. However, she remained behind when that **fateful** shuttle exploded, killing everyone onboard. Afterward, Morgan **assumed** the duties of NASA's Teacher in Space.

2   Morgan spent 20 years working with NASA on the ground but only made her first trip to space in 2007 aboard *Endeavor* space shuttle flight STS-118.

3   Here is part of a longer interview Morgan gave right before this mission. She was about to be the first Teacher in Space to blast off since the horrible *Challenger* **tragedy** in 1986.

Preflight Interview

4   **NASA:** Barbara, STS-118 will mean a lot of things to a lot of people, but probably not more than it will for kids around the world who will be watching you as you fly in space. How would you describe the mission to kids and what your role and duties are on the flight?

5   **MORGAN:** Well, my first word would be "exciting." Actually, it's more than a word. Exciting, interesting, amazing, and fun. We are going to the International Space Station; we call it an assembly mission. We are going to the International Space Station to help finish building it. In our cargo bay, or in the back end of the shuttle, we're taking up a couple of big pieces that are part of the station. One is part of the support structure that's going to hold more of the **solar arrays**, and one is the **stowage** platform that's going to hold a bunch of spare equipment that will be used eventually on station.

72   Unit 3 ▪ Reading Informational Text: Key Ideas and Details

---

Words to Know

General Academic Vocabulary
assumed (*v.*): took on
fateful (*adj.*): connected to the occurrence of something important or terrible
tragedy (*n.*): terrible event; disaster

Domain-Specific Vocabulary
flight deck (*n.*): the area where the astronauts sit to control the space shuttle
solar array (*n.*): a set of solar panels, which store energy from sunlight
stowage (*n.*): storage

Working with Word Meaning Ask students to sort the vocabulary into categories, such as things astronauts do and tools they use.

KEY IDEAS AND DETAILS

6   Those are two of our major things that we're going to be doing. <u>We'll be transferring all the things over that they need and bringing the things that they don't need back home with us.</u> I'll have many different duties, so I'll just tell you about a couple of them. I'll be one of the robotic arm operators, so I'll be using the space shuttle arm and the space station arm to help us move some of these pieces of equipment as we attach them onto the station. And I'll be helping on the **flight deck**, coming home, or during what we call "entry" of the space shuttle back to Earth.

7   **NASA:** Kids always love spaceflight. What should they pay particular attention to on your flight? What should they be looking for? And ultimately, what do you think they're going to learn from this mission?

8   **MORGAN:** You're going to laugh at this, but what I really want them to do is to pay attention to themselves and to look very deep within themselves and dig up all the questions that they can that they have about our world, our universe, and about space exploration. Because this is all about (learning,) and we're here to help and we want to know from them—what is it that they really want to know and learn? Because this is their future and it's open-ended for them. I also hope that they'll see an ordinary person doing the things that they can be doing.

CITE EVIDENCE

C A **summary** is made up of central ideas without a lot of details. Double underline the sentence in Morgan's response that does the best job of summarizing the mission. How would you summarize what Morgan says in the rest of the paragraph about her duties on the shuttle?

D Being aware of key, or important, words as you read will help you determine central ideas. What does Morgan say is the key reason kids should pay attention to her mission? Circle the key word in her answer.

Comprehension Check

Why is Barbara Morgan so excited about this mission?

Barbara Morgan in the weightlessness of space

Unit 3 ■ Reading Informational Text: Key Ideas and Details   **73**

Guided Instruction

CITE EVIDENCE

C Be sure students notice the beginning of paragraph 6, where Morgan sums up the two major goals of her mission: delivering things that are needed and taking away things are not needed. Her other duties are operating the robotic arm and helping on the flight deck. Students should see that a summary statement is brief and has the most important information.

D Have students read Morgan's response in paragraph 8 that says why her mission is important. The sentence "Because this is all about learning . . . " should help students see why the word *learning* is a key to one of the central ideas in this interview.

Comprehension Check

Sample Answer: Morgan is excited because she has been with NASA a long time, and this is her first opportunity to go into space.

Answer Explanation: As students read in paragraph 2, Morgan had been working with NASA on the ground for 20 years before she finally got to go into space. And if her mission were successful, she would be the first teacher in space.

Support English Language Learners

The interview format will provide some challenges and opportunities for English language learners. Because this is a transcript of an interview, the language is slightly less orderly than if Morgan's remarks had been written or prepared in advance. Some of the sentences are made longer as Morgan circles back to clarify what she is saying. There are many appositions and pauses. Demonstrate how Morgan's responses sound in a natural, conversational speaking mode. This will help model the rhythms of natural speech being captured in print.

Guided Instruction

CITE EVIDENCE

A Have students reread paragraph 10 to find the word that Morgan repeats four times. This word explains why Morgan signed up with NASA, but it also says something about Morgan's enthusiastic point of view.

B Students should notice in paragraph 12 that Morgan makes two points about Christa McAuliffe. First, she brought the world to her classroom—as a good teacher to her students. Second, she brought teachers to the attention of the world—showing the good that teachers do. It is clear that Morgan talks about McAuliffe in a very positive and respectful way, which shows that she thinks very highly of McAuliffe.

Review: Drawing Inferences

Paragraph 15 contains the first mention in this interview of the *Challenger* and *Columbia* accidents. Because students may not be familiar with these events, ask what they can infer about the accidents based on the information in the text. (Both were serious accidents that led to a national debate about the safety of space exploration; both caused the deaths of astronauts on board the shuttles.)

DETERMINING CENTRAL IDEAS

Guided Instruction

Barbara Morgan, Teacher and Astronaut *continued*

WORDS TO KNOW

documented

long-standing

seize

tribulation

CITE EVIDENCE

A Paying attention to repeated words is important in determining the central ideas of a text. Circle the word in paragraph 10 that expresses Morgan's main reason for signing up with NASA.

B What two things did Christa McAuliffe accomplish, according to Morgan? Underline them. Summarize Morgan's views of McAuliffe.

9 **NASA:** Let's go back a little bit in history and trace the path that took you to this point in your career, from teacher in McCall, Idaho, to astronaut. Why did you sign up to do this in the first place all those many years ago?

10 **MORGAN:** Well, when the Teacher in Space program was started, I was sitting at home, it was after school, it was about five o'clock . . . and the President came on the news and announced that they were going to send a teacher in space. I shot straight up and said, "Wow!" As you know, teachers all across the country did! What a great opportunity! Because as teachers, we're always looking for opportunities to bring the world to our classroom, to gain more experiences, gain more knowledge about our world so that we can make our classroom a better place for our kids. And, it was a tremendous opportunity. And, as all teachers, we don't pass up those opportunities.

11 **NASA:** That summer day in 1985 when you and your fellow candidates were at the White House and Christa McAuliffe was announced as the Teacher in Space, you were announced as her backup, what feelings did you have?

12 **MORGAN:** We were all really excited and really thrilled to be doing what we were doing. Christa was, is, and always will be our "Teacher in Space," our first teacher to fly. She truly knew what this was all about—not just bringing the world to her classroom—but also helping . . . helping to show the world what teachers do and what all the good teachers do across our country day in and day out.

13 **NASA:** Isn't that really the whole point of you flying in space as an Educator Astronaut, to show that there are no boundaries to kids, that there are no limitations, that the opportunities are there if they would just wish to **seize** them?

14 **MORGAN:** Absolutely.

15 **NASA:** Certainly the **tribulations** have been well **documented** over the past two decades, most recently the *Columbia* accident. After that, after all of this, and after reliving the *Columbia* accident and all of the memories and the shadows of *Challenger* all over again, did it cause you at all to rethink your goal to fly in space, and to fly as an educator to carry out this **long-standing** dream of yours, of Christa, of your fellow educators?

74 Unit 3 ■ Reading Informational Text: Key Ideas and Details

---

Words to Know

General Academic Vocabulary

documented (*adj.*): recorded in documents, as with evidence

long-standing (*adj.*): in place for a long time

seize (*v.*): to take hold of something

tribulation (*n.*): a severe trouble or difficulty

Working with Word Meaning Ask students to restate these definitions in their own words and write exemplar sentences for each.

KEY IDEAS AND DETAILS

16 **MORGAN:** I'm going to answer that in a couple of ways because both *Challenger* and the *Columbia* have caused me to think, and it caused all of NASA to think. First of all, it caused us to think about what are we doing wrong, and how can we make it better, how can we make spaceflight safer because it is risky business, but we want to make it as safe as we can. All the astronauts, all of NASA, have been working really hard and will continue to work hard to try to make spaceflight as safe as we can possibly make it. It also caused me to really think, both *Challenger* and *Columbia*, about what's really important. In both situations, we had kids watching adults, and they watch adults. Kids learn a lot from watching adults. It's not just what we say, but it's what we do, and, kids were watching to see what the adults do in a terrible, terrible situation. What I thought was really important for kids to see is that we figure out what's wrong, we fix it, and we move on, and we keep the future open for our young people. *And I just thought that that was really important, and feel that's really important today.* I'll feel that's important forever.

Comprehension Check

Why might Barbara Morgan be afraid to fly into space? Is she?

CITE EVIDENCE

C Double underline some of the conclusions that NASA drew from the *Challenger* tragedy.

D Put a box around Morgan's key point about the most important thing to come from the *Challenger* tragedy.

E Put an asterisk next to the sentences that show Morgan's emphasis on the key point she made. Summarize Morgan's ideas about why her "long-standing dream" of flying in space is important.

Guided Instruction

CITE EVIDENCE

C Have students refer to paragraph 16, where Morgan discusses how NASA responded to the *Challenger* tragedy. Tell students that NASA used the information to improve safety going forward; however, students should realize that space travel will always involve risk.

D Language in a text sometimes signals a central idea or important point to come. As an example, guide students to where Morgan says, "What I thought was really important . . ." Ask students to identify this signal before boxing the key point.

E Students should be able to identify the repetition of the word *important* in paragraph 16 as emphasizing Morgan's point. Connect this idea to what Morgan hopes to learn from space exploration and what she hopes to model for students.

Comprehension Check

Sample Answer: Morgan has seen how dangerous space travel can be. But she seems excited about the chance to go to space and doesn't seem afraid.

Answer Explanation: Students should recall from reading paragraph 16 that Morgan is aware of the *Challenger* and *Columbia* accidents and has given them thought. However, she keeps herself focused on the possibilities of going to space, thinks it is an important thing to do, and remains optimistic.

Differentiate Instruction

Have proficient readers help those who are struggling with reading the text. Put students into two groups and have them re-create the interview. Have the struggling students read the questions from NASA as written. Have the proficient students take the role of Barbara Morgan. However, instead of having them read her answers, ask them to summarize. This activity will give the proficient students a chance to stretch while making the interview more accessible for students who are having trouble.

Determining Central Ideas

Guided Practice

Recap Reading Selection

Have students recall what they have learned so far about Barbara Morgan, the NASA "Teacher in Space," who was interviewed before a mission to the International Space Station. Let students know that next they will learn what Morgan values about education.

Read and Practice

Have partners take turns reading the selection as you circulate to provide support. Circulate among students and ask them to find stated ideas and to draw inferences using Cite Evidence callouts A and B. Provide additional scaffolding as needed, using the suggestions below.

CITE EVIDENCE

A Direct students' attention to paragraphs 18 and 20. Be sure that students notice that Morgan does not see learning as a one-way street. She is not just in the classroom to help students learn; she is also there to learn herself.

B If students have difficulty identifying Morgan's ideas about the benefits of space exploration, have them reread paragraph 20. The parallel structure of the sentences in the paragraph should also help students identify the related ideas. Students' opinions on whether the benefits of space exploration outweigh the risks should be supported by evidence and examples.

DETERMINING CENTRAL IDEAS

Guided Practice

Barbara Morgan, Teacher and Astronaut *continued*

WORDS TO KNOW

chemist

decade

perceived

singular

CITE EVIDENCE

A How can you tell how Morgan feels about learning? Underline evidence in paragraphs 18 and 20.

B How does Morgan emphasize the benefits over the risks of space exploration? With a partner, count the benefits and put an asterisk by each of them. Does Morgan convince you that the benefits outweigh the risks? Explain.

17 **NASA:** One of the things I'm struck by is that the roles are reversed: the teacher is being taught how to fly in space here, and has been over the course of all these years. Is Barbara Morgan a good student?

18 **MORGAN:** I hope I'm a good student. One thing is, like anything else, the more you put into it, the more you're going to get out of it. Actually, yes, I've been a student here at NASA, but, teachers are also students in their own classroom. <u>That's one of the challenges and one of the rewards of being a classroom teacher is that you're there helping other people learn, and every day you're learning yourself.</u>

19 **NASA:** Why is it worth the risk for humans to fly in space? And, what is really the benefit of the risk of putting an educator in space?

20 **MORGAN:** The risks are the same for an educator or a physician or an engineer or a pilot or a **chemist**, anyone else who flies in space.* <u>We're doing it to learn.</u>* We're doing it to explore,* we're doing it to discover.* We're doing it to help make this world a better place, and* we're doing it to help keep those doors open for our young people so that they can, they can do it, too.

21 **NASA:** What kind of a support system is in place in your family to go through two **decades** of this **singular** goal of yours?

22 **MORGAN:** Well, my family knows that space exploration is really important. My husband and both our boys would love to fly, too.

23 **NASA:** What do you see as the similarities between what astronauts and teachers do, and how will your mission be **perceived** as a benefit for the education process in schools, do you think?

Words to Know

General Academic Vocabulary

decade (*n.*): a ten-year period

perceived (*v.*): understood

singular (*adj.*): unique or extraordinary

Domain-Specific Vocabulary

chemist (*n.*): a scientist who works with chemicals

Working with Word Meaning Have students meet with partners, and use the words to tell a brief anecdote about a topic of interest.

24 **MORGAN:** Astronauts and teachers learn and share; they explore; they discover; and then they go learn and share some more. And that's what this is all about.

Comprehension Check

1. What are two of the central ideas in Morgan's interview so far?

   (a.) learning and opportunity

   b. risk and reward

   c. assembly and cargo

   d. limitations and boundaries

2. How does Morgan develop the idea that she is a student as well as a teacher?

   a. by explaining how she will share her experiences in space when she returns to the classroom

   b. by describing how important a role model Christa McAuliffe was to her

   c. by comparing herself to a physician, an engineer, a pilot, and a chemist

   (d.) by reminding the interviewer that she learns from her students as much as they learn from her

3. One conclusion that readers can draw about Morgan is that she looks to the future with a sense of

   a. uncertainty.

   (b.) excitement.

   c. worry.

   d. overconfidence.

4. Which is the best summary of the interview so far?

   a. Morgan loves learning and teaching.

   b. Morgan was lucky not to be on the *Challenger* shuttle.

   (c.) Morgan is a teacher who is excited to go into space.

   d. Morgan is a mother with a supportive family.

5. How does Morgan's conclusion about the similarities between teachers and astronauts help you understand one of the central ideas of the text? Use evidence from the text. If you need more space to write, continue on another sheet of paper. When you are finished, compare answers with a partner.

   Sample answer: Morgan says that teachers and astronauts share an interest in learning, sharing, discovering, and exploring. Astronauts bring new discoveries to the world. Morgan states that teachers should "gain more knowledge about our world so that we can make our classroom a better place." Morgan makes a clear connection between learning and sharing. This supports the central idea that her experiences as a teacher have helped prepare her to be successful as an astronaut.

Unit 3 ■ Reading Informational Text: Key Ideas and Details **77**

Discussion Skills

Have students think about the question *Why do you think Morgan is willing to take big risks for the sake of exploring new frontiers?* Encourage students to quote Morgan's words in support of their answers. Suggest the following stems for them to try out as they have this discussion:

• *Morgan's statement about _____ supports my idea about _____.*

• *Morgan says _____, and that means _____.*

• *When Morgan says _____, she is implying that _____.*

Guided Practice

Comprehension Check

Answer Explanations:

1. Students should recognize that A is the correct answer because "learning and opportunity" are the two ideas that Morgan returns to repeatedly.

2. Although choices A and B sound plausible, they are not details that appear in the interview. Choice C does not provide evidence to match Morgan's statement. Therefore, choice D is the answer.

3. Students who have understood the text should immediately eliminate choices A and C. Morgan's words in the interview repeatedly stress excitement, not overconfidence, about the future, so choice B is the correct answer.

4. Students should realize that all the answer choices give true statements, but choice C includes the two most important points in the interview.

5. Students should understand that Morgan sees going to space as a learning opportunity. They should support their responses and opinions by citing textual evidence.

Writearound

Use a group-work technique to generate summaries and reinforce the skill of recognizing central ideas. Give each group the same sentence starter, such as *Barbara Morgan really wants to . . .* on a sheet of paper. Have the first group member write a sentence and pass it on to the next group member. Have the group continue until they feel they have a good summary. Bring the whole class together to compare each smaller group's summary.

Independent Practice

Recap Reading Selection

Ask student volunteers to list some things that they have learned about Barbara Morgan so far. Be sure they include the ideas that Morgan is a teacher who was selected to train as an astronaut. She trained with the crew of the *Challenger*, and after its deadly crash, became NASA's second Teacher in Space. She trained for twenty years before being selected for a mission to the International Space Station and was excited to go despite the dangers. She sees space as another place of learning, like the classroom.

Read and Apply

Have students read this section independently as you circulate. Ask them to read aloud so you can see if they are reading fluently. You can also use the support below to help students who are having difficulty.

CITE EVIDENCE

A Paragraph 26 concerns Morgan's childhood, so students should look there for the two experiences that inspired her interest in space.

B Students should be able to find several examples of Morgan's positive attitude in paragraph 28. Ask them to tell some of the specific words or phrases that show this attitude, such as "look forward to" and "better and better and better."

DETERMINING CENTRAL IDEAS

Independent Practice

Barbara Morgan, Teacher and Astronaut *continued*

WORDS TO KNOW

inherent
momentary
propelled
sustenance
telescope

CITE EVIDENCE

A What were the two main experiences that inspired Morgan as a child? Underline that information.

B Put an asterisk by places in paragraph 28 that show Morgan's positive attitude. What central idea of the text do these examples point to?

25 **NASA:** Did you just have an **inherent** interest in space at all? Did you follow the Neil Armstrong thing that so many astronauts say **propelled** them to want to specifically become an astronaut?

26 **MORGAN:** Absolutely, I was always interested in looking up at the stars when we'd go camping and as a Girl Scout. My folks, when we were very young, got us a little **telescope** for Christmas, and we had that out and would look up at the stars. I was always interested in what's out there. And then, yes as the space program was being born, we were glued to the TV when we first landed on the Moon and the flights leading up to that, and yes, that was very much a part of my growing up. I didn't even consider that that would be something that I could do, so that wasn't part of what I thought I would be doing. Part of that, too, was because the [lack of] opportunities then for women. I'm so glad now that's not the case anymore.

27 **NASA:** What kind of a mark do you think you will have left on education when this is all said and done? Is it going to be a lasting mark, or is this just a **momentary** blip on the radar screen in history? How can you make your flight an impact flight that will have **sustenance** for years to come with the lessons that you will have provided from the mission itself and what you're going to be doing up in orbit?

28 **MORGAN:** NASA's been doing excellent education, both on the ground and from orbit. By "education" I mean providing opportunities for students and teachers to get involved and to both experience and to contribute to space exploration goals. This is just one of many, many steps along the way. I really look forward to coming back and helping with what comes next, and what comes next, and what comes next. Education is never-ending. It can get better and better and better.

29 **NASA:** In that sense, is education very much like space itself—limitless? No boundaries?

Words to Know

General Academic Vocabulary

inherent (*adj.*): existing as a natural part of someone or something
momentary (*adj.*): lasting only for a moment; brief
propelled (*v.*): pushed in a direction
sustenance (*n.*): the state of being sustained, or kept going, for a long period

Domain-Specific Vocabulary

telescope (*n.*): a tool used to magnify objects

Working with Word Meaning Have students team up to play 20 Questions. Ask partners to take turns thinking of words while the other asks indirect questions in order to guess which word it is.

KEY IDEAS AND DETAILS
Independent Practice

30 **MORGAN:** Absolutely.

31 **NASA:** Barbara Morgan, educator astronaut, mission specialist, shuttle *Endeavour*, STS-118, thank you so much.

32 **MORGAN:** Thank you.—www.nasa.gov

Comprehension Check (MORE ONLINE) **sadlierconnect.com**

1. Which words show that Morgan is interested in being part of a team?

   a. *women* and *history*

   b. *contributing* and *helping*

   c. *education* and *program*

   d. *interested* and *opportunities*

2. Based on this passage, what can you conclude about Morgan?

   a. She is fearless.

   b. She learns quickly.

   c. She is calm under pressure.

   d. She is enthusiastic about her job.

3. Which of the following would NOT be necessary in a summary of the text?

   a. Morgan wants to inspire children to learn.

   b. Morgan hopes to bring attention to her fellow teachers and their work.

   c. Morgan's husband and sons are very supportive of her goals.

   d. Morgan became a Teacher in Space in 1986.

4. Education is a central idea of this interview. How does Morgan define it?

   a. getting involved in an experience

   b. studying quietly alone

   c. reading books on different subjects

   d. learning from role models

5. Think again about the central ideas of this text. What makes Morgan a good representative for NASA's Teacher in Space program? Give reasons, using evidence from the text.

   Sample answer: Morgan is an excellent representative. She shows how education and space exploration are based on similar values. She wants students to get involved. She shares with others her excitement about space and her love of learning.

Unit 3 ■ Reading Informational Text: Key Ideas and Details   79

Extend Thinking: Hypothesize

Barbara Morgan says that her mission to the International Space Station involved bringing up equipment, including solar arrays, but she doesn't say what those are used for. She also says that another part of her mission will be to bring home things that are not needed on the Space Station. Challenge students to come up with a hypothesis for one or both of these information gaps. Then have students check the NASA Web site to confirm their ideas.

Follow up by having students discuss their finding in small groups or as a whole class. Remind students to use language appropriate for class discussions.

Independent Practice

Comprehension Check

Answer Explanations:

1. Students should see that the words *contributing* and *helping* suggest the involvement of others and support the idea of being part of a team.

2. All are possible answers, but students should choose D because they have seen many examples of Morgan's enthusiasm.

3. Choice C is the only detail that is not related to the central ideas of learning and going into space.

4. Based on the information throughout the interview, students should be able to determine that "getting involved in an experience" is how Morgan defines education.

5. Students' answers will vary, but all should be supported with specific evidence from the text.

Critical Comprehension

Challenge students to think more deeply about the text and to support their answers with evidence from the text.

How might students benefit from having a teacher like Barbara Morgan? (Students might say that it would be exciting to have a teacher who is so interested in exploring space and pushing the boundaries of what we know. Also, they might say it would be fun to study the solar system with a real astronaut.)

Assess and Respond
If students have trouble answering the questions in the Comprehension Check,
Then ask them to work in small groups to discuss the answers and benefit from their peers' insights.

Guided Instruction

OBJECTIVE
Analyze the relationships between ideas, people, and events in a text.

Genre: Feature Article

Feature articles are longer articles that treat a subject in depth, going beyond basic facts to explore questions, such as *how* or *why*.

Set the Purpose

Have students give examples of how people, events, and ideas can influence each other, by using information from Barbara Morgan's interview. *What factors led to Morgan going into space?*

Model and Teach

Read or have volunteers read the selection and callouts as the class follows along. Model effective strategies for responding to the callouts by using the suggestions below.

CITE EVIDENCE

A Students should realize that traveling to Mars when the distance between Earth and Mars is shortest would be the most practical plan in terms of time, fuel, and cost.

B Students can find several facts about the weather and atmosphere on Mars in paragraph 4.

ANALYZING TEXTS
Guided Instruction

WORDS TO KNOW

circumference
compound
dissipate
mass
plummet

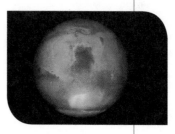

> **Analyzing a text** means understanding how its people, events, and ideas relate to and influence each other.

CITE EVIDENCE

A **Analyzing a text** means paying close attention to its details. Underline the information about the distance between planets that is important to consider when planning a mission to Mars.

B Which weather and atmospheric conditions will influence how astronauts prepare for Mars's climate? Put asterisks by two pieces of relevant information.

Destination Mars
(Genre: Feature Article)

1   After landing on the moon, landing on a planet seems to be the next logical step. Of our two neighbors, Venus and Mars, Mars is the logical choice. The surface of Venus is too hot—hot enough to melt metal. Mars is colder than Earth, which is less challenging. Even so, nearly 50 years after landing on the moon, we still haven't made it there!

2   Mars is visible in the night sky and has been known to humans since ancient times as the Red Planet. It is red because its surface is full of iron oxide, the same **compound** that colors blood and rust. In fact, the planet was named after the ancient Roman god of war due to its blood-red color.

3   Mars is the fourth planet from the sun, which makes it Earth's next-door neighbor. It's not a close neighbor, though, since Mars is about 36 million miles away from Earth at the closest point in their orbits. When the two planets are at their furthest distance, on opposite sides of the sun, Mars is closer to 250 million miles away. Obviously, then, any mission to Mars would have to be timed to take advantage of the shorter distance.

No Place Like Home

4   Mars, being farther from the sun, is colder than Earth. *Although its temperatures can reach 80 degrees Fahrenheit at the warmest point on the warmest day, it can also **plummet** to more than 100 degrees below zero. The coldest place that humans regularly inhabit is Oymyakon, Russia. There the average winter temperature is minus 58 degrees Fahrenheit. *On Mars the temperature drops dramatically because the atmosphere is thinner than on Earth. A thinner atmosphere allows heat to **dissipate** quickly. The atmosphere here on Earth holds heat in and also protects us from certain kinds of radiation; the thinner atmosphere on Mars does not.

Words to Know

General Academic Vocabulary
dissipate (*v.*): to scatter; spread out and away
plummet (*v.*): to drop suddenly and quickly

Domain-Specific Vocabulary
circumference (*n.*): the length of the outer boundary of a circle
compound (*n.*): a combination of chemical elements
mass (*n.*): the substance and weight of an object

Working with Word Meaning Have students use images or diagrams to help them visualize the meaning of each new word.

Guided Instruction

5   It's not only the cold temperatures and radiation that can harm humans on Mars. The atmosphere on Mars is missing oxygen, which means that the air is poisonous for Earthlings to breathe. <u>Humans would need to have life-support systems, radiation protection, and defense from below-freezing temperatures to survive on Mars.</u>

What Goes Up

6   Mars is smaller than Earth. The **circumference** around Earth's equator is about 25,000 miles, while the circumference around Mars is about 13,000 miles. Therefore, another big difference between the two planets is connected to the force of <u>gravity</u> on each. As Earth is bigger and has more **mass**, the gravity on Earth is stronger than the gravity on Mars. On the Red Planet, you would be able to jump higher and throw a ball farther, which would make you much better at basketball! Your shape wouldn't look any different, but your weight would be reduced by about one-third. You might even be an inch or so taller with less gravity pulling you toward the planet's center. However, there would be a big price to pay if you ever returned to Earth.

7   The force of Earth's gravity pulling on us creates muscle strength even when we are still. When the force of gravity is reduced, your muscles don't have to work as hard, so they begin to shrink. This includes your heart, which is also a muscle. You might feel like Superman going from Earthling gravity to Martian gravity, but the reverse could be deadly!

8   Considering all the differences between the two planets, any mission that included humans would have to be very carefully planned.

Comprehension Check

Why is planning a manned trip to Mars so much more difficult than sending robot probes?

CITE EVIDENCE

C What would astronauts need to explore the surface of Mars? Double underline that information.

D Circle the evidence that shows that Mars is smaller than Earth. Why does this fact matter? Underline the word that answers this question.

E When analyzing a text, focus on how important ideas impact the people involved. What issues related to gravity could be problematic for astronauts? Put a box around that information.

Guided Instruction

CITE EVIDENCE

C Reinforce the Idea that analyzing a text involves close reading and attention to detail. Be sure that students read attentively to the end of paragraph 5 to identify the requirements for human exploration of Mars.

D Analyzing a text also means understanding how a text's details relate to each other. After reading paragraph 6, students should understand that there is a relationship between a planet's size and its mass, which affects the strength of the force of gravity on its surface. This information would have implications for anyone planning to visit Mars.

E Guide students to read paragraph 7 carefully to find details about how gravity affects the human body.

Comprehension Check

Sample Answer: Robots aren't alive, so they don't need the air, water, and food that astronauts would require on a manned trip. Also, robots can stand higher and lower temperatures. Finally, it's possible to leave probes in space without trying to bring them back.

Answer Explanation: Students should realize that sending humans on a mission to Mars is much more difficult than using robot probes because humans need supplies and must be kept safe.

Support English Language Learners

Scientific terms may not be as difficult for native speakers of Latinate languages, such as Spanish or French. Many scientific terms have Latin roots, which means that many are cognates. Explain to students that cognates are words that have the same or a similar spelling or that share a common root. Here are some examples you can share with native Spanish speakers:

- *circunferencia*—circumference
- *atmósfera*—atmosphere
- *planetas*—planets
- *órbita*—orbit

Challenge students to keep a list of all the cognates they find.

Guided Instruction

CITE EVIDENCE

A In paragraph 9, the author explicitly states the Mars Society mission. Students should realize that the Mars Society is trying to simulate the experience of staying on Mars by setting up training centers in remote desert locations.

B Guide students to paragraph 10 for details about the tools used to measure the crewmembers' stress and mood, including a questionnaire, a computer assessment, scales and profiles of behaviors, and physical measures.

Review: Determining Central Ideas

On pages 82–83, the sections "How Do We Measure Stress and Mood?," "Does Music Reduce Stress?," and "Does Exercise Improve Mood?" all point to an important central idea. Ask students to identify that central idea. (Knowing factors that affect and improve stress and mood is important for future exploration of Mars, which will involve people living together in cramped conditions for long periods.)

ANALYZING TEXTS
Guided Instruction

WORDS TO KNOW

genre
invigorating
isolated
marshal
philanthropist
suborbital

CITE EVIDENCE

A How is the Mars Society contributing to future exploration of Mars? Underline this information.

B What tools did the researchers use to measure the crew's stress and mood responses? Circle that information.

82

Destination Mars *continued*

Training on the Ground

9   A group called the Mars Society is preparing for human exploration of Mars. The Mars Society is using small research bases established in desert terrains on Earth to study how people might live and work on Mars. As part of this project, a team of college students stayed at the Mars Desert Research Station in Hanksville, Utah. These students were there to research factors that might affect a team's stress levels and mood while **isolated** together inside a small living space for two weeks.

How Do We Measure Stress and Mood?

10   The first thing the team had to do was figure out how to measure the crewmembers' state of mind. One tool used was a questionnaire that asked crewmembers how they felt. Another was a computer assessment for measuring such functions as attention span, memory, reaction time, and decisionmaking. Scales and profiles gave descriptions the team could match to observable behaviors. Lastly, the team could measure physical indicators, such as blood pressure and heart rate. One of the goals was to see which tools worked best.

Does Music Reduce Stress?

11   One member of the team performed a study on the effect of music. The experiment exposed subjects to five different **genres** of music. These were played twice over a 10-day period. For three days no music was played. Those music-free days came at the beginning, middle, and end of the experience. The preliminary results showed that the crewmembers had the lowest blood-pressure measurements and heart rates on the days when country music was played, even though several crewmembers claimed to dislike that type of music. All of the crewmembers preferred days with some kind of music rather than no music at all.

Words to Know

General Academic Vocabulary

genre (*n.*): style; type
invigorating (*adj.*): energizing
isolated (*adj.*): separated from others; alone
marshal (*v.*): to bring together; gather
philanthropist (*n.*): a person who gives money to do good works

Domain-Specific Vocabulary

suborbital (*adj.*): not having the altitude to reach orbit

Working with Word Meaning Have students restate these definitions in their own words.

KEY IDEAS AND DETAILS

Does Exercise Improve Mood?

12   Another factor studied was the effect of exercise on mood. In a Mars mission, exercise would be important to combat muscle loss, an effect of reduced gravity. The experiment compared the effects on mood after an <u>advanced workout</u> versus the effects after a moderate workout. The results first showed a negative reaction to the advanced workout and a positive reaction to the moderate workout. Over time, however, those feelings reversed. The advanced workout felt less intense over time and the moderate workout became less **invigorating**. Preliminary conclusions show that increasing workout intensity keeps workouts satisfying.

Beyond NASA

13   The Mars Society is not the only private group to get involved in space innovation. In the past, governments were the only organizations that could **marshal** enough money, talent, and resources to pull off such a large endeavor. Today, both private companies and individuals are funding space projects.

14   The era of private manned space travel began in 2004. The brainchild of a **philanthropist**, engineer, and pilot, *SpaceShipOne* was the first privately developed reusable launch vehicle and winner of a $10 million prize. (A reusable vehicle is the key to making space trips more affordable.)

15   This means it's only a matter of time before space tourism becomes a workable business. Space tourism began when a few wealthy people paid millions for a ride into space. A Russian spaceship took these privileged passengers to the International Space Station. Soon companies will offer **suborbital** rides to anyone with a few hundred thousand dollars or so to spare.

Comprehension Check

Based on your analysis of the text, how long will it take before humans are able to overcome the issues involved with traveling to Mars? Explain your answer.

Guided Instruction

CITE EVIDENCE

C Double underline the factor that experiments show might reduce stress and improve the mood of Mars explorers.

D What new technology is necessary for space tourism to become a real business? Circle your answer.

E Put a box around the information that tells how space tourism got started.

The International Space Station

Guided Instruction

CITE EVIDENCE

C Drawing conclusions is an important part of analyzing a text. Guide students to the result of the experiment in paragraph 12: Over time, the crew reported feeling more invigorated by the advanced workouts.

D Have students scan paragraph 14 for the type of technology that could make space travel "more affordable."

E Students should look for the key phrase "space tourism" as they read the last two paragraphs on page 83. Ask students to consider the appeal of space tourism and its effect on the long-term goal of reaching distant planets.

Comprehension Check

Sample Answer: It will be many years before humans reach Mars. There are still some difficult problems to solve.

Answer Explanation: Students should be able to see from the information they have analyzed in this section that many problems related to humans' physical and emotional health, among other issues, must be studied and resolved before humans are ready to go to Mars.

Differentiate Instruction

Make some of the ideas discussed in the section about the Mars Society training program more concrete for students by showing them examples of questionnaires, scales, and profiles for stress and mood. Point out that participants fill out the questionnaires, while scales and profiles are tools for observing participants. Show them how heart rate and blood pressure might be measured. Then let students propose an experiment of their own to measure stress and mood. Help them connect their ideas to what happened on the Mars Society research base.

Guided Practice

Recap Reading Selection

Ask students to recall what is challenging about the conditions on Mars and how some people are preparing to go there.

Read and Practice

Have partners take turns reading the selection as you circulate to provide support. Circulate among students and ask them to find stated ideas and to draw inferences using Cite Evidence callouts A and B. Provide additional scaffolding as needed, using the suggestions below.

CITE EVIDENCE

A Students who are reading attentively should see that sentence 2 of paragraph 16 cues the more complete answer to this question, found at the end of paragraph 16 and the beginning of paragraph 17.

B Suggest that students create a T-chart or Venn diagram to determine the differences in the two missions, as explained in paragraphs 18–20. If students need help, have them focus on the goals of the two missions, how they will be funded, and who will participate.

ANALYZING TEXTS
Guided Practice

Destination Mars continued

WORDS TO KNOW
cosmic
disorder
entrepreneur
impaired
scout

CITE EVIDENCE

A People who travel to Mars might have to worry about their thinking skills. Underline two reasons that support this idea.

B With a partner, consider the private missions to Mars (paragraphs 18–20). Put asterisks by the differences between the two missions. Then discuss which mission is more likely to succeed.

Danger Ahead

16   Mars is the dream destination of many would-be space travelers. However, there are two big issues: the psychological effects of extreme isolation and the dangers of **cosmic** radiation. Mars500 was designed to test the effects of a simulated Mars voyage. An international crew was sealed in a spaceship-like environment for 520 days and monitored. Most of the crew developed sleep **disorders** that caused **impaired** thinking.

17   Experiments done with cosmic radiation showed that certain particles cause brain damage in mice. Of course, we can't be sure radiation would affect people the same way. Unfortunately, it's difficult to protect astronauts from these particles, since the particles can travel through almost anything.

Against the Odds

18   Despite these risks, a U.S. millionaire and rocket scientist has started the Inspiration Mars Foundation.* Its goal is a manned mission to Mars in 2018.* The plan is to fly by Mars rather than land on the planet.* The voyage would last about 500 days.* The Foundation is looking for a married couple to serve as the crew. Many have already applied.* The group still needs to raise more money to make the mission happen.

19   A company founded by a Dutch **entrepreneur**, Mars One is taking a different approach.* This group plans to generate the money it needs by turning the mission into a reality show.* The ambition is greater, as well, since this group plans to start a human colony on Mars by 2023. Tens of thousands of people have already applied for a one-way ticket to the Red Planet.* The company is planning its first launch, of equipment only, for 2016.

20   Two years later, a rover will **scout** the best location, and six living units will be sent up in 2021, according to the plan.* In

84

© 2013 Bryan Versteeg/Mars One

Words to Know

General Academic Vocabulary

disorder (*n.*): disease; disability
entrepreneur (*n.*) a person who starts his or her own business
impaired (*adj.*): not working correctly
scout (*v.*): to search for

Domain-Specific Vocabulary

cosmic (*adj.*): having to do with space or the cosmos

Working with Word Meaning Have students create scenarios based on vocabulary word pairs, such as "cosmic entrepreneur" or "impaired scout."

2023, the first humans would land.* Of course, the plan can work only if people around the world remain interested in watching this mission on TV, since the mission depends on money generated by television advertising.

21 Because it's so risky, NASA is not planning on any manned trips to Mars until 2030.

Comprehension Check

1. How does understanding different organizations' plans for private Mars missions help readers?

   a. Readers can better understand how much such a mission will cost.

   b. Readers can explore the problems with each organization's plan.

   c. Readers can imagine traveling to Mars on one of the missions.

   d. Readers can consider different solutions to the challenges of a Mars mission. *(circled)*

2. Of all the organizations preparing for a trip to Mars, which has the most problems to solve?

   a. the Mars Society

   b. Mars One *(circled)*

   c. NASA

   d. the Inspiration Mars Foundation

3. We can't be sure if cosmic radiation will harm humans because

   a. no experiments have been conducted.

   b. the results were negative.

   c. the results were positive.

   d. the experiment wasn't conducted on humans. *(circled)*

4. The dates in 2016, 2018, and 2023 were probably chosen because

   a. that's when Mars and Earth will be closest. *(circled)*

   b. that's how long it will take to raise the money needed.

   c. that's how long it will take to get ready.

   d. that's when the space radiation will be reduced.

5. Why might the ideas in this text influence people to choose one of the private companies instead of NASA? Discuss your answer with a partner, citing text evidence.

   Sample answer: According to the text, the private companies have a variety of innovative ideas for manned Mars programs and are pushing to get to Mars soon. NASA, on the other hand, is moving more slowly and is much more concerned about the risk. People who are attracted by the innovative ideas and are willing to take the risks might choose one of the private companies instead of NASA.

Discussion Skills

Put students in groups to discuss their ideas about a mission to colonize Mars. Group members should prepare in advance by identifying at least three key problems that a Mars colony would have to solve. Assign group roles, such as Facilitator, Timekeeper, and Notetaker, and have each group develop a comprehensive list of problems and potential solutions. Remind students to ask questions of one another and to keep the discussion on track. At the end of the discussion, have groups share their lists with the class, and develop a class list of problems and solutions. Ask students if they would be willing to volunteer to live on a Mars colony.

Comprehension Check

Answer Explanations:

1. While all of the answer choices sound viable, D is the one that most broadly covers the advantages of understanding all of the missions.

2. Colonizing Mars is the most ambitious and complex plan, so students should see that Mars One has the most problems to solve.

3. In paragraph 17, students read that the experiments were done on mice, not humans. Therefore, D is the correct answer.

4. To answer this item correctly, students must remember that the distance between Earth and Mars varies because of the planets' orbits, and that it is desirable to travel to Mars when the two are closest.

5. Answers will vary, but students must support their response with evidence from the text.

Peer Collaboration

You might have students do a think-pair-share so that peers can support each other in responding to callout B on page 84 and Comprehension Check question 5 on page 85. Ask students to finalize their answers and then share them with a partner. Students should ask questions as needed and then make changes to their answers based on the discussion with their partner. Finally, ask pairs to report their answers to the whole group, keeping in mind the discussion rules established in Unit 2.

Independent Practice

Recap Reading Selection

Ask students to discuss why sending people to Mars is the next logical goal of space exploration. Have them list some of the challenges of sending humans there, and have them sum up the efforts that are underway that they have read about so far.

Read and Apply

Have students read this section independently as you circulate. Ask them to read aloud so you can see if they are reading fluently. You can also use the support below to help students who are having difficulty.

CITE EVIDENCE

A Be sure students understand that the Soviet *Mars 2* mission failed when the unmanned craft crash-landed. One possible explanation for that failure is that the mission was rushed. The successful U.S. mission that took place four years later helps provide evidence for this conclusion.

B Students should understand that the information gathered during one mission helped scientists plan the next mission. The *Viking* missions sent information from Mars's orbit that was used to plan the missions to explore the planet's surface. Information from the surface led to more specific questions about water, life, and the planet's core.

ANALYZING TEXTS

Independent Practice

Destination Mars continued

WORDS TO KNOW
- artifact
- deposit
- refined
- sedimentary
- transmitted

Robots in Space

22   Even though NASA is not ready to plan a manned mission to Mars, it has sent many probes and rovers to study the planet. Over the years, these machines have become more **refined** and complex. You might even call them robots. Here's a short history of what has been accomplished so far.

23   *Mars 2*, the first unmanned craft that made it to the Red Planet, was sent up by the Soviets in 1971. The mission failed when *Mars 2* was destroyed in a crash landing, but it became the first human **artifact** left on another planet.

24   NASA had the first successful landing with the Viking Program in 1975, which included *Viking 1* and *Viking 2*. Each craft had an orbiter and a lander. All parts performed better than expected and **transmitted** data from the Martian orbit and ground for several years.

25   In 1996, NASA's *Pathfinder* delivered a micro-rover called *Sojourner* to the surface. *This mission, building on what was learned from *Viking*, was much more efficient and cost the government much less.

CITE EVIDENCE
A Did the Soviets rush the *Mars 2* mission? Underline evidence you can use to answer this question.

B Put asterisks by details that tell you how each mission built on the one before it. Discuss what the progress of unmanned Mars missions reveals about NASA's goals.

26   Large rovers *Spirit* and *Opportunity* followed, reaching Mars in 2003. As information about the planet was gathered, the missions became more specific. *Spirit* was designed to explore the Gusev Crater and look for evidence that liquid water may have once been present there. *Opportunity* was designed to explore the Meridiani Planum, an area that includes iron-rich mineral **deposits**.

27   The rover *Opportunity* discovered a rock with markings that scientists think may have been made by flowing water because they look similar to markings on certain **sedimentary** rocks here on Earth. In 2007 the *Phoenix* mission explored the polar region of Mars and the next year was able to confirm the existence of frozen water in the soil.

Words to Know

General Academic Vocabulary
refined (*adj.*): precise or exact

Domain-Specific Vocabulary
artifact (*n.*): an object of historical interest made by humans
deposit (*n.*): a natural collection of a substance, usually a mineral
sedimentary (*adj.*): made of sand compacted together
transmitted (*v.*): sent by signal

Working with Word Meaning Have students work in pairs to write a brief story using all of the words.

KEY IDEAS AND DETAILS
Independent Practice

28   The most recent rover to go to Mars is *Curiosity*, which was sent in 2012. It has already retrieved a core sample that includes all the necessary building blocks for life! Yet another robotic mission is planned for 2016. The *InSight* mission will drill down into the surface to learn more about the planet's core.

29   It will be interesting to see whose boots walk the dusty red soil first. Will it be NASA's slow and steady progress, or one of the bold space entrepreneurs?

Comprehension Check   (MORE ONLINE) **sadlierconnect.com**

1. Why has NASA sent so many unmanned missions to Mars?

   a. They haven't landed successfully.

   b. They haven't found evidence of life yet.

   c. Astronauts fear the Red Planet.

   d. They keep making new discoveries. ✓

2. What led to the discovery of water on Mars?

   a. exploring the polar region ✓

   b. seeing the markings on rock

   c. digging into the planet's core

   d. finding iron-rich mineral deposits

3. Which Mars mission will benefit most from the discovery of water?

   a. a fly-by mission

   b. a colony mission ✓

   c. a rover mission

   d. a 500-day mission

4. The discovery by *Curiosity* means that

   a. there was definitely life on Mars.

   b. there is life somewhere on Mars.

   c. there is no more to learn about possible life on Mars.

   d. there is more to learn about possible life on Mars. ✓

5. Would the *Curiosity* mission have been as successful if the other missions had not gone before it? Explain your answer, using evidence from the text.

   Sample answer: *Curiosity* would not have been as successful without the knowledge gained from the earlier missions. The other missions brought back information from the surface of Mars and helped scientists know where to look for water and where to take the best samples. They also found ways to increase efficiency and reduce costs, making it much easier to send another rover.

Independent Practice

Comprehension Check

Answer Explanations:

1. Students should see that choices B and D are both true, but D is correct because NASA's goal is not specifically to find evidence of life on Mars.

2. Have students recall from paragraph 27 that rock markings inspired the polar mission, which confirmed water's existence.

3. Students should understand that a colony mission would need water to support the people living on Mars, so it would benefit most.

4. Choices A, B, and C are too broad and unequivocal to be true. As students have already learned, each new discovery on Mars generally leads to further exploration.

5. Students' answers will vary, but each response should be supported with evidence from the text.

Critical Comprehension

Challenge students to think more deeply about the text and to support their answers with evidence from the text.

Which mission to Mars is most likely to tells us things we don't yet know about the planet? (Students may respond that a colony mission would give the most new information about Mars and would be most likely to lead to new discoveries.)

Assess and Respond
If students have trouble answering the questions in the Comprehension Check,
Then ask them to return to the text and highlight information that can help them answer the questions.

Speaking and Listening Presentation

Have students prepare a presentation about reaching a challenging goal, in the spirit of President Kennedy's speech. Remind students to plan by setting milestone goals and deadlines.

Presenters should include facts and details about the goal and how it can be accomplished, using multimedia or visual elements to support their points; adapt their language for a formal presentation; speak clearly; and maintain eye contact with their listeners. At the end of the presentation, presenters should answer questions and acknowledge listeners' ideas.

Listeners should listen attentively and ask questions.

OBJECTIVES

- Use textual evidence to support an analysis of both explicit and inferred information from the text.
- Identify two or more ideas that are central to the text and analyze how the author develops them. Summarize the text.
- Analyze the relationships between ideas, people, and events in a text.

Genre: Explanatory Text and Policy Statement

Remind students that explanatory text provides information and often explains a process. Tell students that the policy statement included in this selection was created so U.S. citizens and other interested people around the world could see America's plans and goals for space exploration.

Path Options

You may want to do a close reading with students; if so, use the supports provided on these pages. Or, you may wish to have students read the text independently and apply the skills learned in this unit. In either case, students should read the text more than once to facilitate understanding and to be able to answer the Comprehension Questions correctly.

Our National Space Policy

(Genre: Explanatory Text and Policy Statement)

1   Part of every U.S. president's job is to set space policy. During the election season, presidential candidates talk about their goals for space exploration. Voters decide if they agree with those goals. Space policy may not seem like an important issue during an election because other issues get a lot more attention in the media.

2   In fact, some people are not in favor of more space exploration. They feel that the government has more important business and should focus on helping people. Space programs cost the government many millions of dollars, taking money away from other things government could be doing. However, people might be surprised to learn what else we get for that money in addition to knowledge and a sense of achievement.

3   In order to pull off a mission to space, a huge amount of research needs to be done.

This research takes place in all kinds of areas, such as engineering, biology, weather, communications, computer technology, and more. Many inventions that come out of this research have applications beyond the space program. Here are a few benefits that have come from the space program. Some of these advances were developed by NASA, and some were developed by private companies that were commissioned by NASA.

For Your Health

4   NASA, along with doctors and a technology company, developed a lifesaving heart pump for patients awaiting heart transplants. The ventricular assist device (VAD) can keep people alive and active until an organ donor is found.

5   Before the invention of the ear thermometer, taking your temperature meant sitting for several minutes with a mercury-filled glass tube under your tongue. Modern ear thermometers, developed with NASA's assistance, take your temperature in two seconds. They use the same infrared-detection technology that astronomers use to measure the temperature of distant stars.

6   Originally created for NASA, space robotic technology is now adding comfort and function to artificial limbs. Advances include artificial muscle systems with robotic sensing and movement. In addition, NASA's temper foam technology can be used to create natural-looking limbs that have the soft feel of flesh. The foam also provides cushioning that makes prosthetics more comfortable for people to wear.

Support English Language Learners

Help students read this selection by giving them a walkthough of its major sections. Say: *This is the introduction; it tells us what a space policy is, and then it leads to a discussion of the benefits of the U.S. space program.* For each section, give a brief summary of the type of information included. Students may need to translate into their first language some specialized or scientific terms, such as "heart pump," "medical thermometer," and "artificial limb."

KEY IDEAS AND DETAILS

For Safety and Convenience

7 Speaking of temper (memory) foam, you may have seen the mattresses or pillows that spring back when you touch them. That foam was developed by NASA to improve safety during crashes. It's now being used in safety features for cars, airplanes, amusement park rides, sports equipment, and more. The primary quality of the foam is its ability to absorb energy, which can soften impacts. That feature also makes it very comfortable to sink into. It is even used to make luxurious dog beds!

8 A tool company used *Apollo* and *Gemini* mission technologies to make cleaning easier. NASA required a portable, self-contained drill capable of extracting core samples from below the lunar surface. A computer program optimized the design of the drill's motor and reduced its need for power. That computer program made the cordless miniature vacuum cleaner possible.

For the Environment

9 A NASA-sponsored coalition of companies, government groups, universities, and nonprofits helped create improvements to solar power cells, making them both lighter and more effective. These new solar cells allow people to reduce the costs and pollution associated with traditional energy sources. The coalition's original goal was to create solar power sources without adding weight to unmanned aircraft.

10 NASA technology is being used to clean petroleum-based pollutants from water. The basic technology is thousands of microcapsules—tiny balls of beeswax with hollow centers. Water cannot get inside the microcapsule, but oil is absorbed right inside. The beeswax spheres float on the water's surface. In this way, oil spills can be captured before they settle into the water, damaging sea life and the ocean floor.

11 Water purification is an important part of space missions. Water is heavy to carry, so any water carried onboard needs to be recycled multiple times. NASA engineers in collaboration with private companies developed a water purification system for the astronauts living on the International Space Station. This system can turn wastewater from respiration, sweat, and urine into drinkable water. It's also used to help people all over the world who lack clean water. The system can provide drinkable water from even badly polluted sources.

12 Did you know NASA's excess rocket fuel can be used to destroy land mines? Instead of dumping this fuel as waste, NASA shares it with a company that gets rid of land mines. A device with a battery-operated electric match ignites solid rocket fuel placed on the mine. The fuel burns a hole in the mine's case and also burns up the explosive inside, so the mine is safely disarmed.

A man searches for land mines.

Support First Reading

Circulate to check and support students' understanding. Use the following comprehension and strategy check-ins as needed.

Check-in Questions

- *Who decides on the space policy for the nation?* (The President of the United States decides on the space policy.)
- *Which inventions mentioned in the text impact people's health?* (the heart pump, the ear thermometer, and robotics and temper foam for artificial limbs)
- *What is the special property of memory foam that makes it a good material for safety equipment and comfortable beds?* (It absorbs energy.)
- *What two problems are solved with a battery operated match?* (using up extra solid rocket fuel and getting rid of land mines)

Review: Drawing Inferences

Have students find a clue in paragraph 2 that tells what some people would prefer the government spend money on rather than the space program. ("They feel that the government . . . should focus on helping people.")

Differentiate Instruction

To be sure that all students can be successful with this selection, give students who cannot read it independently the option of hearing the text read aloud. In addition, some students will need help with the hyphenated descriptors, such as *mercury-filled* (filled with mercury), *infrared-detection* (able to detect heat), and *NASA-sponsored* (hired by NASA), and will also need definitions for difficult words such as *limbs* (arms and legs), *microcapsules* (tiny containers), *purification* (cleaning), and *ignites* (lights on fire).

Close Reading

Check-in Questions

- *How do the new inventions mentioned on these pages help the economy?* (When new products are invented, new companies are created to make and sell these things, so more people have jobs. When those people get paid, they spend their money on other things.)

- *What is the next mission to space, according to the National Space Policy?* (The next mission is 2025, to go beyond the Moon to an asteroid.)

- *In what way does NASA hope to protect the country?* (NASA will try to reduce the risk from unexpected impact from near-Earth objects.)

Review: Determining Central Ideas

Review with students that central ideas are often repeated in a text; for example, the author of this text refers to partnerships repeatedly, which suggests that they are a central idea. Ask the class to name as many of the kinds of partnerships NASA hopes to form as possible. (Partnerships include international partners, private sector partners, academic partners, and industrial partners.)

Review: Analyzing Texts

After students read page 91, remind them that analyzing a text means understanding how the people, ideas, and events in it interact. Have students explain how the mission to an asteroid is supposed to work. (A robot probe would capture the asteroid and tow it into the moon's orbit. Astronauts would fly to the moon's orbit to study the asteroid.)

CLOSE READING

Our National Space Policy *continued*

And More!

13   Space technology has contributed to improvements or new products in all kinds of fields, from photography and art restoration to infant care and clothing manufacturing. In addition, NASA advances spurred technology that has led to smaller and smaller electronic devices, such as cell phones.

14   All these new products are great for individuals, but they also help the economy in general. New companies are created, and more people are hired. Of course, part of their paychecks goes to buy more things. In a way, then, some of the money spent on space exploration makes its way back to us all.

15   Probably the greatest benefit of the space program is its ability to inspire children's imagination. By motivating students to study science, technology, engineering, and math, our society will advance. The wonders of tomorrow will come from the students we are educating now. They will make devices that we cannot even imagine today.

16   So what is NASA's mission? It's inside the United States Space Policy document. These are the guidelines that were given to NASA by President Obama.

90

Guidelines for Space Science, Exploration, and Discovery

- NASA shall set far-reaching exploration milestones. By 2025, begin crewed missions beyond the Moon, including sending humans to an asteroid. By the mid-2030s, send humans to orbit Mars and return them safely to Earth.

- NASA shall continue the operation of the International Space Station (ISS), in cooperation with its international partners, likely to 2020 or beyond.

- NASA shall seek partnerships with the private sector to enable safe, reliable, and cost-effective commercial spaceflight capabilities and services for . . . the ISS.

- NASA shall implement a new space technology development working with industry, academia, and international partners . . . that can increase the capabilities, decrease the costs, and expand the opportunities for future space activities.

- NASA shall conduct research and development in support of next-generation launch systems, including new U.S. rocket engine technologies.

- NASA shall maintain a sustained robotic presence in the solar system to: conduct scientific investigations of other planetary bodies; demonstrate new technologies; and scout locations for future human missions.

- NASA shall continue a strong program of space science for observations, research, and analysis . . . to enhance knowledge of the cosmos, . . . understand the conditions that may support the development of life, and search for planetary bodies and Earth-like planets in orbit around other stars.

Strategic Reading

Remind students that there are strategies they can use if they are having difficulty understanding a complex text. One strategy is to reread any parts that are giving them trouble. Tell them to go back to the point where they last understood the text and reread slowly and carefully from there. Remind students to use text features, such as subheadings, boldfaced definitions, and illustrations, to help them make sense of the material. Another strategy is to read ahead. Glancing ahead may provide context that helps students make sense of the text they have already read.

If students try rereading and reading ahead and still have trouble understanding the text, they may need to request additional support.

KEY IDEAS AND DETAILS

- And NASA shall pursue capabilities . . . to detect, track, catalog, and characterize near-Earth objects to reduce the risk of harm to humans from an unexpected impact on our planet and to identify potentially resource-rich planetary objects.

Going to an Asteroid?

17 Did you notice the goal of sending humans to an asteroid by 2025? NASA is also working with the University of Arizona on a mission called OSIRIS-REx in which a robot probe would approach and take samples of an asteroid named Bennu. Then the probe would tow the asteroid into the Moon's orbit, where astronauts can study it.

18 Bennu is a 500-ton asteroid in a near-Earth orbit. That might sound enormous, but Bennu is small enough to burn up in Earth's

atmosphere. It is rated 0 on the Torino Scale, used to measure how dangerous an asteroid might be to Earth. The OSIRIS-REx mission may help us learn to deflect more dangerous asteroids in the future.

The asteroid Bennu

19 Bennu is also rich in carbon, the building block of life on Earth. Scientists hope that it may help answer questions about why Earth is abundant in carbon, unlike other planets.

20 In less than 100 years, humans will have gone from gazing at the stars to capturing asteroids—and the possibilities for future knowledge from and exploration of space are as boundless as the universe itself.

Comprehension Check

1A. The space technology we use is mostly developed by

- **a.** NASA.
- **b.** private companies.
- **c.** NASA and private companies working together.
- **d.** neither NASA nor private companies.

1B. What phrase from the text supports the answer to Part A?

- **a.** "new companies are created"
- **b.** "a NASA-sponsored coalition"
- **c.** "originally created for NASA"
- **d.** "NASA technology"

2A. What can you infer about most advances in new space technology?

- **a.** They are a result of problem solving.
- **b.** They are a result of wasteful spending.
- **c.** They are an attempt to recycle waste.
- **d.** They are lucky accidents.

2B. What sentence from the text best supports the answer to Part A?

- **a.** "Did you know NASA's excess rocket fuel can be used to destroy land mines?"
- **b.** "NASA technology is being used to clean . . . pollutants from water."
- **c.** "Modern ear thermometers . . . take your temperature in two seconds."
- **d.** "[Memory] foam was developed by NASA to improve safety."

Unit 3 ■ Reading Informational Text: Key Ideas and Details **91**

Research to Build Knowledge

Students may wish to find out more about NASA's missions. Challenge them to find more specific information about NASA's future plans. You may wish to group students with similar interests. Have them gather information from multiple sources, using effective search terms, and choose credible sources. Remind students to give credit to their sources, following standard forms of citation. Then give students an opportunity to share their findings with the class.

Multiple Readings for Critical Comprehension

Have students reread and annotate this selection. Then pose questions that focus on critical comprehension.

- *What kind of mission to space generally happens before a mission includes humans?* (Robot probes go first to collect information that will help scientists keep humans safe.)

- *What is one of the main things that people are looking for in space?* (signs of life, information that might give clues about the formation of Earth)

Self-Select Text

As preparation for Connect Across Texts, have students choose one selection from this unit and reread it independently. Students can access full .pdf versions of some selections at **sadlierconnect.com**.

Comprehension Check

Begin scoring students' performance of unit skills with this Comprehension Check and continue through Connect Across Texts on page 94. Use students' scores to determine their readiness for the Unit 3 Review on page 96.

Multiple-Choice Questions: *1 point each*

1A. The text states several times that NASA has been working with partners.

1B. Students should understand that the phrase "NASA-sponsored coalition" means that NASA has initiated working with other groups on its missions.

2A. The text describes several instances of space technology being developed to solve a specific problem.

2B. Protecting astronauts during a crash is an example of problem solving.

Multiple-Choice Questions, continued: *1 point each*

3A. Choice C expresses a big idea that relates to the text, while choices A and B are details.

3B. Students can reason that the U.S. president is an important person, and if creating space policy is part of the president's job, it must be an important thing to do.

4A. Choice A is sometimes a by-product of space technology development, but it is not a goal of the Space Policy. Choices C and D are not mentioned in the Space Policy.

4B. The Space Policy states goals for exploration and research. Partners help NASA reach those goals, but partnership is not one of the goals.

5A. The Space Policy deals with asteroids in two ways. One is to study them, and the other is to protect Earth from impacts. Only one of these is mentioned among the answer choices.

5B. Asteroids are near-Earth objects that could impact Earth, so NASA detects and tracks them. Students should understand that a near-Earth impact could cause a lot of damage.

Short-Answer Questions: *2 points each* (10 points total)

Item 6 Rubric

2	Student correctly states memory foam's key quality and explains why it has so many uses.
1	Student states memory foam's key quality but does not explain its uses well.
0	Student cannot explain memory foam's key quality or uses.

CLOSE READING

3A. Which of the following is a main idea that is supported by the text?

  a. Space exploration is very expensive.

  b. Some people are not in favor of a space policy.

  c. It's important to have a space policy.

  d. all of the above

3B. What detail from the text best supports the answer to Part A?

  a. Other issues get more attention than space policy.

  b. The U.S. president sets space policy.

  c. NASA's mission is stated in the Space Policy document.

  d. The space program inspires students to study science and engineering.

4A. What is the main reason for having a space policy?

  a. to advance consumer products

  b. to set goals for exploration and research

  c. to make rules for how to treat alien life

  d. to spend more money helping people

4B. What detail from the text does NOT support the answer to Part A?

  a. "NASA shall continue a strong program of space science . . ."

  b. "NASA shall seek partnerships with the private sector . . ."

  c. "NASA shall set far-reaching exploration milestones."

  d. "NASA shall conduct research and development in support of next-generation launch systems . . ."

5A. Which part of the nation's policy addresses asteroids?

  a. "maintain a sustained robotic presence in the solar system"

  b. "detect, track, catalog, and characterize near-Earth objects"

  c. "seek partnerships with the private sector"

  d. "continue the operation of the International Space Station"

5B. Which words from that part of the policy are a clue to answer Part A?

  a. "near-Earth objects, impact"

  b. "Earth-like planets, life"

  c. "decrease costs, expand opportunity"

  d. "launch systems, engine"

6. What is the key quality of temper (memory) foam, and why does it have so many uses? Explain.

Sample answer: The foam is able to absorb energy, so it works as a cushion. This makes excellent padding for safety equipment and can make furniture and artificial limbs more comfortable. Also, its springiness can make artificial limbs feel more realistic.

Extend Thinking: Formulate a Plan

Invite students to formulate a future space policy for a time when humans have the technology to explore farther into space than is now possible. Have students analyze and imitate the language of the National Space Policy by creating a series of "shall" statements that sets goals, and then briefly explain how those goals will be met. Consider having students share their ideas in small groups and then present them to the whole class.

KEY IDEAS AND DETAILS

7. What is an asteroid, and why does NASA want to study one?

Sample answer: An asteroid is a space rock. It is a piece of evidence from when the solar
system was formed and may hold clues about Earth's past. Studying asteroids may also
help scientists figure out ways to deal with asteroids that threaten Earth.

8. Summarize how the OSIRIS-REx mission to study an asteroid is supposed to work.

Sample answer: The OSIRIS-REx mission will first send a robotic probe to the asteroid to
take samples. Then the probe will tow the asteroid into the moon's orbit. After that,
another spaceship will take astronauts to the asteroid, where they can study it.

9. Write a paragraph summarizing the text that tells how events in space research
have positively affected everyday people's lives. Explain your answer using
evidence from the text. Use a separate piece of paper if you need more space for
your answer.

Sample answer: The research needed for space exploration has led to many inventions
and technological advances that have uses beyond the space program. People in the U.S.
and elsewhere have benefited from products and improvements in the fields of health
and medicine, safety, caring for the environment, and more. Convenience products such
as memory foam mattresses and ear thermometers are available to the average
consumer; more importantly, NASA technology is helping to address larger problems
such as land mine disposal and the lack of clean water in countries around the world.

10. Below are three claims that one could make based on the United States Space Policy.

- The United States is mainly committed to protecting its own interests in space.
- The United States supports cooperative efforts in the exploration of space.
- The United States intends to transfer responsibility for space exploration from the
  government to private organizations.

A. Underline the claim that is supported by the most relevant and sufficient evidence
within the Space Policy excerpt.

B. On a separate piece of paper, write two facts that best provide evidence to support
the claim you underlined in Part A.

Two of the guidelines in the United States Space Policy encourage cooperative efforts, and
NASA is cooperating with the University of Arizona on the OSIRIS-REx mission.

Unit 3 ▪ Reading Informational Text: Key Ideas and Details **93**

Item 7 Rubric

2	Student correctly defines *asteroid* and gives a thorough explanation of the purpose for studying one.
1	Student gives only one reason for studying asteroids.
0	Student cannot give any reasons for studying asteroids.

Item 8 Rubric

2	Student includes all steps of the mission: to capture the asteroid, tow it into moon's orbit, and study it there.
1	Student includes at least two steps.
0	Student includes only one step.

Item 9 Rubric

2	Student writes an accurate summary of the text and includes supporting evidence.
1	Student writes an adequate summary and includes some supporting evidence.
0	Student's summary omits most of the important information from the text.

Item 10 Rubric

2	Student identifies correct claim and two solid pieces of supporting evidence.
1	Student identifies correct claim and only one solid piece of supporting evidence.
0	Student identifies incorrect claim.

Differentiate Instruction

Certain students may benefit from modeling of the two-part question format. Have them choose the correct answer for the first question below (choice a) and then show how that answer is supported only by choice b in the second question.

Why does NASA plan to keep using robots to explore space?

a. They can send back information without risking any lives.

b. They can conduct scientific investigations better than humans.

Which detail supports the answer above?

a. Robots will maintain a sustained presence in the solar system.

b. Robots will scout locations for future human missions.

Theme Wrap-Up

Lead students in a group discussion on the theme of new frontiers. *Where are the places left for humans to explore? What do people hope to find?* (Students should understand that all of space beyond the moon is left to explore.)

Connect Across Texts: 4 *points* Review Reading Selections

Put students into four groups, giving each group the responsibility to summarize one of the four reading selections in this unit. Ask a volunteer from each group to briefly summarize the selection for the class.

Support a Claim

Review the directions on page 94 of the Student Book. Be sure students understand that they are to list information from each text to support its claim.

Graphic Organizer Rubric

4	Student identifies key information in all four selections to support the claim.
3	Student identifies key information in three of the four selections to support the claim.
2	Student identifies key information in two of the four selections to support the claim.
1	Student identifies key information in one of the four selections to support the claim.
0	Student is unable to identify key information to support the claim for any of the selections.

Support Essential Question Discussion

Have students reread the Essential Question. Challenge them to finish this sentence: *Finding and analyzing the key ideas and details in a text helps me to . . .*

If students have difficulty finishing that sentence, prompt them by asking why understanding a text requires they do more than simply read the words.

CONNECT ACROSS TEXTS

Support a Claim

In this unit you've read an explanatory text and speech about the Space Race, an astronaut interview, a feature article about going to Mars, and guidelines from the United States Space Policy. Think about the claim below and how these selections might support that claim. In the chart, list key details and important points from the texts to use as evidence. Then write a brief essay in which you use the information in the chart to support the claim. Use a separate sheet of paper if you need more room to write. Be prepared to discuss your ideas with the class.

Selection 1
- scientific knowledge from space exploration
- technological advances in aeronautics, computing, and so on
- prestige of being first nation to the moon

Selection 3
- space program has led to the possibility of space tourism
- private companies are now able to invest in space travel and exploration

CLAIM: The United States has benefited in many ways from the space program.

Selection 2
- inspiring children to achieve
- working with other nations on the International Space Station

Selection 4
- research and technologies developed for and with the space program have led to many beneficial products

Return to the Essential Question

How can readers find and analyze central ideas in a text?

In small groups or as a class, discuss the Essential Question. Think about what you have learned about drawing inferences; determining central ideas; and analyzing interactions among people, events, and ideas in a text. Use evidence from the four texts in this unit to answer the question.

94 Unit 3 ■ Reading Informational Text: Key Ideas and Details

---

Assess and Respond (pages 91–94)

If	Then
Students scored 0–10 points, they are **Developing** their understanding of unit skills...	Provide students with reading support and more extensive modeling and practice of skills.
Students scored 11–17 points, they are **Improving** their understanding of unit skills...	Review students' scores to pinpoint skills that students need more help with, and offer targeted instruction.
Students scored 18–24 points, they are **Proficient** in their understanding of unit skills...	Have these students move on. They are ready for the formal assessment at the end of the unit.

LANGUAGE

Greek and Latin Roots

Guided Instruction Knowing common **Greek and Latin roots** can help you determine the meaning of unfamiliar words. See if you can recognize an unfamiliar word's root (the core of the word). Some words have more than one root.

Root	Origin	Meaning
astro / aster	Greek	star
cosmo	Greek	universe
lab	Latin	work
lun	Latin	moon
micro	Greek	small
miss / mit	Latin	send
naut	Greek	sailor
port	Latin	carry
sol	Latin	sun
techno	Greek	skill
therm	Greek	heat
trans	Latin	across

Examples:
- **atmosphere** (Greek: *atmo* is "air," *sphere* is "ball or globe")
  The **atmosphere** is like a globe of air around Earth.
- **manufacture** (*manu* is Latin for "hand," *fact* is Latin for "make")
  Before machines, to **manufacture** something was to make it by hand.

Guided Practice Use the Greek and Latin roots from the chart above to complete the sentences below.

1. The astro ___naut___ trained and was ready for her space mission.

2. Solar panels are a green energy ___techno___ logy.

3. The plan is to capture an ___aster___ oid and put it in ___lun___ ar orbit.

Independent Practice What other words with Greek and Latin roots can you find in the Close Reading selection? Write them on another piece of paper. Are there any other words you know with these roots? Add them. Write three sentences using some of the words on your list.

Unit 3 ▪ Reading Informational Text: Key Ideas and Details   **95**

Support English Language Learners

Students who speak Latinate languages may recognize some of the Latin roots; however, it's possible that they have never thought of breaking up words in this way. Help students who are having trouble by giving them the word list below and asking them to circle the root inside each word.

mission (*miss*)	technology (*techno*)	cosmic (*cosmo*)
solar (*sol*)	lunar (*luna*)	microscope (*micro*)
astronomy (*astro*)	transmit (*trans/mit*)	thermometer (*therm*)
asteroid (*aster*)	laboratory (*lab*)	nautical (*naut*)

OBJECTIVE
Use Greek and Latin roots to determine word meanings.

Guided Instruction

Have students review the Guided Instruction section on page 95 in the Student Book. Be sure they understand that a root is a word part—the core of the word that often has a prefix, a suffix, or an ending added to it. By learning some common roots that came into English from Greek and Latin, students will have a way to unlock the meanings of many words that are made from these roots.

Guided Practice

As students advance to the practice sentences, remind them to use the clues embedded in the sentences to determine the missing word roots. For example, "space mission" is a clue to the root that completes the word "astronaut."

Independent Practice

If students have difficulty finding words with Greek and Latin roots in the Close Reading, give them a chance to work with a partner or in a small group. (Possible answers: *astronomers, collaboration, commissioned, important, microcapsules, missions, opportunities, portable, support, thermometer, transplants*)

Apply to Reading

Have students work in groups to scan the other selections for additional Greek and Latin roots. They might find in their Student Books the words *cosmonaut* (page 66), *missile* (page 68), *atmosphere* (page 80), *cosmic* (page 84), and *transmitted* (page 87).

Unit Summary

At this point in the unit, students have read a text about the Space Race, an excerpt from President Kennedy's famous speech; an interview with Barbara Morgan, NASA's Teacher in Space; a feature article about Mars and different possible missions to take humans there; and an excerpt from the U.S. National Space Policy. Students have also learned how to draw inferences, find central ideas, and analyze texts. They have learned and practiced how to use Greek and Latin roots to determine word meanings. Students should now be ready to take this unit review.

Introduce the Review

Explain to students that they will read two related passages that continue the theme of "new frontiers." Instruct students to read the passages carefully and return to them as needed while they answer questions 1–10 on pages 97–98.

Answer Explanations (pages 97–98)

Scoring: When scoring students' work, assign one point for each multiple-choice question and two points for each short answer question, for a total of 20 points.

1A. Students should realize that the space elevator is an alternative to rockets, not satellites or space stations.

1B. Once students determine that an elevator would replace rockets, they can see that only choice D explains why.

Read the following texts that include implied ideas; multiple central ideas; interactions among people, events, and ideas; and words with Greek and Latin roots. Then answer the questions on pages 97 and 98.

Going Up: Space Elevator

1 For the entire space age so far, we have depended on rocket technology for getting out of the grip of Earth's orbit. Rockets have to burn a tremendous amount of fuel to overcome the force of Earth's gravity. It is one of the most difficult and expensive parts of space travel. What if there were another way?

2 The space elevator was once an idea in a science-fiction story, and now some engineers think it is possible. From a platform in the sea, a cable would stretch into space. Climbing machines attached to the cable would transport people and supplies into Earth's orbit for much less money than it costs to send up spacecraft.

3 The trick is to find a substance strong enough to use to make the cable. Carbon nanotubes are the material being considered. A carbon nanotube is a configuration of carbon atoms arranged in a pattern like a soccer ball. Carbon nanotubes are nearly as light as air and are as flexible as plastic, but

they are also 100 times stronger than steel. Although carbon nanotubes are incredibly strong when woven into small strands, engineers are still working on longer strands. They are trying to weave a thread made of millions of carbon nanotubes. It's like trying to weave a rope from a pile of powder.

4 In the meantime, one of the companies working on this problem is going to try to build a space elevator on the moon first. They believe it will work with existing technology. The moon's gravity is much weaker than Earth's, and without an atmosphere, the moon has no weather. So, it might become a shortcut from the International Space Station to the moon.

5 Some people are less optimistic about the carbon nanotube breakthrough necessary to tether a space elevator to Earth. However, that's not the only issue that makes the idea of a space elevator unlikely.

Going Nowhere: Space Elevator

1 The motion from solar wind, the gravitational pull of the sun and moon, and the climbers themselves could cause the cable to vibrate like a plucked guitar string. Of course, there could be a way to dampen the cable's motion, but that's more technology to develop.

2 Another issue is that satellites and space junk could crash into the cable. New satellites could have technology that would allow them to dodge the cable, but existing satellites and space junk would be a risk. Despite these issues, even skeptics admit that the idea just might work on the moon.

Self-Assessment: Progress Check

Have students return to the Progress Check on page 61 of their book. Point out the boxes underneath the arrow that says "After Unit 3," and have students answer the questions again. Have them assess how well they have grasped the important skills and concepts in this unit.

You may wish to instruct students to write a number in the box to show how they rate their ability with each skill, using a scale of 0–2, with 0 meaning they do not understand the skill at all, 1 meaning they understand the skill but have trouble applying it, and 2 meaning they understand and can apply the skill without difficulty.

UNIT 3 REVIEW

Circle the letter next to the best answer choice.

1A. Which of the following would a space elevator make unnecessary?

  a. rockets

  b. orbiting satellites

  c. travel to the moon

  d. the International Space Station

1B. What details from "Going Up: Space Elevator" support the answer to Part A?

  a. Carbon nanotubes are difficult to weave together.

  b. Orbiting satellites might crash into the space elevator.

  c. A space elevator might be built on the moon.

  d. People have always used rockets to get out of Earth's orbit.

2A. Which of the following is a reasonable inference, based on both texts?

  a. There is no way that a space elevator can ever be made to work.

  b. Any alternatives to the space elevator would have to solve the same basic problems.

  c. A space elevator is the only way to transport things into space inexpensively.

  d. Humans will never stop searching for a way to travel into space more cheaply.

2B. What information from the texts supports the answer in Part A?

  a. A space elevator will be easier to build on the moon.

  b. Rockets are expensive and burn a lot of fuel.

  c. A cable would be attached to a platform in the sea.

  d. Scientists have to find a way to dampen the cable's motion.

3A. Which of the following is a central idea of "Going Up: Space Elevator"?

  a. Carbon nanotubes are 100 times stronger than steel.

  b. The space elevator might be a shortcut from the ISS to the moon.

  c. The space elevator is an idea from science fiction.

  d. The space elevator might be easier to build on the moon.

3B. What detail from the text supports the answer to Part A?

  a. The gravitational pull of the sun could make a cable vibrate.

  b. Some people think it is possible to build a space elevator.

  c. The moon has no atmosphere and no weather.

  d. Climbing machines would move up and down a cable.

4A. What is a quality of carbon nanotubes that makes them a good option for a space elevator cable?

  a. They are inexpensive.

  b. They are arranged in a pattern.

  c. They have almost no weight.

  d. They are made from powder.

4B. What evidence from "Going Up: Space Elevator" supports the answer to Part A?

  a. A carbon nanotube is a configuration of carbon atoms.

  b. Carbon nanotubes are nearly as light as air.

  c. Carbon nanotubes are 100 times stronger than steel.

  d. Carbon nanotubes are hard to weave into long strands.

Unit 3 ▪ Reading Informational Text: Key Ideas and Details   **97**

Answer Explanations (pages 97–98)

2A. Students should realize that the same basic problems have to be solved for any type of transportation into space.

2B. Only choice B mentions a problem that would also have to be addressed by an alternative to the space elevator.

3A. Students should realize that choice D is a central idea, while the others are details.

3B. Once students recognize that the big idea is building the elevator on the moon, they can see that a lack of weather and atmosphere support this idea.

4A. From the text, students can see that the tubes are light, flexible, and strong, but only one of those qualities is listed among the answers: almost no weight.

4B. "Carbon nanotubes are nearly as light as air" is another way to say that they have almost no weight.

5A. Students should understand from reading both texts that nanotube technology is very new, and we will need time to see if it can work.

5B. The statement that engineers are still working on longer strands shows that carbon nanotube technology is not ready to use yet.

Test-Taking Tips

Explain that the two-part questions give students an opportunity to check their answers. Point out that if there doesn't seem to be a good answer in part 2 of the question, it might be because their answer in the first part of the question is incorrect.

After answering both parts of a question, encourage students to go back and reread their answers to make sure there is a connection between them.

Unit 3 Review

Answer Explanations

6A. Students should recognize the roots *trans* and *port* from their study of word roots.

6B. The phrase "take materials into space" helps show the connection between the roots *trans* and *port*.

Item 7 Rubric

2	Student identifies one or more problems with building the space elevator and a technology breakthrough that might solve it.
1	Student identifies a breakthrough that could help the space elevator.
0	Student does not cite a breakthrough.

Item 8 Rubric

2	Student gives a complete summary of the text.
1	Student gives a partial summary.
0	Student fails to summarize any of the major ideas in the text.

Item 9 Rubric

2	Student infers that many problems have to be solved before a space elevator can be built.
1	Student infers some problems that need to be solved.
0	Student does not infer that problems need to be solved.

Item 10 Rubric

2	Student recognizes advantages stated in the text and add inferences of his or her own.
1	Student recognizes at least one reasonable advantage of having a space elevator.
0	Student cannot suggest even one reasonable advantage.

UNIT 3 REVIEW

5A. Which claim about nanotube technology is supported by both texts?

  a. This technology is ready to use.

  b. This technology has not been proven.

  c. This technology cannot possibly work.

  d. This technology is too expensive to build.

5B. Which statement provides evidence for the claim above?

  a. The idea comes from a science-fiction story.

  b. Carbon nanotubes are being considered.

  c. Engineers are still working on longer strands.

  d. It's like trying to weave a rope from a pile of powder.

6A. Which word from "Going Up: Space Elevator" contains the Latin roots for *across* and *carry*?

  a. *International*

  b. *transport*

  c. *technology*

  d. *nanotubes*

6B. Choose the idea from the text that could be expressed using the answer to Part A.

  a. A space elevator would be less expensive than using rockets.

  b. Solar wind can make a space cable vibrate.

  c. Carbon atoms can be arranged in a pattern.

  d. The space elevator would be used to take materials into space.

7. What breakthroughs in technology might improve the space elevator's chances?

Engineers will have to develop a cable, probably made from carbon nanotubes, that is long enough, strong enough, and stable enough.

8. Briefly summarize "Going Up: Space Elevator."

A space elevator, made from a carbon nanotube cable, would make space travel easier and less expensive. However, the required technology is not yet advanced enough.

9. What inference can you draw from "Going Nowhere: Space Elevator" about how soon a space elevator might exist on Earth? Support your inference.

Sample answer: A space elevator is unlikely to be built anytime soon. Even if the right cable could be developed, the possibility of collisions with older satellites and space junk remains.

10. What would be the biggest impact of a space elevator? Explain.

Sample answer: The biggest impact would be opening up space. Because a space elevator could transport people and supplies into orbit for less money, space exploration would become more affordable. The cost savings could fund more space missions and encourage space tourism and permanent space colonies.

Analyze Student Scores

16–20 pts Strong	Student has successfully learned and applied the skills in this unit. Review any errors with the student, and explain them if necessary.
10–15 pts Progressing	Student is struggling with one or more of the skills in this unit. Identify the specific skills that are problematic to target additional instruction.
0–9 pts Emerging	Student is having trouble understanding most of the skills in this unit. Student may need to work through the unit again with a higher level of individual support.

Introducing UNIT 4

In this unit about new frontiers in technology, you will learn how to write an informative/explanatory essay. In this type of essay, your primary purpose is to communicate information—that is, to explain something that your readers may not know.

Your essay should be complete and well presented. Break your topic down in a way that will help readers grasp it better. Explain each important point clearly, and connect the points with transitions. Include facts, details, and examples to support your ideas. Consider strategies such as defining, comparing, and cause-effect analysis to help explain the topic. Headings and graphics, too, can help make information clear.

Progress Check Can I?

Before Unit 4 / After Unit 4

- [ ] Introduce a topic clearly.
- [ ] Use an appropriate strategy to organize ideas and information.
- [ ] Use formatting and graphics to make information clear.
- [ ] Develop a topic with facts, details, and examples.
- [ ] Use a formal style in my writing.
- [ ] Include appropriate transitions to link ideas.
- [ ] Choose precise language.
- [ ] Use commas correctly when punctuating phrases and clauses.
- [ ] Recognize and correct misplaced modifiers.
- [ ] Understand and use figurative language.

Unit 4 ■ Text Types and Purposes: Write Informative/Explanatory Texts

Student Page 99

Progress Check

The Progress Check is a self-assessment feature that students can use to gauge their own progress. Before students begin work on Unit 4, have them check the boxes next to any item that they feel they can do well. Explain that it is fine if they don't check any of the boxes. Tell them that they will have an opportunity to learn about and practice all of these items while studying the unit. Let them know that near the end of the unit they will have a chance to reconsider how well they can do each item on this list.

Before they begin their Unit 4 Review (see page 111 of this guide), you will be prompted to have students revisit this page. You can use this information to work with students on any items they don't understand before they tackle the Review.

HOME ◆ CONNECT...

In this unit, your child will learn to **write to explain or inform** effectively. Your child will **organize** relevant facts and details and share them clearly. Help your child with these skills by working together to **select and analyze the content** of good examples of informative writing. You may wish to point out well-written explanations in newspaper or magazine articles, manuals, and other nonfiction sources. Together, discuss how the explanations are developed and why they are clear.

Help your child acquire knowledge about topics that spark his or her interest. Together, look for and discuss print sources and reliable online sources of information. Ask questions to prompt more comprehensive explanation; for example, ask your child what he or she learns from **quotations, examples,** and **graphics** in the text. Encourage your child to use **precise language** when responding and to link ideas with **transitions**.

Activity: Explore with your child the unit theme: "New Frontiers in Technology." Together, research and discuss areas in which people are pushing the boundaries of knowledge and innovation in areas such as genetic research, alternative energy, and robotic technology. You and your child might choose one area of exploration and create a timeline that shows major milestones and breakthroughs in that field, ending with anticipated next steps for the future.

IN THIS UNIT, YOUR CHILD WILL...

- Learn to write an informative/explanatory text that introduces a topic, organizes information logically, and ends with a conclusion.
- Use facts, details, and examples to develop a topic.
- Use text features such as headings and graphics to help communicate information.
- Include transitions to link ideas.
- Choose precise language and a formal style.
- Use commas correctly with phrases and clauses.
- Recognize and correct misplaced modifiers.
- Understand and use figurative language.

WAYS TO HELP YOUR CHILD

Have your child practice communicating information about topics he or she already knows well. For example, you might ask for step-by-step instructions for operating an electronic device, or your child might share information about a sport, hobby, or other interest. Talk about the information that your child shared and where you need more information to answer your remaining questions.

ONLINE
For more Home Connect activities, continue online at sadlierconnect.com

100   Unit 4 ■ Text Types and Purposes: Write Informative/Explanatory Texts

Student Page 100

HOME ◆ CONNECT...

The Home Connect feature is a way to keep parents or other adult family members apprised of what their children are learning. The key learning objectives are listed, and some ideas for related activities and discussions are included.

Explain to students that they can share the Home Connect page with their parents or other adult family members in their home. Let students know how much time the class will be spending on this unit so they can plan their time accordingly at home.

Encourage students and their parents to share their experiences using the suggestions on the Home Connect page and the Home Connect activities at **sadlierconnect.com**. You may wish to make a place to post some of this work.

UNIT PLANNER

Theme: New Frontiers in Technology	Focus
WRITING MODEL *pp. 102–104*	*Five-Minute Meals*
WRITING ACTIVITY *p. 105*	**ORGANIZATIONAL STRUCTURE:** Outline
LANGUAGE MINI-LESSONS *pp. 106–109*	• Phrase and Clause Placement • Misplaced Modifiers • Figurative Language: Metaphor and Simile • Figurative Language: Hyperbole and Personification
SPEAKING AND LISTENING *p. 110*	Discuss the Essential Question
UNIT 4 REVIEW *pp. 111–112*	Writing Process Summary

Objective(s)

Write an informative/explanatory text about a topic with ideas and information that have been selected, analyzed, and organized.

Introduce the topic logically and develop it with ideas, facts and details, using transitions and precise language and a conclusion that supports the information.

- Understand how to use and punctuate clauses and phrases, avoiding misplaced modifiers.
- Understand the different types of figurative language and how to use them.

Engage in a respectful, collaborative discussion with peers.

Unit Assessment

- Unit 4 Review *pp. 111–112*

Additional Assessment Options

- Performance Task 1 *pp. 311A–320*
  (ALSO ONLINE)
- Performance Task 2 *pp. 321A–330*
  (ALSO ONLINE)

Optional Purchase:

- iProgress Monitor (ONLINE)
- Progress Monitor Student Benchmark Assessment Booklet

(ONLINE) Digital Resources

- Home Connect Activities
- Additional Practice
- Teacher Resources
- iProgress Monitor (optional purchase)

Go to SadlierConnect.com to access your Digital Resources.

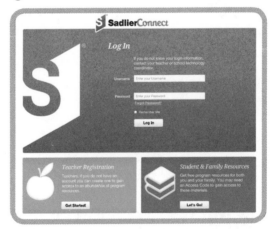

For more detailed instructions see page T3.

LEARNING PROGRESSIONS

In this unit, students will learn how to write an informative/explanatory essay on a topic that interests them. In order to learn the skills necessary to craft an informative essay, students will further develop skills learned in the sixth grade. They should be aware that they will further build on these skills when they reach the eighth grade.

Introducing the Topic and Organizing Ideas

- By the end of the sixth grade, students should be able to introduce a topic and organize ideas by using strategies such as definition and classification as well as formatting, graphics, and multimedia.

- In the seventh grade, students learn to introduce a topic and preview what is to follow, as well as organize ideas by using strategies, formatting, and multimedia to aid reader comprehension.

- Eighth graders will learn to introduce a topic, preview what is to follow, organize ideas into broader categories, and use formatting, graphics, and multimedia to aid reader comprehension.

Developing the Topic

- Sixth and seventh graders learn to develop topics with relevant facts, definitions, vivid details, quotations, and other information.

- In the eighth grade, students continue learning to develop a topic with relevant, well-chosen facts, definitions, examples, details, and other information.

Using Language

- In grades six, seven, and eight, students learn to use appropriate transitions, precise language, and domain-specific vocabulary when writing informative/explanatory essays.

Writing a Conclusion

- Sixth-grade students should be able to provide a concluding statement that follows from the information presented.

- Seventh and eighth graders will be able to write a concluding statement that provides additional support for the information presented in the essay.

Text Types and Purposes: Write Informative/ Explanatory Texts

Essential Question:
How can writers present information effectively?

Unit 4 ■ Text Types and Purposes: Write Informative/Explanatory Texts **101**

Essential Question:
How can writers present information effectively?

In this unit, students will learn to introduce a topic in an informative/ explanatory essay and develop it with well-organized facts, examples, and other information.

Theme: New Frontiers in Technology

Students will continue their investigation of the theme "new frontiers" by thinking about technology that has helped us explore outer space, as they read and analyze an informative/ explanatory essay writing model.

Curriculum Connection: Science

Students will use what they have already learned about the problem-solving nature of technology as they work on their own informative/ explanatory essays.

Connect Reading to Writing

Remind students that they read two explanatory texts in Unit 3: *A Man on the Moon* (Student Book pages 64–71) and *Our National Space Policy* (Student Book pages 88–91). Review how each author organized the text's information by using subheads.

Writing Handbook

If students need extra practice with writing an informative/explanatory essay, refer them to the *Writing Handbook* on pages 299–310 in their Student Books. The *Writing Handbook* gives students detailed instruction on planning, drafting, revising, and editing their writing. They will also find tips on producing, publishing, and presenting their writing.

OBJECTIVES

- Write an informative/explanatory text with ideas and information that have been selected, analyzed, and organized.
- Introduce the topic logically and develop it with ideas, facts, and details, using transitions and precise language and a conclusion that supports the information.

Introduce: Organizational Structure

Draw attention to the outline. Ask students to look for the key elements as you read the Student Model together.

Analyze a Student Model

TITLE: Inform students that title should give information about the topic.

INTRODUCTION: Point out how the writer states the topic in the first sentence and previews the information to come.

WRITE INFORMATIVE/EXPLANATORY TEXTS

CREATING AN ORGANIZATIONAL STRUCTURE

Alex used an outline like the one below to organize his essay.

TITLE
- Gives readers an interesting clue about the topic

INTRODUCTION
- Introduces the topic, using a formal style
- Gives a preview of what is to come in the essay

INFORMATION ORGANIZED BY IDEA
- Develops the topic by grouping and exploring ideas related to it

Read a Student Model

Alex is a student in Mr. Paulson's seventh-grade Language Arts class. Mr. Paulson gave Alex's class an assignment to write an explanatory essay about a modern technology that has changed our lives on Earth. Mr. Paulson expects the essays to be written clearly and to be well organized. Think about a technology that you might choose when you write your own informative/explanatory essay.

Five-Minute Meals

A technology that has changed our lives is the microwave oven. It offers people a very different way to cook. Before microwave ovens existed, the only way to heat food was with a gas or electric oven. Traditional ovens take time to heat up, time to cook the food, and more time to cool down. Microwave ovens cook food very quickly and stay cool inside after the food is done.

Quick Cooking

The main benefit of this new technology is saving time. You can make dinners and snacks quickly. Meals that used to take 45 minutes or more to heat up now take just a few minutes. However, there are some kinds of cooking you can't do in a microwave oven. You can't grill or fry foods, and you can't brown the outside of foods, either. Still, you can steam vegetables in the microwave oven, you can "bake" a potato, and you can even make a small cake in a mug!

102   Unit 4 ■ Text Types and Purposes: Write Informative/Explanatory Texts

---

Genre: Informative/Explanatory Text

Remind students that the purpose of an informative/explanatory text is to inform readers, so it is important to present information in a clear and organized way. Transitions between ideas should be clear and should help keep the text focused. Clear writing means that word choice should be precise and exact. The style should be formal, with no slang or humor to distract readers from the topic.

As students work on their informative/explanatory texts, suggest that they ask themselves, "Am I explaining this information clearly? What might be confusing to someone who has no knowledge of this topic?"

How Does It Work?

Microwave ovens use electromagnetic waves to cook food. Electromagnetic waves include radio waves, light waves, and X-rays. Food is made up of different types of molecules, including water molecules. When food is heated in a microwave, the water molecules inside the food are displaced by the electromagnetic waves. The waves agitate the water molecules, causing them to rotate at different speeds.

As the water molecules inside the food begin to rotate at increasing speeds, energy is created. The food absorbs the microwave energy, and that energy heats the food inside and out. The particles within the food absorb this energy at the same time. Consequently, unlike food cooked in a traditional oven, all of the food inside a microwave is cooked at the same temperature, at the same time.

Microwave Safety

Microwave ovens are safer than hot ovens as long as you follow a few safety rules. Do not use metal in the microwave because metal can cause dangerous sparks. Use microwave-safe containers only, and if you're not sure, glass or ceramic containers are best. Some kinds of plastic can begin to melt in the microwave, and you don't want plastic to get into your food. Be careful when you remove food from the microwave, especially if it comes in a pouch, as microwave popcorn does. Hot steam rushing out of the pouch can be hot enough to burn you.

FORMATTING

Make ideas clear by using headings to show how your ideas are organized.

TRANSITIONS

Link your ideas, so the reader can follow your logic. Alex uses the word *Consequently* to show a cause-and-effect link.

Circle another transition word or phrase under Quick Cooking *on page 102.*

FACTS AND DETAILS

Alex includes many facts and details in this essay.

Underline examples of facts and details in this paragraph.

PRECISE LANGUAGE

Use precise language that names exact things and ideas. Also, use words that describe actions specifically, such as the word *rushing.*

Put an asterisk next to three examples of precise language in paragraph 1.

Analyze a Student Model

INFORMATION ORGANIZED BY IDEA: Point out how each paragraph in the essay focuses on one central idea that is supported by facts, definitions, examples, and details.

FORMATTING: Explain to students that formatting features, such as subheads, help make the organizational structure clear by telling the reader what information is going to be covered in each section. Have students use the essay's subheads to determine each paragraph's central idea. Note that subheads are set apart from the body of the paragraph and in boldfaced type. These formatting choices make it easier to see the overall organization of the essay.

TRANSITIONS: Review how transitions help link related ideas. Model identifying the transition word in paragraph 2 on page 102: *I'm going to look for a word that connects two ideas and that could be removed without changing what the sentence means.*

FACTS AND DETAILS: Let students know that the facts and details in an informative/explanatory text should come from reputable sources. If a writer knows a topic well, he or she can be considered a reliable source. Be sure that students notice how the facts and details relate to the central idea in each section.

PRECISE LANGUAGE: Using precise language means choosing specific words rather than vague ones. This is especially important when explaining a technical process. Model this concept when students have identified the precise language in the section "How Does It Work?" The writer uses the technical term "electromagnetic waves" and then lists the types of electromagnetic waves. Choosing the wrong words would make the explanation incorrect, and choosing general words would make the explanation less clear.

Support English Language Learners

English language learners may not have a large vocabulary of transition words and phrases. Help them build up some synonyms for words they might already know. Share the list below with them.

and: also, in the same way, in addition

but: however, in contrast, on the other hand

for example: for instance, specifically, to illustrate

so: therefore, consequently, thus

finally: in conclusion, in the end, to summarize

Analyze a Student Model

GRAPHICS: Explain to students that graphics often appear in informative/explanatory texts because they can convey information in a visual way. Ask students to compare the written directions embedded in the text with the graphic and label on page 104. Ask them to notice which direction was easier for readers to comprehend.

CONCLUSION: Ask students to describe how the concluding section at the end of the essay "wraps up" the essay's ideas in a way that is satisfying for the reader. Point out how the final statement sums up the central idea of the entire essay.

Evaluate a Writer's Work

Begin a group discussion about Alex's informative/explanatory essay. Remind students that the purpose of this genre is to convey information. Ask students to discuss how effective Alex was in sharing information about his subject. Have students consider this question: *What do I know now about microwave ovens that I didn't know before?* Ask students to share their thinking.

Model: Organizational Structure

Ask students to think about how an outline would show the underlying structure of Alex's essay. Post the outline template that appears on page 105. Point out that well-written essays have a strong organizational structure, which requires brainstorming and planning.

Before students fill in the outline based on the Student Model, remind them to review the margin notes that appear with the essay. Have students fill in the main sections of the outline, using the subheads for guidance.

WRITE INFORMATIVE/EXPLANATORY TEXTS

Chilly or Sore?

Microwave ovens have other uses besides cooking, too! They are great for warming up a heating pad, which you can use to soothe sore muscles or warm up cold toes. If you don't have a heating pad, it's easy to make one. Put some uncooked rice inside a clean cotton tube sock and sew the end closed. If you want a pleasant scent, mix some dried herbs in with the rice. You can also sprinkle the rice with vanilla extract or your favorite scented oil. Your heating pad only takes a minute or two in the microwave to get warm.

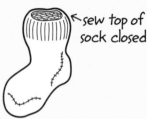
←sew top of sock closed

Some people might say that microwave ovens are not as exciting an invention as computers or the Internet. That may be true, but microwave technology has made it possible for people all over the world to have safe and quick access to hot meals without having to use fire. You can't beat a microwave oven for heating things up without wasting time or energy!

GRAPHICS

Make some information easier to understand by putting it in a chart or showing it in a diagram.

Circle information in the text that is also shown in the diagram.

CONCLUSION

Alex's conclusion sums up the central idea of his essay.

Double underline the statement that summarizes the essay's central idea.

Review: Analyzing Texts

Remind students that in Unit 3 they learned how to analyze an informative text by looking for the relationships among ideas, individuals, and events. Explain to students that this skill will also be helpful in writing an informative/explanatory text. In order to share information about a subject, students must think about these kinds of relationships and be able to communicate them.

Ask students to talk with a partner about the relationship between people and events in Alex's essay about microwave ovens. They should see that people are interested in speed and convenience. This interest led to the popularity and widespread use of microwave ovens, which are a convenient and fast method of cooking.

Use this outline to organize your informative/explanatory essay for the Unit 4 Review on page 111. Then write your first draft on a separate sheet of paper. Remember to use a formal style and to develop the topic with a variety of facts and details. Also, think about which precise words and transitions will help make your ideas and information clear.

Title _____

I. **Introduction**

    a. Topic: _____

II. **Supporting Resources**

    a. First paragraph: information about _____

       1. Fact or detail _____

       _____

       2. Fact or detail _____

       _____

    b. Second paragraph: information about _____

       1. Fact or detail _____

       _____

       2. Fact or detail _____

       _____

    c. Third paragraph: information about _____

       1. Fact or detail _____

       _____

       2. Fact or detail _____

       _____

III. **Conclusion**

    _____

    _____

Unit 4 ▪ Text Types and Purposes: Write Informative/Explanatory Texts **105**

Create: Organizational Structure

Brainstorming

Writers write informative/explanatory texts about subjects they know well—either from their own experience or from their research. As a class, brainstorm a list of topics about a modern technology that has changed our lives on Earth. Post the list for students to consider as they plan their essays.

Planning

Students will use the outline on page 105 to plan their writing. They should first decide on a technology to write about. Students should:

- List three central ideas about the technology.
- Identify facts and details that they will use to elaborate.

Drafting an Informative/ Explanatory Essay

Direct students to consult their outlines as they draft their essays on a separate sheet of paper. Be sure that students have an introduction, three central ideas, relevant supporting facts and details, and a conclusion.

Introduce the Writing Process

Remind students that good writing happens in stages. After prewriting and drafting, they will revise and edit their essays. For more on the writing process, see the *Writing Handbook* on page 299.

Assess and Respond
If students have difficulty identifying three central ideas about their topic,
Then have them find a partner who knows less about the subject and can ask questions about it. This will help the student see what information a reader will need.

Differentiate Instruction

Some students may not feel they have enough knowledge about a technological topic to explain it. Ask students to consider choosing a form of technology that they interact with daily, such as smartphones, music players, or televisions. If they don't feel comfortable with those topics, then have them choose any other type of product they use and can write about knowledgeably. Point out to students that they should choose a topic with some complexity because a very simple subject leaves little to explain.

OBJECTIVE
Understand how to use and punctuate clauses and phrases, avoiding misplaced modifiers.

Guided Instruction

Help students understand that phrases do not look like sentences because they have no verb. Dependent clauses are incomplete sentences because they have a subject and verb but cannot stand alone. A comma is needed after a long introductory phrase or a dependent clause that appears at the beginning of a sentence. Point out the examples.

Guided Practice

Ask students if they can identify the dependent clauses in the first two sentences. Take a moment to discuss why a clause's position in the sentence matters.

Independent Practice

Tell students that a long introductory phrase includes one or more prepositions (*near, at, on, around*). Dependent clauses often begin with words such as *if, when, after, although, because, unless, while, since, from, even if.*

Assess and Respond

If students need help finding introductory phrases and dependent clauses,

Then have them circle the sentence part that could stand alone. The remaining part is the phrase or clause.

LANGUAGE

Phrase and Clause Placement

Guided Instruction A **phrase** is a group of words that functions together as a single part of speech, such as a noun or adjective. A **clause** is a phrase that has a subject and verb. A dependent clause cannot stand alone. When you begin a sentence with a long phrase or a dependent clause, follow it with a comma.

- **Comma needed**

  On Monday evenings after 5:00, the museum is closed. (long introductory phrase)

  Because we're in a hurry, let's heat the soup in the microwave. (dependent clause first)

- **No comma needed**

  After dinner we looked at the stars. (short introductory phrase)

  The star party is at 10:00 P.M. *because the sky will be dark by then.* (dependent clause at end)

Guided Practice Read each sentence carefully. Underline the introductory phrase or dependent clause, and add commas where needed. (Not every sentence has an introductory element or needs a comma.)

1. When my favorite television show comes on, I'll watch it eagerly.
2. Alicia Perez gave a speech after she was elected class president.
3. At some time between midnight and dawn, an asteroid will pass by Earth.

Independent Practice Write four original sentences, two with a long introductory phrase and two with a dependent clause at the beginning. Add commas where needed.

1. Sample answer: From the beginning to the end, this novel was a great adventure.

2. Sample answer: In the event of lightning, come inside immediately.

3. Sample answer: After everyone returns from the hike, we'll serve lunch.

4. Sample answer: If you are going to the store, please pick up some apples.

Support English Language Learners

Prepositions that can be demonstrated (*near, under, beside, over, inside, outside, next to*) are not especially difficult for English language learners to master. But other prepositions can be tricky because they do not translate easily between languages, such as prepositions of time (*on Saturday, at 2 P.M., in the afternoon*) and prepositions of place (*at home, in school, on First St.*).

Writing long introductory phrases for the independent practice portion of this lesson is a good opportunity for students to practice using some of these tricky prepositions.

Misplaced Modifiers

Guided Instruction A word or phrase often **modifies**, or describes, another word in the same sentence. Make sure, however, that the modifying word or phrase is in a place that makes sense. In the examples below, the modifier has a double underline and the word it modifies has a single underline.

The <u>new</u> <u>children's</u> toys were scattered in the yard. (incorrect)

The children's <u>new</u> <u>toys</u> were scattered in the yard. (correct)

José gave the bicycle to his <u>cousin</u> <u>with silver handlebars</u>. (incorrect)

José gave the <u>bicycle</u> <u>with silver handlebars</u> to his cousin. (correct)

I saw a double <u>rainbow</u> <u>going outside after the storm</u>. (incorrect)

<u>Going outside after the storm</u>, <u>I</u> saw a double rainbow. (correct)

Guided Practice Each modifying word or phrase in the following sentences has a double underline. Study each sentence and then answer the questions.

1. I was sad when I heard about my <u>broken</u> friend's leg.

   What does the word seem to modify? _____friend_____

   What should the word modify? _____leg_____

2. Wearing an old shirt, Bryan gave his speech <u>with a big stain on it</u> in class.

   What does the phrase seem to modify? _____speech_____

   What should the phrase modify? _____shirt_____

3. Rochelle was surprised by her cat <u>trying to do her math homework</u>.

   What does the phrase seem to modify? _____cat_____

   What should the phrase modify? _____Rochelle_____

Independent Practice Rewrite the sentences above so that each modifying phrase is placed correctly. Reword sentences if necessary.

1. I was sad when I heard about my friend's broken leg.

2. Wearing an old shirt with a big stain on it, Bryan gave his speech in class.

3. Trying to do her math homework, Rochelle was surprised by her cat.

Unit 4 ■ Text Types and Purposes: Write Informative/Explanatory Texts **107**

OBJECTIVE
Understand how to use and punctuate clauses and phrases, avoiding misplaced modifiers.

Guided Instruction

Be sure that students understand why it is important to put a modifying word or phrase next to the word that it describes. If the word or phrase is in the wrong place or if the word it modifies is missing, then the sentence will be incorrect or confusing for the reader.

Guided Practice

Help students recognize the word that is supposed to be modified. Then ask them if the modifying word or phrase is next to it. If not, the sentence is not correct.

Independent Practice

Once students are able to recognize the word that the modifying word or phrase refers to, they should be able to rewrite the sentences correctly. In each case, moving the modifying phrase will correct the sentence.

Assess and Respond
If students have trouble determining which word in the Independent Practice sentences should be modified,
Then have students work with partners to answer the questions, "What is broken?", "What has a stain?", and "Who is trying to do homework?"

Differentiate Instruction

Help students understand how the position of a modifying word or phrase affects the meaning of a sentence. Give pairs of students note cards, and have them write each word from the first Guided Practice sentence on a separate card. Tell students to place the cards face up on a desk, and manipulate them to reproduce the sentence on the page. Then have them move the card with the word *broken* to different positions within the sentence. Students should read the sentence aloud each time they move the word to a new position to determine which version of the sentence makes the most sense.

OBJECTIVE

Understand the different types of figurative language and how to use them.

Guided Instruction

Explain that similes and metaphors are two ways to compare unlike things, but similes draw attention to the comparison by using the word *like* or *as*, while metaphors state or imply that one thing is another. Students should understand that a metaphor is a bolder claim but is not meant literally.

Guided Practice

As students read the practice sentences, have them scan for the words *like* and *as* to distinguish the similes from the metaphors. Remind them that a metaphor need not use the word *is* to make a comparison.

Independent Practice

Remind students that their similes should use the word *like* or *as* to make a comparison, and their metaphors should make the bolder claim. When students write their own similes and metaphors, instruct them to think about two things that don't seem alike but share one important quality.

Assess and Respond

If students have trouble finding two things to compare when writing their original similes and metaphors,

Then ask them to choose an object and a quality. Set up a Venn diagram to help them brainstorm a dissimilar item that shares this one quality.

LANGUAGE

Figurative Language: Metaphor and Simile

Guided Instruction **Figurative language** adds interest to writing by inviting readers to imagine things in new ways. Metaphors and similes are types of figurative language that compare two essentially unlike things. A **metaphor** makes the comparison directly, sometimes by using the word *is*, whereas a **simile** uses the words *like* or *as* to show the comparison.

- *The microwave is a dark club where food molecules dance.* (metaphor)

- *Let's explore microwave ovens, those dark clubs where food molecules dance.* (metaphor)

- *Microwave ovens, unlike traditional ovens, cook like race cars.* (simile)

Guided Practice Write whether the figurative language in each sentence is a simile or a metaphor.

1. We still haven't been to Mars, that red stoplight in the sky. ___metaphor___
2. Music was the vitamin that gave them strength. ___metaphor___
3. His forehead was as hot as fire. ___simile___
4. My stomach growled like a monster in a horror film. ___simile___
5. The dentist looked into the patient's open cave of a mouth. ___metaphor___

Independent Practice Turn these comparisons into sentences by using a metaphor or simile, as marked. Then write two original sentences that use these techniques.

1. Space tourism/an amusement park ride (metaphor)
   Sample answer: Space tourism will be an amusement park ride in the sky.

2. A hot sidewalk/frying pan (simile)
   Sample answer: Walking on a hot sidewalk is like being in a frying pan.

3. A day with no chores/a birthday present (metaphor)
   Sample answer: A day with no chores is a gift, an extra birthday present.

4. Answers will vary.

5. Answers will vary.

Differentiate Instruction

Many English idioms use figurative language to make their point. Because English language learners often struggle with unfamiliar idioms, place them in pairs with proficient speakers. Have the pairs discuss the literal and figurative meanings of idioms and expressions, such as "eat like a bird," "I'm all ears," and "fit as a fiddle." Many lists of English idioms are available on the Internet.

In turn, English language learners can share with their partners or with the class some common idioms of their native language.

Students can also consult online dictionaries to find meanings of idiomatic expressions; these sites frequently include sound files that model correct pronunciation.

Figurative Language: Hyperbole and Personification

Guided Instruction **Figurative language** stretches the meaning of words in order to entertain readers and make them think. Types of figurative language include **hyperbole** (exaggeration) and **personification** (giving human qualities to an object or animal).

- *Microwave ovens can cook dinner <u>in a second</u>.* (hyperbole)

- *A microwave oven <u>can lend you a hand</u> when you want to cook food quickly.* (personification)

Guided Practice Write whether each sentence contains hyperbole or personification.

1. The cat gave me a lecture when his dinner was late. <u>personification</u>
2. We'll be ten years older by the time we get out of this traffic! <u>hyperbole</u>
3. These family photographs tell us stories about the past. <u>personification</u>
4. My handwriting is harder to read than earthworm tracks. <u>hyperbole</u>
5. The skyscraper was so tall that birds couldn't fly over it. <u>hyperbole</u>
6. The spring wind danced through the trees. <u>personification</u>

Independent Practice Complete each sentence with personification or hyperbole, as indicated. Then write two original sentences, using each of these techniques once.

1. The launch pad <u>melted</u> as the rockets fired. (hyperbole)
2. The meal was so delicious that our taste buds <u>giggled</u>. (personification)
3. The prizewinning pumpkin was so large that <u>it wouldn't fit in the house</u>. (hyperbole)
4. The old chair <u>groaned</u> as the boy bounced on it. (personification)
5. <u>Answers will vary.</u>
6. <u>Answers will vary.</u>

Unit 4 ■ Text Types and Purposes: Write Informative/Explanatory Texts **109**

OBJECTIVE
Understand the different types of figurative language and how to use them.

Guided Instruction

Make it clear to students that all figurative language is, by definition, not meant to be taken literally. Hyperbole can be easy to identify as figurative language because it is so exaggerated. Personification can be more subtle; identifying it requires the reader to ask, "Can that object or animal literally do what this sentence is saying?"

Guided Practice

Have a student volunteer read aloud the first practice sentence, and then ask, *Can cats really lecture, or is lecturing something only people do?* Students should be able to see this is an example of personification. Ask them if anything in the second sentence is being exaggerated. (time) They should realize that the sentence is an example of hyperbole.

Independent Practice

Instruct students to make sure the sentences using hyperbole express an exaggerated idea. The sentences using personification should have an object or animal act in a human way.

Assess and Respond

If students have trouble remembering the difference between personification and hyperbole,

Then discuss the words' parts and their meanings. Point out that personification involves a thing acting like a person. Explain that *hyper* is from a Greek word meaning "over" or "beyond."

Peer Collaboration

Have students self-select one of the following activities and work collaboratively on it in a small group for ten minutes.

- Write a poem from the point of view of a common object, such as a chair or toothbrush.

- Write a verse or two for a song by using all four figurative language techniques taught on pages 108 and 109.

- Go on a figurative language hunt in the Student Model. ("on the other hand"; "can't be beat")

OBJECTIVE
Engage in a respectful, collaborative discussion with peers.

Discuss the Essential Question

Copy and distribute the "Did I?" checklist available on **sadlierconnect.com**.

Leading the Class Discussion

1. Remind students to review the subheads in Alex's essay.

2. Have students look for facts and details in each section.

3. Have students identify precise language and transitions.

SPEAKING AND LISTENING

Discuss the Essential Question

How can writers present information effectively?

Prepare for a class discussion about the Essential Question by responding to the questions below. Support your point of view with reasons and examples.

1. How did Alex organize information about his topic?

Sample answer: Alex grouped his information so facts and details that support the same idea are together in a paragraph. He explained what microwave ovens are, how they work, how to use them safely, and how to use them for something other than cooking.

2. What facts and details did Alex use to develop the essay?

Sample answer: Alex explained that microwaves heat food, the difference between a microwave and a traditional oven, why microwaves are so convenient, the effect of putting metal in a microwave, and a process for making a microwave heating pad.

3. What kind of language did Alex use to discuss concepts and connect ideas?

Sample answer: He used precise terms like *electromagnetic waves, radio waves, light waves,* and *X-rays* to help explain how microwave ovens work. The transitions *however, still,* and *consequently* helped to show relationships between ideas.

Use your notes above as you discuss the Essential Question with your class or in small groups. Use the organizer below to record your ideas and what you hear in the discussion. Follow the discussion rules on the "Did I?" checklist (page 58).

Ideas I Agree or Disagree With		Questions I Asked
SideText		
SideText		
New Ideas I Had During Discussion		**Questions I Answered**

Discussion Skills

Remind students that when making claims during discussions they should try to be clear about their ideas and support their claims with factual information and text evidence. As listeners, students should respectfully request evidence, clarification, elaboration, rephrasing, and examples as needed. Here are some questions students can ask:

- *Where in the text does it say that . . . ?*
- *Can you restate/elaborate . . . so I can understand?*
- *It would help to know the source of this information.*

UNIT 4 REVIEW

Read this introductory paragraph from a student informative/explanatory essay, and answer the questions below.

> (1) A modern technology that has changed our lives is the GPS, or global positioning system. (2) In the old days, people needed paper maps or directions to keep from getting lost. (3) Today, if you are driving in a car to a new place, riding on a boat, or hiking in the woods, an electronic GPS device can guide you on your way. (4) A GPS device can tell you where to find a restaurant or gas station in your car.

1. Which of the following is an example of informal language?

   a. changed our lives

   b. paper maps

   c. in the old days

   d. gas station

2. Which of the following is the best way to correct sentence 4?

   a. A GPS device can tell you, in your car, where to find a restaurant or gas station.

   b. A GPS device in your car can tell you where to find a restaurant or gas station.

   c. A restaurant or gas station can be found in your car by a GPS device.

   d. In your car, a restaurant or gas station can be found by a GPS device.

3. Which is the clearest example of precise language from the text?

   a. modern technology

   b. global positioning system

   c. deep in the woods

   d. can guide you on your way

4. Which of the following details would best help develop this topic?

   a. GPS technology has decreased in cost since its invention.

   b. Some hikers prefer using maps to a GPS.

   c. A detailed GPS map can display a user's current location.

   d. Another technology is the smartphone.

5. Based on this introduction, which heading would you NOT expect to see in this essay?

   a. How a GPS Works

   b. Developments in GPS Technology

   c. How to Use a GPS

   d. Why GPS Technology Is Overrated

6. Which transition word or phrase would make sense at the beginning of sentence 4?

   a. Furthermore,

   b. On the other hand,

   c. To begin with,

   d. Nevertheless,

Unit 4 ■ Text Types and Purposes: Write Informative/Explanatory Texts   **111**

Introduce the Review

Explain to students that this review will give them an opportunity to apply the language and writing skills they have studied and practiced in this unit.

Language Skills Summary

Let students know that they are going to use what they have learned about phrases and clauses and figurative language to make their writing better.

- Have students explain when a comma is needed with a dependent clause and an introductory phrase.
- Ask students how to tell if a modifier is misplaced or dangling.
- Ask students to list four types of figurative language.

Self-Assessment: Progress Check

Have students revisit the Progress Check on page 99 and compare their answers now to the answers they gave before they started Unit 4.

Answer Explanations

Scoring: 5 points each for items 1–10; 50 points for essay.

1. Students should identify "in the old days" in sentence 2 as an example of informal language.

2. Students should recognize that "in your car" should follow the phrase it modifies: "A GPS device."

3. Precise language involves referring to something by its exact or technical name.

4. Answer choice C is most closely related to the topic of the essay.

5. Answer choice D contradicts the first sentence in the essay.

6. *Furthermore* is a transition word that suggests that an idea is being continued.

Test-Taking Tips

Give students the following reminders and tips to help with taking assessments that include a paragraph or essay with numbered sentences.

- The numbers appear in parentheses at the start of each sentence. The test questions often refer to a sentence in the essay by number.
- Read the entire paragraph (or essay) first. Then when a question asks about a numbered sentence, look for that number and reread the sentence again.
- Underline information in the paragraph or essay that helps answer a question.

Answer Explanations

7. Students should see *like* as a clue to the simile in the third sentence.

8. Students should recognize that only humans give advice.

9. Students should understand that you, not the GPS, know about this technology.

Item 10 Rubric

2	**5 pts.** Student writes a conclusion that follows from information presented.
1	**2–3 pts.** Student writes a conclusion partially based on information presented.
0	**0 pts.** Student fails to write a conclusion related to information presented.

Writing Process Summary

Remind students that planning can help them organize their ideas before they draft. Revising and editing help make the draft better.

Planning and Drafting

Have students revisit their outline and draft (page 105). Have them check that the draft includes all items in the outline.

Informative/Explanatory Text Rubric

4	**50 pts.** The text has a clear introduction and structure and uses transitions, precise language, subheads, and graphics. It has few or no editing errors.
3	**40 pts.** The text includes the key elements but has minor errors.
2	**30 pts.** The text is missing one or more key elements and has errors that interfere with meaning.
1	**20 pts.** The text is unfinished and shows a lack of understanding of required elements.
0	**0 pts.** The assignment was not attempted.

UNIT 4 REVIEW

Read these next two paragraphs from the student informative/explanatory essay, and answer the questions below.

(1) One of the benefits of a GPS device is that it can give directions out loud. (2) When you are driving, you need to keep your eyes glued to the road. (3) Hearing the directions out loud is like having a copilot while you drive. (4) Spoken directions are also helpful when riding a bike or even walking. (5) You can program the address, and the GPS directions can guide you there.

(6) You still may have times when a GPS device gives you wrong directions despite knowing about this technology. (7) However, it usually is the mapping software, not the GPS, that gives you bad advice. (8) GPS signals bounce off of satellites and give coordinates that describe your current location. (9) These coordinates are plugged into the mapping software. (10) If there's a glitch in the software, or the maps are out of date, then the directions can go very wrong.

7. Underline the sentence in the first paragraph that includes a simile.

8. Circle the number of the sentence in the second paragraph that includes an example of personification.

9. Find the misplaced modifier in sentence 6, and write the sentence correctly here. Despite knowing about this technology, you still may have times when a GPS device gives you wrong directions.

10. Write a conclusion for this essay. Sample answer: GPS technology can be very helpful for getting around. It can make following directions safer by giving them out loud. But it is not always accurate, since its software can be old or have errors. Maybe it will become more reliable over time.

Assignment: On a separate piece of paper, provide a final draft of the essay you began on page 105. Use what you learned about phrases and clauses, modifiers, and figurative language in the Language section of this unit. Think about how you and your classmates answered the Essential Question. Check your outline to be sure you have organized your ideas well. Be sure to use precise language and transitions. End with a concluding statement.

Digital Connection: Using Multimedia

Once students are finished writing their essays, they can add multimedia features to them. Have students go online to look for images, videos, and audio that will help bring their essays to life. They can even turn their essays into a series of slides.

If possible, display students' work on an interactive whiteboard, or set up a projector connected to a computer so that students can share their multimedia presentations with the class. If you have a class Web site, post students' presentations on it so family members can see them.

Introducing UNIT 5

Literary texts almost always involve a conflict of some kind. If you've ever had an argument with a friend, you've experienced conflict. Conflict can also occur between you and an object. Remember the last time your computer crashed? Sometimes you experience conflict with nature, too—for example, when you have to work outdoors on a day so hot that even the thought of going outside makes you sweat. In this unit, you will read stories, poems, and dramas about characters who face conflict as they work toward a goal.

To make stories interesting and exciting, authors use elements of craft and structure. For example, they consider the sounds and connotations of words. They decide if literal language or a figure of speech is the better way to express an idea. Authors also consider a work's structure, or how it is put together. For example, is a poem a better way to tell a particular story than a play or a traditional short story might be? And what about the characters in the story—what are their points of view, and why are their differences important?

Learning about these elements will help you understand and enjoy the stories that you are about to read.

Progress Check Can I?

Before Unit 5 / **After Unit 5**

- [ ] Determine the figurative and connotative meanings of words and phrases. [ ]
- [ ] Analyze the impact of rhymes and other repeated sounds on a poem, short story, or play. [ ]
- [ ] Explain how the form or structure of a drama or poem affects its meaning. [ ]
- [ ] Analyze how an author develops the points of view of characters or narrators in a text. [ ]
- [ ] Interpret figures of speech, including allusions, in context. [ ]

Unit 5 ■ Reading Literature: Craft and Structure

Student Page 113

HOME ◆ CONNECT...

The Home Connect feature is a way to keep parents or other adult family members apprised of what their children are learning. The key learning objectives are listed, and some ideas for related activities and discussions are included.

Explain to students that they can share the Home Connect page with their parents or other adult family members in their home. Let students know how much time the class will be spending on this unit so they can plan their time accordingly at home.

Encourage students and their parents to share their experiences using the suggestions on the Home Connect page and the Home Connect activities at **sadlierconnect.com**. You may wish to make a place to post some of this work.

Progress Check

The Progress Check is a self-assessment feature that students can use to gauge their own progress. Before students begin work on Unit 5, have them check the boxes next to any item that they feel they can do well. Explain that it is fine if they don't check any of the boxes. Tell them that they will have an opportunity to learn about and practice all of these items while studying the unit. Let them know that near the end of the unit they will have a chance to reconsider how well they can do each item on this list.

Before they begin their Unit 5 Review (see page 148 of this guide), you will be prompted to have students revisit this page. You can use this information to work with students on any items they don't understand before they tackle the Review.

HOME ◆ CONNECT...

When reading stories, your child needs to remember that many words have **connotative meanings**; that is, the words affect readers' emotions. Read part of a story with your child, and talk about the ways that its words affect your emotions. Discuss how the effect would be different if the author had used more "neutral" words—for example, the word *tasty* instead of the word *scrumptious*, or the word *confidence* instead of the word *arrogance*.

Although dramas and poems can tell stories, they have different structures, and **their structure affects their meaning**. For example, a poem with strong rhythm and rhyme feels very different from a haiku. In a play, the effect of a soliloquy differs from the effect of regular dialogue. Read a short story with your child. Talk about how you would feel if the story were presented as a poem.

At the heart of most stories is a conflict, and that conflict often occurs when characters have **different points of view**. Ask your child to think of a story in which the characters have strongly differing opinions. Why is that difference important to the story?

IN THIS UNIT, YOUR CHILD WILL...

- Read literary selections, including poems, a drama, a work of historical fiction, and an adventure story.
- Determine the meanings of words and phrases, including figurative and connotative meanings.
- Analyze the effect of rhymes and repeated sounds on a text.
- Analyze how the form or structure of a poem or drama affects the work's meaning.
- Analyze how an author develops and contrasts characters' points of view.
- Interpret figures of speech, including allusions.
- Compare and contrast ideas across four selections on the theme of sources of conflict.

WAYS TO HELP YOUR CHILD

Listen to the words and phrases your child uses, and identify connotative meanings of which he or she may be unaware. You can also play a game: Say a word and have your child suggest a synonym with a strong positive or negative connotation. Together, explore the connotative meaning of each word.

Conversation Starter: Ask your child to recall a conflict that he or she has experienced—for example, a disagreement with a friend or sibling, a challenge when playing a sport, or a difficult decision. Then recall a conflict that you have experienced. Together, identify the source of each conflict and how the conflict was resolved. Discuss what each of you learned from the experience.

ONLINE
For more Home Connect activities, continue online at sadlierconnect.com

114 **Unit 5** ■ Reading Literature: Craft and Structure

Student Page 114

UNIT PLANNER

Theme: Sources of Conflict	Focus
ANALYZING LITERARY LANGUAGE *pp. 116–123*	*A Valentine; Annabel Lee* **GENRE:** Poetry **LEXILE®:** NP* **WORDS TO KNOW:** luminous, talisman, amulet, sabre, scintillating, eloquent, seraph, coveted, highborn, kinsman, bore, sepulchre, demon, dissever, tomb, sounding
ANALYZING DRAMATIC STRUCTURE *pp. 124–131*	*The Longest Walk* **GENRE:** Drama **LEXILE®:** NP* **WORDS TO KNOW:** demonstrating, bill, legislator, treaty, transcendentalist, civil disobedience, dais, heritage, trek, restricting, agitated, temporary, rally, intense, authority, acknowledge, philosophy, perpetuate, conscientious
ANALYZING POINT OF VIEW *pp. 132–139*	*Race to the Golden Spike* **GENRE:** Historical Fiction **LEXILE®:** 990L **WORDS TO KNOW:** entrepreneurship, transform, construction, immigrant, commencing, mutually, founded, federal, allocated, colleague, arduous, duration, manual, spike, promontory, summit, so-called, crevasse, considerable
CLOSE READING *pp. 140–145*	*Toward the Unknown River* **GENRE:** Adventure—Based on Actual Events **LEXILE®:** 1010L
CONNECT ACROSS TEXTS *p. 146*	Compare and Contrast Texts
LANGUAGE *p. 147*	Figurative Language
UNIT 5 REVIEW *pp. 148–150*	*Rehearsing with a Friend, An Entry from Gwen's Diary* **GENRE:** Drama, Diary Entry **LEXILE®:** NP*

*Selections comprising more than 50% non-standard or non-conforming prose do not receive a Lexile measure, merely the NP code.

Objective(s)

Determine the meaning of words and phrases and analyze the impact of rhymes and repetition in a poem.

Analyze how a drama's or poem's form or structure contributes to its meaning.

Examine how an author develops and contrasts the points of view of different characters in a story.

- Determine the meaning of words and phrases and analyze the impact of rhymes and repetition in a poem.
- Analyze how a drama's or poem's form or structure contributes to its meaning.
- Examine how an author develops and contrasts the points of view of different characters in a story.

- Interpret figures of speech, including allusions, in context.

Unit Assessment

- Unit 5 Review *pp. 148–150*
- Unit 5 Performance Task   ONLINE

Additional Assessment Options

- Performance Task 1 *pp. 311A–320*
  ALSO ONLINE
- Performance Task 2 *pp. 321A–330*
  ALSO ONLINE

Optional Purchase:
- iProgress Monitor   ONLINE
- Progress Monitor Student Benchmark Assessment Booklet

ONLINE   Digital Resources

- Home Connect Activities
- Unit Performance Task
- Additional Practice
- Full-Length Reading Selections
- Teacher Resources
- iProgress Monitor (optional purchase)

Go to SadlierConnect.com to access your Digital Resources.

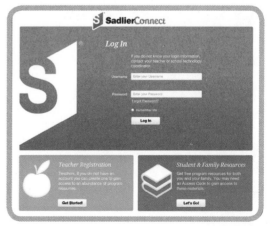

For more detailed instructions see page T3.

LEARNING PROGRESSIONS

In this unit, students will learn how the craft and structure of a literary text contribute to their understanding of it. The skills that students learn in this unit build upon the skills they learned during the sixth grade. Likewise, the skills students learn this year will provide a foundation for the skills they will develop in the eighth grade.

Analyzing Literary Language

- By the end of sixth grade, students should be able to determine the meaning of words and phrases as they are used in a text and analyze the impact of a specific word choice on meaning.

- In seventh grade, students will analyze the impact of rhymes and other repetitions of sounds in poems, stories, and drama.

- During eighth grade, students will continue to build on their literary language skills, while also analyzing analogies and allusions to other texts.

Analyzing Dramatic Structure

- While in sixth grade, students will analyze how a particular sentence, chapter, scene, or stanza fits into the overall structure of a text.

- In seventh grade, students will look at how a drama's or poem's structure contributes to its meaning.

- During eighth grade, students will compare and contrast the structure of two different texts and analyze how the differing structure of each contributes to its meaning.

Analyzing Point of View

- By the end of sixth grade, students will be able to explain how an author develops the point of view of the narrator or speaker in a text.

- During seventh grade, students will analyze how an author contrasts the points of view of different characters or narrators.

- While in eighth grade, students will analyze how differences in points of view of the characters and the audience create suspense or humor.

Reading Literature: Craft and Structure

UNIT 5

Essential Question:
How do authors use language, structure, and characters to create meaning?

Essential Question:
How do authors use language, structure, and characters to create meaning?

In this unit, students will learn about the craft and structure of literature, specifically the impact of rhymes and other repetitions of sounds in poems, how a drama's structure contributes to its meaning, and how the author contrasts the different points of view of the characters in a story.

Theme: Sources of Conflict

Students will read selections that have to do with the sources of conflicts, including a poem that tells a tragic love story, a drama about a famous protest march made by Native Americans in 1978, and historical fiction about the race to complete the transcontinental railroad.

Curriculum Connection: Social Studies

Students will learn about Henry David Thoreau and civil disobedience, the Native American civil rights movement, and the hardships endured by workers during the building of the transcontinental railroad.

Vocabulary Overview

General Academic Vocabulary

acknowledge, agitated, allocated, amulet, arduous, authority, bore, colleague, commencing, conscientious, considerable, construction, coveted, dais, demon, demonstrating, dissever, duration, eloquent, founded, heritage, highborn, immigrant, intense, kinsman, luminous, manual, mutually, perpetuate, rally, restricting, sabre, scintillating, sepulchre, seraph, so-called, sounding, talisman, temporary, tomb, transform, trek

Domain-Specific Vocabulary

bill, civil disobedience, crevasse, entrepreneurship, federal, legislator, philosophy, promontory, spike, summit, transcendentalist, treaty

Guided Instruction

OBJECTIVE
Determine the meaning of words and phrases and analyze the impact of rhymes and repetition in a poem.

Genre: Poetry

Explain to students that poetry expresses feelings and ideas with carefully chosen words. Tell students that poetry often includes sound devices such as rhyme or other repetitions of sounds to create certain effects.

Set the Purpose

Help students understand the purpose for learning the reading skill by asking: *How do the repetitions of sounds in the poem affect you as a reader?*

Model and Teach

Read or have volunteers read the selection and callouts as the class follows along. Model effective strategies for responding to the callouts by using the suggestions below.

CITE EVIDENCE

A Point out that rhymes repeat the ending sound of a word. Encourage students to find the word that has the same ending sound as *eyes* (*lies*).

B Explain that the poet may give instruction to the reader directly. Have students look for words that are synonyms for *searching*.

ANALYZING LITERARY LANGUAGE

Guided Instruction

WORDS TO KNOW
- amulet
- eloquent
- luminous
- sabre
- scintillating
- talisman

Poets carefully choose words and phrases for their impact on readers. Look for different kinds of **literary language**, and analyze both their meaning and their impact on the poem.

CITE EVIDENCE

A One type of literary language that poets often use is **rhyme** at the ends of lines. Rhyming words help give a poem its structure and rhythm. Find and underline a word at the end of one of the first four lines that rhymes with *eyes* in line 1.

B Edgar Allan Poe wrote "A Valentine" as a love poem to a woman whose identity he keeps secret. The poem is also a **riddle**—a challenge for readers to find the woman's name hidden in the poem. Double underline any details in lines 1–9 that suggest that readers should search for a name hidden in the poem.

A Valentine
by Edgar Allan Poe
(Genre: Poetry)

For her this rhyme is penned, whose **luminous** eyes,
  Brightly expressive as the twins of Leda,
Shall find her own sweet name, that nestling lies
Upon the page, enwrapped from every reader.
5 Search narrowly the lines! they hold a treasure
  Divine, a **talisman**, an **amulet**
That must be worn at heart. Search well the measure—
The words—the syllables. Do not forget
The trivialest point, or you may lose your labor:
10 And yet there is in this no Gordian knot
Which one might not undo without a **sabre**,

Words to Know

General Academic Vocabulary

amulet (*n.*): an object that has symbolic meaning; a charm
eloquent (*adj.*): expressive; meaningful
luminous (*adj.*): shining
sabre (*n.*): a type of sword
scintillating (*adj.*): dazzling; brilliant
talisman (*n.*): an object believed to have magical or protective properties

Working with Word Meaning Have students explain in their own words what each of the Words to Know means.

CRAFT AND STRUCTURE

If one could merely comprehend the plot.
Enwritten upon the leaf where now are peering
   Eyes **scintillating** soul, there lie *perdus*[1]
15 Three **eloquent** words oft uttered in the hearing
 *Of poets, by poets—as the name is a poet's, too.
Its letters, although naturally lying
   Like the knight Pinto, Mendez Ferdinando,
   Still form a synonym for Truth.— Cease trying!
20   You will not read the riddle, though you do the
   best you can do.

[1]*perdus* French for "lost"

Comprehension Check

How does knowing that the poem is an acrostic affect its
meaning as well as your experience when reading it?

Guided Instruction

CITE EVIDENCE

C "A Valentine" is a special kind of poem called an **acrostic**. The words of an acrostic are written so that certain letters spell out a hidden word or name. Circle the first letter of the first line, the second letter of the second line, the third letter of the third line, and so forth. What name is spelled out?

D Poets use **repetition** of sounds and words to emphasize ideas and create rhythm. In lines 5 and 7 of the poem, the poet repeats the word *search*. Put an asterisk next to a line on page 117 that contains repetition. What effect does the repetition have on the poem?

E The denotation of a word is the word's literal meaning. The **connotation** of a word is the idea or emotional quality that it suggests. Put a box around the word near the end of the poem that literally means "to come to an end" but that has a connotative meaning of "to stop suddenly or abruptly."

Guided Instruction

CITE EVIDENCE

C Help students understand the need to return to the beginning of the page to start circling the letters, and encourage them to be careful to follow the pattern described—to circle the first letter in line 1, the second letter in line 2, the third letter in line 3, and so on. With students, write the letters that you have circled and divide them into three names (*Frances Sargent Osgood*).

D With students, find the word that is repeated in line 16 (*poet*). Discuss the effect the repetition of the word has on the poem, especially given the fact that the hidden name is the name of a poet.

E Encourage students to look for the word that is a synonym for *stop*. When students have found *cease*, discuss the connotative and denotative meanings and how they affect the meaning of the poem.

Comprehension Check

Sample Answer: Knowing that the poem is an acrostic makes me search for clues about how to solve the riddle of the name. It also makes me look for clues about this person and why the poet hides this name in the poem.

Answer Explanation: Students should find that solving the acrostic may make them more aware of each word and its importance to the meaning of the poem.

Listening and Viewing

Have students view the drawing as you read the poem aloud. Ask: *Who does the woman in the picture represent?* (the woman for whom Poe wrote the poem) *Is the woman working to solve the puzzle?* (She seems to enjoy the tribute.) *What does this imply about the tone of the last line?* (It is playful.)

Support English Language Learners

Students who are learning English may overlook some of the sound repetitions in poetry if they do not recognize that different letter combinations can make the same sound (for example, *eyes*, *lies*). Have students work with peers to read the poem aloud, paying special attention to rhymes and other repetitions of sounds.

Guided Instruction

CITE EVIDENCE

A Lead students to find that the last two lines include exaggeration about Annabel Lee. Discuss with them what the poet might intend by this exaggeration, and whether it would really be possible that someone "lived with no other thought/Than to love and be loved" by another person.

B Point out to students that in each of the lines, one word is repeated (*child* in line 7, *loved* in line 9).

C You may wish to read the second stanza aloud to students, emphasizing the beginning consonant sounds in lines 9 and 10. Point out that the poet may use more than one kind of repetition in the same line or lines.

ANALYZING LITERARY LANGUAGE
Guided Instruction

WORDS TO KNOW
bore
coveted
highborn
kinsman
sepulchre
seraph

CITE EVIDENCE

A **Figurative language** has a meaning beyond its literal meaning. One kind of figurative language is **hyperbole**, or exaggeration. Circle two lines in stanza 1 that exaggerate something about Annabel Lee. What does this hyperbole mean?

B Recall that one kind of literary language is the repetition of sounds and words to impact meaning. Underline the words in two lines in stanza 2 that demonstrate repetition.

C A poet who writes a series of words that begin with the same letter or sound creates a kind of repetition called **alliteration**. Put a box around the line in stanza 2 that shows alliteration, and name the consonant sound that is repeated.

Annabel Lee
by Edgar Allan Poe
(Genre: Poetry)

It was many and many a year ago,
  In a kingdom by the sea,
That a maiden there lived whom you may know
  By the name of Annabel Lee;
5 And this maiden *she* lived with no other thought
  Than to love and be loved by me.

I was a *child* and *she* was a *child*,
  In this kingdom by the sea,
But we *loved* with a *love* that was more than *love*—
10   I and my Annabel Lee—
With a love that the wingèd **seraphs** of Heaven
  Coveted her and me.

Words to Know

General Academic Vocabulary
bore (*v.*): carried
coveted (*v.*): became jealous of
highborn (*adj.*): aristocratic; of noble family
kinsman (*n.*): relative
sepulchre (*n.*): tomb
seraph (*n.*): angel

Working with Word Meaning Have students draw pictures to represent the meanings of the words.

CRAFT AND STRUCTURE

And this was the reason that, long ago,
  In this kingdom by the sea,
15 A wind blew out of a cloud, chilling
  My beautiful Annabel Lee;
So that her **highborn kinsmen** came
  And **bore** her away from me,
To shut her up in a **sepulchre**
20 In this kingdom by the sea.

Comprehension Check

What effect does the repetition of words and sounds create in stanzas 1 and 2 of the poem?

CITE EVIDENCE

D There are other ways to repeat sounds. In **assonance**, the same vowel sound repeats within or at the end of a series of words. For example, listen for the repeated long-*A* sound in "It's a sh**a**me I didn't get any m**ai**l tod**ay**." In line 15, put a box around the words that demonstrate assonance.

E In **consonance**, the same consonant sound repeats within or at the end of a series of words, as in "The tru**ck** hit a ro**ck** near the thi**ck**et." Circle the words in line 16 that are an example of consonance. Which of those words is repeated in each stanza of the poem, and why?

CITE EVIDENCE

D With students, read line 15, paying attention to the repeated sounds in *out* and *cloud*.

E Have students read line 16 out loud, listening for the *l* sound repeated at the end of the word *beautiful* and *Annabel*. With students, review the poem to see which of the two words appears in each stanza (*Annabel*). Discuss with them that the poet includes the name of the beloved character in the title and each stanza of the poem, and talk about the effect produced by the repetition of the character's name.

Comprehension Check

Sample Answer: The rhyme and repetition in stanzas 1 and 2 create a lulling sound with a strong, calm rhythm.

Answer Explanation: Students should be able to recognize that the rhyming of long vowel sounds *o* and *e*, along with the repetition of the words *many*, *love*, and *child*, create a sound that is lilting and has a strong rhythm.

Digital Connection: Poetry in Performance

Give students the opportunity to go online to discover and compare different readings of "Annabel Lee." For example, at an online video portal, students may listen to the different readings performed by various actors. They may compare how each performer emphasizes repeated sounds and where they use pauses to manipulate the listener's attention.

After listening to various performers' readings, students may wish to perform their own reading of "Annabel Lee," using some of their favorite effects from the performances they have heard.

Analyzing Literary Language

Guided Practice

Recap Reading Selection

Have students recall what they learned from the first part of the poem about where the narrator and Annabel Lee lived and what happened to Annabel Lee.

CITE EVIDENCE

A Remind students that *assonance* is the repetition of vowel sounds within a series of words. Discuss with them the repetition of the short *i* sound in the words *killing* and *chilling* and how those words and their sounds affect the reader.

B Discuss with students that supernatural beings are not found in nature nor are they explainable by science, and remind students that *hyperbole* is exaggeration. By stating that not even supernatural beings (*demons* and *angels*) could tear the narrator from his love, the poet adds to the otherworldly, exaggerated effect.

C Lead students to look at the last two lines of the poem and have them use context to determine that *dissever* means "to separate." Discuss with them that the narrator is saying nothing can separate the two souls and that they have become as one.

Guided Practice

Annabel Lee *continued*

WORDS TO KNOW
demon
dissever

CITE EVIDENCE

A Double underline the words at the end of stanza 4 that create assonance. How is this assonance meant to affect readers?

B Circle the two details in stanza 5 that refer to supernatural beings. How do these details help create hyperbole?

C Underline the word in stanza 5 that literally means "to separate." Discuss the connotative meaning of the word and what it suggests about the speaker's feelings for Annabel Lee.

The angels, not half so happy in Heaven,
  Went envying her and me—
Yes!—that was the reason (as all men know,
  In this kingdom by the sea)
25 That the wind came out of the cloud by night,
  <u>Chilling</u> and <u>killing</u> my Annabel Lee.

But our love it was stronger by far than the love
  Of those who were older than we—
  Of many far wiser than we—
30 And neither the angels in Heaven above,
  Nor the **demons** down under the sea,
Can ever **dissever** my soul from the soul
  Of the beautiful Annabel Lee;

Words to Know

General Academic Vocabulary
demon (*n.*): evil spirit
dissever (*v.*): to cut apart

Working with Word Meaning Have students use each of the words above in a brief conversation with a partner.

CRAFT AND STRUCTURE
Guided Practice

Comprehension Check

1. Which lines create an example of rhyme at the ends of lines?

   a. lines 21 and 30

   b. lines 22, 24, and 26 *(circled)*

   c. lines 23, 27, and 32

   d. lines 27, 30, and 32

2. Lines 28–29 are an example of

   a. denotation.

   b. connotative meaning.

   c. repetition of words. *(circled)*

   d. consonance.

3. Which group of words from stanza 5 helps create hyperbole?

   a. our love

   b. stronger by far *(circled)*

   c. those who were older

   d. the beautiful Annabel Lee

4. Which word from stanza 5 has a connotation of "evil and frightful"?

   a. soul

   b. angels

   c. dissever

   d. demons *(circled)*

5. Lines 28 and 29 both end with the word *we*—a combination of rhyme and repetition. Why did the poet make that choice of literary language? With a partner, discuss how that choice helps you understand what the speaker is thinking and feeling in this stanza.

Sample answer: This literary language emphasizes the bond between the speaker and Annabel Lee and also reinforces the speaker's claim that the love he and Annabel Lee shared was special to them and different from anyone else's kind of love. The repeated word *we* contrasts their love with the love of people who are older and people who are wiser.

Unit 5 ■ Reading Literature: Craft and Structure **121**

Comprehension Check

Answer Explanations:

1. Students should recall that rhymes are the repetitions of ending sounds of a series of words, as in lines 22, 24, and 26 (*me, sea,* and *Lee*) Therefore, B is the correct answer.

2. Students should recognize the repetition of the words *Of, than,* and *we* and identify that the best answer is choice C, *repetition of words.*

3. Students should recall that *hyperbole* is a kind of exaggeration, and recognize that choice B, *stronger by far,* is the best answer.

4. Students should recognize that a word's connotation is the associations that it brings to mind, and recognize that choice D, *demons,* is the best answer.

5. Students should also recognize that the repetition of the word *we* emphasizes the narrator and Annabel as one, having a single viewpoint. They may also note that *we* sounds the same as *wee,* which emphasizes how the two characters are small or weak compared to those who are older and wiser.

Turn and Talk

Encourage partners to quickly discuss the text, using callouts B and C on page 120 and question 5 on page 121 of the Student Book. Have students ask questions as needed and develop their answers in a quick chat with their partners. Finally, have partners present their answers to the whole group, contributing to the whole-class discussion.

Discussion Skills

Have students think about the question *How does Poe use words with fearful connotations to emphasize his narrator's love?* Encourage students to find specific words to support their answers. Suggest the following stems for them to try out as they have this discussion:

• *The word _____ connotes _____.*

• *The words ____ and ____ make me think that the narrator is _____.*

• *When the narrator uses the words ____ and ____, it makes me think his love is _____.*

Independent Practice

Recap Reading Selection

Have students recall what they have read so far about the narrator and Annabel Lee. Ask students to recall what caused Annabel Lee's death. Tell them they will continue to read about the effect her death had on the narrator and how he lives with his grief.

Read and Apply

Have students read the selection independently as you circulate. Ask them to read aloud so you can see if they are reading fluently. You can also use the support below to help students who are having difficulty.

CITE EVIDENCE

A Choral read and have students listen for words with the long *i* sound (*rise, I, bright, eyes, night-tide, I, lie, by, side, my, life, bride*). Remind students that *assonance* is repetition of a vowel sound in a series of words. Ask students why Poe may have used assonance in this section of the poem. Discuss how the long *i* sound also appears in the word *cry* and intensifies feeling in the poem.

B Discuss with students the emotional effect of lines 40 and 41. Have them pay attention to the break in rhythm that the word *sepulchre* adds. Have them identify emotions evoked in the lines. Choral read the lines, stressing the alliteration in the words *sepulchre*, *sea*, and *sounding sea*. Discuss possible reasons Poe didn't include the word *sepulchre* in line 41; suggest that *tomb* provides a more regular rhythm for the last line.

WORDS TO KNOW

sounding

tomb

CITE EVIDENCE

A Underline each word in stanza 6 that has a long-*I* sound. Why does the poet use so much assonance here?

B What is the emotional effect of lines 40–41? Circle the words in those lines that create alliteration. Why does the poet not repeat the word *sepulchre* in line 41?

For the moon never beams, without bringing me dreams

35 Of the beautiful Annabel Lee;

And the stars never <u>rise</u>, but I feel the <u>bright eyes</u>

Of the beautiful Annabel Lee;

And so, all the <u>night-tide</u>, I lie down <u>by</u> the <u>side</u>

Of <u>my</u> darling—my darling—<u>my</u> life and <u>my</u> bride,

40 In her (sepulchre) there by the (sea—)

In her **tomb** by the **(sounding** sea.)

Words to Know

General Academic Vocabulary

sounding (*adj.*): rumbling; booming

tomb (*n.*): grave; place where a person is buried

Working with Word Meaning Encourage students to state the meaning of *tomb* and *sounding* in their own words. Have them pay special attention to the specific contextual meaning of the multiple-meaning word *sounding*. Have them use each word in a sentence.

CRAFT AND STRUCTURE
Independent Practice

Independent Practice

Comprehension Check — MORE ONLINE — sadlierconnect.com

1. In the final stanza (lines 34–39), how does the poet's literary language change?

  a. He does not rhyme any other words with Annabel Lee's name.

  b. He rhymes some words within lines as well as at ends of lines.

  c. He does not include any repetition of words.

  d. His only rhymes come from repeated words.

2. Which group of words in lines 38–39 shows that the poet is using hyperbole?

  a. all the night-tide

  b. I lie down

  c. my darling—my darling

  d. my bride

3. Which set of words from the poem demonstrates consonance?

  a. rise, lie, life, bride

  b. loved, child, cloud

  c. beams, bringing, beautiful

  d. eyes, side, bride

4. Which statement does NOT describe the connotation of the word *tomb*?

  a. *Tomb* suggests the finality of death.

  b. *Tomb* creates a feeling of closure.

  c. *Tomb* reminds readers that everyone will die.

  d. *Tomb* suggests that the person died peacefully.

5. With a partner, discuss different types of repetition and the reasons that a poet might use them. Then analyze how the poet uses repetition in this final stanza. Tell what is repeated and where it occurs. Describe what the repetition means to this stanza and to the poem as a whole.

Sample answer: A poet may use repetition of words, phrases, lines, and different types of sounds to create musical effects, to call attention to a certain idea or image, or to create a thread that binds a long poem together. In the final stanza of "Annabel Lee," the poet repeats sounds, including rhyme (lines 38–39), assonance (line 36), consonance (line 34), and alliteration (lines 40–41). He begins some lines with the words *Of [the]*, some with the word *And*, and the final two with the words *In her*. He also repeats *never* (lines 34 and 36), *sea* (lines 40 and 41), and *my darling* (line 39) and even an entire line (lines 35 and 37). Repetition makes this stanza the most emotional of the entire poem and reminds readers of how deeply the speaker feels the loss of Annabel Lee.

Unit 5 ■ Reading Literature: Craft and Structure   **123**

Extend Thinking: Hypothesize

Ask students to reread the last stanza of the poem and have them discuss what they believe the narrator really means. Have them discuss, for example, whether or not they believe that the narrator goes to the tomb of Annabel Lee and sleeps there every night. If he does sleep there, what does that say about the narrator? Ask them to discuss other possibilities (for example, the narrator's thoughts or *affections* might lie with Annabel Lee, or the narrator himself might be dying). Encourage students to defend their ideas explicitly, using evidence from the text for support.

Comprehension Check

Answer Explanations:

1. Students should be able to identify the repetition of sounds and therefore recognize that the best answer is choice B.

2. Since it is unlikely that the narrator would lie down near his dead bride for the entire night, choice A is the best answer.

3. Students should know *consonance* is repeated ending consonant sounds, so the best answer choice is B, *loved, child, cloud*.

4. Students should know that *tomb* has dark connotations, so the best answer is choice D.

5. Students should be aware of the way repetition dramatizes the narrator's experiences.

Critical Comprehension

Challenge students to think more deeply about the text and to support their answers with evidence from the text.

Ask: *How is the relationship between the narrator and Annabel Lee different by the end of the poem?* (By the end, she is not only dead, she is his bride.)

Assess and Respond
If students have trouble answering questions in the Comprehension Check,
Then lead them in underlining repetitions in the poem, reviewing literary terms, and discussing how different types of repetitions affect the tone of the poem.

Guided Instruction

OBJECTIVE
Analyze how a drama's or poem's form or structure contributes to its meaning.

Genre: Drama

A drama is a piece of fiction meant to be performed. A list of characters at the start tells the reader who will be included in the story. Stage directions help set the scene and explain the characters' feelings and actions. In drama, characters speak directly to each other.

Set the Purpose

Tell students that plays have a different structure from poetry or stories. Direct them to look at page 124. Ask: *What do you see about the form of this first page of the play that looks different from a poem or a story?* Ask them to speculate about why drama might be constructed in this special way.

Model and Teach

Read or have volunteers read the selection and callouts as the class follows along. Model effective strategies for responding to the callouts by using the suggestions below.

CITE EVIDENCE

A Have students locate the act and scene number directly following the list of characters.

B Help students find the most important event mentioned in the paragraph of stage directions—the arrival of the Longest Walk.

ANALYZING DRAMATIC STRUCTURE

Guided Instruction

WORDS TO KNOW
bill
demonstrating
legislator
treaty

> A series of connected scenes and acts creates the structure of a play, or drama. A drama's **structure** contributes to its meaning.

CITE EVIDENCE

A The **events** that make up a drama are divided into acts and scenes that provide **structure**. Circle the act and scene number of this section of the play.

B Events in a drama may be expressed in **stage directions**, **dialogue**, or both. Underline the event described in the opening italicized paragraph.

The Longest Walk
(Genre: Drama)

CAST OF CHARACTERS
LILY WILSON, an 18-year-old girl
JAYSON WILSON, her 12-year-old brother
KIM STONEFISH, Lily's best friend
LAURA, a Native American protestor
POLICEMAN
HENRY DAVID THOREAU, American author
MRS. WILSON, mother of Lily and Jayson

ACT I, SCENE 1

1 **SETTING:** *It is 3:00 on a hot, overcast afternoon—July 15, 1978—in Washington, D.C. JAYSON is at home with LILY and KIM, who recently finished their first year at college. They are all watching a live news report on television. The big story of the day is the arrival in the nation's capital of the Longest Walk, a peaceful protest march for Native American rights that began five months and 3,200 miles ago in San Francisco, California.*

KIM *(under her breath, almost whispering):* Wow.

LILY: There must be more than a thousand people marching: Native American activists, African American community leaders, politicians . . . And there's that movie star—what's his name?

JAYSON *(bored):* Who cares? It's just another protest march.

5 **LILY** *(irritated):* Jayson, you have a lot to learn. Those Native Americans have marched on foot to Washington, D.C., from San Francisco! It's taken them months. *(to herself)* Can you imagine walking across the entire country?

Words to Know

General Academic Vocabulary
demonstrating (*v.*): protesting

Domain-Specific Vocabulary
bill (*n.*): a proposed law
legislator (*n.*): lawmaker
treaty (*n.*): an agreement between two groups, especially when they have been in conflict

Working with Word Meaning Have students draw pictures to show the meaning of each word.

CRAFT AND STRUCTURE

JAYSON: What are they protesting, anyway?

LILY *(impatiently):* They're **demonstrating** against the way that Native Americans are being treated by the government.

JAYSON: What's been so terrible for them?

KIM *(with passion):* Where do I begin? First, some members of Congress have introduced **bills** that would close some Native American schools and hospitals. There are also efforts to force Native Americans to pay taxes on reservation land. And to add insult to injury, some **legislators** want to abolish rights established by **treaties**—treaties that were signed years ago by both sides!

10　**LILY** *(impressed):* Wow, Kim, you really care about this!

KIM: Well, I *should* care—I'm half Lenni Lenape.

JAYSON: What does that mean?

KIM: The Lenni Lenape are a Native American group. My people originally lived in what is today New York, New Jersey, Pennsylvania, and Delaware.

LILY: Oh, right! Now I remember from history class: The Lenape were renamed the Delaware by the English.

15　**KIM:** Exactly! And we go back further than that. It was the Lenni Lenape who sold Manhattan to some Dutch settlers!

(They continue to watch the coverage of the march. KIM is especially quiet.)

KIM *(pondering):* You know what? <u>I want to go down there and join the march.</u>

LILY *(aghast):* Are you crazy? There are so many people, not to mention that it's probably 100 degrees outside. And I saw a lot of police there, Kim. You could get in trouble!

Comprehension Check

In what way does Act I, Scene 1, introduce the drama? What details set the scene? Cite specifics from the text.

Guided Instruction

CITE EVIDENCE

C At the beginning of each scene, the playwright tells you the **setting**, or time and place, of the scene. Double underline the time and place of this scene.

D Structure gives drama meaning, but so do the characters who experience the events. In the Cast of **Characters**, put a box around the names of the three characters introduced in this scene.

E How a character reacts to an event moves a drama's story forward. Underline Kim's reaction to watching the march. What might she do next? Why?

CITE EVIDENCE

C Help students locate the sentence that tells the setting of the play at the beginning of the stage directions.

D With students, name the characters that have been introduced in the scene. Have students find the names in the cast of characters.

E With students, read over Kim's lines that occur as she is watching TV. Have students underline the sentence that tells what she would like to do. Have students predict what she will do next. (She will go to the march.) Discuss with them why she might want to attend, given her Lenni Lenape background.

Comprehension Check

Sample Answer: It introduces three main characters discussing a demonstration. A problem is posed right away, since Kim wants to go to the march and Lily doesn't think she should. The details about a Native American march in 1978 and the fact that the characters are watching the protest on TV help set the scene.

Answer Explanation: Students learn about Kim, Lily, and Jayson through the cast of characters, the stage directions, and the dialogue. Students find out about the Native American march through the stage directions and the dialogue. The problem is shown through dialogue.

Support English Language Learners

Some of your English language learners may have experienced similar feelings of unfairness or injustice to those alluded to in this selection. If so, seize the opportunity to engage them as resources for the class as a whole. Invite them to share and/or elaborate on their experiences, and help them draw analogies to the experiences of the characters in the play. Provide sentence stems such as the one below to assist them in discussing their experiences in relation to the play.

My experience was (like/unlike) (Kim's/Lily's/Jayson's) because _____.

Guided Instruction

CITE EVIDENCE

A Have students locate the information where Act I, Scene 2 takes place by looking at the information next to "Setting."

B Read with students to find the information in the stage directions about Laura at the bottom of page 126 and in the stage directions next to her dialogue on page 127. Discuss with students that the dialogue reveals that Laura is initially cautious but warm, and that she is a participant in the march.

Review: Analyzing Literary Language

Remind students that authors use language purposefully to achieve specific effects in their writing. For instance, an author may repeat words or sounds in a piece of literature to emphasize or reinforce an idea or emotion. Have students look at Kim's first speech on page 125. Lead them to recognize that Kim repeats the word *treaties* in the last sentence. Ask: *What is the effect of the repetition?* (It shows Kim's anger.)

ANALYZING DRAMATIC STRUCTURE

Guided Instruction

The Longest Walk *continued*

WORDS TO KNOW
civil disobedience
dais
heritage
transcendentalist
trek

CITE EVIDENCE

A When and where does Act I, Scene 2, take place? Double underline details about setting that appear in the text.

B The introduction of a new character is an important structural event in a drama. Circle any details about Laura that appear in stage directions. Then discuss what you learn about Laura from dialogue.

KIM: Lily, remember reading Henry David Thoreau in English class? He was the American **transcendentalist** whose essay *On Civil Disobedience* talks about exactly what we're up against! Thoreau said, "A people, as well as an individual, must do justice, cost what it may." *(pointing at the television)* Those marchers are my people, and I'm an individual!

20 **LILY** *(with a sigh):* Then I'm going with you. *(grabbing Jayson's hand):* I promised Mom I'd look after you, Jayson, so you're coming, too!

ACT I, SCENE 2

SETTING: <u>An hour later, on a path leading to the steps of the United States Capitol,</u> Native American protesters are shouting and holding signs that say, "The Longest Walk, 1978" and "Support Indian Resistance." JAYSON, LILY, and KIM can barely hear each other over the noise.

JAYSON *(pointing):* What's that flag?

KIM *(shouting):* It's the flag of the American Indian Movement.

*(The marchers begin to turn their attention to a man on a **dais** in front of the steps. Just then, LAURA, an older woman in a wheelchair approaches them.)*

126   Unit 5 ■ Reading Literature: Craft and Structure

Words to Know

General Academic Vocabulary
dais *(n.)*: a raised platform
heritage *(n.)*: something one is born to
trek *(n.)*: a long walk or journey

Domain-Specific Vocabulary
civil disobedience *(n.)*: political action in which participants peacefully break laws as a form of protest
transcendentalist *(n.)*: a philosopher who believes that true meaning lies beyond ordinary experiences

Working with Word Meaning
Have students use the words in sentences.

CRAFT AND STRUCTURE

25 **LAURA** (*suspiciously*): May I ask what you all are doing here?

LILY (*warmly*): Hi! I'm Lily, this is my brother Jayson, and this is my friend Kim. We're here to support the protest.

LAURA (*clearly relieved*): Oh, that's great! I was afraid you might be journalists! My name is Laura.

KIM (*laughing*): Journalists? We're college students! My **heritage** is Lenni Lenape, so I just had to come down and show my support.

LAURA: Lenape? (*brightening*) Well then, as a fellow Lenape, I say to you, *Hohoh!*

30 **JAYSON:** What does that mean?

KIM (*grinning*): In the Lenape language, it's an expression of joy!

LILY (*pointing into the distance*): Laura, who is that speaking?

LAURA: That's one of our leaders. He helped organize the march. I'll introduce you. He and many others have worked for so long to organize this walk. And quite a walk it was—you know, only about twenty Native Americans actually made the entire **trek**. Many of us joined the march along the way in other American cities. (*to KIM*) How did you hear about it?

(*KIM is about to reply when she suddenly hears a commotion in front of them. She sees police guiding a group of protestors toward their location.*)

35 **POLICEMAN** (*shouting*): All right now—back up, folks! We don't want any trouble today!

* (*As the group is forced toward KIM and her friends, the protestors become impatient. Other marchers, until now just quietly listening to the speaker, become upset as well. Suddenly, a disturbance breaks out, and KIM is separated from her friends.*)

LILY (*calling out while holding tightly to JAYSON*): Kim! KIM!

Comprehension Check

How do the two scenes in Act I fit together? In what way does their structure give meaning to the drama?

Guided Instruction

CITE EVIDENCE

C A drama may have other structures within its larger form. For example, a **soliloquy** is a speech made to the audience in which a character's thoughts are revealed. A **monologue** is a long speech delivered by one character to another. An **epilogue** is the final section of a play after events have been resolved. Put a box around the monologue in this scene.

D A playwright may build suspense by introducing an event that leaves readers wondering what will happen. Put an asterisk next to the suspenseful event in this scene.

E Underline the stage direction that tells how Lily reacts to being separated from Kim. Is this a good place to end Act I?

Guided Instruction

CITE EVIDENCE

C Help students locate Laura's monologue in the middle of page 127. One way to identify a monologue is to look for a large chunk of uninterrupted speech by one character.

D Have students reread Act I, Scene 2 to identify the event that creates the most suspense when Kim is separated from her friends.

E After locating the stage direction that tells how Lily reacts, discuss with students that ending Act I here creates suspense and makes readers or an audience want to know what happens next, which will be revealed in the next act.

Comprehension Check

Sample Answer: In the first scene, we meet the characters and find out about the Long March. In the second scene, the characters are at the Long March, and by the end of the scene, one character could be in danger.

Answer Explanation: The plot in a drama generally builds throughout a play until the conflict is resolved. In the first scene the situation is set up, and in the second scene a real problem develops.

Differentiate Instruction

Students who are struggling with callouts D and E may benefit from hearing Act I, Scene 2, including the stage directions, read by fluent readers. After listening to the scene's reading, students can discuss which part of the play had the most suspense and whether the scene ended in an appropriate place.

Guided Practice

Recap Reading Selection

Have students recall what has happened to the characters so far in the play—especially Kim, who at the end of Act I, Scene 2 was separated from her friends at the protest. Let students know that they will continue to read the play to learn what happens to Kim, her friends, and the rest of the protesters.

Read and Practice

Have partners take turns reading the selection as you circulate to provide support. Ask students to respond to Cite Evidence callouts A and B. Provide additional scaffolding as needed, using the suggestions below.

CITE EVIDENCE

A Have students look closely at the italicized text in the middle of page 128 to find the stage directions that tell how Kim reacts to being restricted.

B Have students look for a new boldfaced name on the page (Henry David Thoreau). Once they find the new character, work with them as they read to learn more about Thoreau. Have students identify descriptions of him in the stage directions ("as if he were a ghost. His eyes are intelligent and intense, but warm"). Then discuss with students what they learn from Thoreau's words about his ideas regarding the individual and the authority of the state.

ANALYZING DRAMATIC STRUCTURE

Guided Practice

The Longest Walk *continued*

ACT II, SCENE 1

SETTING: *Twenty minutes later, KIM and the other protestors, fuming with frustration, are standing behind a line of police officers who are* **restricting** *the movement of the group.*

LILY *(to LAURA):* Why are the police holding those people back like that?

40 **LAURA:** They have to make sure no one gets hurt. Some of those folks were getting pretty **agitated**, so I think it was a good idea for the police to separate them from the rest of the crowd. Don't worry—it's only **temporary**.

JAYSON: Temporary? What do you mean? What about Kim?

LILY: We can't stay for the entire **rally**. My mom will be home soon, and we have to get back before she arrives!

(LILY scans the crowd and finally sees KIM standing patiently and helplessly *behind the row of police.)*

KIM *(*her head down, speaking softly to herself*):* Me and my bright ideas! How long are they going to keep me here? I could use a Good Samaritan just about now!

45 *(Suddenly, she hears a voice in front of her.)*

HENRY DAVID THOREAU *(Lights come up on him suddenly,* as if he were a ghost. His eyes are intelligent *and* **intense***, but warm):* A people, as well as an individual, must do justice, cost what it may.

KIM *(looking up, stunned):* Whaaa…? *(hesitatingly and quietly)* M-M-Mr. Thoreau? *(Clearly she is the only person who can see or hear him. She takes a breath, realizing she is about to speak to her mentor.)* I'm scared, Mr. Thoreau, but I think that what the government is doing to Native Americans is unjust.

THOREAU: There will never be a really free and enlightened State until the State comes to recognize the individual as a higher and independent power, from which all its own power and **authority** are derived, and treats him accordingly.

WORDS TO KNOW

agitated
authority
intense
rally
restricting
temporary

CITE EVIDENCE

A Underline the stage directions that tell how Kim reacts to being restricted by the police.

B In this scene, another new character is introduced. Circle the name of the character, and double underline what you learn about him. Do you learn about him from stage directions, dialogue, or both?

128   Unit 5 ■ Reading Literature: Craft and Structure

Words to Know

General Academic Vocabulary

agitated *(adj.)*: upset
authority *(n.)*: the right to tell others what to do
intense *(adj.)*: having or showing great strength or feeling
rally *(n.)*: public gathering; demonstration
restricting *(v.)*: holding back; containing
temporary *(adj.)*: not permanent; of short term

Working with Word Meaning Have students explain each word's meaning in their own words. Then have them write a short paragraph using as many of the words as they can.

CRAFT AND STRUCTURE

Guided Practice

KIM *(nodding):* Yes, exactly! That's what you wrote in *On Civil Disobedience*. I love that essay. I want Native Americans to be treated with the respect they deserve, and I know you do, too.

50 **THOREAU:** I please myself with imagining a State at last which can afford to be just to all men, and to treat the individual with respect as a neighbor. *(He steps back out of spotlight, into the darkness.)*

Comprehension Check

1. Which of the following best describes Laura's response to Lily's question?

   a. Laura is angry at the police.

   b. Laura believes the police aren't doing enough to protect people.

   c. Laura feels the police are doing their job.

   d. Laura thinks Lily is overreacting.

2. About how much time has passed since the first scene of the play?

   a. an hour

   b. twenty minutes

   c. an hour and twenty minutes

   d. two days

3. In this scene, we learn about Laura's beliefs from

   a. stage directions only.

   b. dialogue only.

   c. both stage directions and dialogue.

   d. neither stage directions nor dialogue.

4. What is the main event of this scene?

   a. Jayson asks what *temporary* means.

   b. Lily finally finds Kim in the crowd.

   c. Henry David Thoreau appears and speaks to Kim.

   d. Laura expresses her opinion about the police.

5. How is the introduction of the character of Thoreau different from the introduction of Laura in the previous scene? Discuss with a partner how Thoreau impacts the meaning and your understanding of the play. Explain your answer with details from the text.

   Sample answer: Thoreau is an even more important character to Kim than

   Laura is. Kim quoted Thoreau in Act I, Scene 1, so clearly he means a lot to her.

   His presence gives Kim the chance to express her beliefs for the reader, which

   are very important to the meaning of the play as a whole.

Comprehension Check

Answer Explanations:

1. Students should recognize that Laura is explaining to Lily why the police had to act the way that they did, so choice C is the best answer.

2. Students should be able to locate the information on the passage of time in the stage directions for Act I, Scene 2 and Act II, Scene 1. They should identify that choice C, *an hour and twenty minutes*, is the best answer.

3. Since there are no stage directions that tell about Laura, students should recognize that choice B, *dialogue only*, is the best answer.

4. Since Henry David Thoreau is both a new and an unexpected character, students should recognize that the best answer is choice C, *Henry David Thoreau appears and speaks to Kim*.

5. Students should also recognize that while the character of Laura is supposed to be a real person in the scene, Thoreau appears only to Kim. His words seem to come from his writings, which Kim has read.

Numbered Heads Together

Have students work in groups of four, and have them call out their numbers from one to four. Ask groups to put their heads together to answer the following question within five minutes: *How do you think Thoreau's appearance to Kim affects her?* After five minutes, call a number. Have students with that number stand and answer the question. Discuss answers with the class.

Discussion Skills

Have students practice discussion and presentation skills by having them work in small groups to speak about Thoreau and the role of the individual in society. Assign each group to discuss what they have learned from the play about Thoreau's ideas and have them decide whether they agree with these ideas as they understand them. Each group should prepare a short speech or presentation to explain their ideas.

Remind students to look back through the play to see how the ideas inspire characters.

Independent Practice

Recap Reading Selection

Have students recall what has happened so far to Kim in the play. Ask students if they can recall Thoreau's ideas that inspired Kim to action. Let students know that they will continue to read about what happens to Kim and her friends.

Read and Apply

Have students read the selection independently as you circulate. Ask them to read aloud so you can see if they are reading fluently. You can also use the support below to help students who are having difficulty.

CITE EVIDENCE

A After you explain to students that a soliloquy is a long speech that a character gives directly to the audience, they should be able to find Kim's soliloquy on page 130.

B Make sure that students find Thoreau's response to Kim in the middle of page 130. Have students reread Kim's soliloquy. Then make sure that student partners understand that this experience has helped Kim decide that she believes in protest but not in breaking the law.

ANALYZING DRAMATIC STRUCTURE

Independent Practice

The Longest Walk *continued*

WORDS TO KNOW

acknowledge
conscientious
perpetuate
philosophy

CITE EVIDENCE

A Reread the definition of the word *soliloquy* on page 127. Circle the name of the character who presents a soliloquy in this scene.

B Underline the dialogue that shows Thoreau's response to Kim's words. What has Kim learned from this experience? Discuss your answer with a partner.

(KIM) *(to the audience)*: America is long overdue to **acknowledge** Native Americans as the original American people. They are entitled to live freely on the land their ancestors lived on, cared for, and loved for thousands of years.

I believe in the **philosophy** that people should take a stand when their government creates bad policies, but I don't believe that it's right to break the law.

For example, I understand the argument that people **perpetuate** bad government when they pay federal taxes while opposing that government's policies. To quote Henry David Thoreau: "Those who, while they disapprove of the character and measures of a government, yield to it their allegiance and support are undoubtedly its most **conscientious** supporters, and so frequently the most serious obstacles to reform."

I appreciate what this means, but I prefer peaceful protest as a way of showing civil disobedience. *(She turns back toward the spot where THOREAU spoke to her.)*

55 **THOREAU** *(reappearing in the light, smiling)*: I ask for, not at once no government, but at once a better government.

(With that remark, THOREAU disappears. KIM is brought back to reality by the voice of the POLICEMAN.)

POLICEMAN: All right—rally's over. Everyone can go.

(KIM races toward LILY, JAYSON, and LAURA.)

LILY: Kim, thank goodness you're all right! I don't know how you got through that all by yourself!

60 **KIM** *(smiling to herself)*: Well, I wasn't exactly by myself....

EPILOGUE

SETTING: *An hour later, LILY, JAYSON, and KIM are back at the Wilsons' home. Just then, MRS. WILSON enters.*

MRS. WILSON: I'm home! Hello, Kim; it's nice to see you again. So, what did you all do today?

JAYSON *(starting to blurt it out)*: We—

130   Unit 5 ■ Reading Literature: Craft and Structure

Words to Know

General Academic Vocabulary
acknowledge (*v.*): to admit to be real or true
conscientious (*adj.*): careful; exacting
perpetuate (*v.*): to keep something going; to support

Domain-Specific Vocabulary
philosophy (*n.*): system of belief

Working with Word Meaning Encourage students or partners to come up with one or more synonyms for each word.

LILY (*slapping her hand over his mouth*): We watched the march on television. It's called "The Longest Walk," and it was really impressive. Some Native Americans marched thousands of miles to protest their mistreatment by the government.

65 **MRS. WILSON** (*pausing, and then*): "A people, as well as an individual, must do justice, cost what it may."

JAYSON (*with amazement*): Mom, you just quoted Thoreau!

(*THE END*)

Comprehension Check   **MORE ONLINE** sadlierconnect.com

1. Which of the following is NOT true about the soliloquy in this scene?

   a. The speaker is the only character in the scene.

   b. The speaker is expressing personal thoughts and beliefs.

   c. The speaker is addressing the audience.

   d. The speaker's remarks are very brief.

2. Which stage direction could you add before Lily's dialogue in paragraph 59?

   a. (*relieved*)

   b. (*confused*)

   c. (*curious*)

   d. (*upset*)

3. The Epilogue is very short because

   a. Mrs. Wilson is not an important character.

   b. Thoreau has already disappeared.

   c. the play's main events have already been resolved.

   d. it presents a funny moment instead of a serious one.

4. Which is NOT a way that the Epilogue contributes to the play's meaning?

   a. It signals that the play is about to end.

   b. It tells the audience that Lily, Jayson, and Kim reached home safely.

   c. It provides an opportunity for Mrs. Wilson's character to express a belief.

   d. It creates a suspenseful ending.

5. What is the meaning of this play? How does the structure of the play contribute to that meaning? Give evidence for your answer.

   Sample answer: The play shows how Kim explores her beliefs. In the first scene, Kim's heritage is revealed, along with her belief in the mission of the march and in Thoreau's ideas. In the second scene, Kim acts on her beliefs but must face the consequences. Thoreau helps her do that in Act II. The Epilogue tells Kim that Thoreau's beliefs are shared by more people than she thought.

Unit 5 ■ Reading Literature: Craft and Structure   **131**

Extend Thinking: Investigate

After students read about Thoreau's ideas and how they affect Kim in the play, encourage them to read more about one of his ideas, such as civil disobedience, and conduct research to learn more about it. Students may research how different groups or movements have been inspired by Thoreau's ideas, and how they put them to use.

Have students present their findings in a paper or multimedia presentation.

Independent Practice

Comprehension Check

Answer Explanations:

1. Students should recognize that Kim is not the only character in the scene, which means that the best answer is choice A.

2. Students should understand that Lily was worried about Kim, and so the best answer is choice A, *relieved*.

3. Review with students that an Epilogue takes place after the action of a play, so the best choice is C.

4. Students should recognize that the play does not end in suspense, so that the best answer is choice D.

5. Students should also recognize that Kim's soliloquy gives her a chance to explain her beliefs in some detail.

Critical Comprehension

Challenge students to think more deeply about the text and to support their answers with evidence from the text. Ask: *If Kim had not been separated from her friends, would she have reached the same conclusions?* (probably not)

Assess and Respond
If students have trouble answering the questions in the Comprehension Check,
Then lead them in highlighting the different parts of the play referred to in the questions, reviewing literary terms and discussing what happens in each section.

Guided Instruction

OBJECTIVE
Examine how an author develops and contrasts the points of view of different characters in a story.

Genre: Historical Fiction

Explain to students that if a story is historical fiction, it takes place in the past and uses real details about a historical period as part of the story.

Set the Purpose

Help students understand the purpose for reading by asking: *How can you tell how a character feels about something? How do you identify whether two characters feel the same way about something?*

Model and Teach

Read or have volunteers read the selection and callouts as the class follows along. Model effective strategies for responding to the callouts by using the suggestions below.

CITE EVIDENCE

A Help students find the reference to Abraham Lincoln in the second paragraph and Paul's feelings about Lincoln. Paul's love for Lincoln is his point of view.

B With students, read the fourth paragraph and help students find the word (*brave*) that tells the narrator's point of view.

WORDS TO KNOW
commencing
construction
entrepreneurship
immigrant
mutually
transform

An author develops different **points of view** for various characters. Comparing these points of view can help the reader undersand a story's events from different perspectives.

CITE EVIDENCE

A The **point of view** of a character refers to that character's feelings about various topics and events. Underline the text that reveals Paul's point of view about Abraham Lincoln.

B The "voice" that tells the story (but often is not an actual character) is the story's narrator. A narrator can also have a point of view. In paragraph 4, circle a phrase that shows the narrator's point of view about the veterans who fought on the Union side in the Civil War.

Race to the Golden Spike
(Genre: Historical Fiction)

1   Paul Kelley looked up at the blazing sun and squinted. Then he looked out across the land and considered his position. He was working on one of the greatest feats of ingenuity, engineering, and **entrepreneurship** in the history of the world!

2   The United States desperately needed a railroad that could cross the continent and, in so doing, **transform** the nation's entire way of life. The late president Abraham Lincoln—how Paul had loved that man—had authorized a transcontinental railroad back in 1862, but it had taken years to get started.

3   Now its **construction** was underway in earnest, and Paul and his fellow workers felt lucky to be a part of it. Nearly all the men on the team he was working with were Irish **immigrants**. They were young men, some still in their teens, others with families back East, and many of them veterans of the War Between the States. Fought for the Union, they did; they fought for the end of slavery, for Mr. Lincoln, and for their own futures in a *United* States. That was the only outcome they would accept.

4   The Union won the war, of course, and now these brave, able-bodied young men were back at work on behalf of their country, building an iron road—a nearly 2,000-mile iron road that would bring the country together in a way never before imagined.

A Transcontinental Race

5   What kept Paul and his co-workers going (other than the pitiful wages they were being paid) was that the construction of the transcontinental railroad was a competition—a race

---

Words to Know

General Academic Vocabulary
commencing (*v.*): beginning
construction (*n.*): building
immigrant (*n.*): a newcomer to a country or area
mutually (*adv.*): done together
transform (*v.*): to change completely

Domain-Specific Vocabulary
entrepreneurship (*n.*): development of a new business

Working with Word Meaning Challenge students to create a single sentence that contains all of the words.

between two well-established railroad companies: the Central Pacific Railroad and the Union Pacific Railroad.

6   Each company was responsible for half the line, with the Central Pacific starting in Sacramento, California, and heading east, and the Union Pacific **commencing** in Omaha, Nebraska, and moving west. They were racing toward each other, the plan being to meet at a **mutually** chosen spot in Utah, where the final railroad stake would be pounded into the ground. Then the railroad would be done, and horse-drawn wagons for the journey would be a thing of the past.

Working for the Union Pacific Railroad

7   Although Paul was proud to be a part of this massive American project, his work was not easy. The days were long and hot. He missed his wife and young son back in Massachusetts.

8   But Paul thought back to the months immediately after the war's end, when those who were lucky enough to have survived suddenly found themselves without a purpose. Fighting for the Union had been their job, but now they were civilians again.

9   As soon as the war was over, thousands of men answered the call for workers on the transcontinental railroad. <u>They were truly grateful for the work.</u> It was more than two years since Paul had arrived in Omaha, and he knew he had about that many more still to go. He hadn't seen his family since.

10   Paul also had been hearing rumors that the men who ran the Union Pacific were corrupt. They were getting rich off the manual labor of hard-working veterans! And sometimes wages were late. At least the U.P. was hiring American workers; the Central Pacific was using almost entirely Chinese labor.* Paul didn't like that one bit. It was more motivation to win this transcontinental race.

Comprehension Check

What aspects of working on the transcontinental railroad does Paul like? What parts does he not like? Support your answer with text evidence for Paul's point of view on his work.

CITE EVIDENCE

C How does the narrator feel about the amount of money Paul and the men are earning? Put a box around a detail in the text that gives you the answer.

D Double underline the veterans' point of view about having a job on the railroad project.

E Authors will **develop**—or may even change—a character's point of view about a topic as a story unfolds. Place an asterisk beside the sentence that shows Paul's point of view of Chinese workers. What might change his mind about them?

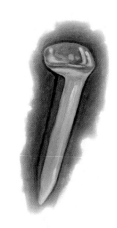

CITE EVIDENCE

C Remind students that words with strong connotations help readers determine point of view. They should be able to identify that the word *pitiful* has strong negative connotations.

D Help students understand that this question asks about the point of view of all the workers, not just Paul, and not the men who ran the Union Pacific. They should be able to locate the sentence in the fourth paragraph that explains the men's feelings.

E Students should be able to locate the sentence in the last paragraph on the page that indicates Paul's viewpoint on Chinese workers being hired. ("Paul didn't like that one bit.") Students should recognize that this is a negative viewpoint, and that how the workers accomplish their work could affect Paul's view.

Comprehension Check

Sample Answer: Paul is proud to be part of the work on building the great railroad, as told in the third paragraph. He likes being part of the competition to reach the meeting spot first. He doesn't like being away from his family.

Answer Explanation: The third paragraph states that "Paul and his fellow workers felt lucky to be a part of it." The fifth paragraph states that competition is what keeps the men going. Finally, the seventh paragraph states that "[he] missed his wife and young son."

Support English Language Learners

Some of the words in the story may be difficult for native speakers of Latinate languages, such as Spanish or French. Many words used here have Latin roots, and many are cognates. Explain to students that cognates might be spelled the same way as a word they are familiar with or may share a root with such a word. Below are some examples of cognates you can share with native Spanish speakers.

authorize—*autorizar*   construction—*construccion*

immigrant—*immigrante*   labor—*laborar*

Guided Instruction

CITE EVIDENCE

A Read with students the paragraph under the head "Chinese Immigrant Workers" to find a detail the narrator includes about the mountain. If students are unfamiliar with the word *massive*, encourage them to use a dictionary to find its meaning.

B Reread the last paragraph with students. Help them realize that in the first two sentences, the narrator is talking about how Chinese workers would be the solution for the Central Pacific. Then have them locate the words used that reveal the narrator's point of view (*their salvation*).

Review: Analyzing Dramatic Structure

Review with students that drama has a different structure from other forms of literature. Authors of drama use features such as a cast of characters and stage directions to set the scene for the reader. In fiction, the narrator or the characters themselves serve that purpose by describing the setting and even the feelings and emotions of the characters. Ask students: *In this story, how are we made aware of the feelings, emotions, and opinions of Paul and Shin Lu? How do we know the setting for the action in the story? How might this information have come to us differently were this story to be written in the form of a drama?* (Students may respond that the narrator informs us about the characters' thoughts and feelings. In a drama, stage directions may serve the same purpose.)

WORDS TO KNOW
allocated
arduous
colleague
federal
founded

CITE EVIDENCE

A Double underline the details that show the narrator's point of view about the Sierra Nevada Mountains.

B To make a story more interesting, authors may **contrast the points of view** of various characters (including the narrator). Put a box around a detail that reveals the narrator's point of view about Chinese workers. In what way does this contrast with Paul's point of view?

Race to the Golden Spike continued

The Central Pacific Railroad

11   The Central Pacific Railroad began building its side of the transcontinental railroad in Sacramento, California. In fact, the entire project originated there in the mind of a California-based railroad engineer, Theodore Judah. Building a railroad is expensive, however, and Judah had to raise big sums of money for the project. He found in Sacramento five businessmen who saw great potential in the project. In 1861, these people **founded** the Central Pacific Railroad.

12   The idea for a transcontinental railroad had already been receiving attention from politicians in Washington, D.C. (including President Lincoln), and it was not too long before **federal** money was **allocated** to the effort. Armed with this support, Judah and his **colleagues** went to work. Little progress was made during the Civil War, mostly because potential workers were away, fighting as soldiers; but by the war's end in 1865, both the Central Pacific and the Union Pacific were rapidly laying their tracks.

Chinese Immigrant Workers

13   The Central Pacific, however, had a problem that the Union Pacific did not. The Central Pacific's half of the railroad would have to cut through the <u>majestic</u> but massive Sierra Nevada Mountains. The company's owners faced <u>a serious problem:</u> Where could they find workers willing to do such **arduous** labor?

14   The men who ran the Central Pacific found their answer in the Gold Rush; indeed, it turned out to be [their salvation]. Chinese laborers who had originally been lured to California by the Gold Rush were hired by the thousands to work on the western half of the transcontinental railroad. In 1865, some 7,000 Chinese were working on the project; that number rose to 14,000 by 1867.

134

Words to Know

General Academic Vocabulary

allocated (*v.*): assigned when resources are divided up
arduous (*adj.*): difficult; hard
colleague (*n.*): coworker; person in a similar position
founded (*v.*): began or started a business or other large effort

Domain-Specific Vocabulary

federal (*adj.*): part of or from the national government

Working with Word Meaning Have students use the words in sentences.

CRAFT AND STRUCTURE

Working in America

15 One such Chinese worker, Shin Lu, had been toiling in the harsh conditions of the Sierra Nevadas all winter. He was excited to be working in America on a project of this scope. He had heard from the other Chinese workers that this was to be the first transcontinental railroad in the entire world.

16 It was exciting to be in a new place, yet Lu missed his family terribly. His mother and father thought he was out of his mind to accept such a project—it was so far away from home—but he needed the work, and many of his friends were also going.

17 The worst part, Lu believed, was how dangerous the work was. First of all, they were using large amounts of explosives. Black gunpowder, homemade liquid nitroglycerin—you name it, they were using it. There was no other way to blast tunnels through the mountains.

18 (However, he appreciated how the Chinese workers had shown ingenuity) by developing a system by which a worker could be lowered down in a basket alongside a cliff to place an explosive on the wall of rock. After lighting it, the worker would be hauled up. It was the best way to blast through solid rock, but it was dangerous, and sometimes the explosion would go off before the man returned to the top. Some of his friends had been killed in such accidents.

19 Lu wondered if there were Chinese workers laboring for the other company, the Union Pacific. The Central Pacific managers kept saying the Union Pacific was the enemy, but Lu didn't see it that way. To him, they were all working toward a common goal: uniting the coasts of the United States.

Comprehension Check

Compare and contrast Lu's and Paul's points of view about working on the transcontinental railroad. What opinions do they share? On what do they differ? Cite evidence.

Unit 5   Reading Literature: Craft and Structure   **135**

Guided Instruction

CITE EVIDENCE

C Put an asterisk by a detail in paragraph 16 that expresses an opinion that Shin Lu shares with Paul.

D In terms of his work, what is Lu proud of? Circle a key detail in paragraph 18 of the text.

E Underline the two sentences in paragraph 19 that express Lu's point of view about the Union Pacific workers. In what way do Lu and Paul view each other differently?

Guided Instruction

CITE EVIDENCE

C Comparing characters' points of view can mean finding that they feel the same about some things. Students should understand that both Paul and Shin Lu feel excited and homesick.

D Make sure that students read paragraph 18 carefully. If students understand that the question refers to Shin Lu's pride in the work done by the men of the Central Pacific (not just his own work), they should be able to recognize the detail in the first sentence.

E Students will probably see that what makes characters interesting and unique is their differing viewpoints. Make sure students understand that Shin Lu's company, the Central Pacific, hires Chinese workers. Have students refer to page 133 to see how Paul feels about Chinese workers.

Comprehension Check

Sample Answer: Shin Lu and Paul share excitement about working on the big project and they share the feeling of being homesick. They differ in their feelings about the race. While Paul resents the Chinese workers and wants to beat the Central Pacific, Shin Lu feels that both are working toward a common goal. He does not see the Union Pacific workers as the enemy.

Answer Explanation: Paragraph 7 states Paul's feelings of pride and homesickness. Shin Lu's similar feelings are stated in paragraphs 16 and 17. Paul's competitive and negative feelings toward the Chinese workers are shown in paragraph 10, while Shin Lu's more accepting emotions toward the Union Pacific are explained in paragraph 19.

Differentiate Instruction

You can help students better understand Paul's and Shin Lu's experiences by showing them a map of the country. First, explain where Paul and his colleagues are by outlining the path that the workers on the Union Pacific took building the railroad through Omaha. Next, show first where the Gold Rush in California was. Then point out where the workers on the Central Pacific had to blast through the Sierra Nevada mountains, and outline their path through present-day Nevada. Finally, point out on the map where the railroads met in present-day Utah.

Guided Practice

Recap Reading Selection

Ask students to recall how Paul and Shin Lu feel about the race across the continent and some of the hardships they have experienced.

Read and Practice

Have partners take turns reading the selection as you circulate to provide support. Ask students to respond to Cite Evidence callouts A and B. Provide additional scaffolding as needed, using the suggestions below.

CITE EVIDENCE

A Students not reading carefully may look for the detail about the Sierra Nevada mountains in paragraph 20. However, if students read on, they should be able to locate Shin Lu's point of view at the end of paragraph 20 and beginning of paragraph 21.

B Remind students that they can look for the answer in the page across from the question (page 137). Make sure students read through the end of the letter to find the positive words in the last sentence.

ANALYZING POINT OF VIEW

Guided Practice

Race to the Golden Spike *continued*

A Letter from Shin Lu to His Mother

July 22, 1868

Dear Mother,

20   We continue to make our way across the hot, dry desert of a place the Americans call Nevada. The heat is indescribable, and tonight I feel exhausted, but I'm in it for the **duration**.

21   For all its faults, however, the flat expanse of Nevada is much preferred to the mountains of the Sierra Nevadas. I cannot stop thinking about last winter; indeed, I don't know how I survived it. Beyond the cold and the snowstorms, digging icy soil and drilling through cold, black rock was (the hardest **manual** labor I have ever done in my life.)

22   (It was extremely frustrating work,) too, because no sooner would we cut a tunnel through a hillside than a mountain's worth of snow would come crashing down on us. Avalanches were a frequent event. I lost count of how many workers died.

I miss you.

Shin Lu

A Letter from Paul Kelley to His Famiy

January 7, 1869

Dearest Catherine and Daniel,

23   I haven't the words to express how much I miss you two.

24   Our work continues here, and they have changed my job: Now I am laying actual track and no longer building culverts, the water pipes that run underneath the railroad. Daniel, my boy, you would have such fun pounding in those railroad **spikes** with me!

WORDS TO KNOW

duration

manual

spike

CITE EVIDENCE

A Circle two details that give evidence of Lu's point of view about working in the Sierra Nevada Mountains.

B In Paul's letter, underline any statement that reveals his hope for the future. Has he expressed this hope in the past? Explain.

136   Unit 5 ■ Reading Literature: Craft and Structure

Words to Know

General Academic Vocabulary

duration (*n.*): length of time that something takes or lasts
manual (*adj.*): done by hand; physical

Domain-Specific Vocabulary

spike (*n.*): pointed piece of metal like a giant nail

Working with Word Meaning Have students draw pictures to show the meanings of the words.

CRAFT AND STRUCTURE
Guided Practice

25   This job is truly an example of man versus nature. Everyone is anticipating the Wasatch Mountains in Wyoming, which are coming next. The mountains will be very difficult to cut through. So far, we have been lucky with the flatlands of Nebraska, but now we face an entirely new challenge.

26   Just the same, I feel closer to the finish line than ever before—and that means that I will see you soon!

Love, Paul (Daddy)

Comprehension Check

1. Which statement best describes Lu's point of view in his letter?

   a. He is thrilled to be working on the project.

   (b.) He has become weary of the project.

   c. He is inspired by the places he's seen.

   d. He is tired but is finding the work to be easier.

2. Which of the following does Lu NOT mention in his letter?

   a. the Nevada desert

   b. the Sierra Nevada Mountains

   (c.) the ingenuity of his fellow workers

   d. the difficult manual labor

3. In their letters, both workers express thoughts about

   a. how flat Nevada is.

   (b.) how much they miss their families.

   c. how grateful they are to be working.

   d. how dangerous the work is.

4. What is Paul's point of view about working in the Wasatch Mountains?

   a. He wishes he could stay in Nebraska.

   b. He doubts his team will be successful.

   c. He thinks the work will be fun.

   (d.) He thinks the work will be difficult.

5. With a partner, discuss how Lu's and Paul's opinions regarding their work have changed. How does contrasting "then" and "now" help you understand the story? Give evidence for your answer.

   Sample answer: Because the points of view in their letters are different from what they once felt, I understand how difficult the life of a transcontinental railroad worker was. In his letter, Lu does not mention any positive aspects of the experience. Earlier, he appreciated his colleagues' ingenuity and felt excited about taking part in historic work. Paul, too, does not mention anything about feeling proud and lucky to be on the project, as indicated before.

Unit 5 ■ Reading Literature: Craft and Structure   **137**

Comprehension Check

Answer Explanations:

1. Since Lu mentions being exhausted, students may incorrectly choose D. However, his weary tone and harsh memories should lead them to the correct answer, B.

2. If students have read carefully, they know that Lu mentioned no positive aspects of the job, so they will recognize the correct answer is C.

3. Since both letters are to family members and both Lu and Paul miss their families, students should recognize the correct answer, B.

4. Since Paul sounds apprehensive, students may incorrectly choose A or B. However, Paul does not make either of these statements in the letter, so the correct answer is D.

5. Students may also note that contrasting "then" and "now" allows them to see changes in viewpoint over time.

Reciprocal Teaching

Have students work in groups of four. Give one notecard to each group member. On the notecard will be one of the following words: *Summarizer*, *Questioner*, *Clarifier*, or *Predictor*. Explain that after reading a section, the Summarizer will note key ideas, the Questioner will pose questions about anything that is unclear, the Clarifier will try to give insight about things that are confusing, and the Predictor will suggest what may happen next. Have students reread the text so far. At the end of the first two pages, have students perform their roles. Then have students switch roles to read the next two pages. Students should continue in this way to the completion of the story.

Discussion Skills

Provide students with opportunities to practice discussion and presentation skills by having them portray the roles of transcontinental railroad workers, either for the Union Pacific or the Central Pacific. Put students in small groups and have members discuss the hardships and challenges of their company's task. Then have groups prepare a short speech that a worker might have given at the celebration in Utah. The speech should include thanks to coworkers and stories about the worker's experiences. Groups should choose one member to deliver the speech. Remind students to look back through the reading selection to gather information to use in their speeches.

Analyzing Point of View

Independent Practice

Recap Reading Selection

Have students recall what they have read so far about Paul, Shin Lu, and the transcontinental railroad. Ask students to name what Lu found to be the most difficult task. Let students know that they will next read about the race to the finish.

Read and Apply

Have students read the selection independently as you circulate. Ask them to read aloud so you can see if they are reading fluently. You can also use the support below to help students who are having difficulty.

CITE EVIDENCE

A Remind students that the narrator may indicate his or her own opinion or emotion by using a descriptive word with a strong connotation. Read paragraph 27 with them, and help them locate the word that tells the narrator's feelings (*money-hungry*).

B Students may need to refer back to page 133 to find how Paul feels about Chinese workers earlier in the story. With that in mind, have them reread paragraph 30 to locate Paul's change of heart. Discuss with students that at first, Paul resents any Chinese workers being hired. By the end of the story, however, he realizes these workers have made a valuable contribution.

WORDS TO KNOW
considerable
crevasse
promontory
so-called
summit

Toward the Finish Line

27   By the spring of 1869, it was clear that both companies were nearing the finish line. Naturally, there was fierce competition to finish first. These were money-hungry companies, after all, and the one that controlled a greater portion of the transcontinental railroad would have a financial advantage when goods started to travel by train. It took the United States Congress to step in and select a meeting place: a site in Utah Territory called **Promontory Summit**.

The Central Pacific and the "Big Fill"

28   Shin Lu and the other Chinese laborers had worked themselves to the bone, but Lu's spirits had been brighter ever since the finish came into sight. They had one last job to do: the **so-called** Big Fill. The head of the Central Pacific made a last-minute change to their route, and so a deep **crevasse** had to be filled in with soil. Lu and the others went right to work, and their efforts allowed the Central Pacific to reach Promontory Summit first. Lu was overwhelmed with pride.

The Union Pacific and the "Big Trestle"

29   The Union Pacific had its own final project: the "Big Trestle." Trestles are big metal frames that support railroad tracks that run across valleys or rivers. Paul Kelley and his team raced to erect a temporary structure so the Union Pacific effort wouldn't be delayed. The workers finished on May 5, and the Union Pacific reached Promontory Summit. They came in second, but in the end it didn't matter; it was still a great achievement.

CITE EVIDENCE
A Circle the term the narrator uses to express a point of view about the two railroad companies.

B Underline Paul's point of view about Chinese workers after he sees the "Big Fill." How does his point of view change?

30   Paul had heard about the "Big Fill" and wanted to see it for himself. He couldn't believe his eyes: That job had taken **considerable** effort! When he thought about the thousands of Chinese workers who labored on this and so many other parts of the railroad, Paul decided that they had done well.

138   Unit 5 ■ Reading Literature: Craft and Structure

Words to Know

General Academic Vocabulary
considerable (*adj.*): significant
so-called (*adj.*): known as

Domain-Specific Vocabulary
crevasse (*n.*): crack in a rock or mountain
promontory (*n.*): high point; overlook
summit (*n.*): top; peak

Working with Word Meaning Have students use images or diagrams to help them visualize the meaning of each new word.

CRAFT AND STRUCTURE

The Golden Spike

31   On May 10, 1869, representatives from the two great railroad companies were present when a commemorative golden spike was hammered into the ground. Paul Kelley was there, exhausted but smiling. Shin Lu looked with satisfaction at the railroad he had helped build. It had all been worth it, he thought.

Comprehension Check   **MORE ONLINE** sadlierconnect.com

1. Shin Lu's point of view grows more positive in this last part of the story because

   a. he finally meets Paul Kelley.

   (b.) the project comes to a successful end.

   c. he gets to hammer in the golden spike.

   d. he is proud of his work on the "Big Trestle."

2. About which subject does Paul change his point of view at the end of the story?

   a. the Sierra Nevada Mountains

   b. the "Big Fill"

   (c.) the Chinese laborers

   d. the Central Pacific Railroad

3. In the section "The Golden Spike," which word or phrase is evidence of the narrator's point of view about the two companies?

   (a.) great

   b. commemorative

   c. golden

   d. worth it

4. About which fact does the narrator feel "in the end it didn't matter"?

   a. The Union Pacific came in first.

   (b.) The Central Pacific came in first.

   c. The "Big Trestle" was a temporary structure.

   d. The workers received low wages.

5. How can a change in a character's point of view give a story meaning and strengthen its conclusion? Specifically, how does the change in Paul's opinion give this story a satisfying ending?

   Sample answer: A change in a character's point of view shows that the story's

   events have affected that character. In Paul's case, he realizes that the

   successfully completed railroad was in part thanks to people who, while

   different in some ways, shared a common goal with him and worked as hard

   as he did to achieve it. This common goal was a central theme. An ending in

   which Paul remained bigoted would not have felt true to that theme.

Unit 5 ■ Reading Literature: Craft and Structure   **139**

Speaking and Listening Presentation

Have students prepare a presentation about the Transcontinental Railroad's effects on the United States. Remind them to plan for the presentation with milestone goals and deadlines. Students should: 1) include facts and details about how the U.S. was affected, using multimedia or visuals to support their points; 2) adapt their language for a formal presentation; 3) speak clearly and maintain eye contact; 4) answer questions and acknowledge others' ideas, eliciting responses from students of different cultural backgrounds. Listeners should listen attentively and ask questions.

Comprehension Check

Answer Explanations:

1. If students have read carefully, they should recognize that only choice B applies for Shin Lu.

2. Students may lean toward choice D, believing that Paul has changed his mind about the Central Pacific. However, Paul's earlier views were about Chinese workers, so choice C is correct.

3. Only choice A applies to the companies themselves.

4. Choice A is factually incorrect and, though C and D are mentioned in the story, the narrator only applied the phrase "in the end it didn't matter," when writing about the race. Therefore, choice B is correct.

5. Students may also note that a change in Paul's viewpoint makes him more sympathetic.

Critical Comprehension

Challenge students to think more deeply about the text and to support their answers with evidence from the text. Ask: *Which group did more dangerous work, the Central Pacific or the Union Pacific?* (The Central Pacific did more dangerous work.)

Assess and Respond

If students have trouble answering the questions in the Comprehension Check,

Then ask them to reread the story, paying attention to which character does what and how each feels about what he does.

Close Reading

OBJECTIVES

- Determine the meaning of words and phrases and analyze the impact of rhymes and repetition in a poem.

- Analyze how a drama's or poem's form or structure contributes to its meaning.

- Examine how an author develops and contrasts the points of view of different characters in a story.

Genre: Adventure—Based on Actual Events

Explain to students that adventure stories tell about exciting situations in which characters often find themselves in danger. Tell them that this particular selection is based on the true story of former president Theodore Roosevelt's explorations in Brazil. The characters depicted are real people except for Kermit Roosevelt's friend Jack.

Path Options

You may want to do a close reading with students; if so, use the supports provided on these pages. Or, you may wish to have students read the text independently and apply the skills learned in this unit. In either case, students should read the text more than once to facilitate understanding and to be able to answer the Comprehension Questions correctly.

CLOSE READING

Toward the Unknown River

(Genre: Adventure—based on actual events)

1   "I've never felt a hotter, more humid day in all my life," young Jack Arthur muttered to himself as he drew his hand across his sweaty brow. He was just 18 years old, trekking through *Mato Grosso*, the "great wilderness" of western Brazil. Jack and his companions had been traveling for weeks but were barely halfway to their destination: the *Dúvida*, or so-called River of Doubt.

2   Jack was a guest of his pal Kermit Roosevelt, himself only 19 and the son of Colonel Theodore Roosevelt, the wildly popular former president of the United States.

3   "Jack, old chum," Kermit had asked him last fall, slapping his hand on Jack's shoulder, "how would you like to go on a journey of a lifetime with my father and me?"

4   Jack, like all Americans, was familiar with Theodore Roosevelt's outdoor adventures and Herculean feats of derring-do. For example, the president's African safari, taken shortly after he left office, was a major event in the newspapers.

5   This trip, a scientific exploration of an unexplored tributary of the Amazon River in Brazil, had received its share of attention, too.

6   Jack loved the outdoors—he and Kermit were both accomplished athletes at Harvard College—so he readily agreed to the invitation. They received permission from their professors to take some time off.

7   Now it was months after their arrival in the South American country of Paraguay, and the past weeks had been unbelievably arduous. Jack thought back to how it began.

Team of Explorers

8   It was a few days after New Year's Day, 1914, when Jack, Kermit, Colonel Roosevelt, and the rest of the team gathered at the Paraguay River to begin the journey to the River of Doubt. There was no simple or direct way to reach the *Dúvida*, but everyone seemed confident about getting there via the Paraguay River, which ran through the wild and dense Brazilian jungle.

9   It was a remarkable team of travelers who would be undertaking this odyssey. Colonel Roosevelt had brought along a secretary as well as his friend Father Zahm, a priest. There were also some American naturalists who wanted to study the plants and animals of the Amazon.

140   Unit 5 ▪ Reading Literature: Craft and Structure

Support English Language Learners

Students who are learning English may have difficulty with some of the old-fashioned words and phrases in the story. Preview the meaning of these words with students before they read.

Words: *pal* (friend); *chum* (friend)

Phrases: *feats of derring-do* (brave or fearless actions); *soldiered on* (persevered, continued)

CRAFT AND STRUCTURE

10   The Brazilian team was headed by Colonel Cândido Rondon, an experienced explorer and traveler. Assisting him was a group of *camaradas*, Brazilian workers who would carry supplies and set up tents.

The Paraguay River

11   It was immediately apparent to Jack that he and the others were not going to simply canoe down the Paraguay to the start of the River of Doubt.

12   For one thing, the river was shallow in some places, making it difficult to negotiate. Barges loaded with five tons of baggage and supplies were so heavy they couldn't move.

13   Quite often the river thinned out and gave way to areas of marsh and jungle. The explorers had to get out and use their long knives to slash their way through the vegetation. The *camaradas* lifted the canoes over their heads and followed close behind.

Mato Grosso

14   They had completed the main stretch of the Paraguay weeks ago, and now they were in the middle of *Mato Grosso*. Jack couldn't believe how hot and humid it was: It was early January, but the sun beat down on them without mercy. But the steamy heat was nothing compared to the insects.

15   Jack had read about the legendary insects of *Mato Grosso*, but he didn't believe until he saw for himself butterflies as big as birds, bumblebees and wasps, and bloodthirsty mosquitoes nipping at any patch of exposed skin. Swatting them was a Sisyphean task; the mosquitoes just kept coming back.

16   But the "great wilderness" was beautiful, too. Jack had never seen a palm tree, much less the tall specimens he spied along the riverbank. There were flowers, too, including orchids of the brightest colors imaginable. Less appealing were the snakes; indeed, an anaconda could squeeze a person to death, people said.

17   Overhead, little monkeys hung from vines, and lime-green parakeets darted by. At one point, Kermit turned back toward Jack and smiled, as if to say, "Enjoy it, pal."

18   Days turned into weeks as they alternately canoed and hiked toward a little Brazilian town that would serve as their launching point for the River of Doubt. The heat and humidity remained unbearable, and fresh water to drink and bathe in was scarce. Food was an issue, as well; there weren't any large animals to hunt. Everyone on the team was hungry, and Jack had eaten enough monkey stew to last him a lifetime.

Approaching the River of Doubt

19   By the end of February, the travelers were exhausted and still had not reached the beginning of the River of Doubt. Jack wondered if it was even worth continuing, but he, like the rest of the team, soldiered on.

20   One of the most treacherous aspects of their river journey was the abundance of waterfalls. They varied in size, but all were dangerous to the men in their fragile, hand-carved wooden canoes.

141

Support First Reading

Circulate to check and support students' understanding. Use the following comprehension and strategy check-ins as needed.

Check-in Questions

- *Which members of the exploration team carry supplies and set up tents?* (the *camaradas*)
- *How do the travelers try to reach the River of Doubt?* (by traveling on the Paraguay River)
- *Name three things that made travel difficult in Mato Grosso.* (insects, heat, and lack of food)

Review: Analyzing Literary Language

Review once again with students that authors seek to achieve specific effects through the purposeful use of literary language. Remind them that one such use is the effect known as *alliteration*, or the repetition of beginning sounds in words. Ask: *How does the alliteration in paragraph 15, line 3 affect that section of the story?* (The author repeats the b-sound at the beginning of three words: <u>b</u>utterflies as <u>b</u>ig as <u>b</u>irds, which calls the reader's attention to the comparison.)

Differentiate Instruction

Create mixed groups of struggling and more proficient readers. Give each group a copy of the Check-in Questions, and have group members reread together and work to answer the questions. Then have the group discuss and create a brief summary of what has happened in the story so far.

CLOSE READING

Check-in Questions

- *What do Jack, Kermit, and Colonel Roosevelt do once they reach the River of Doubt?* (They continue their exploration.)

- *What new challenges does the group face on the River of Doubt?* (Colonel Roosevelt injures his leg, which becomes infected. He also gets malaria.)

- *How does the Brazilian government thank the group?* (It names one section of the River of Doubt "Rio Roosevelt" and another section "Rio Kermit.")

Review: Analyzing Dramatic Structure

Remind students that the structure of a work of literature influences the way we come to understand its meaning. Ask: *Why might the author include Jack singing "America the Beautiful" near the end of this section of the story?* (It shows how Jack is coping with the difficult surroundings and remembering home. It also shows a bond developing between Jack and the *camaradas*.)

Review: Analyzing Point of View

Review with students that point of view is a particular character's perspective or opinion about the events in a story. Ask: *Which character's point of view about the journey is most strongly expressed in the story? What is his point of view?* (Jack's point of view is most strongly expressed; he generally finds the journey difficult.)

Toward the Unknown River *continued*

21 The final days approaching the River of Doubt really were the most miserable that Jack had ever endured. A few team members had nearly drowned in the river. The heat and humidity would not abate. Torrents of rain poured down, leading some expedition members to joke that they should start building an ark.

22 Through it all, Jack noted, Colonel Roosevelt and Kermit rarely lost their humor. The rotund ex-president was full of Falstaffian wit and jollity, even in the toughest of conditions. It seemed to Jack that Kermit was totally fed up but hid it from his father, preferring to force a smile in spite of his discomfort.

23 One particularly hot afternoon, with horseflies biting his neck and his shirt soaked with sweat, Jack's mind wandered. He thought of a new song he had heard at school, shortly before leaving for Paraguay. Jack began singing "America the Beautiful" softly to himself:

24 *O beautiful for spacious skies,*
For amber waves of grain,
For purple mountain majesties
Above the fruited plain!

America! America!
God shed His grace on thee,
And crown thy good with brotherhood
From sea to shining sea!

25 Two young *camaradas*, feverish from the heat, looked at him with a smile on their faces. Though they spoke no English, they understood what it meant to be homesick.

Traveling the River of Doubt

26 At long last, on February 27, 1914, the team reached the River of Doubt. Some members of the team refused to go any farther on the journey and begged off. Colonel Roosevelt, Kermit, Jack, Colonel Rondon, and a few *camaradas* continued, however. They had come this far, Jack mused, so they had to finish.

27 The weeks that followed, canoeing down the *Dúvida*, featured more of the same: heat, humidity, insects, and lousy food. The small team would canoe until the rapids became too dangerous; then they would take to the riverbank and hike until the river calmed.

28 There was, however, a new crisis. Colonel Roosevelt had injured his leg, and a bad infection had set in. Even worse, he was showing symptoms of malaria, a serious tropical disease. It became almost impossible for him to walk during those parts of the journey when the river was too rough. Roosevelt repeatedly told his son and Rondon to leave him behind, but they refused to do so.

142

Strategic Reading

Remind students that they can use different strategies if they are having difficulty comprehending a text. One such strategy is to make a mental image of what is happening in the story. Authors often use descriptive language that can help readers visualize people and places that are unfamiliar. Encourage students to reread the text, taking time to "make a movie" or "paint a picture" in their minds using details from the text. This strategy will help students visualize and comprehend better.

CRAFT AND STRUCTURE

29   Jack was never more proud of his friend than he was in the weeks that followed. Kermit tended to his father's every need as the group slowly made its way down the River of Doubt.

30   "This river is aptly named," Jack remarked to Kermit one particularly dreary day. "I have my doubts that we are going to make it to the end." Kermit had to nod in agreement.

31   Colonel Roosevelt eventually recovered, however; and one day in late March, Colonel Rondon surprised him with an announcement. On behalf of the Brazilian government, he was naming a section of the River of Doubt *Rio Roosevelt*, or "Roosevelt River." Furthermore, a smaller tributary was declared *Rio Kermit*. Jack stood by as the two Roosevelt men, stunned and proud, accepted the honor.

32   By late April the team of exhausted travelers had reached a small town from which they could travel to the larger town of Manáos. From there, they could arrange for a return to North America.

33   Jack Arthur completed his studies at Harvard University alongside his friend, Kermit Roosevelt. The two young men never forgot their adventure down "the largest unknown river in the world."

Comprehension Check

1A. What does the hyperbole in paragraph 18 exaggerate?

(a.) the travelers' hunger

b. the friendliness of the Brazilians

c. the amount of time that was passing

d. the lack of clean water

1B. Which words from the text support the answer to Part A?

a. "town that would serve as their launching point"

b. "Days turned into weeks"

(c.) "enough monkey stew to last him a lifetime"

d. "Food was an issue, as well"

2A. What is the denotation of the word *trekking*?

a. canoeing down a wide river

b. hiking up a mountain

c. retreating from a challenge

(d.) going on a long, difficult journey

2B. Which word from the text relates to the meaning of the word *trekking* by connoting a sense of duty?

a. recovered

(b.) soldiered

c. continued

d. reached

Unit 5 ■ Reading Literature: Craft and Structure   **143**

Research to Build Knowledge

Students may wish to learn more about Theodore Roosevelt. Have students research different periods of the president's life. For example, students might be interested in Roosevelt's participation in the Spanish American War, his service as governor, his role as vice president under McKinley, or his presidency. You may wish to group students with similar interests. Have them gather information from multiple sources, using effective search terms, and choose credible sources over less reliable ones. Remind students to give credit to their sources, following standard citation forms. When they are finished, have students share their findings with the class.

Multiple Readings for Critical Comprehension

Have students reread and annotate this selection, then pose questions that focus on critical comprehension.

What can you infer about Kermit's feelings about the trip as it continues? (Kermit keeps up good spirits but grows frustrated as the trip goes on.)

Jack does not seem to enjoy the journey. Why did Jack agree to the trip? (He wanted to travel with his friend Kermit, but also with Roosevelt.)

Self-Select Text

As preparation for Connect Across Texts, have students choose one selection from this unit and reread it independently. Students can access full .pdf versions of some selections at **sadlierconnect.com**.

Comprehension Check

Begin scoring students' performance of unit skills with this Comprehension Check and continue through Connect Across Texts on page 146. Use students' scores to determine their readiness for the Unit 5 Review on page 148.

Multiple-Choice Questions: *1 point each*

1A. The last sentence of the paragraph includes hyperbole, which clearly refers to the travelers' hunger. Choice A is correct.

1B. Since students are looking for exaggeration, they should recognize that only choice C is a reasonable answer.

2A. Remind students that a word's denotation is its dictionary meaning, choice D.

2B. Point out that a word's connotation includes the associations we bring to it, so choice B, *soldiered,* is correct.

Close Reading

Multiple-Choice Questions, continued: *1 point each*

3A. The only detail given about the *camaradas* as the journey continues supports answer choice D.

3B. If students recall that Jack sang "America the Beautiful" when he was homesick, they should identify the correct answer, D.

4A. Although the narrator makes it clear that Kermit generally keeps up good spirits, when Jack expresses concern, Kermit agrees. Choice C is correct.

4B. If students recall that Kermit agrees with Jack's worries, they should be able to see that choice A is correct.

5A. Students may be tempted to choose A, since the *camaradas* do smile at Jack when he sings. However, they smile because they recognize he is homesick, like they are. Choice C is correct.

5B. None of the word choices besides choice B, "America," is repeated in the excerpt of the song.

Short-Answer Questions: *2 points each* (10 points total)

Item 6 Rubric

2	Student identifies how Jack's point of view is different from Kermit's for most of the story, and what changes.
1	Student identifies either Jack's or Kermit's point of view but does not identify the other.
0	Student cannot identify Jack's point of view or Kermit's.

CLOSE READING

3A. As the journey becomes longer, what is the point of view of the *camaradas*?

  a. They are eager to befriend the natives.

  b. They are ready to revolt against Rondon.

  c. They are excited for the next challenge.

  (d.) They are very homesick.

3B. What detail from the text supports the answer to Part A?

  a. They choose not to go down the *Dúvida*.

  b. They carry canoes over their heads.

  c. They nurse Colonel Roosevelt back to health.

  (d.) They smile at Jack when he sings.

4A. The author develops Kermit's point of view over the course of the trip by showing that Kermit

  a. is unhappy throughout the trip.

  b. slowly becomes excited about the trip.

  (c.) expresses concern near the end of the trip.

  d. never shows doubt about the trip.

4B. Which event in the text supports the answer to Part A?

  (a.) "Kermit nodded in agreement."

  b. "Kermit . . . slapping his hand on Jack's shoulder."

  c. "Kermit tended to his father's every need."

  d. "The two young men never forgot their adventure."

5A. How does the song relate to what is happening at that moment in the story?

  a. Jack and the *camaradas* become friends.

  b. Jack thinks that the river is beautiful.

  (c.) Jack feels very homesick.

  d. Jack is suffering in the heat and humidity.

5B. Which word in the song is repeated?

  a. beautiful

  (b.) America

  c. grace

  d. brotherhood

6. In what way is Jack's point of view different from Kermit's for most of the story? What changes toward the end? Cite evidence from the text.

  Sample answer: Jack is miserable for the entire story. He complains about the heat and is tired of eating monkey stew. He even has doubts that they'll complete the trip. Kermit, by contrast, is in a good mood for much of the trip. At the end, however, he joins Jack in having doubts about finishing the adventure.

144   Unit 5 ■ Reading Literature: Craft and Structure

Extend Thinking: Hypothesize

Have students work in small groups. Ask students to discuss the following question: *How might this story be different if, instead of telling an adventure story, the author wanted to argue that Theodore Roosevelt should never have taken this journey?* Have students think about how the text's structure might change, how text features such as illustrations and section headings might be different, and what details would probably be expanded upon.

Copyright © by William H. Sadlier, Inc. All rights reserved.

144   Unit 5 ■ Reading Literature: Craft and Structure

CRAFT AND STRUCTURE

7. In the section "*Mato Grosso*," where does the author use alliteration? Write the alliterative phrase, and then explain how it impacts that part of the story.

Sample answer: In paragraph 15, the author describes the insects as *butterflies as big as birds, bumblebees and wasps, and bloodthirsty mosquitoes*. The use of alliteration (sound of the letter *B*) draws attention to the unusual insects and to Jack's amazement at them.

8. How are the lyrics to "America the Beautiful" structured? How do they contribute to the meaning of the song?

Sample answer: The lyrics appear in two groups of lines. The first group (the stanza) describes America's physical beauty. The second group (the chorus) expresses a prayer for America and the hope that Americans will come together in brotherhood. The chorus gives meaning to the stanza, which is simply a description.

9. Write a paragraph analyzing the structure of the story. Use text evidence to show how the story's overall meaning is impacted by its form. Use a separate piece of paper if necessary.

Sample answer: After an introductory chapter, each remaining chapter tells about a section of the journey. In this way, the structure parallels the journey itself. Jack sings "America the Beautiful" around the middle of the story, which highlights the length of the trip and his homesickness. The story ends with two exciting events: Roosevelt's illness and the naming of the rivers. The final paragraph reveals that Jack and Kermit survived the trip and stayed friends.

10. Reread the first sentence of the story. Then answer these questions.

A. What does this sentence reveal about Jack's point of view regarding the journey?

Sample answer: The sentence suggests that Jack feels frustrated or unhappy but that he doesn't want to share his feelings openly.

B. Explain how the literary language in the sentence leads you to that answer.

Sample answer: The hyperbole in the phrase *never felt a hotter, more humid day in my life* indicates Jack's great discomfort, as does the negative connotation of *sweaty brow*. The author's choice of the word *muttered* instead of the more neutral word *said* suggests that Jack is frustrated but does not want anyone to hear him saying so.

Unit 5 ■ Reading Literature: Craft and Structure **145**

Item 7 Rubric

2	Student identifies alliteration and explains its impact.
1	Student identifies alliteration but not its impact.
0	Student does not identify alliteration in "Mato Grosso."

Item 8 Rubric

2	Student explains lyrics' structure and their contribution to song's meaning.
1	Student explains lyrics' structure but not contribution to song's meaning.
0	Student doesn't explain lyrics' structure or contribution to song's meaning.

Item 9 Rubric

2	Student analyzes story's structure and its impact.
1	Student analyzes story's structure but not its impact.
0	Student cannot analyze story's structure or its impact.

Item 10 Rubric

2	Student correctly analyzes points of view and literary language.
1	Student analyzes either point of view or literary language.
0	Student doesn't analyze point of view or literary language.

Differentiate Instruction

Certain students may benefit from hearing the short-answer items read aloud. After you or a volunteer read(s) the question to those students, make sure that the students understand what they are supposed to do. Allow students to ask questions about directions they find confusing. Review any academic words students may not understand, such as *cite*, *alliteration*, and *impacted*.

Theme Wrap-Up

Lead students in a group discussion of sources of conflict. Ask: *What are some major sources of conflict in life? How do people seek to overcome conflict?* Students should understand that sources of conflict in the unit have included love, death, struggle for equal rights, and surviving in nature.

Connect Across Texts: *4 points*
Review Reading Selections

Have students work in small groups to discuss how the characters in "Annabel Lee," "Race to the Golden Spike," and "Toward the Unknown River" found themselves in conflict with nature.

Compare and Contrast Texts

Review the directions on page 146. Be sure students understand that the outer circles should show details about each of the selections, and that the inner circles should show what details are shared.

Graphic Organizer Rubric

4	Student identifies details about man's conflict with nature in three selections and indicates which selections share details.
3	Student identifies details about man's conflict with nature in three selections, but does not indicate shared details.
2	Student identifies details about man's conflict with nature in two of the selections.
1	Student identifies details about man's conflict with nature in one selection.
0	Student is unable to provide details about man's conflict with nature in any selection.

Support Essential Question Discussion

Have students reread the Essential Question. Ask them to discuss the following: *Analyzing language, structure, and characters helps me to find meaning in a story.*

CONNECT ACROSS TEXTS

Compare and Contrast Texts

In this unit, you've read texts in which characters face conflict. In "Annabel Lee," "Race to the Golden Spike," and "Toward the Unknown River," humans wrestle with natural forces in some way. Complete the Venn diagram with details from these selections. Then write a brief essay in which you use the details to compare and contrast how the selections explore the conflict of "man vs. nature." Use a separate sheet of paper if you need more room to write. Be prepared to discuss your ideas with the class.

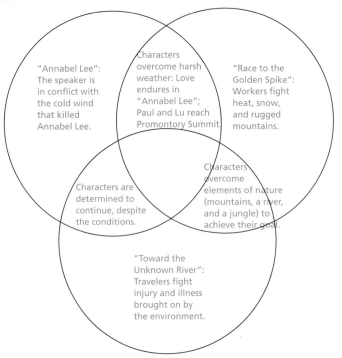

"Annabel Lee": The speaker is in conflict with the cold wind that killed Annabel Lee.

Characters overcome harsh weather: Love endures in "Annabel Lee"; Paul and Lu reach Promontory Summit.

"Race to the Golden Spike": Workers fight heat, snow, and rugged mountains.

Characters are determined to continue, despite the conditions.

Characters overcome elements of nature (mountains, a river, and a jungle) to achieve their goal.

"Toward the Unknown River": Travelers fight injury and illness brought on by the environment.

Return to the Essential Question

How do authors use language, structure, and characters to create meaning?

In small groups or as a class, discuss the Essential Question. Think about what you have learned about literary language, dramatic and poetic structure, and point of view. Use evidence from the texts in this unit to answer the question.

Assess and Respond (pages 143–146)

If	Then
Students scored 0–10 points, they are **Developing** their understanding of unit skills …	Provide students with reading support and more extensive modeling and practice of skills.
Students scored 11–17 points, they are **Improving** their understanding of unit skills …	Review students' scores to pinpoint skills that students need more help with, and offer targeted instruction.
Students scored 18–24 points, they are **Proficient** in their understanding of unit skills …	Have these students move on. They are ready for the formal assessment at the end of the unit.

Figurative Language

Guided Instruction A **figure of speech** is a phrase or expression that uses words in a nonliteral way. Figures of speech can add interest and deeper meaning to a text. Some figures of speech are **allusions**; that is, they refer to a story from literature, mythology, or the Bible. Interpreting allusions will help you better understand and enjoy what you read. Below are some examples of allusions that are used in this unit's selections.

Allusion	Origin	Meaning
Falstaffian	literature (Shakespeare)	jolly, bold, witty, and fat
Gordian knot	Greek mythology	a very difficult problem or puzzle
Good Samaritan	the Bible	someone who unexpectedly helps a person in need

Guided Practice In the following sentences, allusions are underlined and their origins are given. On the lines, write the meaning of each allusion. Use context or a print or online dictionary to help you if necessary.

1. Jack, like all Americans, was familiar with Theodore Roosevelt's . . . <u>Herculean</u> feats of derring-do. (Greek mythology) _____ difficult; requiring a lot of effort

2. And <u>to add insult to injury</u>, some legislators want to abolish rights established by treaties . . . . (literature [Aesop's fables]) _____ making a bad situation even worse

Independent Practice In the following sentences, underline the allusion. Then research its origin, and tell what it means in your own words.

1. It was a remarkable team of travelers who would be undertaking this <u>odyssey</u>. (Greek) literature; a long and difficult journey

2. Torrents of rain poured down, leading some expedition members to joke that they should start <u>building an ark</u>. the Bible; a joke about a great flood coming

3. Swatting them was a <u>Sisyphean task</u>; the mosquitoes just kept coming back. (Greek) mythology; a task that is repeated over and over

Unit 5 ▪ Reading Literature: Craft and Structure **147**

OBJECTIVE
Interpret figures of speech, including allusions, in context.

Guided Instruction

Have students review the Guided Instruction section on page 147. Make sure that students understand that an allusion may use a word that is in a different form from its use in the original source. For example, Shakespeare's Falstaff is the source for the word "Fallstaffian." By reviewing these examples of allusions, students will become aware of a new way to find the meanings of words that come from literary, biblical, or mythological sources.

Guided Practice

As students move to the practice section, encourage them to read the whole sentence to help with context for the meaning. Encourage them to name the character or story that relates to the allusion to help unlock its meaning.

Independent Practice

If students have difficulty identifying the allusions, let them work with a partner. Pairs can work together to find the origins of the allusions.

Apply to Reading

Have students look for allusions as they reread "A Valentine" and "Annabel Lee."

They might find *twins of Leda* (p. 116), *Gordian knot* (p. 116), *seraphs of Heaven* (p. 118) and *demons* (p. 120).

Support English Language Learners

In some cases, English language learners may recognize words and phrases that allude to familiar mythological, biblical, or literary sources in their first language. Point out similar words and phrases to Spanish speakers to help them recognize allusions. Then have them identify more allusions in Spanish and English that come from shared sources.

- herculean—*hercúleo*
- cut the Gordian knot—*cortar el nudo gordiano*
- Good Samaritan—*el buen samaritano*
- demon—*demonio*

Unit Summary

At this point in the unit, students have read poetry about love by Edgar Allen Poe; they have read a drama about a real Native American protest in the 1970s; they have read historical fiction about two workers building the transcontinental railroad, and they have read an adventure based on a real journey to the Amazon that Theodore Roosevelt undertook with his son and his son's friend. Students have also learned how to analyze literary language, analyze dramatic structure, and analyze point of view. They have learned and practiced how to use allusions to interpret figures of speech. Students should now be ready to take the unit review.

Introduce the Review

Explain to students that they will read two related passages that continue the theme *sources of conflict*. Instruct students to read the passages carefully and return to them as needed while they answer questions 1–10 on pages 149 and 150.

Answer Explanations (pages 149–150)

1A. Students should realize that only choice B is treated with hyperbole.

1B. Once students realize that Jeremy uses hyperbole, they should recognize that choice D is the correct answer.

2A. Students may need to reread to find the repetition in Gwen's haiku. Once they locate the repetition, they should recognize the correct choice, C.

2B. If students read question 2A carefully, they should be able to identify that choice A is the correct answer.

UNIT 5 REVIEW

Read the following texts that include literary language, dramatic and poetic structures, differing points of view, and literary allusions. Then answer the questions on pages 149 and 150.

Rehearsing with a Friend

CAST OF CHARACTERS

JEREMY, a 13-year-old boy
GWEN, a 13-year-old girl

SETTING: *In the present day, JEREMY is at home, practicing his trumpet for a contest the next weekend. The musical piece his teacher, Mr. Green, has selected for him is written for trumpet and piano. Jeremy's friend GWEN will accompany him on the piano. They've been rehearsing for 90 minutes.*

1 **GWEN:** Jeremy, I don't think this section should go quite as fast as you're playing it. It doesn't sound right.

2 **JEREMY** *(irritated)*: I'm playing what's printed on the page: "quickly." *(sharply)* I already practiced this part with Mr. Green.

3 **GWEN** *(gently)*: Jeremy, I wish you wouldn't disregard my opinion. If we play this section *too* quickly, the music won't make any sense. *(She puts her hands on the piano keys.)* Here, let me show you what I mean—

4 **JEREMY** *(exploding)*: Gwen, I haven't got time to argue with you! I like how I'm playing this section, and Mr. Green agrees with me! *(taking a breath)* Look, I've come in second place in this contest for the past three years. If I'm runner-up again, I'll die! I *have* to win this year, and I know how to do it. I've been working on this for months with Mr. Green, and my interpretation of this section stands—quickly, slowly, whatever!

5 **GWEN** *(calmly closing the lid of the piano)*: Jeremy, I don't like working like this. It's not creative; it's not fun. I'll talk to you later— after you've calmed down.

(Gwen leaves.)

An Entry from Gwen's Diary

Dear Diary,

Today was a tough day. I was flattered when Jeremy asked me to accompany him on his trumpet for the contest, but rehearsing with him has not been fun. He can be a real Jekyll and Hyde: Some days he's very agreeable and open to my suggestions, and other days he doesn't want to hear from me.

I'm willing to hang in there as long as it takes, but I'm starting to think I'll need the patience of Job to get through this coming week. I wrote a poem—a Japanese *haiku*, in fact—that expresses how I feel.

*Friendship can survive:
Even when friends disagree,
Friends can still be friends.*

Self-Assessment: Progress Check

Have students return to the Progress Check on page 113 of their books. Point out the boxes under the arrow that says "After Unit 5," which is where they can answer the questions again. Have them respond to the questions again in order to assess how well they have grasped the important skills and concepts in this unit.

You may wish to have students work in small groups as they review the questions. Group members may discuss what they feel they have mastered and what skills they still need to practice. Students may volunteer to help each other learn to apply the skills without difficulty.

UNIT 5 REVIEW

Circle the letter next to the best answer choice.

1A. The hyperbole in the drama exaggerates

    a. how quickly Jeremy is playing.

    b. how badly Jeremy wants to win.

    c. how well Jeremy is playing.

    d. how much Gwen dislikes Jeremy.

1B. Which statement supports the answer to Part A?

    a. "I've been working on this for months . . . "

    b. "I don't like working like this."

    c. "Gwen, I haven't got time to argue with you!"

    d. "If I'm runner-up again, I'll die."

2A. How does repetition impact the meaning of "An Entry from Gwen's Diary"?

    a. It reveals how much Jeremy's remarks have hurt her.

    b. It expresses how strong her opinion is about the music.

    c. It emphasizes that she wants to remain friends with Jeremy.

    d. It shows that she does not wish to continue to work with Jeremy.

2B. What part of Gwen's diary entry supports the answer to Part A?

    a. her repetition of "friends" in the *haiku*

    b. her comparison of Jeremy to Jekyll and Hyde

    c. her reference to "the patience of Job"

    d. her statement that she was flattered by Jeremy

3A. What does *exploding* in the stage directions suggest about that moment in the drama?

    a. Jeremy is angry and impatient.

    b. Jeremy is playing too fast.

    c. Jeremy has thought out his position.

    d. Jeremy is not feeling any pressure.

3B. What denotation of the word *exploding* provides evidence for Part A?

    a. explaining

    b. speaking casually, as with a friend

    c. racing ahead

    d. blurting out suddenly

4A. What does the allusion *the patience of Job* in Gwen's diary entry mean for her future?

    a. Gwen doesn't need more patience with Jeremy than she already has.

    b. Gwen will need a lot of patience to deal with Jeremy in the days ahead.

    c. Gwen will have to work hard to keep from losing Jeremy's friendship.

    d. Gwen should schedule two 15-minute rehearsals with Jeremy.

4B. What evidence from Gwen's diary entry supports the answer to Part A?

    a. Gwen wrote a poem to express her feelings.

    b. Gwen was flattered to be asked to accompany Jeremy.

    c. Gwen doesn't like playing with Jeremy.

    d. Gwen says she's "willing to hang in there as long as it takes."

5A. What is Jeremy's point of view about the upcoming contest?

    a. He just wants to perform well, regardless of the outcome.

    b. He wishes that Mr. Green had helped him prepare better.

    c. He cannot bear the thought of losing the contest.

    d. He wishes he weren't playing with Gwen.

Unit 5 ■ Reading Literature: Craft and Structure   **149**

Test-Taking Tips

Explain that the two-part questions give students an opportunity to check their answers.

Point out that if students have a hard time figuring out the correct answer to part 1 of the question, they should read on to part 2. After reading all of the answer choices to both parts, students may understand the focus of the question better.

After answering both parts of a question, encourage students to go back and read their answers to make sure there is a connection between them.

Answer Explanations (pages 149–150)

3A. Students may find it helpful to reread the drama to find *exploding* in context. Then they will see that choice A is correct.

3B. Students should recall that *denotation* refers to a word's dictionary definition. With that knowledge, they should then choose D.

4A. *The patience of Job* refers to the Biblical story of Job, who underwent many hardships. Even students who are unfamiliar with this story should be able to choose B as the correct answer based on context clues.

4B. Although A, B, and C may be true of Gwen, only choice D supports Part A.

5A. Students may choose D because of Jeremy's anger toward Gwen, but he seems to be emotional because of the contest. Therefore, choice C is correct.

5B. If students understand that Jeremy is upset about the contest, they should be able to recognize that the correct choice is A.

6A. Students may be confused because both monologues and soliloquies are long speeches made by a single character. However, students should remember that soliloquies are spoken directly to the audience, and so the correct choice here is B.

6B. If students understand the difference between a monologue and a soliloquy, they should understand that choice D is correct.

Answer Explanations

Item 7 Rubric

2	Student circles the alliterative paragraph and explains its effect.
1	Student either circles the correct paragraph or explains the effect of the alliteration.
0	Student neither circles the alliterative paragraph nor explains its effect.

Item 8 Rubric

2	Student explains the allusion and uses it to explain Gwen's meaning.
1	Student either explains the allusion or examines Gwen's meaning.
0	Student does not explain the allusion or what Gwen means.

Item 9 Rubric

2	Student explains the haiku's impact and how the entry would be different with a longer poem.
1	Student can either explain the haiku's impact or explain what Gwen means.
0	Student cannot explain the impact of the haiku nor explain what Gwen means.

Item 10 Rubric

2	Student can identify Gwen's point of view and compare it to Jeremy's.
1	Student can identify Gwen's point of view but not Jeremy's.
0	Student cannot identify Gwen's point of view.

UNIT 5 REVIEW

5B. Which statement from the text provides evidence for the claim above?

- **a.** "I have to win this year"
- **b.** "Mr. Green agrees with me!"
- **c.** "I like how I'm playing this section"
- **d.** "Gwen, I haven't got time to argue with you!"

6A. Which of the following terms correctly describes paragraph 4 of the drama?

- **a.** epilogue
- **b.** monologue
- **c.** soliloquy
- **d.** stage directions

6B. What evidence from the text supports the answer to Part A?

- **a.** Jeremy is alone on stage while he speaks.
- **b.** The text tells what Jeremy does, not what he says.
- **c.** The drama's conflict has been resolved.
- **d.** Jeremy is expressing his feelings directly to another character.

7. Find the paragraph in the drama that contains alliteration. Then explain the effect of that alliteration.

Sample answer: The alliteration (the repeated sound of the letter *P*) in paragraph 2 highlights and emphasizes Jeremy's impatience and irritation with Gwen. When I read this paragraph, I can feel Jeremy's frustration.

8. Gwen's statement *He can be a real Jekyll and Hyde* is an allusion to a story in which the respectable Dr. Jekyll takes a potion that turns him into the evil Mr. Hyde. How does that allusion help you understand what Gwen means?

Sample answer: The allusion refers to Jeremy's changeable mood. Gwen describes how Jeremy is sometimes open to her thoughts but sometimes shuts her out.

9. The poem that Gwen writes is a *haiku*—a three-line Japanese poem. What is the impact of the *haiku* on Gwen's diary entry? How might the entry be different if she had written a long poem with rhymed lines?

Sample answer: The haiku has a gentle feeling that captures Gwen's sincere hope that she and Jeremy will reconcile. A long, rhymed poem would seem more formal and perhaps not as sincere.

10. How is Gwen's point of view developed over the course of the drama and the diary entry? As part of your answer, analyze the ways in which her point of view differs from Jeremy's.

Sample answer: Gwen begins by gently making a suggestion to Jeremy about the music. Her point of view is that he is playing it too fast. At the end of the drama, she walks out and writes in her diary that she is willing to help Jeremy but that he's difficult to work with. Jeremy stubbornly sticks to his point of view about the music.

Analyze Student Scores

16–20 pts Strong	Student has successfully learned and applied the skills in this unit. Review any errors with the student, and explain them if necessary.
10–15 pts Progressing	Student is struggling with one or more of the skills in this unit. Identify the specific skills that are problematic to target additional instruction.
0–9 pts Emerging	Student is having trouble understanding most of the skills in this unit. Student may need to work through the unit again with a higher level of individual support.

Introducing UNIT 6

In this unit about sources of conflict, you will learn how to write an evidence-based text. This type of writing uses evidence—in the form of facts, details, and examples—to inform readers about a topic. In this unit the writing is about an historical conflict, an event in the past that caused an important disagreement between people.

You can write about an historical conflict, too. You will probably start with research so that you can write knowledgeably about the conflict. After creating an introduction in which you identify your topic, you will develop that topic by sharing your information in an organized, interesting way. For example, you may want to start with background information that will help readers understand your topic. Then you will present an explanation that uses facts, details, and examples to support your ideas. Use precise, formal language so that readers will view your essay as a reliable source of information. Finally, wrap up your discussion with a conclusion that explains how the conflict was resolved or how it affected the world we live in today.

 Progress Check *Can I?*

Before Unit 6		After Unit 6
☐	Write an evidence-based text about an historical conflict.	☐
☐	Organize my ideas and information in a way that makes sense for my topic.	☐
☐	Use evidence from informational texts (such as facts, details, and examples) to support my ideas.	☐
☐	Use precise language and a formal writing style.	☐
☐	Write sentences that have different structures.	☐
☐	Use standard English capitalization, punctuation, and spelling in my writing.	☐

Unit 6 ■ Text Types and Purposes: Write Evidence-Based Texts

Student Page 151

HOME ✦ CONNECT...

The Home Connect feature is a way to keep parents or other adult family members apprised of what their children are learning. The key learning objectives are listed, and some ideas for related activities and discussions are included.

Explain to students that they can share the Home Connect page with their parents or other adult family members in their home. Let students know how much time the class will be spending on this unit so they can plan their time accordingly at home.

Encourage students and their parents to share their experiences using the suggestions on the Home Connect page and the Home Connect activities at **sadlierconnect.com**. You may wish to make a place to post some of this work.

Progress Check

The Progress Check is a self-assessment feature that students can use to gauge their own progress. Before students begin work on Unit 6, have them check the boxes next to any item that they feel they can do well. Explain that it is fine if they don't check any of the boxes. Tell them that they will have an opportunity to learn about and practice all of these items while studying the unit. Let them know that near the end of the unit they will have a chance to reconsider how well they can do each item on this list.

Before they begin their Unit 6 Review (see page 163 of this guide), you will be prompted to have students revisit this page. You can use this information to work with students on any items they don't understand before they tackle the Review.

HOME ✦ CONNECT...

In this unit, your child will learn to **write an evidence-based informative/explanatory text** about an historical conflict. This type of writing uses **researched evidence from trustworthy sources** to explain something to readers. An informative/explanatory text uses a structure that helps readers understand the topic, including an **introduction**; paragraphs that **develop the topic** with facts, details, **examples,** and other supporting evidence; and a **conclusion** that explains the results of the conflict. An evidence-based text uses **precise, formal language** to clearly convey information.

Describe an historical conflict to your child. If possible, show him or her historical photos or visit a museum exhibit about the conflict. Explain what each side wanted and how each side viewed the other. Describe how the conflict played out and what its final outcome was. Point out to your child how you use evidence to support your ideas about the conflict.

Activity: Explore with your child the unit theme: "Sources of Conflict." Together, research and make a list of important conflicts that people have faced in the past. Remember that some of these conflicts may have taken the form of wars, but many did not. Then choose a conflict to research further. Together, explore why the conflict arose and how it was resolved. Create a three- or four-panel drawing that summarizes the conflict.

IN THIS UNIT, YOUR CHILD WILL...

- Learn how to write an evidence-based text about an historical conflict.
- Use a variety of trustworthy sources to research and gather information.
- Organize ideas effectively, including using a clear introduction and strong conclusion.
- Develop a topic by incorporating various kinds of evidence (such as details, facts, and examples) that support key points.
- Use precise words and a formal writing style.
- Write using a variety of sentence styles: simple, compound, complex, and compound-complex.
- Use standard English capitalization, punctuation, and spelling.

WAYS TO HELP YOUR CHILD

Have your child describe a conflict he or she has read about or experienced. Ask your child to think about how each side viewed the issue, what each side wanted to happen, what each side thought about the other, and what each side was willing to do to get its way. Have an informal debate in which you argue one side of a conflict and your child argues the other.

ONLINE
For more Home Connect activities, continue online at sadlierconnect.com

152   Unit 6 ■ Text Types and Purposes: Write Evidence-Based Texts

Student Page 152

UNIT PLANNER

Theme: Sources of Conflict	Focus
WRITING MODEL *pp. 154–156*	*Better Lives for All*
WRITING ACTIVITY *p. 157*	**ORGANIZATIONAL STRUCTURE:** Outline
LANGUAGE MINI-LESSONS *pp. 158–161*	• Simple, Compound, Complex, and Compound-Complex Sentences • Standard Capitalization, Punctuation, and Spelling
SPEAKING AND LISTENING *p. 162*	Discuss the Essential Question
UNIT 6 REVIEW *pp. 163–164*	• Language Skills Summary • Writing Process Summary

Objective(s)

Write a well-organized evidence-based text that includes evidence, facts, or quotations.

Introduce the topic logically; develop it with facts and evidence, using appropriate transitions, precise language, and a supporting conclusion.

- Understand simple, compound, complex, and compound-complex sentence structures.
- Use standard English capitalization, punctuation, and spelling correctly.

Engage in a respectful, collaborative discussion with peers; be prepared for the discussion and participate.

Unit Assessment

- Unit 6 Review *pp. 163–164*

Additional Assessment Options

- Performance Task 1 *pp. 311A–320*
  ALSO ONLINE
- Performance Task 2 *pp. 321A–330* **ONLINE**

Optional Purchase:
- iProgress Monitor **ONLINE**
- Progress Monitor Student Benchmark Assessment Booklet

ONLINE Digital Resources

- Home Connect Activities
- Additional Practice
- Teacher Resources
- iProgress Monitor (optional purchase)

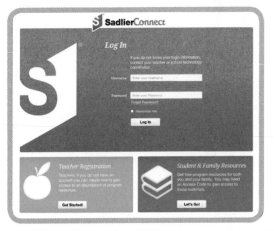

Go to SadlierConnect.com to access your Digital Resources.

For more detailed instructions see page T3.

LEARNING PROGRESSIONS

In this unit, students will learn how to write an evidence-based text. The skills that students learn in this unit build upon the skills they learned during the sixth grade. Likewise, the skills students learn this year will provide a foundation for the skills they will develop in the eighth grade.

Organizing an Essay

- By the end of the sixth grade, students should be comfortable organizing information in their writing, using strategies such as comparison/contrast or cause/effect.

- In the seventh grade, students will increase their ability to use these strategies to organize information in their writing and support a claim.

- By the time they finish the eighth grade, these organizational skills should be a natural part of students' writing.

Finding and Using Evidence

- In the sixth grade, students learn to develop a topic with facts, definitions, and examples.

- In the seventh and the eighth grades, students will increase their proficiency in finding evidence from trustworthy sources and incorporating this evidence into their writing as facts, examples, details, and quotations.

Using Language

- Sixth-grade students work on using transitions, precise language, and correct standard English in their writing.

- Throughout the seventh and the eighth grades, students will continue to improve these skills. They will be expected to use transitions, correct English, and a formal style in their written work.

Writing a Conclusion

- Sixth-grade students should be able to provide a conclusion that follows from the information presented.

- Seventh- and eighth-graders should be able to write conclusions for their essays that follow from the information presented and add to that information in a meaningful way.

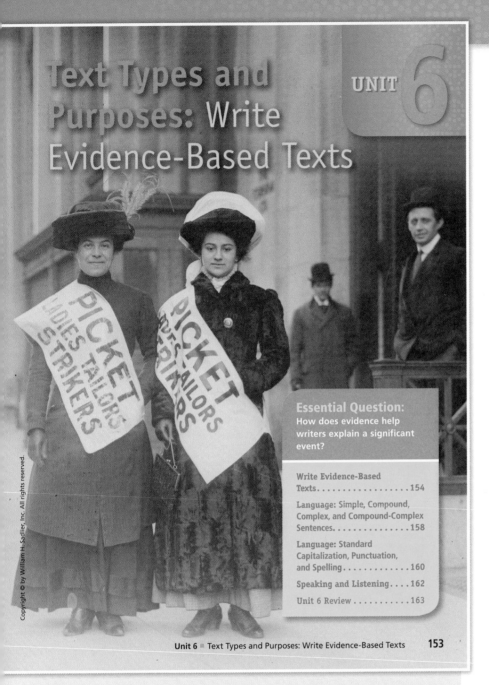

Text Types and Purposes: Write Evidence-Based Texts

UNIT 6

Essential Question:
How does evidence help writers explain a significant event?

Writing Handbook

If students need extra practice with writing an evidence-based essay, refer them to the *Writing Handbook* on pages 299–310 in their Student Books. The *Writing Handbook* gives students detailed instruction on planning, drafting, revising, and editing their writing. They will also find tips on producing, publishing, and presenting their writing.

Essential Question:
How does evidence help writers explain a significant event?

In this unit, students will learn to examine a topic and find evidence from other texts to support their ideas in a well-organized evidence-based essay.

Theme: Sources of Conflict

Students will continue their examination of sources of historical conflict. Moving on from man vs. nature, they will examine a conflict between people as they read and analyze an evidence-based essay writing model.

Curriculum Connection: Social Studies

As they read the writing model, students will have an opportunity to examine how an historical conflict changed American society. As students write their own evidence-based texts, they can explore the impact of other historical conflicts.

Connect Reading to Writing

Remind students that they read fictional accounts of historical conflicts in Unit 5 in *The Longest Walk* (Student Book pages 124–131) and *Race to the Golden Spike* (Student Book pages 132–139). Explain that even these fictional pieces used real facts to tell their stories. In this unit, students will be using historical facts and evidence to support their claims in an evidence-based essay.

OBJECTIVES

- Write a well-organized evidence-based text that includes evidence, facts, or quotations.
- Introduce the topic logically; develop it with facts and evidence, using appropriate transitions, precise language, and a supporting conclusion.

Introduce: Organizational Structure

Draw students' attention to the outline. Ask them to look for the key elements as you read the Student Model together.

Analyze a Student Model

TITLE/INTRODUCTION: Both elements orient the reader to the topic and the writer's claim.

HEADINGS: Note the headings. Explain that headings help the writer organize information and help readers know what each section of the essay is about.

CREATING AN ORGANIZATIONAL STRUCTURE

Jillian used an outline like the one below to organize her writing so that it explains the causes and outcomes of an historical conflict between factory owners and workers.

TITLE
- Gives readers a clue about the nature of the conflict.

INTRODUCTION
- Introduces the topic and previews what Jillian will discuss in the essay.

HEADINGS
- Help show the organization of the text.

BACKGROUND
- Jillian includes information that will help readers better understand the historical issue.

WRITE EVIDENCE-BASED TEXTS

Read a Student Model

Jillian is a student in Mrs. Herrera's seventh-grade Language Arts class. Mrs. Herrera gave the class an assignment: to write an evidence-based text about an historical conflict. For this evidence-based text, Jillian must research to find facts, details, and examples to explain her topic. As you read her writing, think about an historical conflict that you might write about in your own evidence-based text.

Better Lives for All

Today, most workers in the United States enjoy safe working conditions, weekend time off, and a limit to the numbers of hours in a workday. However, when the United States first became industrialized in the late 1800s, workers faced dangerous conditions and long hours for low pay. By joining together, forming labor unions, and struggling for many years, workers were able to create better lives for themselves and for workers who came after them.

Background: Changing America

In the first half of the nineteenth century, most Americans worked on farms. After the Civil War, industrialization grew rapidly, and more and more people—including women, children, and immigrants—left the farms and went to work in factories in the cities. Factory owners grew eager to profit as much as possible, no matter how poor the working conditions they created. At that time there were few laws to protect workers.

Genre: Evidence-Based Text

Explain to students that an evidence-based text is one that makes a claim and then supports it with facts and evidence. The intent is both to inform and persuade a reader, but this type of text does not rely on the emotional appeals that may be found in an opinion piece. Instead, an evidence-based text gives evidence—from trustworthy sources—to support its writer's claim.

As students work on their evidence-based texts, suggest that they ask themselves, "Do I have enough evidence to show that my claim is true?" and "How can I prove that my claim is true?"

Working Conditions

Workers usually had to work long hours for low pay. For example, teenage girls working in New York City's clothing factories in the early 1900s had to work six days a week, thirteen hours a day, with only a half-hour lunch break. Some workers were locked into their buildings and denied opportunities to go to the bathroom. Most workers were paid only $6.00 a week, but they still had to pay for their own sewing supplies.

Labor Unions

American workers began to form unions in the 1860s. The Knights of Labor was the first national union that accepted all workers in industry. Other unions, such as the American Miners' Association and the National Labor Union, were also formed. Workers began to speak out and to strike, or refuse to work, in order to draw attention to their demand for an eight-hour workday.

The Haymarket Riot

Factory owners disliked strikes, which cost them money and often ended in violence and riots. The worst of these was the Haymarket Riot in Chicago in 1886. During a union strike, several people were injured in clashes with the police. The next day, the strikers held a demonstration. Someone threw a bomb, and the police shot back. Both civilians and police were killed, and although eight men were arrested, the real culprit was never found. This riot led many people to mistrust labor unions, particularly the Knights of Labor, which was blamed for the violence.

— **EVIDENCE**

Use evidence—that is, relevant facts, details, examples, and other information—to support your ideas. The evidence should come from trustworthy sources that you have researched.

Jillian states an important idea in the first sentence of this paragraph. Underline the evidence that supports that idea.

— **DEFINITIONS**

Readers may not be familiar with words that are specific to your subject. Include definitions when needed.

Find and circle the definition of strike.

— **CAUSE AND EFFECT**

There are many strategies that can help explain a topic. The cause-and-effect strategy shows readers why events happened and what the results were.

Put a box around two effects of the Haymarket Riot, as Jillian explains it.

Analyze a Student Model

BACKGROUND: Remind students that once they have researched an historical conflict, they will know information about it that their classmates do not. In order for readers to understand their essay, they will need to give background information about the topic. Ask students to consider what background this essay gives them about the conditions that led to the rise of labor unions.

EVIDENCE: Review with students the types of evidence, adding anecdotes and statistics (numerical information) to the types listed in the Student Book. Discuss how to identify reliable sources for evidence, such as books, published nonfiction pieces, or trustworthy Web sites, and remind students that they will need to carefully choose which pieces of evidence and which facts to include in their essays to support their claims.

DEFINITIONS: Defining unfamiliar terms is part of providing background information that makes the topic comprehensible to readers.

CAUSE AND EFFECT: Point out that essays often employ more than one organizational strategy. This essay is organized chronologically, which allows the writer to describe how this historical conflict unfolded over time. Additionally, the "Haymarket Riot" section is organized to show a cause-and-effect relationship between the riot and its results.

Support English Language Learners

English language learners may need support to understand some of the topic-specific vocabulary in this essay and may need additional background information on the changes America went through as the country became industrialized. Help students by defining terms such as *industrialization, labor union, strike, garment factory,* and *sweatshop* before you read through the essay. Then read through the essay with students, stopping after each paragraph to clarify, to summarize, and to offer additional background information as needed.

Analyze a Student Model

TRANSITIONS: Including appropriate and well-chosen transitions is essential to connect the ideas in an essay into a comprehensible whole as well as to give writing a sense of flow.

MULTIMEDIA: Encourage students to think about images and graphics that would enhance their evidence-based essays. Remind students that images can help readers connect to the past and charts or graphs can help readers understand information.

STYLE/CONCLUSION: A formal style avoids slang and incorrect grammar or sentence structure and uses a formal tone. Explain to students that a formal style gives writers credibility and helps readers understand their points.

The conclusion in this essay shows the effect of this historical conflict today. It completes the chronological order by stating current conditions and the final effects of the causes the labor unions worked for.

Evaluate a Writer's Work

Have students work in pairs to evaluate Jillian's evidence. Remind students that an evidence-based essay must use facts to support its ideas. Ask: *Does Jillian support her claim and her ideas with facts? Are there parts of the essay where she needs more evidence?* Have volunteers share their ideas.

Model: Organizational Structure

Display the outline template that appears on page 157. Explain that well-written evidence-based texts have strong organizational structure requiring brainstorming and planning. Help students find clues that reflect a chronological order to the essay. Have students fill in the outline, using the subheads for guidance.

WRITE EVIDENCE-BASED TEXTS

TRANSITIONS

Transitional words and phrases can help connect ideas within paragraphs and between paragraphs. These connections can include a change in time or place, a contrast, an additional idea, and more.

Double underline two transitions in this paragraph.

MULTIMEDIA

Multimedia items, such as photographs, help bring the text to life for readers. This image of the Triangle Shirtwaist Factory fire emphasizes the reality of this tragedy.

Box the information in the text that this image helps bring to life.

STYLE/CONCLUSION

Jillian uses a formal style in her writing, using clear language and avoiding personal opinion. The conclusion wraps up the topic by showing some results of the conflict she has described in this text.

Circle the results Jillian describes.

The Garment Workers' Strike

<u>Almost 25 years later</u>, workers were still struggling for their rights. Women working in New York's garment factories—often called "sweatshops"— went on strike in 1909. These women bravely faced arrest and even violence, and they won some victories. <u>However</u>, some women went back to work at the Triangle Shirtwaist Factory without a union agreement. This factory was the scene of a horrible tragedy in 1911, when 129 women, most in their teens and twenties, were killed after a fire broke out. Factory owners had locked the exit doors to keep workers from taking too many breaks.

Conclusion

The horrible events at the Triangle Shirtwaist Factory helped bring attention to the abuse of workers. With this attention, and with further union strikes, more and more safety standards for workers were slowly implemented in the twentieth century. The eight-hour workday was finally instituted for most workers in 1938. The fight for workers' rights that started with the Industrial Revolution continues to benefit workers to this day.

156 Unit 6 ▪ Text Types and Purposes: Write Evidence-Based Texts

---

Review: Analyzing Point of View

Remind students that in Unit 5 they learned how authors develop the point of view of characters in the text. Explain that in this unit, they will write an essay that reveals their own point of view. In order to make a claim about an historical conflict, students must develop an opinion about that conflict and share their point of view through their writing.

Ask students to look for sentences that reveal Jillian's point of view about the role of labor unions in developing worker safety over the past century and a half. They should see that Jillian's point of view is that labor unions are useful and help make situations better for American workers. Point out, however, that her point of view is supported by evidence in this type of essay.

Use this outline to organize your evidence-based text for the Unit 6 Review on page 164. Then write your first draft on a separate sheet of paper. Remember to supply relevant information that develops the topic and supports your ideas. In addition, use a formal writing style, precise words, and appropriate transitions.

Title _____

I. **Introduction**

   a. Topic: _____

II. **Subtopics and Evidence**

   a. First paragraph: information about _____

     1. Fact, detail, or example _____

     _____

     2. Fact, detail, or example _____

     _____

   b. Second paragraph: information about _____

     1. Fact, detail, or example _____

     _____

     2. Fact, detail, or example _____

     _____

   c. Third paragraph: information about _____

     1. Fact, detail, or example _____

     _____

     2. Fact, detail, or example _____

     _____

III. **Conclusion**

   _____

   _____

Unit 6 ■ Text Types and Purposes: Write Evidence-Based Texts   **157**

Create: Organizational Structure

Brainstorming

Students may be intimidated by the idea of identifying an historical conflict to write about. Suggest that students consider modern issues that concern them (these may have historical roots), talk with older family members, or look through history books to get ideas. Once they have identified a topic, students will need to research it to learn more.

Planning

Students will use the outline on page 157 to plan their writing. Students should first develop their claim about the historical conflict and then select facts and evidence that support their claim. Remind students to think about the best organizational structure to share their information and ideas.

Drafting an Evidence-Based Essay

Direct students to consult their outlines as they draft their essays on separate paper. Be sure that students have an introduction, a claim, background information about the conflict, supporting evidence, and a conclusion.

Introduce the Writing Process

Remind students that good writing happens in stages. After prewriting and drafting, they will revise and edit their essays. For more on the writing process, see the *Writing Handbook* on page 299.

Assess and Respond
If students have difficulty identifying a conflict to write about,
Then help them brainstorm current conflicts that interest them. Help them identify earlier conflicts that are connected to the modern ones or similar to them.

Differentiate Instruction

Some students may have difficulty developing a claim about an historical conflict. Help students by having them research the conflict about which they will be writing and making a list of important facts about the conflict. Then have students discuss their conflicts with a partner. Each student should explain the conflict and its opposing sides; then their partner should ask questions about it. Encourage students to ask questions such as the ones below in order to help their partners develop their claims.

Whose side would you have been on in the conflict?

What would have happened if this conflict had not taken place?

How has this conflict impacted American or world society today?

OBJECTIVE

Understand simple, compound, complex, and compound-complex sentence structures.

Guided Instruction

Make sure students understand that these sentence structures are different due to the number of independent and dependent clauses, not due to length or the complexity of the ideas the sentence contains.

Then go over the instruction and examples on this page with students. You might write the examples on the board or on a large piece of paper and underline the independent and dependent clauses in different colors. Help students count the different types of clauses in each example sentence and connect this count to the appropriate sentence structure.

To test your students' understanding of these different sentence structures, ask volunteers to select some random sentences out of a novel or other book in the classroom and write them on the board. As a class, work through identifying the dependent and independent clauses in the sentence and the corresponding sentence structure. You could choose to make this exercise into a bingo-style game.

LANGUAGE

Simple, Compound, Complex, and Compound-Complex Sentences

Guided Instruction There are four basic structures of English sentences. The structures depend on the number of independent and dependent clauses in a sentence. An **independent clause** can stand as a complete sentence on its own. A **dependent clause** needs to be connected to an independent clause in order to make sense.

- A **simple sentence** is made of one independent clause.

  The dog whined for her dinner.   *The storm grew stronger.*

- A **compound sentence** has more than one independent clause. These clauses are joined by one of the coordinating conjunctions: *and, but, or, nor, for, so,* and *yet*.

  The dog whined for her dinner, but she did not scratch at the door.

  The storm grew stronger, and it soon became a hurricane.

- A **complex sentence** has one independent clause and one or more dependent clauses. The clauses are joined by subordinating conjunctions (such as *after, although, because, before, if, since, unless, until, when,* and *while*) or by relative pronouns (such as *that, which,* and *who*). The independent clause does not have to come first in the sentence; sometimes the dependent clause comes first.

  The dog whined for her dinner until her owner finally got out the dog food.

  When its winds passed 74 miles per hour, the storm was classified as a hurricane.

  Our soccer team just played a game that was one for the record books.

- A **compound-complex sentence** has two or more independent clauses and one or more dependent clauses. This type of sentence may include relative pronouns and both types of conjunctions. The clauses can appear in any order.

  The dog whined for her dinner until her owner finally got out the dog food, and then she began to bark excitedly.

  When its winds passed 74 miles per hour, the storm was classified as a hurricane, and people prepared for its landfall.

  If you haven't heard, our soccer team just played a game that was one for the record books, so we should celebrate the big win.

Differentiate Instruction

If students have trouble understanding independent and dependent clauses, help them analyze sample sentences by identifying the subjects, verbs, and objects in each clause. Then guide them to circle and identify any subordinating and coordinating conjunctions.

Once students have become comfortable identifying different clauses, help them underline and double underline the types in the sample sentences, then guide them to identify which sentence structures are being used.

Guided Practice In the sentences below, underline each independent clause. Double underline each dependent clause. Then classify each sentence as simple, compound, complex, or compound-complex.

1. <u>Since we had no sunscreen</u>, we bought some on our way to the beach. ____complex____

2. This yellow house is the largest one on our block. ____simple____

3. My family left the fair at 8:00, so we missed the fireworks display. ____compound____

4. I was really tired on the class trip <u>until we saw the dinosaur bones at the museum</u>. ____complex____

5. <u>Before the car wash</u>, Tanya made signs and Gabe signed up volunteers. ____compound-complex____

Independent Practice Add your own writing to the clauses below to create the kind of sentence described in parentheses.

1. When the lights suddenly went out, (complex) _____
   Sample answer: everyone in the class screamed.

2. Tyler bought that book yesterday, (compound) _____
   Sample answer: and now he has already finished it.

3. We took a canoe trip down the river, (compound-complex) _____
   Sample answer: but we carried our canoes when the water was too shallow.

4. Maria opened another window (complex) _____
   Sample answer: because she wanted more fresh air in the house.

5. As the meteorite blazed over our town, (compound-complex) _____
   Sample answer: all of the dogs howled, and many people were frightened.

Unit 6 ■ Text Types and Purposes: Write Evidence-Based Texts   **159**

Guided Practice

Help students identify the independent and dependent clauses in each sentence. You may wish to list subordinating and coordinating conjunctions on the board or somewhere where the class can easily refer to them, or use this strategy and add a simple definition of each sentence structure.

If students have difficulty, encourage them to begin by examining the sentences to look for subordinating and coordinating conjunctions. This should help them break down the clauses in each sentence.

Independent Practice

Students may enjoy sharing their completed sentences with the class. You can choose some of these sentences to write on the board and then have a different student identify the clauses and conjunctions. Remind students to take care to use commas between any coordinate adjectives.

Assess and Respond

If students have difficulty completing the Independent Practice,

Then model completing one or more of the sentences, showing your thought process as you consider how to create the type of sentence structure requested.

Support English Language Learners

English language learners may have difficulty understanding the ramifications of coordinating and subordinating conjunctions. Review these conjunctions with students and guide them to think about the relationships between ideas that these conjunctions are used to show.

Then go over the sentences in the Guided Practice with students. Encourage them to circle any conjunctions they see, and discuss the relationship between ideas that each conjunction creates in the sentence.

OBJECTIVE
Use standard English capitalization, punctuation, and spelling correctly.

Guided Instruction

The information on this page may be familiar to many students. Remind them that, no matter how advanced they become in their writing, it is important to pay attention to the basics. Point out that sloppy capitalization, punctuation, and spelling will make their writing look untrustworthy. It is important to make standard English a habit in their writing.

Go over the instruction on this page with students. It may help students to be engaged with the information if you ask for their suggestions before you begin. For the Capitalization section, ask: *When do you capitalize words?* Make a list of their answers, and then compare them to the instruction. For the Punctuation section, ask: *When do you use a period at the end of a sentence? When do you use a question mark?* and so on. Then go through the instruction. For the Spelling section, write each group of easily confused words on the board and ask students to identify their meanings. Then compare students' answers to the instruction.

LANGUAGE

Standard Capitalization, Punctuation, and Spelling

Guided Instruction When you write, remember to use standard, correct English capitalization, punctuation, and spelling. When you do, you make your writing easier for readers to understand and enjoy.

- **Capitalization**

  It is standard to always capitalize the first word of a sentence. English capitalization also includes the names of people, places, days of the week, and months; the pronoun *I*; and titles, such as book or movie titles. Titles can be either underlined or italicized.

  Alejandra will visit her cousins in Houston in July.

  I saw the movie Annie for the first time last Wednesday.

- **Punctuation**

  The use of punctuation depends on the structure of the sentence, but every sentence needs punctuation at the end. End punctuation includes periods, which identify statements; question marks, which identify questions; and exclamation points, which show emphasis. Within a sentence, commas are used to separate ideas, such as the name of a person being spoken to, long introductory phrases, or dependent clauses. A semicolon can be used to separate closely related independent clauses in the same sentence.

  Until Pam hit a home run, our team was facing a certain loss.

  At the end of the recital, give your sister that bouquet of flowers.

  Do you want spaghetti for supper, Evan, or would you rather have lasagna?

  It's very hot out today; how I wish for some cooler weather!

- **Spelling**

  Be careful to spell correctly, especially with words that sound like other words. Note these examples.

  there (over there) / *they're* (they are) / *their* (belonging to more than one person)

  it's (it is) / *its* (belonging to *it*)

  where (location) / *wear* (put on, as clothes)

  whose (to whom something belongs) / *who's* (who is)

  except (all but this one) / *accept* (agree to do or take)

Differentiate Instruction

Some students may need more detailed instruction on standard capitalization, punctuation, and spelling. Go over the sample sentences on this page carefully with students. Ask them to identify the capitalized terms and the punctuation marks; then explain why each term is capitalized and the function of each punctuation mark in the sentence. Model the thought process of a reader or writer who encounters these terms and punctuation marks. For the Spelling section, write on the board and read aloud sample sentences that use each easily confused word. Encourage students to practice by writing sentences of their own, reminding students to spell words correctly.

Guided Practice Rewrite each sentence to correct errors in capitalization, punctuation, and spelling.

1. from the attic to the basement the house was dark and quiet

From the attic to the basement, the house was dark and quiet.

2. Who's Hat is this on the chair.

Whose hat is this on the chair?

3. what a great time paul and i had at the lincoln park zoo

What a great time Paul and I had at the Lincoln Park Zoo!

4. because she would leave early friday morning alicia packed for her trip to california on thursday night

Because she would leave early Friday morning, Alicia packed for her trip to California on Thursday night.

5. naomi worked at an animal shelter in martinsville in june now she wants a career that will let her work with animals all the time

Naomi worked at an animal shelter in Martinsville in June; now she wants a career that will let her work with animals all the time.

Independent Practice Write a response for each of the directions below. Be sure to use standard capitalization, punctuation, and spelling.

1. Ask your friend if you may borrow her book. Call your friend and the book by name.

Sample answer: Chandra, may I borrow your copy of A Wrinkle in Time?

2. Ask the name of the new student across the room.

Sample answer: Who's that new girl over by the bookshelves?

3. Explain why you were late to school last week. Name the day of the week you were late, and start the sentence with the word *because*.

Sample answer: Because my mother's car broke down, I was late to school Wednesday.

4. Use *there*, *they're*, and *their* in a compound sentence.

Sample answer: I invited Scott and Helen to go to the park with me, but they're going there with their grandparents on Saturday.

5. Use two spelling words from page 160 to tell what only one person was willing to do.

Sample answer: Except for Brandon, my friends were unwilling to accept a role in the school play.

Guided Practice

Encourage students to look over each sentence first to identify the errors, and then rewrite it. Suggest they ask themselves: *Is the first word capitalized? Are names and titles capitalized? Is there end punctuation? Does the sentence need commas to separate ideas? Are the correct easily-confused words used?* It may help students to mark corrections on the sentence before rewriting it.

Independent Practice

After students have completed the Independent Practice, have them trade papers with a partner. Partners should examine each other's work for errors in standard written English.

Assess and Respond

If students have trouble with easily confused words that use contractions,

Then explain that the apostrophe stands for a missing letter. Write sentences using *they're* and *it's* on the board and have students read them out loud, substituting *they are* and *it is* for the contractions.

Peer Collaboration

Place students in pairs. Students should take turns briefly sharing a personal experience or summarizing a book or movie. The listener should transcribe the story, using correct capitalization, punctuation, and spelling. Students may need to make a quick transcription and then go back and edit the story; or, if possible, students can record each other's stories and work from the recordings. Finally, each student should read the transcribed story back to their partner.

OBJECTIVE

Engage in a respectful, collaborative discussion with peers; be prepared for the discussion and participate.

Return to the Essential Question

Distribute the "Did I?" checklist available on **sadlierconnect.com**.

Leading the Class Discussion

Have students tell Jillian's evidence. Ask students what Jillian wanted to accomplish and why she needed evidence.

SPEAKING AND LISTENING

Return to the Essential Question

How does evidence help writers explain a significant event?

Prepare for a class discussion about the Essential Question by responding to the questions below. Support your point of view with reasons and examples. Be sure to follow the rules for participating in an effective class discussion.

1. What kind of evidence did Jillian use to show why many people in the early 1900s faced very difficult working conditions?

   Jillian presented facts and details about how America changed after the Civil War to explain the move of workers to factories in the cities. She gave examples of the conditions the workers faced, such as long hours, low pay, and great danger.

2. What evidence did Jillian use to support the idea that there was conflict between workers and factory owners?

   Jillian provided facts about the formation of unions, the Haymarket Riot, and the garment workers' strike to support the idea that the conflict between workers and factory owners lasted a long time and could be violent at times.

3. Why is this evidence a necessary part of Jillian's text?

   This evidence helps readers understand the topic in detail. It also supports Jillian's idea that labor unions were needed to help give all workers better lives.

Use your notes above as you discuss the Essential Question with your class or in small groups. Use the organizer below to record your ideas and what you hear in the discussion. Follow the discussion rules on the "Did I?" checklist on page 58.

	Ideas I Agree or Disagree With	Questions I Asked
agree		
disagree		

New Ideas I Had During Discussion	Questions I Answered

162 Unit 6 ■ Text Types and Purposes: Write Evidence-Based Texts

---

Discussion Skills

Encourage students to move beyond thinking about whether or not they agree with an opinion to consider if the speaker has evidence for his or her opinions. Remind students to ask their peers politely to explain their answers and to give evidence for their opinions. Students should also evaluate others' opinions on their own. Encourage students to use visual displays in their discussion for clarity when necessary, and remind them to use precise language in their evaluations and discussion. Encourage them to ask themselves:

- *Does the evidence support this opinion?*
- *Can I think of any counter-examples or contradicting facts?*
- *What is the source of this evidence?*

UNIT 6 REVIEW

Read this draft of an introductory paragraph and a background paragraph from a student's evidence-based text, and answer the questions below.

The Salem Witch Trials

(1) One of the most dramatic and strange conflicts in early American history happened when the people of Salem, Massachusetts, executed nineteen people for witchcraft and arrested many more. (2) This witch hysteria was begun by a few girls. (3) Though today we know that this conflict cannot be blamed on witches, there are still many different ideas about why it happened.

How the Witch Hysteria Began

(4) The world of the 1690s was very different from the world we know today. (5) The deeply religious Puritans of this time feared witchcraft and the possible presence of witches. (6) In February 1692, two girls began having mysterious fits, screaming and throwing things. (7) When the doctor diagnosed them as being attacked by witches, hysteria began.

1. What is the topic of this text?
   a. witches
   b. the Salem Witch Trials *(circled)*
   c. Puritan New England
   d. modern disagreements about history

2. Based on the information in the introduction, what will the text NOT include?
   a. a definite cause for the witch hysteria *(circled)*
   b. a description of the witch trials conflict
   c. ideas about why the trials happened
   d. evidence about this conflict

3. Sentence 1 is a
   a. simple sentence.
   b. compound sentence.
   c. complex sentence. *(circled)*
   d. compound-complex sentence.

4. Sentence 5 develops the topic by helping readers understand that
   a. the Puritans were religious.
   b. the Puritans thought witches were real. *(circled)*
   c. the people of the time were called Puritans.
   d. there were witches in Salem.

Introduce the Review

Explain to students that this review will give them an opportunity to apply the language and writing skills they have studied and practiced in this unit.

Language Skills Summary

Let students know that they are going to use what they have learned about sentence structure and the use of correct capitalization, punctuation, and spelling to make their writing better.

- Ask students to explain the type of clauses each sentence structure (simple, compound, complex, and compound-complex) includes.
- Ask students to name three common types of words that must be capitalized.
- Ask students when a comma should be used in a sentence.

Self-Assessment: Progress Check

Have students revisit the Progress Check on page 151 and compare their answers now to the answers they gave before they started Unit 6.

Answer Explanations

Scoring: 5 points each for items 1–10; 50 points for essay.

1. Students should use the title and introduction to identify the topic of this essay.
2. Students can use sentence 3 to identify choice A as correct.
3. Students should be able to identify the independent and dependent clause in sentence 1 and to identify it as a complex sentence.
4. Students should see that sentence 5 is a supporting detail.

Test-Taking Tips

Give students the following reminders and tips to help with taking assessments that include a paragraph or essay with numbered sentences.

- Read the title and headers on both pages before you begin. This helps you understand what the text will be about and what parts of it you'll be reading.
- Read the text on the first page and answer the questions. Most multiple choice questions will apply to the text on the same page.
- Expect written, short-answer questions to cover a more general understanding of the text. You may need to refer to text on another page to answer.

Answer Explanations

5. Students can conclude that no punctuation should be added.

6. Students should identify choice D as the appropriate word.

7. Students should circle *fungus* as a more precise replacement.

8. Students should identify "fits and hallucinations" as the effects.

9. Answers should join the sentences with appropriate conjunctions.

Item 10 Rubric

2	**5 pts.** Student ends topic satisfactorily, connects conflict to present.
1	**2-3 pts.** Student ends topic but doesn't connect to present.
0	**0 pts.** Student fails to end topic.

Writing Process Summary

Remind students that planning helps organize the draft. Revising and editing help make the draft better.

Planning and Drafting

Have students check that their draft includes all items in the outline (p. 157).

Evidence-Based Text Rubric

4	**50 pts.** Text includes introduction and background, makes claim supported by evidence, uses transitions, precise language, correct English.
3	**40 pts.** Text includes key elements; only minor errors.
2	**30 pts.** Text missing key elements or evidence, has errors that interfere somewhat with meaning.
1	**20 pts.** The text is unfinished and/or has errors that show a lack of knowledge of the event or that interfere with meaning.
0	**0 pts.** The assignment was not attempted.

Read another paragraph from the student evidence-based text and answer the questions below.

> **Possible Causes**
>
> (1) Some scientists today think that the people of Salem were affected by accidentally eating something called ergot. (2) This (fungus) can cause fits and hallucinations. (3) Perhaps the girls ate it and then imagined seeing witches. (4) Some historians think that there were social causes. (5) These historians note that the first people to be blamed for the witchcraft were poor women who were not accepted by their society.

5. What type of punctuation should be added to sentence 5?

a. a comma   c. a semicolon
b. a question mark   **d. none**

6. What transitional word or phrase could be added at the beginning of sentence 4?

a. Furthermore,   c. As a result,
b. In fact,   **d. However,**

7. In sentence 2 above, circle the word that is a more precise replacement for the word *something* in sentence 1.

8. In the paragraph above, underline the effects of eating ergot.

9. Combine and revise sentences 2 and 3 to form a compound-complex sentence.

Sample answer: This fungus can cause fits and hallucinations, so if the girls ate it, they might have imagined seeing witches.

10. Write a conclusion for this text.

Sample answer: The precise cause of the witch hysteria in Salem remains uncertain, but there is no doubt that it caused chaos in this early American town. Even today, the events in Salem remind us of the power that fear can have over people.

Assignment: On separate paper, provide a final draft of the evidence-based text you began on page 157. Use what you learned about sentence structures and standard English capitalization, punctuation, and spelling in this unit. Think about how you and your classmates answered the Essential Question. Check your outline to be sure you organized your ideas well. Be sure to use precise language and transitions. End with a concluding statement that wraps up the topic well.

Digital Connection: Photographic Evidence

Have students make a poster of photographic evidence that supports their claim. Students should write their claim in the middle of the poster and then surround the claim with photographic evidence that supports their point of view. To find historical photos, students can search on the Library of Congress Web site. If the historical conflict they discuss is too far in the past to have available photos, students may be able to find pictures of illustrations, movie stills, or pictures that show the conflict's modern repercussions. Encourage students to write a caption for each image.

Introducing UNIT 7

In this unit about earth and sky, you will see how authors use language and organization to express ideas and information. Nonfiction texts are often meant to inform; that is, authors write nonfiction in order to educate readers about a particular topic. However, authors sometimes write nonfiction to express an opinion about a topic, as well, and to support that opinion with facts.

Nonfiction texts consist of many genres, including web articles, technical texts, scientific texts, and explanatory texts. In this unit, you will read an example of each. Within each text, you will learn ways in which people study the earth and the sky. As you read, consider how each author organizes information and chooses language to make his or her presentation clear and interesting. Ask yourself what the author thinks is important and what point of view he or she is expressing. Finally, explore each text a bit further by thinking about how you can identify those essential features of the text. What do your answers tell you about what makes an effective informational text?

Before Unit 7 → | Progress Check **Can I?** | After Unit 7 →

☐ Analyze the effect of word choice on a text's tone and meaning. ☐

☐ Analyze how an author organizes information and uses that organization to develop ideas in a text. ☐

☐ Follow and understand a multistep experiment. ☐

☐ Determine an author's point of view and purpose in a text. ☐

☐ Use context clues to help figure out the meanings of unfamiliar words and phrases. ☐

Unit 7 ■ Reading Informational Text: Craft and Structure

Student Page 165

Progress Check

The Progress Check is a self-assessment feature that students can use to gauge their own progress. Before students begin work on Unit 7, have them check the boxes next to any item that they feel they can do well. Explain that it is fine if they don't check any of the boxes. Tell them that they will have an opportunity to learn about and practice all of these items while studying the unit. Let them know that near the end of the unit they will have a chance to reconsider how well they can do each item on this list.

Before they begin their Unit 7 Review (see page 200 of this guide), you will be prompted to have students revisit this page. You can use this information to work with students on any items they don't understand before they tackle the Review.

HOME ◆ CONNECT...

 Today's students must learn to analyze a constant flow of information, including analyzing both content and an author's writing choices. As you work through this unit, help your child to look carefully at the writing choices each author has made. Questions like "How does that word affect the meaning of this paragraph?" or "How do you think the author feels about this subject?" can increase understanding of an author's **point of view** and **purpose**.

An author's **word choices** and choice of **organizational structure** can offer insight into the meaning of a text. As you read a scientific or technical text, ask your child to describe how the information is presented (for example, in steps or as a discussion of causes and effects). Discuss why the author might have organized the text that way.

The ability to **follow a multistep procedure** can indicate how well your child is following the structure of some scientific or technical texts. This unit includes an experiment for your child to follow. Work together on the experiment, checking each other's understanding of the procedure.

🐾 **On the Go:** In your travels around the community, find opportunities for you and your child to discuss the ecology of the area or ways in which weather conditions have affected the area. Together, choose a topic from your discussions and draft the text for a feature story that might be part of a local news broadcast. You even may want to refine the text, film the report, and share it with the family.

IN THIS UNIT, YOUR CHILD WILL...

- Read four nonfiction selections, including a web article, a technical text, a scientific text, and an explanatory text.
- Determine word meanings and how word choices affect a text.
- Analyze how an author's way of organizing a text contributes to the effectiveness of the text as a whole.
- Follow a step-by-step procedure related to an experiment or technical task.
- Determine an author's point of view and purpose.
- Use context to figure out the meanings of unfamiliar words and phrases.
- Compare and contrast ideas across four selections on the theme of earth and sky.

WAYS TO HELP YOUR CHILD

Help your child focus on how point of view can be an inherent element of information reporting. See if your child can identify implied points of view, or opinion, while watching different news broadcasts. At the end of a report, ask him or her to identify both the subject of the story and the reporter's opinion on that subject. Discuss how your child came to those conclusions.

ONLINE
For more Home Connect activities, continue online at sadlierconnect.com

166   Unit 7 ■ Reading Informational Text: Craft and Structure

Student Page 166

HOME ◆ CONNECT...

The Home Connect feature is a way to keep parents or other adult family members apprised of what their children are learning. The key learning objectives are listed, and some ideas for related activities and discussions are included.

Explain to students that they can share the Home Connect page with their parents or other adult family members in their home. Let students know how much time the class will be spending on this unit so they can plan their time accordingly at home.

Encourage students and their parents to share their experiences using the suggestions on the Home Connect page and the Home Connect activities at **sadlierconnect.com**. You may wish to make a place to post some of this work.

UNIT PLANNER

Theme: Earth and Sky	Focus
ANALYZING WORD MEANINGS *pp. 168–175*	*Satellites and the Global Positioning System* **GENRE:** Web Article **LEXILE®:** 1090L **WORDS TO KNOW:** sophisticated, encrypted, constellation, receiver, trilateration, sphere, electromagnetic, atomic, nanosecond, environmental, preservation, aviation, pertinent, timely, measure, smartphone, cellular, innovation
ANALYZING TEXT STRUCTURE *pp. 176–183*	*Hurricanes: Earth's Most Violent Storms* **GENRE:** Technical Text **LEXILE®:** 1060L **WORDS TO KNOW:** hurricane, atmospheric, evaporation, eye, classified, storm surge, apprised, infrared, relative humidity, saturation, hygrometer, condensation, bulb, theorized, propulsion, ventured, awe
ANALYZING POINTS OF VIEW *pp. 184–191*	*Our Fragile Ecosystem: The Importance of Preserving the Wetlands* **GENRE:** Scientific Text **LEXILE®:** 1140L **WORDS TO KNOW:** contiguous, ecosystem, aqueous, estuary, watershed, prolific, waterfowl, safeguard, filtration, toxin, integral, viable, wholesale, depleted, mandated, equilibrium, invaluable, native, contaminant, urban sprawl
CLOSE READING *pp. 192–197*	*Satellites: Bridging the Gap from Earth to Sky* **GENRE:** Technical Text **LEXILE®:** 1100L
CONNECT ACROSS TEXTS *p. 198*	Support a Claim
LANGUAGE *p. 199*	Context Clues
UNIT 7 REVIEW *pp. 200–202*	*The Hurricane Hunters* *The Science of "Space Weather"* **GENRE:** Explanatory Text **LEXILE®:** 1000L

Essential Question: How do authors use language and organization to express
a point of view?

UNIT 7

Objective(s)

Determine the meanings of words and phrases in a text, and analyze how word choice impacts tone.

Analyze the way in which an author chooses to organize a text.

Analyze how an author expresses his or her point of view in an informational text.

- Determine the meanings of words and phrases in a text, and analyze how word choice impacts tone.

- Analyze the way in which an author chooses to organize a text.

- Analyze how an author expresses his or her point of view in an informational text.

Use context clues to decipher word meanings.

Unit Assessment

- Unit 7 Review *pp. 200–202*
- Unit 7 Performance Task   ONLINE

Additional Assessment Options

- Performance Task 1 *pp. 311A–320*
  ALSO ONLINE

- Performance Task 2 *pp. 321A–330*
  ALSO ONLINE

Optional Purchase:

- iProgress Monitor   ONLINE

- Progress Monitor Student Benchmark Assessment Booklet

ONLINE Digital Resources

- Home Connect Activities
- Unit Performance Task
- Additional Practice
- Full-Length Reading Selections
- Teacher Resources
- iProgress Monitor (optional purchase)

Go to SadlierConnect.com to access your Digital Resources.

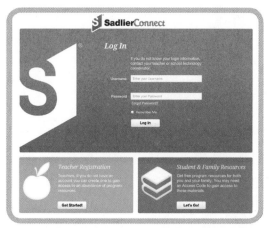

For more detailed instructions see page T3.

LEARNING PROGRESSIONS

In this unit, students will learn how language and organization in informational texts contribute to their understanding of a text. The skills that students learn in this unit build upon the skills they learned during the sixth grade. Likewise, the skills students learn this year will provide a foundation for the skills they will develop in the eighth grade.

Analyzing Word Meanings

- Sixth-grade students should have finished the year with the ability to determine the meanings of words in a text, including figurative, connotative and technical meanings.

- While in the seventh grade, students continue developing their skills by analyzing the impact of word choice on meaning and tone.

- In the eighth grade, students will enhance their skills by learning to cite and more completely analyze analogies and allusions presented within a given text.

Analyzing Text Structure

- Proficient sixth-graders should have learned how specific sections of a text fit into the overall structure, and how those sections contribute to the development of ideas in the text.

- In the seventh grade, students continue to develop their skills by analyzing the overall structure an author uses to organize a text.

- Students will extend this skill in the eighth grade by analyzing, in detail, the structure of a specific paragraph in a text, including the role of specific sentences in developing a key concept.

Analyzing Points of View

- By the end of the sixth grade, students should have learned how to determine an author's point of view, and explain how it is conveyed in a text.

- Seventh-graders deepen their understanding of informational texts by determining how an author distinguishes his or her position from that of others.

- In the eighth grade, students will be responsible for understanding how an author responds to conflicting viewpoints or evidence.

Reading Informational Text: Craft and Structure

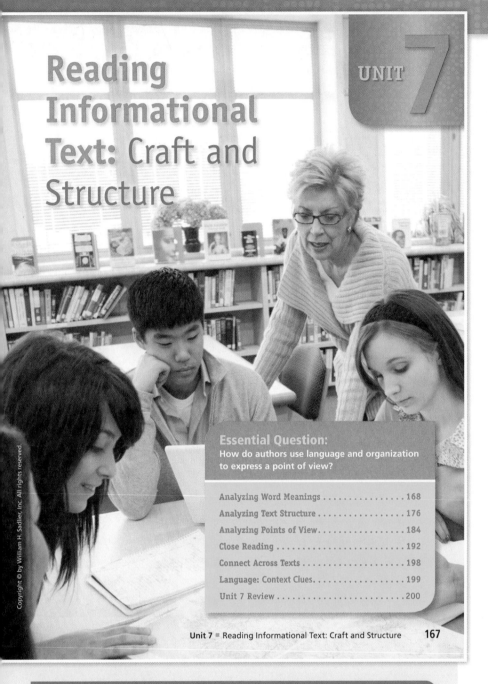

Essential Question:
How do authors use language and organization to express a point of view?

In this unit, students will learn how language and organization in informational texts help contribute to their understanding of a text. Specifically, students will learn to analyze word meanings, text structure, and points of view in order to better understand the information contained within the text.

Theme: Earth and Sky

Students will read informative texts relating to the theme, including a Web site article about GPS technology, a technical text about the science behind predicting hurricanes, a scientific text about the preservation of the wetlands, and a technical text about satellites.

Curriculum Connection: Science

The selections in this unit are all based on the science involved in researching and understanding events and occurrences in nature. Students will learn about the science behind satellite technology, the study of hurricanes, and the preservation of endangered environments.

Essential Question:
How do authors use language and organization to express a point of view?

Unit 7 ■ Reading Informational Text: Craft and Structure   **167**

Vocabulary Overview

General Academic Vocabulary

apprised, aqueous, awe, bulb, classified, contiguous, depleted, encrypted, environmental, equilibrium, innovation, integral, invaluable, mandated, measure, nanosecond, native, pertinent, preservation, prolific, safeguard, sophisticated, sphere, theorized, timely, toxin, ventured, viable, waterfowl, wholesale

Domain-Specific Vocabulary

atmospheric, atomic, aviation, cellular, condensation, constellation, contaminant, ecosystem, electromagnetic, estuary, evaporation, eye, filtration, hurricane, hygrometer, infrared, propulsion, receiver, relative humidity, saturation, smartphone, storm surge, trilateration, urban sprawl, watershed

Guided Instruction

OBJECTIVE

Determine the meanings of words and phrases in a text, and analyze how word choice impacts tone.

Genre: Web Article

Explain to students that a Web article is an informative article that appears on a Web site. It is typically written in a more conversational style, making it easier for readers to understand.

Set the Purpose

Help students understand the purpose for understanding the reading skill by asking: *What are some of the ways readers can determine the meanings of words in an informational text?*

Model and Teach

Read or have volunteers read the selection and callouts as the class follows along. Model effective strategies for responding to the callouts by using the suggestions below.

CITE EVIDENCE

A Explain to students that technical text uses language that is specific to the subject. Help students identify the words *GPS*, *coordinates*, and *receivers* as technical terms.

B Inform students that figurative language includes words that can have double meanings or that create a picture for the reader. Guide students to identify the word *constellation* as an example of figurative language.

ANALYZING WORD MEANINGS

Guided Instruction

WORDS TO KNOW

constellation

encrypted

receiver

sophisticated

To be an effective reader, you must understand the **meanings of words and phrases** that an author chooses. In addition, seeing the effect of an author's word choices will help you understand a text better.

CITE EVIDENCE

A Informational texts often include **technical words**, or words specific to the topic, in order to inform readers. In paragraph 2, underline three examples of technical words.

B Even when presenting scientific facts, an author may choose to use **figurative language** to make an interesting comparison. In paragraph 3, circle a word whose figurative meaning compares GPS satellites to stars.

Satellites and the Global Positioning System

(Genre: Web Article)

By Randolph Sims Magnusson, Editor, *Tech Times Daily*
www.techtimesdaily.net/satellites_and_gps

1   Picture this: You are in a car with your parents, on vacation, and you are close to reaching your destination. You and your parents know you are in the right area. However, you do not know, specifically, how to get to your intended stopping place. Luckily, you realize that there is no need to panic. Your dad turns on a device, types in the address of your destination, and gets detailed directions from an electronic voice. You may not realize it, but you and your parents have just interacted with one of the largest and most **sophisticated** technological operations in use today.

What Is GPS?

2   *GPS* stands for *Global Positioning System*. Typically, we use it to mean both the GPS receivers—or small units that transmit directions, coordinates, and time—and the large network of satellites that orbit Earth and transmit signals to those receivers. The Global Positioning System was originally conceived and operated by the United States military. It used **encrypted** signals to broadcast location. It was employed extensively during the Persian Gulf War in 1991. Then, in 1995, the U.S. government opened up the Global Positioning System for civilian use. This move allowed nonmilitary people the chance to use military satellites to find directions and locations.

3   The United States government owns and operates a constellation of 27 satellites that orbit Earth, making up the Global Positioning System. Of this number, 24 satellites are actually in use, while the rest are held as back-up in case a satellite fails.

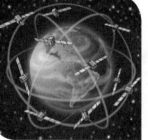

Words to Know

General Academic Vocabulary
encrypted (*v.*): placed in code
sophisticated (*adj.*): complex or intricate

Domain-Specific Vocabulary
constellation (*n.*): group of objects in the sky
receiver (*n.*): object that receives and processes signals

Working with Word Meaning Encourage students to restate the definitions in their own words and then use each word in a sentence.

CRAFT AND STRUCTURE

4   These satellites weigh about 2,000 pounds each. They orbit Earth at a rate of 7,000 miles an hour, which allows each satellite to completely circle the planet twice in a 24-hour period. Each of the 24 satellites moves in a fixed orbit that keeps it from crashing into other satellites and allows its position around Earth to be known at all times.

What Is Trilateration?

5   Think back to your fictional family vacation. This time, imagine that your dad does not have his GPS **receiver** with him. Instead, in order to isolate your location, you must ask the people around you to tell you where you are.

6   When you ask the first person to tell you where you are, she answers, "You are 1,400 miles from Fargo, North Dakota." You get out your map and draw a circle, with Fargo at the center. The circle covers every place that lies within 1,400 miles of Fargo. This leaves a lot of possibilities!

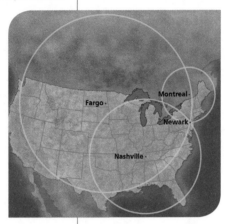

7   You decide to ask another person for help. This time, the gentleman answers, "You are 874 miles away from Nashville, Tennessee." You draw a second circle on your map, this time with Nashville at the center, extending out 874 miles. Now you are starting to refine your search. You notice the two places where the two circles intersect. These are the only two possibilities for your location.

8   You then ask one more person for help. The teenager answers, "You are 366 miles from Montreal, Canada." You draw one more circle, with Montreal at the center. Now, instead of multiple points of intersection, you see only one, at Newark, New Jersey. You have just identified your location.

Comprehension Check

The author of this text chooses words that help create a formal tone. Look again at the words or phrases you put a box around in paragraphs 7 and 8. What are some words you could replace these with in order to create a more informal tone?

CITE EVIDENCE

C Word meanings can affect the **tone** of a text. Look closely at the last sentence in paragraph 5. Put a box around the two words that create a more formal, educational tone for the sentence.

D In paragraph 7, the author uses a technical term meaning "to meet." Put an asterisk next to the word that means "to meet."

E Think about the tone of paragraphs 7 and 8. Put a box around three words or phrases that help create a more formal tone in these paragraphs.

Unit 7 ■ Reading Informational Text: Craft and Structure   **169**

CITE EVIDENCE

C Explain to students that tone refers to how an author approaches a text. In an informative text, authors often use a formal tone to explain facts. Guide students to the words *isolate* and *location* as examples of formal tone.

D Have students look for context clues in paragraph 7 that help them narrow the word *intersect* as meaning *to meet*.

E Direct students to look for words that give the text a more formal tone.

Comprehension Check

Sample Answer: Some of the formal language in paragraphs 7 and 8 includes the words *extending*, *refine*, and *identified*. These words could be changed to the words *stretching*, *narrow*, and *found* to create a more informal tone.

Answer Explanation: Students should have already identified examples of the formal language in these paragraphs. They should replace these words with synonyms that would create a more informal tone in the text.

Listening and Viewing Skills

Have students look at the diagram on page 169 while you or a student volunteer reads aloud paragraphs 5–8. Then have students compare the details in the diagram to those in the text. Ask them to identify how the details in the diagram enhance the explanation of the word *trilateration* given in the text.

Support English Language Learners

Technical language can be a distinctly challenging area for English language learners, particularly on first reading a text. In order to help students better comprehend the meaning of the text, language-specific instruction should be done prior to the first reading. Have students scan the text, highlighting words with which they are unfamiliar. Then help students create vocabulary cards that they can use while reading the text. Each card should include the unfamiliar word, a definition of the word, an example sentence using the new word, and a picture or other visual representation of the word to help cue the students' understanding.

Guided Instruction

CITE EVIDENCE

A Students should look for information that describes a technical process; in this case, using three intersecting locations to narrow down a single point. Help students identify the word *trilateration* as the technical term for this process.

B Remind students that technical language refers to the specialized language of a field of study. Help students identify the two sentences that describe the technical requirements for 3-D trilateration.

Satellites and the Global Positioning System *continued*

WORDS TO KNOW

atomic

electromagnetic

nanosecond

sphere

trilateration

CITE EVIDENCE

A You can sometimes figure out meanings of technical words based on processes described in the text. Paragraph 9 introduces a technical term for the process of drawing intersecting circles, described earlier in the section. Circle that term.

B Paragraph 11 uses technical words to describe satellite positioning. Underline the two sentences that explain the requirements for 3-D trilateration.

9 This method of identification, known as **trilateration**, is very similar to the way that GPS maps locations—although the satellite system works much more quickly! The biggest difference between the map method and the way GPS works is that the map method is 2-D, or two-dimensional, trilateration. This means that you are working with flat surfaces rather than three-dimensional objects. GPS receivers use 3-D, or three-dimensional, trilateration to find people or objects.

How Does 3-D Trilateration Work?

10 Three-dimensional trilateration works very similarly to two-dimensional trilateration. Instead of circles, however, the mapping process involves **spheres**. Picture the circles you drew on your imaginary map. This time, instead of circles, visualize spheres; instead of a flat map, visualize the spheres in space, with the possible locations touching many different points on Earth.

11 When these spheres intersect, locations on Earth's surface can be identified. Unlike 2-D trilateration, it takes four spheres to truly pinpoint an exact position. In fact, Earth itself could act as the fourth sphere: You could eliminate any points in space and just use those that intersect on Earth's surface. GPS typically uses four satellites, however, in order to identify the location more accurately. For any given location on Earth there are always four satellites in Earth's orbit that are in the correct position to use for GPS navigation.

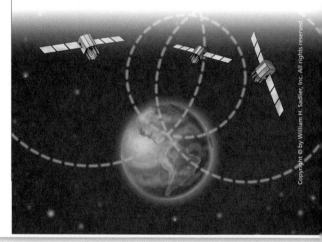

170

Words to Know

General Academic Vocabulary

nanosecond (*n.*): 1/1,000,000,000 of a second

sphere (*n.*): a ball or rounded, ball-like form

Domain-Specific Vocabulary

atomic (*adj.*): having to do with atoms, the tiny, basic building blocks of matter

electromagnetic (*adj.*): associated with the electric and magnetic fields, and their interactions with one another

trilateration (*n.*): the process of using three data points to figure out a location

Working with Word Meaning Encourage students to illustrate each vocabulary word and to describe each picture, using the vocabulary word.

CRAFT AND STRUCTURE

How Does a GPS Determine Location?

12   As we have seen, a GPS receiver works by finding its location in relation to four orbiting satellites. To determine its location, the GPS needs two important pieces of information: where each satellite is and its distance away from the GPS receiver. The GPS receiver gets this information from the satellites themselves.

13   GPS satellites regularly send signals as high-frequency **electromagnetic** radio waves—fancy language for waves that travel at the speed of light. A signal includes information about the satellite's position and the exact time that the signal is sent. The GPS receiver picks up the signal and then calculates how long the signal took to travel from the transmitting satellite to the GPS receiver. Given that the speed of light is 186,000 miles per second, you can see that it does not take long for the signal to reach the GPS receiver. This means that GPS receivers need access to measurements of time reported in tiny units.

14   The **atomic** clock is the most precise tool in existence for keeping time. It notes time to the nearest *nanosecond. The time on each satellite's atomic clock is sent in each signal transmission. Ideally, a GPS receiver would also have an atomic clock for determining the time difference from when the signal was sent to when it was received. Unfortunately, an atomic clock costs $50,000–$100,000. This means that a GPS receiver must use a plain quartz clock such as you might have at home.

15   To solve the problem of the differences in precision between the atomic clock and its quartz clock, the GPS receiver analyzes the time signals from each of the four GPS satellites. This tells the receiver how far off the "true time" its clock is and allows the receiver to compensate when it does its calculations.

Comprehension Check

How can understanding technical words help you read the rest of this article?

Guided Instruction

CITE EVIDENCE

C In this web article, the author occasionally makes some word choices to create a less formal tone. In paragraph 13, put a box around the words that create a less formal tone.

D In paragraph 14, a unit of measurement for extremely small periods of time is mentioned. Put an asterisk next to this technical term.

E In paragraph 14, the author uses the technical term for the type of clock that would be used in a typical home setting. Double underline this word. Why does the author offer an explanation of the types of clocks used by GPS units?

Guided Instruction

CITE EVIDENCE

C Remind students that Web articles are typically written for the general population to read—authors understand that they need to make the information accessible for everyone. Help students identify the language in the first sentence of paragraph 13 that is more casual in tone.

D Have students look for the technical term that refers to a unit of measurement. Students should identify the word *nanosecond* in the second sentence.

E Explain to students that they are looking for a technical term that describes a typical clock, rather than an atomic clock. Sample answer: *GPS units use time to coordinate location. Understanding how GPS works also involves understanding how GPS receivers calculate time.*

Comprehension Check

Sample Answer: In an article that describes a technical process, some of the specific tools can only be referred to through technical language. Readers must understand the meaning of the technical terms in order to comprehend the information being presented in the text.

Answer Explanation: Students should think about the kind of language they would use to describe a familiar process, like searching the Internet. Even familiar actions can require technical language to describe them, like *Internet*, *Web site*, or *username*. Help students recognize that, without understanding these technical terms, it would be very difficult to understand the process.

Digital Connection: Using Online Tools

Online satellite mapping apps can provide students with interesting opportunities for working with satellite and GPS technology. Have students use one of these apps to complete the activities below.

- Have students use the app to map due north from their location. Then, have students experiment with walking to various points away from due north, and plotting those points in the app.

- Have students map certain places of interest (school, home) or routes (routes of famous explorers, personal vacations) using GPS coordinates and the app.

- If you have them available, use GPS coordinates and the app to follow a GPS "scavenger hunt" around the school.

Guided Practice

Recap Reading Selection

Have students recall what they have read so far in the selection. Prompt them to review the information already presented in the text, including information about how GPS receivers use satellite positioning to determine coordinates. Let students know that next they will be reading about practical applications of GPS technology.

Read and Practice

Have partners take turns reading the selection as you circulate to provide support. Circulate among students and ask them to respond to Cite Evidence callouts A and B. Provide additional scaffolding as needed, using the suggestions below.

CITE EVIDENCE

A Have students read paragraph 16 to identify technical language in the text. Have students work with a partner to identify the word *velocity* as a technical term meaning *speed*.

B Encourage students to read paragraph 18 aloud, to a partner. As one student reads, have their partner write down the words they hear that represent examples of technical language. Have students discuss the impact this type of language has on the tone of the text.

ANALYZING WORD MEANINGS

Guided Practice

WORDS TO KNOW

aviation

environmental

pertinent

preservation

CITE EVIDENCE

A In paragraph 16, the author uses a technical word meaning "speed." Put a box around the word.

B With a partner, underline examples of technical language that appear in paragraph 18. Discuss the effect these word choices have on the tone of the text.

Satellites and the Global Positioning System *continued*

Why Does Time Matter So Much?

16   Remember the information a GPS receiver needs in order to pinpoint its location: the position of at least three satellites and the distance between the receiver and each of those satellites. Since satellites send radio signals with the velocity of the speed of light, the GPS receiver can determine the distance to each satellite by calculating the time it takes each signal to reach Earth.

17   The receiver is able to get and analyze signals from all the GPS satellites at the same time, then use trilateration to determine its position. And assuming the GPS receiver is in your hand or mounted on your car dashboard, you then know your position, too!

So, How Does GPS Help Me?

18   Besides giving you directions and telling you where you are, GPS technology has many other applications. These include aviation, public safety, disaster aid, and **environmental preservation**.

19   The use of GPS in **aviation** may be one of the most important applications of the technology. Pilots track their routes using the Global Positioning System, leading to greater accuracy in flight patterns and landing times and increased safety and efficiency in the air. Not only do the people flying and directing the planes benefit, but the passengers do as well.

20   In a disaster, whether natural (such as a tornado) or man-made (such as a building collapse), time is of the essence. Relief officials must be able to get to potential victims quickly and safely. GPS tracking gives emergency service providers an accurate representation of all **pertinent** landmarks, roadways, and bodies of water.

21   In 2005, GPS became a key member of the rescue team after Hurricane Katrina and Hurricane Rita attacked the Gulf Coast. In both cases, emergency services personnel were able to enter the affected areas with complete knowledge of the landmarks they would encounter. GPS technology saved valuable minutes, so that emergency workers could focus on the victims instead of their surroundings.

Words to Know

General Academic Vocabulary

environmental (*adj.*): having to do with nature and the natural world

pertinent (*adj.*): relevant; having to do with the matter at hand

preservation (*n.*): protection; keeping something safe from harm

Domain-Specific Vocabulary

aviation (*n.*): the design, production, and use of aircraft

Working with Word Meaning Encourage students to find synonyms and antonyms for each of the words and to use them in sentences based on the text.

CRAFT AND STRUCTURE
Guided Practice

Comprehension Check

1. Throughout the selection, the author mentions important applications of GPS technology. Based on your reading, what does *applications* mean?

   a. requests for employment

   b. medical treatments

   c. hard work

   d. uses for something

2. In paragraphs 19–21, the author gives evidence for the idea that GPS technology has several applications by discussing all of the following EXCEPT

   a. tourism.

   b. disaster aid.

   c. aviation.

   d. public safety.

3. Which of the following passages contains figurative language?

   a. "Since satellites send radio signals with the velocity of the speed of light . . . "

   b. "The use of GPS in aviation may be one of the most important applications of the technology."

   c. "In 2005, GPS became a key member of the rescue team after Hurricane Katrina and Hurricane Rita attacked the Gulf Coast."

   d. ". . . so that emergency workers could focus on the victims instead of their surroundings."

4. In paragraph 20, the word *representation* refers to

   a. a lawyer.

   b. a map.

   c. a demonstration.

   d. a satellite.

5. With a partner, discuss why the author may have chosen to use both technical and casual language in this web article. What effect does this mix have on the tone of the article? What does this mix suggest about the author's intended audience?

   Sample answer: The author uses both kinds of language to appeal to a wide
   Internet audience. The tone is mostly formal, since a large amount of technical
   language has to be used. However, in order to appeal to the Internet readers
   who are likely uninformed on this topic, the text also includes casual language
   to create a more friendly, engaging tone.

Comprehension Check

Answer Explanations:

1. Students should gather from the context that the best choice for the meaning of the word *applications* is choice D.

2. The author discusses uses for GPS in the areas of disaster aid, aviation, and public safety, making choice A the correct answer.

3. Students should remember that figurative language paints a picture, evidenced in the word *attacked* in choice C.

4. Students should note that paragraph 20 discusses GPS receivers and mapping coordinates, making choice B the correct choice.

5. Students should refer to both the genre of the text, and the type of language being used. Students should note that an informative text typically requires some formal and technical language, where a Web article must also appeal to a wider, perhaps uninformed, audience.

Writearound

Have students create a writearound summary of the first two sections of the selection. Place students in groups of four, and provide them with a sentence starter: *GPS technology represents an important advancement because . . . .* Have one student finish the sentence and then pass the paper to the right. Students should read the sentence(s) passed to them and then add one of their own. Four summaries of the text will emerge.

Discussion Skills

Have students practice discussion skills by having them talk about ways in which they have seen the impact of GPS technology on modern life. Have students work in pairs to create a position statement about the impact of GPS technology. Have students cite evidence from the text to back up their positions. Then, direct each pair to join with another pair in the class to discuss and debate their ideas. Ask one group to present the conclusions of their discussion in front of the class. Finally, lead a class discussion about how well the small group discussion incorporated details from the text.

Independent Practice

Recap Reading Selection

Have students recall what they have read so far about GPS technology. Ask students to name some of the ways GPS technology can benefit everyone. Let them know that they will be reading about the future of GPS technology in the rest of the selection.

Read and Apply

Have students read this section independently as you circulate. Ask them to read aloud so you can see if they are reading fluently. You can also use the support below to help students who are having difficulty.

CITE EVIDENCE

A Guide students to read paragraph 22 carefully, looking specifically for technical terms. If students are struggling, have them first identify all technical language in the paragraph. Then have them narrow down to the two terms that relate to natural processes, using context for reference.

B Students should look to the end of the paragraph for the appropriate technical terms. Sample answer: *The paragraph discusses the shift from military GPS to civilian. The author uses formal language in order to continue to match the language of the text to the subject matter.*

Satellites and the Global Positioning System *continued*

WORDS TO KNOW
cellular
innovation
measure
smartphone
timely

22   A third application of GPS technology lies in its usefulness in maintaining the environment. One of the greatest obstacles in environmental preservation has always been the lack of **timely** information. GPS allows environmentalists to identify and observe patterns, including those that can have devastating ecological consequences. Furthermore, GPS allows for accurate tracking of man-made environmental disasters, like oil spills and fires. Scientists can track the long-term consequences of these disasters and, ideally, put preventative **measures** into place.

What Is the Future of the Global Positioning System?

23   If you have ever used a **smartphone** to find your location or get directions, you are already a part of the future of GPS. What once was used only for military purposes has now become a common technology used by civilians as well as by military personnel. However, these are not the only applications that GPS may hold for the future.

24   One of the anticipated innovations in GPS is the invention of a GPS technology that works indoors. Right now, if you are using the map on your smart phone inside a building, you are not actually tapping into the global satellite system. Instead, your phone is using the positions of the **cellular** towers around you to make an approximation. In the future, we can expect to see GPS technology applied to both indoor and outdoor systems.

25   A more creative application for the future is the possibility of self-driving cars. Someday you may be the passenger while sitting in the driver's seat of your own car! By using GPS to navigate self-driven vehicles, scientists hope to eliminate human error on the roadways. Doing so could lead to a significant decrease in both traffic and accidents, especially in major metropolitan areas.

26   The Global Positioning System is a technological **innovation** that many people today take for granted. It allows for the kinds of precise location services, directional mapping, and

CITE EVIDENCE

A In paragraph 22, the author uses two technical terms that mean "natural" or "biological." Put a box around each of those terms.

B In paragraph 23, circle the terms the author uses for "members of the armed forces" and "people who do not work in a certain profession." Why does the author choose these terms rather than using more informal language?

Words to Know

General Academic Vocabulary
innovation (*n.*): new idea; invention
measure (*n.*): step; procedure
timely (*adj.*): available at the right moment

Domain-Specific Vocabulary
cellular (*adj.*): relating to the system that uses radio waves to communicate telephone signals
smartphone (*n.*): a phone that includes a hand-held computer for Internet access, e-mail, and so on

Working with Word Meaning Have students come up with examples and/or nonexamples for each word.

environmental tracking that were not possible 100 years ago. Now we can see not only where we are but also where we are going, in clear, exact images. Through GPS, the possibilities of satellite-directed technologies are as endless as human imagination!

Comprehension Check   MORE ONLINE sadlierconnect.com

1. Define the phrase *ecological consequences* (paragraph 22).

   a. financial difficulties

   b.) effects on nature

   c. personal concerns

   d. atmospheric changes

2. Which word in paragraph 25 means "to plan and travel on a given course"?

   a. self-driven

   b. metropolitan

   c. eliminate

   d.) navigate

3. In the final section of this web article, which of the following is NOT one of the "anticipated innovations in GPS"?

   a. improved transportation safety

   b.) improved national defense

   c. more widespread use of GPS

   d. an "indoor" GPS system

4. In the conclusion to this article, the author uses figurative language to compare the possibilities of GPS to

   a. the interior of a building.

   b. a cleaned-up environment.

   c.) people's creativity.

   d. an automobile.

5. In this web article, the author uses technical language in very specific places. When does the author use technical language, and why? What impact does word choice have on the overall tone of this article?

   Sample answer: The author uses technical language when relaying information

   about the subject matter. That use makes sense because the concepts behind

   satellites and GPS are technical subjects and are best described in appropriate,

   related language. By using technical words, the author creates a text that is

   both informative and accessible for a web-based audience.

Extend Thinking: Critique

Have students prepare a short critique of the article. Have them analyze the author's style and tone by asking the following questions: *Does the author strike a balance between formal and informal tone? Is the information presented in an accessible way for Internet readers? Is there any place in the text that seems to be indicative of author bias toward the subject? If so, what bias does the author exhibit?* Have students volunteer to present their ideas to the class.

Comprehension Check

Answer Explanations:

1. Students should recall that the word *ecological* refers to natural processes, so the logical answer is choice B.

2. The third sentence in paragraph 25 discusses using GPS to drive, or choice D, navigate.

3. The military uses of GPS are discussed earlier in the selection. Therefore, choice B, is the correct answer.

4. In paragraph 25, the author refers to a "creative application" of GPS technologies, leading to the logical conclusion that choice C is correct.

5. Student answers should refer to the fact that the author uses technical language specifically when information about GPS technologies is being conveyed. The student should note that this allows the author to present the information with the appropriate vocabulary, while still making the subject accessible to a wider audience.

Critical Comprehension

Challenge students to think more deeply about the text and to support their answers with evidence from the text.

Ask students: *Can you think of any other technologies that were created for government or business use, but have become part of our everyday lives?* (Answers will vary, but may include cargo pants, military vehicles, duct tape, computers, and microwaves.)

Assess and Respond
If students have trouble answering Comprehension Check question 5,
Then lead them to highlight the area in the text where the author uses technical language. Have them pay attention to the effect technical vocabulary has on their reading of the text.

Guided Instruction

OBJECTIVE
Analyze the way in which an author chooses to organize a text.

Genre: Technical Text

A technical text is a very specific kind of informative writing. The author uses key technical language in order to explain a subject, and avoids the use of casual vocabulary, humor, or figurative language.

Set the Purpose

Have students reflect on the process of giving directions to another person. Ask: *When you are giving someone directions, is it important to organize the steps they need to take in a certain order? Why or why not?*

MODEL AND TEACH

Read or have volunteers read the selection and callouts as the class follows along. Model effective strategies for responding to the callouts by using the suggestions below.

CITE EVIDENCE

A Explain to students that the word *sequential* is another word for *step-by-step*. Guide them to highlight the step-by-step processes in paragraph 3.

B Help students understand that "causal" refers to a cause and effect relationship. Help them identify the causal explanation of weather conditions leading to the formation of a hurricane.

ANALYZING TEXT STRUCTURE
Guided Instruction

WORDS TO KNOW
atmospheric
evaporation
eye
hurricane

Authors of technical texts use **text structure** to present material in an organized way. Common structures include **sequential, comparative,** and **causal.**

CITE EVIDENCE

A Authors who use a **sequential structure** describe steps in the order in which they occur. Put a box around the block of text that illustrates sequential organization.

B A **causal structure** shows how one event causes another. In paragraph 4, underline the sentence that shows a causal relationship between paragraphs 3 and 4.

Hurricanes
Earth's Most Violent Storms
(Genre: Technical Text)

1   **Hurricanes** are among the greatest weather phenomena on our planet. They can be as large as 600 miles across and can reach wind speeds of up to 200 miles per hour. The strength and force of a hurricane can have devastating consequences for those in its path. Furthermore, the aftereffects of a powerful hurricane can linger for years.

2   One of the earliest written records of a hurricane came from Christopher Columbus in 1494, and people have been documenting hurricane movements ever since. Today, scientists have moved beyond tracking hurricanes to studying the complex processes that lead to the development of hurricanes. In this way, scientists hope to be better able to predict both the occurrence of hurricanes and the intensity that a particular hurricane will achieve.

Understanding Hurricane Conditions

3   Three basic **atmospheric** and environmental conditions must be present in order for a hurricane to develop:

a. First, warm oceanic temperatures cause sufficient heat and moisture to develop in the atmosphere.

b. Next, seawater **evaporation** combines with heat and energy to propel the movements of the hurricane.

c. Then, a strong wind pattern near the surface of the ocean causes the air to turn inward upon itself.

4   When all three requirements are met, conditions are ripe for the presence of a hurricane. Both the Atlantic and eastern Pacific Oceans see these conditions most frequently in late summer. In the Atlantic Ocean, the peak hurricane season runs from June 1 until November 30. In the eastern Pacific, it runs from May 15 until November 30.

176

Words to Know

Domain-Specific Vocabulary

atmospheric (*adj.*): of the atmosphere, the layer of air that surrounds Earth

evaporation (*n.*): the natural process in which water is drawn up into the air

eye (*n.*): the calm center of a hurricane

hurricane (*n.*): a large storm that develops over the ocean but can move inland

Working with Word Meaning Have students draw images of each word and then trade their images with a partner who must guess the vocabulary word illustrated.

CRAFT AND STRUCTURE
Guided Instruction

5   Simply having the presence of these conditions is not enough, however, to guarantee the development of a hurricane. The atmospheric conditions must first undergo a variety of processes before the intense power of a hurricane can be fully generated.

The Stages of Hurricane Development

Stage 1: Evaporation

6   During the first stage of development, warm water rises upward from near the surface of the ocean. The water temperature must be greater than 80 degrees Fahrenheit for this to occur. The rising water causes evaporation, creating an area of low pressure below and leading to higher levels of humidity. This provides energy for the hurricane to develop.

Stage 2: Wind Force

7   Once the warm air has risen, air begins to circulate and spiral. Air with higher pressure collides with air with lower pressure. Moisture is forced upward. As the "old" air is pushed upward, "new" air continues to swirl into the area of evaporation, creating a constant cycle of air pressure.

Stage 3: Cloud Formation

8   As the warm, moist air rises, it cools. The water in the air then begins to form clouds. The clouds shift with the movement of the air above the surface. As the system spins and builds, the clouds begin to spin and build, as well. The storm system grows, gaining more and more power as warm air and moisture are forced upward from the surface of the ocean.

Stage 4: Wind Rotation

9   The combination of strong winds and evaporation causes the air to spiral. The air begins to spin faster, resulting in the development of an **eye** in the center of the growing storm. Inside the eye, the air pressure is very low. Conditions are calm and clear. Outwardly, however, the storm becomes ever more powerful, as higher air pressure rotates around and into the eye of the storm.

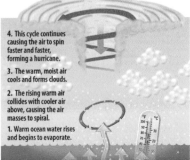

4. This cycle continues causing the air to spin faster and faster, forming a hurricane.

3. The warm, moist air cools and forms clouds.

2. The rising warm air collides with cooler air above, causing the air masses to spiral.

1. Warm ocean water rises and begins to evaporate.

CITE EVIDENCE

C   On this page, the author clearly details a sequential structure. Put an asterisk by each step in the sequence.

D   In paragraph 7, the author notes the importance of "a constant cycle of air pressure." Double underline the cause of this cycle.

E   In paragraph 9, double underline two sentences that show a causal relationship. How do a sequential structure and a causal structure work together in this part of the text?

Comprehension Check

How does the illustration of the steps in the development of a hurricane contribute to your understanding of the text?

Guided Instruction

CITE EVIDENCE

C Remind students that they are looking for a step-by-step description. Guide them to identify the various stages of hurricane formation as a sequential explanation.

D Help students identify key words in causal relationships: *as, therefore, consequently, resulting.* Have students look for phrases that include these words. This should help them identify the last sentence in paragraph 7 as illustrating a causal relationship.

E Remind students to look for the key words and phrases that indicate causality. In paragraph 9, guide students to the key word *resulting* and the corresponding cause and effect.

Comprehension Check

Sample Answer: The illustration shows, visually, the complicated steps described in the article. It helps the reader picture the sequence occurring, rather than just reading about it.

Answer Explanation: Students should consider how the illustration reinforces the information being presented in the text.

Review: Analyzing Word Meanings

Paragraph 3 illustrates the consistent use of technical language found in the text. Have students identify some of the technical terms they find in the paragraph, and then define those terms, based on context. Technical terms chosen should include: *atmospheric, environmental, oceanic, evaporation.*

Support English Language Learners

An important factor in identifying sequential and causal relationships is an understanding of the grammatical structures that help indicate these relationships. This can be difficult for English language learners, who may still be struggling with decoding these structures. Help English language learners by isolating these structures in separate instruction. Have students create written "cue cards" illustrating these structures. On one card, have students draw examples of the different ways sequential information can be presented: numbered, bulleted, offset, and inline with other text. On another card, have students write some of the key words that help cue causality, and then include an example sentence using each.

Guided Instruction

CITE EVIDENCE

A Explain to students that information presented using a comparative structure makes a comparison between one object and another. Guide students to look at the inset box under paragraph 12. In this box, hurricane categories are explained based on the wind speeds and storm surges of each. The increasing degrees of hurricane power are indicated based on how they compare with other categories.

B Inform students that subheadings are an important part of a technical text. They tell the reader what will be discussed in the next section. In this way, the reader is able to prepare for the types of technical language that will be used, and to create context for unfamiliar words. Help students identify the subhead "Hurricane Classification."

ANALYZING TEXT STRUCTURE

Guided Instruction

Hurricanes Earth's Most Violent Storms *continued*

WORDS TO KNOW

apprised

classified

infrared

storm surge

CITE EVIDENCE

A Information that has a **comparative structure** shows how details are similar to or different from each other. Put a box around the block of information on this page that focuses on technical differences among hurricanes.

B Throughout this technical text, the author has provided clear direction as to how each subsection will be organized. Circle the two lines of text that help readers recognize the structure of this page.

The Stages of Hurricane Development (continued)

Stage 5: Dissipation

10   As the hurricane reaches land, it begins to weaken. Without the evaporation cycles of the ocean waters, hurricanes lose the conditions needed to build force, and the system dissipates. However, it is often days before the hurricane completely dies out. It will typically move farther inland, leaving extensive rain and wind damage in its wake.

Hurricane Classification

11   The intensity and strength of the storm determines its official title. As the winds spiral, reaching speeds of up to 38 miles per hour (mph), the storm is officially **classified** as a "tropical depression." When the strength of the winds in the storm reaches 39 mph, the storm is called a "tropical storm." Once the winds hit 74 mph, the tropical storm officially becomes a hurricane. Scientists refer to all hurricane-like events as "tropical cyclones." This term includes hurricanes, typhoons, and cyclones.

12   Scientists also classify hurricanes according to their size and strength. The storm classification also indicates how much damage the storm can be expected to cause once it reaches land. This damage is assessed according to the height of the **storm surge**—that is, the rise of the ocean water onto the shoreline. The classifications are as follows:

- Category 1: wind speeds of 74–95 mph; storm surge heights of 4–5 feet
- Category 2: wind speeds of 96–110 mph; storm surges of 6–8 feet
- Category 3: wind speeds of 111–130 mph; storm surges of 9–12 feet
- Category 4: wind speeds of 131–155 mph; storm surges of 13–18 feet
- Category 5: wind speeds greater than 155 mph; storm surges greater than 19 feet in height

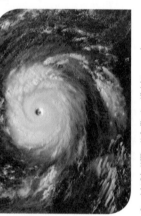

Words to Know

General Academic Vocabulary

apprised (*v.*): informed

classified (*v.*): placed in a group or category

Domain-Specific Vocabulary

infrared (*adj.*): heat-sensing

storm surge (*n.*): flood of ocean water onto land during a hurricane

Working with Word Meaning Have students restate the vocabulary words in their own terms and then write a sentence using each.

CRAFT AND STRUCTURE

13   Although Category 4 and 5 hurricanes are comparatively rare, they cause considerable destruction whenever they reach land. <u>Hurricane Katrina</u>, a <u>Category 4</u> hurricane, hit the Gulf Coast of the United States in 2005, leaving behind it communities shattered by its sheer force. Katrina reached <u>400 miles across</u> and hit <u>wind speeds of more than 125 mph</u>. <u>Storm surges from Katrina reached 14 feet high in some coastal areas and more than 28 feet high in New Orleans, Louisiana</u>. More than 1,800 people died, either during the storm or as neighborhoods attempted to recover in the weeks following Katrina's arrival. It is estimated that Katrina caused some $81 billion in property damage.

Studying Hurricanes

14   In an effort to better understand and predict the movements of hurricanes, scientists study the creation, life cycle, and intensity of the storms. Meteorologists, or scientists who study atmospheric processes, use satellite technology to gather remote data on hurricanes. Additionally, scientists look at surface data gathered by specially equipped aircraft. Weather centers track and monitor hurricanes and other extreme weather events in order to keep the public **apprised** of developing concerns.

15   One of the most important methods of gathering data on hurricanes is through the use of weather satellites. These satellites track the movements of hurricanes, as well as atmospheric changes that occur within the storms. The satellites monitor cloud movements and air circulation patterns. They also track the rainfall, air speed, and precipitation generated by the storm. Typically, weather satellites are equipped with **infrared** sensors. These sensors allow meteorologists to monitor temperatures in the hurricane. Within the last 15 years, scientists have been able to use these data to identify important patterns in hurricane intensity and relative humidity.

CITE EVIDENCE

C In paragraph 13, the author adds more specific details to the comparison of wind speeds and storm surges than in the previous paragraph. Underline the details that further illustrate this comparison.

D In paragraphs 14 and 15, the author changes the structure of the text. Circle the text that specifies you are reading a new section of the piece. What purpose do these two paragraphs serve in the overall structure of the text?

Comprehension Check

So far, how has the structure of the text helped you understand the topic of hurricanes?

CITE EVIDENCE

C Have students reread paragraph 13, looking specifically for facts that relate to the categorization of hurricanes. Help them look for any references to hurricane size, wind speed, and the effects of storm surges that will help the reader better understand hurricane classification.

D Guide students to look for the subheading that delineates the next section of the text. Sample answer: *Paragraphs 14 and 15 serve as an introduction to the next main section of the piece. They are a break from the sequential steps outlined throughout the rest of the article.*

Comprehension Check

Sample Answer: The text is structured sequentially, comparatively, and causally, presenting the steps in hurricane development and the causes of each step, and a comparison between the categories of hurricanes. This helps better illustrate the overall process.

Answer Explanation: Students should be able to articulate how the text is organized—sequentially, comparatively, and causally. They should explain that these types of organization help the reader better comprehend the technical information being presented in the text.

Differentiate Instruction

Help struggling students better understand text structures and relationships by creating an illustrated chart of each type. Across the top, have students write the words *Structure*, *Definition*, and *Example*. Under the heading *Structure*, students should indicate each of the structures illustrated in the text (comparative, sequential, and causal). Under *Definition*, students should give a definition of the structure, in their own words. Under *Example*, students should write or draw a familiar example of the type of structure. For instance, under *Sequential*, a student could write down the correct order of steps to make a sandwich. This will help activate the students' prior knowledge when deciphering structures in a text.

Guided Practice

Recap Reading Selection

Ask students to recall some of the different ways they have seen the text structured so far, as well as some of the facts they have learned about how hurricanes form. Tell students that they will be reading about relative humidity in the next section.

Read and Practice

Have partners take turns reading the selection as you circulate to provide support. Circulate among students and ask them to respond to Cite Evidence callouts A and B. Provide additional scaffolding as needed, using the suggestions below.

CITE EVIDENCE

A Have students meet with a partner to reread and discuss the structure of paragraphs 16–19. They should look, specifically, at the function of subheadings and titles in the portion of the text.

B Students should work with a partner to identify the sentence that introduces the step-by-step procedure on this page. Partners should then discuss how they would complete the experiment and why the author may have included it in the text.

Hurricanes *Earth's Most Violent Storms continued*

WORDS TO KNOW
bulb
condensation
hygrometer
relative humidity
saturation

CITE EVIDENCE

A This page is organized with one main heading, one subheading, and one title. Identify and underline each of these items.

B Circle the sentence that introduces the step-by-step procedure on this page. Discuss with a partner how you would complete the experiment and why the author included the experiment in the text.

Relative Humidity

16   The term **relative humidity** refers to the amount of water that is actually in the air. The rate of evaporation of water into the atmosphere is not consistent. As evaporation speeds up or slows down, the percentage of water in the air changes. This percentage is called relative humidity.

17   When meteorologists calculate relative humidity, they look at the rate of evaporation in the atmosphere. They then compare this rate of evaporation to the maximum, or **saturation**, rate for the existing temperature. They make this calculation using a special device called a **hygrometer**. When the relative humidity is at 100%, the air is full of water. As more water evaporates, an equal amount of water condenses, or collects. You can see evidence of **condensation** in the presence of clouds and fog.

18   Conversely, a lower percentage of relative humidity indicates that water is evaporating more quickly than it is condensing. Desert climates experience very low percentages of relative humidity and very high speeds of evaporation.

19   **Learn About Relative Humidity** Relative humidity can be better understood through a simple, at-home experiment:

Temperature and Relative Humidity

Materials Needed:
- two household thermometers
- paper towels or pieces of cloth
- water at room temperature
- paper and pen for recording results

Procedures

a. Place one of the thermometers on the work surface. This is the dry **bulb** thermometer.

b. Thoroughly wet the piece of cloth or paper towel in the water.

c. Wrap the wet cloth around the bulb end of the other thermometer. This is the wet bulb thermometer.

d. Place the wet bulb thermometer near the dry bulb thermometer.

e. Record the temperatures indicated on each thermometer.

f. Wait 5 minutes.

Words to Know

General Academic Vocabulary

bulb (*n.*): a rounded part, especially at the end of a cylinder

Domain-Specific Vocabulary

condensation (*n.*): process in which water collects into clouds or fog

hygrometer (*n.*): instrument that measures humidity

relative humidity (*n.*): a measure of the amount of moisture in the air, based on moisture possible at a given temperature

saturation (*n.*): the state of being as full of liquid as possible

Working with Word Meaning Have students write the Words to Know and their definitions on individual index cards or separate sheets of paper. Then have students sort the words into categories, such as *Weather Instruments* and *Hurricane Development*.

CRAFT AND STRUCTURE
Guided Practice

g. Record the temperature on each thermometer again.

h. Continue to record the temperatures in 5-minute intervals. Do this for a total of 20 minutes or until the wet bulb temperature holds steady.

Comprehension Check

1. Which organizational structure has appeared in this article so far?

a. comparative

b. sequential

c. causal

d. all of the above

2. What is the author's purpose in including the subsection "Learn About Relative Humidity"?

a. to encourage young readers to pursue a career in meteorology

b. to provide a hands-on representation of a scientific concept

c. to demonstrate advanced scientific theories through experimentation

d. to indicate a change in the overall structure of the text

3. What is the purpose of the illustration on page 180?

a. to show what the experiment should look like when performed correctly

b. to reveal to readers the results of the experiment

c. to emphasize that many tools that meteorologists use are quite simple

d. none of the above

4. The experiment on pages 180–181 has a structure that is primarily

a. comparative.

b. sequential.

c. causal.

d. all of the above

5. Suppose you did not perform the experiment on these pages. Would merely reading about the experiments be as effective as conducting the experiments yourself? What do the experiments contribute to the text? Compare answers with a partner and explain your thoughts.

Sample answer: It would be effective just to read about the experiment.

The experiment is simple and easy to visualize, and there is a clear connection

between it and the concept of relative humidity. It contributes to

understanding the text as a whole.

Guided Practice

Comprehension Check

Answer Explanations:

1. Students should recall that all three types of structures have appeared in the text, making choice D the best answer.

2. Students should have discussed, with a partner, the author's purpose in including an experiment in the text. Based on this discussion, students should note that the best answer is choice B.

3. Students should note that the illustration shows how the experiment looks when completed, leading to choice A as the best answer.

4. The experiment is presented as a step-by-step process, making choice B the correct answer.

5. Answers may vary. Students should present reasons for why it is, or is not, effective to read about the experiment rather than actually following it.

Turn and Talk

Read aloud Comprehension Check question 5 on page 181. Then have students immediately turn to the person on their right to discuss it. Tell students to work together to come up with an answer. Invite volunteers to share their answers with the class.

Discussion Skills

Place students in groups to discuss the uses of each type of text structure presented in the lesson. Have students think about which type of text lends itself best to each type of structure, and what kinds of writing would not pair well with a specific structure. Have students divide up roles in the group, including Facilitator, Timekeeper, Recorder, and Presenter. Remind students to ask questions and brainstorm ideas, keeping the discussion going throughout. At the end of the discussion, have students share their ideas with the class.

Analyzing Text Structure

Independent Practice

Recap Reading Selection

Have students discuss how subheadings can help readers better understand the ideas presented in an informative text. Then ask them to summarize what they have learned about relative humidity. Let students know that they will be reading about the relationship between relative humidity and hurricane formation.

Read and Apply

Have students read this section independently as you circulate. Ask them to read aloud so you can see if they are reading fluently. You can also use the support below to help students who are having difficulty.

CITE EVIDENCE

A Students should use their understanding of text structure to circle the subheading above paragraph 22.

B Students should look for text that indicates a causal relationship. Sample answer: *The final two paragraphs serve as the summary for the whole article.*

WORDS TO KNOW

awe

propulsion

theorized

ventured

CITE EVIDENCE

A Paragraphs 22 and 23 relate to the relative humidity experiment. Circle the text that indicates this relationship.

B Double underline a causal relationship in paragraph 24. What purpose do paragraphs 24 and 25 serve in the overall structure of this text?

Interpreting the Data

20   Look at the differences between the temperatures recorded for the wet bulb thermometer and the dry bulb thermometer. A large difference between the temperatures means that evaporation is occurring quickly. Consequently, the relative humidity in the air is low.

21   A small difference between the temperatures means that the water around the wet bulb is not evaporating quickly. The air is already heavy with moisture. Any new water attempting to enter the atmosphere must become condensation. The percentage of relative humidity is high.

Hurricanes and Relative Humidity

22   Since hurricanes develop through the evaporation of warm moisture into the air, scientists have **theorized** that hurricane intensity may be related to relative humidity. In 2012, scientists from NASA's Jet **Propulsion** Laboratory in Pasadena, California, published the results of an eight-year study. The study analyzed the relationship between hurricane intensity and relative humidity.

23   After studying data gathered between 2002 and 2010, scientists determined that hurricanes that intensify quickly exist in environments with higher levels of relative humidity. In contrast, hurricanes that were weakening did so in environments with lower levels of relative humidity. These data represent one of the first times scientists have **ventured** to study the intensity of hurricane systems rather than just the storms' development and life cycle.

24   Hurricanes present one of the most awesome displays of nature's fury on Earth. From their initial stages of development, through their slow movement across the ocean, <u>they are studied by scientists so that we might have a better understanding of these amazing storms.</u>

15°C   10°C   5°C

25% Relative humidity   50% Relative humidity   100% Relative humidity

---

Words to Know

General Academic Vocabulary

awe (*n.*): a strong feeling of admiration for something grand or powerful

theorized (*v.*): made an educated, informed guess or judgment

ventured (*v.*): attempted; tried

Domain-Specific Vocabulary

propulsion (*n.*): a means of pushing something forward

Working with Word Meaning Have students work with a partner to create a short, one-paragraph narrative using these Words to Know.

CRAFT AND STRUCTURE
Independent Practice

25   The better we understand hurricanes, the more we can predict their behaviors and, therefore, provide sufficient warning to those in their path. With continued study and greater understanding, perhaps someday we can find ways to avoid the destruction of a hurricane without lessening our **awe** of its power.

Comprehension Check

MORE ONLINE sadlierconnect.com

1. Overall, how is the information in this technical text presented?

   a. sequentially

   b. comparatively

   c. causally

   d. none of the above

2. What is the author's purpose for summarizing the experiment in paragraphs 20 and 21?

   a. to encourage readers to complete the experiment

   b. to relate the results of the experiment to the overall topic of the article

   c. to present theories that could be explored through an additional experiment

   d. to give an opinion about ideas related to the experiment

3. Throughout the text, the author indicates changes in topic through the use of

   a. large section headings.

   b. subsection headings.

   c. titles for special elements.

   d. all of the above

4. What is the main purpose of the diagrams and photographs included in the text?

   a. to keep readers interested in the subject matter

   b. to provide visual support for the concepts being discussed

   c. to introduce readers to new and unfamiliar ideas

   d. to change the structure of the text

5. How did the overall structure of this text contribute to your understanding of the material? Cite evidence to support your answer.

Sample answer: The author structured the text so that the organization was clear from start to finish. Overall, the information was presented sequentially, although there were instances of comparative analysis (as in the hurricane categories) and causal relationships (as in the stages of hurricane development). The use of a step-by-step procedure (the experiment) to explain a concept helped me understand the material, too.

Unit 7 ■ Reading Informational Text: Craft and Structure   **183**

Extend Thinking: Investigate

Have students discuss the conditions that led up to the disasters surrounding Hurricane Katrina, and the continuing consequences still seen in the Gulf Coast region. Have students work in small groups to discuss the challenges faced by Americans living in the Gulf Coast region during Hurricane Katrina, and how unexpected events contributed to the catastrophe. Allow students to refer to the National Oceanic and Atmospheric Administration Web site for further information.

At the end of the discussion, have each group summarize their conclusions in a short presentation to the rest of the class.

Independent Practice

Comprehension Check

Answer Explanations:

1. Although all three types of structures are used, students should note that choice A, *sequentially*, is used far more often than the others.

2. Choice B provides the only explanation that describes how the structures of the text relate to the information.

3. The author uses all of the elements given as options, so choice D is correct.

4. Throughout the text, students have discussed the purpose of illustrations and diagrams to support the text. Choice B is the best answer.

5. Students should note that the text is structured to allow for easy comprehension of the topics. Students should mention that most of the text is structured sequentially, but includes instances of comparative and causal analysis, as well.

Critical Comprehension

Challenge students to think more deeply about the text and to support their answers with evidence from the text.

Ask students: *Why do you think it is important for scientists to understand more about the nature of hurricanes?* (Answers will vary, but should include ideas about the need for people to be able to better predict when hurricanes will occur, and what effect they will have.)

Assess and Respond

If students have trouble answering the questions in the Comprehension Check,

Then lead them to look for instances of comparative, causal, and sequential structures, as well as large subheadings that describe the information in the text.

Guided Instruction

OBJECTIVE
Analyze how an author expresses his or her point of view in an informational text.

Genre: Scientific Text

A scientific text provides information and facts based on scientific research and experimentation. Scientific text presents fact-based information. However the author's bias may be present.

Set the Purpose

Lead students in a discussion of how an author's point of view can affect his or her handling of a subject. Ask: *How can an author's point of view affect the way the author writes about certain subjects?* Ask students to provide examples.

Model and Teach

Read the selection and callouts as the class follows along. Model effective strategies for responding to the callouts by using the suggestions below.

CITE EVIDENCE

A Explain to students that author bias and opinion is often present in informative texts. Tell students that authors typically use facts to provide evidence for their opinions. Have students look for facts that back up the author's position in paragraph 1.

B Read paragraph 2 with students. Have them identify which sentence sounds more like opinion than fact. Have students put an asterisk next to that sentence in the text.

ANALYZING POINTS OF VIEW

Guided Instruction

WORDS TO KNOW
- aqueous
- contiguous
- ecosystem
- estuary
- watershed

> Some scientific texts include statements of the author's **point of view**, or **position**, regarding the topic. Critical readers must determine whether a given statement is a **fact**, an **opinion**, or a **reasoned judgment**.

CITE EVIDENCE

A Authors use **facts**—details that can be proven—to support their personal **points of view,** or **positions**. Underline two facts in paragraph 1 that support this author's point of view.

B Authors who want to express an **opinion**—a statement that can be supported but with which people can disagree—often do so early in a text. Put an asterisk next to the sentence in paragraph 2 that expresses this author's opinion about what people should think.

Our Fragile Ecosystem
The Importance of Preserving the Wetlands
(Genre: Scientific Text)

1   It is estimated that before the coming of European colonists in the 1600s, more than 220 million acres in what is now the United States were wetlands. Since then, it has <u>lost over 50% of</u> these wetlands. In 2009, there were <u>only 110 million acres of</u> wetlands in the **contiguous** United States (the lower 48 states).

2   An area of 110 million acres may seem like a great deal of space devoted to wetlands. However, quite the opposite is true. Consider how your life would change if you were to lose 53% of the space in your house, or if you had to sleep on only 53% of your bed every night. The way you now live would be vastly altered, and not for the better. In the same way, the widespread destruction of the wetlands in the United States is, even now, having painful effects on our environment. If we do not continue to work toward preservation, those effects will worsen with time. The wetlands represent a unique and important element in Earth's ecosystems.* If we want to maintain the delicate balance that exists among natural areas, then preservation of the wetlands should be at the top of our environmental priorities.

What Is a Wetland?

3   The definition of a wetland environment would appear to be quite simple: an **ecosystem** that is neither dry land, nor water, but a combination of both. However, the political battle

---

Words to Know

General Academic Vocabulary

aqueous (*adj.*): of water, or containing water; watery
contiguous (*adj.*): next to one another; touching

Domain-Specific Vocabulary

ecosystem (*n.*): the system of animals, plants, and other organisms that interact in an environment
estuary (*n.*): area where a river meets the sea
watershed (*n.*): the network of streams and rivers that flow into a lake or ocean

Working with Word Meaning Have students work with a partner to play a game using the Words to Know: one student draws a representation of the word and the other guesses the word.

CRAFT AND STRUCTURE

12 surrounding the preservation of the wetlands has blurred the meaning. To date, more than 50 different definitions have been assigned to the wetland ecosystems in the United States.

4 A widely accepted definition comes from the United States Army Corps of Engineers. This group is responsible for maintaining the provisions of the Clean Water Act that apply to the wetlands. The Corps definition states, "Wetlands are inundated or saturated by surface or groundwater at a frequency and duration sufficient to support . . . a prevalence of vegetation typically adapted for life in saturated soil conditions." In simpler terms, a wetland is an ecosystem that balances both **aqueous** and dry conditions. This balance results in plant and animal life that is specifically adapted for the unique wetland environment.

5 Wetlands are located in almost every one of the lower 48 states. California and Kentucky, however, have seen a much greater decrease in their wetland areas. Both of those states now have less than 20% of their original wetland regions. Similarly, the Florida Everglades, the largest wetland environment in the world, has lost more than 60% of its functional area.

6 It is estimated that the United States continues to lose between 70,000 and 90,000 acres of wetlands every year. As more people settle in coastal areas, the increased need for development threatens natural resources. We move nearer to unique environments because we want to be a part of the natural phenomena that produce such beauty. However, if we are not careful, we may forget to preserve the very thing we love.

Types of Wetlands

Coastal Wetlands

7 There are two main types of wetlands: coastal and inland. Coastal wetlands are located on the eastern and western coasts of the United States. They include both saltwater and freshwater **estuaries** that are located along a coastal **watershed**. About 40% of the wetlands in the United States are coastal wetlands, and 81% of those are located in the southeastern United States.

Comprehension Check

In this scientific text, what point of view does the author express? Why does the author take this position?

Guided Instruction

CITE EVIDENCE

C Authors use statements of fact in an argument meant to show a **reasoned judgment**—a carefully thought-out position about the topic. Circle two such statements of fact in paragraph 5.

D Authors may attempt to show that they are making a reasoned judgment by presenting facts and opinions together. In paragraph 6, underline the two statements of fact. Then put a box around the opinion that is based upon these facts.

Guided Instruction

CITE EVIDENCE

C Explain to students that authors present reasoned judgments when they detail facts that can be used as evidence for a position statement. Guide students to the two fact statements located at the end of paragraph 5.

D Help students understand that one way authors present convincing positions is by combining fact and opinion. Help students identify each in paragraph 6.

Comprehension Check

Sample Answer: In this text, the author is expressing the opinion that the wetlands are vital components of Earth's ecosystem that are being destroyed. The author believes that we must actively work to preserve the wetlands.

Answer Explanation: Students should be able to distinguish the author's position within the text. Students should note that the author believes the wetlands are important, and that they are in dire need of preservation.

Support English Language Learners

English language learners may benefit from a more hands-on approach to delineating fact from opinion in this selection. Create a large chart with the words *Fact* and *Opinion* written across the top. On small cards, write various statements from the texts that are clearly indicative of either fact or opinion. (Attach tape to the back of the card, or use self-adhesive notes.) Read the statement aloud. Then have students place the card with the statement under the correct heading on the chart. Talk about why the statement is either fact or opinion and what kinds of features help distinguish one from the other.

Guided Practice

Recap Reading Selection

Remind students that they have read about the destruction of the wetlands and their importance in the ecosystem. Have them recall the way the author intersperses opinion with fact. Tell them that they will be reading about what is currently being done in order to preserve the wetlands.

Read and Practice

Have partners take turns reading the selection as you circulate to provide support. Ask students to respond to Cite Evidence callouts A and B. Provide additional scaffolding as needed, using the suggestions below.

CITE EVIDENCE

A Have students work with partners to identify the opinion statement in paragraph 16.

B Have students work with a partner and read paragraph 17 aloud. As one partner reads, the other should be following and listening for the names of government agencies involved in wetland preservation efforts. Students should then discuss why the author includes the names of these government agencies, and what effect their inclusion has on the reader's opinions.

ANALYZING POINTS OF VIEW

Guided Practice

Our Fragile Ecosystem The Importance of Preserving the Wetlands *continued*

WORDS TO KNOW

depleted
equilibrium
mandated
viable
wholesale

CITE EVIDENCE

A Underline the sentence in paragraph 16 that is not a statement of fact.

B Put an asterisk next to the names of the two federal agencies the author includes to show a reasoned judgment. Discuss with a partner the effect of the inclusion of these agencies on your opinion of the topic.

Current Efforts in Preservation

16   From the 1950s until the 1970s, the United States experienced record losses in wetland acreage. During that period, the United States lost, on average, 458,000 acres of **viable** wetland each year. The realization that the country could be headed for the **wholesale** elimination of an entire ecosystem led to increased efforts to protect and preserve our country's wetlands. And those efforts have had some success. By 2009, wetland loss had gone from 458,000 acres each year to approximately 14,000 acres each year. While these numbers represent significant improvement, more should be done, for the wetlands are still being **depleted**.

17   Currently, the *Environmental Protection Agency (EPA) and the *Army Corps of Engineers are leading federal efforts to preserve this valuable environment. In 1948, an early version of what came to be known as the Clean Water Act was passed. It **mandated** that the federal government enact procedures dedicated to preserving and maintaining our nation's water resources. Today, the EPA and the Army Corps of Engineers work together to ensure that **equilibrium** in the wetlands is maintained. In addition, both groups focus on balancing the desires of commercial interests against the still-diminishing wetlands.

18   State and local governments also play a significant role in helping to preserve the wetlands. In order to assist local governments in this mission, the EPA awards Wetland Program Development Grants to local community groups dedicated to the preservation of wetlands. The EPA's Five Star Restoration Challenge Grant Program provides funding to groups looking to restore already damaged wetland ecosystems.

19   To date, these programs have supported nearly 600 wetland preservation and restoration projects and have awarded more than $30 million in funds for wetland improvement. In total, almost 9,000 acres of wetland have been restored or improved through these federal grant programs.

Words to Know

General Academic Vocabulary

depleted (*v.*): used up
equilibrium (*n.*): a state of balance
mandated (*v.*): stated as a law or rule
viable (*adj.*): able to live or grow correctly
wholesale (*adj.*): extensive

Working with Word Meaning Have students work in small groups to play a game of vocabulary charades. One student should act out a word from the list, chosen at random, while the others try to guess which word is being presented. Continue until each student has had a turn to act.

CRAFT AND STRUCTURE
Guided Practice

Comprehension Check

1. Which of the following techniques helps support the author's point of view?

   a. loaded language

   b. inclusion of helpful details

   c. use of reasoned judgment

   d. all of the above

2. The author's position is supported by a text structure in which

   a. only statements of opinion are included.

   b. only statements of fact are included.

   c. facts and opinions are both presented.

   d. opposing opinions are presented.

3. In paragraph 16, the phrase *the wholesale elimination of an entire ecosystem* is best described as an example of

   a. avoidance.

   b. inclusion.

   c. loaded language.

   d. reasoned judgment.

4. What is the best explanation of the purpose for paragraphs 17–19?

   a. They show readers that the problem of wetland preservation is now under control.

   b. They inform readers that some help for the problem has come from the government.

   c. They help readers understand that the problem is best handled by the government.

   d. They encourage readers to apply for federal grants and solve the problem themselves.

5. Work with a partner to list some facts or questions that the author may have avoided in order to keep the focus on his or her point of view.

   Sample answer: The author may have avoided including a discussion of the circumstances that led to the depletion of the wetlands, acknowledging sources to back up the figures listed in the text, and mentioning any other opinions regarding the issue.

Unit 7 ■ Reading Informational Text: Craft and Structure **189**

Guided Practice

Comprehension Check

Answer Explanations:

1. Students have already identified examples of all three types of techniques in the text, making choice D the best answer.

2. Students should be aware that the author uses both fact and opinion in the text, making choice C the correct answer.

3. The words *wholesale elimination* would trigger an emotional response in the reader. Therefore, choice C is the correct answer.

4. Paragraphs 17–19 provide the reader with information about government efforts in wetlands preservation, making choice B the correct answer.

5. Although the author includes a great number of facts about the state of the wetlands, he or she does not provide any information about opposing viewpoints regarding the cause and solutions. By leaving out these facts, the author acknowledges and reinforces only one opinion on the subject.

Peer Collaboration

Have students do a Think-Pair-Share to discuss the answer to Comprehension Check question 5. Students should write their own answer to the question and then share it with a partner. Partners should discuss their answers and then make any changes based on their partner's feedback. Ask volunteers to share their answers with the class.

Discussion Skills

Have students meet in small groups to discuss this question: *Do you agree with the author that the preservation of the wetlands is vital to maintaining Earth's ecosystem?* Encourage students to quote from the text, or to note opposing viewpoints, in support of their answers. Suggest the following sentence stems for students to use in their discussion.

- *The author's statement about _____ supports my opinion that _____.*
- *I agree with the author's opinion that _____, based on _____.*
- *I disagree with the author's opinion that _____, based on _____.*

Independent Practice

Recap Reading Selection

Remind students that they have been reading about the preservation of the wetlands. Have students summarize the information they read in the last section. Tell students that they will be reading about ways private citizens can help with preservation efforts.

Read and Apply

Have students read this section independently as you circulate. Ask them to read aloud so you can see if they are reading fluently. You can also use the support below to help students who are having difficulty.

CITE EVIDENCE

A Students should identify the bullet points that create offset text, highlighting the information for the reader.

B Students should look for words that elicit an emotional response and sway the reader to the author's position.

ANALYZING POINTS OF VIEW

Independent Practice

Our Fragile Ecosystem The Importance of Preserving the Wetlands *continued*

WORDS TO KNOW

contaminant

invaluable

native

urban sprawl

CITE EVIDENCE

A Put a box around the change in organizational structure on this page.

B Circle examples of loaded language in paragraph 21. What does this language tell you about the author's point of view?

20   However, it will take more than just federal monies to help preserve the integrity of the country's inland and coastal wetlands. Private citizens must also work to protect these **invaluable** resources. Individuals can help by taking some of the following actions:

- Plant **native** vegetation in order to avoid introducing any potentially harmful species of plant into the environment.
- Avoid using fertilizer and pesticides in personal gardening and landscaping. Work to avoid adding chemical **contaminants** to the water supply.
- Volunteer with a local conservation group to help preserve a wetland, stream, or other body of water.
- Work with a community group to help restore a local endangered wetland. Look into getting funding through the federal programs already mentioned, as well as state and local agencies.
- Find out if your local government sponsors an adopt-a-wetland program, and then get involved!

21   The wetlands are one of our most important ecosystems. They house essential elements of the environment that cannot be found elsewhere. They serve to protect and preserve other natural surroundings through flood control and filtering. They provide necessary lifelines for hundreds of unique and vital plant and animal species. And they play important roles in commercial industries worldwide.

Words to Know

General Academic Vocabulary

invaluable (*adj.*): extremely valuable; beyond price

native (*adj.*): from the area; local

Domain-Specific Vocabulary

contaminant (*n.*): pollutant

urban sprawl (*n.*): the uncontrolled spread of cities and development into country areas

Working with Word Meaning Have students replace each of the Words to Know in the text with a synonym and/or antonym. Have partners discuss how the substitutions change the meaning of the text.

CRAFT AND STRUCTURE

22   As a country, we cannot afford to lose such a critical resource. Since the European settlement of the United States in the 1600s, the wetlands have been a target for the negative consequences of **urban sprawl**, leading to the elimination of over a hundred million acres. We cannot let this happen again.

Comprehension Check   MORE ONLINE **sadlierconnect.com**

1. In what way does paragraph 20 present a contrast to paragraphs 17–19?

    a. It suggests that the government has secret reasons for not doing more for the environment.

    b. It reveals ways in which the Clean Water Act has failed to solve the problem.

    c. It encourages readers not to think that only the government can solve the problem.

    d. none of the above

2. For what main purpose does the author include a bulleted list in paragraph 20?

    a. to show readers that they, too, can help solve the wetlands problem

    b. to show readers that there are other opinions on the central issue

    c. to remind readers that many wetlands remain threatened or endangered

    d. to blame readers for not helping solve the problem in the past

3. Which statement best represents the author's overall point of view on the preservation of the wetlands?

    a. There are enough wetland ecosystems to support future generations.

    b. The wetlands are an essential ecosystem that must be preserved.

    c. The wetlands have been in danger for so long that they cannot be saved.

    d. Private citizens must rely on government entities to preserve wetlands.

4. Which statement best describes the purpose of paragraph 21?

    a. It condemns industry for polluting wetlands.

    b. It challenges readers to get involved in wetland preservation.

    c. It repeats information from the author's introduction.

    d. It summarizes the reasons that wetlands are valuable.

5. Is the use of loaded language appropriate for a scientific text? Defend your position.

Sample answer: It depends on the author's purpose for the scientific text.
In this case, the author's purpose is to persuade readers of the need to do more
to preserve American wetlands. The author presents facts to support that
point of view but also uses some loaded words to express the seriousness
of the problem and his or her strong desire to see the problem solved.

Unit 7 ■ Reading Informational Text: Craft and Structure   **191**

Comprehension Check

Answer Explanations:

1. Paragraphs 17–19 present information about government preservation efforts, whereas paragraph 20 discusses private efforts. Choice C is the only answer that indicates this.

2. The author offsets the text in order to affirm a point with the reader—to show readers that they, too, can help solve the wetlands problem. Choice A is the best answer.

3. After reading the text, students should see that choice B best describes the author's position in the selection.

4. Paragraph 21 summarizes the author's position. Consequently, choice D is the correct answer.

5. Loaded language can be used appropriately in a scientific text when it is used to persuade the reader regarding the importance of a position based on the facts and evidence presented in the text.

Critical Comprehension

Challenge students to think more deeply about the text and to support their answers with evidence from the text.

Ask students: *Has your reading of the text caused you to either develop an opinion, or change your opinion about the preservation of the wetlands? Why or why not?* (Answers will vary, but should include references to the persuasive techniques employed by the author.)

Assess and Respond

If students have trouble answering question 5 of the Comprehension Check,

Then have them go back and find examples of loaded language in the selection, thinking about whether or not the language fits in with the overall text.

Speaking and Listening Presentation

Have students prepare a presentation about a current ecological concern or event of natural significance. Have students plan by creating a timeline with clear goals for completing their presentation. Presenters should include facts and details about their subject, using multimedia or visual elements as support; adapt their language for a formal presentation; speak clearly; and maintain eye contact with their listeners. At the end of the presentation, presenters should answer questions and acknowledge listeners' ideas. Listeners should listen attentively and ask questions. Elicit responses from students of different cultural backgrounds.

CLOSE READING

OBJECTIVES

- Determine the meanings of words and phrases in a text, and analyze how word choice impacts tone.
- Analyze the way in which an author chooses to organize a text.
- Analyze how an author expresses his or her point of view in an informational text.

Genre: Technical Text

Remind students that a technical text is one in which the author uses technical language to present information about a subject, while avoiding use of informal or conversational language.

Path Options

You may want to do a close reading with students; if so, use the supports provided on these pages. Or, you may wish to have students read the text independently and apply the skills learned in this unit. In either case, students should read the text more than once to facilitate understanding and to be able to answer the Comprehension Questions correctly.

Satellites
Bridging the Gap from Earth to Sky
(Genre: Technical Text)

1 In 1957, the Soviet government (the government that ruled Russia and several other countries in Asia and Eastern Europe at that time) launched *Sputnik I*, the first satellite to orbit Earth. Although the Soviet government kept the launch under tight secrecy, we now know that *Sputnik I* was a metal sphere, 23 inches around and 184 pounds in weight. Onboard, the satellite carried a thermometer, a battery, a radio transmitter, and nitrogen gas. The satellite orbited for 92 days, until it was pulled into Earth's gravity and destroyed upon reentry.

2 The Soviet accomplishment was incredible, and the launch of *Sputnik I* was the impetus for a competition with the United States for leadership in space exploration. By today's standards, however, *Sputnik I* was a highly simplistic craft, with very little utility in space. Today, satellites are a vital, if often unrecognized, presence in our daily lives. Without the presence of satellites orbiting above us, some of our common amenities—weather reports, news and information distribution, and even cable television—would cease to exist.

Anatomy of a Satellite

3 A satellite is any object that orbits, or circles, Earth or another astronomical body. The term *satellite*, however, is typically taken to mean a man-made object placed into orbit for a specific purpose. Building and launching satellites can cost anywhere from $50 million to $400 million, and they are usually custom-made devices. The exception is the series of satellites that make up the Global Positioning System. These 27 satellites are almost exact copies of each other, in order to better facilitate consistent function.

4 A typical satellite is composed of six fundamental elements:

a. Satellite Housing—the outside container of the satellite. The housing is either square or cylindrical, depending on the type of stabilizing system employed to keep the satellite in orbit. Solar cells, used to power the satellite, are mounted to the housing, as is the communications antenna.

b. Power System—solar-powered, battery-powered, or both. Satellites must maintain a constant source of electricity in order to function properly.

c. Antenna System—to provide for tracking and communications. The antenna system receives electronic signals necessary for positioning.

d. Control System—the command center of the satellite. The control system monitors all of the satellite functions and receives and transmits data signals from Earth.

e. Station Keeping—keeps the satellite in orbit. The station keeping uses thrusters to maintain the correct orbit. When the thrusters run out of fuel, the satellite stops working.

f. Transponders—help maintain strong signals between Earth and the satellite.

192   Unit 7 ■ Reading Informational Text: Craft and Structure

Support English Language Learners

Provide English language learners with an introduction to the text by having them first identify any unknown vocabulary in the text. Have students create a glossary of unknown words so that they can easily define them as they are reading. Pair English language learners with more fluent students, and have them work on creating their glossaries together. In addition to writing definitions, have students use each word in an example sentence to aid comprehension.

CRAFT AND STRUCTURE

5   The main function of a satellite is to transmit and receive signals. A signal, called an uplink, is sent from Earth's surface to the satellite. The signal frequency is called a gigahertz (GHz) range signal. The satellite transmits this signal to the appropriate receiving stations back on Earth. This type of transmission is called a downlink. Only those receiving stations within the satellite's functional area can accept and transmit the downlink.

Types of Satellites

6   Although most satellites are made of the same elements, arising from the same basic functionalities, a wide variety of satellites orbit Earth. They are classified according to their intended function, the type of orbit they maintain, and their altitude above Earth.

Satellite Function

7   Satellites maintain a variety of roles and allow for a large number of practical applications on Earth. These include the following:

- Weather satellites: aid in identifying and forecasting weather patterns
- Military satellites: used for military purposes—use is typically secret, not disclosed to the general public
- Rescue satellites: receive and transmit distress calls
- Scientific satellites: aid in scientific research (One of the best known of these is the Hubble Space Telescope.)
- Communications satellites: facilitate voice and data transmission
- Navigational satellites: pinpoint locations and guide directions (The Global Positioning System includes a series of navigational satellites.)
- Broadcast satellites: transmit television signals

- Earth observation satellites: track changes in Earth's systems

8   Besides differing in function, satellites can differ in the type of orbit they maintain in space. The orbit of a satellite is the pattern by which the satellite circles Earth. The two orbital patterns are either circular or elliptical (egg-shaped). The point on the orbital path that is closest to Earth is called the perigee; the point that is farthest away is called the apogee.

Satellite Orbit

9   There are three basic types of satellite orbits:

- Geostationary orbits: Geostationary orbits, also known as geosynchronous or synchronous orbits, are orbital patterns in which the satellite maintains a stable position above a spot on Earth's surface. In order to maintain consistent functionality, broadcast satellites follow geostationary orbits.
- Asynchronous orbits: Satellites in asynchronous orbits pass a spot on Earth's surface at different times during the day. Observation satellites usually follow asynchronous orbit patterns.
- Polar orbits: During a polar orbit, the satellite flies low in the atmosphere and passes over each pole (North and South) in the course of one revolution. Polar orbiting satellites include those used for photography and mapping.

Unit 7 ■ Reading Informational Text: Craft and Structure   **193**

Support First Reading

Circulate to check and support students' understanding. Use the following comprehension and strategy check-ins as needed.

Check-in Questions

- *What is the main function of a satellite?* (Satellites transmit and receive signals.)
- *How are satellites classified?* (Satellites are classified by function, orbit, and altitude above the Earth.)
- *What type of technology employs navigational satellites?* (Navigational satellites are used with GPS transmissions.)
- *What is the difference between geostationary and asynchronous orbits?* (Geostationary orbits are those in which the satellite maintains one position above a point on the Earth's surface. Asynchronous orbits pass a point on Earth's surface at different times during the day.)

Review: Analyzing Word Meanings

Have students practice identifying examples of technical language and defining it within the text. Tell students to work with a partner to find examples of technical text in paragraphs 5–9. Then, ask students to work together to write definitions for the types of technical language they found.

Differentiate Instruction

Help struggling readers by having them preview the text before reading. Have students scan the first two pages, looking for examples of technical text. Then have students work alone or with a partner to define the unfamiliar language. Students should reread the text to aid comprehension, replacing the unfamiliar words with more familiar terms.

Check-in Questions

- *What is the technical word that means "height above Earth's surface"?* (altitude)

- *What type of structural relationship does the author use to describe the different classifications of satellite altitude?* (The author describes a comparative relationship between the altitude measurements.)

- *What type of text structure does the author use in describing satellite launches?* (The author uses sequential structure to explain what happens at each step of the launch.)

Review: Analyzing Text Structure

Have students practice identifying the different types of text structure. Have them find examples of comparative, sequential, and causal structure in the first three pages of the selection.

Review: Analyzing Points of View

Have students think about ways the author might have inserted loaded language or opinion in the text. Have students choose one paragraph to rewrite as a position statement rather than as a strictly technical text.

CLOSE READING

Satellites: Bridging the Gap from Earth to Sky *continued*

Satellite Altitude

10   The height of the satellite above Earth's surface is its altitude. Different orbiting altitudes are needed for different types of satellites. Satellite altitudes are generally divided into the following three categories:

  a. Low altitude orbit: 0 to 1,200 miles above Earth: Observation satellites usually orbit at this altitude band. These satellites are used for capturing images, from mapping to geologic movements. This classification also includes search-and-rescue satellites, used for relaying emergency distress signals from aircraft and ships.

  b. Medium altitude orbit: about 1,200 to 22,000 miles above Earth: This altitude is used by the Global Positioning System, or GPS. The GPS is a series of 27 satellites maintained by the United States government. These satellites are used to determine exact locations.

  c. High altitude (geostationary) orbit: 22,236 miles above Earth's equator. Weather satellites that aid in both the tracking and the forecasting of weather patterns use a high geosynchronous orbit. Communications satellites also orbit Earth at this altitude.

194

Getting into Orbit

11   Satellites get into space, and into orbit, through a two-step process: the launch phase and the injection phase. Each phase has a very specific role in introducing the satellite into Earth's gravitational pull.

Launch Phase

12   During the launch phase, the satellite is attached to either an expendable rocket or to a space shuttle. Expendable rockets shoot straight up into Earth's atmosphere. When the correct altitude and orbital speed are reached, the rocket releases the satellite into a temporary elliptical orbit.

13   Shuttle launches used to be one of the most common methods of getting a satellite into orbit. During a space shuttle launch, the satellite is attached to the space shuttle. When the shuttle reaches the correct altitude, the satellite and shuttle detach from each other, and the satellite goes into temporary orbit.

Injection Phase

14   The object injection phase places the satellite into a permanent orbital pattern. During the injection phase, the satellite apogee kick motors fire, moving the object into its intended circular orbital pattern.

15   Satellites are able to stay in orbit due to the balance between velocity and gravitational force. Velocity is the speed the satellite would travel if it were moving in a straight line. Without gravity, the velocity of the satellite would cause it to travel straight into space. Without velocity, gravity would cause the satellite to fall back to Earth. The combination of the two keeps the satellite in orbit.

Strategic Reading

Encourage students to reread any portion of the text that they have trouble understanding. If, after reading a segment of the text, students find they did not comprehend the material, have them go back through the text and read it again slowly and carefully. It can also help to vary the way the student is reading, switching from reading aloud to silent reading, and vice versa.

If students employ rereading as a comprehension strategy and still have trouble understanding the text, encourage them to ask for help from a teacher or classmate.

CRAFT AND STRUCTURE

16   Once used only for military purposes, satellites have become an integral part of life on Earth. Satellites play a role in practically everything—from communications to emergency services to television signals. Without satellites, we would miss many of the applications we consider essential to our daily lives. Understanding satellites—their operation and use—allows us a greater insight into the ways in which Earth and sky are becoming ever more connected in today's world.

Comprehension Check

1A. The technical meaning of the word *orbit* is

(a.) a path in space.

b. to compass an area.

c. the scope of an event.

d. a sphere of influence.

1B. Which sentence from the text does NOT provide a clue to the answer for Part A?

a. "The term *satellite*, however, is typically taken to mean a man-made object placed into orbit for a specific purpose."

b. "The station keeping uses thrusters to maintain the correct orbit."

c. " . . . satellites can differ in the type of orbit they maintain in space."

(d.) "Different orbiting altitudes are needed for different types of satellites."

2A. Which statement represents the author's point of view?

a. Humans should attempt to lessen their use of satellite technology.

b. Satellites serve no viable purpose in today's society.

(c.) Satellites are a crucial element in life on Earth today.

d. Satellite technology is an invasion of personal privacy.

2B. Which sentence from the text best supports the answer to Part A?

(a.) "Today, satellites are a vital . . . presence in our daily lives."

b. "By today's standards, however, *Sputnik I* was a highly simplistic craft . . ."

c. "A satellite is any object that orbits, or circles, Earth."

d. "These satellites are used to determine exact locations."

Research to Build Knowledge

Students may be interested in learning more about satellite functions and applications. Challenge students to identify and research one of the ways that satellite technology makes life on Earth more convenient. You may want to have students review the text to identify applications of satellite technology. Students can work together in small, cooperative-learning groups to gather credible and reliable information from multiple sources. Remind students to credit their sources and to use multimedia aids when they present their findings to the class.

Multiple Readings for Critical Comprehension

Have students read and annotate this selection. Then pose questions that focus on critical comprehension.

- *What benefit does the author believe readers will get from studying satellite technology?* (The author states that satellite technology has become an integral part of life on Earth and that people should be aware of their myriad functions.)

- *How does the article relate to the unit theme of Earth and Sky?* (Satellites are objects in the sky that affect life on Earth.)

Self-Select Text

As preparation for Connect Across Texts, have students choose one selection from this unit and reread it independently. Students can access full .pdf versions of some selections at **sadlierconnect.com**.

Comprehension Check

Begin scoring students' performance of unit skills with this Comprehension Check and continue through Connect Across Texts on page 198. Use students' scores to determine their readiness for the Unit 7 Review on page 200.

Multiple-Choice Questions: *1 point each*

1A. The text describes an orbit as *a path in space*.

1B. Choice D describes orbiting altitude but does not give context for the meaning of the word.

2A. The author discusses the importance of satellite technology in the final paragraph of the text.

2B. Choice A is the only statement that relates to the conclusion in 2A.

Multiple-Choice Questions, continued: *1 point each*

3A. Paragraph 4 lists the main parts of a satellite.

3B. The topic heading cues the reader that the section will describe the various components of a satellite.

4A. Paragraph 5 describes the function of an uplink, as detailed in choice C.

4B. Choice B is the sentence from the text that describes the definition of the word *uplink*.

5A. The text under the heading **Getting Into Orbit** details sequentially how satellites get from Earth to an orbital pattern above Earth.

5B. Choice B refers to a two-step process indicating sequential structure.

Short-Answer Questions: *2 points each* (10 points total)

Item 6 Rubric

2	Student names the type of structure and describes how it appears in the text.
1	Student names the type of structure but does not indicate how it is used in the text.
0	Student indicates neither the type of structure nor how it is used in the text.

CLOSE READING

3A. What is the purpose of the list in paragraph 4?

   a. to make a comparative analysis of different types of satellites

   b. to explain the components of a satellite

   c. to indicate that the other text is of lesser importance

   d. to show how satellites are built according to a series of steps

3B. Which element of text structure supports the answer to Part A?

   a. the organization of paragraphs 1 and 2

   b. the use of subsections on page 193

   c. the topic heading **Anatomy of a Satellite**

   d. the comparison between *Sputnik I* and modern satellites

4A. The technical term *uplink* refers to

   a. a signal transmission from a satellite to Earth's surface.

   b. a connection maintained between similar types of satellites.

   c. a way of providing a satellite with information.

   d. an element of the orbital pattern of a satellite.

4B. Which sentence from the text best supports the answer to Part A?

   a. "The signal frequency is called a gigahertz (GHz) range signal."

   b. "A signal, called an uplink, is sent from Earth's surface to the satellite."

   c. "The main function of a satellite is to transmit and receive signals."

   d. "Besides differing in function, satellites can differ in the type of orbit they maintain in space."

5A. The text that appears under the heading **Getting into Orbit** has a structure that is primarily

   a. sequential.

   b. comparative.

   c. causal.

   d. none of the above

5B. Which sentence from the text best supports the answer to Part A?

   a. "Shuttle launches used to be one of the most common methods of getting a satellite into orbit."

   b. "Satellites get into space, and into orbit, through a two-step process: the launch phase and the injection phase."

   c. "Each phase has a very specific role in introducing the satellite into Earth's gravitational pull."

   d. "Expendable rockets shoot straight up into Earth's atmosphere."

Extend Thinking: Initiate a Debate

Have students engage in a classroom debate about the use of technology and its potential impacts on Earth and on space. Break students into debate teams and provide the teams with a prompt, such as: *The advent of satellite technology has been one of the greatest technological advancements known to humankind.* Have each team take a pro or con position, research their ideas, and then present them in a proctored debate.

CRAFT AND STRUCTURE

6. Describe the organizational structure of the list of satellite functions in paragraph 7.

   Sample answer: The list is organized comparatively. The types of satellite functions are listed and then described to show how each type differs in function from the others.

7. Based on your reading, define the technical term *synchronous orbit*.

   Sample answer: Satellites in a synchronous orbit maintain position over a fixed point on Earth's surface.

8. Think about the effect of word meanings and structure. How would you describe the tone of this text?

   Sample answer: The tone of this text is both formal and informative. The author uses a significant amount of technical language, with the goal of informing and educating readers about the functions of satellites.

9. Based on your reading, define the technical terms *apogee* and *perigee*.

   Sample answer: *Apogee* is the point on a satellite's orbital path that is farthest from Earth. *Perigee* is the point on the satellite's orbital path that is closest to Earth.

10. Below are three statements from the text.

    ■ Without satellites, we would miss many of the applications we consider essential to our daily lives.

    ■ Without velocity, gravity would cause the satellite to fall back to Earth.

    ■ The object injection phase places the satellite into a permanent orbital pattern.

    A. Underline the statement that represents the author's point of view.

    B. Find two more statements in the text that illustrate a point of view that the author holds. Write them here.

    Sample answers: "One of the best known of these is the Hubble Space Telescope" (paragraph 7); "Today, satellites are a vital, if often unrecognized, presence in our daily lives" (paragraph 2)

Unit 7 ■ Reading Informational Text: Craft and Structure   **197**

Short-Answer Questions: *2 points each*

Item 7 Rubric

2	Student correctly defines the term *synchronous orbit*.
1	Student attempts to define the term but leaves out key points.
0	Student does not attempt to define the term.

Item 8 Rubric

2	Student identifies formal tone and provides evidence.
1	Student defines tone but does not provide evidence.
0	Student does not identify formal tone of the text.

Item 9 Rubric

2	Student correctly defines the terms *perigee* and *apogee*.
1	Student attempts to define the terms but leaves out key points.
0	Student does not attempt to define the terms.

Item 10 Rubric

2	Student correctly discerns author's position in first statement and provides two further examples from the text.
1	Student identifies opinion in first statement or provides further examples.
0	Student neither identifies opinion nor provides examples.

Theme Wrap-Up

Lead students in a discussion on the theme of Earth and sky. Ask: *How can technology help connect Earth and sky? In what areas do you see examples of this technology in your own life?* (Students should address some of the technologies described in the unit.)

Differentiate Instruction

Help students recognize the connection between Part A and Part B of the two-part comprehension questions on pages 195–196. If students are struggling with answering the initial half of each question pair, have them answer the question in Part B, first. Guide students to understand that the second question always refers explicitly to the text and that this textual material should help lead them to an answer for Part A.

Connect Across Texts: *4 points*
Review Reading Selections

Have students work in groups of four to review the unit's reading selections. Have students go back through each selection, identifying the main theme of the text, finding examples of formal, figurative, and technical language, and looking for ways the author's point of view may be expressed in the text.

Support a Claim

Review the directions on page 198. Make sure students understand that they are to list information about the author's point of view in each of the four selections they have read.

Graphic Organizer Rubric

4	Student analyzes the author's point of view in all four selections.
3	Student analyzes the author's point of view in three of the selections.
2	Student analyzes the author's point of view in two of the selections.
1	Student analyzes the author's point of view in one of the selections.
0	Student is unable to analyze the author's point of view in any of the selections.

Support Essential Question Discussion

Have students reread the Essential Question. Challenge them to finish this sentence: *Understanding how authors use language and organization in a text helps me to . . .*

If students have difficulty finishing the sentence, prompt them by asking how the type of language in a text can affect a reader's perception and understanding of the author's point of view.

CONNECT ACROSS TEXTS

Support a Claim

In this unit you've read a web article about the use of satellites in GPS technology, a technical text detailing the development of hurricanes, an opinion-based scientific text on the preservation of the wetlands, and another technical text on how satellites work. Think about how the authors were able to incorporate their own points of view into each of these texts. In the chart, list details that help you understand the author's point of view in each selection. Then write a brief essay comparing the addition of point of view in each of the selections. Use a separate sheet of paper if you need more room to write. Be prepared to discuss your ideas with the class.

Satellites and the Global Positioning System
- author describes many benefits of GPS
- author cites real-world applications of the technology
- author does not present a downside to the use of the technology

Our Fragile Ecosystem
- author makes opinion on preservation of wetlands very clear
- author uses positive descriptors to describe the wetlands and negative descriptors to describe their destruction

> To help present their point of view within a text, authors make specific language choices and choices about what facts to include or omit.

Hurricanes: Earth's Most Violent Storms
- author structures the text in sequential order
- text is very information-oriented, with little opinion inserted
- author seems to support technology to study and predict hurricanes

Satellites: Bridging the Gap from Earth to Sky
- author details applications of satellite technology
- author presents the use of technology as a positive development
- author gives a great deal of positive information about satellites

Return to the Essential Question

How do authors use language and organization to express a point of view?

In small groups or as a class, discuss the Essential Question. Think about what you have learned about the power of word meanings, text structure, and point of view in a text. Use evidence from the four texts in this unit to answer the question.

Assess and Respond (pages 195–198)

If	Then
Students scored 0–8 points, they are **Developing** their understanding of unit skills. . .	Provide students with reading support and more extensive modeling and practice of skills.
Students scored 9–17 points, they are **Improving** their understanding of unit skills. . .	Review students' scores to pinpoint skills that students need more help with, and offer targeted instruction.
Students scored 18–24 points, they are **Proficient** in their understanding of unit skills. . .	Have these students move on. They are ready for the formal assessment at the end of the unit.

Context Clues

Guided Instruction When you come across an unfamiliar word or phrase, look for context clues that may help you figure out the meaning. **Context clues** are bits of helpful information that appear near the word or phrase in question. There are four types of context clues:

- **Definition:** The unfamiliar word is defined in the sentence in which it appears. *The teacher expected complete* deference, *or respect, from her students.* (*Respect* is the definition of *deference*.)

- **Antonym:** The opposite meaning of the unfamiliar word is given. *Jeffrey's room was* immaculate, *but his sister Allison's room was* messy. (*Messy* is an antonym of *immaculate*.)

- **Synonym:** A word similar in meaning to the unfamiliar word is given. *That* mammoth *dog was so large that his head reached up to my waist.* (*Mammoth* and *large* have very similar meanings.)

- **Inference:** The meaning of the unfamiliar word is not stated explicitly. *Diego's* tenacity *helped him win the debate.* (You can infer that *tenacity* means *stubbornness*.)

Guided Practice In each of the sentences below, study the word in **bold** type. Identify the type of context clue being used and then define the word.

1. Typically, we use it to mean both the GPS **receivers**—or small units that transmit directions, coordinates, and time—and the large network of satellites . . .
   definition; Receivers are small units that transmit directions.

2. Once the warm air has risen, air begins to **circulate** and spiral.
   synonym; Circulate means "to spiral."

3. Similar to coastal wetlands, inland wetlands are also home to many different **species** of waterfowl, marine life, and plants.
   inference; Species means "different types of wildlife."

Independent Practice Find these words in the Close Reading selection (pages 192–195). Use context clues from the selection to help define each word.

1. impetus (page 192, paragraph 2) _incentive or drive_

2. applications (page 193, paragraph 7) _uses_

3. detach (page 194, paragraph 13) _separate_

4. insight (page 195, paragraph 16) _understanding_

OBJECTIVE
Use context clues to decipher word meanings.

Guided Instruction
Have students review the Guided Instruction on page 199. Help them understand that context clues are bits of information contained around an unknown word, which are helpful in providing clues to the meaning of the word. By familiarizing themselves with the four types of context clues, students will be better able to determine word meanings based on context material.

Guided Practice
Have students use the information presented about the four types of context clues to define the unknown terms presented in each sentence.

Independent Practice
Have students work alone or in small groups to identify the words within the selections and to define them using context clues. Remind students to look for cues indicating which type of context clue is being used.

Apply to Reading
Have students work in groups to find more unfamiliar words within the text, and define them based on context. They might identify the words *three-dimensional* (page 170), *rotation* (page 177), *saturated* (page 185), and *facilitate* (page 192).

Support English Language Learners

A think-aloud strategy is one way teachers can help English language learners understand context clues. Read the text with the students, having them follow along as you read aloud. When you come to a word that you suspect may be difficult, stop reading the text. Go through the process aloud of using context clues to determine the meaning of the word. When you have arrived at an appropriate meaning, ask students to describe the steps you took to comprehend the word based on its context. Continue reading the selection, modeling strategies for the students each time you come across potentially challenging vocabulary.

Unit Summary

In this unit, students have read a Web article, technical texts, and a scientific article. They have learned about the importance of understanding man's interactions with Earth and the sky, including the uses of satellites in space, the need for more in-depth study of hurricanes, and the importance of preserving the wetlands. Students have learned to analyze word meanings, analyze text structure, and analyze an author's point of view. They have also practiced working with context clues to determine word meanings. Students should now be ready to take this unit review.

Introduce the Review

Explain to students that they will read two related passages that continue the theme of "Earth and Sky." Instruct students to read the passages carefully and return to them as needed while they answer questions 1–10 on pages 201–202.

Answer Explanations (pages 201–202)

Scoring: When scoring students' work, assign one point for each multiple-choice question and two points for each short-answer question for a total of 20 points.

1A. Students should use evidence from the text to decipher the author's point of view about the bravery of the Hurricane Hunters.

1B. Students should be able to identify the words "dangerous" and "violent" as examples of loaded language in choice C.

UNIT 7 REVIEW

Read the following texts that include word meanings and text structures that help define an author's point of view. Then answer the questions on pages 201 and 202.

The Hurricane Hunters

1 Meteorologists predict hurricanes using various tools, such as satellites, infrared sensors, and on-ground monitoring systems. However, a special government group, known as the Hurricane Hunters, does more: It undertakes the dangerous job of flying into violent storms to gather vital, current information about hurricanes.

2 Hurricane Hunters fly directly into the eye of the hurricane. There, the atmosphere is calm and clear. However, the winds on the outer shell of the hurricane can reach speeds of 200 mph. Before Hurricane Hunters can reach the eye of the storm, they must first brave those violent outer winds.

3 Once inside the storm, Hurricane Hunters gather data through their planes' onboard instruments. They also use a specialized piece of equipment called a dropsonde. A dropsonde is a small tube containing data-collecting instruments and a radio transmitter. The tube is attached to a parachute. Hurricane Hunters then release the dropsonde into the exact center of the eye of the hurricane. Just before the dropsonde reaches the water below, it sends all of the information gathered to the computer systems on the aircraft. In this way, Hurricane Hunters are able to gather data about the intensity of the storm.

The Science of "Space Weather"

1 Monitoring and predicting weather patterns is about more than weather systems seen on Earth. In fact, "space weather" is becoming an increasingly important area of scientific research.

2 "Space weather" refers to weather effects created by the interaction of the sun and Earth, in space. These interactions create geomagnetic "storms." Geomagnetic storms impact Earth's systems in a number of ways, including the following:

  • Satellite disruption: When a satellite hits a geomagnetic storm, the solar particles in the storm can damage the apparatus. As a result, satellite services can be disrupted, both in space and on Earth.

  • Electric power disturbances: Entire power grids can be downed by a geomagnetic storm. By monitoring space weather, scientists are able to warn power companies of impending storms. The power companies can then take action to minimize or avoid service outages.

3 In today's world, many of our vital systems are run by electronic, computer-based technologies. With this in mind, the research being done by space weather scientists is of ever-increasing importance. Through their work, we someday may be able to avoid the potential for a complete shutdown of our most vital systems.

Self-Assessment

Have students return to the Progress Check on page 165 of their Student Book. Have students answer the Progress Check questions again, this time marking the "After Unit 7" boxes. Have students respond to the questions to determine how much progress they have made during the unit.

Then have students meet with partners to discuss what they have learned during the unit. Have students go through each Progress Check question with their partner, offering information about which selections and activities covered the various skills.

UNIT 7 REVIEW

Circle the letter next to the best answer choice.

1A. Which statement best expresses the author's point of view about the Hurricane Hunters?

    a. They are the best meteorologists.

    (b.) They are brave people doing necessary work.

    c. They could do a better job if they had better equipment.

    d. They are gathering data that may turn out to be unimportant.

1B. Which loaded language from "The Hurricane Hunters" supports the answer to Part A?

    a. "Meteorologists predict hurricanes"

    b. "gather data through their planes' onboard instruments"

    (c.) "undertakes the dangerous job of flying into violent storms"

    d. "satellites, infrared sensors, and on-ground monitoring systems"

2A. The information in paragraphs 2 and 3 of "The Hurricane Hunters" is structured

    a. causally.

    (b.) sequentially.

    c. comparatively.

    d. none of the above

2B. Which word or group of words from those paragraphs does NOT support the answer in Part A?

    a. Just before

    b. they must first brave

    (c.) However

    d. Once inside the storm

3A. What is the meaning of *geomagnetic*?

    a. pertaining to the sun and the oceans

    (b.) pertaining to Earth and the sun

    c. pertaining to Earth and the solar system

    d. pertaining to the sky and the sun

3B. In which paragraph from "The Science of 'Space Weather'" is the meaning of the term defined?

    a. paragraph 1

    (b.) paragraph 2

    c. paragraph 3

    d. It is not defined in the text.

4A. What is the author's point of view on the study of "space weather"?

    a. It does little to help weather forecasters on Earth.

    b. It was not important until the latter part of the twentieth century.

    (c.) It is an essential new field of research.

    d. It is based on flawed science.

4B. Which phrase from "The Science of 'Space Weather'" supports the answer to Part A?

    a. "predicting weather patterns is about more than weather systems seen on Earth"

    b. "scientists are able to warn power companies of impending storms"

    c. "solar particles in the storm can damage the apparatus"

    (d.) "'space weather' is becoming an increasingly important area of scientific research"

5A. According to paragraph 2 of "The Science of 'Space Weather,'" an *apparatus* is

    (a.) a mechanical device.

    b. a spacecraft.

    c. a vehicle.

    d. an electronic disruption.

5B. Which word in paragraph 2 best helps define the term?

    a. geomagnetic

    (b.) satellite

    c. space

    d. power

Answer Explanations (pages 201–202)

2A. Paragraphs 2 and 3 present the information in a step-by-step pattern, indicating a sequential structure.

2B. The word *however* is not typically indicated for sequential relationships.

3A. Students should break the word into its parts: *geo-* and *magnetic-*, in order to decipher the meaning of the word.

3B. Choice B correctly identifies the second paragraph as the one in which the term in Part A is defined.

4A. In the selection, the author discusses the importance of studying space weather.

4B. In choice D, the author clearly states his opinion.

5A. Students should look to context clues to correctly define the word *apparatus* as a *mechanical device*.

5B. The word *satellite*, choice B, relates most directly to the term *apparatus*.

6A. Based on context clues, the term *transmitter* means a *signaling device*.

6B. Choice C best relates to the words *signal* and *transmitter*.

Test-Taking Tips

Explain to students that the two parts of the questions that appear on pages 201–202 and elsewhere in the unit are related. In each case, part A asks a question about a text, and Part B asks students to identify text evidence that supports the answer they gave in Part A. If students are struggling to answer the paired questions, have them read both questions before answering either. Advise students to work backward, looking for the statement in Part A that is supported by the text evidence in Part B.

Unit 7 Review

Answer Explanations

Item 7 Rubric

2	Student identifies and supports a point of view about the text.
1	Student identifies point of view only.
0	Student does not identify point of view in the text.

Item 8 Rubric

2	Student compares and draws conclusions about the use of language and tone in both texts.
1	Student does not compare tone and language in their answer.
0	Student does not attempt to answer the question.

Item 9 Rubric

2	Student identifies and describes a structural element that would relate directly to the text.
1	Student identifies a structural element that does not relate to the text.
0	Student does not provide information about an additional structural element.

Item 10 Rubric

2	Student compares and contrasts the information presented in the two texts.
1	Student compares or contrasts the information in the texts, but does not do both.
0	Student does not compare and contrast the texts.

UNIT 7 REVIEW

6A. What is the meaning of the technical term *transmitter* in paragraph 3 of "The Hurricane Hunters"?

a. part of a hurricane
b. an atmospheric instrument
c. a signaling device
d. part of a plane

6B. Which context clue from the text helped you determine the answer to Part A?

a. "their planes' onboard instruments"
b. "reaches the water below"
c. "sends all of the information"
d. "computer systems on the aircraft"

7. Based on what you have read, why does the author believe that research into "space weather" is important?

Sample answer: It is important because geomagnetic storms can disrupt the electronic systems related to many basic functions of life on Earth.

8. Given what you know about word meanings and structure, which of the two texts would you call more formal in tone? Why?

Sample answer: "The Science of 'Space Weather'" is more formal. The author uses bullet points to give important facts and includes a large amount of technical vocabulary. In contrast, "The Hurricane Hunters" focuses as much on the human aspect of the science as the research itself.

9. What is one type of organizational or structural element that could be added to "The Science of 'Space Weather'" to help show the concepts more clearly?

Sample answers: a chart, a graph, an illustration, or an experiment on solar storms

10. How does the scientific research described in "The Hurricane Hunters" differ from that described in "The Science of 'Space Weather'"? How is it the same?

Sample answer: "Hurricane Hunters" focuses on data gathered directly by people; "The Science of 'Space Weather'" focuses on data gathered remotely. Both texts focus on the way technology can help predict natural occurrences.

Analyze Student Scores

16–20 pts Strong	Student has successfully learned and applied the skills in this unit. Review any errors with the student, and explain them if necessary.
10–15 pts Progressing	Student is struggling with one or more of the skills in this unit. Identify the specific skills that are problematic to target additional instruction.
0–9 pts Emerging	Student is having trouble understanding most of the skills in this unit. Student may need to work through the unit again with a higher level of individual support

Introducing UNIT 8

In this unit about earth and sky, you will learn how to write a research report. When you write a research report, your primary goal is to search multiple places for information that answers your question about a particular subject, and then to put your findings together in a clear and organized way.

Your research report should be thorough and well developed. Research your subject and take note of the information that answers your specific research question. Record the sources where you found the information so you can share them with your readers. Break your subject down in a way that will help readers understand it better. Explain each important point clearly, and include facts, details, and examples to support your ideas. Make sure to use formal language and to pay attention to writing conventions. At the end of your report, cite your sources so your reader knows your information is reliable.

Progress Check   *Can I?*

Before Unit 8		After Unit 8
☐	Conduct research to answer a question.	☐
☐	Gather relevant information from outside sources.	☐
☐	Introduce a topic clearly.	☐
☐	Use an appropriate strategy to organize ideas and information.	☐
☐	Develop a topic with facts, details, and examples.	☐
☐	Maintain a formal style.	☐
☐	Write a strong conclusion.	☐
☐	Understand and use verbal phrases correctly.	☐
☐	Recognize and correct dangling modifiers.	☐

Unit 8 ■ Research to Build and Present Knowledge: Write Research Reports

Student Page 203

HOME ✦ CONNECT...

The Home Connect feature is a way to keep parents or other adult family members apprised of what their children are learning. The key learning objectives are listed, and some ideas for related activities and discussions are included.

Explain to students that they can share the Home Connect page with their parents or other adult family members in their home. Let students know how much time the class will be spending on this unit so they can plan their time accordingly at home.

Encourage students and their parents to share their experiences using the suggestions on the Home Connect page and the Home Connect activities at **sadlierconnect.com**. You may wish to make a place to post some of this work.

Progress Check

The Progress Check is a self-assessment feature that students can use to gauge their own progress. Before students begin work on Unit 8, have them check the boxes next to any item that they feel they can do well. Explain that it is fine if they don't check any of the boxes. Tell them that they will have an opportunity to learn about and practice all of these items while studying the unit. Let them know that near the end of the unit they will have a chance to reconsider how well they can do each item on this list.

Before they begin their Unit 8 Review (see page 215 of this guide), you will be prompted to have students revisit this page. You can use this information to work with students on any items they don't understand before they tackle the Review.

HOME ✦ CONNECT...

In this unit, your child will learn to **research and present knowledge** in a well-developed **research report**. Your child will **gather** relevant facts and details and clearly **organize** them in a structured report. Help your child with these skills by working together to find reliable **sources** of information, both in print and online. Together, discuss what makes each source credible and how it can be used in a research report.

Help your child find a topic that will spark his or her interest. For example, you might brainstorm ideas about how environmental and geological changes can have unforeseen consequences. Ask questions to prompt a more comprehensive explanation; for example, ask your child what he or she learns from **quotations, examples,** and **graphics** in each source. Encourage your child to use **formal language** when crafting written responses, and to follow appropriate conventions while writing a report.

Activity: Explore with your child the unit theme, "earth and sky." Together, research and discuss how changes in Earth's environmental structures can have long-reaching, and often unexpected, consequences. You and your child might choose one area of change or concern in your local community and discuss the causes and effects of the event. Make a cause-and-effect chart with your child, and complete the activity by discussing how human impact on the environment can have both positive and negative effects on future generations.

204   Unit 8 ■ Research to Build and Present Knowledge: Write Research Reports

IN THIS UNIT, YOUR CHILD WILL...

- Learn to write an informative or explanatory text that introduces a topic, organizes information logically, and ends with a conclusion.
- Conduct a short research project to answer a question, drawing on several sources, both in print and online.
- Draw evidence from informational texts to support analysis, reflection, and research.
- Produce clear and coherent writing.
- Use formal language as appropriate.
- Use verbal phrases correctly.
- Recognize and correct dangling modifiers.

WAYS TO HELP YOUR CHILD

Have your child practice finding reliable sources of information. For example, you might compare an article from an online encyclopedia with an opinion piece from the local paper. Talk about what makes the encyclopedia article a more credible source of facts, and how your child can identify those sources that are appropriate for research purposes.

ONLINE
For more Home Connect activities, continue online at **sadlierconnect.com**

Student Page 204

UNIT PLANNER

Theme: Earth and Sky	Focus
WRITING MODEL *pp. 206–208*	*The Dust Bowl*
WRITING ACTIVITY *p. 209–210*	**ORGANIZATIONAL STRUCTURE:** Outline
LANGUAGE MINI-LESSONS *pp. 211–213*	• Verbals and Verbal Phrases • Dangling Modifiers
SPEAKING AND LISTENING *p. 214*	Discuss the Essential Question
UNIT 8 REVIEW *pp. 215–216*	• Language Skills Summary • Writing Process Summary

Objective(s)

Write a research report with a coherent structure, appropriate language, and supporting facts and information.

Correctly format a research report, focusing on the organization of ideas, concepts, and information.

- Identify verbals and verbal phrases and define their functions within a sentence.

- Recognize and correct misplaced and dangling modifiers.

Engage in a well-informed, collaborative discussion with peers.

Unit Assessment

- Unit 8 Review *pp. 215–216*

Additional Assessment Options

- Performance Task 1 *pp. 311A–320*
  (ALSO ONLINE)

- Performance Task 2 *pp. 321A–330*
  (ALSO ONLINE)

Optional Purchase:

- iProgress Monitor (ONLINE)

- Progress Monitor Student Benchmark Assessment Booklet

(ONLINE) Digital Resources

- Home Connect Activities
- Additional Practice
- Teacher Resources
- iProgress Monitor (optional purchase)

Go to SadlierConnect.com **to access your Digital Resources.**

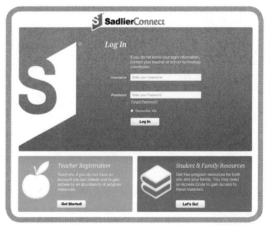

For more detailed instructions see page T3.

LEARNING PROGRESSIONS

In this unit, students will learn how to write a research report. The writing skills that students learn in this unit build upon the skills they learned during the sixth grade. Likewise, the skills students learn this year will provide a foundation for the skills they will develop in the eighth grade.

Introducing a Topic and Organizing Ideas

- By the end of the sixth grade, students should be able to introduce a topic and organize ideas by using such strategies as definition and classification, and using formatting, graphics, and multimedia to help readers' comprehension.

- During the seventh grade, students will learn to introduce a topic and preview what is to follow, as well as organize information by using strategies and formatting, graphics, and multimedia to aid readers' comprehension.

- Eighth-graders build on those skills by learning to introduce a topic and organizing the information in broader categories while also using formatting, graphics, and multimedia.

Developing Ideas

- In the sixth and the seventh grades, students work to develop a topic with relevant facts, definitions, details, examples, and quotations from experts.

- Eighth-grade students build on those skills by learning to carefully select relevant facts, definitions, details, examples, and quotations from experts.

Using Precise and Formal Language

- In the sixth, the seventh, and the eighth grades, students learn to use precise language to express their ideas, explain topics, and inform readers.

- Students in the sixth, the seventh, and the eighth grades learn to establish and maintain a formal style by using Standard English to write a research report.

Creating a Conclusion

- Sixth-graders will have learned to craft a conclusion that summarizes the information presented in the text.

- In the seventh and the eighth grades, students will learn how to write a conclusion that follows from and supports the information or explanation presented in the text.

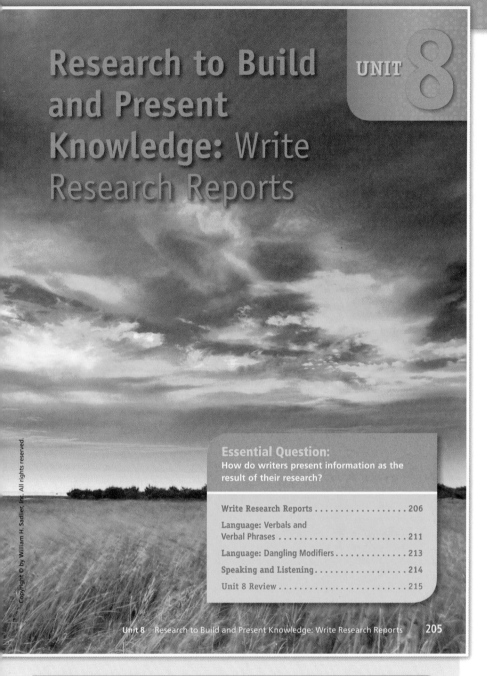

Research to Build and Present Knowledge: Write Research Reports

UNIT **8**

Essential Question:
How do writers present information as the result of their research?

Essential Question:
How do writers present information as the result of their research?

Unit 8 Research to Build and Present Knowledge: Write Research Reports **205**

Writing Handbook

If students need extra practice with writing a research report, refer them to the *Writing Handbook* on pages 299–310 in their Student Books. The *Writing Handbook* gives students detailed instruction on planning, drafting, revising, and editing their writing. They will also find tips on producing, publishing, and presenting their writing.

Essential Question:
How do writers present information as the result of their research?

In this unit, students will learn to write a research report by using appropriate techniques to research, develop, and support a topic.

Theme: Earth and Sky

Students will continue their exploration of the theme of "Earth and Sky" by learning about human interactions with nature as they read and analyze a model research report.

Curriculum Connection: Science

Students will use what they have already learned about the science involved in events that occur in nature while they work on their own research reports.

Connect Reading to Writing

Remind students that in Unit 7, they explored the technologies that enable humans to learn more about Earth and the sky. Review how the authors of *Satellites and the Global Positioning System* (Student Book pages 168–175) and *Hurricanes: Earth's Most Violent Storms* (Student Book pages 176–183) used logical text structures to convey information to the reader.

OBJECTIVES

- Write a research report with a coherent structure, appropriate language, and supporting facts and information.

- Correctly format a research report, focusing on the organization of ideas, concepts, and information.

Introduce: Organizational Structure

Draw attention to the graphic organizer. Ask students to look for the key elements as you read the Student Model together.

Analyze a Student Model

INTRODUCTION: Guide students to notice how Eliza's introduction introduces the topic explicitly in the first paragraph and lets readers know that the rest of her report will focus on some causes and effects of the Dust Bowl.

WRITE RESEARCH REPORTS

CREATING AN ORGANIZATIONAL STRUCTURE
Eliza used an outline to organize the information in her research report. It shows what main ideas and supporting information will be in each paragraph.

Title _____
I. **Introduction**
    a. Topic: _____
    b. Preview Information _____
II. **Supporting Resources**
    a. First paragraph: information about _____
        1. Fact or detail _____
        2. Example _____
    b. Second paragraph: information about _____
        1. Fact or detail _____
        2. Example _____
    c. Third paragraph: information about _____
        1. Fact or detail _____
        2. Example _____
III. **Conclusion**
        _____

INTRODUCTION
- Introduces the topic clearly
- Previews the information to come

TRANSITIONS
The transition word "Therefore" shows a cause-and-effect link.

ORGANIZATION OF INFORMATION
Eliza develops the topic by presenting information chronologically, or according to a timeline of the topic.

Read a Student Model

Eliza is a student in Mrs. Mariel's seventh-grade Language Arts class. Mrs. Mariel gave Eliza's class an assignment: to write a research report about an environmental or geological change on Earth. Mrs. Mariel expects the reports to be written clearly and to be well organized. Think about an environmental change that you might choose when you write your own research report.

The Dust Bowl

In the United States, the period from 1931 until 1940 was known as the Great Depression. This economic collapse forced millions of Americans to leave their homes to look for work. The Great Plains region was particularly devastated. Years of poor farming practices led to what is now known as the Dust Bowl, which seriously affected both the land and the people. Therefore, understanding the causes and effects of the Dust Bowl, and how the land eventually recovered from it, is essential to avoiding a repeat of this catastrophe.

History of the Dust Bowl

In 1862, Congress passed the Homestead Act, encouraging Americans to settle in the Great Plains. The act gave a parcel of land to anyone who could make it productive. By 1890, almost six million people had signed up. Wheat was one of the major crops of the farming community.

Genre: Research Report

Remind students that a research report is an informational text in which a writer summarizes, synthesizes, and analyzes information he or she has gained through researching a topic. Writers of research reports present not only facts but also their ideas about the topic, which are shaped by their research.

As students work on their own research reports, guide them to be aware of the need for a logical organizational structure. Have students ask themselves, "Does my report present important facts, details, and other evidence in a way that makes sense for readers?" Remind students to use subheads and other text features to help with readers' comprehension.

Poor Soil Management

Unfortunately, these lands were being (tilled and ploughed) without any attention to the potential harm to the enormous grasslands of the Great Plains. The new crops, like (wheat), that were being introduced into the soil had shallow root systems, making them particularly (vulnerable) to climate changes. The soil was overworked and began to (erode). Then, in 1931, a (drought) struck the region. An area already experiencing the overwhelming financial consequences of the Great Depression was now faced with the loss of its only source of (economic stability).

Devastating Consequences

The lack of water caused the soil, already loose from overuse, to turn into dust, which was then blown by the wind into raging dust storms. The worst storms brought dust that covered the area like snow. <u>People had trouble breathing, and railway travel was stopped until workers could shovel the dust off of the tracks. Houses were boarded up, and every opening to the outside was sealed. People described the conditions as blizzard-like, with streetlights so covered by the dust that it looked like dusk in the middle of the day.</u>

Many farming families were forced to leave the area because of the dust. With failed crops, lost homes, and rampant sickness brought on by the blowing dust, people moved either further west or back to their families in the east. The areas most affected by the Dust Bowl lost up to 60 percent of their population as farming communities were destroyed.

PRECISE LANGUAGE

Eliza uses precise language— nouns and verbs that give her readers a clear and specific idea of the information she wants to communicate.

Circle at least two examples of precise language in the first paragraph on this page.

GIVE RELEVANT INFORMATION

Eliza thoroughly researched her subject, so she was able to give important facts about the causes and effects of the Dust Bowl.

FACTS, DETAILS, AND EXAMPLES

Eliza includes key facts and concrete details necessary to explain her topic. Then she supports them with examples.

Underline three examples that support the fact that dust "covered the area like snow."

FORMAL STYLE

Research reports should use a formal, academic style, avoiding slang, contractions, and personal statements by the writer.

Analyze a Student Model

TRANSITIONS: Explain that transitions make connections between ideas clearer. Point out to students the function of the transition word *therefore* on page 206.

ORGANIZATION OF INFORMATION: Remind students that chronological order is a logical structure to use when writing about historical topics. By using chronological order, writers describe events in the order in which they occurred.

PRECISE LANGUAGE: Tell students that precise language involves using exactly the right words to explain or describe something. Help students identify examples of precise language in the first paragraph on page 207.

GIVE RELEVANT INFORMATION: Explain to students that Eliza most likely left out many facts she learned during her research because she wanted to focus only on those most relevant to her topic. Remind students to choose their facts and details thoughtfully.

FACTS, DETAILS, AND EXAMPLES: Facts and details are essential to a research report, whose purpose is to inform about a topic. Guide students to locate in Eliza's report important facts and details about effects of the Dust Bowl.

FORMAL STYLE: Inform students that research papers require them to use a formal style of writing. Their reports should not include any informal or conversational language or slang. Instead, students should use Standard English to express their ideas. Point out for students the difference in how they speak when among their friends versus the expectations for their language in a formal paper.

Support English Language Learners

Help English language learners understand the model essay by providing background information on the essay topic and preparing them to read its topic-specific vocabulary. Read with students the first paragraph, in which the Dust Bowl is introduced, and tell them that the term refers to the parts of Texas, Oklahoma, Kansas, Colorado, and New Mexico affected in the 1930s by drought, loss of topsoil, and massive dust storms. Help students by defining terms such as *homestead, erosion,* and *drought* before reading the essay.

Then read through the essay with students, stopping after each paragraph to clarify and summarize what it says and to offer additional background information as needed.

Write Research Reports

Analyze a Student Model

GRAPHICS: Explain that images and graphics, such as diagrams, maps, charts, graphs, and tables, present information visually and therefore can enhance the writer's words. Ask students how Eliza's choice of image of a dust storm helps their understanding of the Dust Bowl.

CONCLUSION: Remind students that a conclusion in a research report should summarize the presented information as well as confirm the writer's main findings and ideas.

INCLUDE A LIST OF SOURCES: Tell students that they must provide a list of sources in their research reports. Explain that a list of sources lets readers know that the report's sources of information are credible and reliable. The list also makes clear that the writer is not attempting to plagiarize anyone else's work.

Evaluate a Writer's Work

Have students break into small groups to discuss how the Student Model presents and synthesizes information about the Dust Bowl. Have each group identify one passage that exemplifies the formal language that should be used in a research report. Have students share their ideas with the class.

Model: Organizational Structure

Ask students to think about how Eliza could have used an outline to organize her facts and details. Post the outline template that appears on page 210. Point out that well-written research reports have a strong organizational structure. Before students fill in the outline based on the Student Model, remind them to review the notes that appear in the margins of Eliza's research report.

WRITE RESEARCH REPORTS

GRAPHICS

In an historical research report, images can help the reader better understand the topic.

CONCLUSION

Eliza's conclusion summarizes the central idea of her report.

Place an asterisk next to the statement that summarizes the report's central idea.

INCLUDE A LIST OF SOURCES

Citing sources shows the reader that your information is both credible and reliable— that is, that your information comes from trustworthy, expert sources.

Rehabilitation

In 1935, the federal government established the Soil Conservation Service, which showed farmers how to use better farming techniques. At the same time, the Shelterbelt Project began. Areas of trees were planted on farms to help stop erosion and to block the blowing dust. As farmers came back into the Dust Bowl region, new techniques and more environmentally friendly practices were put into place, and the soil began to return to its pre-drought conditions.

By 1938, the drought had begun to diminish. In 1935, almost 50 million acres of land in the Great Plains were covered in eroded soil. By 1939, fewer than 10 million acres were still seeing severe conditions. During the 1940s, normal rainfall returned, and crops and grasslands once again covered the Great Plains. However, those affected by the Dust Bowl would be forever changed.*That disaster illustrated how people must not abuse the land but instead work responsibly to preserve it for future generations.

Sources

"Dust Bowl During the Great Depression." American Memory Timeline. Classroom Presentation Teacher Resources. Library of Congress Home. Web. 13 Aug. 2013.

Gibson, Arrell M. "Dust Bowl." Encyclopedia Americana. Grolier Online. Web. 8 Aug. 2013.

Hurt, R. Douglas. "Dust Bowl." The New Book of Knowledge. Grolier Online. Web. 12 Aug. 2013.

Worster, Donald. Dust Bowl: The Southern Plains in the 1930s. New York: Oxford University Press, 1979. Print.

208 Unit 8 ■ Research to Build and Present Knowledge: Write Research Reports

---

Review: Analyzing Text Structure

Remind students that they learned in Unit 7 to analyze sequential, causal, and comparative text structures in informational texts. Tell them that knowing this skill will help them as they prepare their own research reports. They will need to determine the most logical structure (or structures) to convey the information about their topics.

Remind students that a writer might use more than one organizational structure in his or her report. Have students discuss the text structures Eliza used in the Student Model. Work together to identify the parts of the text that explain cause-and-effect relationships, use chronological order, and compare and contrast ideas.

Use index cards like the ones below to take notes for your research report on an environmental or geological change on Earth. You may use print or digital sources to find information. You will then use these notes to create your outline on page 210.

Environmental or geologic change: _____

Source 1
Summarize or paraphrase information:

Source 2
Summarize or paraphrase information:

Source 3
Summarize or paraphrase information:

Unit 8 ■ Research to Build and Present Knowledge: Write Research Reports   **209**

Peer Collaboration

Having students work in teams on their research reports can help them learn how to conduct research effectively and work collaboratively. Suggest that students work in groups of three or four to explore different aspects of the same topic. For example, one student could research the science of meteorology while another explores the history of meteorology, and a third learns about new weather forecasting technology. Students should work together to find source materials, organize information, and develop conclusions. Finally, students could collaborate on a class presentation, complete with visuals.

Create: Note-Taking

Collecting Sources

Inform students that writers can find information from print sources, such as books, magazines, and newspapers, and from online sources, such as Web sites, databases, and digital reference materials.

If students will be using the Internet for their research, guide them through the steps required to conduct an online search. Suggest appropriate search engines, and explain how to create an effective search term. Also, be sure to discuss how to identify sources that are credible and current.

Taking Notes

Tell students how to use the index cards on page 209 to take notes. Explain that they should consult at least three sources related to their topic. They should write the title of a source at the top of one card and then record facts and details from the source onto the card. Remind students to use their notes to guide them as they complete the outline on page 210.

Summarizing and Paraphrasing Information

If necessary, review the difference between summarizing and paraphrasing. Summarizing involves condensing information to its most important ideas. Paraphrasing means restating an idea in one's own words.

Citing Sources

Remind students to write down the publication information for each source on their note cards.

Assess and Respond
If students have trouble summarizing and paraphrasing their sources,
Then have them work with a partner to orally retell what the source says while the partner writes down what they say.

Create: Organizational Structure

Brainstorming

Students will be most interested in researching topics that have some relevance for them. As a class, brainstorm ideas for research papers that cover the theme of Earth and sky. Post the list for students to reference as they decide on topics.

Planning

Students will use the outline on page 210 to plan their writing. They should first decide on topics and then think about how they will introduce the topics. Remind students that they should base their organizational structures on the information they find during their research.

Drafting a Research Report

Tell students to consult their outlines as they write the first draft of their reports on a separate sheet of paper. Be sure that students are presenting a well-researched topic and using an appropriately formal style for a research report.

Introduce the Writing Process

Remind students that good writing happens in stages. After prewriting and drafting, they will revise and edit their research reports. For more on the writing process, see the *Writing Handbook* on page 299.

Assess and Respond

If students have difficulty organizing their information into an outline,

Then have them create a cluster diagram with the research topic at the center and relevant facts surrounding it. Have students work in pairs to "translate" the information from the diagram into the outline.

Use an outline like the one below to organize your research report on an environmental or geological change on Earth. Then write a first draft of your research report on a separate sheet of paper. You will use this draft to write your final research report in the Unit 8 Review section on page 216.

Title _____

I. **Introduction**

   a. Topic: _____

   b. Preview information: _____

II. **Supporting Resources**

   a. First paragraph: information about _____

     1. Fact or detail _____

     _____

     2. Example _____

     _____

   b. Second paragraph: information about _____

     1. Fact or detail _____

     _____

     2. Example _____

     _____

   c. Third paragraph: information about _____

     1. Fact or detail _____

     _____

     2. Example _____

     _____

III. **Conclusion**

   _____

   _____

Differentiate Instruction

Students who are not linear thinkers may have trouble filling in the outline on page 210. If this is the case, consider allowing students to use an alternate graphic organizer, such as a content map, a flowchart, or a time line to help them organize their ideas. (You can find examples of these organizers online, and, if time allows, demonstrate how to use them with the class.)

Point out that the advantage of the outline is that it helps students see how the ideas in the paper will flow and build from the beginning (the introduction) to the end (the conclusion). Encourage students to use more than one graphic organizer if it helps them feel more confident about planning and organizing their reports.

LANGUAGE

Verbals and Verbal Phrases

Guided Instruction A **verbal** is a verb form that is used as a noun, adjective, or adverb. For example, in the sentence *Jogging is good exercise*, you can see that "jogging" is formed from the verb "to jog." It is not the verb of this sentence, however; it is a noun functioning as the subject of the sentence. There are three kinds of verbals in English: gerunds, infinitives, and participles. A **verbal phrase** is made up of a verbal and the words (modifiers and complements) that go with it.

- A **gerund** is a verb form that ends in *–ing* and functions as a noun. A **gerund phrase** is made up of a gerund and the words that go with it. A gerund or gerund phrase can do anything in a sentence that a noun can do.

  Gardening is an enjoyable way to spend time outdoors. (gerund as subject)

  I enjoy skiing more than any other sport. (gerund as direct object)

  Walking to school can be faster than riding the bus. (gerund phrase as subject)

  Fear kept me from crossing the rope bridge. (gerund phrase as object of preposition)

- An **infinitive** is the *to* form of a verb, such as *to see, to laugh,* and *to sleep.* An **infinitive phrase** is made up of an infinitive and the words that go with it. An infinitive or infinitive phrase can function as a noun and can do anything in a sentence that a noun can do. An infinitive or infinitive phrase can also function as an adjective or an adverb in a sentence.

  To laugh brings great joy. (infinitive as noun/subject)

  He wants to win a motocross championship. (infinitive phrase as noun/direct object)

  That was an effort to be proud of. (infinitive phrase as adjective modifying *effort*)

  I'll try to show I can do a good job. (infinitive phrase as adverb modifying *try*)

- A **participle** is a verb form that functions as an adjective. Most participles end in *-ing* or *-ed.* A **participial phrase** is made up of the participle and the words that go with it.

  Grinning, Heather accepted the award. (participle modifying *Heather*)

  Spattered with mud, Grant walked slowly back to the locker room. (participial phrase modifying *Grant*)

  The birds flying overhead are seagulls. (participial phrase modifying *birds*)

Unit 8 ■ Research to Build and Present Knowledge: Write Research Reports   **211**

OBJECTIVE
Identify verbals and verbal phrases and define their functions within a sentence.

Guided Instruction

Guide students as they work through the instruction on verbals and verbal phrases. Help them identify each of the three types of verbals and determine their function in a sentence. Read aloud the example sentences and guide students to look closely at what the verbals and verbal phrases do.

Guide students to take note of these cues that indicate verbals and verbal phrases:

- Gerunds end in *–ing* and function as nouns.

- Infinitives always begin with the word *to.*

- Participles end in *–ing* or *–ed* and function as adjectives.

If necessary, review the relevant parts of speech (nouns, adverbs, and adjectives) and how they function in a sentence.

To show how verbals or verbal phrases function, write one of the example sentences on the board. Then cross out the verbal or verbal phrase and replace it with a "regular" noun, adverb, or adjective. Example:

To laugh brings great joy.

Summertime brings great joy.

Remind students to use the example sentences as models as they work through the Guided Practice and Independent Practice exercises on page 212.

Support English Language Learners

Comprehending verbals and verbal phrases will be difficult for many English language learners who do not have a strong understanding of the structure of the English language. Assist students by having them work in small groups to categorize a list of verbals and verbal phrases you provide. Have students prepare a sheet of paper by drawing a three-column chart with these headings: *Gerund, Infinitive,* and *Participle.* Then on the board, write a list of four or five different verbals and verbal phrases. Have students copy each verbal or verbal phrase into the correct column of the chart. Remind students to compare the verbals or verbal phrases to the examples that appear on page 211.

OBJECTIVE

Identify verbals and verbal phrases and define their functions within a sentence.

Guided Practice

Have students work alone or with partners to identify the type of verbal or verbal phrase indicated in italics in each practice sentence. Remind students to refer back to the example sentences on page 211 if they have trouble. Also, write the following information on the board:

- Gerund/Gerund phrase = noun
- Infinitive/Infinitive phrase = noun OR adjective OR adverb
- Participle/Participial phrase = adjective

Independent Practice

Once students are able to recognize the verbals and verbal phrases, they should be able to determine each word's or phrase's function in a sentence. If necessary, review the functions of subjects, direct objects, and the objects of prepositions in a sentence.

Assess and Respond

If students struggle to determine the functions of verbals and verbal phrases,

Then write these questions on the board: *What is the part of speech? What does it do in the sentence?* Encourage students to answer the questions for each item.

LANGUAGE

Guided Practice For each sentence below, identify the words in italics as a *gerund, gerund phrase, infinitive, infinitive phrase, participle,* or *participial phrase.*

1. Josh left school early *to go to his dental appointment.* ___infinitive phrase___

2. *Hang gliding* is the next best thing to flying like a bird. ___gerund___

3. *Grunting,* the football player fumbled the ball as he was tackled. ___participle___

4. Marion couldn't imagine *reading another book like the scary one she had just finished.* ___gerund phrase___

5. My former home, *seeming smaller than it had when I was young,* stood across the street. ___participial phrase___

6. After this tiring weekend I just want *to rest.* ___infinitive___

7. *Amazed by the performance,* the crowd cheered and applauded the singer. ___participial phrase___

Independent Practice Tell whether the italicized verbal phrase in each sentence is a gerund phrase, an infinitive phrase, or a participial phrase. Then tell the phrase's part of speech (*noun, adjective,* or *adverb*). If the verbal phrase is a noun, tell its function in the sentence (*subject, direct object, object of a preposition*). If the verbal phrase is an adjective or adverb, tell what word the phrase modifies.

1. I can't stand *going to bed early on weekends!* ___gerund phrase, noun, direct object___

2. For Jackie, housework was a chore *to be avoided.* ___infinitive phrase, adjective, modifies chore___

3. The blue vase, *bumped by the careless shopper,* crashed to the floor. ___participial phrase, adjective, modifies vase___

4. The last bus left *to go to the stadium.* ___infinitive phrase, adverb, modifies left___

5. *Being first in line at lunch* is always my goal. ___gerund phrase, noun, subject___

6. *Gliding silently beneath the water's surface,* the shark approached the swimmers. ___participial phrase, adjective, modifies shark___

Differentiate Instruction

Help struggling students by focusing on sentence structure. Begin by having students write out the first two Independent Practice sentences on a sheet of paper. After giving students different colored highlighters, read the sentences aloud, stopping after each word to identify its part of speech or function in the sentence. Students should highlight each part of speech in a different color; for example, nouns are pink, verbs are orange, adjectives are yellow, and adverbs are green. After students have color-coded two of the sentences, lead a discussion of the patterns they notice. For example, modifying phrases tend to be very close to the word they modify.

LANGUAGE

Dangling Modifiers

Guided Instruction Phrases and clauses should be placed in a sentence so that they relate directly to the words they modify. You have already learned about **misplaced modifiers**. Now you will learn about **dangling modifiers**. A **dangling modifier** is a phrase that modifies a word not clearly stated in the sentence.

- **Dangling Modifier**

  Turning the corner, *the house came into view*. (Incorrect: Who or what was turning the corner?)

  Turning the corner, *I caught sight of the house*. (Correct: Now you can tell who or what the phrase is modifying.)

  After seeing the movie, *the book is sure to be great*. (Incorrect: Who saw the movie?)

  After seeing the movie, *I can't wait to read the book, which is sure to be great*. (Correct: Now you can tell who or what the phrase is modifying.)

Guided Practice Read each sentence below and underline the dangling modifier.

1. Being excused from soccer practice, home is a good place to relax.
2. The test score was terrible, not having studied the chapter.
3. While writing my essay for class, the dog sat in my lap.
4. When riding my bike down the street, a tree branch fell onto a car.

Independent Practice Correct each of the sentences above. Make sure the modifying phrase is correctly placed next to the word that it modifies.

1. Sample answer: Being excused from soccer practice, I thought home would be a good place to relax.

2. Sample answer: Not having studied the chapter, I knew my test score would be terrible.

3. Sample answer: While writing my essay for class, I let the dog sit in my lap.

4. Sample answer: When riding my bike down the street, I saw a tree branch fall onto a car.

Recognize and correct misplaced and dangling modifiers.

Guided Instruction

Explain to students that dangling modifiers can confuse readers because readers cannot tell which word is supposed to be modified. Guide students through the example sentences on page 213. Tell students that readers assume that modifiers are near the word they describe. Lead students in a discussion about why sentences with dangling modifiers are confusing.

Guided Practice

Have students work alone or in pairs to underline the dangling modifiers in each sentence. (If students need help, point out that all the modifying phrases use *-ing* words.)

Independent Practice

Have students correct the sentences in the Guided Practice section of the page. Explain that, in revising, students might have to add the subjects that are meant to be modified, as well as other clarifying words.

Assess and Respond
If students are having difficulty correcting dangling modifiers,
Then ask them clarifying questions, such as: *Who was excused from soccer practice?* and *Who did not study the chapter?*

Peer Collaboration

Model a think-aloud to demonstrate the thought process behind revising sentences with dangling modifiers. Start with the first Independent Practice sentence. Say: *Hmm. Home is a place. It could not have been excused from soccer practice. I don't see any other possible subject in the sentence. I will have to add one, so the sentence might read this way: Being excused from soccer practice, I thought home would be a good place to relax.* Then have students work in mixed-ability pairs to complete the rest of the Independent Practice items. Tell students to read each item and then talk about it, following your example. If necessary, the more proficient student can offer hints or strategies for determining what the modifiers describe.

OBJECTIVE
Engage in a well-informed, collaborative discussion with peers.

Discuss the Essential Question

Copy and distribute the "Did I?" checklist available on **sadlierconnect.com**.

Leading the Class Discussion

Guide students to use the Student Model to review Eliza's organizational structure, facts and detials, and use of formal, academic language

---

SPEAKING AND LISTENING

Discuss the Essential Question

How do writers present information as the result of their research?

Prepare for a class discussion about the Essential Question by responding to the questions below. Support your point of view with reasons and examples, and follow the discussion rules you learned earlier in this book.

1. How did Eliza organize information about her topic?

Sample answer: Eliza grouped her information so that facts and details that supported the same idea went together in a paragraph. Further, she described the events surrounding the Dust Bowl chronologically, first showing the causes, then the effects, and finally the solution to the problem.

2. What facts and details did Eliza use to develop the report?

Sample answer: Eliza described the events of the Dust Bowl. She discussed what led up to the Dust Bowl, the consequences of mismanaging the soil, and how the government stepped in to help fix the problem.

3. What kind of language did Eliza use to discuss concepts and connect ideas?

Sample answer: Eliza used formal language. She wrote in third person, and made sure that her writing style was academic, rather than conversational.

Use your notes above as you discuss the Essential Question with your class or in small groups. Use the organizer below to record your ideas and what you hear in the discussion. Follow the discussion rules on the "Did I?" checklist (page 58).

	Ideas I Agree or Disagree With	Questions I Asked
agree		
disagree		

New Ideas I Had During Discussion	Questions I Answered

Discussion Skills

Place students in groups and then assign each Discuss the Essential Question topic from page 214. Students should discuss their question and then present their findings to the class. Remind students to follow the rules of collegial discussions and to ask for clarification, rephrasing, and examples from their peers.

Then have students give a brief class presentation based on their discussions. They should recap Eliza's research report and use an informal visual aid, such as a chart of the organizational structure of the text. Students should use appropriate language in their presentations to the class.

UNIT 8 REVIEW

Read this draft paragraph from a student research report and answer the questions below.

> (1) Glacier National Park encompasses over 1,000,000 acres in northwest Montana. (2) Under pressure from influential leaders of the time, the area was established as a national park on May 11, 1910. (3) At the time, there were almost 150 glaciers present within the park. (4) However, the glaciers are going away far more rapidly than scientists had once predicted. (5) Today, there are only twenty-five glaciers larger than twenty-five acres left in the park.

1. Which of the following does this introduction NOT accomplish?

   a. establishing the topic to be examined

   b. using specific details to support claims

   c. explaining the cause of the main problem

   d. placing the analysis in an historical period

2. Which of the following is the dangling modifier in sentence 2 meant to modify?

   a. the area of the park

   b. the government

   c. the influential leaders

   d. the park's glaciers

3. Which is the clearest example of a concrete detail from the text?

   a. "the glaciers are going away"

   b. "encompasses over 1,000,000 acres"

   c. "established as a national park"

   d. none of the above

4. Which of the following details would best help develop this topic?

   a. The park is a famous hiking destination.

   b. Many visitors take aerial tours of the park.

   c. The largest glaciers will vanish by 2030.

   d. Some European parks feature glaciers.

5. Based on this introduction, which of the following is NOT a heading that you might expect to see in this essay?

   a. Climate Change in Glacier National Park

   b. Glacier Recession in Glacier National Park

   c. The Changing Face of Glacier National Park

   d. Visitor Activities in Glacier National Park

6. How would you change sentence 4 to achieve a more precise, formal style?

   a. correct the dangling modifier

   b. replace *going away* with *disappearing*

   c. replace *rapidly* with *fast*

   d. remove the comma after *However*

Unit 8 ■ Research to Build and Present Knowledge: Write Research Reports **215**

Test-Taking Tips

Give students the following reminders and tips to help with taking assessments that include reading passages:

1. Tell students to make sure they read the text in its entirety before attempting to answer any questions.

2. Point out that sentences in the text are numbered and that these numbers will often appear in the assessment questions.

3. Tell students that, if they are struggling, they should look closely at each answer choice and eliminate those that are obviously wrong before narrowing down the other choices.

Introduce the Review

Explain to students that this review will give them an opportunity to apply the language and writing skills they have studied and practiced in this unit.

Language Skills Summary

Inform students that they will be using what they have learned about verbals, verbal phrases, and dangling modifiers to enhance their writing.

- Have students list and describe the types of verbals and verbal phrases.

- Have students explain what a dangling modifier is and why it is confusing.

Self-Assessment: Progress Check

Have students revisit the Progress Check on page 203 and compare their answers now to the answers they gave before they started Unit 8.

Answer Explanations

Scoring: 5 points for each item 1–10; 50 points for the final essay.

1. Students should determine that the introduction does not explain the cause of the problem.

2. Students should recognize that the phrase "Under pressure . . . the time" modifies the government.

3. Students should remember that concrete details state specific facts.

4. Students should choose the detail that relates to the text.

5. Students should understand that the text does not relate to visitor activity in Glacier National Park.

6. Students should replace casual language with formal language.

Answer Explanations

7. Students should remember that participial phrases end in *–ing* and function as adjectives.

8. Students should look for the words that connect facts or ideas.

9. Students should scan the text for the use of the word *to* in an infinitive phrase.

Item 10 Rubric

2	**5 pts.** Student writes a conclusion that follows from and supports details in the text.
1	**2–3 pts.** Student writes a conclusion that is related to the text but does not support details in it.
0	**0 pts.** Student does not write a conclusion.

Writing Process Summary

Remind students that planning can help them organize their ideas before they draft. Revising and editing help make the draft better.

Planning and Drafting

Have students revisit their graphic organizer and draft (page 210). Have them check that the draft includes all items in the graphic organizer.

Research Report Rubric

4	**50 pts.** The text has an introduction and organizational structure and uses precise language to relate relevant facts.
3	**40 pts.** The text includes the key elements but contains minor errors in editing.
2	**30 pts.** The text is missing one or more key elements and contains minor errors in editing.
1	**20 pts.** The text is unfinished and shows a lack of understating of nonfiction narrative style.
0	**0 pts.** The assignment was not attempted.

UNIT 8 REVIEW

Read these next two paragraphs from the student research report and answer the questions below.

(1) A glacier is a large mass of snow and ice that moves over land. (2) Glaciers form when fallen snow stays in one place long enough to form ice. (3) The ice then compacts into a slowly moving mass. (4) The largest glaciers can reach up to 62 miles in width. (5) Moving like slowly flowing rivers, glaciers usually advance only a few inches each day, if at all.

(6) In Glacier National Park, the largest glaciers are melting more quickly than would naturally be expected. (7) Glaciers are a good measure of climate changes. (8) Colder average temperatures lead to glacier growth, while warmer temperatures result in a decrease in glacier size. (9) Currently, long-term measurements in Glacier National Park show an increase in average summer temperatures. (10) Many scientists believe that these changes are a direct effect of global climate change, and that the consequences of melting glaciers could be significant for life on Earth.

7. What sentence in paragraph 1 includes a participial phrase? _____ 5 _____

8. What sentence in paragraph 2 contains a transition word? _____ 9 _____

9. Which sentence on this page contains an infinitive? _____ 2 _____

10. Write a conclusion for this report. Use a separate sheet of paper if necessary.
Sample answer: The number of glaciers in Glacier National Park has decreased significantly in the past 100 years, and it continues to do so. Scientists can't yet predict the long-term effects of this change.

Assignment: On separate paper, provide a final draft of the research report you began on page 209. Use what you learned about verbal phrases and dangling modifiers in the Language section of this unit. Think about how you and your classmates answered the Essential Question. Check your outline to be sure you organized your ideas well. Be sure to use relevant facts and concrete details and correct writing conventions. Cite your sources. End with a strong conclusion.

216   Unit 8 ■ Research to Build and Present Knowledge: Write Research Reports

---

Digital Connection: Incorporating Graphics

Once students have completed their research reports, encourage them to use digital tools to create graphics—such as charts, tables, or timelines—that they can incorporate into the body of their paper. The graphics should display data or provide visuals that enhance but not overpower their words. Allow students time to use word-processing software to format their papers and incorporate the graphic components. Then have student post their papers to an approved Web site or blog so that their classmates and families can see their work.

Introducing UNIT 9

Do you like to read stories that take place in the past? Many stories about people who lived in the past are based on actual historical events. In this unit, you will read not only fictional stories based on historical events but also historical accounts of those events.

It is fun to read historical fiction, and it is even more enlightening to watch the movie version of an historical story and compare it to the original text. Did the filmmaker follow the text very closely, or is the film quite different? This skill of comparing and contrasting is also useful for analyzing historical fiction and first-person nonfiction accounts of events. Like a filmmaker, an author may decide to alter history in order to make the story more dramatic. The words that an author uses are also an important part of enjoying and understanding historical fiction. An author may use words associated with a certain period of history. He or she also may choose words for their connotation, or emotional meaning, to make a story exciting.

Exploring various elements of craft and structure makes reading fictional texts more enjoyable. Let's see what we find as we explore these tales of the past!

Progress Check — Can I?

Before Unit 9 / After Unit 9

- [ ] Compare and contrast a written story with a film that is based on the same story.
- [ ] Determine the meanings of words and phrases that are related to social studies and history.
- [ ] Compare and contrast a piece of historical fiction with an historical account of the same time period.
- [ ] Compare and contrast primary and secondary sources that are about the same topic.
- [ ] Understand the different connotations of words that have similar meanings.

Unit 9 ■ Reading Literature: Integration of Knowledge and Ideas

Student Page 217

Progress Check

The Progress Check is a self-assessment feature that students can use to gauge their own progress. Before students begin work on Unit 9, have them check the boxes next to any item that they feel they can do well. Explain that it is fine if they don't check any of the boxes. Tell them that they will have an opportunity to learn about and practice all of these items while studying the unit. Let them know that near the end of the unit they will have a chance to reconsider how well they can do each item on this list.

Before they begin their Unit 9 Review (see page 244 of this guide), you will be prompted to have students revisit this page. You can use this information to work with students on any items they don't understand before they tackle the Review.

HOME ◆ CONNECT...

The Home Connect feature is a way to keep parents or other adult family members apprised of what their children are learning. The key learning objectives are listed, and some ideas for related activities and discussions are included.

Explain to students that they can share the Home Connect page with their parents or other adult family members in their home. Let students know how much time the class will be spending on this unit so they can plan their time accordingly at home.

Encourage students and their parents to share their experiences using the suggestions on the Home Connect page and the Home Connect activities at **sadlierconnect.com**. You may wish to make a place to post some of this work.

HOME ◆ CONNECT...

Your child undoubtedly has some favorite movies, so ask whether any of those movies were **based on a written story**. Go over a list of his or her favorite movies, looking for examples. Talk about how the movies are different from the original texts.

It can be a fascinating exercise to take a story that is based on an historical event and compare it to an actual **first-person historical account** of the same event. Encourage your child to talk about how he or she includes or leaves out details when telling stories about events in which he or she has had a part.

Your child probably knows the definitions of most of the words he or she uses, but those words' **connotative meanings** may be less familiar. Explain to your child that words have cultural and emotional meanings as well as literal, "dictionary" definitions. With your child, think of words that have particularly potent connotative meanings. (Adjectives are a great place to start.) Talk about the situations in which these words would be used.

Conversation Starter: Ask your child to share a personal story about something that happened to him or her in the past. Then ask your child to imagine making a movie based on that story. Would your child change the story to make the movie more exciting? If so, how, and how much? Discuss the events of the story. You may even want to create an outline storyboard for key moments in this imaginary movie.

IN THIS UNIT, YOUR CHILD WILL...

- Compare a written story to a movie version of the story.
- Read and comprehend domain-specific terms having to do with social studies and history.
- Compare a work of historical fiction to an historical account of the same time period.
- Compare a primary source and a secondary source that deal with the same topic.
- Understand the connotations of multiple words that have the same definition.

WAYS TO HELP YOUR CHILD

Play a game with your child in which you take turns thinking of words with strong connotative meanings but similar definitions. Start with a "mild" word like *big*, for example, and encourage your child to work up toward words like *huge* or *colossal*. Pause as you play to discuss how the connotative meanings would affect the way readers would interpret a description of a story.

ONLINE
For more Home Connect activities, continue online at sadlierconnect.com

218   Unit 9 ■ Reading Literature: Integration of Knowledge and Ideas

Student Page 218

UNIT PLANNER

Theme: Tales of the Past	Focus
COMPARING AND CONTRASTING VERSIONS *pp. 220–227*	*The Last of the Mohicans; Exciting* Mohicans *Diverges from the Novel* **GENRE:** Historical Fiction; Movie Review **LEXILE®:** 1370L; 1130L **WORDS TO KNOW:** expanse, repose, stoicism, wary, diverges, steed, animated, soldiery, meager, exuberance, hue, sultriness, accouterment, emblem, musket, sage, rude, buckskin, sinew, agile, garb
COMPARING AND CONTRASTING HISTORICAL ACCOUNTS *pp. 228–235*	*Journal of a British Officer* **GENRE:** Historical Account **LEXILE®:** 1040L **WORDS TO KNOW:** colony, enabled, confirm, aspect, league, estimation, prospect, altered, portion, incident, evidence, occurred, sentry, physical, canopy, hide, corded, intricate, provocation
CLOSE READING *pp. 236–241*	*A Plains Family Moves West; Great* Plains; *Across the Plains in 1844* **GENRE:** Historical Fiction; Movie Review; Historical Account **LEXILE®:** 1100L; 1020L
CONNECT ACROSS TEXTS *p. 242*	Support a Claim
LANGUAGE *p. 243*	Word Meanings
UNIT 9 REVIEW *pp. 244–246*	*Great* Plains (continued); *Joe's Letter To His Grandmother* **GENRE:** Review; Letter **LEXILE®:** 1020L

Essential Question: How can different media and forms of a text affect our understanding?

UNIT 9

Objective(s)

- Compare and contrast a literary work to its filmed version.
- Find the meanings of terms that relate to history and social studies.

Compare a fictional account of an historical event to a nonfiction historical account of the same event.

- Compare and contrast a literary work to its filmed version.
- Find the meaning of terms that relate to history and social studies.
- Compare a fictional account of an historical event to a nonfiction historical account of the same event.

Identify the different connotations of words with similar definitions.

Unit Assessment

- Unit 9 Review *pp. 244–246*
- Unit 9 Performance Task (ONLINE)

Additional Assessment Options

- Performance Task 1 *pp. 311A–320*
  (ALSO ONLINE)
- Performance Task 2 *pp. 321A–330*
  (ALSO ONLINE)

Optional Purchase:

- iProgress Monitor (ONLINE)
- Progress Monitor Student Benchmark Assessment Booklet

(ONLINE) Digital Resources

- Home Connect Activities
- Unit Performance Task
- Additional Practice
- Full-Length Reading Selections
- Teacher Resources
- iProgress Monitor (optional purchase)

Go to SadlierConnect.com to access your Digital Resources.

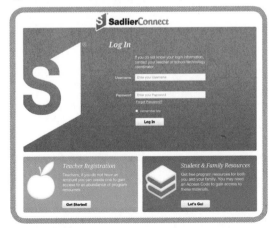

For more detailed instructions see page T3.

219B

LEARNING PROGRESSIONS

In this unit, students will learn to compare and contrast versions of a text. The skills that students learn in this unit build upon the skills they learned during the sixth grade. Likewise, the skills students learn this year will provide a foundation for the skills they will develop in the eighth grade.

Comparing and Contrasting Versions

- In sixth grade, students will compare and contrast reading a literary text to listening to or viewing a version of the text, including contrasting what they "see" and "hear" when reading to what they perceive when they listen or watch.

- In seventh grade, students will build on their ability to compare and contrast a literary text to its audio, filmed, staged, or multimedia version by analyzing the effects of techniques that are unique to each medium.

- Students in eighth grade will analyze the extent to which a filmed or live production of a story or drama stays faithful to or departs from the text or script.

Comparing and Contrasting Historical Accounts

- By the end of sixth grade, students will be able to compare and contrast texts in different forms or genres in terms of their approaches to similar themes and topics.

- Seventh-grade students will compare and contrast a fictional portrayal of a time, place, or character and an historical account of the same period in order to understand how fiction authors use or alter history.

- Students in eighth grade will analyze how a modern work of fiction draws on themes, patterns of events, or character types from myths, traditional stories, or religious works.

Reading Literature: Integration of Knowledge and Ideas

Essential Question:
How can different media and forms of a text affect our understanding?

Essential Question:
How can different media and forms of a text affect our understanding?

In this unit, students will learn about the integration of knowledge and ideas, specifically how to compare and contrast different versions and forms of a literary work and how to compare an historical account to a fictional portrayal.

Theme: Tales of the Past
Students will read selections related to historical events, including an excerpt from the novel *The Last of the Mohicans*, a movie review of the film adaptation of that novel, and an historical account about the war that is the focus of the book. In addition, they will read historical fiction about 19th century travelers on the Oregon Trail and a review of a film based on that story.

Curriculum Connection: Social Studies
Students will learn about the French and Indian War, which took place from 1754 until 1763. In this conflict, Great Britain fought the French and France's Native American allies over territory and control in North America. Students will also learn about the struggles of pioneering families who moved westward on the Oregon Trail.

Vocabulary Overview

General Academic Vocabulary

accouterment, agile, altered, animated, aspect, confirm, corded, diverges, emblem, enabled, estimation, evidence, expanse, exuberance, garb, hide, hue, incident, intricate, league, meager, occurred, physical, portion, prospect, provocation, repose, rude, sage, sinew, steed, sultriness, wary

Domain-Specific Vocabulary

buckskin, canopy, colony, musket, sentry, soldiery, stoicism

Guided Instruction

OBJECTIVES
• Compare and contrast a literary work to its filmed version.
• Find the meanings of terms that relate to history and social studies.

Genre: Historical Fiction and Movie Review

Explain to students that historical fiction is fiction set in an era of time in the past. A movie review evaluates different aspects of a film.

Set the Purpose

Help students understand the purpose for learning the reading skill by asking *Why would a filmmaker change aspects of a novel when adapting it for film?*

Model and Teach

Read the selection and callouts as the class follows along. Model effective strategies for responding to the callouts by using the suggestions below.

CITE EVIDENCE

A Discuss the meaning of *ally* (a person or group who cooperates in a common cause with another).

B Use context to discuss the meaning of *tomahawk* in paragraph 2 (a type of weapon).

COMPARING AND CONTRASTING VERSIONS

Guided Instruction

WORDS TO KNOW
diverges
expanse
repose
stoicism
wary

You can **compare a written story to its film version** and analyze the techniques the filmmakers used in creating the adaptation. Also, when reading historical fiction, look for **terms that relate to history and social studies.**

CITE EVIDENCE

A The word *ally* often is a **word related to history**. In the introduction, circle a form of this word and draw boxes around details that offer clues to its meaning. What does the word *ally* mean?

B Find and underline the history term *tomahawk*. Then, using context clues, give a simple definition of the word *tomahawk*.

The Last of the Mohicans
(Genre: Historical Fiction)

*In 1757, a war was raging in North America between Britain and France over who would control the vast **expanses** of the continent. The name "French and Indian War" identifies the two groups allied against the British.*

James Fenimore Cooper's novel The Last of the Mohicans *was published in 1826. It begins with a threat to Fort William Henry, under the command of Colonel Munro. Munro's daughters, Cora and Alice, demand to go to him despite what will be a dangerous journey through a forest populated with native tribes allied with the French.*

Cora and Alice are escorted by Major Duncan Heyward and a native scout named Magua. In this excerpt, Heyward is introduced to Magua.

1   His eyes fell on the still, upright, and rigid form of the "Indian runner" … Although in a state of perfect **repose**, and apparently disregarding, with characteristic **stoicism**, the excitement and bustle around him, there was a sullen fierceness mingled with the quiet of the savage that was likely to arrest the attention of much more experienced eyes than those which now scanned him, in unconcealed amazement.

2   The native bore both the tomahawk and knife of his tribe; and yet his appearance was not altogether that of a warrior. On the contrary, there was an air of neglect about his person, like that which might have proceeded from great and recent exertion, which he had not yet found leisure to repair.

3   His eye, alone, which glistened like a fiery star amid lowering clouds, was to be seen in its state of native wildness. For a single instant his searching and yet **wary** glance met the wondering look of the other, and then changing its direction, partly in cunning, and partly in disdain, it remained fixed, as if penetrating the distant air.

220

Words to Know

General Academic Vocabulary

diverges (*v.*): splits apart from
expanse (*n.*): open area
repose (*n.*): rest
wary (*adj.*): cautious; slow to trust

Domain-Specific Vocabulary

stoicism (*n.*): paying no attention to pain or difficulty; uncomplaining

Working with Word Meaning Encourage students to restate these definitions in their own words and to write their own example sentences.

INTEGRATION OF KNOWLEDGE AND IDEAS

Exciting *Mohicans* Diverges from the Novel

(Genre: Movie Review)

1   Director Michael Mann has delivered an exciting film adaptation of James Fenimore Cooper's novel *The Last of the Mohicans*, but it takes liberties with the story's plot and characters.

2   The film **diverges** from the novel right from the start. <u>A key early scene in which Major Duncan Heyward is introduced to his scout, Magua, is much more developed in the book.</u> Cooper offers a thorough description of Magua as seen through the eyes of Heyward. Embedded in the major's description are stereotypes typical of Cooper's time, and they add to the racial tension that pervades the novel.

3   In the corresponding scene in Mann's film, Magua steps out of the dark shadows and reveals himself to Heyward. The costume and makeup team have matched Cooper's description of Magua well. <u>Actor Wes Studi communicates the character's stillness and apparent lack of feeling.</u> The most effective moment in this scene is the look Magua gives Heyward at the end: a perfect mix of curiosity and disdain.

Comprehension Check

Which filmmaking techniques does the movie reviewer explicitly mention? What aspects of filmmaking are implied? Cite specifics.

Guided Instruction

CITE EVIDENCE

C Find the words *repose* and *stoicism* in paragraph 1 on page 220, and double underline them. Then find the sentence in the movie review on this page that describes how the film captured these words, and double underline that sentence.

D When a **written story is adapted into a film**, the **screenwriter** may not follow the story exactly. In paragraph 2 of the movie review on this page, underline one way in which the film and the novel—the written story—are different.

E A film's **costume and makeup designers** are responsible for representing the characters visually. In the movie review, put an asterisk by the reviewer's statement about how the character of Magua appears in the film in comparison to his description in the novel. What does the **actor** playing Magua add to the character?

Guided Instruction

CITE EVIDENCE

C After students have located *repose* and *stoicism* in paragraph 1, use context to discuss the meaning of the words with them. Direct students to look at paragraph 3 in the movie review to find how the actor who played Magua captured the qualities of *repose* and *stoicism*.

D With students, read paragraph 2 of the movie review. The first sentence clues students to look for a difference between the treatments, and the second sentence explains in which scene the different treatment occurs.

E Help students locate the sentence that describes how the costume and makeup team have treated the character's appearance. Students may suggest that the actor who plays Magua adds to the character's depth through the look he gives Heyward.

Comprehension Check

Sample Answer: The reviewer explicitly refers to directing, acting, costuming, and makeup. Indirectly, the reviewer refers to lighting and screenwriting.

Answer Explanation: In paragraph 1, the reviewer mentions the name of the director. The reviewer calls attention to acting, costuming, and makeup in paragraph 3. The writer implicitly refers to screenwriting in paragraph 2 ("A key early scene . . . is much more developed in the book,") and to lighting in paragraph 3 ("Magua steps out of the dark shadows . . . ").

Support English Language Learners

Students learning English may benefit from additional opportunities to build background on the French and Indian War. Use a map to show students sites where famous battles took place, especially Fort Ticonderoga and Fort William Henry in New York State. Explain that American colonists still considered themselves British at the time and fought against France and their Native American allies. Show a time line indicating when British colonists first established permanent colonies in America and including significant events in colonial America up to and beyond the French and Indian War, pointing out that this war took place before the American Revolution.

Guided Instruction

CITE EVIDENCE

A Through context, students should be able to identify that the outpost, Fort William Henry, is the characters' destination. If necessary, have students look up the meaning of the word *outpost* (a military post at a distance from the main force).

B Students may be confused about what is different in the character of Alice, since paragraph 5 on page 223 states that she is well cast. However, if they read carefully they should be able to identify that the actress does not have blue eyes as the character does in the book. Help students locate in paragraph 6 on page 223 how Cora's character in the film seems different from the character in the novel.

C Students should be able to identify the sound description (*silently*) in paragraph 8 on page 223. The novel excerpt does not specify anything about the sound of this scene.

Listening and Viewing Skills

Read paragraph 5 on page 222 as students listen. Have them look at the photo of the character Alice near paragraph 5 on page 223. Discuss differences between the description of Alice in the novel and how she appears in the photograph. Ask about the emotions that she shows in each. (Alice smiles in the novel but looks serious in the photograph.) What does this difference in emotions add to your understanding of the character? (She is not simply gracious and happy; she can be serious and perhaps even angry.)

WORDS TO KNOW
animated
exuberance
meager
soldiery
steed

CITE EVIDENCE

A The word *outpost* is a social studies term. Find the word in the introduction on this page and then, in the same paragraph, put an asterisk next to a term that refers to the same thing. What is an outpost?

B The movie review mentions the importance of **casting**, or selecting actors. In paragraphs 5 and 6 of the movie review on page 223, underline the ways that the actresses playing Cora and Alice differ from the characters' descriptions in the novel.

C The use of **sound** is a critical technique in moviemaking. In paragraph 8 of the movie review on page 223, put a box around a word that describes the sound of this scene. How does the sound of this scene compare to its description in the novel?

Cora, Alice, Heyward, and other British soldiers begin their long journey on horseback through the forest to*Fort William Henry. Accompanying them to that outpost is Magua, who rides up ahead.

4   A young man . . . conducted to their **steeds** two females, who, (as it was apparent by their dresses, were prepared to encounter the fatigues of a journey in the woods.)

5   [Alice] . . . and she was the more juvenile in her appearance, though both were young, permitted glimpses of her dazzling complexion, fair golden hair, and bright blue eyes . . . The flush which still lingered above the pines in the western sky was not more bright nor delicate than the bloom on her cheek; nor was the opening day more cheering than the **animated** smile which she bestowed on the youth, as he assisted her into the saddle.

6   [Cora] . . . concealed her charms from the gaze of the **soldiery** with a care that seemed better fitted to the experience of four or five additional years. It could be seen, however, that her person, though molded with the same exquisite proportions, of which none of the graces were lost by the (traveling dress) she wore, was rather fuller and more mature than that of her companion.

7   . . . [Alice] was the first to dash aside the slight branches of the bushes, and to follow the runner along the dark and tangled pathway . . . after which they emerged from the broad border of underbrush which grew along the line of the highway, and entered under the high but dark arches of the forest.

8   In a few moments a colt was seen gliding, like a fallow deer, among the straight trunks of the pines; and, in another instant, [Magua] came into view, with as much rapidity as he could excite his **meager** beast to endure . . . Until now this personage had escaped the observation of the travelers.

Words to Know

General Academic Vocabulary
animated (*adj.*): full of life or spirit; lively
exuberance (*n.*): enthusiasm; excitement and eagerness
meager (*adj.*): small or weak; puny
steed (*n.*): horse

Domain-Specific Vocabulary
soldiery (*n.*): soldiers; members of the army

Working with Word Meaning Ask students to share examples for each word.

INTEGRATION OF KNOWLEDGE AND IDEAS

Exciting *Mohicans* Diverges from the Novel *continued*

4   One of the many responsibilities of a film director is casting the right actors. The scene in which Colonel Munro's two daughters, Cora and Alice, prepare for their journey proves this point. The actors offer a strong sense of who these two young women are.

5   The role of the younger sister, Alice, is particularly well cast. <u>The luminous young actress Jodhi May does not have Alice's blue eyes (as described in the novel)</u>, but she brings a childlike **exuberance** to the role. When she expresses to Heyward her naïve hope that they shall see some "red men" during their journey in "the wilderness," we understand her character at once.

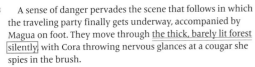

6   Cora, as played by Madeleine Stowe, is another example of how the film varies from the book. <u>Cora is supposed to be an older, darker-skinned half sister to Alice. In the film, Stowe is all fair skin and youthful loveliness.</u>

7   Compliments must be paid to the exquisite period costumes the women wear. The tension between their riding dresses—still elegant, despite their practicality—and the rawness of the forest is tangible.

8   A sense of danger pervades the scene that follows in which the traveling party finally gets underway, accompanied by Magua on foot. They move through <u>the thick, barely lit forest silently</u> with Cora throwing nervous glances at a cougar she spies in the brush.

Comprehension Check

How does the reviewer's description of the film version affect your understanding of the excerpts from the novel? Give an example to support your answer.

223

Guided Instruction

Guided Instruction

CITE EVIDENCE

D **Lighting** is an important filmmaking technique. Even in an outdoor scene lit by the sun, the **cinematographer** is responsible for how light or dark the scene is. In paragraph 7 of the novel on page 222, double underline two descriptions of the light. Then, in paragraph 8 of the movie review, double underline how that aspect of the film has been handled.

E Circle the movie review's description of Cora's and Alice's dresses, which are part of the film's costume design. Then circle any details about the dresses in the novel excerpt on page 222. Are the movie costumes similar to or different from the novel's descriptions?

CITE EVIDENCE

D After students locate the phrases on page 222, direct them to paragraph 8 on page 223 to locate the description of light in the movie scene.

E Direct students to paragraph 6 of the novel excerpt to find a description of Cora's and Alice's dresses. Then have them focus on paragraph 7 in the review to find descriptions of the movie costumes. Discuss with students that the movie costumes are different from their description in the novel. The novel implies that the dresses are mainly practical garments, but the review states that they are "exquisite."

Comprehension Check

Sample Answer: Because the movie review is more succinct and much shorter than the original novel, the review helps me better understand what is going on in the novel.

Answer Explanation: Students might use the following examples as evidence for their answer: on page 223, the reviewer includes three brief descriptive statements that suggest what is happening and explain what the characters are thinking and seeing. In paragraph 5, the actress playing Alice is described as having "a childlike exuberance." In paragraph 7, we are told that "the rawness of the forest is tangible." And in paragraph 8, we are told that the party "move through the thick, barely lit forest silently."

Digital Connection: Read or Research

Students who are interested in reading more of the novel can download the text of *The Last of the Mohicans*, which is in the public domain and readily available for free on the Internet. Alternately, students may enjoy using Internet resources to learn more about the French and Indian War, which was a part of the Seven Years' War between Great Britain and France. When students have read the novel or researched the period, have them share what they have learned with the rest of the class.

Guided Practice

Recap Reading Selection

Have students recall what they have read so far about Cora, Alice, and Magua. Prompt them to tell what they remember about how the movie differs from the novel. Let students know that they will next be reading about three new characters in the book.

Read and Practice

Have partners take turns reading the selection as you circulate to provide support. Circulate among students and ask them to respond to Cite Evidence callouts A and B. Provide additional scaffolding as needed, using the suggestions below.

CITE EVIDENCE

A Direct students to paragraph 9 on page 225 to find the sound of the scene (there is no dialogue). Then have them reread paragraph 9 on page 224 to find the sounds in the novel. Discuss with students that the written novel describes "the low voices of the men;" in the film, the scene is without dialogue.

B Point out that a lighting description may tell about an aspect of color (such as hue or intensity) without naming the actual shade. This should help students locate the phrase in paragraph 9 of the novel that has to do with color. If necessary, tell them that they will find more than one example of description of color in both the novel and the review.

COMPARING AND CONTRASTING VERSIONS

Guided Practice

The Last of the Mohicans *continued*

WORDS TO KNOW
accouterment
emblem
hue
musket
sage
sultriness

CITE EVIDENCE

A In the movie review on page 225, put an asterisk by a phrase that describes the sound of the scene. How is the sound of this scene different in the written story on this page?

B The cinematographer determines not only what is light and dark but also the **colors** in the film. Double underline any detail in the novel excerpt that mentions color. Then double underline in the movie review on page 225 any phrases that describe colors. Discuss with a partner how these decisions shape this scene.

Soon Cora, Alice, Heyward, and Magua will encounter three men: an older man named Chingachgook, his son Uncas, and a white hunter named Hawkeye. Chingachgook and Uncas are Mohican, a native tribe, and they are the last Mohicans known to survive. This excerpt describes both the forest and Chingachgook; the following page describes Hawkeye.

9   On that day, two men were lingering on the banks of a small but rapid stream ... the vast canopy of woods spread itself to the margin of the river, overhanging the water, <u>and shadowing its dark current with a deeper **hue**</u>. The rays of the sun were beginning to grow less fierce ... Still that breathing silence, which marks the drowsy **sultriness** of an American landscape in July, pervaded the secluded spot, interrupted only by the low voices of the men, the occasional and lazy tap of a woodpecker, the discordant cry of some gaudy jay, or a swelling on the ear, from the dull roar of a distant waterfall.

10   ... One of these loiterers showed the <u>red skin</u> and wild **accouterments** of a native of the woods. [Chingachgook's] body ... presented a terrific **emblem** of death, drawn in <u>intermingled colors of white and black.</u> His closely shaved head ... was without ornament of any kind ... A tomahawk and scalping knife, of English manufacture, were in his girdle. ...

Words to Know

General Academic Vocabulary

accouterment (*n.*): accessory; piece of equipment
emblem (*n.*): symbol; sign
hue (*n.*): color
sage (*n.*): wise and learned person who gives advice to others
sultriness (*n.*): damp heat

Domain-Specific Vocabulary

musket (*n.*): an early type of rifle

Working with Word Meaning Have partners restate each word's meaning in their own words and then use the word in conversation.

INTEGRATION OF KNOWLEDGE AND IDEAS

Guided Practice

Exciting *Mohicans* Diverges from the Novel *continued*

9   There is an early chapter in the novel that the film version does not include in which the characters of Hawkeye, Chingachgook, and Uncas are described in detail. In its place, the film shows a brief scene with no dialogue in which the men discover that a group of rival natives are on their way to ambush Heyward and the other travelers. The scene is breathtaking. It recreates a forest so dense that direct sunlight cannot break through. <u>The vegetation is colored in darker, not lighter, shades of green.</u>

10   Chingachgook is instantly recognizable as an Indian of the period. He is clothed from head to toe (<u>we therefore have no idea if his chest bears a black-and-white "emblem of death," as the novel describes</u>), and the full hair on his head ends in a long black ponytail. For weapons, he carries a long **musket** and a tomahawk. He appears older than his companions but does not suggest the old **sage** from the book.

Comprehension Check

1. One detail about Chingachgook that both the novel and film mention is his

   a. ponytail.   **c.** musket.

   (b.) tomahawk.   **d.** shaved head.

2. Which detail from the novel, if filmed, would be the responsibility of the cinematographer?

   a. "his closely shaved head was without ornament of any kind"

   b. "that breathing silence . . . pervaded the secluded spot"

   c. "the dull roar of a distant waterfall"

   (d.) "the rays of the sun were beginning to grow less fierce"

3. Paragraph 9 mentions a chapter from the novel not included in the movie. Who would be responsible for such a decision?

   a. the actors

   b. the cinematographer

   (c.) the screenwriter

   d. the casting director

4. Which of the following words is a term from history or social studies?

   a. hue

   b. landscape

   c. vegetation

   (d.) musket

5. Discuss with a partner which technique of filmmaking was the most crucial in adapting this section of the novel. Cite specifics in your argument.

Sample answer: Cinematography is the most important technique in adapting this section because it sets the scene's mood. Since this scene is about an ambush, the cinematographer had to figure out how to portray the dark woods as ominous.

Discussion Skills

Put students in groups to discuss their ideas about the challenges of adapting a novel for film. Group members should prepare by identifying at least three key challenges that the director of a film adaptation would have to solve. Assign group roles, such as Facilitator, Timekeeper, Notetaker, and Reporter, and have each group develop a comprehensive list of challenges and potential solutions. Remind students to ask questions of one another and to keep the discussion on track. At the end of the discussion, have Reporters share their groups' list with the class. Develop a class list of challenges and solutions.

Comprehension Check

Answer Explanations:

1. Encourage students to read the paragraphs in both the novel and the movie review that describe Chingachgook. They should be able to find that B, *tomahawk*, is the best answer.

2. Students have learned that the cinematographer determines lighting in a scene, so they should recognize that D, *the rays of the sun were beginning to grow less fierce*, is the best choice.

3. Based on what they have learned in this unit, students shoud recognize that the screenwriter would be responsible for adapting a novel into a script and therefore would choose which scenes to omit and which to include. Therefore, C is the correct answer.

4. Since students know that history and social studies deal with how human beings behave in society, they should recognize that D, *musket*, is the best answer.

5. Students' opinions as to the most crucial aspect of filmmaking for this section may vary, but they should support their choice with reasoning and specific evidence from the texts.

Turn and Talk

Pose the following question: *Given what you have read from the novel and what you have read about the movie, would you rather read the entire novel or see the film?* Have partners quickly discuss the question. Then have volunteers share their answers, explaining their reasoning.

Comparing and Contrasting Versions

Independent Practice

Recap Reading Selection

Have students recall what they have read so far about the novel and the movie. Ask students if they can recall the names of the three new characters who were introduced in the last two pages (Hawkeye, Chingachgook, and Uncas). Let students know that they will next read more about Hawkeye.

Read and Apply

Have students read this selection independently as you circulate. Ask them to read aloud so you can see if they are reading fluently. You can also use the support below to help students who are having difficulty.

CITE EVIDENCE

A If students are having difficulty, direct them to paragraph 15 on page 226 and paragraph 11 on page 227. Discuss with students that the descriptions of Hawkeye's eyes are different; in the novel they are said to be "small, quick, keen, and restless," and in the review they are said to have "an expression of calm alertness."

B Students should be able to locate the word *beads* that relates to *wampum*. They may suggest that *wampum* is a type of bead. A dictionary will give more specifics, telling students that *wampum* is made from polished mollusk shells.

COMPARING AND CONTRASTING VERSIONS

Independent Practice

WORDS TO KNOW
agile
buckskin
garb
rude
sinew

CITE EVIDENCE

A Underline in the novel excerpt and in the review any words or phrases that describe Hawkeye's eyes. How are these descriptions similar and different? Cite evidence from the text.

B The word *wampum* is a social studies term. Circle any words in paragraph 12 on page 227 that offer a clue as to its meaning. Then give a meaning in your own words, and check it in a print or online dictionary.

The Last of the Mohicans *continued*

11 . . . the other [man] exhibited, through the mask of his **rude** and nearly savage equipments, the brighter, though sun-burned and long-faced complexion of one who might claim descent from a European parentage.

12 The frame of the white man, judging by such parts as were not concealed by his clothes, was like that of one who had known hardships and exertion from his earliest youth.

13 He wore a hunting shirt of forest green, fringed with faded yellow, and a summer cap of skins which had been shorn of their fur. He also bore a knife in a girdle of wampum, like that which confined the scanty garments of [Chingachgook], but no tomahawk.

14 His moccasins were ornamented . . . while the only part of his under dress which appeared below the hunting frock was a pair of **buckskin** leggings, that laced at the sides, and which were gartered above the knees, with the **sinews** of a deer. A pouch and horn completed his personal accouterments. . . .

15 The eye of [Hawkeye] was small, quick, keen, and restless, roving while he spoke, on every side of him, as if in quest of game, or distrusting the sudden approach of some lurking enemy.

Words to Know

General Academic Vocabulary
agile (*adj.*): moving and jumping easily; quick and well-coordinated
garb (*n.*): clothing; style of clothing
rude (*adj.*): roughly made; not fancy or refined
sinew (*n.*): tendon

Domain-Specific Vocabulary
buckskin (*adj.*): made from the skin of a deer

Working with Word Meaning Have students draw pictures for the words.

INTEGRATION OF KNOWLEDGE AND IDEAS

Independent Practice

Exciting *Mohicans* Diverges from the Novel *continued*

11   The great British actor Daniel Day-Lewis is well cast as Hawkeye. His lean frame and long face support his portrayal of a white man raised by Indians who is stern and steady yet physically **agile**. In this scene with Chingachgook and Uncas in the forest, he practically dances over the moss-covered rocks in the stream as he looks for clues left by the rival group. His eyes carry an expression of calm alertness.

12   Hawkeye presents more fine work from the film's costume designer. He wears traditional native **garb**, including a long, pale deerskin garment similar to a smock. He keeps a knife tied to his belt and carries a musket over his shoulder. He wears buckskin leggings and wampum beads in his hair.

13   Uncas, the son of Chingachgook, is played by Canadian actor Eric Schweig. Schweig portrays him as every bit the eager, "youthful warrior" of the novel.

Comprehension Check   MORE ONLINE sadlierconnect.com

1. Which two items of Hawkeye's costume appear in both the novel and the film?

   a. a knife and buckskin leggings

   b. a green shirt and animal skin cap

   c. a musket and moccasins

   d. a pouch and wampum beads

2. Which technique of filmmaking is NOT mentioned in the movie review?

   a. costume design

   b. casting

   c. sound

   d. acting

3. All of the following terms from the novel come from social studies EXCEPT

   a. buckskin leggings.

   b. complexion.

   c. moccasins.

   d. wampum.

4. Which of the following characteristics of Hawkeye is mentioned only in the novel?

   a. his long face

   b. his being a white man

   c. his alertness

   d. his sun-burned skin

5. Choose any two film techniques and analyze what effect they have on the film.

   Sample answer: By re-creating native clothing and accessories for each character,

   the costume designer helped express their distinctiveness. The cinematographer

   decided how to use natural sunlight to create a dark, dense forest.

Independent Practice

Comprehension Check

Answer Explanations:

1. Students reading carefully should find that only A, *a knife and buckskin leggings*, are items in both the novel and the film.

2. C, *sound*, is the correct answer. The review does not mention or evaluate the film techniques of capturing or creating sound.

3. Students should know that social studies is the study of human societies. B, *complexion*, is not a societal artifact and is the best answer.

4. Students may need to reread paragraph 11, page 226, to find that D, *his sun-burned skin*, is the best answer.

5. Students can choose any of the film techniques mentioned in the movie review. They should support their responses with specific examples from the review.

Critical Comprehension

Challenge students to think more deeply about the text and to support their answers with evidence from the text.

Why does the cinematographer use dark lighting? (to re-create the sense of a canopied forest and to suggest danger)

Assess and Respond

If students have trouble answering the questions in the Comprehension Check,

Then lead them in highlighting the section of the text referenced in the question, rereading carefully, and discussing how different film techniques affect the film.

Extend Thinking: Apply Concepts

Encourage students to think about other books they have read that have been turned into movies. These could include anything from picture books to novels for young adults. Have students form groups based on the books and movies they choose. Then have students use what they have learned in this unit to compare and contrast the written and filmed versions. Ask students to work together to create a presentation of their comparisons.

Guided Instruction

OBJECTIVE
Compare a fictional account of an historical event to a nonfiction historical account of the same event.

Set the Purpose

Tell students to think about the difference between a fictional and a nonfiction account of the same event. Ask: *What might be different? What might be the same?*

Genre: Historical Account

An historical account is nonfiction writing about an historical event by a witness or participant. This selection, while not an actual historical account, imitates the kind of source documentation that James Fenimore Cooper could have used for creating *The Last of the Mohicans*.

Model and Teach

Read or have volunteers read the selection and callouts as the class follows along. Model effective strategies for responding to the callouts by using the suggestions below.

CITE EVIDENCE

A Students may need to be reminded to refer to the title to find the word *Journal*.

B Direct students to paragraph 5 and help them to locate the event that occurs in the novel.

COMPARING/CONTRASTING HISTORICAL ACCOUNTS

Guided Instruction

WORDS TO KNOW

aspect

colony

confirm

enabled

A fictional account of an historical event can be compared to a nonfiction historical account of the same event.

CITE EVIDENCE

A A **primary source** is a firsthand account or other document created at the time of an historical event, such as a letter, journal, or official record. A **secondary source,** such as a textbook or magazine article, uses primary source material to interpret and analyze an event. This selection is not a real primary source, but it mirrors the type of source James Fenimore Cooper might have used. Circle the word on this page that suggests it is a type of primary source.

B Authors of historical fiction research **historical accounts** of events to make their stories believable. In this way, an author adapts and "uses" history to tell a story. Underline in paragraph 5 an historical detail that this work shares with *The Last of the Mohicans*.

(Journal) of a British Officer
(Genre: Historical Account)

1   **July 22, 1757** Today, after months of fighting on the western front of the **colony** of Pennsylvania, I arrived at my present location of Fort Edward in New York, where I have entered into the service of General Daniel Webb as an officer of the British army.

2   It is an extremely tense time. The war with the French and their native allies has been going on for more than three years. The British have suffered several recent failures, and many noble lives have been lost. The other soldiers and I are perplexed, for we know the French are fewer in number; we suspect it is their alliance with the various native groups that has **enabled** them to pressure us so.

3   Tomorrow General Webb will travel to Fort William Henry to **confirm** what has been rumored: groups of Frenchmen and natives are waiting on Lake George to attack the fort. He will meet with Lieutenant Colonel George Munro, who is in charge there.

4   **July 29, 1757** General Webb returned today with confirmation of the worst: the French are indeed gathering near Fort William Henry and have every intention of attacking. I fear another devastating loss for our side, and so I imagine General Webb will be asked by Munro to send support.

5   **July 30, 1757** Today brought an unusual turn of events. I was summoned to the office of General Webb wherein I witnessed the arrival of an officer whose name I could not discern. General Webb has ordered this officer to Fort William Henry as part of an official party for the purpose of accompanying the sister and niece of a Major Drummond, who serves with Colonel Munro at the fort. The sister insists on being with her brother at the fort. General Webb ordered me to go along.

Words to Know

General Academic Vocabulary

aspect (*n.*): characteristic; part or side

confirm (*v.*): to check that something is true

enabled (*v.*): allowed; let happen

Domain-Specific Vocabulary

colony (*n.*): far-off area immigrated into and/or controlled by a country

Working with Word Meaning In pairs, have one student choose a vocabulary word and define it in his or her own words. The other student guesses the word. Then have partners switch roles.

INTEGRATION OF KNOWLEDGE AND IDEAS

6   General Webb also asked a local native—a*Huron—to accompany us. This native is responsible for intercepting the message that contained the plot to attack Fort William Henry. He is to be our runner, scout, and guide through the forest, which is no doubt full of enemy natives. The Huron are supposedly allied with the French, but this man is loyal to the British crown, I am told.

7   I watched the native scout very closely as he stood before my commanding officer: he hardly moved, which was odd, especially for a fleet-footed runner. Of course all the natives claim to be runners, it's some sort of privilege, though I admit it is one of many **aspects** of natives I have yet to understand.

8   My concern grew as I gazed at him, for the scout had an evil look to him. He's dangerous, capable of unexpected behavior, I thought. I watched the officer's face, too; he looked as suspicious as I was. At one point General Webb addressed the native directly, and the native replied in English. I was astonished; it was inflected with a strong accent, but English it was.

9   His countenance was alert, as if ready for battle. He had piercing dark brown eyes that stared straight ahead and moved only when General Webb addressed him. The look he gave my commander upon their introduction seemed to express confidence.

10   <u>The native's overall appearance was sharp and neat, and his manner of dress made a strong impression. His chest was partially bare, covered on the left side by a woven blanket. The skin on his face was smooth, dark, and unmarked; I had expected to see evidence of war paint, yet I did not. He carried a musket, a knife, and a tomahawk.</u>

Comprehension Check

How does what you learn about the native scout's appearance and behavior compare to what you learn about Magua in James Fenimore Cooper's novel?

Guided Instruction

CITE EVIDENCE

C   A primary source can help establish the time and place of an event. Box in paragraph 1 the date of the journal entry and where the author is located on that date.

D   What detail about the native in paragraph 6 is not the same as the one in the excerpt from Cooper's novel on page 220? Put an asterisk next to it.

E   Double underline details the author gives about the native scout's physical appearance. How does this description compare to the description of Magua in Cooper's novel?

229

Guided Instruction

CITE EVIDENCE

C   If students have difficulty, help them locate the date at the beginning of paragraph 1 and the author's current location as stated in the first sentence.

D   Help students recognize that, while the novel states that Magua is a native, it does not say that he is a Huron.

E   Direct students to the description of the native's appearance in paragraph 10. Discuss with students that here, the writer says the scout is "sharp and neat," but in Cooper's novel, Magua is said to have an "air of neglect" about him.

Comprehension Check

Sample Answer: In his novel, Cooper notes Magua's wildness, which highlights that Magua and Heyward are different. In the journal, the writer places more emphasis on the potential danger that the scout poses.

Answer Explanation: Cooper describes Magua using the following phrases: "the quiet of the savage," "a sullen fierceness," and his eye's "state of native wildness." The British officer, on the other hand, writes that "the scout had an evil look to him," and that "He's dangerous . . ."

Support English Language Learners

Comparing one more text to the excerpt of the novel may seem difficult for English learners. They may benefit from using a Venn diagram, listing what is the same in both the journal and the novel in the common area, and listing what is unique in each text in the separate areas. Have students add to the diagram as they continue to read.

Guided Instruction

CITE EVIDENCE

A Reread paragraph 13 with students. Discuss with students that Cooper includes the detail of the young woman smiling, but he does not portray her in a negative light, as the British officer does.

B Remind students that opinions sometimes contain expressions of feelings. Help students locate the writer's opinion in the first sentence of the paragraph.

Review: Compare and Contrast Versions

Supposing that this journal account were an historical source used by James Fenimore Cooper, have students locate an incident on this page that is also used in the movie *The Last of the Mohicans*, according to the movie review. Discuss with them why this particular incident was included in the movie. (In paragraph 12, the author writes: "I overheard her expressing to another soldier her excitement at the prospect of going through the 'wilderness,' as she called it, and she said she also hoped to meet 'red men.'" This incident probably was included in the movie because it reveals the extent of the younger woman's lack of experience.)

COMPARING/CONTRASTING HISTORICAL ACCOUNTS

Guided Instruction

WORDS TO KNOW

altered
estimation
incident
league
portion
prospect

CITE EVIDENCE

A Underline any words or phrases that describe the author's opinion of young Anna's behavior as she mounts her horse. Are any of these details similar to those used in Cooper's novel? Explain.

B Primary sources often reveal the personal opinions of their authors. Secondary sources, like biographies, often try to be unbiased. Circle the journal author's personal opinion of the native scout in paragraph 17.

Journal of a British Officer *continued*

11   **July 31, 1757** I write this at the end of the first day of our journey through the forest accompanying the woman and her daughter. We marched a number of **leagues**—so many I cannot remember now—and at last reached an area that was suitable for camping. At the moment I can hear the buzzing of insects all around me.

12   In the privacy of this journal I can report how totally insufferable both of these women are. The daughter, Anna, is the worse of the two: she is very young, 15 years old at my **estimation**, and her behavior reveals someone who is totally naïve in the ways of the world. I overheard her expressing to another soldier her excitement at the **prospect** of going through the "wilderness," as she called it, and she said she also hoped to meet "red men." How the soldier kept from rolling his eyes I'll never know. She would do better to hope *against* meeting any natives; they are dangerous savages.

13   As I lifted her into her saddle, <u>she smiled at me with a false, forced charm. She has bright blue eyes which she no doubt employs to charm young men, but I am not that young. I did nothing more than my duty.</u>

14   Her mother is about thirty-five years old and carries a world-weariness of more years than that. She made no effort to connect with me—friendly or otherwise—as I helped her

---

Words to Know

General Academic Vocabulary

altered (*v.*): changed
estimation (*n.*): approximate calculation; judgment
incident (*n.*): event; thing that happened
league (*n.*): a unit of distance equal to about 3 miles
portion (*n.*): segment; piece of the whole
prospect (*n.*): idea; possibility

Working with Word Meaning Have students name words with similar meanings for each of the vocabulary words.

INTEGRATION OF KNOWLEDGE AND IDEAS

into her saddle. Indeed, she seemed to resent my attempt, and I must confess this actually endeared her to me.

15 I'm curious to meet Major Drummond after meeting his sister. Mrs. Hill (for that is her name) is heavy of form, with dark hair and a complexion more olive than fair. She has on her face the lines of one who has not always had an easy life, but she carries herself with dignity.

16 *The older woman rode ahead of young Anna, following our commander and the scout, who rode a powerful steed. I followed them in the rear at some distance; my duty being to keep the marching officers in their lines. If Anna's mother felt any trepidation at venturing further into the forest her face did not betray it, though I admit to noticing her glance from time to time into the thick brush—no doubt in response to the sudden movement of a wild animal.

17 The native scout never left my sight at any time, and I must admit that this impressed me and I felt some admiration for him. Though I suppose it could be argued that the scout's job is to stay far enough ahead of the group to be an effective protector, it comforted me that I could keep our entire travelling party in sight. At times the path became very narrow and the arrangement of the soldiers had to be **altered**, but the men did so at my direction without complaint.

18 The **portion** of the journey that we accomplished today was uneventful, I'm pleased to report. Not a single native person was sighted, although there was a startling moment when a young horse cut across our path. The men were alert after that **incident**, to be sure.

Comprehension Check

How does the information about the woman and her daughter in this journal entry differ from the information in the section of Cooper's novel that begins on page 222? What conclusion can you draw about why Cooper's details are different? What might he be trying to achieve?

Unit 9 ■ Reading Literature: Integration of Knowledge and Ideas   **231**

CITE EVIDENCE

C Place an asterisk by the sentence in the journal that tells who rides in front. Is this detail the same in Cooper's novel? If so, explain whether Cooper might have altered such a detail to serve his purposes in his novel.

D Double underline in paragraph 17 the detail about the native scout that differs from the description of Magua in Cooper's novel.

E A secondary source like Cooper's novel uses and interprets facts from a primary source. In the novel, Cooper describes a colt "gliding" among the trees. Box the sentence in paragraph 18 of the journal that this detail might have been based on.

CITE EVIDENCE

C Students may need to refer to page 222 to find which young woman rides first in the novel. Discuss with students that Cooper has the younger woman ride first instead of the older woman, as described in the journal. He may have wanted to emphasize Alice's youth, eagerness, and naiveté.

D Encourage students to look at paragraph 8 on page 222 to help them find the detail that is different about the native in the journal.

E Reread paragraph 18 with students. Point out that, although the horse cutting across a path sounds quite different from "gliding," this is likely the incident Cooper used.

Comprehension Check

Sample Answer: Cooper alters some details for the sisters in his novel, such as their relationship and ages. He adapts the daughter's excitement about going into the forest for Alice. The details Cooper does not adapt—the mother's weariness and attitude, for example— are probably left out because he wishes to paint a more positive portrait of his characters.

Answer Explanation: While the women in the journal are mother and daughter, in the novel they are sisters and closer in age. The journal writer, on page 230, describes the mother as being "about thirty-five years old" and carrying "a world-weariness of more years than that." He also describes her, in paragraph 15, as being "heavy of form." It may be that Cooper thought a younger, less world-weary character would be more sympathetic.

Differentiate Instruction

Encourage students who benefit from visual instruction to draw a picture of the older woman as described in the journal on this page, and of the older sister (*Cora*) described in the excerpt from the novel on page 222. Ask students to pay attention to the details in the text as they draw. When they are done, they can compare their drawings. Students may want to repeat this activity based on other characters mentioned in both the journal and the novel.

Guided Practice

Recap Reading Selection

Have students recall what has happened so far to the group traveling from Fort Edward to Fort William Henry. Explain that they will continue to read about the group during its next day of travel.

Read and Practice

Have partners take turns reading the selection as you circulate to provide support. Circulate among students and ask them to respond to Cite Evidence callouts A and B. Provide additional scaffolding as needed, using the suggestions below.

CITE EVIDENCE

A If students need help, explain that primary sources are more apt to use words like *I* or *we* and to express an opinion. Then help them locate the sentence.

B Help students locate the description of the light and color in paragraph 10 on page 224 so that they can compare it to the description here. Discuss with students that the novel's description makes the reader aware of how the trees block the sunlight; the journal is describing colors at sunset; both texts are telling how the color changes.

COMPARING/CONTRASTING HISTORICAL ACCOUNTS

Guided Practice

WORDS TO KNOW
canopy
evidence
occurred
physical
sentry

CITE EVIDENCE

A Circle a phrase in paragraph 21 that suggests that this journal is a primary source.

B Underline in paragraph 23 a detail about the colors of the forest that is similar to the one that Cooper uses in his novel. What is the effect in Cooper's novel of describing these colors? Is the effect similar or different here?

Journal of a British Officer *continued*

19   **August 1, 1757** Our second day through the forest is complete, another large sum of leagues travelled. Today there was concern that we would run into hostile natives—that was the idea delivered by our scout, for at one point he rode ahead and returned a short while later with a look of concern on his face.

20   He is trained, as all runners are, to look for telltale signs of native activity, including rocks that have been overturned in a stream, or disturbance of the surrounding vegetation. I also know that he looks closely at the moss that grows on the top of rocks to see if it has been trampled upon.

21   He claimed to have seen such **evidence**, so we were on high alert the entire day. I sensed concern among the two women, but by nightfall no event had **occurred** and we decided to take our chances and set up camp in a clearing; there is, of course, always the chance of a nighttime attack, but our **sentries** stand guard all night.

22   I would be remiss if I did not include here an account of the forest itself; not that I think I shall ever forget it. It has astonishing **physical** beauty; to begin with, the trees are so tall one can barely see their tops, and the branches that grow closer to the ground arc out at such an angle as to create a **canopy**. It creates a sensation of having a roof over one's head despite the obvious fact that one is out of doors.

23   Sunlight barely reaches the forest's floor, which is covered in leaves and pine needles. At the end of the day, the colors of the forest become darker hued, with greens appearing almost blue, and blues becoming purple.

Words to Know

General Academic Vocabulary
evidence (*n.*): proof; signs
occurred (*v.*): happened; took place
physical (*adj.*): related to the substances something is made of

Domain-Specific Vocabulary
canopy (*n.*): overhanging covering
sentry (*n.*): a soldier posted to stand guard or keep watch

Working with Word Meaning Have students use their own words to tell the meanings of the vocabulary words.

24   The sounds of the forest are almost entirely created by its animal and insect residents; birds are calling, bees are buzzing, squirrels jump from branch to branch and shuffle leaves underfoot. Sometimes one can even hear the rush of a river or waterfall in the distance, but other than that, the forest is a silent place.

Comprehension Check

1. Which of the following would be an example of a secondary source?

  a. letters from Anna to her uncle

  (b.) a biography of General Webb

  c. Major Drummond's birth certificate

  d. the aunt's diary

2. Which detail described in the journal is similar to one Cooper uses in his novel?

  (a.) Sometimes the native scout rides ahead.

  b. The journey took more than a day.

  c. The native scout checks rocks to see if they have been overturned.

  d. Squirrels jump from branch to branch.

3. Which statement about the relationship between the journal and the novel is true?

  a. The novel gives more detail about how Magua scouts for natives.

  (b.) Both texts contain vivid descriptions of the forest.

  c. Neither text is concerned with the women's feelings about the journey.

  d. Only the journal describes the sounds of the forest.

4. Which elements of paragraph 22 suggest that the text is a primary source?

  a. It has a first-person point of view.

  b. The author speaks of his own role as a writer.

  c. The author includes his reaction to what he sees.

  (d.) All of the above.

5. Which details from this section of the primary source are similar to those Cooper used? Which are different? Work with a partner and discuss why this might be so and how it affects your understanding of the story.

> Sample answer: Cooper does not include the details about the scout riding
>
> ahead and scouting for natives, but his novel does include many of the details
>
> about the forest—its beauty, colors, and sounds. Cooper may have left out the
>
> detail about the native doing his job successfully because it seems that Cooper
>
> does not want the reader to see Magua in a positive light.

Unit 9 ▪ Reading Literature: Integration of Knowledge and Ideas   **233**

Discussion Skills

Have groups of students discuss the following question: *What are the benefits of reading historical fiction vs. historical accounts?* Encourage students to use evidence from *The Last of the Mohicans* and the journal entry to support their ideas. Remind students to follow rules established in Unit 2 for discussion. Encourage them to promote discussion by asking questions and making comments that will move the discussion forward.

Guided Practice

Comprehension Check

Answer Explanations:

1. Students who understand that primary sources are firsthand accounts should be able to identify that the secondary source is B, *a biography of General Webb*.

2. Students may need to scan the excerpt and the journal before identifying that the best answer is A.

3. Though students may incorrectly guess that the answer is A, *The novel gives more detail about how Magua scouts for natives*, there is no evidence for that in the excerpt. Instead, the best choice is B, *Both texts contain vivid descriptions of the forest*.

4. Students may be inclined to circle A when they see that the text has a first-person point of view, but if they read on, they will identify that the paragraph uses all of the first-person elements listed.

5. Students may also recognize that the descriptions of the women vary, and that Cooper is generally more positive in his portrayal.

Grouping Options

Pair students who are having difficulty with the Comprehension questions with more proficient learners. Allow the more proficient learner to model finding answers for the struggling learner.

Independent Practice

Recap Reading Selection

Ask student volunteers to review what the scout has conveyed to the group. Let students know that they will read about the group's meeting with a European man raised by natives.

Read and Apply

Have students read this selection independently as you circulate. Ask them to read aloud so you can see if they are reading fluently. You can also use the support below to help students who are having difficulty.

CITE EVIDENCE

A Reread paragraphs 12–15 of the novel with students, and point out that there is no description of Hawkeye's hair. Prompt students to pay attention to the color of Hawkeye's clothing in the novel as compared to that of his counterpart in the journal entry.

B Point out that dates often appear at the beginning of each journal entry.

COMPARING/CONTRASTING HISTORICAL ACCOUNTS

Independent Practice

WORDS TO KNOW

corded

hide

intricate

provocation

CITE EVIDENCE

A Review paragraphs 12–15 in Cooper's novel. Then underline in paragraphs 27 and 28 of the journal details about the white man's physical appearance that are different for the character of Hawkeye in the novel.

B Recall that primary sources give specific dates for events. Circle the date on which the travelling party encountered the white man and the native man.

Journal of a British Officer *continued*

25 [**August 2, 1757**] We were nearly finished with our journey today when we suddenly came upon two men in the woods. One was a native, and one was white. To say our travelling party was stunned at the sight of them would be an understatement. Immediately my men raised their muskets in defense, but the white man called out in clear English that he was not our enemy.

26 Only later did I learn the legend of the white man: he was apparently raised by natives. Under what circumstances he found himself in such a position I do not know, but I must admit hearing this explanation explained much about his appearance.

27 This man is the most peculiar blend of white European and native I have ever seen. His face was long and narrow and his skin a light color, yet red with sunburn. It was evident from his sunburn that he lived most of his life outdoors. His long black hair was tied neatly in a ponytail.

28 His clothing was the strongest evidence of his native roots; he wore garments made from animal **hides**. He wore a long shirt of a dark brown color. He had buckskin leggings on his long legs, laced along their sides. There were animal skin moccasins on his feet as well.

29 He was clearly a man of considerable physical strength; he was lean and broad shouldered, and his bare forearms were **corded** with muscle and veins.

30 The other man was native, as I have said. I am not certain of his association; one soldier said Mohican, another said Huron, but I sensed no connection between him and our scout.

234

Words to Know

General Academic Vocabulary

corded (*adj.*): lined with cord or cord-like lines

hide (*n.*): skin of a large animal

intricate (*adj.*): detailed; complex

provocation (*n.*): reason to take offense or be angry

Working with Word Meaning Ask students to name which word or words have to do with clothing or objects and which word or words have to do with human emotion.

31 His appearance was most remarkable; his front was without a garment, and visible was a large black-and-white tattoo so **intricate** I cannot describe it. He carried a hand-woven basket that he handled nervously. In fact, his energy was very active; his eyes moved as if he were ready to strike us at the smallest **provocation**.

Comprehension Check   MORE ONLINE sadlierconnect.com

1. Which of the following details does the journal offer that the novel does not?

  a. the meaning of the native man's tattoo

  b. the fact that one of the men is of white European descent

  (c.) the fact that the native man carries a hand-woven basket

  d. the color of the white man's hunting shirt

2. Which statement correctly compares the descriptions of Hawkeye in the novel and the white man in the journal?

  a. The descriptions are totally identical.

  b. Only the journal's description treats Hawkeye as a comical character.

  c. Only the novel's description mentions clothing details.

  (d.) Both descriptions suggest that Hawkeye knows how to live off the land.

3. The character of Hawkeye is probably based on a man like the white man in the journal. In which text do we learn that Hawkeye can speak English?

  (a.) only in the journal

  b. only in the novel

  c. in both the journal and the novel

  d. in neither the journal nor the novel

4. What detail about Chingachgook's tattoo in the novel is different from that in the journal?

  (a.) that it is an emblem of death

  b. that it is black and white

  c. that it is on Chingachgook's chest

  d. that it is so small it can hardly be seen

5. How might the sections of James Fenimore Cooper's novel be different if he had used the same details provided in the journal? Cite specifics.

  Sample answer: Cooper's descriptions are not too different from those in the

  journal; however, if Cooper had used the fact that the white man spoke

  English, that might have made Hawkeye appear less wild. Also, the detail

  about the native's hand-woven basket is interesting; it could have provided

  yet another detail about Chingachgook's character.

Speaking and Listening Presentation

Have students prepare a presentation about the natives in New York State during the French and Indian War. Remind students to plan by setting milestone goals and deadlines. Presenters should include facts and details about the topic, using multimedia or visual elements to support their points; adapt their language for a formal presentation; speak clearly; and maintain eye contact with their listeners. At the end of the presentation, presenters should answer questions and acknowledge listeners' ideas.

Independent Practice

Comprehension Check

Answer Explanations:

1. The journal does not tell the tattoo's meaning. In both the journal and novel, one man is of European descent. In both he has a colored hunting shirt, so the best answer is C.

2. Students should infer that since Hawkeye has grown up with the natives, he can live off the land. Choice D is correct.

3. Students may need to review the descriptions of Hawkeye in the novel before identifying the correct answer, A.

4. Since choice D is false and the details in choices B and C are covered in both the journal and novel, the correct answer is A.

5. Students should recognize that Cooper included details such as the fact that Hawkeye doesn't speak English, which is a big difference between the two versions.

Critical Comprehension

Challenge students to think more deeply about the text and to support their answers with evidence from the text. Ask: *Which character is more fully described in the journal than the excerpt?* (the native scout Magua)

Assess and Respond
If students have trouble answering the Comprehension Check questions,
Then ask them to return to the text and highlight information that can help them answer the questions.

OBJECTIVES

- Compare and contrast a literary work to its filmed version.
- Find the meaning of terms that relate to history and social studies.
- Compare a fictional account of an historical event to a nonfiction historical account of the same event.

Genre: Historical Fiction, Movie Review, and Historical Account

Remind students that historical fiction tells made-up stories that take place in the past. Then explain that this story takes place in the United States during the 1840s, when pioneers were moving westward. Have students recall that a movie review evaluates the storytelling, cinematography, acting, lighting, and other technical aspects of a film. Talk with students about historical accounts, or primary-source writing about events that took place long ago. Remind students that writers of historical fiction may use historical accounts for information and ideas.

Path Options

You may want to do a close reading with students; if so, use the supports provided on these pages. Or, you may wish to have students read the text independently and apply the skills learned in this unit. In either case, students should read the text more than once to facilitate understanding and to be able to answer the Comprehension Check Questions correctly.

A Plains Family Moves West

By Peter McMann-Farningsworth

(Genre: Historical Fiction)

1   Norma pulled her hat down over her head to the tip of her slender nose and tried to fall asleep. She was exhausted, and the setting sun beaming in through the rear opening of the covered wagon was keeping her awake. She and her four sisters and three brothers were squeezed into the wagon bed, four on each side, and they had to sleep sitting up. She was thirteen years old—not old by any means, but the oldest of the eight children.

2   It was August 1, 1844, and Norma and her family were relocating to Oregon from their home in Missouri. Her mother, Sarah, had weak lungs, and doctors had suggested that the cool forest air of the Pacific Northwest would alleviate her suffering, which included violent fits of coughing. Norma saw how gaunt her mother's face was, however, and sadly suspected that something much worse was ailing her. Upon hearing the doctors' recommendations, Ronald, Norma's loyal and loving father, set in motion plans to move the family from Platte County, Missouri, to Oregon.

Departure

3   Norma thought back to the day their family packed up two wagons and bade their friends and neighbors goodbye. The occasion had an air of a celebration to it, but Norma could not say why. She knew well that the journey promised to be unbelievably difficult; for one thing, they would have to brave the elements of summer, including an unrelenting sun as well as violent July thunderstorms. Even less predictable than the weather were the Indians, who did not favor white people traversing their lands.

4   They would not be alone, however, as theirs was not the only family desiring to relocate from the dry plains of Missouri to somewhere greener. Other families, packed into their own wagons, came together in one long wagon train, divided into companies.

Journey

5   The first few weeks, Norma admitted, were rather fun. They stopped every night and set up a camp where they would eat and sleep. The other families' children were friendly and fun; the adults played instruments and sang. One of the boys, Jed, a lanky lad of sixteen, asked Norma to dance one evening. She looked to her mother for permission, and Sarah gave it with a wink.

Challenges

6   One particularly hot day, the cattle were pulling the wagon by their yokes when one of the bulls collapsed. Norma's father called out to Captain Shaw, a slim young army

236   Unit 9 ■ Reading Literature: Integration of Knowledge and Ideas

---

Support English Language Learners

Help English language learners build background knowledge about the time period and events that provide the context for all three texts in this lesson. Use a map such those available on the park service Web site to show students the path pioneers followed from Missouri to Oregon. Discuss with students what they might already know about the Oregon Trail and what they imagine life was like for travelers on this route.

INTEGRATION OF KNOWLEDGE AND IDEAS

officer taking his own family to Oregon, who was leading their company.

7   Captain Shaw led the company toward a river where the cattle could drink and rest. When they were refreshed, the beasts did not want to resume the trip—in fact, they appeared not to want to move at all. Captain Shaw had to prod the steers until they began ambling back up to the main road.

8   A worse incident involved poor, sick Sarah. One afternoon, the caravan was traveling by a river when the cattle pulling the first wagon suddenly took off down the riverbank and overturned the wagon. It so happened that day that Sarah was riding up front with Captain Shaw, who was driving.

9   The force of the crash threw Sarah into the air, and she landed hard on her right side. Ronald rushed to her in a panic. He and Captain Shaw carried her thin frame to the second wagon, from which Norma and her siblings were watching anxiously.

10   The company would have to stop and wait for a doctor; luckily enough, there was a surgeon farther up in the train.

11   This surgeon set Sarah's broken arm in a splint and ordered her to remain in the wagon bed for the remainder of the trip. Ronald looked at his wife and then looked west toward the sun. He was determined to deliver his family to their new home.

Great *Plains*
(Genre: Movie Review)

1   The new film *Plains Family* is a stunningly realistic look at the difficult journey American pioneer families took in the mid-nineteenth century. Its director, Annabel Nancy Jackson, deserves praise for her full-blooded yet restrained interpretation of Q. Wayne Sumner's magnificently straightforward screenplay, which is based on Peter McMann-Farningsworth's historical novel *A Plains Family Moves West*.

2   Jackson and her cinematographer, Paul Weymouth Daniels, have clearly worked hard to create the gorgeous images of the American West that permeate the film.

3   The opening shot shows young Norma peering out the back of her family's covered wagon early one evening. Jackson cuts to what the character is looking at, namely an incredible sunset rich in reds, oranges, and even purples.

4   Perhaps more impressive is how Daniels has lit the nighttime camp scenes. Most of the time, the characters are lit only by the flickering embers of the dying campfire. The lighting successfully heightens the drama of the scene.

Unit 9 ■ Reading Literature: Integration of Knowledge and Ideas   **237**

Support First Reading

Circulate to check and support students' understanding. Use the following comprehension and strategy check-ins as needed.

Check-in Questions

- *Why did Norma and her family decide to move to Oregon?* (Norma's mother, Sarah, needs to move for her health.)
- *How did Sarah get injured on the trip?* (The wagon she was riding in overturned, and she broke her arm.)
- *What aspect of filmmaking does the movie review focus on?* (The movie review focuses on the cinematography in the film.)
- *Why is Q. Wayne Sumner important to the movie?* (Q. Wayne Sumner is the screenwriter.)

Review: Comparing and Contrasting Versions

Ask students how the beginning of the story and movie are both similar and different. (The story opens as Norma looks out the back of the wagon, annoyed because the light keeps her awake. The movie also opens with Norma looking back, but instead of showing her annoyance, it focuses on the beautiful sunset.)

Differentiate Instruction

Pair struggling readers with more proficient readers. Allow the more proficient readers to read the text aloud to the struggling readers. Let partners ask and answer questions about the text.

Students may also benefit from previewing unfamiliar words and phrases in the text, such as the following:

halting place (stopping place)

forced march (a march that is longer than usual or made in more difficult conditions)

come to terms (to accept a situation)

Close Reading

Check-in Questions

- *How are the first weeks' traveling different in the historical account from the historical fiction?* (In the historical account, everyone is sick. In the historical fiction, the first weeks are fun.)

- *Why, in the historical account, does the narrator's father call on Captain Shaw for help?* (He needs help handling oxen.)

- *How do the travelers amuse themselves in the evenings?* (They listen to people playing instruments, and they talk around the campfire.)

Review: Comparing and Contrasting Historical Accounts

How is the account of the family beginning their journey different in the historical account and in the historical fiction? (*In the historical account, everyone is sad to see the emigrants leave, while in the historical fiction, "the occasion had an air of celebration . . . "*)

Review: Finding Meaning of History and Social Studies Terms

Use context to determine the meaning of *emigrated* in paragraph 1 of the historical account. Look for a related word on the page. (*Emigrated* means to leave one area or country for another. *Emigrants* in paragraph 3 is related.)

CLOSE READING

Across the Plains in 1844

by Catherine Sager Pringle

(Genre: Historical Account)

1   My father was one of the restless ones who are not content to remain in one place for long. Late in the fall of 1838, we emigrated from Ohio to Missouri. Our first halting place was on Green River, but the next year we took a farm in Platte County. Father engaged in farming and blacksmithing, and he had a wide reputation for ingenuity. Anyone who needed to have something made or mended sought his shop.

2   The promise of a more healthful climate induced my mother to favor a further move to Oregon. Immigration was the theme all autumn, and we decided to start for Oregon. Late in 1843 Father sold his property and moved us near St. Joseph, and in April 1844 we started across the plains. The first encampments were a great pleasure to us children. We were three girls and two boys, ranging from the baby girl to be born on the way to the older boy, hardly old enough to be much help.

Starting on the Plains

3   We waited several days at the Missouri River. Many friends came that far to see the emigrants start on their long journey; there was much sadness at the parting, and it was a sorrowful company that crossed the Missouri that bright spring morning.

4   The motion of the wagon made us all sick, and weeks passed before we got used to it all. Rain came down and required us to tie down the wagon covers, and that increased our sickness by confining the air we breathed.

5   Our cattle recrossed in the night and went back to their winter quarters. This caused delay in recovering them and a weary, forced march to rejoin the train. This was divided into companies, and we were in the company commanded by William Shaw. Soon after starting, Indians raided our camp one night and drove off several cattle. The animals were pursued but never recovered.

6   Soon everything went more smoothly, and our train made steady headway. The weather was fine, and we enjoyed the journey pleasantly. There were several musical instruments among the emigrants, and these sounded clearly on the evening air when camp was made and merry talk and laughter resounded from almost every campfire.

Incidents of Travel

7   We had one wagon, two steady yoke of old cattle, and several of young and not well-broken ones. Father, who was no ox driver, had trouble with these until one day he called on Captain Shaw for assistance. It was furnished by the good captain's prodding the refractory steer until they were glad to come to terms. Reaching buffalo

238

Strategic Reading

The sentence structure and vocabulary in the historical account may be difficult for less proficient readers. Encourage these students to ask for help when they have trouble understanding what they are reading. Ask for volunteers to answer students' questions and to help steer them toward additional appropriate strategies they can use when they are struggling.

INTEGRATION OF KNOWLEDGE AND IDEAS

country, Father got someone to drive his team and then joined the hunt, for he knew the importance of supplying our company with meat. He not only killed the great bison but often also brought home an antelope that had fallen at his unerring aim—something not often acquired by ordinary marksmen.

8   Soon after crossing South Platte, the unwieldy oxen ran on a bank and overturned the wagon, greatly injuring our mother. She lay long insensible in the tent put up for the occasion.

9   On August 1 we nooned in a beautiful grove on the north side of the Platte. We had by this time gotten used to climbing in and out of the wagon when in motion. When performing this feat that afternoon, however, my dress caught on an axle helve, and I

was thrown under the wagon wheel, which passed over and badly crushed my leg before Father could stop the team.

10   He picked me up and saw the extent of the injury when the injured limb hung dangling in the air.

11   In a broken voice he exclaimed, "My dear child, your leg is broken all to pieces!" The news soon spread along the train, and a halt was called. A surgeon was found and the limb set; then we pushed on the same night to Laramie, where we arrived soon after dark. This accident confined me to the wagon the remainder of the long journey.

Comprehension Check

1A. What does *yoke* mean in paragraph 6 of "A Plains Family Moves West"?

    a. a wooden bar attached to the necks of cattle

    b. a shade that shields cattle from the sun

    c. a brace that supports the legs of cattle when they get tired

    d. a large wooden wheel

1B. Which detail from the historical fiction selection supports the answer to Part A?

    a. "when one of the bulls collapsed"

    b. "one particularly hot day"

    c. "the cattle were pulling the wagon"

    d. "Norma's father called out to Captain Shaw"

2A. The text by Catherine Sager Pringle is

    a. a primary source.

    b. a secondary source.

    c. both a primary and secondary source—a mix of the two.

    d. neither a primary nor a secondary source.

2B. Which of the following supports the answer to Part A?

    a. The story is written in the third person.

    b. The story is written in the first person.

    c. The story does not establish a time or place.

    d. The story analyzes a primary source.

Unit 9 ■ Reading Literature: Integration of Knowledge and Ideas   **239**

Research to Build Knowledge

Students may wish to find out more about the journeys that people took to Oregon in the mid-19th century. Challenge them to find primary sources, secondary sources, and documentaries about the topic. You may wish to group students with similar interests together. Have them gather information from multiple sources, using effective search terms, and choose credible sources over less reputable ones. Remind students to give credit to their sources, following standard forms of citation. Then give students an opportunity to share their findings with the class.

Multiple Readings for Critical Comprehension

- Have students reread and annotate this selection. Then pose questions that focus on critical comprehension.

- *What kind of information might a fiction author use from an historical account?* (A fiction author might use incidents or the location of events.)

- *In which of the texts does the journey seem most unpleasant?* (The historical account seems the most unpleasant.)

Self-Select Text

As preparation for Connect Across Texts, have students choose one selection from this unit and reread it independently. Students can access full .pdf versions of some selections at **sadlierconnect.com**.

Comprehension Check

Begin scoring students' performance of unit skills with this Comprehension Check and continue through Connect Across Texts on page 242. Use students' scores to determine their readiness for the Unit 9 Review on page 244.

Multiple-Choice Questions: *1 point each*

1A. Students should use context to find the meaning of *yoke*, which will show them that the best answer is A.

1B. After reading paragraph 6, students should recognize that choice C is the most reasonable answer.

2A. Students who know that a primary source is a firsthand account of events will find that A is correct.

2B. Firsthand accounts are usually written in the first person. Choice B is correct.

Multiple-Choice Questions, continued: *1 point each*

3A. In the historical account, the narrator did not mention dancing. Choice A is correct.

3B. The movie review and the historical account do not give many details about the mother, so the mother's action "gave (permission) with a wink" supports choosing the fiction (choice D).

4A. "A Plains Family Moves West" (choice B) gives more details in general about the mother.

4B. Choice B quotes a sentence from the historical fiction that indicates what is wrong with Norma's mother.

5A. The movie reviewer mentions the colors of the sunset as well as scenes filmed in firelight, so students should recognize C as the correct choice.

5B. Students may skim the movie review again to locate a place where the review is *not* about lighting. Choice A is correct.

Short-Answer Questions: *2 points each (10 points total)*

Item 6 Rubric

2	Student can explain the significance of both terms.
1	Student can explain why one term is important to selection.
0	Student cannot explain why either term is important.

Item 7 Rubric

2	Student clearly cites two examples of how description affects understanding.
1	Student gives one example of how reviewer's description affects understanding.
0	The student cannot provide an explanation.

3A. Which selection reveals that Sarah approves of Norma's dancing?

- **(a.)** "A Plains Family Moves West"
- **b.** "Across the Plains in 1844"
- **c.** both selections
- **d.** neither selection

3B. Which detail from the text supports the answer to Part A?

- **a.** "merry talk and laughter resounded"
- **b.** "She lay long insensible in the tent"
- **c.** "There were several musical instruments among the emigrants"
- **(d.)** "gave it with a wink"

4A. Which statement about the relationship between the historical fiction selection and the historical account is accurate?

- **a.** The main character in both selections is named Norma.
- **(b.)** Only the fiction selection identifies the mother's specific illness.
- **c.** Only the fictional account deals with the dangers posed by Indians.
- **d.** Only the historical account establishes the year of the family's move.

4B. What evidence supports the answer to Part A?

- **a.** "The promise of a more healthful climate induced my mother to favor a further move"
- **(b.)** "Her mother, Sarah, had weak lungs"
- **c.** "did not favor white people traversing"
- **d.** "Late in the fall of 1838, we emigrated from Ohio to Missouri"

5A. Which of these filmmaking jobs does the movie reviewer mention?

- **a.** acting
- **b.** sound
- **(c.)** lighting
- **d.** costumes

5B. Every paragraph from the movie review gives evidence for the answer to Part A EXCEPT

- **(a.)** paragraph 1.
- **b.** paragraph 2.
- **c.** paragraph 3.
- **d.** paragraph 4.

6. Why are terms such as *wagon train* (paragraph 4 of the historical fiction), and *Missouri River* (paragraph 3 of the historical account) important to these selections?

Sample answer: These selections are tied to history and so need to include terms that help give readers a sense of the historical setting. The word *wagon train* is a term that evokes a certain era in American history. The term *Missouri River* locates a specific scene in a specific geographical location at that time.

Extend Thinking: Evaluate

Have students reread the historical fiction and the historical account. Ask them to evaluate decisions that the fiction author made about what to include from the historical account and what to change. As a class, make a list of these decisions. Then go through the list and discuss what effect each of the decisions had on the fiction. Was the tone of the story affected? Was the plot different? Were different values highlighted?

INTEGRATION OF KNOWLEDGE AND IDEAS

7. How does the reviewer's description of the film affect your understanding of the historical fiction selection? Cite specifics in your explanation.

Sample answer: The reviewer's praise for the film's "straightforward" screenplay helps

me imagine the story as very simple and clear as I read it. The reviewer's explanation of

how the minimal lighting in the campfire scene is used for dramatic effect helps me

imagine that scene when I read it.

8. Imagine another primary source related to Catherine Sager Pringle's historical account. Suggest how it might impact the story if the author of the fiction selection were to use it.

Sample answer: Letters from a member of the party would be another useful primary

source. The fiction selection might then draw upon another point of view of the events.

For example, perhaps there would be more detail about other events such as the

Indian raid.

9. Analyze the effect that the cinematographer's work had on the film *Plains Family*. Support your answer with examples from the movie review.

Sample answer: The cinematographer not only helped create beautiful images of the

West (especially the scenes with sunsets), but he also helped create dramatic tension

in the campfire scene by lighting the characters with just a dying fire.

10. Identify two details from Pringle's story that Peter McMann-Farningsworth, the author of "A Plains Family Moves West," either altered or left out. Write a paragraph discussing the effect of these omissions. Cite specifics in your answer.

Sample answer: McMann-Farningsworth gave Norma more siblings than appear in

Pringle's account. The effect is to dramatize how crowded it was in the wagon bed and

therefore how difficult the journey was. Additionally, he did not include incidents having

to do with heavy rainfall, which Pringle mentions; instead, he focused on the more

"personal" difficulty of Sarah's injury.

Unit 9 ■ Reading Literature: Integration of Knowledge and Ideas **241**

Item 8 Rubric

2	Student can identify another possible primary source and describe its impact on story.
1	Student can name another primary source but not how it might impact fiction.
0	Student is unable to suggest another primary source or how it might impact fiction.

Item 9 Rubric

2	Student names effect of cinematographer's work and gives two examples.
1	Student names one effect of cinematographer's work.
0	Student cannot name an effect of cinematographer's work.

Item 10 Rubric

2	Student names two details of changes and identifies effect on story.
1	Student names one detail that the fiction author changes, along with the effect.
0	Student cannot name any details or effect of changes.

Theme Wrap-Up

Lead students in a group discussion regarding the theme of tales of the past. Ask: *What kinds of tales do people like to read? How do primary sources help fiction writers tell the tales?* (Students may note that people like adventure stories about periods in history. Primary sources serve as research and material for fiction writers.)

Differentiate Instruction

Reluctant readers may benefit from hearing the short-answer items read aloud. After you or a volunteer read(s) the question to those students, make sure that the students understand what they are supposed to do. Allow students to ask questions about directions they find confusing. Review any academic words students may not understand, such as *evidence*, *altered*, and *omissions*.

Connect Across Texts: *4 points*
Review Reading Selections

Put students into three groups. Give each group the responsibility for gathering key details about setting in the historical fiction, the journals, or the movie reviews. Have a volunteer from each group give an overview of the information the group has gathered.

Support a Claim

Review directions on page 242 of the Student Book. Help students understand that they are to list key details from selections to support the central claim.

Graphic Organizer Rubric

4	Student identifies key details in all six selections to support the central claim.
3	Student identifies key details in most of the six selections to support a central claim.
2	Student identifies key details in half of the six selections to support a central claim.
1	Student identifies key details in at least one of the six selections to support a central claim.
0	Student is unable to identify key details to support the central claim for any selection.

Support Essential Question Discussion

Have students reread the Essential Question. Have them complete the sentence: *Different media can affect our understanding of a past event by…"* Encourage students to discuss which medium best highlights which details.

CONNECT ACROSS TEXTS

Support a Claim

In this unit you've read two works of historical fiction, two journals, and two movie reviews. Think about the claim below and how these selections might support that claim. In the chart list key details that serve as evidence. Then write a brief essay in which you use the information in the chart to support the claim. Be prepared to discuss your ideas with the class.

Authors and filmmakers have to help audiences understand the historical setting of a story or film.

Historical Fiction Selections
- *The Last of the Mohicans*: The author describes the undeveloped forest and the Indians of that time in great detail but also presents tensions between British and Indian characters.
- "A Plains Family Moves West": The author specifies dates and places to establish setting, he notes the fear of Indian attacks, and he details two episodes whose difficulties probably would not have been as severe if they had happened more recently.

Journal Selections
- "Journal of a British Officer": The author dates the entries and provides many firsthand details relating to the French and Indian War.
- "Across the Plains in 1844": The author details episodes that reveal the difficulties of traveling by wagon train and the simple pleasures found along the way; she also refers to farming, blacksmithing, and hunting.

Movie Review Selections
- "Exciting *Mohicans* Diverges from the Novel": The reviewer frequently praises the authentic costuming in *The Last of the Mohicans* and notes the "stereotypes typical of Cooper's time."
- "Great *Plains*": The reviewer praises *Plains Family* for its "stunningly realistic look" at the pioneer experience and the cinematographer's skill at capturing both the nature of the American West and the pioneers' camp scenes.

Return to the Essential Question

How can different media and forms of a text affect our understanding?

In small groups or as a class, discuss the Essential Question. Think about what you have learned about how written stories compare to their film versions, about history and social studies terms, and about the way that historical fiction can use and alter historical facts provided by primary sources and nonfiction accounts. Use evidence from the texts in this unit to answer the question.

Assess and Respond (pages 239–242)

If	Then
Students scored 0–10 points, they are **Developing** their understanding of unit skills …	Provide students with reading support and more extensive modeling and practice of skills.
Students scored 11–17 points, they are **Improving** their understanding of unit skills …	Review students' scores to pinpoint skills that students need more help with, and offer targeted instruction.
Students scored 18–24 points, they are **Proficient** in their understanding of unit skills …	Have these students move on. They are ready for the formal assessment at the end of the unit.

LANGUAGE

Word Meanings

Guided Instruction Many words have both a **denotation** and a **connotation**. A word's denotation is its literal definition, the definition found in a dictionary. A word's connotation refers to the emotions and ideas readers associate with the word. The chart below shows the connotations of different words from "A Plains Family Moves West," all of which have a similar denotation.

Word	Connotation	Use in the Text
slender	elegant and graceful	"the tip of her slender nose . . . "
gaunt	sickly	"Norma saw how gaunt her mother's face was . . . "
lanky	long-limbed; awkward	"Jed, a lanky lad of sixteen . . . "
slim	attractive and fit	"Captain Shaw, a slim young army officer . . . "
thin	perhaps unwell; not full enough	"Captain Shaw carried her thin frame to the second wagon . . . "

Guided Practice Complete each sentence with a word from the chart. Think about the word's connotation when choosing the word.

1. Will may not be eating enough; he's too ___thin___.

2. She must be working out; she looks ___slim___ and healthy.

3. I have a basketball player's build; I'm tall and ___lanky___.

Independent Practice Replace the underlined word in the sentence with a synonym with a different connotation. Tell how the meaning of the sentence changes.

"Today brought an <u>unusual</u> turn of events."

Sample answer: *Amazing* has a positive connotation, so it would describe a day of wonderful events rather than a day of strange events.

"My concern grew as I gazed at him, for the scout had an <u>evil</u> look to him."

Sample answer: *Unfriendly* would suggest that the scout doesn't like or want to be approached by other people. *Evil* implies that the scout is capable of harmful actions.

Unit 9 ■ Reading Literature: Integration of Knowledge and Ideas   **243**

OBJECTIVE
Identify the different connotations of words with similar definitions.

Guided Instruction

Have students review the Guided Instruction section on page 243. Make sure they understand that a word's connotations have to do with negative or positive emotions associated with the word. By paying attention to the different connotations that words with similar definitions have, students will expand their ability to comprehend text.

Guided Practice

As students move to Guided Practice, have them note the shared definition, or denotation, of the words in the chart. (*They all describe someone who is not overweight.*) Have students review the words' connotations and how they are used in the text. Then have them read each sentence and think about the feeling it conveys as they choose the word with the right connotation.

Independent Practice

If students have difficulty, suggest they work with a partner. Other possible synonyms for *unusual* include *strange* and *bizarre*, which both have more negative connotations. A possible synonym for *evil* is *foul*, which makes the scout sound physically repugnant.

Apply to Reading

Have students work in groups to find and discuss the impact of other words that have similar denotations but different connotations. For example, they might find *stoicism*, *quiet*, and *stillness* on pages 220 and 221.

Support English Language Learners

English language learners may benefit from using another approach when learning about connotation. Suggest that students work in pairs. Have them reread the chart in Guided Practice. Then have them draw a picture of a person who is *slender*, a picture of a person who is *gaunt*, a picture of a person who is *lanky*, a picture of a person who is *slim*, and a picture of a person who is *thin*. Have partners review each other's pictures and discuss the emotions each word and picture brings to mind. Then have partners fill in sentences 1–3 together.

Unit Summary

At this point, students have read tales of the past, including an excerpt from *The Last of the Mohicans*, a movie review of the film adaptation, and an historical account of the events covered in the novel. They have also read a story about a family on the Oregon Trail, a review of a movie based on the story, and an historical account of the events covered in the story. Students have also learned to compare and contrast different versions of a story and to look for words related to history and social studies. They have learned to compare and contrast historical accounts and how to recognize differences in connotation among words that have the same denotation. Students should now be ready to take this unit review.

Introduce the Review

Explain to students that they will read two related passages with the theme "tales of the past." Have students read the passages carefully and return to them as needed while they answer questions 1–10 on pages 245–246.

Answer Explanations (pages 245–246)

Scoring: When scoring students' work, assign one point for each multiple-choice question and two points for each short answer question, for a total of 20 points.

1A. Students having difficulty should review the story, movie review, and letter to find the correct answer choice, B.

1B. Students should recognize that when people are in pain, they often scream; choice A is correct.

2A. Students who understand that primary sources include journals and letters will identify that the correct choice is A.

Reread "A Plains Family Moves West." Then read the continuation of the "Great *Plains*" movie review and the letter below. Think about the differences between a written story and its filmed version and between primary sources and secondary sources. Answer the questions on pages 245 and 246.

Great *Plains* (continued)

1 Director Annabel Nancy Jackson has assembled a fine ensemble of actors to play the principal roles in *Plains Family*, but she misses the mark in a few places.

2 Paige Carlsberg, in her feature film debut, is an interesting choice for the main character of Norma. Carlsberg is too old for the role; Norma is supposed to be 12 years old, and the actress looks at least 18. Yet the age difference does the film a favor, for Carlsberg infuses Norma with a toughness and grit that the original novel frankly misses.

3 Completely miscast, however, is Aaron Richards as Captain Shaw. The character is supposed to be a tall, handsome young farmhand who helps save the life of Sarah. Instead Jackson has cast a short, middle-aged veteran actor who comes off as much too gruff. Shaw is supposed to be a sympathetic character, but the casting spoils any chance of that.

4 Brief mention must go to the marvelous young actors playing Norma's siblings. Tate Myers is a standout as young Joe.

Joe's Letter to His Grandmother

August 3, 1844

Dear Grandmother,

1 I don't want you to worry too much, but Mother has been injured on our journey to Oregon. The day before yesterday, the two cattle pulling one of our wagons broke loose of the yoke and ran off down a steep embankment toward the South Platte River.

2 With the yoke loose, the falling tongue up front broke as the wagon tumbled down the bank, which in turn caused the entire wagon to flip over. The force of the event caused the jockey box to come loose as well, throwing bolts, nails, and tools all over the place.

3 Mother was thrown from the driver's seat where she was sitting with Father. She fell hard on her right side and screamed. Father leapt down heroically at once, lifted her up, and carefully carried her to a nearby wagon. Luckily, a surgeon from farther up the train came to help. He set Mother's arm in a splint and told her to rest.

4 Please know that other than this unfortunate accident, the trip has been fine—even fun, sometimes. I love going to the trading posts, where Father buys supplies and hears the news. In fact, I'm at a trading post now, and I'll mail this letter to you from here.

Love, Joe

Self-Assessment: Progress Check

Have students return to the Progress Check on page 217 of their book. Point out the boxes underneath the arrow that says "After Unit 9," which is where they can answer the questions again. Have them respond to the questions again in order to assess how well they have grasped the important skills and concepts in this unit.

You may wish to instruct students to write a number in the box to show how they rate their ability with each skill, using a scale of 0–2, with 0 meaning they do not understand the skill at all, 1 meaning they understand the skill but have trouble applying it, and 2 meaning they understand and can apply the skill without difficulty.

UNIT 9 REVIEW

Circle the letter next to the best answer choice.

1A. In which selection do we learn that Sarah was in pain after she was thrown from the wagon?

  a. "A Plains Family Moves West"

  b. "Joe's Letter to His Grandmother" ✓

  c. the movie review "Great *Plains*"

  d. No selection tells this detail.

1B. Which statement supports the answer to Part A?

  a. "fell hard on her right side and screamed" ✓

  b. "she misses the mark in a few places"

  c. "she was sitting with Father"

  d. "the crash threw her into the air"

2A. Which of the following statements about primary and secondary sources is true?

  a. Authors of primary sources often reveal personal opinions. ✓

  b. Encyclopedia articles often contain their author's opinion.

  c. A newspaper article, if written well, will express an opinion.

  d. Opinions in primary sources are useless to authors of secondary sources.

2B. Which choice is a personal opinion that indicates that "Joe's Letter" is a primary source?

  a. "Mother was thrown from the driver's seat"

  b. "two cattle . . . broke loose"

  c. "He set Mother's arm in a splint"

  d. "the trip has been fine—even fun, sometimes" ✓

3A. The social studies term *jockey box* refers to

  a. a box containing food.

  b. a box upon which the driver sits.

  c. a box containing tools. ✓

  d. a box containing money.

3B. Which detail from Joe's letter is a clue to the answer to Part A?

  a. Mother was thrown from the driver's seat.

  b. Bolts, nails, and tools flew everywhere. ✓

  c. Two cattle broke loose of the yoke.

  d. The falling tongue broke.

4A. A primary source may do all of the following EXCEPT

  a. establish the time of an event.

  b. establish where an event took place.

  c. offer a first-person account of an event.

  d. gather facts from multiple sources. ✓

4B. What detail does NOT help establish the time and place of "Joe's Letter"?

  a. He is on a journey to Oregon.

  b. A surgeon set Mother's arm. ✓

  c. Father buys supplies at the trading posts.

  d. The date of the letter is August 3, 1844.

5A. According to the film reviewer, the actress playing Norma was

  a. simply superb.

  b. older than the role indicated. ✓

  c. an example of perfect casting.

  d. wearing the wrong costume.

5B. What evidence supports the answer to Part A?

  a. "Paige Carlsberg . . . is an interesting choice"

  b. "Norma is supposed to be 12 years old"

  c. "Carlsberg infuses Norma . . . with a toughness and grit"

  d. "Carlsberg is too old for the role" ✓

Unit 9 ■ Literature: Integration of Knowledge and Ideas **245**

Test-Taking Tips

Encourage students to read questions slowly and carefully, rereading the relevant selection as necessary to help figure out the correct answer. When students are working on a two-part question, encourage them to read both parts of the question so that they can make sure their pair of answers are related and make sense.

Answer Explanations (pages 245–246)

2B. Choices A, B, and C do not contain personal opinion, so students should recognize that D is correct.

3A. Students may need to reread "Joe's Letter" to find context that will help them determine the meaning of *jockey box*. Choice C is correct.

3B. If students have reread "Joe's Letter" they will recognize that bolts and tools flew everywhere when the jockey box came loose, so B is correct.

4A. Students who understand that a primary source is a firsthand account will be able to recognize that choice D is correct.

4B. Have students who are unsure if B or C is correct think about which situation indicates something happened in the past. Students should recognize that we no longer shop at trading posts. Choice B is correct.

5A. Students who reread the review will find that though the reviewer was positive about the actress playing Norma, he or she does write that the actress was older than indicated. Choice B is correct.

5B. Though choices A–C all concern the actress playing Norma, choice D best supports the idea that she is older than the role required.

6A. Students should be able to use context in Joe's letter to identify that *tongue* meets the definition. Choice C is correct.

6B. Students should be able to identify that only choice C gives context for the definition in 6A.

Answer Explanations

Item 7 Rubric

2	Student identifies connotations of both words and explains how understanding would change.
1	Student identifies connotation of one word, but can't explain change in understanding.
0	Student is unable to identify or explain.

Item 8 Rubric

2	Student explains how the analysis helps reader understand more than one character in the story.
1	Student identifies analysis of one character, and explains contriubution to understanding the character in the story.
0	Student is unable to explain how the analysis helps reader understand character in the story.

Item 9 Rubric

2	Student identifies more than one detail from letter and includes how the author alters some details.
1	Student identifies one detail from the letter that the author uses.
0	Student is unable to identify any details the author uses.

Item 10 Rubric

2	Student is able to tell how the meaning of the sentence would change for each synonym.
1	Student is able to identify how one or two of the synonyms would affect the sentence.
0	Student is unable to identify how the sentence would change with any of the words.

UNIT 9 REVIEW

6A. In Joe's letter, what social studies term means "a long piece of wood that connects a covered wagon to a yoke"?

a. yoke
b. embankment
c. tongue ⟵
d. splint

6B. What text supports the answer to Part A?

a. "toward the South Platte River"
b. "the event caused the jockey box to come loose"
c. "the falling tongue up front broke as the wagon tumbled" ⟵
d. "I'm at a trading post now"

7. How would readers have a different understanding of the following sentence if the word *tender* were used instead of the word *sympathetic*?

Shaw is supposed to be a sympathetic character, but the casting spoils any chance of that.

Sample answer: *Tender* has a gentle connotation; it would imply that Captain Shaw's character is supposed to be kind and sensitive. The word *sympathetic* works better because the character is supposed to be likeable, but not beyond that.

8. How does the film reviewer's analysis of the actors and their performances help you understand the characters in the original story?

Sample answer: Knowing that the actress playing Norma is tougher and the actor playing Captain Shaw is less sympathetic than the same characters in the story helps me better understand what those story characters are supposed to be like.

9. How does the author of "A Plains Family Moves West" use details from the historical event described in "Joe's Letter to His Grandmother"? Does he alter any details from Joe's letter? Explain and give details.

Sample answer: The author uses many of Joe's details; for example, Sarah was thrown on her right side, and Father helped her. He does alter whom Mother was sitting with and who helped her. In the story, she sits with Captain Shaw, and both he and Father help her.

10. Read this line from "Joe's Letter to His Grandmother":

. . . other than this <u>unfortunate</u> accident, the trip has been fine—even fun . . .

Consider the following synonyms for *unfortunate*, and tell how the meaning of the sentence would change in each instance: *disastrous, hopeless, inappropriate*.

Sample answer: *Disastrous* gives the sense of a very serious incident; Sarah's injury would qualify. The word *hopeless* is very emotional; it would make Joe's grandmother think that Sarah might never recover. The word *inappropriate* suggests a lack of emotion in a letter that otherwise expresses Joe's feelings quite well.

246   Unit 9 ▪ Literature: Integration of Knowledge and Ideas

Analyze Student Scores

16–20 pts Strong	Student has successfully learned and applied the skills in this unit. Review any errors with the student, and explain them if necessary.
10–15 pts Progressing	Student is struggling with one or more of the skills in this unit. Identify the specific skills that are problematic to target additional instruction.
0–9 pts Emerging	Student is having trouble understanding most of the skills in this unit. Student may need to work through the unit again with a higher level of individual support.

Introducing UNIT 10

In this unit about tales of the past, you will learn how to write an opinion piece, also called an argument. In this piece, you will thoroughly research an event from the past that you find interesting. Then you will shape and support an opinion about this event to inform and persuade your readers.

In your first paragraph, introduce your topic and explain your claim, or your position on the topic, to readers. Next, make sure readers understand the topic by giving background information. In the body of the essay, support your claim with logical reasoning and evidence from informational texts found in reliable sources. Use language that clarifies the relationships among your claims, reasons, and evidence, and that maintains a formal style. Acknowledge opposing claims, and argue against them. Finally, write a conclusion that follows from and supports your argument.

Progress Check Can I?

Before Unit 10 / After Unit 10

☐ Write an opinion piece about an event from the past. ☐

☐ Acknowledge and argue against opposing claims. ☐

☐ Make a claim and support it with logical reasoning and evidence. ☐

☐ Draw evidence from trustworthy informational sources. ☐

☐ Correctly punctuate coordinate and cumulative adjectives. ☐

☐ Use language to express ideas precisely and concisely. ☐

Unit 10 ■ Text Types and Purposes: Write Opinion Pieces

Student Page 247

Progress Check

The Progress Check is a self-assessment feature that students can use to gauge their own progress. Before students begin work on Unit 10, have them check the boxes next to any item that they feel they can do well. Explain that it is fine if they don't check any of the boxes. Tell them that they will have an opportunity to learn about and practice all of these items while studying the unit. Let them know that near the end of the unit they will have a chance to reconsider how well they can do each item on this list.

Before they begin their Unit 10 Review (see page 259 of this guide), you will be prompted to have students revisit this page. You can use this information to work with students on any items they don't understand before they tackle the Review.

HOME◆CONNECT...

In this unit, your child will learn about **writing an opinion piece** about an event from the past. Explain that this type of writing **includes a claim** based on the writer's opinion and must back up that claim with **relevant evidence and logical reasoning**. Your child must use trustworthy **sources** to find evidence to support the claim he or she writes about. Additionally, your child will be asked to acknowledge and **address opposing claims** about the topic.

Work with your child to develop the skills necessary for success in this unit. Describe to your child an event from the past about which you have an opinion. Give background information so that he or she can understand the event, and elaborate on your opinion. Point out to your child how you use evidence and logical reasoning to support your claim about the event. Model how to acknowledge and refute opposing claims. Then put your opinion piece in writing for your child to study and explore.

Activity: Explore the unit topic, "tales from the past," with your child. Work together to make a timeline showing past events that people had strong opinions about, such as the Civil War. Discuss whether opinions are still divided on these events, and why. Pick two or three events your child is interested in and brainstorm ideas that could support his or her claim in an opinion piece on this event.

IN THIS UNIT, YOUR CHILD WILL...

- Learn how to write an opinion piece about an event from the past.
- Introduce a claim and acknowledge opposing claims.
- Support an argument with evidence and logical reasoning.
- Use trustworthy sources to gather information about a topic.
- Incorporate information from texts as evidence for an argument.
- Conclude an essay with a section that follows from and supports the argument.
- Write in a formal style that includes the correct punctuation of coordinate and cumulative adjectives, and that expresses ideas precisely and concisely.

WAYS TO HELP YOUR CHILD

Hold a debate with your child on an event from the past (either from history or from your family's past). You and your child should argue different sides. Take time to prepare by listing evidence and logical reasoning that supports each side. You may choose to have another family member moderate the debate and declare who better supported his or her claim.

ONLINE
For more Home Connect activities, continue online at sadlierconnect.com

248   Unit 10 ■ Text Types and Purposes: Write Opinion Pieces

Student Page 248

HOME◆CONNECT...

The Home Connect feature is a way to keep parents or other adult family members apprised of what their children are learning. The key learning objectives are listed, and some ideas for related activities and discussions are included.

Explain to students that they can share the Home Connect page with their parents or other adult family members in their home. Let students know how much time the class will be spending on this unit so they can plan their time accordingly at home.

Encourage students and their parents to share their experiences using the suggestions on the Home Connect page and the Home Connect activities at **sadlierconnect.com**. You may wish to make a place to post some of this work.

UNIT PLANNER

Theme: Tales of the Past	Focus
WRITING MODEL *pp. 250–252*	*Preserving our Natural Heritage*
WRITING ACTIVITY *p. 253*	**ORGANIZATIONAL STRUCTURE:** Outline
LANGUAGE MINI-LESSONS *pp. 254–257*	• Coordinate and Cumulative Adjectives • Expressing Ideas Precisely and Concisely
SPEAKING AND LISTENING *p. 258*	Discuss the Essential Question
UNIT 10 REVIEW *pp. 259–260*	• Language Process Summary • Writing Process Summary

Essential Questions: How can writers support an analysis of a text?

UNIT 10

Objective(s)

Write a well-organized opinion piece that supports its claim with evidence.

Introduce the claim within a logical format and develop it with facts and evidence from literary or informational texts, using appropriate transitions and formal language with a conclusion that supports the information presented.

- Differentiate between coordinate and cumulative adjectives and punctuate them correctly.
- Use precise and concise language.

Engage in a respectful, collaborative discussion with peers.

Unit Assessment

- Unit 10 Review *pp. 259–260*

Additional Assessment Options

- Performance Task 1 *pp. 311A–320*
  (ALSO ONLINE)
- Performance Task 2 *pp. 321A–330*
  (ALSO ONLINE)

Optional Purchase:

- iProgress Monitor (ONLINE)
- Progress Monitor Student Benchmark Assessment Booklet

(ONLINE) Digital Resources

- Home Connect Activities
- Additional Practice
- Teacher Resources
- iProgress Monitor (optional purchase)

Go to SadlierConnect.com to access your Digital Resources.

For more detailed instructions see page T3.

LEARNING PROGRESSIONS

In this unit, students will learn how to write an opinion piece. The skills that students learn in this unit build upon the skills they learned during the sixth grade. Likewise, the skills students learn this year will provide a foundation for the skills they will develop in the eighth grade.

Making a Claim

- By the end of the sixth grade, students should have learned how to introduce a claim.

- Seventh-grade students develop their skills of introducing a claim and acknowledging opposing arguments.

- In the eighth grade, students will learn to distinguish their own claims from opposing claims.

Organizing Evidence

- Sixth-grade students learned to support claims with clearly organized reasons and evidence.

- In the seventh and the eighth grades, students will increase their proficiency by organizing their supporting evidence in a logical manner.

Making Connections

- In the sixth grade, students learned to support claims by using words, phrases, and clauses to clarify the relationships among claims and reasons.

- Seventh- and eighth-grade students continue to improve these skills by clarifying relationships among claims, reasons, evidence, and counterclaims.

Writing Conclusions

- Sixth-grade students should be able to provide a conclusion that follows from the information presented.

- Seventh- and eighth-graders should be able to write conclusions that follow from the information presented and support the claim being made.

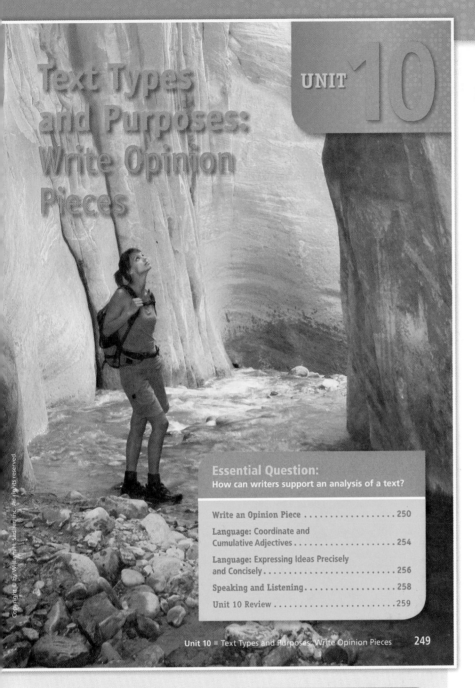

Text Types and Purposes: Write Opinion Pieces

UNIT **10**

Essential Question:
How can writers support an analysis of a text?

Essential Question:
How can writers support an analysis of a text?

Write an Opinion Piece 250

**Language: Coordinate and
Cumulative Adjectives** 254

**Language: Expressing Ideas Precisely
and Concisely** 256

Speaking and Listening 258

Unit 10 Review 259

Unit 10 ■ Text Types and Purposes: Write Opinion Pieces   **249**

Copyright © by William H. Sadlier, Inc. All rights reserved.

Writing Handbook

If students need extra practice with writing an opinion piece, refer them to the *Writing Handbook* on pages 299–310 in their Student Books. The *Writing Handbook* gives students detailed instruction on planning, drafting, revising, and editing their writing. They will also find tips on producing, publishing, and presenting their writing.

Essential Question:
How can writers support an analysis of a text?

In this unit, students will learn to write an opinion piece that uses logical reasoning and a clear organizational structure to support its claims.

Theme: Tales of the Past

Students will continue their exploration of tales of the past by thinking about their own perspectives on world-shaping events as they read and analyze an opinion piece writing model.

Curriculum Connection: Social Studies

Students will continue to think about the past as they choose an historical event about which to write an opinion piece. Students will have a chance to explore these historical events more closely as they research and then develop opinions about them.

Connect Reading to Writing

Remind students that they read in Unit 9 different types of texts about the same historical events in *The Last of the Mohicans* and *Exciting* Mohicans *Diverges from the Novel* (Student Book pages 220–227) and *Journal of a British Officer* (Student Book pages 228–235). Explain that these texts showed different perspectives on the same historical period. In this unit, students will be able to describe in an opinion piece their own perspectives on an historical event.

Unit 10 ■ Text Types and Purposes: Write Opinion Pieces   **249**

OBJECTIVES

- **Write a well-organized opinion piece that supports its claim with evidence.**
- **Introduce the claim within a logical format and develop it with facts and evidence from literary or informational texts, using appropriate transitions and formal language with a conclusion that supports the information presented.**

Introduce: Organizational Structure

Draw attention to the outline. Ask students to look for the key elements as you read the Student Model together.

Analyze a Student Model

INTRODUCTION: Help students identify the claim the writer makes in the introduction. Remind them that opinion pieces must present a claim, or clearly stated argument, about the topic.

BACKGROUND: Point out how the background information supports Marley's claim that these parks are part of America's natural heritage and should be preserved.

Read a Student Model

Marley is a student in Ms. White's seventh-grade Language Arts class. Ms. White gave Marley's class an assignment to write an opinion piece based on an event from the past. For this opinion piece, Marley must make a strong claim and then support it with clear reasons and relevant evidence. As you read Marley's essay, think about an historical event that you might choose to write about in your own opinion piece.

CREATING AN ORGANIZATIONAL STRUCTURE

Marley used an outline like the one below to organize her essay and support her argument.

Title ______

I. Introduction
   a. Claim: ______
   b. Give necessary background information on the topic: ______
II. Support Claim
   a. Logical reasoning about ______
      1. Facts and evidence ______
      2. Facts and evidence ______
   b. Logical reasoning about ______
      1. Facts and evidence ______
      2. Facts and evidence ______
   c. Logical reasoning about ______
      1. Facts and evidence ______
      2. Facts and evidence ______
   d. Opposing claim(s) to address: ______
      1. Facts to address opposing claim ______
      2. Facts to address opposing claim ______
III. Conclusion

INTRODUCTION
- Introduces the topic and presents the writer's claim

BACKGROUND
- Includes background information for the reader. This is especially important when discussing an historical issue with which the reader may not be familiar.

FORMAL STYLE
- Includes academic language
- Avoids slang, contractions, and personal statements
- Uses complete sentences and clear explanations

Preserving our Natural Heritage

Today, some people think that the natural world is there to be exploited and developed. Of course, there are places where development is reasonable. However, America's National Parks are far more valuable when preserved. The development that threatened what is now Grand Canyon National Park shows that designating these unique areas as national parks is essential to preserving America's heritage.

Background

For almost a century, America had no national parks. However, the discovery of California's Yosemite Valley in 1851 led many to advocate that the area be preserved so that it could be enjoyed by generations to come. In 1890, after Yellowstone became America's first national park, Yosemite was finally designated one, too. America's national parks now number in the hundreds.

Copyright © by William H. Sadlier, Inc. All rights reserved.

Genre: Opinion Piece

Explain to students that an opinion piece gives a writer an opportunity to express his or her opinion about a topic. Students should realize that an effective opinion piece is not simply an expression of the writer's likes or dislikes. The writer must support his or her ideas with such evidence as reasons, facts, and examples.

As students work on their own opinion pieces, suggest they ask themselves, "What reasons can I give to readers so that they will agree with my opinion? What evidence can I use to support my claim and convince readers that I am right?"

The Grand Canyon

One of America's most amazing parks is Grand Canyon National Park, an incredible one-mile-deep canyon visited by nearly five million people a year. Even those who have not visited it are familiar with images of the deep canyon and the layers of rocks that reveal geological history from the ancient past. According to the (National Park Service website,) the park also contains human artifacts from nearly 12,000 years ago and is home to many species of plants and animals, including the rare California Condor.

The Need for Parks

*Some might believe that these natural areas would be preserved even if they were not designated parks—that people's respect for them would prevent destruction and development. This is not true. In the 1860s, tourists who wanted to see Niagara Falls had to pay private landowners who claimed every good spot for viewing the natural wonder. In Arizona, the Mesa Verde cliff dwellings suffered looting and vandalism until the area became a national park.

The Grand Canyon

When President Theodore Roosevelt hoped to make the Grand Canyon a national park, he was opposed by local miners, settlers, and ranchers. Although he named the canyon a national monument in 1908, mining was still allowed, and hotel owner Ralph Cameron claimed the most scenic spots. <u>Cameron built hotels, charged travelers tolls and high fees, and tried to build two dams and a platinum mine in the park.</u>

SOURCES

Make sure the sources you use are credible. Trustworthy sites include .gov sites and reliable information providers such as news organizations and universities.

Circle the source the author cites in this paragraph.

ADDRESS OPPOSING CLAIMS

Acknowledge opposing claims—what people who disagree with you might say—and present evidence against them.

Put an asterisk next to the opposing claim in this paragraph.

LOGICAL REASONING

Use logical reasoning supported by evidence to strengthen your argument.

Underline the evidence that supports Marley's argument that President Roosevelt faced opposition.

Analyze a Student Model

FORMAL STYLE: Writers use a formal style if they want their writing to be taken seriously. Guide students to recognize Marley's use of formal style. Help them understand how it makes her sound like an authority on her topic.

SOURCES: Make a list with students of types of trustworthy sources they can consult when writing about historical events, such as newspaper articles of the time they are writing about, history books, and biographies. Guide them to see how Marley identifies one of those sources in her essay.

ADDRESS OPPOSING CLAIMS: Tell students that they need to acknowledge arguments against their claim. By doing so, they can show that they fully understand their topic. Then they can provide convincing evidence against the opposing claim. Point out how Marley articulates an opposing claim in the section "The Need for Parks" and then gives a compelling reason why it does not hold up.

LOGICAL REASONING: Help students understand that logical reasoning involves the conscious application of logic to one's thought processes. Instead of presenting a claim based on feelings or instinct, students should, like Marley, find concrete evidence in support of their claim and present it in a logical fashion. Point out how at the bottom of page 251, Marley identifies three facts that support her argument. She employs them at a logical point in her argument to support her claim about President Roosevelt.

Support English Language Learners

Help English language learners by modeling your thought process aloud as you read the essay. After reading aloud the title and claim, pause to explain what the essay is arguing. Then pause after reading aloud each section to summarize how the section supports the claim. Break down the logical reasoning and evidence and explain how these elements work to support the main claim of the essay.

After you have modeled this strategy for the first two pages, encourage students to share their own thought processes as you read the final page of the opinion piece.

Write an Opinion Piece

Analyze a Student Model

CONNECT EVIDENCE: Writers of opinion pieces want to make their arguments as clear as possible so that readers will follow their ideas. Typically, they use transition words such as *and*, *but*, *instead*, *yet*, and *so* to show the connections between ideas or between their claims, reasons, and evidence.

LOGICAL ORGANIZATION: Point out how the writer uses subheads to organize the information in her essay. Each section of the essay focuses on a different aspect of her topic. Have students scan the essay's subheads and draw a conclusion about her claim based on them. (The writer believes in protecting our national parks.)

CONCLUSION: Tell students that the conclusion of an opinion piece often restates the essay's claim. Point out that in this essay, Marley also includes a call to action that tells readers how they should respond to her argument. Although a call to action is not appropriate for every issue, it helps readers know what they should take away from the essay.

Evaluate a Writer's Work

Begin a group discussion about whether Marley's opinion piece is persuasive. Have students ask: *Does Marley state a clear opinion about the topic? Does she back up her claim with convincing evidence? Does she answer the opposing claims effectively?*

Model: Organizational Structure

Ask students to think about how an outline would show the underlying structure of Marley's essay. Post the outline template that appears on page 253. Before students fill in the outline based on the Student Model, remind them to use the essay's margin notes and subheads for guidance.

WRITE AN OPINION PIECE

CONNECT EVIDENCE

Use clear transition words, phrases, and clauses to connect your claims, reasons, and evidence.

Underline the word Marley uses to connect past images of the canyon to the reason for preserving it as a national park.

LOGICAL ORGANIZATION

Organize the information logically, and use subheads throughout the essay to make the organization clear and to create unity among sections and arguments.

Box the subhead that makes it clear that Marley has moved from an historical discussion of national parks to a modern one.

CONCLUSION

The conclusion of an opinion piece must follow from and support the essay's argument. Many opinion pieces end with a call to action to tell readers what they should do in response to this issue.

Circle the call to action in this conclusion.

> Now that the Grand Canyon has become a national park, its trails are open to everyone. It is no longer cluttered with hotels, dams, or mines. <u>Instead</u>, the canyon is an incredible monument to history. The layers of its walls preserve a record of the past, and the canyon itself provides a safe home for native plants and animals. And it protects evidence of the ancient cultures that once lived there. If the canyon were developed, it would lose its majesty and primitive beauty; it would simply become like everywhere else.
>
> **Threats Today**
>
> Being declared a national park is no guarantee that a piece of wilderness will be safe forever. Today, national parks face threats from many sources, including invasive foreign plants and animal species, development on park borders, decreasing supplies of fresh water, and air pollution. Ironically, the park's popularity itself poses a threat: park visitors damage vegetation and leave trash behind, and sightseeing flights and boat rides cause disturbance and noise pollution.
>
> **Our Parks, Our Responsibility**
>
> America has a responsibility to protect the Grand Canyon and other national parks for future generations. We must not let these national treasures be developed or exploited. Tell those who want more development in our parks, or who want to reduce park funding, that our national resources must be protected. We would lose invaluable aspects of America if we no longer possessed these incredible parks.

Review: Comparing and Contrasting Versions

Remind students that in Unit 9 they learned how to compare and contrast different versions of the same event. Explain that this skill will be useful as they write an opinion piece about something that happened in the past. Students will have to compare and contrast evidence to determine their opinions about their topic. They will also need to compare and contrast their own views against other people's views in order to prepare for counterarguments.

Ask students to talk about how Marley compares and contrasts her opinion with that of her opponents and how she uses the different ideas about how our national parks should be managed as evidence in support of her opinion.

Use this outline to organize your opinion piece about an event in the past for the Unit 10 Review on page 259. Be sure to draw evidence from literary and informational sources and to make connections between them to support your claim. Then write your first draft on another sheet of paper.

Title _____

I. **Introduction**

    a. Claim: _____

    b. Give necessary background information on the topic: _____

    _____

II. **Support Claim**

    a. Logical reasoning about _____

        1. Facts and evidence _____

        2. Facts and evidence _____

    b. Logical reasoning about _____

        1. Facts and evidence _____

        2. Facts and evidence _____

    c. Logical reasoning about _____

        1. Facts and evidence _____

        2. Facts and evidence _____

    d. Opposing claim(s) to address: _____

    _____

        1. Facts to address opposing claim _____

        2. Facts to address opposing claim _____

III. **Conclusion**

    _____

    _____

Unit 10 ■ Text Types and Purposes: Write Opinion Pieces   **253**

Differentiate Instruction

Help students understand the structure of an opinion paper by having small groups work together to orally analyze the parts of Marley's essay. Ask one student to state the claim of the essay. Ask others to summarize the background information and identify types of supporting evidence. Challenge another student to explain how the writer handles opposing claims and yet another to summarize the conclusion. Once the students have completed their analysis, lead a group discussion about how each part of the essay contributed to the whole. Ask: *Would the essay have been stronger or weaker without a particular part? Why?*

Create: Organizational Structure

Brainstorming

Students may have difficulty identifying an historical event to write about. Encourage students to use different strategies to find an event that interests them, such as by looking at historical images online and discussing past events with family members who experienced them. Students may also be able to find diaries and journals that describe historical events.

Planning

Students will use the outline on page 253 to plan their writing. Students should first develop their claim about the historical event and then identify facts and evidence that support their claim. Remind students to consider opposing claims, and think about why some people have had different opinions on the subject.

Drafting an Opinion Piece

Direct students to consult their outlines as they draft their essays on separate paper. Be sure that students have an introduction, a claim, supporting evidence, a section that addresses opposing claims, and a conclusion.

Introduce the Writing Process

Remind students that good writing happens in stages. After prewriting and drafting, they will revise and edit their essays. For more on the writing process, see the *Writing Handbook* on page 299.

Assess and Respond
If students have difficulty forming an opinion about an event of the past,
Then encourage them to describe the event to a partner. The partners should ask questions such as: *Was that a good idea?* or *What would you have done?* to help them formulate an opinion.

OBJECTIVE
Differentiate between coordinate and cumulative adjectives and punctuate them correctly.

Guided Instruction

Make sure students understand that no comma should be placed between an adjective and the noun it modifies unless there is a series of coordinate adjectives. However, when a cumulative adjective and a noun together make a unit, there is no need to insert a comma before the cumulative adjective even if it is among a series of adjectives.

With students, go through the instruction and examples on page 254. As you discuss coordinate adjectives, you may choose to write each word of an example sentence on separate cards that are large enough for students to see. Arrange the cards on the board to reflect the sentence as it appears on the page. Then rearrange only the adjectives, and ask students to determine if the sentence's meaning has changed at all. When the adjectives are coordinate adjectives, the meaning of the sentence will not change.

Go over the tests described in the text for distinguishing coordinate and cumulative adjectives. Suggest that students might also ask themselves "What is that?" about an object and then notice whether they answer with a cumulative adjective and noun or a noun alone. For example: *What is that? It's an electric car. It's a toy boat. It's a ballet dancer.*

Coordinate and Cumulative Adjectives

Guided Instruction A string of adjectives is punctuated differently in a sentence depending on whether it uses **coordinate** or **cumulative** adjectives.

■ **Coordinate adjectives** are adjectives that each separately modify the noun they come before. When a sentence contains a string of coordinate adjectives, the adjectives are separated by commas.

The lazy, green, winding river was full of silver fish.

The fierce, hungry, strong lion took down a zebra.

Each adjective separately describes the noun. The river is lazy *and* green *and* winding; the lion is fierce *and* hungry *and* strong. The adjectives could be rearranged in the sentence and the meaning would remain the same.

■ However, **cumulative adjectives** are formed when an adjective joins with the noun it comes before to make a unit.

ruby slippers

deserted island

young child

Since the adjective and noun have formed a unit, there should not be a comma between the preceding adjective and the unit.

She was excited to wear the sparkling ruby slippers.

They landed on a mysterious deserted island.

The happy, excited young child opened the present.

■ It can be difficult to determine the difference between coordinate and cumulative adjectives. Test by considering:

If the adjectives in the sentence can be rearranged and still make sense in the sentence, they are coordinate.

If the adjectives can be joined by the word "and" and still make sense, the adjectives are more likely to be coordinate.

254   Unit 10 ■ Text Types and Purposes: Write Opinion Pieces

---

Support English Language Learners

English speakers will probably have a natural ear for cumulative adjectives because they will have heard them used throughout their lives. But distinguishing between coordinate and cumulative adjectives may be difficult for English language learners. Remind English language learners to ask themselves these questions:

• *Does removing the adjective change your idea of what the noun is?*

• *Does the adjective make the noun more specific?*

• *If I told someone else about the noun, which adjective would I use to make him or her know what I meant?*

Guided Practice Rewrite the sentences below, adding commas where necessary.

1. The wild untrained dog splashed mud all over me.

   The wild, untrained dog splashed mud all over me.

2. My friend lives in that big old rundown house.

   My friend lives in that big, old, rundown house.

3. The exhausted airline passengers trudged off the plane.

   The exhausted airline passengers trudged off the plane.

4. I spilled hot chunky spicy soup all over the white tile floor.

   I spilled hot, chunky, spicy soup all over the white tile floor.

5. The long dirty hot hike finally came to an end at a sparkling blue lake.

   The long, dirty, hot hike finally came to an end at a sparkling blue lake.

Independent Practice Write one sentence using coordinate adjectives and one sentence using cumulative adjectives for each prompt.

Describe something you saw at the aquarium.

1. I saw a large, hungry, dangerous shark.

2. I saw a school of beautiful flying fish.

Describe a story or article you recently read.

3. I read a long, boring, difficult article on bird flu.

4. I read an exciting fantasy story about mythological creatures.

Describe a meal you enjoyed.

5. I enjoyed the spicy, crunchy, tasty tacos.

6. I enjoyed the buttery dinner rolls.

Unit 10 ▪ Text Types and Purposes: Write Opinion Pieces **255**

OBJECTIVE
Differentiate between coordinate and cumulative adjectives and punctuate them correctly.

Guided Practice

Help students distinguish between the coordinate and cumulative adjectives in the Guided Practice sentences by encouraging them to read the sentences aloud to a partner. Then students should read them again with the adjectives in a different order. Students should ask each other questions about the sentence, such as *What kind of dog?* for item 1; *What kind of house?* for item 2, and so on. Explain to students that hearing the sentences and the answers to the questions said aloud will help them understand which nouns and adjectives combine to form a unit.

Independent Practice

Invite students to share their completed sentences with the class. Write several of these sentences on the board without commas. Then ask volunteers to add commas, as appropriate.

Assess and Respond
If students have difficulty completing the Independent Practice,
Then help them brainstorm cumulative adjectives that they might encounter in each situation, such as *giant squid*, *historical novel*, or *cold cereal*.

Differentiate Instruction

Help students understand cumulative adjectives by writing the following pairs of words on the board: *American flag, haunted house,* and *stuffed animal.* Ask how the meaning of each pair of words would change without the adjective. Explain that cumulative adjectives indicate a particular kind of noun.

Then have students list additional adjectives that could modify one of the cumulative adjective units. Write the adjectives in a circle around the adjective unit, and discuss how each adjective modifies the unit rather than the noun alone. For example, different adjectives could modify an American flag as opposed to a flag, a haunted house as opposed a house, and a stuffed animal as opposed to an animal.

OBJECTIVE
Use precise and concise language.

Guided Instruction

Help students understand that effective writers use precise language, or exactly the right words, to convey their ideas, and they avoid repetition and wordiness.

Lead students through the Guided Instruction on page 256. To make the comparison between vague and precise clearer, draw a T-chart on the board. Label one side *Vague* and the other *Precise.* Then write *large vehicles* and *road* on the vague side, and *trucks*, *buses*, and *highway* on the precise side. Ask volunteers to explain why the words on the precise side are easier to imagine.

Suggest that as students review their own writing, they try to picture exactly what they want to describe. Then they should use words that readily convey their ideas to their readers.

Remind students that wordy sentences are likely to leave them breathless when read aloud. Invite a volunteer to read aloud a wordy example sentence and its concise version and to comment on the difference in reading them aloud. Encourage students to test their own writing by reading it aloud. If they run out of breath before they reach the end of a sentence, they should consider ways to make it more concise.

Finally, point out the relationship between precise and concise language. Sentences that use precise language are likely to be concise because they make thoughtful use of language.

LANGUAGE

Expressing Ideas Precisely and Concisely

Guided Instruction Writers should use language that expresses their ideas **precisely**, choosing the exact words to communicate their meanings. Writers should also share their ideas **concisely**. This means avoiding wordiness and redundancy. Wordiness is using too many words to describe something, and redundancy is saying the same thing more than once.

■ **Precise Language**

Choose the right word to share your meaning. Think carefully about the nouns and verbs that you choose.

Vague: *I saw many large vehicles on the road.*

Precise: *I saw many trucks and buses on the highway.*

Vague: *She jumped over the rock and walked quickly up the path.*

Precise: *She sprang over the rock and dashed up the path.*

To use precise language in your own writing, make sure you understand the meanings and connotations of the words you use. Choose the word that means exactly what you want to say, and try to stick to words that you're familiar with and understand.

■ **Concise Language**

To write concisely, keep your sentences sharp and to the point. Decide what you want a sentence to say and say it directly.

Wordy: *There is the belief among some people that all teenage boys and girls should experience paid employment.*

Concise: *Some people believe all teenagers should have a job.*

Redundant: *The giant trees were very tall and towered far above us.*

Concise: *The trees towered far above us.*

The best way to check for wordiness and redundancy is in the revision phase of your writing. Reread your work and note anywhere that the writing slows down. Revise these sections to say more directly what you want to share with the reader. Avoid language that puts your ideas in an unnaturally or overly formal style, and state your ideas simply and straightforwardly.

Differentiate Instruction

Help struggling writers understand the importance of precise and concise language by writing these sentences on the board:

- *The garden bed was a prickly tangle of roses and blackberry bushes.*
- *The governor addressed the crowd from the podium.*

Ask students to work together to revise these sentences "backwards" in order to make them vague, wordy, or redundant. Have volunteers share their revised sentences with the class. Then lead a brief discussion on why the original versions are examples of effective writing.

Guided Practice Rewrite each sentence to correct the error identified in parentheses.

1. (wordiness) All people on all the seven continents should gravely consider this issue.
Sample answer: Everyone should think seriously about this issue.

2. (vague language) The big house was old.
Sample answer: The ancient mansion was crumbling and deserted.

3. (redundancy) The hot, blazing sun shone down on the overheated runners, making them very hot.
Sample answer: The blazing sun overheated the runners.

4. (vague language) The furniture was ugly.
Sample answer: The hideously upholstered couch, broken-down chairs, and table carved with gargoyles jarred their eyes.

5. (wordiness) This is just one problem of the many, many problems that people have caused for the lions, elephants, giraffes, and zebras who live on the savannah.
Sample answer: This is just one of the many problems humans have caused for the animals on the savannah.

Independent Practice Revise this paragraph to convey its ideas precisely and concisely.

Long ago, in the previous century in the 1940s, there was a terrible event. This event was when many Japanese Americans who were living peacefully in the United States were forcibly interned in internment camps by the United States government. Because the United States was at war with Japan, the government believed that people in the U.S. who were of Japanese descent might be sympathetic to Japan's side of the global conflict in which these two countries were engaged. Innocent men, women, children, and old people were put into the camps and lived in bad conditions for no reason.
Sample answer: In the 1940s, when the United States and Japan were at war, many Japanese Americans were placed in internment camps by the U.S. government. The government was afraid these people might be sympathetic to Japan. People of all ages were placed in the camps and lived in unpleasant conditions, even though they had done nothing wrong.

Unit 10 ■ Text Types and Purposes: Write Opinion Pieces **257**

OBJECTIVE
Use precise and concise language.

Guided Practice
Make sure students understand that the problem in each Guided Practice sentence is identified in parentheses. Encourage students to revise by asking themselves: *What does the writer want to say in this sentence? How can I say it more precisely or concisely?* Students can use these questions to help them revise the sentences.

Independent Practice
Suggest that students read the Independent Practice paragraph all the way through before thinking about making changes. Suggest that students mentally summarize the paragraph before they revise it. That will help them focus on the most important ideas they need to convey. If time allows, challenge students to come up with the most concise version possible—that still makes sense and conveys the original ideas. Write that version on the board. Compare it to the original.

Assess and Respond
If students have difficulty completing the Independent Practice,
Then have students read the paragraphs aloud to themselves or to a partner. Instruct students to listen for places where the language in the paragraph is wordy, redundant, or vague.

Peer Collaboration

Have students apply what they have learned about precise and concise language to their opinion piece. After students have written a first draft, have them meet with partners to examine each other's writing for vague language, wordiness, or redundancy. Suggest that, as they review, students use different colored pencils or highlighters to identify each problem. Allow students time to share and discuss the reviewed drafts. Students should explain their comments and ask probing questions to help their partner improve his or her writing.

OBJECTIVE
Engage in a respectful, collaborative discussion with peers.

Discuss the Essential Question

Copy and distribute the "Did I?" checklist available on **sadlierconnect.com**.

Leading the Class Discussion

1. Ask students to restate Marley's claim.

2. Have students to scan the text for evidence.

3. Have students review the text for examples of informational texts.

SPEAKING AND LISTENING

Discuss the Essential Question

How can writers support an analysis of a text?

Prepare for a class discussion about the Essential Question by responding to the questions below. Support your points of view with reasons and examples.

1. How did Marley support her claim with logical reasoning and evidence?

Sample answer: Marley showed what happened to other sites that were not designated National Parks, and described what happened to the Grand Canyon before it was designated a park. She showed the importance of the national park designation in protecting nature and history.

2. How did Marley address opposing claims in her essay?

Sample answer: Marley mentioned one opposing claim in her introduction and then addressed another in a full paragraph later in the essay. She used evidence to show that these claims are not true.

3. Did Marley's analysis of informational texts work to support her argument?

Sample answer: Marley's analysis of informational texts provided the evidence that she needed to support her claim and address opposing claims.

Use your notes above as you discuss the Essential Question with your class or in small groups. Use the organizer below to record your ideas and what you hear in the discussion. Follow the discussion rules on the "Did I?" checklist (page 58).

Ideas I Agree or Disagree With		Questions I Asked
agree		
disagree		
New Ideas I Had During Discussion		Questions I Answered

Discussion Skills

Remind students that when they make claims about Marley's essay in discussion groups, they must use logic and clear language to clearly delineate their points. They should also support their claims with evidence from the text, such as details and examples. Remind students that in discussion, they should: present evidence that is logical and based on reason rather than on emotions; present an abundance of evidence; and speak clearly and in a respectful tone so that listeners who might not initially agree with them will listen thoughtfully.

UNIT 10 REVIEW

Read this draft of an introductory paragraph and body paragraph from a student essay and answer the questions below.

Altamont Pass: A Terrible Idea

(1) In the 1970s, Americans began to look at alternative energy sources, such as wind energy. (2) A wind farm was built in California's Altamont Pass, known for its strong winds. (3) However, it was built in the wrong place, which led to the deaths of thousands of raptors, or hunting birds. (4) Some people think that the jobs and clean energy that resulted were worth the death of these birds, but clean energy should be cleaner than this wind farm. (5) Altamont Pass should never have been built.

(6) Altamont Pass is indeed an important source of clean energy for California. (7) However, the pass is also where many different type of birds hunt, such as Golden Eagles, Red-tailed Hawks, and Burrowing Owls. (8) According to Sierra Club information, several of these hunting animals are on the Endangered Species list! (9) It is not right to excuse these rare birds' deaths just because they are being killed by clean energy.

1. In what sentence does the writer acknowledge opposing claims about this issue?

a. 1   **c.** 5

(b.) 4   **d.** 7

2. What is the writer's claim about Altamont Pass?

(a.) It should never have been built.

b. It is a wind farm in California.

c. The birds' deaths are sad but necessary.

d. It kills many different types of birds.

3. Why does the writer cite the Sierra Club?

a. to use precise language

(b.) to provide an expert source

c. to address an opposing argument

d. to provide logical reasoning

4. What precise word would best replace the phrase "hunting animals" in sentence 8?

a. birds   **(c.)** raptors

b. eagles   **d.** prey

Unit 10 ■ Text Types and Purposes: Write Opinion Pieces **259**

Introduce the Review

Explain to students that this review will give them an opportunity to apply the language and writing skills they have studied and practiced in this unit.

Language Skills Summary

Let students know that they are going to use what they have learned about coordinate and cumulative adjectives and the use of precise and concise language to make their writing better.

- Ask students to explain the difference between coordinate and cumulative adjectives.
- Ask students to give examples of precise language to describe their classroom.
- Ask students how to check for wordiness and redundancy in their writing.

Self-Assessment: Progress Check

Have students revisit the Progress Check on page 247 and compare their answers now to the answers they gave before they started Unit 10.

Answer Explanations

Scoring: 5 points each for items 1–10; 50 points for essay.

1. Students should observe that "Some people think . . . but" introduces and counters an opposing claim.

2. Students can use the title and the last sentence of paragraph 1 to determine the writer's claim.

3. Students should recognize that the Sierra Club is cited as an expert source.

4. Students should understand that *raptors* is more precise than *hunting animals*.

Test-Taking Tips

Give students the following tips to help when taking assessments that include a paragraph or essay with numbered sentences.

After you have completed your test,

- check to make sure that you have carefully read and followed all the directions;
- make sure that you have identified an answer for all of the multiple-choice questions—by circling the letters or filling in the bubbles;
- make sure that your handwritten answers to short-answer questions are legible and correctly punctuated.

Answer Explanations

5. Student determines the conclusion needs a call to action.

6. Students should identify choice C as supporting evidence.

7. Students should see that sentence 1 is wordy and repetitive.

8. Students should restate sentence 2 in a formal style.

Item 9 Rubric

2	**5 pts.** Student explains why there have been fewer deaths.
1	**2–3 pts.** Student suggests an explanation that does not support sentence 3.
0	**0 pts.** Student fails to suggest an explanation.

10. Students should insert commas after *beautiful* and *vital*.

Writing Process Summary

Remind students that planning can help them organize their ideas before they draft. Revising and editing help make the draft better.

Planning and Drafting

Have students revisit their outline and draft (page 253). Have them check that the draft includes all items in the outline.

Opinion Piece Rubric

4	**50 pts.** The text includes an introduction, a claim, supporting evidence, and a conclusion. It has no editing errors.
3	**40 pts.** The text includes key elements with only minor errors.
2	**30 pts.** The text is missing key elements and has many editing errors.
1	**20 pts.** The text lacks a clear opinion and is unfinished.
0	**0 pts.** The assignment was not attempted.

Read the conclusion from the student essay and answer the questions below.

> (1) In poems and stories and books, birds often symbolize <u>freedom, and symbolize escape, and these symbols encourage us to fly beyond our limitations.</u> (2) We should fly beyond the need for energy that will harm Earth and its creatures. (3) Recently, there have been fewer raptor deaths at Altamont Pass. (4) We can't improve our planet's health if we harm these beautiful vital predatory birds.

5. How could the writer improve this conclusion?

a. include a reference to literature

b. restate the argument

c. include a picture of a raptor

d. include a call to action

6. What facts could the writer provide to serve as evidence for the claim?

a. numbers of wind turbines at Altamont Pass

b. types of birds in California

c. numbers of birds killed by the turbines

d. other causes of death for endangered birds

7. Underline the sentence that is redundant in this conclusion.

8. Restate sentence 2 in a formal style.
Sample answer: For the sake of our natural habitats, humans must abandon destructive energy sources.

9. What explanation would support the statement in sentence 3?
Sample answer: An explanation of what has led to fewer recent raptor deaths.

10. Punctuate the adjectives in sentence 4 correctly.
beautiful, vital, predatory birds

> **Assignment:** On separate paper, provide a final draft of the essay you began on page 253. Use what you learned about punctuating adjectives and writing concisely and precisely. Think about how you and your classmates answered the Essential Question. Check your outline to be sure you organized your ideas well. End with a conclusion that follows from and supports your claim.

Digital Connection: Posting an Historical Drama

Have students work in small groups to write a one-act play based on an historical event they explored in one of their opinion pieces. The play should also convey their opinions about the topic.

After writing the play, students should perform it and make a video recording to share with the class. If you have access to a school or class Web site, post the videos for students to share with their families and the school community.

Introducing UNIT 11

The word *transformation* refers to some sort of major change. Transformations can be scientific, such as when a caterpillar turns into a butterfly, or they can be social, such as when a nation undergoes a revolution. In this unit, you're going to read about different kinds of world transformations.

Integrating what you know with your reading skills makes reading nonfiction texts much more pleasurable. One way to approach a nonfiction text is to see if there is an audio, video, or multimedia version of it so you can compare the two versions. Even when the text is the same, its meaning is affected by the medium, or method of communication, it is presented in. Some nonfiction texts offer arguments about a certain topic. In such cases, it is a good idea to read a text that offers the opposite point of view and then compare the arguments. Whichever side of the argument you are reading, always look to see if the writer has supported his or her claim with strong reasoning and evidence.

Progress Check Can I?

Before Unit 11 / **After Unit 11**

- ☐ Compare a text to an audio, video, or multimedia version of it. ☐
- ☐ Evaluate an argument in terms of the soundness of the evidence that supports it. ☐
- ☐ Analyze how two authors writing about the same topic emphasize different evidence. ☐
- ☐ Identify an author's point of view, based on loaded language and the inclusion of particular facts. ☐
- ☐ Integrate visual information with other information in a text. ☐
- ☐ Distinguish among facts, opinions, and reasoned judgments. ☐
- ☐ Determine the central ideas of a text. ☐
- ☐ Use the relationship between words to help understand their meaning. ☐

Unit 11 ■ Reading Informational Text: Integration of Knowledge and Ideas

Student Page 261

HOME ◆ CONNECT...

The Home Connect feature is a way to keep parents or other adult family members apprised of what their children are learning. The key learning objectives are listed, and some ideas for related activities and discussions are included.

Explain to students that they can share the Home Connect page with their parents or other adult family members in their home. Let students know how much time the class will be spending on this unit so they can plan their time accordingly at home.

Encourage students and their parents to share their experiences using the suggestions on the Home Connect page and the Home Connect activities at **sadlierconnect.com**. You may wish to make a place to post some of this work.

Progress Check

The Progress Check is a self-assessment feature that students can use to gauge their own progress. Before students begin work on Unit 11, have them check the boxes next to any item that they feel they can do well. Explain that it is fine if they don't check any of the boxes. Tell them that they will have an opportunity to learn about and practice all of these items while studying the unit. Let them know that near the end of the unit they will have a chance to reconsider how well they can do each item on this list.

Before they begin their Unit 11 Review (see page 296 of this guide), you will be prompted to have students revisit this page. You can use this information to work with students on any items they don't understand before they tackle the Review.

HOME ◆ CONNECT...

IN THIS UNIT, YOUR CHILD WILL...

- Compare a text to an audio or video version of it.
- Evaluate an argument or claim in terms of its evidence and reasoning.
- Analyze how two authors writing about the same topic emphasize different evidence in support of their claims.
- Identify loaded language and understand how it reveals an author's point of view.
- Integrate visual information with information in a text.
- Distinguish among facts, opinions, reasoned judgments, and speculation.
- Use word relationships to figure out the meaning of words.

Your child will likely understand that when someone gives a speech on television, the speech had to be written down first. A concept that may be new, however, is that a text's medium impacts its meaning. Ask your child how a **written text changes when it is delivered by a speaker**. To get started with the concept, ask how the words of a play change when actors act them out. Then talk about other kinds of texts that are performed or delivered, such as speeches.

Your child may have engaged in arguments with siblings or friends. Encourage him or her to talk about winning or losing arguments and what the outcome had to do with how well he or she **reasoned in support of his or her position**. When two people are arguing about something, each must present strong reasoning and evidence in order to convince the other.

When your child encounters an unfamiliar word, looking at other, **related words like synonyms or antonyms** can be helpful. Brainstorm pairs of synonyms and antonyms with your child. Talk about how related words help with understanding meaning.

WAYS TO HELP YOUR CHILD

Discuss with your child the difference among facts, opinions, and reasoned judgments. Explain that facts can be verified and that opinions are personal beliefs. Reasoned judgments are opinions supported by evidence. Offer examples of each from your personal life and then have your child do the same.

Activity: Play a game with your child in which you try to think of as many different kinds of transformations as possible. Encourage your child to think about changes that happen in science, history, and current events. Your child may also think about big changes in his or her own life—such as starting a new school or moving from one city to another.

ONLINE
For more Home Connect activities, continue online at sadlierconnect.com

262 Unit 11 ■ Reading Informational Text: Integration of Knowledge and Ideas

Student Page 262

UNIT PLANNER

Theme: World Transformations	Focus
COMPARING MEDIA PRESENTATIONS *pp. 264–271*	*The 40th Anniversary of D-Day/Reconsidering Reagan* **GENRE:** Speech/Reaction to a Speech **LEXILE®:** 990L; 900L **WORDS TO KNOW:** tyranny, sheer, desolate, oratorical, bagpipes, valor, anecdote, buoyancy, beachhead, liberation, devised, evoke, affinity, daunting, reconciliation, vow, forsake
EVALUATING ARGUMENTS *pp. 272–279*	*What Forests Offer Us* **GENRE:** Web Article (Opinion Piece) **LEXILE®:** 1130L **WORDS TO KNOW:** deforestation, forestry, timber, renewable resource, hectare, biofuel, processed food, plantation, sustainable, hydroelectric dam, water cycle, generate, watt, decimation, erosion, secondary forest, primary forest
ANALYZING THE PRESENTATION OF IDEAS *pp. 280–287*	*Save the World's Forests* **GENRE:** Scientific Text (Opinion Piece) **LEXILE®:** 1120L **WORDS TO KNOW:** restraint, unassailable, refute, forest canopy, archipelago, peat, subsidizing, fertilizer, indigenous, marvel, gloss over, permit, gaudy, greenhouse gases, combatant, carbon footprint, biodiversity
CLOSE READING *pp. 288–293*	*Deeply Flawed Book/ Dark Wyoming* **GENRE:** Letter to the Editor/Movie Review **LEXILE®:** 1100L
CONNECT ACROSS TEXTS *p. 294*	Compare and Contrast Texts
LANGUAGE *p. 295*	Word Relationships
UNIT 11 REVIEW *pp. 296–298*	*Cloud Computing: An Interview* *Cloud Computing: An Opinion* **GENRE:** Interview/Opinion **LEXILE®:** 1000L

Objective(s)
Compare and contrast a text to its presentation in another medium.
Evaluate an argument or claim in terms of its reasoning and evidence.
Analyze how two authors writing about the same topic emphasize different evidence in support of their claims.
• Compare and contrast a text to its presentation in another medium. • Evaluate an argument or claim in terms of its reasoning and evidence. • Analyze how two authors writing about the same topic emphasize different evidence in support of their claims.
Use the relationship between words to help understand their meaning.

Unit Assessment

• Unit 11 Review *pp. 296–298*

• Unit 11 Performance Task ONLINE

Additional Assessment Options

• Performance Task 1 *pp. 311A–320*
  ALSO ONLINE

• Performance Task 2 *pp. 321A–330*
  ALSO ONLINE

Optional Purchase:

• iProgress Monitor ONLINE

• Progress Monitor Student Benchmark Assessment Booklet

ONLINE Digital Resources

• Home Connect Activities

• Unit Performance Task

• Additional Practice

• Full-Length Reading Selections

• Teacher Resources

• iProgress Monitor (optional purchase)

Go to SadlierConnect.com to access your Digital Resources.

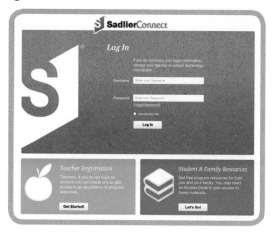

For more detailed instructions see page T3.

263B

LEARNING PROGRESSIONS

In this unit, students will learn how the integrate information presented in different formats or media by comparing and contrasting them. The skills that students learn in this unit build upon the skills they learned during the sixth grade. Likewise, the skills students learn this year will provide a foundation for the skills they will develop in the eighth grade.

Comparing Media Presentations

- By the end of the sixth grade, students will know how to integrate information presented in different media or formats to develop an understanding of a topic.

- In the seventh grade, students will compare and contrast a text to an audio, video, or multimedia version of the text and analyze the portrayal in each medium.

- Eighth-grade students will look at the advantages and disadvantages of different media for presenting a particular topic.

Evaluating Arguments

- In the sixth grade, students will evaluate the argument and specific claims in a text, looking at which claims are supported by reasons and evidence and which claims are not.

- Seventh-grade students will build on the argument evaluation skill, looking at whether the reasoning in an argument is sound and whether the evidence is relevant and good enough to support the claim.

- By the end of the eighth grade, students will be able to trace and evaluate the arguments and claims in a text, analyzing the reasoning and evidence, and recognizing when irrelevant evidence is introduced.

Analyzing the Presentation of Ideas

- Sixth-grade students will compare one author's presentation of events with another author's presentation.

- By the end of the seventh grade, students will know how to analyze the writing of two or more authors on the same topic and understand how different evidence or different interpretations of facts shape their presentations of key information.

- In the eighth grade, students will be able to analyze two or more texts that provide conflicting information on the same topic, identifying where the texts disagree on facts or interpretation.

Reading Informational Text: Integration of Knowledge and Ideas

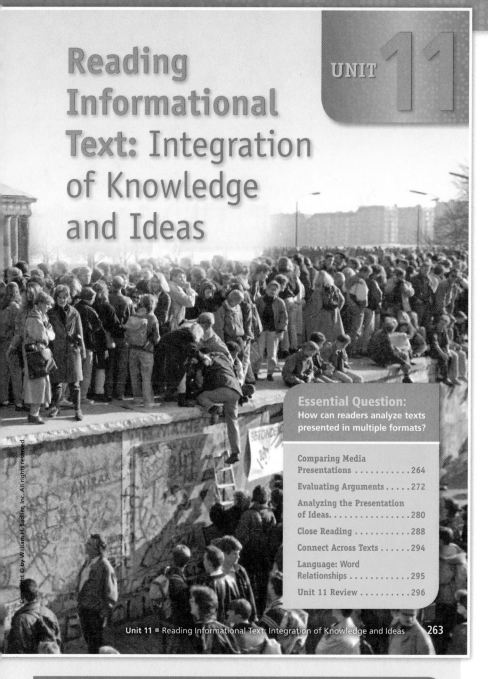

Essential Question:
How can readers analyze texts presented in multiple formats?

Essential Question:
How can readers analyze texts presented in multiple formats?

Unit 11 ■ Reading Informational Text: Integration of Knowledge and Ideas **263**

In this unit, students will learn about the integration of knowledge and ideas, specifically how to compare media presentations on a topic, evaluate arguments in one or more texts, and analyze the presentation of ideas.

Theme: World Transformations

Students will read selections related to the topic of the changing world, including a speech given by Ronald Reagan on the 40th anniversary of D-Day, a Web article that argues for deforestation and a science article that argues against it, a review of a book about the Johnson County War, and a review of a movie based on the book.

Curriculum Connection: Social Studies

Students will learn about why President Ronald Reagan was known as a great communicator and will read different interpretations of events during the Johnson County War in 19th-century Wyoming.

Curriculum Connection: Science

Students will read arguments for and against deforestation.

Vocabulary Overview

General Academic Vocabulary

affinity, anecdote, bagpipes, buoyancy, combatant, daunting, decimation, desolate, devised, evoke, fertilizer, forsake, gaudy, generate, gloss over, marvel, peat, permit, plantation, reconciliation, refute, restraint, sheer, subsidizing, timber, unassailable, valor, vow

Domain-Specific Vocabulary

archipelago, beachhead, biodiversity, biofuel, carbon footprint, deforestation, erosion, forest canopy, forestry, greenhouse gases, hectare, hydroelectric dam, indigenous, liberation, oratorical, primary forest, processed food, renewable resource, secondary forest, sustainable, tyranny, water cycle, watt

Comparing Media Presentations

OBJECTIVE
Compare and contrast a text to its presentation in another medium.

Genre: Speech/Reaction to a Speech

Explain to students that a speech is a text that is written to be delivered orally to an audience. A reaction to a speech is a review of the speech based on its text and delivery.

Set the Purpose

Help students understand the purpose for learning the reading skill by asking: *How can you compare two different media presentations of a text?*

Model and Teach

Read or have volunteers read the selection and callouts as the class follows along. Model effective strategies for responding to the callouts by using the suggestions below.

CITE EVIDENCE

A Help students locate the word "Speech" near the title of the text. Explain that a speech exists as a text but is performed in front of an audience.

B Students should be able to pick out the date from the text on the page. Explain that the date of the invasion is a fact, so it can be verified.

WORDS TO KNOW
desolate
oratorical
sheer
tyranny

> The **medium**, or form of communication, by which information is delivered can affect the meaning of the information itself.

CITE EVIDENCE

A **Media** are the means by which information is delivered. Public officials like presidents deliver information in a variety of media, such as audio, video, newspapers, and Internet sites. Place an asterisk by the word that tells you what medium this text is in.

B Texts will contain **facts**, which are true pieces of information that can be verified; **opinions**, which express personal beliefs; and **reasoned judgments**, which are opinions that are supported by evidence. Underline a fact that tells when D-Day occurred.

The 40th Anniversary of D-Day

Excerpt of remarks by President Ronald Reagan, June 6, 1984

(Genre: *Speech)

1   We are here to mark that day in history when the Allied armies joined in battle to reclaim this continent to liberty. For four long years, much of Europe had been under a terrible shadow. Free nations had fallen, Jews cried out in the camps—millions cried out for liberation. Europe was enslaved, and the world prayed for its rescue. Here in Normandy the rescue began. Here the Allies stood and fought against **tyranny** in a giant undertaking unparalleled in human history.

2   We stand on a lonely, windswept point on the northern shore of France. The air is soft, but forty years ago at this moment, the air was dense with smoke and the cries of men, and the air was filled with the crack of rifle fire and the roar of cannon. At dawn, on the morning of the 6th of June, 1944, 225 Rangers jumped off the British landing craft and ran to the bottom of these cliffs. Their mission was one of the most difficult and daring of the invasion: to climb these **sheer** and **desolate** cliffs and take out the enemy guns. . . .

3   The Rangers looked up and saw the enemy soldiers at the edge of the cliffs shooting down at them with machine guns and throwing grenades. And the American Rangers began to climb . . . Soon, one by one, the Rangers pulled themselves over the top, and in seizing the firm land at the top of these cliffs, they began to seize back the continent of Europe. Two hundred and twenty-five came here. After 2 days of fighting, only 90 could still bear arms.

Words to Know

General Academic Vocabulary
desolate (*adj.*): lonely and gloomy
sheer (*adj.*): straight and deep

Domain-Specific Vocabulary
oratorical (*adj.*): having to do with speaking and making speeches
tyranny (*n.*): unrestrained abuse of power and authority by a government

Working with Word Meaning Have students paraphrase the definitions of each word. Encourage them to use the words in example sentences.

INTEGRATION OF KNOWLEDGE AND IDEAS

Reconsidering Reagan

Transcript of a television interview

(Genre: Reaction to a Speech)

1 **RON BLAKE, journalist:** Tonight my guest is presidential historian Nancy Busch Jameson, and she specializes in the presidency of Ronald Reagan. I want to begin with what may be Reagan's finest **oratorical** achievement: the speech he gave on the fortieth anniversary of D-Day. Let's watch a video clip.

(video clip of Reagan speaking)

2 **NANCY BUSCH JAMESON, historian:** Ron, I was actually at this speech in person and I remember feeling at the time that it was going to be a speech—and a delivery of a speech—for which Reagan would be long remembered.

3 But first, let's be clear: the speech works extremely well even if you just read it on paper. Reagan's gift for word choice is apparent; for example, he uses the word *prayed*, and that is such a Reagan-esque word, if you will. Reagan liked to evoke his religious faith during tough times.

4 Listening to the video, however, shows how he emphasized words effectively. A good example is the way he stressed *unparalleled*; his delivery of that word really communicates that what happened on D-Day was special and unique in history.

5 His phrasing is wonderful, too: he pauses slightly before he says "and the cries of men," which highlights the emotional meaning of that phrase.

Comprehension Check

How does Reagan's delivery of the speech affect the impact of the words? Cite some specifics from the interview.

Unit 11 ■ Reading Informational Text: Integration of Knowledge and Ideas **265**

Guided Instruction

CITE EVIDENCE

C Double underline a word in Reagan's speech that is effective both as written and as spoken, according to Nancy Busch Jameson.

D Circle a word and a phrase in the speech that Jameson mentions as examples of effects that one can get only from listening to Reagan's delivery.

E Box the aspects of Reagan's delivery mentioned in the interview that Jameson says are particularly effective. What other information could you get from watching a video of Reagan's speech?

CITE EVIDENCE

C Direct student attention to the word *prayed* in paragraph 1 on page 264. Point out that Jameson uses this as an example of "Reagan's gift for word choice," and claims "the speech works extremely well even if you just read it on paper."

D After reviewing Jameson's comments in paragraphs 4 and 5 of "Reconsidering Reagan," help students locate the words in paragraphs 1 and 2 of the speech.

E Lead students to understand that "Reagan's delivery" refers to how he spoke the words. Help them find the words that describe his effective delivery in paragraphs 4 and 5. Discuss with students that watching a video would provide information on President Reagan's facial expressions and body language.

Comprehension Check

Sample Answer: President Reagan's way of pausing and emphasizing certain words brings out their meanings. For example, emphasizing *unparalleled* brings attention to the specialness of the event.

Answer Explanation: In paragraph 4, Jameson states that President Reagan "emphasized words effectively," and goes on to discuss how he stressed the word *unparalleled*. In paragraph 5, Jameson states that President Reagan's "phrasing is wonderful, too." She uses the example of his pausing slightly before saying "and the cries of men," noting that this "highlights the emotional meaning of that phrase."

Support English Language Learners

English language learners may benefit from specific vocabulary support to facilitate discussion of the events discussed in President Reagan's speech. Remind students that the speech commemorated the 40th anniversary of D-Day, a crucial day in World War II. Show students the location of Normandy in France on a map of Europe. Explain that on D-Day, forces from the United Kingdom, Canada, and the United States, along with Free French troops, sought to take back territory from the German occupying forces. Provide vocabulary support for terms such as *invasion*, *occupy*, *fortress*, *amphibious*, *troops*, *front*, and *launch*.

Guided Instruction

CITE EVIDENCE

A Help students locate the word *valor* in the first sentence of paragraph 1.

B Students may have difficulty because the task is not simply to find one loaded word, but a whole story that is set up to evoke both smiles and awe in the listeners.

Listening and Viewing Skills

Read aloud paragraph 8 of President Reagan's speech and have students look at the photograph on this page. Have students guess what the photograph represents. Students may correctly volunteer that the statue represents a memorial to Bill Millin, the piper in President Reagan's story. Explain that the statue stands near Sword Beach in Normandy and pays tribute not only to Millin, but to all the Allied soldiers who fought that day.

COMPARING MEDIA PRESENTATIONS

Guided Instruction

WORDS TO KNOW

anecdote

bagpipes

buoyancy

valor

CITE EVIDENCE

A A speaker's point of view is revealed in a number of ways, one of which is the use of **loaded language**. Loaded language consists of words and phrases that have highly emotional connotations beyond their literal meanings. For example, the word *champions* in paragraph 5 has a connotation that these men were heroes. Circle a loaded word in paragraph 9 that has a connotation of "noble courage."

B Loaded language is often used to persuade an audience to feel a certain way about something. Put a box around a section of loaded language that is humorous but is meant to make the audience appreciate one soldier's remarkable modesty in the face of war.

The 40th Anniversary of D-Day *continued*

4   Behind me is a memorial that symbolizes the Ranger daggers that were thrust into the top of these cliffs. And before me are the men who put them there.

5   These are the boys of Pointe du Hoc. These are the men who took the cliffs. These are the champions who helped free a continent. These are the heroes who helped end a war.

6   Gentlemen, I look at you and I think of the words of Stephen Spender's poem. You are men who in your "lives fought for life . . . and left the vivid air signed with your honor."

7   I think I know what you may be thinking right now—thinking "we were just part of a bigger effort; everyone was brave that day." Well, everyone was. Do you remember the story of Bill Millin of the 51st Highlanders? Forty years ago today, *British troops were pinned down near a bridge, waiting desperately for help. Suddenly, they heard the sound of **bagpipes**, and some thought they were dreaming. Well, they weren't. They looked up and saw Bill Millin with his bagpipes, leading the reinforcements and ignoring the smack of the bullets into the ground around him.

8   Lord Lovat was with him—Lord Lovat of *Scotland, who calmly announced when he got to the bridge, "Sorry I'm a few minutes late," as if he'd been delayed by a traffic jam, when in truth he'd just come from the bloody fighting on Sword Beach, which he and his men had just taken.

9   There was the impossible valor of the *Poles who threw themselves between the enemy and the rest of Europe as the invasion took hold, and the unsurpassed courage of the *Canadians who had already seen the horrors of war on this coast. They knew what awaited them there, but they would not be deterred. And once they hit Juno Beach, they never looked back. . . .

266   Unit 11

Words to Know

General Academic Vocabulary

anecdote (*n.*): brief story describing an event or person

bagpipes (*n.*): musical instrument made of a bag and connected pipes, often played in Scotland

buoyancy (*n.*): lightness; cheerfulness

valor (*n.*): boldness in facing danger; bravery

Working with Word Meaning Have students draw pictures to represent the meaning of each vocabulary word.

INTEGRATION OF KNOWLEDGE AND IDEAS

Reconsidering Reagan *continued*

6   **NANCY BUSCH JAMESON:** In the video clip of this section, we experience more of Reagan's oratorical skills.

7   The **anecdote** about Lord Lovat is classic Reagan; he had such a marvelous sense of humor and often peppered his speeches with it. And yet the humor is a device; it serves to make us chuckle but it also highlights a serious point about how these men maintained incredible humility in the face of extraordinary events. It's a section that reads just as well as it sounds, I might add.

8   I'm struck by Reagan's pace in the clip you just showed. He moves on steadily and never rushes. He had such a good touch; you feel the weight of what he's saying, yet there's a lightness and **buoyancy** as well. He's very listenable.

9   The physical setting of the speech is so effective, too. When Reagan speaks repeatedly of "these cliffs" and then you see the wind whipping around him with the English Channel in the background, the stories in the speech really come alive.

Comprehension Check

How does learning about the various aspects of Reagan's speech help you understand its meaning? Cite specifics from the interview as part of your answer.

CITE EVIDENCE

C Another way a speaker expresses a point of view is by **including—or omitting—particular facts about a topic**. For example, Reagan mentions the contributions of countries other than the United States. Find those nationalities in the speech and place an asterisk next to them. What does their inclusion tell you about Reagan's point of view of D-Day?

D Underline in Jameson's remarks the effects that one can get only from watching the video (or listening to the audio) of Reagan's delivery of the speech.

CITE EVIDENCE

C In the text of President Reagan's speech, help students find the word *British* in paragraph 7, *Scotland* in paragraph 8, *Poles* and *Canadians* in paragraph 9. Discuss with them that President Reagan seems to believe that the United States doesn't deserve all the credit for the victory at Normandy, and he wants to acknowledge the other allied forces.

D Direct students to paragraph 8 in President Reagan's speech. Point out that listeners could react to the *pace* and the *lightness and buoyancy* of President Reagan's delivery simply by listening to an audio recording of the speech. However, they would need to see a video of the speech to understand the impact of the setting (mentioned in paragraph 9).

Comprehension Check

Sample Answer: President Reagan's word choice, phrasing, and pace all help me understand the importance of D-Day. For example, his pace is steady, but serious. Also, his use of humor underlines the humanity of soldiers.

Answer Explanation: On page 265, in paragraph 3, Jameson mentions how President Reagan had a "gift for word choice," and "liked to evoke his religious faith during tough times." In paragraph 5, Jameson mentions, "His phrasing is wonderful, too." In paragraph 8 on page 267, speaking of President Reagan's pace, Jameson states that he "moves on steadily and never rushes." She brings attention to his use of humor and how it helps us understand "how these men maintained incredible humility in the face of extraordinary events."

Unit 11 ■ Reading Informational Text: Integration of Knowledge and Ideas   **267**

Digital Connection: Primary Sources Online

Encourage students to view a video of President Reagan giving the entire speech at Normandy before an audience of Rangers. The speech is available online. Have students note where President Reagan pauses and where the audience seems to be the most moved. Discuss with students whether they agree with Jameson's assessment of President Reagan's delivery as having a "lightness and buoyancy." Explain that in the later part of the speech, President Reagan discusses American foreign policy of his day, implying that the countries that were Allies during World War II must still stand together for freedom and oppose the forces of communism and totalitarianism. Have students analyze how President Reagan ties all of these ideas together.

Comparing Media Presentations

Guided Practice

Recap Reading Selection

Have students recall what they have read from President Reagan's speech commemorating D-Day and Nancy Busch Jameson's reactions to the speech.

Read and Practice

Have partners take turns reading the selection as you circulate to provide support. Circulate among students and ask them to respond to Cite Evidence callouts A, B, and C. Provide additional scaffolding as needed, using the suggestions below.

CITE EVIDENCE

A Discuss with students that President Reagan's purpose in using the word *boys* is to make the audience feel the youth, innocence, and vulnerability of the soldiers.

B Students should recognize that the boxed phrases in paragraph 13 evoke small town America, with their imagery of Americans on the "home front" reacting to news of the D-Day invasion.

C On page 269 Jameson mentions President Reagan's effective use of the liberty bell as a patriotic symbol. Students working with partners may find that, depending on their delivery, they can emphasize how unusual the action of ringing the Liberty Bell was, or they can tie this action to the religious actions mentioned directly before.

COMPARING MEDIA PRESENTATIONS

Guided Practice

WORDS TO KNOW

affinity

beachhead

devised

evoke

liberation

CITE EVIDENCE

A Reagan's use of the word *boys* in paragraph 10 is an example of loaded language. What is his purpose in using this word? Circle a phrase with a strong emotional connotation.

B Put a box around the loaded language in paragraph 13 that evokes a feeling of people living in small town America.

C Review what Jameson says on page 269 about patriotic symbols, and then underline a phrase in paragraph 13 that would have an impact in both written and spoken media. Then work with a partner and practice speaking this phrase out loud with different pace, phrasing, and emphasis.

The 40th Anniversary of D-Day *continued*

10   Forty summers have passed since the battle that you fought here. You were young the day you took these cliffs; some of you were hardly more than boys, (with the deepest joys of life before you.) Yet, you risked everything here. Why? Why did you do it? What impelled you to put aside the instinct for self-preservation and risk your lives to take these cliffs? What inspired all the men of the armies that met here? We look at you, and somehow we know the answer. It was faith and belief; it was loyalty and love.

11   The men of Normandy had faith that what they were doing was right, faith that they fought for all humanity, faith that a just God would grant them mercy on this **beachhead** or on the next. It was the deep knowledge—and pray God we have not lost it—that there is a profound, moral difference between the use of force for **liberation** and the use of force for conquest. You were here to liberate, not to conquer, and so you and those others did not doubt your cause. And you were right not to doubt.

12   You all knew that some things are worth dying for. One's country is worth dying for, and democracy is worth dying for, because it's the most deeply honorable form of government ever **devised** by man. All of you loved liberty. All of you were willing to fight tyranny, and you knew the people of your countries were behind you.

13   The Americans who fought here that morning knew word of the invasion was spreading through the darkness back home. They fought—or felt in their hearts, though they couldn't know in fact, that in Georgia they were filling the churches at 4 a.m, in Kansas they were kneeling on their porches and praying, and in Philadelphia they were ringing the Liberty Bell. . . .

268

Words to Know

General Academic Vocabulary

affinity (*n.*): fondness for; connection to

devised (*v.*): thought up; created

evoke (*v.*): to cause people to think about; to call up memories or feelings about

Domain-Specific Vocabulary

beachhead (*n.*): base established on an enemy's shore during an invasion

liberation (*n.*): the act of setting a nation or area free

Working with Word Meaning Encourage students to come up with synonyms for each word.

INTEGRATION OF KNOWLEDGE AND IDEAS

Reconsidering Reagan *continued*

Guided Practice

10 **NANCY BUSCH JAMESON:** In this section, as before, Reagan **evokes** religion; however it's interesting to hear how he also weaves in the Liberty Bell. Reagan had a strong **affinity** for America's patriotic symbols, and here he connects one to religious images in a subtle but effective way.

11   Seeing the video of the speech after all these years also reminds me that Reagan's voice had a very natural gentleness to it, and that he rarely shouted or bellowed as some politicians do—he didn't need to!

Comprehension Check

1. Jameson mentions Reagan's gentle voice. In what medium would you NOT experience this aspect of his delivery?

    a. a video of his second inaugural address

    b. a sound clip from his first State of the Union address

    (c.) a poster from his 1984 reelection campaign

    d. a television interview with a journalist

2. What aspect of Reagan's delivery does Jameson mention in this section of her interview?

    (a.) volume

    b. pace

    c. body language

    d. humor

3. Which of the following is an opinion, and not a reasoned judgment, of Jameson's?

    (a.) Reagan did not need to shout.

    b. Reagan rarely shouted.

    c. Reagan's voice was gentle.

    d. Reagan had an affinity for patriotic symbols.

4. Which fact reinforces the religious theme in Reagan's speech?

    a. D-Day involved 156,000 Allied troops.

    b. A radio journalist broadcasted a D-Day report from the deck of a naval ship.

    c. More than 9,000 Allied soldiers died on the first day of the D-Day invasion.

    (d.) People in the United States attended church services on D-Day.

5. Why is it important to distinguish among facts, opinions, and reasoned judgments when you read about history? Consider the question with a partner and then tell why.

    Sample answer: In order to get a clear and accurate idea of what happened

    during an historical event, one must know the facts. However, reasoned

    judgments of historians can add important insight. Unsupported opinions are

    less useful, but can be interesting.

Unit 11 ▪ Reading Informational Text: Integration of Knowledge and Ideas   **269**

Discussion Skills

Group students to discuss their ideas about the most important aspects of a speech. Members should prepare by identifying at least three areas of importance, such as 1) text, 2) spoken delivery, and 3) body language. Assign roles, such as Facilitator, Timekeeper, Note-taker, and Reporter, and have each group develop a list of items for each area. For example, for "Text," students might include "word choice," "anecdote," and "repetition." Remind students to ask each other questions, and to keep the discussion on track. Afterwards, have Reporters share their groups' lists with the class. Develop a class list of important aspects of a speech.

Comprehension Check

Answer Explanations:

1. Students should easily see that President Reagan's voice could be heard in a video, a sound clip, and a television interview, but not in a poster.

2. Jameson states that President Reagan "rarely shouted," which points to choice A.

3. The details that President Reagan rarely shouted, that he had a gentle voice, and that he had an affinity for patriotic symbols, can all be verified by listening to and reading his speeches. However, whether or not he was so authoritative that he did not need to shout is a matter of opinion.

4. Students should recognize that only the fact that people attended church services supports the religious theme of President Reagan's speech.

5. Answers will vary, but students should understand that, because facts are generally agreed upon and can be verified through evidence, they teach us what is generally agreed upon. When reading reasoned judgment, we read an author's point of view that is based on evidence. Opinions use the least amount of evidence of the three.

Jigsaw

Put students into groups of three to work together as a jigsaw team. That means each member of the team is responsible for one of the two pages from each set (Student Book pages 264–265, pages 266–267, or pages 268–269). Have students reread their sections and make one comparison between the speech text and the reaction to the video. Have each group choose one comparison to share with the whole class.

Comparing Media Presentations

Independent Practice

Recap Reading Selection

Have students recall what they have read so far in President Reagan's speech and Jameson's reaction to the speech. Ask students if they can recall the patriotic symbol President Reagan includes in his description of what some of the people in the United States did on June 6, 1944. (rang the Liberty Bell) Explain that next they will read the end of the speech and Jameson's reaction to it.

Read and Apply

Have students read this selection independently as you circulate. Ask them to read aloud so you can see if they are reading fluently. You can also use the support below to help students who are having difficulty.

CITE EVIDENCE

A Students should identify that the word *shield* has a connotation of protection against violence, and the words *freedom*, *prosperity*, and *peace* have a highly positive connotation of a thriving society.

B Help struggling students see that the use of the words *you* and *your* in the last sentence of paragraph 16 signal direct address. President Reagan is addressing the people and governments of the European democracies who fought with the United States in World War II.

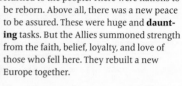

COMPARING MEDIA PRESENTATIONS

Independent Practice   The 40th Anniversary of D-Day *continued*

14   When the war was over, there were lives to be rebuilt and governments to be returned to the people. There were nations to be reborn. Above all, there was a new peace to be assured. These were huge and **daunting** tasks. But the Allies summoned strength from the faith, belief, loyalty, and love of those who fell here. They rebuilt a new Europe together.

15   There was first a great **reconciliation** among those who had been enemies, all of whom had suffered so greatly. The United States did its part, creating the Marshall Plan to help rebuild our allies and our former enemies. The Marshall Plan led to the Atlantic alliance—a great alliance that serves to this day as (our shield for freedom, for prosperity, and for peace....)

16   We are bound today by what bound us 40 years ago, the same loyalties, traditions, and beliefs. We're bound by reality. The strength of America's allies is vital to the United States, and the American security guarantee is essential to the continued freedom of Europe's democracies. <u>We were with you then; we are with you now. Your hopes are our hopes, and your destiny is our destiny.</u>

17   Here, in this place where the West held together, let us make a **vow** to our dead. Let us show them by our actions that we understand what they died for. Let our actions say to them the words for which [U.S. Army general] Matthew Ridgway listened: "I will not fail thee nor **forsake** thee."

18   Strengthened by their courage, heartened by their [valor], and borne by their memory, let us continue to stand for the ideals for which they lived and died.

19   Thank you very much, and God bless you all.

WORDS TO KNOW

daunting

forsake

reconciliation

vow

CITE EVIDENCE

A Circle in paragraph 15 a phrase made up of a list of loaded words. What is the connotation of the phrase? What is Reagan's purpose for including these particular words?

B Direct address is a powerful method of relating one's point of view to one's audience. Underline the sentences in paragraph 16 in which Reagan directly addresses his audience.

270   Unit 11 ■ Reading Informational Text: Integration of Knowledge and Ideas

---

Words to Know

General Academic Vocabulary

daunting (*adj.*): difficult and frightening; intimidating

forsake (*v.*): forget; abandon

reconciliation (*n.*): process of becoming friends again

vow (*n.*): solemn promise

Working with Word Meaning Have partners review each word's meaning and then use the word in conversation.

INTEGRATION OF KNOWLEDGE AND IDEAS

Reconsidering Reagan *continued*

12 **NANCY BUSCH JAMESON:** Here we get a few good examples of how Reagan used lists of loaded words to great effect. As I was listening to him pause slightly between each of the words "faith, belief, loyalty, and love" when describing what the Allies leaned on for support, I thought, I love how Reagan does that! He also uses repetition very effectively in this section; he repeats words and phrases for emphasis. This entire speech demonstrates that Reagan was a great communicator.

Comprehension Check

MORE ONLINE **sadlierconnect.com**

1. Which phrase from the speech is NOT an example of Reagan's use of repetition?

   a. "We were with you then; we are with you now."

   b. "Your hopes are our hopes, and your destiny is our destiny."

   c. "The United States did its part, creating the Marshall Plan." ✓

   d. "We are bound today by what bound us 40 years ago . . . We're bound by reality."

2. Which statement expresses a reasoned judgment by Jameson?

   a. Ronald Reagan was a great communicator. ✓

   b. In the speech, Reagan often repeats words.

   c. She loves how Reagan pauses slightly.

   d. Reagan uses lists of loaded words.

3. Which of the following can be experienced only by watching or listening to the speech?

   a. Reagan's use of repetition

   b. Reagan's pausing between lists of words ✓

   c. Reagan's making references to religion

   d. Reagan's use of loaded language

4. Which fact is excluded from this part of Reagan's speech?

   a. The United States created the Marshall Plan.

   b. The Marshall Plan led to the Atlantic alliance.

   c. The Atlantic alliance was in effect 40 years after D-Day.

   d. The former Soviet Union was strongly opposed to the Marshall Plan. ✓

5. Analyze the effectiveness of Reagan's words in both written and spoken media. In what way do the words work solely on the page? What does Reagan's oral delivery add to them? Is one more effective than the other? Cite specifics from the text.

   Sample answer: Reagan's words do work as written. For example, listing words together like "faith, belief, loyalty, and love" shows what the Allies leaned on for support. However, the speech was written to be spoken and is most effective this way. Reagan's pace, phrasing, volume, and emphasis on certain words bring out the meaning of, for example, the quote from General Ridgway.

Independent Practice

Comprehension Check

Answer Explanations

1. Students should recognize repetition in A ("we" and "with you"), in B ("your" and "our"), and in D ("We are bound").

2. Because items B and D are facts and C expresses an opinion, choice A is correct.

3. Since repetition, references to religion, and loaded language can all be read, the correct answer is B.

4. Students should know that Reagan mentions the creation of the Marshall Plan and Atlantic alliance still in effect 40 years later. Therefore, D is correct.

5. Students should choose examples from the speech to show how the words work on the page, and specifics from Jameson's reaction to support what Reagan's oral delivery adds. Students may conclude that watching the speech is more effective than reading the text.

Critical Comprehension

Challenge students to think more deeply about the text and to support their answers with evidence from the text.

Ask students: *Why does President Reagan use repetition?* (to add emphasis and to make the ideas memorable)

Assess and Respond

If students have trouble answering the questions in the Comprehension Check,

Then lead them in highlighting the section of the text referenced in the question, rereading carefully, and discussing how the speech effectively pays tribute to World War II veterans.

Extend Thinking: Apply Concepts

Have students work in groups to read another presidential speech, such as Bill Clinton's speech commemorating the 50th anniversary of the Normandy invasion. Then have them watch a video of the speech. Have students note how the speaker uses pacing, volume, and phrasing to enhance the speech. Remind them to distinguish among fact, opinion, and reasoned judgment. Ask them to evaluate and hypothesize reasons for audience reactions. Have a volunteer from each group present their findings.

Evaluating Arguments

Guided Instruction

OBJECTIVE
Evaluate an argument or claim in terms of its reasoning and evidence.

Genre: Web Article/Opinion Piece

A Web article is a nonfiction text that appears on the Internet. An opinion piece states the author's view, supported by facts and other types of evidence.

Set the Purpose

Have students think about how they make an argument. Ask: *What kinds of evidence do you use? Do you state your opinion clearly?*

Model and Teach

Read or have volunteers read the selection and callouts as the class follows along. Model effective strategies for responding to the callouts by using the suggestions below.

CITE EVIDENCE

A Explain to students that a claim is a point that is made to support an argument. Help students locate the author's claim in paragraph 1. Note that the claim is stated very directly, using the words "I believe that . . . "

B Help students understand that the sentence containing details about the forest industry is about economic conditions and can easily be verified.

EVALUATING ARGUMENTS

Guided Instruction

WORDS TO KNOW
deforestation
forestry
hectare
renewable resource
timber

> When a writer is making an argument, you should look for **sound reasoning**, as well as **specific evidence that offers support** for the writer's claim.

CITE EVIDENCE

A A piece of writing that offers an argument should **state a specific claim** plainly and clearly. Put an asterisk next to the sentence that contains Alvarado's specific argument.

B Writers who are making arguments will provide **facts** to support their claims. A fact is a true piece of information that can be verified. Underline in paragraph 2 an economic fact that supports the claim that forest industries are vital to many.

272

What Forests Offer Us
By Ricardo Z. Alvarado, MS in Forestry

http://www.futureofforestry.net/What_Forests_Offer_Us/index.html

(Genre: Web article/opinion piece)

1   Amidst all the talk of how damaging **deforestation** is to the environment, there are few voices speaking out in favor of the practice.*I am posting this article because I believe that the clearing of forested land, despite its drawbacks, is actually a "necessary evil." Earth's forests provide land, resources, and jobs upon which millions of people all over the world depend every day.

2   To begin with, forest-related industries employ 60 million people, according to United Nations estimates. These include **forestry**, which is the management of forests, as well as the logging, timber, and paper industries. Every year, nearly $300 billion in forest products are traded around the world. The economic livelihood of many poor communities depends heavily on forest resources. Combating deforestation endangers these communities.

Logging

3   The logging industry involves cutting down trees and turning them into usable **timber**. Timber is an important raw material used to build homes and buildings. Wood is also a significant energy source; in rural societies, it is burned for heat and to cook food. Wood is of course also used to make paper. Trees must be cut down in order for them to be used.

4   The logging industry has shown a commitment to what is termed "selective logging," which is the cutting down of only selected trees. In this way, entire forests are not decimated—only the most desirable trees are harvested. It is also important to note that

---

Words to Know

General Academic Vocabulary
timber (*n.*): wood; lumber

Domain-Specific Vocabulary
deforestation (*n.*): removal of forests and trees
forestry (*n.*): care and management of forests and the businesses that use them
hectare (*n.*): an area of land equal to about 2 ½ acres
renewable resource (*n.*): resource of which more can be grown or produced

Working with Word Meaning Have students draw pictures and graphs to show the meaning of the words.

INTEGRATION OF KNOWLEDGE AND IDEAS

trees are a **renewable resource**, which means they can be replanted and grown back. In recent years, many countries have engaged in the practice of large-scale tree replanting. This practice has resulted in a drop in the number of **hectares** of forest being lost every year, according to a United Nations study.

Cattle Ranching

5   When forested land is deliberately cleared, it is usually for an important reason. One such reason is for cattle ranching. In the rural areas of many countries, the raising of cattle for meat is a vitally important economic practice. Raising cattle requires many acres of land on which the cattle may roam, and so the felling of trees is sometimes necessary.

6   In Brazil—a country with a population of 200 million—cattle ranching is essential to the economy. <u>Brazil is the world's largest producer and exporter of beef, which accounts for an important portion of its annual exports of $242 billion.</u> Brazil's (impressive) cattle ranches, located in sections of cleared Amazon rainforest, are spread out over 283,000 square miles. Cutting down areas of the Brazilian rainforest in order to support Brazil's cattle-ranching industry is entirely justified. In fact, since 2003, Brazil's economy has boomed, thanks in large part to the growth of its beef cattle industry.

Agriculture

7   For many countries, agriculture also depends on clearing forested land. For example, in El Salvador, coffee is an important crop grown on land that was previously forested. Thousands of hectares of "coffee forests" are used to produce this important crop and employ many people. A full ten percent of El Salvador's economy is agriculture. Coffee is important to the economies of many Central American countries; some 2.5 million acres of Central American forest has been cleared for coffee farming. It is an important use of deforested land.

Comprehension Check

Evaluate Alvarado's claim that deforestation is a "necessary evil." Explain your position by citing specific evidence from the opinion piece.

CITE EVIDENCE

C Writers also include their own **opinions** about the subject. An opinion is a personal belief about a topic that is not supported by sound reasoning or substantial evidence. Circle in paragraph 6 a word that expresses Alvarado's opinion about Brazil's cattle ranches.

D An opinion that is supported by substantial evidence is called a **reasoned judgment**. Find a sentence in paragraph 6 that offers reasoning for the assertion that cattle ranching is an important part of Brazil's economy and double underline it.

E As you read an argument, assess whether the writer is using **sound reasoning** and **relevant evidence**. In paragraph 7, there is one sentence that is not relevant to the claim that growing coffee is important and depends on clearing forested land. Draw a box around it. What would be a more relevant fact in this case?

Guided Instruction

CITE EVIDENCE

C Help students locate the word *impressive*, and discuss that it shows a positive value judgment by the author.

D Direct students to sentence 2 in paragraph 6; discuss that it serves as evidence that cattle ranching is essential to the Brazilian economy.

E Help students understand that the boxed sentence is not directly relevant to the argument in paragraph 7. One example of a more relevant fact would be the percentage of El Salvador's agricultural output that is coffee.

Comprehension Check

Sample Answer: I agree with Alvarado's claims that many nations' economies depend on the use of deforested land, but he has not offered any specifics as to how these economies might grow in other ways that do not require deforestation.

Answer Explanation: When assessing whether Alvarado's reasoning is sound and his evidence is relevant and sufficient to support his claim, students might use the following examples as evidence for their answer: Paragraph 6 gives information on the importance of the cattle ranching industry in Brazil, which requires deforestation; paragraph 7 gives information on the importance of the coffee industry in Central America, which also requires deforestation. Despite this evidence, students may feel other possible industries should be explored in order to protect forests.

Support English Language Learners

Students who are learning English may have a difficult time using a dictionary to determine the meaning of unfamiliar words and phrases in the text. Preview the selection's difficult words and phrases, such as the ones below, with students who may benefit, while the rest of the class is using dictionaries to look up unfamiliar words.

raw material (*n.*): the basic material or substance that is used to make something

decimated (*v.*): destroyed

controversial (*adj.*): causing disagreement

vilify (*v.*): speak harshly about someone

Guided Instruction

CITE EVIDENCE

A Help students locate the sentence that begins with, "Studies have shown . . . " Point out that scientific studies are often used to support claims in articles like this.

B Discuss with the students that the word *delicious* describes how the author believes processed foods taste. Not everyone would agree, for example, that mayonnaise is delicious. However, the rest of the claim in the sentence— that palm oil is used in many processed foods—is a true piece of verifiable information. Remind students always to distinguish among fact, opinion, and reasoned judgment.

Review: Comparing Media Presentations

Remind students that when they compare different media presentations, they look at how using different media has an effect on a text. For example, reading a speech will be different from listening to a speaker deliver the same speech. Ask students to imagine that this text is being delivered as a speech. Have them imagine what kind of pacing the author might use, what words he might emphasize, and when his volume might increase. Ask volunteers to read a section of the text as if they are giving a speech.

EVALUATING ARGUMENTS

Guided Instruction

What Forests Offer Us continued

WORDS TO KNOW
biofuel
plantation
processed food
sustainable

CITE EVIDENCE

A Draw an asterisk next to the sentence that offers sound evidence for the assertion that slash-and-burn practices provide environmental benefits.

B Circle the word in paragraph 13 that reveals the writer's claim about processed foods that use palm oil. Then explain why that entire sentence is actually offering a fact.

Benefits of Slash-and-Burn

8   A discussion of the use of deforested land to raise crops is a good opportunity to raise the controversial issue of clearing forests by a method called slash-and-burn.

9   In slash-and-burn, trees are cut down and then burned where they lie on the forest floor. While this may sound like a harsh practice, it is actually full of environmental benefits. *Studies have shown that the ash left behind by the burned trees is an excellent fertilizer. The soil actually benefits from slashing-and-burning.

Palm Oil

10   Previously, I mentioned that many countries participate in large-scale reforestation. Some places actually replace the old trees with different kinds—specific types of trees that provide important economic benefits.

11   In countries like Malaysia and Indonesia, rainforests are being cleared to plant palm trees from which palm oil is then harvested. Palm oil has emerged as one of the world's most important **biofuels**. A biofuel is any fuel that is created from a renewable biological resource. Palm oil is an exciting alternative to fossil fuels. For example, it is being used to run electric plants in Europe.

12   The economies of Malaysia and Indonesia have boomed ever since they concentrated on growing palm trees for the purpose of producing and exporting palm oil. In a sense, it's an environmental trade-off: the clearing of rainforests is compensated by the creation of a clean energy source (palm oil) that reduces dependence on fossil fuels like oil and coal.

274   Unit 11 ■ Reading Informational Text: Integration of Knowledge and Ideas

---

Words to Know

General Academic Vocabulary
plantation (*n.*): a large farm

Domain-Specific Vocabulary
biofuel (*n.*): fuel created from renewable natural resources
processed food (*n.*): food changed from its natural state, usually made in factories
sustainable (*adj.*): able to last a long time, especially by using renewable resources and taking care of the environment

Working with Word Meaning Have partners restate each word's meaning in their own words and then use the word in conversation.

INTEGRATION OF KNOWLEDGE AND IDEAS

13   Furthermore, palm oil is an important part of our daily life, though you may not realize it. It is found in many (delicious) **processed foods** like potato chips, bread, mayonnaise, and ice cream. It is also used in soap, detergent, and paint. Cutting down trees and replacing them with palm trees is a logical practice.

Rubber Trees

14   It's worth mentioning that rubber trees are also big business in many countries. Their development requires the clearing of forested land. The economies of Indonesia, Malaysia, and Thailand all depend on the production of rubber, which is tapped from rubber trees on huge **plantations**. One rubber tree can produce as much as 30 pounds of rubber in one year. As the world's demand for rubber products such as automobile tires increases, these countries feel the benefit.

15   Leading manufacturers all over the world are doing their best to make the production of oil and rubber more **sustainable**. In many countries, these efforts are paying off tremendously. Indonesia, for example, has seen a steep drop in its rate of deforestation in the last 20 years.

Building Boom

16   An obvious reason to deforest land is to build homes and communities for people to live in. While critics have applied the term *urban sprawl* to describe the rapid growth of cities, there are benefits to living in cities and many reasons to encourage their continued expansion.

17   When people's standard of living goes up, they can afford to own their own homes. Further, they often want to move out of the city center and build larger domiciles. This desire for increased living space is legitimate. (The clearing of forested areas for the purpose of developing larger homes and residential areas should be encouraged.)

Comprehension Check

Does Alvarado cite relevant evidence on pages 274 and 275 to support his overall argument that deforestation is necessary? Offer specifics in your answer.

Guided Instruction

CITE EVIDENCE

C Box the sentence in paragraph 15 that expresses an opinion that is not supported by any evidence.

D Double underline the sentence in paragraph 15 that expresses a reasoned judgment that is supported by the sentence that immediately follows it.

E Read the last sentence of paragraph 17 and circle the sentence if it is an unsupported opinion. If it demonstrates reasoned judgment, double underline it. Explain your answer.

A woman taps a rubber tree.

Guided Instruction

CITE EVIDENCE

C Direct students' attention to the first sentence of paragraph 15, and discuss that evidence to support this claim might include a specific action that one leading manufacturer has taken.

D Students should identify that the claim that industry efforts are paying off is supported by the last sentence about Indonesia having a "steep drop in its rate of deforestation . . . "

E The only support the author gives for the claim that we should allow deforestation so that people can live in larger homes that are farther from city centers is that people sometimes want larger homes "out of the city center." This does not serve as sufficient evidence to support the author's opinion that we should encourage deforestation so that people can have the homes they want.

Comprehension Check

Sample Answer: Alvarado cites evidence that clearing forests and using slash-and-burn farming methods help soil; he also cites evidence that different countries benefit economically from deforestation necessary for industries such as palm oil and rubber. However, his claim that we should clear forests so that people can live in larger homes farther from the city is not supported by relevant evidence.

Answer Explanation: In paragraphs 11 and 12, the author discusses that Malaysia and Indonesia clear forests to support the palm oil industry; in paragraphs 14 and 15, Indonesia, Malaysia, and Thailand clear forests to support the rubber industry; in paragraphs 16 and 17, the author discusses deforestation to clear land for homes.

Differentiate Instruction

Discuss with students what they know about the topic of deforestation. Have a note-taker record the ideas. If some students have little knowledge of the topic, work with small groups to research the basics of the topic. Students may benefit from viewing maps and photographs of rainforests and how deforestation has affected those areas. Have different groups share what they have found about deforestation.

Evaluating Arguments

Guided Practice

Recap Reading Selection

Have students recall what they have read so far about the "necessary evil" of deforestation. Let students know that they will read more claims to support the author's idea that clearing forests must continue.

Read and Practice

Have partners take turns reading the selection as you circulate to provide support. Circulate among students and ask them to respond to Cite Evidence callouts A and B. Provide additional scaffolding as needed, using the suggestions below.

CITE EVIDENCE

A Students may be confused by the author's use of the past tense in the first sentence of paragraph 18. Help them understand that the writer intends to continue making claims to support the argument that deforestation can have a positive impact.

B Students should identify that the last sentence in paragraph 19 is an example of reasoned judgment. They should recognize that in order for this sentence to be an opinion, there would have to be a lack of supporting factual evidence.

EVALUATING ARGUMENTS

Guided Practice

What Forests Offer Us *continued*

Hydroelectric Dams

18   I've already cited a number of ways in which the clearing of forested lands is often necessary to improve the lives of the people that exist there.*Another example of this is the building of **hydroelectric dams**, which often requires deforestation.

19   A hydroelectric dam harnesses the incredible power of a raging river and turns it into electricity that can be used by local communities to improve their daily lives. A hydroelectric dam takes advantage of another renewable process—the **water cycle**. When water evaporates, rises, condenses, and then falls as rain, the power supply of a hydroelectric dam is replenished. In this way, <u>hydroelectric dams are environmentally friendly.</u>

20   The building of a hydroelectric dam often requires the clearing—and then flooding—of large areas of forest. The benefits far outweigh the negatives of this practice, however. One example of this is the Three Gorges Dam in China, the world's largest hydroelectric power plant. It is still being completed, but at its peak it will **generate** more than a billion **watts** of power. Not only will millions of people in China have access to affordable energy because of the dam, those same people will be provided with a supply of clean water. Furthermore, the construction of the dam is employing some 250,000 people.

Mining

21   Another practice that concerns opponents of deforestation is mining, because building a mine typically necessitates the removal of many acres of forest. However, the benefits of mining cannot be overlooked. Some might object to the difficult working conditions, but the mining industry employs millions of people all over the world, including 80,000 people in the United States.

22   Mining is also very important to the economies of many South American nations, almost all of which are rich in mineral deposits. Selling mined metals such as gold, silver, copper, tin, and zinc generates significant revenue that can be spent on public works projects like road building.

WORDS TO KNOW

generate
hydroelectric dam
water cycle
watt

CITE EVIDENCE

A Draw an asterisk next to the sentence on this page that clearly states the writer's claim for this section of the text.

B Underline in paragraph 19 the sentence that expresses a reasoned judgment about building hydroelectric dams. Then discuss with a partner how paragraph 19 would have to be different in order for this sentence to be an opinion.

Words to Know

General Academic Vocabulary
generate (*v.*): create; produce

Domain-Specific Vocabulary
hydroelectric dam (*n.*): dam that uses falling water to create electricity
water cycle (*n.*): the cycle in which water evaporates from rivers, lakes, and oceans, falls as rain, and then again evaporates
watt (*n.*): unit in which electricity is measured

Working with Word Meaning Have students make word webs to show words they associate with each vocabulary word.

INTEGRATION OF KNOWLEDGE AND IDEAS
Guided Practice

Guided Practice

23   In the United States, the mining of coal is absolutely vital to coal-rich states like West Virginia and Kentucky. With half of the country's electricity generated from the burning of coal, coal mining must continue despite its effect on forests.

Comprehension Check

1. Which of the following ideas from the text expresses an opinion?

   a. Coal mining must continue, despite what it does to forests.

   b. Many South American countries are rich in mineral deposits.

   c. Half the electricity used in the United States is generated from burning coal.

   d. Mining employs millions of people.

2. Which idea from the text does NOT support the claim that the benefits of clearing forests to build the Three Gorges Dam outweigh the negatives?

   a. The dam will generate billions of watts of power.

   b. The dam will supply clean water.

   c. The dam has created thousands of jobs.

   d. The forest was dying out anyway.

3. Which of the following expresses a fact related to hydroelectric dams?

   a. The power of a raging river is incredible.

   b. Hydroelectric dams are environmentally friendly.

   c. Building a hydroelectric dam often requires clearing forested land.

   d. Building hydroelectric dams improves people's daily lives.

4. Based on the text, which of the following is a reasoned judgment about mining?

   a. Selling mined metals generates revenue.

   b. Coal mining must continue, despite what it does to forests.

   c. Mining revenue can be spent on public works projects.

   d. Coal mining is vital to states like Kentucky.

5. Work with a partner to find examples of facts, opinions, and reasoned judgments on pages 276 and 277. Then explain how identifying facts, opinions, and judgments helps you understand the central claim of the entire article.

   Sample answer: Alvarado's claim that deforestation is a "necessary evil" is supported by the fact that mining employs millions of people. His reasoned judgment that the benefits of hydroelectric dams outweigh their drawbacks also provides support. He is on weaker ground when he expresses the opinion that "coal mining must continue"; he would be wise to discuss how mining could be more environmentally friendly.

Comprehension Check

Answer Explanations

1. Students should recognize that B, C, and D are verifiable, but A is a claim with no evidence to support it.

2. Careful readers will recognize that choice D is not part of the author's evidence.

3. Students may be confused because A, B, and D can be supported with evidence. However, only choice C states true information that can be verified.

4. Students should identify that A and C are facts and B is an opinion. The author supports the claim that mining is vital in states like Kentucky because of the number of jobs it provides and amount of power these states provide the rest of the country.

5. As an example of a fact, students may note "the mining industry employs millions of people all over the world." For reasoned judgment, students may use the author's claim that benefits of hydroelectric dams outweigh negatives, and show how he supports this with facts about Three Gorges Dam. Although the author shows that mining brings jobs and energy, the evidence is not sufficient for him to make the claim that "mining must continue." Students may say that identifying facts, judgments, and opinions help them trace the entire argument, since they all tie to defending deforestation.

Turn and Talk

Have partners discuss the following question: *How is the author effective at supporting his arguments?* (Student answers may vary, but should include specific examples from the text.)

Discussion Skills

Have students think about the question: *Which reason to continue deforestation seems closest to the author's heart?* Encourage students to quote evidence from the text in support of their answers. Suggest the following stems for them to try out as they have this discussion:

- *The author's statement about _____ supports my idea that _____.*
- *The author says _____ and that means _____.*
- *When the author says _____, he is implying that _____.*

Independent Practice

Recap Reading Selection

Have students recall what they read about how deforestation relates to the benefits of dams and mining. Ask students if they can recall the name of the largest hydroelectric power plant. (the Three Gorges Dam in China) Explain that next, students will read about how some companies and governments are taking action to reforest the cleared lands.

Read and Apply

Have students read this selection independently as you circulate. Ask them to read aloud so you can see if they are reading fluently. You can also use the support below to help students who are having difficulty.

CITE EVIDENCE

A Students should recognize that both paragraphs, which discuss Nestlé's efforts to reforest certain areas, support the claim made in paragraph 24 that many companies are working to reforest land.

B In paragraph 27, the author starts with a claim about "The governments . . . making a positive difference." As evidence to support this claim, the author includes Indonesia, where "the government planted an incredible 79 million trees in 2007." He also includes Brazil, where the government "is working with international environmental organizations to slow the rate of deforestation."

EVALUATING ARGUMENTS

Independent Practice

What Forests Offer Us *continued*

WORDS TO KNOW

decimation

erosion

primary forest

secondary forest

CITE EVIDENCE

A What specific claim do the details in paragraphs 25 and 26 support? Draw an asterisk next to the sentence that contains the claim.

B Underline a reasoned judgment the writer makes regarding governmental efforts to fight deforestation. What relevant evidence does the writer offer in support?

278

Reforestation

24   *Despite the efforts of anti-deforestation groups to vilify any company that clears forests as part of its development, the truth is that reforestation is alive and well among many companies.

25   One company that has emerged as a leader in reforestation is Nestlé, which is famous for its chocolate but also manufactures baby food, bottled water, and coffee, among other products. As part of its Creating Shared Value initiative, Nestlé is reforesting areas that have been affected by the production of their food products (coffee and chocolate, especially).

26   In 2011, Nestlé announced a plan to plant 750,000 trees in Malaysia, 100,000 of which would be planted in the first year alone. When all the trees are planted, they will cover an astonishing 2,400 hectares of land.

Government Efforts

27   The governments of many countries whose economies rely on deforested land are making a positive difference as well. For example, in Indonesia, the government planted an incredible 79 million trees in 2007. In Brazil, the government is working with international environmental organizations to slow the rate of deforestation. The work is producing results, too; the rate of deforestation in that country has fallen since 1990. A national law was passed in 2012 that will protect Brazilian forests from **decimation**.

Exotic Trees

28   One reforestation practice that has shown positive results is the planting of exotic trees like eucalyptus trees. Eucalyptus grows quickly and can efficiently replenish the soil with needed nutrients. Also, the quicker replacement trees grow, the better the fight against soil **erosion**.

Secondary Forests

29   In addition to human-driven reforestation efforts, Mother Nature rejuvenates herself by growing **secondary forests**. Secondary forests grow back after a catastrophic event, like a forest fire or flood. A **primary forest**, then, is an original forest that has remained largely untouched by humans.

Words to Know

General Academic Vocabulary

decimation (*n*.): the destruction of a great number of something

Domain-Specific Vocabulary

erosion (*v*.): wearing or washing away

primary forest (*n*.): a forest in its original condition, mostly unaffected by human activities

secondary forest (*n*.): a forest that has grown back after a destructive event

Working with Word Meaning Have students draw pictures or cartoons to demonstrate the possible relationships between vocabulary words.

INTEGRATION OF KNOWLEDGE AND IDEAS

Conclusion

30   No one, including me, denies that deforestation is an environmental problem. It may even be a crisis. Yet let's not completely lose perspective as we tackle this issue. Most of the time, forested land is cleared for important economic reasons. I can only restate my claim even more strongly: deforestation may be an evil, but it is necessary.

Comprehension Check   **MORE ONLINE** sadlierconnect.com

1. Based on the text, which is NOT true about eucalyptus trees?

   a. Eucalyptus grows quickly.

   (b.) Planting eucalyptus does not impact the effects of deforestation.

   c. Eucalyptus replenishes the soil with essential nutrients.

   d. Planting eucalyptus helps combat soil erosion.

2. What claim does the section on secondary forests support?

   (a.) There are a number of ways that deforestation is being slowed.

   b. Deforestation is a serious crisis.

   c. Many companies are concerned about deforestation.

   d. World governments are ignoring the issue of deforestation.

3. Which idea from the text expresses an opinion, as opposed to a reasoned judgment or a fact?

   a. Deforestation may be evil, but it is necessary.

   b. Reforestation is alive and well among many companies.

   (c.) Deforestation may even be a crisis.

   d. Secondary forests grow back after a catastrophic event.

4. Which detail described in the text is irrelevant to the writer's central claim about deforestation?

   a. Most of the time, forested land is cleared for important economic reasons.

   (b.) A primary forest is an original, untouched forest.

   c. Deforestation may be a crisis.

   d. Many companies are engaged in reforestation.

5. Is Alvarado's claim that the benefits of deforestation outweigh its drawbacks a reasoned judgment? Explain your answer with specifics from the text.

   Sample answer: Alvarado provides substantial evidence to support his claim, so
   his claim is an example of reasoned judgment and not opinion. For example, it
   is true that many people rely on the economic strength afforded by industries
   that require deforested land in order to develop and thrive.

Unit 11 ■ Reading Informational Text: Integration of Knowledge and Ideas   **279**

Extend Thinking: Apply Concepts

Have students work in small groups to research one of the industries mentioned in the article. For example, students might choose mining, coffee-growing, hydroelectric power, rubber, or palm oil. Have students look at how their chosen industry has an impact on forests. Encourage students to look for articles defending the industry's role in the environment and for articles that challenge that viewpoint. Ask students to analyze the claims in the articles, looking for facts, opinions, and reasoned judgments. Then have them discuss whether they find the author's arguments effective. Groups may share their work.

Comprehension Check

Answer Explanations

1. Careful readers should recognize that the text states that eucalyptus grows quickly, replenishes the soil, and helps combat soil erosion, so B is correct.

2. B is not true; C may be true, but the section on secondary forests gives "Mother Nature" credit for their growth; and D is untrue, according to paragraph 27. Then choice A is correct.

3. The author gives evidence to support his reasoned judgments presented in choices A and B, and choice D is a verifiable fact. Choice C is an unsupported opinion.

4. The fact that a primary forest is untouched does not support or refute the author's claim that deforestation is necessary. So choice B is correct.

5. Students should understand that the author supports his claim with evidence. They should support their responses and opinions by citing textual evidence.

Critical Comprehension

Challenge students to think more deeply about the text and to support their answers with evidence from the text. Ask: *What arguments could you make to counter the author's claims?* (Students might say we should not clear forests just because people want bigger houses, and that we should find new sources of energy besides coal and hydroelectricity.)

Assess and Respond
If students have trouble answering the questions in the Comprehension Check,
Then ask them to return to the text and highlight information that can help them answer the questions.

Guided Instruction

OBJECTIVE
Analyze how two authors writing about the same topic emphasize different evidence in support of their claims.

Genre: Scientific Text/ Opinion Piece

A scientific text is an informative, nonfiction text on a science topic. An opinion piece includes the author's opinion with evidence to support claims.

Set the Purpose

Help students understand the purpose for learning the reading skill by asking: *Why would two writers considering the same topic emphasize different facts?*

Model and Teach

Read or have volunteers read the selection and callouts as the class follows along. Model effective strategies for responding to the callouts by using the suggestions below.

CITE EVIDENCE

A Help students locate the central claim in the first sentence of paragraph 3.

B Discuss that Alvarado uses the underscored fact to argue that deforestation can continue, while Nguyen argues that there is still too much deforestation to be affected by replanting.

ANALYZING THE PRESENTATION OF IDEAS
Guided Instruction

WORDS TO KNOW
forest canopy
refute
restraint
unassailable

A writer expressing an opinion different from another writer's on the same topic will offer **different evidence** and **interpret the same facts differently.**

CITE EVIDENCE

A A writer's central idea is often found in the first few paragraphs. Draw an asterisk next to the sentence in paragraph 3 that expresses Nguyen's central idea.

B In offering a different opinion on deforestation, Nguyen **interprets facts differently.** Underline in paragraph 8 a point that Alvarado stated that Nguyen challenges.

Save the World's Forests
By Karen X. Nguyen, Ph.D.
(Genre: Scientific Text/Opinion Piece)

1   I have read Ricardo Alvarado's opinion piece on deforestation and I am stunned, outraged, and deeply concerned. Mr. Alvarado points out that the world depends on forests in a variety of ways, but that does not mean that deforestation should be allowed to go on without **restraint**.

2   Mr. Alvarado has a habit of peppering his piece with tidy, **unassailable** truths that sound nice but ignore deeper environmental issues. For example, he says that "trees must be cut down in order for them to be used." This is hardly a disputable fact, but what about deforestation's impact?

3   I will take Mr. Alvarado's claims point by point and **refute** his argument that deforestation is a "necessary evil." Deforestation is wreaking havoc on our environment, and it must be controlled.

Logging

4   Mr. Alvarado's defense of the logging industry involves a discussion of "selective logging." He infers that this practice saves trees. In fact, the opposite is true. "Selective logging" does refer to felling only the most valuable trees, but when these trees are cut down, they usually fall on other trees and bring those down with them.

5   Logging also destroys the **forest canopy**, the protective layer formed by very tall trees that prevents sunlight from hitting the forest floor. The forest canopy keeps the soil moist and the

---

Words to Know

General Academic Vocabulary
refute (*v.*): argue against; disprove
restraint (*n.*): holding back; control
unassailable (*adj.*): unable to be argued with or attacked

Domain-Specific Vocabulary
forest canopy (*n.*): the highest layer of branches and leaves in a forest

Working with Word Meaning Encourage students to restate these definitions in their own words and to write their own example sentences.

INTEGRATION OF KNOWLEDGE AND IDEAS

temperature of the forest cool. Entire species of plants and insects that thrive in cool, moist conditions have been wiped out because forest canopies have been eliminated. The forest canopy also prevents soil erosion by protecting the forest floor from torrential rains.

6   Not only is the cutting down of trees harmful to forests, but logging requires heavy machinery and trucks that crush plants and animals when they drive over the forest floor.

7   Alvarado's solution to the impact of logging is weak. He suggests replanting trees as a way of replenishing lost forests. He neglects to mention that it takes a very, very long time for a forest to grow back to its previous fullness. Reforestation is not a complete solution.

8   Alvarado reports that deforestation is down in some places because "many countries have engaged in the practice of large-scale replanting of trees." Yet the United Nations study he cites shows that overall we are still losing the battle, particularly in South America and Africa. Reforestation will never make a serious dent in the problem of deforestation.

Cattle and Crops

9   Mr. Alvarado's discussion of farmers' and cattle ranchers' need for cleared land makes logical sense, but again, he avoids any of the real impact on forests.

10   To begin with, the practice of slash-and-burn is harmful, not helpful, to forests. Despite his claims about tree ash, clearing forested land in this way leaves thousands of acres of un-farmable, barren land. The soil left behind after burning a forest soon becomes devoid of nutrients.

11   The cleared land is also susceptible to flooding. The trees that had acted as a barrier to storm surges and heavy rains are removed. Small coastal villages in particular have felt the impact of deforestation in this way.

Comprehension Check

How does Nguyen use evidence that differs from Alvarado's to shape her argument thus far? Cite specifics in your answer.

Unit 11 ■ Reading Informational Text: Integration of Knowledge and Ideas   **281**

CITE EVIDENCE

C Nguyen is putting forth a different viewpoint and offers opinions that are different from those of Alvarado. In paragraph 7, box in Nguyen's opinion about reforestation. Then give a summary of her point of view of what logging does to forests.

D You have learned about facts, opinions, and reasoned judgments. **Speculation** is an unsupported conclusion reached by merely guessing. Find the speculation in paragraph 8 and circle it.

E Writers with different viewpoints will also offer and **emphasize different evidence** on a topic to support their opinions. Find in paragraph 10 the evidence about slash-and-burn that Alvarado did not offer and double underline it.

CITE EVIDENCE

C Help students locate Nguyen's opinion in the last sentence of paragraph 7. In summary, Nguyen has stated that selective logging destroys untargeted trees (paragraph 4) and that logging destroys the forest canopy (paragraph 5). Machinery used in logging destroys plants and animals (paragraph 6). Reforestation is slow and cannot provide a total replacement for what has been lost (paragraph 7). Finally, though the pace of deforestation may have slowed, there is still far too much of it, according to Nguyen (paragraph 8).

D Direct students to the last sentence in paragraph 8. Help them understand that, although Nguyen has explained how long it takes for forests to recover, she has neglected to support her opinion with evidence in this paragraph.

E Students should recognize that Alvarado did not state that slash-and-burn "leaves thousands of acres unfarmable."

Comprehension Check

Sample Answer: Nguyen is addressing each area of Alvarado's argument and refuting it with differing evidence and interpretation. For example, she cites the same United Nations study but emphasizes a different fact.

Answer Explanation: Students may include other evidence from Nguyen's text that covers one of Alvarado's claims, such as the existence of "selective logging" (paragraph 4); reforestation as a solution to deforestation (paragraphs 7 and 8); and slash-and-burn agriculture (paragraphs 9–11).

Support English Language Learners

English language learners may benefit from visual support to provide more background for comprehension of this text. Since a fair amount of the discussion of deforestation involves the loss of rainforest, share photographs of rainforests with students. Use examples that show forest canopy shielding the plants and animals from the sun. Have students conduct their own searches for photographs of animals that live in the rainforest, such as the spider monkey, the jaguar, and the macaw. They may also share pictures of the indigenous peoples of the rainforest, such as the Yanomami of Brazil or the Huli in Papua New Guinea. Viewing the photographs should help students understand that loss of the rainforest involves more than just trees.

Guided Instruction

CITE EVIDENCE

A Help students locate Borneo and Sumatra on the map. Then have students find the sentence that discusses Borneo and Sumatra in paragraph 13. Point out the key to the map, and help students understand that the red and orange areas represent areas where deforestation is happening the most quickly. Reread the sentence as students look at the map.

B Work with students to find Nguyen's claim. Discuss that, while Alvarado sees palm oil's popularity as a plus, Nguyen sees it as a threat to forests.

Review: Evaluating Arguments

Remind students that reasoned judgments are supported by evidence, facts are true statements that can be verified, and opinions are someone's viewpoint that is not supported by evidence. Ask students: *Is Nguyen's claim that "Mr. Alvarado's praise of palm oil as a biofuel is misguided" reasoned judgment or merely opinion?* (It is reasoned judgment because she supports the claim with evidence of the environmental dangers of palm oil production.)

ANALYZING THE PRESENTATION OF IDEAS

Guided Instruction

WORDS TO KNOW

archipelago
fertilizer
indigenous
peat
subsidizing

CITE EVIDENCE

A Writers may introduce **visual information** that can be integrated into information presented in the text. On the map, find the islands of Borneo and Sumatra and circle them. Then underline in paragraph 13 a fact about these two islands. Then tell how the map supports what the text states about Borneo and Sumatra.

B In paragraph 14, place an asterisk beside the evidence Nguyen offers about the usefulness of palm oil that differs from Alvarado's statement.

Save the World's Forests *continued*

Case Study: Indonesia

12   One of the countries Mr. Alvarado cites as a beneficiary of clearing forested land is Indonesia. Indonesia is an **archipelago** in Southeast Asia. It is home to more than 251 million people. While much of what Mr. Alvarado says about Indonesia is true—that its economy has benefitted from increased production of palm oil and rubber—he conveniently leaves out the negative impact the palm oil and rubber industries have had on the environment.

13   The rainforests of Indonesia have been cleared for the planting of palm and rubber trees; this is a fact Mr. Alvarado himself offers in his article. What he neglects to mention is that in 2007, the United Nations Environment Program warned that two of Indonesia's islands, <u>Borneo and Sumatra, could see 98% of their rainforests destroyed by 2022.</u>

14   Mr. Alvarado's emphasis on the utility of palm oil (it "is an important part of our daily life," he writes) is also misleading. ＊It is precisely because so many manufacturers use palm oil to make their products (ice cream, detergent, and so forth) that the clearing of forested land continues.

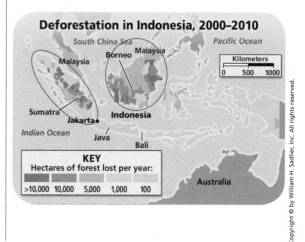

Deforestation in Indonesia, 2000–2010

Words to Know

General Academic Vocabulary

fertilizer (*n.*): a substance used to help plants grow, especially a chemical manure

peat (*n.*): soil that is thick with vegetable matter

subsidizing (*v.*): paying part of the cost for another person or group

Domain-Specific Vocabulary

archipelago (*n.*): group or chain of islands

indigenous (*adj.*): local; native

Working with Word Meaning Have students use images or diagrams to help them visualize the meaning of each new word.

INTEGRATION OF KNOWLEDGE AND IDEAS

A Dangerous Alternative

15   Mr. Alvarado's praise of palm oil as a biofuel is misguided. It's true that palm oil is used as an alternative to fossil fuels, but it presents its own environmental dangers.

16   In Indonesia and Malaysia, much of the land that is cleared to grow palm plantations is peatland. **Peat** is a dark, rich material made up of decayed organisms and is usually added to soil to make it more nutritious. Peatland is 90% water, and when it is drained (or burned), carbon is released into the air. Carbon emissions are the cause of global warming. By 2007, Indonesia was the third-leading producer of carbon emissions in the world.

17   Because of these emissions, many countries have decided to stop **subsidizing**, or helping to pay for, the development of palm oil as an energy alternative. Still others are considering an outright ban on the use of palm oil as a biofuel.

18   Another detail of palm oil deforestation Mr. Alvarado leaves out has to do with the harsh chemical **fertilizers** used to grow the palm trees. These fertilizers damage the surrounding environment. Palm oil has been called an "ecological disaster," and I agree.

Displacing Native People

19   An underreported side effect of deforestation is the displacement of **indigenous** people who live in forests. Very often, indigenous people have no legal ownership of the land they live on. Governments and big corporations can—and do—simply push people off their land and raze it. Displacing indigenous people from their native environment does unimaginable damage to their culture.

Comprehension Check

How does the map that shows deforestation in Indonesia support your overall comprehension of the topic? Explain your answer.

CITE EVIDENCE

C Underline the sentences in paragraph 16 that demonstrate Nguyen's different interpretation of the fact that palm oil is an alternative to fossil fuels.

D Double underline in paragraph 18 the sentence that expresses Nguyen's reasoned judgment about palm oil.

E You should use your own **personal experience**, as well as what you know about **language and culture**, to think analytically. Draw a box around the paragraph on page 283 that deals with a cultural aspect of the problem of deforestation. Then offer in your own words an argument against deforestation from a cultural perspective.

CITE EVIDENCE

C Help students identify the information on peatland's negative impact on the environment. Discuss with students that much of the problem environmentalists have with fossil fuels are their carbon emissions, so Nguyen is pointing out that palm oil does nothing to solve the problem.

D Students should understand that Nguyen has supported her reasoned claim that palm oil is an "ecological disaster" through her discussion of the problems of carbon emissions in palm oil production.

E Sample answer: For people who are indigenous to forests, clearing forests is the same as destroying their home and way of life.

Comprehension Check

Sample Answer: The map shows dramatically how much forest has been lost in Indonesia. This helps me understand how serious the issue is there.

Answer Explanation: Student answers may vary, but should reference the map on page 282 and its depiction of the speed and size of deforestation in Indonesia.

Differentiate Instruction

Pair struggling readers with more proficient readers. Allow the more proficient readers to read the text aloud as the struggling readers follow along. Let partners ask and answer questions about the text.

To cement understanding, have partners make two lists about palm oil, *Pro* and *Con*. Under *Pro*, have them list the positives that Alvarado discusses. Under *Con*, have them write the negatives that Nguyen includes.

Guided Practice

Recap Reading Selection

Have students recall what they have read about the problems of deforestation in the text so far. Tell them that next they will read about the deforestation associated with dams and mines.

Read and Practice

Have partners take turns reading the selection as you circulate to provide support. Circulate among students and ask them to respond to Cite Evidence callouts A and B. Provide additional scaffolding as needed, using the suggestions below.

CITE EVIDENCE

A Students may be confused by the notion of interpreting a fact differently. Explain that two authors might cite the same fact but draw different conclusions from that fact, or an author might choose not to include relevant information related to that fact. In this discussion of deforestation related to building hydroelectric dams, Nguyen includes the fact that "it is common for local populations to be displaced," which Alvarado did not include.

B Students should recognize that the detail about the mining company supports Nguyen's claim that deforestation is a serious concern and should be stopped; even governments that could benefit financially are calling a halt to the practice.

ANALYZING THE PRESENTATION OF IDEAS

Guided Practice

Save the World's Forests *continued*

Dams and Mines

WORDS TO KNOW
gaudy
gloss over
marvel
permit

CITE EVIDENCE

A Underline in paragraph 21 a sentence or phrase that shows that Nguyen is interpreting differently the fact that building a dam requires deforestation.

B What new piece of evidence regarding mining does Nguyen introduce in paragraph 23? Box it and tell how it strengthens or weakens her overall argument about deforestation.

20   Mr. Alvarado's section on hydroelectric dams is interesting, for while he sings their praises as mechanical **marvels** that transform communities—and they are—he conveniently **glosses over** their negative impact.

21   First, he does admit that a hydroelectric dam requires deforestation. When this happens, however, it is common for local populations to be displaced, for their land is needed for the construction of the dam. Second, the construction of a dam requires heavy machinery that damages what land remains. A dam also brings additional roads, which means more cars, which equals pollution. Deforesting land for dams also means loggers using bulldozers and tree cutters.

22   I was impressed that Mr. Alvarado mentioned that sometimes forested land is flooded, rather than cleared, before a dam is built. However, he left out the fact that the flood water can interact with the soil and release harmful gases into the air. He cites a dam's employment of the water cycle as evidence that dams are environmentally friendly. The truth is that they are not.

23   Mining is another industry that Mr. Alvarado is quick to praise. Mining, however, demands extensive deforestation. Indeed, it is not unusual for entire forests to be removed. In 2008, the government of Venezuela courageously denied a **permit** to a huge mining company, Crystallex International Corp., because of "sensitivities surrounding indigenous peoples . . . and the environment." Had it been allowed to go forward, the company would have built the largest gold and copper mines in Venezuela.

An iron mine in Venezuela

284

Words to Know

General Academic Vocabulary

gaudy (*adj.*): tastelessly showy; flashy
gloss over (*v.*): to give a deceptively good appearance to something; to hide the negative aspects of something
marvel (*n.*): an amazing thing
permit (*n.*): official, written permission to do something

Working with Word Meaning In pairs, have one student choose a vocabulary word and define it in his or her own words. The other student guesses the word. Then have partners switch roles.

INTEGRATION OF KNOWLEDGE AND IDEAS

Guided Practice

Urban Sprawl

24   What Mr. Alvarado wrote about the relationship between deforestation and urban sprawl is a good example of his shortsightedness. Mr. Alvarado appears to believe that the desire to live in big, **gaudy** homes is more important than preserving the forest habitats of plants, animals, and insects. Depressingly, deforestation has no hope of decreasing in the coming years.

Comprehension Check

1. Nguyen's central idea about dams is
   - **(a.)** they impact communities in negative ways as well as positive ways.
   - **b.** they are worthy of Alvarado's praise because of their environmental impact.
   - **c.** they are not worth building.
   - **d.** they provide people with jobs.

2. Which of the following pieces of visual information would be most relevant to this section?
   - **a.** a deforestation map of Venezuela
   - **b.** a technical diagram showing how a hydroelectric dam is constructed
   - **(c.)** a chart comparing a city's population with the rate of deforestation
   - **d.** a photograph of the president of Crystallex International Corporation

3. Which key fact is NOT emphasized by either writer?
   - **a.** Building hydroelectric dams requires deforestation.
   - **b.** Before a dam is built, sometimes the forested land is flooded.
   - **(c.)** Many countries practice reforestation.
   - **d.** Hydroelectric dams are mechanical marvels.

4. Which is an example of speculation?
   - **(a.)** Deforestation has no hope of decreasing in the coming years.
   - **b.** Crystallex would have built the largest gold and copper mines in Venezuela.
   - **c.** The construction of a dam requires heavy machinery.
   - **d.** Dams are environmentally friendly.

5. Work with a partner and tell how comparing and contrasting the two writers' claims helps you better understand the topic of deforestation.

   Sample answer: Reading both articles is very useful, as both writers raise good

   points as part of their claims. For deforestation to be fully understood, both its

   positive and negative effects must be considered, and only by reading both

   articles does a reader get a full picture.

Unit 11 ■ Reading Informational Text: Integration of Knowledge and Ideas   **285**

Discussion Skills

Have students think about the following questions: *What is Nguyen's main concern about deforestation? Does Alvarado have the same concern?* Encourage students to find examples to support their answers. Suggest the following stems for them to try out as they talk.

- *Nguyen's main concern about deforestation is _____. Alvarado's main concern seems to be _____.*
- *Nguyen views deforestation as _____, but Alvarado views deforestation as _____.*
- *Nguyen wants to save _____, and Alvarado wants to save _____.*

Guided Practice

Comprehension Check

Answer Explanations

1. In paragraph 20, Nguyen agrees with Alvarado that dams are "mechanical marvels that transform communities." However, she goes on to list several environmental problems with dams. Therefore, A is correct.

2. Students should recognize that for the section "Urban Sprawl," choice C is most relevant.

3. Both authors mention reforestation, but neither emphasizes the pros or cons of the practice.

4. Students should identify that choice A is speculation, since the author has no real way of knowing what the coming years will bring.

5. Student answers may vary, but should include the idea that reading both texts helps them have a fuller understanding of the benefits that industries that clear lands bring and the negatives associated with deforestation.

Numbered Heads Together

Have students work in groups of four, numbering off from one to four. Ask groups to work together for five minutes to answer the following question: *Why do you think Nguyen is "stunned, outraged, and deeply concerned" in reaction to Alvarado's work?* After five minutes, call out a number. Have students with that number share their group's answers. Discuss answers with the class.

Independent Practice

Recap Reading Selection

Have students recall what they learned about the environmental impact of dams and mines, and the effects of urban sprawl. Ask: *What country denied a permit to a huge mining company?* (Venezuela) Explain that next, students will read about the effects of deforestation on global warming and on biodiversity.

Read and Apply

Have students read this selection independently as you circulate. Ask them to read aloud so you can see if they are reading fluently. You can also use the support below to help students who are having difficulty.

CITE EVIDENCE

A Students should recognize that Nguyen's "fact" is more of a reasoned judgment because it must be verified with supporting statements (which she goes on to offer).

B Students should identify that both authors use the word *evil* in their references to deforestation. However, whereas Alvarado calls deforestation a "necessary evil," Nguyen thinks it is unnecessary.

Global Warming

25   My argument is rooted in one central fact: <u>deforestation contributes to global warming</u>. Global warming is the gradual warming of the Earth's temperature due to the release of **greenhouse gases** into the atmosphere. Greenhouse gases are generated by the burning of carbon-based fossil fuels like coal and oil. When they are present in the atmosphere, the surface temperature of the Earth warms. Warmer temperatures cause rising sea levels, changing weather patterns, and many other effects.

26   Earth's forests are a **combatant** to global warming. Trees absorb carbon dioxide, which is a greenhouse gas. If trees are cut down and carbon dioxide is not absorbed, it stays in the air and contributes to global warming.

27   Scientists track the amount of carbon dioxide in the atmosphere by looking at **carbon footprints**. A carbon footprint is the amount of carbon dioxide released into the atmosphere by a population, a place, or an event. Just as we make footprints in wet sand, we make a carbon footprint on the environment when we use carbon-based energy sources. It is estimated that the carbon footprint of four years of deforestation is about the same as the combined carbon footprint of every airplane since those machines were invented—running up until the year 2025! That is an enormous amount of carbon, and it accelerates global warming.

Biodiversity

28   The environmental impact of deforestation does not stop with global warming. Cutting down a rainforest, for example, severely impacts **biodiversity**. It is estimated that nearly half of all plant and animal species exist in rainforests. In addition to fighting the threat of extinction, rainforest life forms are worth protecting because they hold medicinal properties and may help cure disease.

WORDS TO KNOW

biodiversity
carbon footprint
combatant
greenhouse gases

CITE EVIDENCE

A Find the central fact that Nguyen is offering in this section and underline it. Is it truly a fact, or is it a reasoned judgment? Explain your answer.

B Circle a word in Nguyen's conclusion that shows that she and Alvarado agree on one aspect of deforestation. Then tell how her interpretation of this fact departs from Alvarado's.

286   Unit 11 ■ Reading Informational Text: Integration of Knowledge and Ideas

---

Words to Know

General Academic Vocabulary

combatant (*n.*): someone or something that fights against something else

Domain-Specific Vocabulary

biodiversity (*n.*): a great number and variety of plant and animal species in an environment

carbon footprint (*n.*): the amount of carbon dioxide a person, place, or activity releases into the atmosphere

greenhouse gases (*n.*): gases that lead to the warming of Earth's atmosphere

Working with Word Meaning Have students come up with examples and counterexamples for each word.

INTEGRATION OF KNOWLEDGE AND IDEAS

Conclusion

29   Mr. Alvarado argues that deforestation is a "necessary evil" because there are so many human activities that need it in order to succeed. I don't dispute the latter point; however, he omits the downside of deforestation. I've attempted to address it in this article, and I hope the reader will come to agree that deforestation is in fact an (evil) that is unnecessary.

Comprehension Check   (MORE ONLINE) sadlierconnect.com

1. Which evidence emphasized by Nguyen in this section is mentioned by Alvarado in his opinion piece?

   a. Deforestation impacts Earth's biodiversity.

   b. Many human activities require the clearing of forested land.

   c. Deforestation is one of the major culprits of global warming.

   d. Earth's forests combat global warming.

2. Choose the answer that best describes this sentence: *The environmental impact of deforestation does not stop with global warming.*

   a. fact

   b. opinion

   c. reasoned judgment

   d. speculation

3. Which does NOT support Nguyen's reasoned judgment that rainforests are worth saving?

   a. Rainforests are a source of biodiversity.

   b. Animal and plant species living in rainforests face extinction.

   c. Rainforest land has rich, farmable soil.

   d. Rainforest life forms may hold the cure to diseases.

4. Which visual element would be most helpful in explaining carbon footprints?

   a. a photograph of a human footprint

   b. a film showing real-time carbon emissions

   c. a map of Brazil

   d. a product label that estimates that product's carbon footprint

5. Review Alvarado's concluding paragraph on page 279, and summarize how it differs from Nguyen's conclusion on this page.

   Sample answer: Alvarado acknowledges that deforestation may be a crisis, but he feels it is necessary because of the benefits of the human activities that require the clearing of forests. Nguyen comes to the opposite conclusion; deforestation is an ecological crisis and must be stopped. She also objects to Alvarado's leaving out details of deforestation's negative impact on the world in his discussion.

Unit 11 ■ Reading Informational Text: Integration of Knowledge and Ideas   **287**

Comprehension Check

Answer Explanations

1. Students should recognize that both Nguyen and Alvarado state that forested land is essential for certain human activities, so choice B is correct.

2. Students should identify that the statement is a reasoned judgment, given the evidence in Nguyen's text to support it.

3. Careful readers will know that Nguyen lists biodiversity, endangered species, and the possibility that medicinal cures exist there as reasons to save the rainforest, so choice C is correct.

4. Though students may think a product label might be helpful, the correct answer is B. A film would help viewers understand just how much carbon is emitted all the time.

Critical Comprehension

Challenge students to think more deeply about the text and to support their answers with evidence from the text.

Ask students: *How can dams be good and bad for communities?* (Dams bring power and clean water; however, they also displace people and cause pollution.)

Assess and Respond
If students have trouble answering the questions in the Comprehension Check,
Then ask them to reread the text and highlight information that can help them answer the questions.

Speaking and Listening Presentation

Have students prepare a presentation about deforestation in Indonesia. Remind students to plan by setting milestone goals and deadlines. Presenters should include facts and details about the topic, using multimedia or visual elements to support their points; adapt their language for a formal presentation; speak clearly; and maintain eye contact with their listeners. At the end of the presentation, presenters should answer questions and acknowledge listeners' ideas.

OBJECTIVES

- Compare and contrast a text to its presentation in another medium
- Evaluate an argument or claim in terms of its reasoning and evidence.
- Analyze how two authors writing about the same topic emphasize different evidence in support of their claims.

Genre: Letter to the Editor/ Movie Review

Remind students that a letter to the editor expresses a writer's viewpoint on a newsworthy topic. Then explain that this letter to the editor is written in response to the review of a nonfiction book about the 19th-century Johnson County War. The movie review, in which a writer critiques different aspects of a movie, is written about a movie based on the book.

Path Options

You may want to do a close reading with students; if so, use the supports provided on these pages. Or, you may wish to have students read the text independently and apply the skills learned in this unit. In either case, students should read the text more than once to facilitate understanding and to be able to answer the Comprehension Questions correctly.

Deeply Flawed Book

(Genre: Letter to the Editor)

Dear Editor:

1   I was surprised to read in your last issue Marc Sargent's positive review of *Dark Wyoming*, Melissa Christensen's new book about the Johnson County War. I was surprised because the book is not only full of historical errors, but it conjures up a feeling of sympathy for the rich cattle barons of the era that is very misplaced.

2   There has been some very fine recent scholarship about the Johnson County War that Ms. Christensen seems to have missed. Court records, government documents, and contemporary newspaper accounts reveal that the powerful Wyoming cattle barons were not justified in their attack on the local cattlemen of Johnson County. Ms. Christensen's book, however, suggests that they were.

3   I teach a course on the range wars of the American West as part of my curriculum at Beaver Creek Community College, and I feel compelled to correct Ms. Christensen's mistakes.

4   Ms. Christensen devotes the first part of her book to setting the stage for the events of the war. From her point of view, the all-powerful cattle ranchers who raised herds of cattle on huge tracts of land were victims of widespread cattle theft, especially in Johnson County. The cattlemen complained that local authorities were not doing their job sufficiently and that they had no choice but to take matters into their own hands and pursue the thieves.

5   In fact, Johnson County was largely made up of small ranch owners who were doing their utmost to survive. The big cattlemen had overstocked their ranches, creating a supply of steer that market demand could simply not keep up with. The price of beef dropped, and no one was more hurt by this than the small cattle ranchers. Ms. Christensen does not draw this conclusion in her book. She fails to incorporate the experience of the small ranchers into her narrative.

6   When the large cattle barons decided to take matters into their own hands in 1891, they went after a number of suspected thieves, including a man named Nate Champion. Champion allowed his cattle to roam and graze on public land alongside the cattle of the big barons. He was within his legal right to do so, but the barons did not like it. Christensen reports that a local

288

Support English Language Learners

Help English language learners build background knowledge about the context in which the Johnson County War took place. Use online map resources such as those available from the Wyoming State Historical Society to show students the location of the areas over which the battle was fought. Discuss with students what they might already know about cattle ranches in the 19th century and their images of cowboys in the West. Explain that Wyoming had just become a state in 1890, two years before the Johnson County War took place. Tell students that while rich cattle ranchers were used to being able to let their cattle graze on the open range, new settlers and their cattle were competing for the same land.

INTEGRATION OF KNOWLEDGE AND IDEAS

newspaper began running negative stories about Champion, but she does not include the fact that the newspaper was controlled by the cattle barons. In the book, Champion comes off as a guilty party, when in fact, technically he was not.

7   By this point, the cattle barons, organized under a group called the Wyoming Stock Growers Association, had decided to make Champion their number-one target. They organized a group of men to assassinate Champion. The assassination squad engaged Champion at the small cabin in which he lived. Champion fought back and one of the assassins was killed.

8   Christensen's description of the scene in the cabin is a thrilling read, but I doubt the accuracy of her facts. Some details she simply gets wrong. For example, Champion did not have a beard. Other details cannot be verified—like the color of Champion's boots.

9   Furthermore, Christensen's book, which is being advertised as nonfiction, transforms into a work of historical fiction at this point. I appreciate her effort to make the confrontation in Champion's cabin dramatic, but I could do with less excitation and more finely researched storytelling.

10   Another member of the squad was soon captured after the Champion incident. This man told two local ranchers the names of the other members of the group. The big cattle barons were frightened. These two witnesses had enough information to link the barons to the assassination squad. They could be arrested, thrown in jail, or worse.

11   The two witnesses ended up being killed at the hands of the assassination squad, and the people of Johnson County were

outraged. The strongest evidence of their indignation were stories that ran in newspapers friendly to the small ranchers. Again, Christensen has no mention of these reports.

12   Christensen transforms her book yet again at this moment in the story; the trial against Champion's would-be killer feels like a scene out of the movies. Christensen's language is full of detail; we know everything from the size of the courtroom to the type of wood used to construct the judge's bench (mahogany).

13   But despite the addition of all these flourishes, she misses some major points. First, the accused man was named Joe Elliott, not John Elliott. Second, Elliott worked as a detective for the Wyoming Stock Growers Association. That directly linked him to the big cattle barons. She somehow missed this key point in her research, for she strongly implies that the barons and Elliott were disjoined.

14   Her story gets back on track as an invading gang of cattle barons and their men headed straight from the capital city of Cheyenne into Johnson County. Upon receiving intelligence that a group of local ranchers—including Champion—were located nearby, the invaders decided to attack.

Unit 11 ■ Reading Informational Text: Integration of Knowledge and Ideas   **289**

Support First Reading

Circulate to check and support students' understanding. Use the following comprehension and strategy check-ins as needed.

Check-in Questions

• *According to the writer, what is wrong with Christensen's viewpoint in her book?* (She treats the rich cattle owners sympathetically and has little sympathy for small cattle ranchers.)

• *Who was Nate Champion?* (A small ranch owner who allowed his cattle to graze on public lands. Rich cattle owners accused him of theft.)

• *Why does the writer object to the exciting manner in which Christensen tells the story of the confrontation between Champion and those who came to kill him?* (The letter writer believes that the storytelling is "thrilling" but not factual.)

Review: Evaluating Arguments

Remind students that when they read an argument, they should look at what reasoning the author uses and at the evidence that is presented. Have students read the first sentence of paragraph 13. Ask: *Is the writer using reasoned judgment here?* (Yes, because she supports her claim with evidence in the rest of the paragraph.)

Differentiate Instruction

Struggling readers may benefit from having the option of hearing the texts read aloud by a more proficient reader. They may also benefit from discussing the selections with others to ensure understanding of the main ideas in both the letter and the review.

In addition, some students will need help with the more difficult vocabulary in the texts, such as *conjures* (brings forth), *contemporary* (of the same time), *tracts* (areas of land or water), *incorporate* (include), and *compelling* (persuasive).

Check-in Questions

- *Who were the invaders that forced Champion from his cabin?* (cattle ranchers who accused Champion of stealing cattle)

- *According to the writer, what can we infer about why the governor appealed to President Harrison for help?* (The governor sympathized with the cattle barons and did not want them hurt by the angry people outside the cabin.)

Review: Comparing Media Presentations

Remind students that when they compare media presentations, they look at how writers and directors use different aspects of their media to cover the same topic. Ask students: *How does the movie emphasize the difference between the ranchers and the barons through cinematography?* (The movie uses bright sunlight for ranchers and darker colors for the barons.)

Review: Analyzing the Presentation of Ideas

Remind students that when they analyze the presentation of ideas in different media, they look at what the writer or director chooses to include, to emphasize, to reinterpret, and to exclude. Ask: *According to the review, how is the movie different from the book?* (The movie takes the side of the smaller ranchers.)

CLOSE READING

Deeply Flawed Book *continued*

15 Champion was with a friend when the invaders reached his cabin. After his friend was killed, Champion held off the invaders until he was forced from his cabin and struck down. Local citizens arrived in a fury and surrounded the cabin in which the cattle barons' gang were trapped. So began a three-day siege. This was the height of the Johnson County War.

16 The war was not active. The citizen's posse spent most of the three days in a tense state of surveillance. Before they could make their move, however, federal soldiers arrived. The governor had appealed to President Benjamin Harrison himself for help.

17 Christensen is not up to speed with current scholarship yet again. She writes that the governor was ignorant of the situation, but in fact he knew exactly what was happening and was sympathetic to the encircled cattle barons.

18 Christensen gets the main fact related to the resolution of the war correct, but she fumbles the political intrigue that followed. The federal troops arrested the invaders. The governor was not about to let accusations against big cattle barons go forward, so the investigation was stymied.

19 Neither did a trial ever get off the ground. It was too difficult to find a jury, and the financial strain the trial put on Johnson County was too great. Christensen's explanation of the financial challenges is excellent; it's a thorny subject that she gets right.

20 I appreciate that Melissa Christensen has made the story of the Johnson County War exciting to read, but I wish she had paid more attention to historical accuracy. *Dark Wyoming* is a deeply flawed book that does not do its subject justice.

Dark Wyoming

(Genre: Movie Review)

1 Most American history textbooks careen through the range wars of the Old West as quickly as a hurricane's wind. This compelling period of history is largely unknown to most Americans, so Damon Armijo's new film, *Dark Wyoming*, based on Melissa Christensen's book of the same name, is welcome. It is not only a fine film, but it places the Johnson County War in its rightful place as a key event in American history.

2 Armijo has successfully re-created the two worlds of the range war era: the bleak, dusty life of small-scale ranchers, and the realm of wealthy, decadent cattle barons. The scenes featuring the ranchers take place outside in bright, oppressive sunlight. The audience squints its eyes along with them. In contrast, the immoral barons are seen in their offices colored with dark brown woods and burgundy rugs.

3 There is no mistaking Armijo's point of view. The film is firmly on the side of the local ranchers, who are persecuted by the forceful, greedy barons. It's interesting to

290 Unit 11 ■ Reading Informational Text: Integration of Knowledge and Ideas

Strategic Reading

The fact that the texts both describe an historical event, while also describing how that event is portrayed in a book or film, may make these texts challenging for some readers. Remind students that there are strategies they can use when trying to comprehend complex texts. One strategy is to reread text that is confusing. In this case, rereading might prove useful to understand who the different participants were in the Johnson County War. Another strategy is to look for visual clues. The book review includes photographs of cowboys and early settlers that help provide context. The movie review shows posters of actors portraying the ranchers of the time.

INTEGRATION OF KNOWLEDGE AND IDEAS

note that the film diverges from the book in this respect. Christensen's portrait of the barons is more sympathetic.

4   The film has two major sequences: the trial of the attempted murderer of Nate Champion, a local rancher, and the final attack on Champion's tiny cabin in which federal soldiers come to the rescue. I wish I could report that both are excellently done, but only one of them is.

5   The trial scene is interminable; it's like listening to your least favorite relative go on for too long at Thanksgiving dinner.

6   The film's shoot-'em-up climax is thrilling, however. The widescreen shot of the soldiers riding in on horseback is a triumph and it tells the viewer that Champion will be saved.

Dark Wyoming *coming soon!*

7   The uplifting ending is another departure from the book, but it's not uncommon for Hollywood to change a book's ending for a film version. However I couldn't help feeling that the final scene of Champion curling up in front of the fire with his dog rang false, especially in light of the violence that came before. But it's a detail easily forgiven in the larger context of this fine film about a fascinating subject.

Comprehension Check

1A. According to the review, how does the movie portray the cattle barons?

  a. as greedy and evil

  b. as sympathetic

  c. as barely getting by each day

  d. as a powerful force for good

1B. What phrase from the movie review supports the answer to Part A?

  a. "the bleak, dusty life"

  b. "a tense state of surveillance"

  c. "the realm of wealthy, decadent"

  d. "in bright, oppressive sunlight"

2A. The idea about the barons expressed in the Letter to the Editor is that they were

  a. justified in pursuing Nate Champion.

  b. powerless in the local community.

  c. poor victims of local crime.

  d. ruthless manipulators.

2B. What fact from the Letter to the Editor supports the answer to Part A?

  a. Nate Champion was found guilty.

  b. Joe Elliott was linked to the barons.

  c. Nate Champion allowed his cattle to graze on public land.

  d. Johnson County was largely made up of small-ranch owners.

Unit 11 ■ Reading Informational Text: Integration of Knowledge and Ideas   **291**

Research to Build Knowledge

Students may wish to learn more about the Wyoming in the late 19th century. They may choose to research the Johnson County War, the "cattle boom" of 1868-1886, the relationship between settlers and the Plains Indians of Wyoming, or the factors that led Wyoming to allow women to vote. Group students with similar interests together. Have them gather information from multiple sources, using effective search terms, and choose credible sources over less reputable ones. Remind students to credit their sources, following standard forms of citation. Then give students an opportunity to share their findings with the class.

Multiple Readings for Critical Comprehension

Have students reread and annotate this selection, then pose questions that focus on critical comprehension.

• *According to the book, what may be true about Nate Champion?* (He may have been a cattle thief.)

• *Why were cattle barons at odds with owners of small cattle ranches?* (According to the letter, they did not want competition on the open range.)

Self-Select Text

As preparation for Connect Across Texts, have students choose one selection from this unit and reread it independently. Students can access full .pdf versions of some selections at **sadlierconnect.com**.

Comprehension Check

Begin scoring students' performance of unit skills with this Comprehension Check and continue through Connect Across Texts on page 294. Use students' scores to determine their readiness for the Unit 11 Review on page 296.

Multiple-Choice Questions: *1 point each*

1A. Careful readers will recognize that, according to the review, the movie portrays the cattle barons as "immoral," so choice A is correct.

1B. Students who know that *decadent* means "immoral" should know that choice C is correct.

2A. The Letter to the Editor states that "powerful Wyoming cattle barons were not justified in their attack on the local cattlemen," so choice D is correct.

2B. Only choice B is true and points to the manipulation of the cattle barons.

Close Reading

Multiple-Choice Questions, continued: *1 point each*

3A. Since the writer includes a strong personal opinion, choice B is the correct answer.

3B. That the writer expresses a strong opinion is best made clear in choice D.

4A. Students may recognize that A and C are inaccurate since the letter writer criticizes the book. The letter writer does admit the author tells an exciting story, so B is correct.

4B. That Christensen's book does not tell the complete story is most apparent in choice A.

5A. Students should recognize that books can have interesting characters, realistic dialogue, and descriptions of landscapes. Therefore, C is correct.

5B. Students who answer 5A correctly should recognize that B describes camera work that evokes emotion.

Short-Answer Questions: *2 points each (10 points total)*

Item 6 Rubric

2	Student gives two or more examples of evidence.
1	Student gives one example of evidence from the letter.
0	Student cannot provide evidence from the letter.

Item 7 Rubric

2	Student can give two or more examples of how the film differs from the book.
1	Student can give one example of how the film differs from the book.
0	Student can give no specifics on how the film differs from the book.

CLOSE READING

3A. Which of the following characterizes the Letter to the Editor on page 288?

    a. a list of facts and reasoned judgments that stem from those facts

    (b.) a strong personal opinion based on an audience member's reaction

    c. speculation about how a specific work could have been improved

    d. fine scholarship that avoids personal commentary

3B. What phrase from the text supports the answer to Part A?

    a. "The big cattle barons were frightened."

    b. "This was the height of the Johnson County War."

    c. "The federal troops arrested the citizen posse."

    (d.) "I wish she had paid more attention to historical accuracy."

4A. Which statement best summarizes the letter writer's central claim?

    a. *Dark Wyoming* is a brilliant work of historical fiction.

    (b.) *Dark Wyoming* does not tell a complete or accurate story of the Johnson County War.

    c. *Dark Wyoming* should be regarded as the finest book on its subject.

    d. *Dark Wyoming* is a complete failure, for it gets all its details wrong.

4B. Which phrase from the text supports the answer to Part A?

    (a.) "I feel compelled to correct Ms. Christensen's mistakes."

    b. "Christensen transforms her book yet again at this moment in the story."

    c. "Christensen's explanation of the financial challenges is excellent."

    d. "Christensen gets the main fact related to the resolution of the war correct."

5A. How can the medium of film portray an event that a nonfiction text cannot?

    a. by having interesting characters

    b. by having realistic dialogue

    (c.) by using angles and effects to bring out emotion

    d. by describing the landscape's colorful scenery

5B. Which phrase from the movie review supports the answer to Part A?

    a. "The uplifting ending is another departure from the book."

    (b.) "The widescreen shot of the soldiers riding in on horseback is a triumph."

    c. "The trial scene is interminable."

    d. "The film has two major sequences."

Extend Thinking: Evaluate

Have students reread the letter and the review. Ask them to evaluate decisions that the moviemakers made about what to emphasize in their film based on the book and what to change from the book. As a class, make a list of these decisions. Then go through the list and discuss what effect each decision had on the movie, according to the reviewer. Did the plot change? Were different values highlighted?

INTEGRATION OF KNOWLEDGE AND IDEAS

6. What evidence does the Letter to the Editor writer offer to support his claim that Christensen has included errors or avoided certain facts? Offer specifics.

Sample answer: She gets basic facts wrong, such as Joe Elliott's name, and misses others, such as the fact that most of the big newspapers were controlled by the cattle barons. She also mischaracterizes the barons when she portrays them as sympathetic victims.

7. From your interpretation of the movie review, how is the film version of *Dark Wyoming* different from the nonfiction text? In what way are these differences due to the differences between media? Cite specifics.

The film offers a happy ending and generally sides with the small ranchers, which Christensen does not. As a film, it offers rich visuals that support other details, such as the bleak life of the small ranchers and the wealth of the barons.

8. Does the Letter to the Editor writer offer sound reasoning to support his claim that Christensen portrays the cattle barons too sympathetically? Why or why not? Cite specifics.

Sample answer: I think that the letter writer's reasoning is very sound. For example, he cites Christensen's tendency to ignore the reality of the small ranchers' lives, which were tough. Also, the newspapers that depicted the barons as victims of local theft were actually controlled by the barons. This is an important detail she misses.

9. Analyze what the nonfiction text version of *Dark Wyoming* can offer that other versions cannot. Then think about what it would be like to listen to an audiobook of *Dark Wyoming*. What would that version offer? How might it change the meaning of the book?

Sample answer: A book can offer long descriptions of people, places, and events. An audiobook would feature an actor (or actors) reading both the narrative text and the characters' words. This might impact which characters seem sympathetic. The story also might seem more dramatic.

10. How do both the Letter to the Editor writer and the movie reviewer shape their arguments about *Dark Wyoming*? What evidence do they each emphasize to support their claims?

Sample answer: The letter writer's argument is that the text of *Dark Wyoming* is not accurate. He is particularly concerned with Christensen's portrayal of the cattle barons as sympathetic and cites many examples of this. The film reviewer praises the film version, citing ways in which the filmmaking techniques enhance the story. The reviewer does object to the tendency in Hollywood films to change the endings of books to be more upbeat.

Item 8 Rubric

2	Student names more than one piece of evidence.
1	Student names one piece of evidence that the writer uses.
0	Student cannot analyze the letter writer's reasoning.

Item 9 Rubric

2	Student gives more than one example of book's and audiobook's respective advantages. Student tells how meaning might change.
1	Student cites one example each of book's and audiobook's respective advantages.
0	Student cannot cite or explain the advantages of either.

Item 10 Rubric

2	Student names how both writers shape arguments and names evidence they use.
1	Student names how both writers shape arguments but gives only one piece of evidence.
0	Student cannot explain how either shapes their argument.

Theme Wrap-Up

Lead students in a group discussion on the theme of world transformations. Ask: *What kinds of transformations are positive? How can different media depict stories of transformations effectively?* (Students may note that a change from war to peace is positive. Nonfiction books are good for gaining thorough understanding and movies for evoking emotion.)

Differentiate Instruction

Reluctant readers may benefit from hearing the short-answer items read aloud. After you or a volunteer read(s) the question to those students, make sure that the students understand what they are supposed to do. Allow students to ask questions about directions they find confusing. Review any academic words students may not understand, such as *evidence*, *altered*, and *omissions*.

Connect Across Texts

Connect Across Texts: *4 points*
Review Reading Selections

Put students into four groups. Give each group the responsibility to trace the central claims of one of the unit's texts. Have one group analyze the Web article, another the science text, a third the letter to the editor, and the fourth, the movie review.

Compare and Contrast Texts

Review directions on page 294 of the Student Book. Help students understand that they are to list each text's central claim and the reasoning that supports it.

Graphic Organizer Rubric

4	Student identifies the claim and reasoning in all four selections.
3	Student identifies the claim and reasoning of three selections.
2	Student identifies the claim and reasoning of two selections.
1	Student identifies the claim and reasoning in at least one of the four selections.
0	Student cannot name the central claim or reasoning in any of the four texts.

Support Essential Question Discussion

Have students reread the Essential Question. Challenge them to finish this sentence: *Analyzing texts in different formats helps me to . . .*

Encourage students to discuss how different formats can have an impact on the text.

CONNECT ACROSS TEXTS

Compare and Contrast Texts

In this unit you've read texts that offer arguments about a topic. You've learned that it is important to offer specific evidence and sound reasoning to support a claim. Fill in the center column of the chart below with the specific claim from each of the four texts listed. Then fill in the last column with at least one piece of sound reasoning that supports the claim. Make sure this reasoning follows from the texts' main ideas and supporting details. Finally, discuss your completed table in a small group.

Text	Claim	Reasoning
"What Forests Offer Us"	Deforestation is a necessary evil because many needed human activities require the clearing of forested land.	Logging, forestry, mining, and dams all provide jobs and generate economic activity for people.
"Save the World's Forests"	Deforestation should be reduced and controlled. Deforestation causes great harm to the environment.	Deforestation releases carbon into the atmosphere. This practice is causing global warming.
"Deeply Flawed Book": Letter to the Editor	The novel *Dark Wyoming* is riddled with factual errors and suggests an erroneous central claim: that the cattle barons of the range war era were sympathetic characters.	The novel's author ignores recent scholarship that reveals that newspapers of the time were controlled by the cattle barons.
Dark Wyoming: Movie Review	The film version of *Dark Wyoming* beautifully illustrates the contrast between the small ranchers and the cattle barons. An upbeat ending rings false, however.	The small ranchers are depicted in harsh outdoor sunlight; the cattle barons are seen in opulent, comfortable indoor spaces.

Return to the Essential Question

How can readers analyze texts presented in multiple formats?

In small groups or as a class, discuss the Essential Question. Pose questions to your classmates about what they have learned about how written stories compare to versions in other media, how arguments and claims in a text are supported by evidence, and how two or more authors writing about the same topic will emphasize and interpret different evidence. Acknowledge the information your classmates express and, if necessary, ask them to elaborate. Then respond with relevant observations of your own while remaining open to their ideas. Use evidence from the texts in this unit to answer the question.

Assess and Respond (pages 91–94)

If	Then
Students scored 0–10 points, they are **Developing** their understanding of unit skills . . .	Provide students with reading support and more extensive modeling and practice of skills.
Students scored 11–17 points, they are **Improving** their understanding of unit skills . . .	Review students' scores to pinpoint skills that students need more help with, and offer targeted instruction.
Students scored 18–24 points, they are **Proficient** in their understanding of unit skills . . .	Have these students move on. They are ready for the formal assessment at the end of the unit.

LANGUAGE

Word Relationships

Guided Instruction When you have difficulty with the meaning of a word, look for nearby words or phrases that have a relationship to the word. You may find a **synonym**, which is a word that means the same as another word. An **antonym** means the opposite of a word. An **analogy** is a comparison that is made between two words that are alike in some way. Look at the chart below for some examples from this unit's selections.

Word	Related Word(s)	Type	Meaning
decadent	immoral	synonym	corrupt
accuracy	gets wrong	antonym	correctness
careen	as quickly as a hurricane's wind	analogy	to go forward quickly

Guided Practice Read the following sentences from the texts. Circle the word or phrase that is a synonym, antonym, or analogy of the underlined word. Then write the meaning of the underlined word on the line.

1. I appreciate her effort to make the confrontation in Champion's cabin (dramatic,) but I could do with less underline{excitation} and more finely researched storytelling. _____ excitement, drama

2. The trial scene is underline{interminable}; (it's like listening to your least favorite relative go on for too long at Thanksgiving dinner.) _____ unending

3. The governor was not about to let accusations against big cattle barons (go forward,) so the investigation was underline{stymied}. _____ thwarted, obstructed

Independent Practice Read the following sentences from the texts. A word or phrase is underlined. Find the word or term it is related to and tell whether it is a synonym, antonym, or analogy. Write the word and the meaning on the lines.

1. "The people of Johnson County were underline{outraged}. The strongest evidence of their indignation was stories that ran in newspapers friendly to the small ranchers." _____ synonym; *indignation*; anger at something unfair

2. "Just as we make footprints in wet sand, we make a carbon footprint on the environment when we use carbon-based energy sources." _____ analogy; *carbon footprint*; the amount of carbon a person, place, or event produces

---

OBJECTIVE
Use the relationship between words to help understand their meaning.

Guided Instruction

Have students review the Guided Instruction section on page 295 of the Student Book. Review the chart with them to be sure they understand that the "Meaning" column gives a definition for the word on the far left (under "Word"). By paying attention to nearby words that have a relationship to an unfamiliar word, students will have a tool to use to unlock the word's meaning.

Guided Practice

As students move to Guided Practice, have them think about what is being described in each sentence as they look for synonyms, antonyms, and analogies. Once they find the related word, have them use it to write the meaning of the underlined word.

Independent Practice

If students have difficulty, suggest that they work with a partner or in a small group. Point out that sometimes paying attention to sentence structure can help them locate the related word.

Apply to Reading

Have students work in groups to review the selections to look for other examples of word relationships. Ask them to list the related words, the relationships, and the meaning of one of the words. For example, they might find *emphasized* and the synonym *stressed* on page 265. They could use the synonym to find the definition "to give special attention to."

Support English Language Learners

It may be helpful for English language learners to have additional practice with synonyms. Write each vocabulary word below on a separate index card. Then write the synonyms on separate index cards. Place the cards in two separate piles and shuffle the piles. Have students work with partners to match the vocabulary word with its synonym.

Vocabulary Word	Synonym
decimation	destruction
affinity	likeness
valor	courage
gaudy	showy
generate	make

Unit Summary

At this point, students have read a speech delivered by Ronald Reagan on the 40th anniversary of D-Day, and a reaction to that speech; they have read articles for and against deforestation; and they have read a letter criticizing a nonfiction book about the Johnson County War, along with a movie review of a film based on the book. Students have also learned how to compare a text to an audio or video version, evaluate an argument, and analyze how two authors emphasize different evidence on the same topic. They have learned how to use the relationships between words to understand their meaning. They should now be ready to take this unit review.

Introduce the Review

Explain that students will read two related passages that continue the theme of "world transformations." Have students read the passages carefully and refer to them while they answer questions 1–10 on pages 297–298.

Answer Explanations (pages 297–298)

Scoring: When scoring students' work, assign one point for each multiple-choice question and two points for each short-answer question, for a total of 20 points.

1A. Students can reread the interview to find that Koh believes the cloud is transforming work, so B is correct.

1B. Choices A and B refer to the opinion piece. Choice C does not refer to how the cloud changes work, so D is correct.

2A. Though the blogger worries about China, he or she does not say they are currently stealing. B and D refer to Koh's interview, so C is correct.

UNIT 11 REVIEW

Read the following texts that compare a text to its audio version. Evaluate the reasoning behind specific claims and analyze how two different authors approach the same topic. Then answer the questions on pages 297 and 298.

Cloud Computing: An Interview

1 **RADIO HOST:** Tonight we welcome Paula Koh, a technology expert. She's going to tell us about a technology that is changing the way we work. Ms. Koh, can you explain cloud computing?

2 **PAULA KOH:** Well, the cloud is a network of computers that offers a gargantuan amount of space in which enormous amounts of data can be stored. The word *cloud* is used because the data is not stored on physical computers in the user's home or office; it's floating out there like a cloud in the sky. Cloud computing, then, means that businesses can access their data from the cloud, rather than the local computers they keep in the office.

3 **RADIO HOST:** How is it transforming how businesses are working?

4 **PAULA KOH:** It can save a lot of space. For example, employees often need software applications installed on their computers; that software can now be stored on the cloud. Their computers will run faster because the software will run from the cloud.

5 Large computers called servers administer the whole system, and there are also computers just for data storage.

Cloud Computing: An Opinion

1 For today's computer trends blog, I downloaded audio of an interview with Paula Koh, cloud systems expert.

2 Ms. Koh did a good job of explaining cloud computing (although I could barely hear her, the recording was so poor), but she didn't sound excited about it. And of course I couldn't see the diagram she kept referring to.

3 The interviewer also failed to ask her about the drawbacks of the cloud, such as questionable data security.

4 For example, more than 40% of U.S. businesses operating in China are concerned with data theft in China's cloud. I'm sure it's only a matter of time before a business has all its data stolen and experiences a major meltdown.

Self-Assessment: Progress Check

Have students return to the Progress Check on page 261. Point out the boxes underneath the arrow that says "After Unit 11," which is where they can answer the questions again. Have them respond to the question again in order to assess how well they have grasped the important skills and concepts in this unit.

You may wish to instruct students to write a number in the box to show how they rate their ability with each skill, using a scale of 0–2, with 0 meaning they do not understand the skill at all, 1 meaning they understand the skill but have trouble applying it, and 2 meaning they understand and can apply the skill without difficulty.

UNIT 11 REVIEW

Circle the letter next to the best answer.

1A. What is Koh's central claim about cloud computing?

 a. It is unsafe.

 (b.) It is changing the way we work.

 c. It is available only in China.

 d. It is years away from being widely available.

1B. What phrase from the text is evidence that supports the answer to Part A?

 a. "the recording was so poor"

 b. "U.S. businesses operating in China are concerned with data theft"

 c. "employees often need software"

 (d.) "software will run from the cloud"

2A. What is the blogger's central claim?

 a. China is stealing data from U.S. businesses operating there.

 b. Data stored in the cloud is easily accessible.

 (c.) Data stored in the cloud may not be totally secure.

 d. The cloud is made up of a network of computers.

2B. What phrase from the text is evidence that supports the answer to Part A?

 a. "Ms. Koh did a good job of explaining cloud computing"

 b. "I couldn't see the diagram she kept referring to"

 c. "the data is not stored on physical computers in an office"

 (d.) "U.S. businesses operating in China are concerned with data theft"

3A. What is the cloud?

 a. one very large computer

 b. the Internet

 c. a portable storage device

 (d.) a network of computers

3B. Which kind of word relationship did Koh use to explain the cloud?

 a. synonym

 b. antonym

 (c.) analogy

 d. metaphor

4A. What does *gargantuan* mean?

 a. extremely small

 (b.) extremely large

 c. extremely powerful

 d. extremely fast

4B. Rereading paragraph 2, which word relationship can you use to help you with the meaning of *gargantuan*?

 (a.) synonym

 b. antonym

 c. analogy

 d. simile

5A. Look at the diagram. Which of the following is NOT part of the cloud?

 a. servers

 b. storage computers

 (c.) client computers

 d. control nodes

5B. What phrase from the text is evidence that supports the answer to Part A?

 (a.) "rather than the local computers they keep in the office"

 b. "computers called servers administer the whole system"

 c. "employees often need software applications installed on their computers"

 d. "there are also computers just for data storage"

Answer Explanations (pages 297–298)

2B. Only choice D refers to possible security problems.

3A. Students may refer to the interview to find the answer, D.

3B. When Koh says data in the cloud is floating out there "like a cloud in the sky," she is using an analogy.

4A. Students should look for the related word in paragraph 2, which is *enormous*. Therefore, the correct answer is B.

4B. *Enormous* has a definition similar to *gargantuan*, so A is correct.

5A. Students should recognize that servers, databases, and control nodes are in the cloud but client computers are not, so C is correct.

5B. If students have read closely, they will recognize that according to Koh, data is stored in the cloud, not on computers in the office. Therefore, choice A is correct.

6A. The blogger supports the point about data insecurity with a statistic, so choice D is correct.

6B. Careful readers will identify that the blogger supported the reasoned judgment about security with the statistic stated in choice D.

Item 7 Rubric

2	Student identifies blogger's point of view, how he reveals it, examples of loaded language, and one fact the blogger includes.
1	Student identifies blogger's point of view and either how he reveals it, whether he uses loaded language or unique facts.
0	Student cannot identify blogger's point of view, loaded language, or unique facts.

Test-Taking Tips

Encourage students to read questions slowly and carefully, rereading the relevant selection as necessary to help figure out the correct answer. When students are working on a two-part question, encourage them to read both parts of the question so that they can make sure their pair of answers are related and make sense.

Unit 11 Review

Answer Explanations

Item 8 Rubric

2	Student uses text, own experience, and reasoning to write a reasonable response.
1	Student uses only own experience or reasoning to answer question.
0	Student uses poor reasoning and does not tie answer to texts.

Item 9 Rubric

2	Student identifies Koh's argument as having more sound reasoning and uses specifics from the text to support answer.
1	Student states an opinion as to which text is better supported but uses no specifics from the text.
0	Student cannot identify which text is better supported by reasoning.

Item 10 Rubric

2	Student identifies how listening to a recording impacted blogger's view and the benefits of a technical article.
1	Student can identify how listening to a recording impacted blogger's view *or* can identify benefits of a technical article.
0	Student cannot identify how listening to a recording impacted blogger's view. Student cannot identify benefits of a technical article.

UNIT 11 REVIEW

6A. Which of the following does the blogger use to show that he is not alone in his fears about data security?

a. an opinion

b. a fact

c. speculation

(d.) a reasoned judgment

6B. Which phrase from the text supports the answer to Part A?

a. "Ms. Koh did a good job of explaining cloud computing"

b. "she didn't sound excited about it"

c. "it's only a matter of time before a business has all its data stolen"

(d.) "more than 40% of U.S. businesses operating in China are concerned"

7. What is the blogger's point of view about cloud security? How does he reveal it? Does he use any loaded language? Does he offer any facts that Koh did not mention?

Sample answer: The blogger is concerned about the security of data stored on a cloud. He begins by saying that Koh explained the idea well but that she did not mention the topic of security at all. He ends with some loaded language about a future "major meltdown" of an overseas business.

8. Based on both texts, does it seem reasonable that someday a business's cloud will be hacked? Use your own experience and reasoning to answer the question.

Sample answer: It is totally logical that a business may have its cloud hacked at some point in the future. Koh describes data as not being stored on local computers, which seems to be safer to me. And the blogger cites a statistic that many U.S. businesses are already worried about it.

9. Think about both arguments, and tell which is supported by more sound reasoning. Explain your answer with specifics from the text.

Sample answer: I think Koh's argument that the cloud is changing the way businesses work is very well supported. She gives examples of how local computers will run faster and have more storage space available.

10. How does the fact that the blogger listens to a recording of Koh's interview (as opposed to seeing it in person) impact what he thinks of her claim? How would reading a technical article about cloud computing compare with Koh's interview? Explain.

Sample answer: Because the blogger is listening to the interview, he cannot see the diagram and he has a hard time understanding her because the audio is poor. Further, he feels that she is not enthusiastic about the topic. A technical article would probably be more thorough. The medium of an interview limits the information presented to whatever the interviewer asks about.

298　　Unit 11 ▪ Reading Informational Text: Integration of Knowledge and Ideas

Analyze Student Scores

16–20 pts Strong	Student has successfully learned and applied the skills in this unit. Review any errors with the student, and explain them if necessary.
10–15 pts Progressing	Student is struggling with one or more of the skills in this unit. Identify specific skills that are problematic to target additional instruction.
0–9 pts Emerging	Student is having trouble understanding most of the skills in this unit. Student may need to work through the unit again with a higher level of individual support.

STEP 1: Planning.............. 300
STEP 2: Drafting............. 303
STEP 3: Revising............. 304
STEP 4: Editing............. 306
STEP 5: Producing, Publishing,
and Presenting............. 309

WRITING HANDBOOK

This year, you will write narratives, informative/explanatory texts, an opinion piece, an evidence-based essay, and a research report. This handbook is your guide to writing all these types of texts. It takes you through the steps of the writing process, which help you go from ideas to a finished piece of writing. Once you know the steps, you can use them for any kind of writing.

STEP 1 Planning

Suppose you have to write a research report. Writers write research reports to share what they have learned about a topic that interests them. Let's say you want to know more about an activity that is good for the environment, such as composting. The process of good writing begins with planning. For any kind of writing you do, start by asking yourself some questions:

■ **What** am I writing?

You are writing a research report. This type of writing involves identifying questions about a topic, researching the answers in multiple sources, and then sharing what you have learned. You must organize the information in a logical way, provide accurate details, and cite your sources of information. In your report, you should paraphrase, summarize, and quote information from your sources.

■ **Why** am I writing? What is my **purpose**?

Your purpose is your reason for writing. The purpose of a research report is to inform readers. Do this by sharing the relevant information you find during your research. The information you provide should answer the questions that came up during your planning and research.

■ **Who** is my audience? Who will read my writing?

Initially, your audience is your teacher and classmates, but if you decide to publish your paper, your audience will broaden to include anyone who is interested in environmental issues, or specifically interested in composting, such as gardeners.

Planning and Research

■ **Choose a topic that interests you.**

Your first idea may be a broad topic, such as music or scientific discoveries, that has to be narrowed down. Start by thinking about what you already know about the topic. For many informational writing assignments, you cannot rely simply on your own knowledge of a subject, so you must do some research. As you read sources of information, you will likely think of questions to ask about your topic. These questions—and the answers you uncover—will help you focus the topic for your report. If you were writing a fictional narrative, at this stage of the process you might start by thinking about a character and a problem that requires a solution.

■ **Find supporting evidence.**

When you write informational text, you must support your topic with evidence: facts, details, definitions, examples, and quotations from experts. This evidence must come from reliable sources. Reliable sources are writings or quotations from experts in a particular field, found in trustworthy books, periodicals, and Web sites.

The Writing Handbook:
What are the steps in the writing process?

The *Writing Handbook* explains the steps in the writing process. Once students are familiar with the process, they can apply it to all their writing assignments.

Writing Process Overview
Step in the Writing Process
Planning: Assignment/genre; topic; outlining; researching
Drafting: Student model draft
Revising: Working with a partner and a checklist to improve writing
Editing: Correcting mistakes by using proofreading marks

How to Use the Handbook

Use this handbook at the beginning of the school year to introduce students to the writing process. Students can then use it as a reference with any writing unit.

Unit	Genre
2	Nonfictional Narrative
4	Informative/Explanatory Text
6	Evidence-Based Text
8	Research Report
10	Opinion Piece

Step 1: Planning

Assignment/Genre Remind students to consider the genre and purpose of the writing assignment. Point out that the focus of the instruction is a research report. Its purpose is to share information the writer gathered from several sources to answer specific questions about a topic.

Brainstorming Guide students to brainstorm possible topics with a partner or in a small group. Students should choose the topic that best suits their purpose for writing.

Step 1: Planning *continued*

Find Supporting Evidence Remind students that when they write in a nonfictional genre they must include a clearly stated claim or central idea that can be supported by evidence. Guide students to look at the model outline on page 301 and point out that, without supporting facts, a student's paper would simply be a short list of unsubstantiated statements.

Researching Your Topic Model the research process by using a search engine on a classroom computer to do a general search for information about composting. Demonstrate how to find a credible source by refining the search for Web sites ending in .gov, .org, or .edu. Review with students how to access online databases that contain encyclopedias and academic journals. Point out that as students research, they should generate a list of specific questions they want to answer about their topic. They can then narrow their research by looking at credible sources that contain the answers to those questions.

Digital Integration To help students keep track of where and when they find information online, review how to use the bookmarking function on a classroom computer's search engine. Demonstrate how to save online articles as .pdf documents, and show students how to use the highlighting and other text-marking functions to make note-taking easier. Also, show students how to create a working bibliography by copying and pasting URLs and other publication information into a blank document and saving it.

Support English Language Learners Encourage English language learners to use databases and other online resources written in their native language. Doing so will reduce the pressure of having to decode documents written in a language they are less comfortable with, and it will allow them instead to concentrate on explaining their ideas in English. As students become more comfortable in English, challenge them to include more grade-appropriate English-language documents in their research.

Assignment: Planning

Have pairs or small groups of students work together to identify a topic for a research report. Students should then do some general research to learn about their topic, keeping in mind what they have been taught about finding credible sources. They should generate a list of specific questions and work together to outline their ideas. Students should provide one another with feedback about the topic and the value of the supporting evidence they find.

If you were writing a fictional or nonfictional narrative, your details would consist of descriptions of people, places, and things, as well as dialogue.

One way to plan a piece of writing is to make an outline. Here's what an outline for a research report about composting might look like. The outline shows the introduction, the subtopics, and the conclusion. It also notes the sources you used.

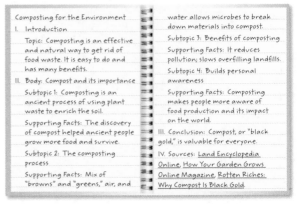

> Composting for the Environment
> I. Introduction
>   Topic: Composting is an effective and natural way to get rid of food waste. It is easy to do and has many benefits.
> II. Body: Compost and its importance
>   Subtopic 1: Composting is an ancient process of using plant waste to enrich the soil.
>   Supporting Facts: The discovery of compost helped ancient people grow more food and survive.
>   Subtopic 2: The composting process
>   Supporting Facts: Mix of "browns" and "greens," air, and water allows microbes to break down materials into compost.
>   Subtopic 3: Benefits of composting
>   Supporting Facts: It reduces pollution; slows overfilling landfills.
>   Subtopic 4: Builds personal awareness
>   Supporting Facts: Composting makes people more aware of food production and its impact on the world.
> III. Conclusion: Compost, or "black gold," is valuable for everyone.
> IV. Sources: Land Encyclopedia Online, How Your Garden Grows Online Magazine, Rotten Riches: Why Compost Is Black Gold.

If you were writing a fictional narrative, your outline would be a chronological sequence of events showing what happens first, next, and last in the story.

DIGITAL TIPS

You can write your outline by hand or by using a word processing program on a computer. A word processing program makes it easier to add and delete text, as well as to change and move text around—which happens a lot in the planning process!

PLANNING TOGETHER

You can work with a partner during the planning stage of any kind of writing. You can brainstorm ideas for topics, as well as ask each other questions to see how much you know (or need to find out) about a topic that interests you.

STEP 1: Planning *(continued)*

Researching Your Topic

The planning step involves finding good sources of information. If you are writing an informational essay, a research report, or an opinion piece, you should present relevant and up-to-date information. This information can come from print or online sources, but those sources must be reliable, accurate, and credible.

■ **Where to Look:** Go to the library or use the Internet to find sources. Find a number of sources and create a good balance of print and online materials. Since virtually anyone can post anything on the Internet, it's a good idea to steer clear of most .com sources unless they represent reputable institutions or publications (city newspapers, established magazines, and the like). The reference database section on your public library's Web site, as well as government (.gov), education (.edu), and many public organization (.org) websites, are usually reliable. Avoid commercial sites, as well as sites that present a one-sided, or biased, point of view.

■ **How to Search:** Use search terms to find appropriate print and online sources. Search terms should be neither too broad nor too narrow. For example, if you were interested in composting at home, *composting* would be too broad as a search term. The more focused search term *composting for beginners* would bring you much closer to the specific information you need. If you already knew something about composting and wanted to focus on a specific method, narrower search terms such as *trench composting* or *worm composting* would bring you more quickly to the information you need. Review the search entries you get by reading the summaries to see which entries best fit what you are looking for.

■ **How to Judge:** Credible sources include respected print and online encyclopedias, newspapers and magazines, professional journals and newsletters, and books and Web sites written by experts. Compare and contrast information in your sources to make sure the information is accurate. Also, notice when a source was published. In general, especially for science and current events topics, you will want to use recent sources to be sure your information is up-to-date.

■ **How to Take Notes:** Take notes on index cards, or create individual files on a computer. Carefully record the source of each note. Paraphrase and summarize the general information. If you find a good quotation, copy it exactly, placing it inside quotation marks. Finally, sort your notes into logical categories that follow your outline.

■ **How to Cite Sources:** As you take notes, be sure to identify the title, author, and publication information of each source. You will need to be able to tell your readers where you got your information. You can use an informal citation, such as: **Author. Title. Publisher. Date. Page number.** For online sources, you will have to identify the source as "Web" and may be asked to include the URL and the date you accessed the information.

RESEARCH TIP

Choose sources that are:
• up-to-date
• written by an expert on the subject
• carefully documented, so that you can verify their credibility and accuracy
• well-written
• unbiased

STEP 2 Drafting

Follow your outline as you write your draft. Get your ideas on the page, and don't worry about spelling and grammar at this point. Writing on a computer will make revising easy later. If you are writing by hand, leave room for revisions by skipping every other line. Here is a draft of a research report about composting.

Composting

Composting is a great way to get rid of plant waste because it is easy to do and has many benefits for the planet.

Composting uses the process that plant materials undergo when they die. Experts think composting is a very old practice. Someone must have discovered that plants grew better in dirt covered by rotting leaves, grass, and manure. Growing more food meant more people could survive long winters or unexpected events.

Compost involves mixing equal amounts of "browns" (carbon-rich dead leaves, wood chips, and manure) and "greens" (nitrogen-rich grass clippings and fruit and vegetable peelings). Add in a little soil, water, and air. Then microbes from the soil begin the process of respiration. They break down the stuff into small parts, releasing carbon dioxide. Over time, a compost pile gets transformed into humus. You can use it to enrich the soil.

One benefit to composting is personal. When people compost, they think about where their food comes from and where it goes. As they add banana peels or moldy bread to a compost pile, they might wonder who grew the food they ate and how and where it was grown.

Composting helps with pollution. The Environmental Protection agency says that "In 2011 alone, more than 36 tons of food waste was generated, with only 4 percent [composted]." The food waste left rotting in landfills generates methane. Also, some cities incinerate their waste. The smoke settles over the land and water and gets into our drinking supplies.

Composting has many benefits and no downside. It reduces pollution. It can inspire people to think about where food comes from. Composting is good for the environment.

STEP 3 Revising

When you revise, you think about how to improve your writing. This step is about checking your ideas and how clearly you have expressed them, not about the finer points of spelling and grammar. Use the items in the checklist below to evaluate your draft. If you are using a computer, read the draft on your screen and enter changes as you go. If you are using a pencil and paper to write, mark up your draft by making notes between the lines and in the margins.

REVISING CHECKLIST

Ideas and Voice
- ☐ Have I developed my ideas by including enough supporting evidence?
- ☐ Have I included accurate and reliable information from my research?
- ☐ Does my writer's voice sound interesting and well informed?
- ☐ Have I conveyed the information in an unbiased and balanced way?

Organization and Coherence
- ☐ Does the beginning introduce the topic clearly?
- ☐ Is the information presented in a logical fashion?
- ☐ Have I used linking words to connect ideas between sentences and across paragraphs?
- ☐ Do I have a concluding section that relates to my topic?
- ☐ Have I combined sentences for better style or to clarify meaning?

Word Choice
- ☐ Have I used specialized terms correctly and checked their definitions?
- ☐ Have I provided definitions for terms readers may not know?
- ☐ Have I avoided using the same words over and over?
- ☐ Have I used formal English and avoided slang or informal language?

REVISING TOGETHER

It is helpful to work with a partner as you revise your writing. Have your partner read your draft and give you feedback. Together, go through the Revising Checklist to identify areas that need revision. Then, read your draft aloud to yourself or to your partner. Determine if you wish to make any more improvements based on the items you checked off in the checklist.

Step 2: Drafting

Encourage students to think about their draft as a "trial run" of their ideas in organized form. They can change and improve it later when they revise.

Time Management/Milestones To help students manage their time well, provide short-term deadlines for the following milestones:

- Complete the planning (research, outline).
- Write the first draft.
- Revise the draft with peers.
- Edit the revised draft.
- Create a clean final copy of the work.
- Produce, publish, or present the final work.

Digital Integration Using a word processing program on a computer can help writers focus on the fluency of their ideas, the ordering of information, and the connections between ideas because they can easily add, move, and delete content and save multiple versions of drafts.

Differentiated Instruction Before students prepare their drafts, have them consult the model first draft "Composting" on page 303. Guide them to see how the student writer followed the organization of his or her outline. Have students carefully follow their own outlines as they begin drafting.

Assignment: Drafting

Meet with students individually to talk about their writing as they draft. If they feel "stuck," remind them that they do not have to get everything right the first time. Guide them to get all their ideas down on paper without worrying about how "perfect" they are before making any changes to the focus of their writing.

Step 3: Revising

Have students use the questions in the Revising Checklist to check their own work, then ask a partner to read the draft and provide feedback based on the checklist. Remind students that the revision stage is the time to focus on organization and the clear expression of ideas.

Peer Review Guide peer reviewers to provide feedback in the form that will best help writers. Reviewers can respond orally, in an email or text, or by using handwritten self-stick notes. Emphasize that constructive criticism is the goal. Writers should remember that feedback is for their consideration and that they can choose which suggested changes to implement.

Step 3: Revising *continued*

Peer Collaboration Tell students that peer collaboration is a good way to get a fresh perspective on their writing. Peer reviewers should encourage and support their partners by asking such questions as:

- *Can you state your central idea more clearly in the introduction?*
- *What other evidence can you use to make this point stronger?*
- *Is there a more concise way to express this idea?*
- *How can you make clearer connections between your ideas?*

Assignment: Revising

Organize students into pairs to review each other's research report drafts. Guide them to use the checklist questions and the "sticky notes" in the margin of the model draft on page 305 as the basis for their constructive feedback. Make sure students use the revising step to focus on the content and organization of their partner's paper.

Step 4: Editing

Have students check off the statements in the Editing Checklist that apply to their writing. In addition, offer students the editing tips below.

Editing Tips

- Read the writing slowly to find mistakes.
- Don't edit for every type of mistake at once. Instead, read the writing four times, once for each heading on the checklist (Sentences, Grammar and Usage, and so on). Each reading should focus on the convention listed.
- Point a finger to one word at a time to check each word.
- Use a blank sheet of paper to cover sentences you have not yet edited as you read.
- Make sure your eyes do not skip from one big mistake to the next big mistake, missing small mistakes in between. Double-check for missing words, such as *it*, *of*, *or*, and *the*.
- Keep a list of your most common editing mistakes and edit for those on a separate reading.
- Have a partner read the draft aloud to catch mistakes in grammar, usage, and sentence structure.

Here is a draft with notes and changes for revisions.
To see the revised draft, turn to page 307.

> I want my title to grab the reader's attention.

Composting ∧ Black Gold for the Planet

Composting is a great way to get rid of plant waste because it is easy to do and has many benefits for the planet.

> My introduction should say something more specific about the benefits of composting.

Composting uses the process that plant materials undergo when they die. Experts think composting is an ancient very old practice. Someone must have discovered that plants grew better in dirt covered by rotting leaves, grass, and manure. Growing more food meant more people could survive long winters or unexpected events. ∧ Today, compost can help people survive by reducing waste and pollution.

> I need to improve the flow of this paragraph.

Compost involves mixing equal amounts of "browns" (carbon-rich dead leaves, wood chips, and manure) and "greens" (nitrogen-rich grass clippings and fruit and vegetable peelings). Add in a little soil, water, and air. Then microbes from the soil begin the process of respiration. They break down the stuff into small parts, releasing carbon dioxide. Over time, a compost pile gets transformed into a dark crumbly material called humus. You can use it to enrich the soil. ∧ Because the material is so dark, rich and full of nutrients, gardeners refer to it as "black gold."

> I want to combine some sentences to get rid of choppiness.

> I need to better explain the phrase "black gold" that's in my title.

One benefit to composting is personal. When people compost, they think about where their food comes from and where it goes. As they add banana peels or moldy bread to a compost pile, they might wonder who grew the food they ate and how and where it was grown.

> I need to switch the order of paragraphs 4 and 5 so the organization is more logical.

Composting helps with pollution. The Environmental Protection agency says that, "In 2011 alone, more than 36 tons of food waste was generated, with only 4 percent [composted]." The food waste left rotting in landfills generates methane. Also, some cities incinerate their waste. The smoke settles over the land and water and gets into our drinking supplies. ^ Cities that incinerate their waste create smoke that gets into groundwater and then into our drinking water.

Composting has many benefits and no downside. It reduces pollution. It can inspire people to think about where food comes from. Composting is good for the environment. Composting truly is as precious as gold because of the value that it provides to the entire planet.

> I need a stronger, more memorable conclusion.

STEP 4 Editing

The editing step is about making your writing correct. Read your revised draft carefully. Use the Editing Checklist below and the Proofreading Marks on page 307 to mark the errors in your draft. Always proofread and correct your own work. Seeing your own mistakes can be difficult, though, so asking a partner to also check your work can help.

EDITING CHECKLIST

Sentences
- ☐ Every sentence is a complete sentence.
- ☐ I have a good mix of simple, compound, and complex sentences.
- ☐ None of my sentences contain a misplaced or dangling modifier.
- ☐ I have not left out any words, and I have deleted any extra words.

Grammar and Usage
- ☐ The subject and verb of every sentence agree.
- ☐ Verb tenses are used correctly and consistently.
- ☐ Pronouns match the nouns they replace.
- ☐ Conjunctions, prepositions, and interjections are used correctly.
- ☐ Correlative conjunctions are used correctly.
- ☐ Linking words and phrases are used correctly to show relationships between ideas.

Mechanics
- ☐ Every sentence begins with a capital letter and ends with the correct punctuation mark.
- ☐ Quotation marks and other punctuation marks are used correctly, and no marks are missing.
- ☐ Commas are used correctly to separate coordinate adjectives, items in a series, and introductory words and phrases from the rest of a sentence.
- ☐ The title and all proper nouns are capitalized.
- ☐ Paragraphs are all indented.

Spelling
- ☐ I have used a print or online dictionary to check spellings I am unsure about.
- ☐ I have correctly used frequently confused words, such as homophones (*their/there/they're; two/to/too; sew/so*).

PROOFREADING MARKS

∧	Add	ℓ	Take out	/	Small letter
⊙	Period	≡	Capital letter	◡	Spelling error
∽	Change order	¶	Indent paragraph	∧	Insert comma

Here are marked edits on a revised draft.

Composting: Black Gold for the Planet

Composting is a great way to get rid of plant waste because it is easy to do and has many benefits for the planet.

Composting uses the ^natural process that plant materials undergo when they die. Experts think composting is an (anceint) practice. Someone must have discovered that plants grew better in dirt covered by rotting leaves, grass, and manure. Growing more food meant more people could survive long winters or unexpected events. Today, compost can help people survive by reducing waste and pollution⊙

Compost involves mixing equal amounts of "browns" (carbon-rich dead leaves, wood chips, and manure) and "greens" (nitrogen-rich grass clippings and fruit and vegetable peelings). Add in a little soil, water, and air. Then microbes from the soil begin the process of respiration, breaking down the stuff into small parts, releasing carbon dioxide. Over time, a compost pile gets transformed into a dark, crumbly material called Humus. You can use it to enrich the soil. Because the material is so dark, rich∧ and full of nutrients, many gardeners refer to it as "black gold."

Composting helps with pollution. The Environmental Protection agency says that, "In 2011 alone, more than 36 tons of food waste was generated, with only 4 percent [composted]." The food left waste rotting in landfills generates methane. Cities that incinerate their waste create smoke that gets into groundwater and then into our drinking water.

¶One benefit to composting is personal. When people compost, they think about where their food comes from and where it goes. As they add banana peels or moldy bread to a compost pile, they might wonder who grew the food they ate and how and where it was grown.

Composting has had many benefits and no downside. It reduces pollution. It can inspire people to think about where food comes from. Composting truly is as precious as gold because of the value that it provides to the entire planet.

Writing Handbook **307**

STEP 4: Editing *(continued)*

Editing Tips

The editing step is your last chance to make sure your writing is complete, coherent, and correct before you hand it in. These tips will help you make sure your writing is the best it can be.

■ **Using Spelling and Grammar Checkers:** When you write on a computer, you might think you can rely on spelling and grammar checkers to catch your errors—but that would be a mistake. If you use a word that is often confused but spell it correctly, your spellchecker probably will not highlight it. For example, if you wrote *The dogs wagged they're tails*, a spell checker probably won't identify *they're* as an error, since it's not misspelled, just not the correct word (*their*). A spellchecker also won't catch proper nouns that are not capitalized. If you leave out a word, the grammar checker might miss that, too. So, double-check for errors, and don't rely on spelling and grammar checkers.

■ **Using Quotations:** Weaving quotations into your own writing is a style issue but one worth thinking about as you edit. Placing a long quotation into the middle of a paragraph can sound awkward, because the author's voice probably sounds very different from your own voice. Instead, integrate quotations smoothly into your own writing:

■ **Original:** To make compost quickly, you want a balance of materials. "The best ratio is one green for every one brown."

■ **Revised:** According to the City of Springfield Waste Management Department's Web site, if you want to make compost quickly, "the best ratio is one green for every one brown."

Be sure that you keep quotation marks around the exact words another writer used, and that you make the source of the quotation clear. Using a quotation without giving credit is plagiarism—taking another writer's words and ideas and passing them off as your own.

■ **Citing Sources:** You will need to provide a list of all the sources you used to write your paper. A Works Cited or Bibliography should appear at the end of the body of your paper. There are several different source citation formats. Your teacher can tell you which one to use. Here are some basic rules:

• List your resources alphabetically by author's last name, or by title if the source has no author.

• Include all the relevant information—author or authors' names, title, publication information, online address.

• Indent all the lines after the first line of each citation.

Here are some source citations from "Composting: Black Gold for the Planet":

"Compost." *The Land Encyclopedia Online.* Land Encyclopedia, 2013. Web. 30 August 2013. <http://www.landencyclopedia.com/checked/topic/90675/compost.>

Freundlich, Calhoun. "Make Composting Work for You." *How Your Garden Grows Online Magazine.* Web. 28 August 2013. <http://www.howyourgardengrows.org/soil/methods_composting/.>

Clampett, Cissy. *Rotten Riches: Why Compost Is Black Gold.* Northampton, MA: Real Organic Matters Publishing Company, 2003. Print.

308 Writing Handbook

Step 4: Editing *continued*

Using Proofreading Marks Tell students that proofreading marks are symbols used to correct small mistakes in writing. Write these sentences on the board. Call on volunteers to use the proofreading symbols to mark the errors.

• *The City was first founded in 1813.*

• *Once settled the city expanded quickly⊙*

• *today, the population is one over million people.*

Digital Integration Point out that when students use a word processor to edit, they can simply make the corrections without having to mark the errors. Because of this, it is a good idea for them to take their edited draft and do a "save as" with a new file name. By making a new file each time they edit, they will create a digital record of the editing process and be able to refer to earlier versions of what they wrote.

Quotations and Citations Encourage students to use a highlighter (or the highlighting function in a word processing program) to identify all the quotations in their draft. Have them meet with a peer to evaluate how well the quotations are integrated into their writing. Students should also consider whether the quoted material would be more effective as a paraphrase. Then have students use a different highlighter color to identify the quotations' sources. Each source should be clearly identified in the same paragraph as the quotation. In-text citations can be done in different ways, such as by simply listing an author's last name and a page reference in parentheses. You may wish to stipulate a style for such citations for your students to follow. Remind students to add any missing source information to their drafts.

Supporting English Language Learners English language learners may struggle with grammar, mechanics, and usage. Pair them with an "editing buddy" who is proficient in English and can quickly check for grammar and punctuation errors. Encourage English language learners to ask questions about the changes their partners make. Make it clear that they can use the corrections to better understand English language conventions.

Assignment: Editing

During the editing step, remind peer collaborators to focus on the clarity and correctness of their partner's writing. Guide students to refer to print or online dictionaries and grammar handbooks as they edit each other's papers.

Step 5: Producing, Publishing, and Presenting

Adding Visuals and Features Explain that students can polish and enhance their written work by selectively using visuals and text features. If students are using a word processing program, suggest that they save a new version of their final draft and then experiment with adding images and subheadings before they submit their work.

Publishing Formats Explain to students that online publishing immediately broadens their potential audience. Point out that online readers want to gather information quickly and without distraction. For that reason, it is important for students to edit their final drafts for conciseness, correctness, and clarity, and to use visuals and text features wisely.

Running Class Presentations Prepare students by giving them a specific presentation date and time limit. Refer students to the *Did I?* checklist from Unit 2 (and the rules below) to guide their conduct during oral presentations.

Speaking and Listening Presentation Guide students to follow these rules for listening and giving feedback:

1. Listen actively to the speaker with care and respect.

2. Ask questions when the speaker invites them. Pose questions that lead to elaboration.

3. Give feedback politely. Focus on the content, not the delivery, of the presentation.

4. Speak one at a time. No yelling or interrupting.

5. Avoid word choices, tone, and gestures that could make the presenter feel criticized.

Evaluations Create an evaluation form that students can use as they prepare their presentations. Have students use the same form to provide feedback for each presentation.

Differentiated Instruction Some struggling writers may be good presenters because they feel more at ease when sharing information orally. Pair them with proficient writers, and have the two work together to rehearse their presentations. Partners should provide each other with feedback about the content and delivery of the presentation.

Assignment: Digital Presentation

Encourage students to use digital technology to present their work. They can publish in digital formats, such as a slide show with music or a blog entry with visuals or even video clips. Tablet users can use apps to create eBooks with text and images. Students can work in teams to use their research reports as the basis for short video documentaries they can edit and post online.

STEP 5 Producing, Publishing, and Presenting

Now that you have edited your writing, making it clear and correct, you can publish it to share it with others. Think about ways you can improve the paper's visual presentation by adding images or text features.

- Photographs and illustrations downloaded from the Internet or created by you can add visual interest.

- Diagrams, graphs, charts, or maps can provide important information that is not easily explained in words. Think about where your writing can benefit from visual support.

- Headings and subheadings can help "chunk" ideas in your paper, making them easier for readers to find, understand, and remember.

- Visuals and text features can enhance your writing, but they can also make your pages more crowded. Don't overdo it! Be sure the way you present your final version best suits your purpose and audience.

- Once you have added the final touches, make a final copy of your paper. You can produce your final copy by using a computer or by neatly writing a clean copy by hand. It's important to show that you care about your work—and your audience—by creating a clean and legible final copy.

Online Publishing and Digital Slide Presentations

Another way to publish your writing is online. Perhaps your class or your school has a Web site where student writing can be published. If so, post the final copy of your work; you can scan in handwritten work if necessary. You might team up with other students to create a class anthology of student writings, or even use a special application to create e-book versions (complete with visuals) of student writings that can be viewed on computers or tablets.

Readers of online media often appreciate brevity, or conciseness. Consider transforming your report into a digital slide presentation. In such presentations, longer informative pieces are summarized and condensed. Each major section gets its own slide, with the most important points presented in bulleted lists.

Here's an example of a slide from "Composting: Black Gold for the Planet." This brief list of facts, along with before-and-after photos of a compost pile, would convey the information to readers effectively.

Process of Composting
- Equal amounts of "browns" and "greens" are mixed with soil, water, and air.
- Microbial respiration breaks down the items into small parts.
- Result is a rich, dark topsoil called humus, or "black gold."

STEP 5: Producing, Publishing, and Presenting *(continued)*

Speaking Tips

Once you finish a piece of writing, you might be asked to share it with classmates in a speech or other oral presentation. Remember that written English and spoken English are different. Follow these rules to make your oral presentation effective.

- Use language that suits your audience and the occasion.

- Speak loudly and clearly so that everyone can hear and understand you.

- Speak in complete sentences, and pause between sentences to show the break in ideas.

- Change the pitch, rate, and volume of your voice to express your ideas.

- Make eye contact with your listeners and watch for audience feedback. If listeners appear confused or bored, change the pace at which you speak.

- If you include visuals, pause to allow your audience to view and respond to them. Clearly explain the connection between the visuals and your topic.

- Ask your listeners if they have any questions after you have finished speaking. Listen carefully and respectfully to the questions. Take time to think before you respond, and then answer politely.

DIGITAL CONNECTION

A digital slide presentation can be a great tool to use during a speech or oral presentation. Show the slides as you speak. Your presentation should expand on the information on the screen. Be sure to rehearse beforehand so that your slides and your talk work together seamlessly.

Listening Tips

When it's your turn to sit in the audience during a classmate's presentation, follow these tips:

- Keep your eyes on the presenter and focus your mind on the ideas.

- Make connections from what you hear to what you already know.

- Take notes. Include questions you want to ask.

- Try to picture what the speaker is describing.

- If you want to ask a question, wait until the speaker is ready. Keep your question brief and direct. Listen carefully to the answer.

Performance Task Overview

The Performance Tasks in *Progress English Language Arts* are designed to determine a student's ability to closely read and understand a complex text, locate textual evidence to support analysis of the text, and create an extended response that shows deep comprehension of the text. Writing prompts in each part of the Performance Task address requirements for creating literary analyses, narratives, or research-based texts. Each Performance Task has three main parts: Literary Analysis, Narrative Writing, and Research Simulation.

Each Performance Task requires students to read thematically related texts in a variety of modes and genres and to respond to two types of assessment items:

- **Selected response items** require students to choose the correct answer from a number of options. Selected response items are divided into two parts: Part A requires students to answer a question related to the content or language of the text; Part B requires students to identify textual evidence that supports the answer to Part A.

- **Constructed response items** require students to create a brief written composition—a literary analysis, a narrative, or a research-based text—in response to a prompt.

You can help your students by introducing the overall topic of the Performance Task, orienting students to the requirements of each part of the task, and communicating helpful reminders that will enable students to approach each part successfully. Once students have completed each part, go over the items and correct responses with them, especially focusing on the connection between textual evidence and acceptable responses.

In **Performance Task 1,** students will read and respond to a series of texts relating to extreme weather and its impact.

- "River Rising" (Drama); "A Katrina Story" (Fictional Narrative)
- "The Cyclone" from *The Wonderful Wizard of Oz* (Fantasy Fiction)
- "Global Dimming" (Informational Article); "Superstorms" (Informational Article)

Specific information about how these texts are used with each section of **Performance Task 1** is shown in the chart at the right.

ONLINE **Digital Resources**

Go to **sadlierconnect.com** to download the following resources for **Performance Task 1:**

Texts:
- "River Rising"; "A Katrina Story"
- "The Cyclone" from *The Wonderful Wizard of Oz*
- "Global Dimming"; "Superstorms"

Answer Keys and Rubrics:
- Literary Analysis Task
- Narrative Writing Task
- Research Simulation Task

RECOMMENDED PACING

Administer the entire Performance Task over a three-day period. Students should complete one part per day, accompanied by instructional support and review. Depending on the amount of class time available, you may want to have students complete their Constructed Response writings at home.

Performance Task 1
PART 1: LITERARY ANALYSIS *(45 minutes)*
TASK Students will respond to questions that require careful analysis of a drama and a fictional narrative. Then they will write a brief literary analysis text in response to a prompt.
SELECTION(S) "River Rising"; "A Katrina Story"
PART 2: NARRATIVE WRITING *(45 minutes)*
TASK Students will respond to questions that require careful analysis of a narrative text. Then they will respond to a prompt by writing a short narrative.
SELECTION(S) "The Cyclone" from *The Wonderful Wizard of Oz*
PART 3: RESEARCH SIMULATION *(45 minutes)*
TASK Students will respond to questions that require careful analysis of an informational article and a government document. Then students will respond to a writing prompt that requires them to synthesize information from the texts.
SELECTION(S) "Global Dimming"; "Superstorms"

There are three parts to this performance task. Your teacher will provide you with copies of one or more reading selections that go with each part.

- "River Rising"   Genre: Drama
- "A Katrina Story"   Genre: Realistic Fiction
- "The Cyclone" from *The Wizard of Oz*   Genre: Fiction
- "Superstorms"   Genre: Informational Article
- "Global Dimming"   Genre: Informational Article

Part 1: Literary Analysis

☐ Carefully read "River Rising" and "A Katrina Story" and take notes about important events, ideas, and details. Then answer Items 1–9 on pages 312–314.

☐ Read the writing prompt in Item 10 on page 314. Review "River Rising" and "A Katrina Story" with the prompt in mind. You will use both passages in this task.

☐ Write an essay on your own paper in response to the prompt.

Part 2: Narrative Writing

☐ Carefully read "The Cyclone," an excerpt from *The Wizard of Oz*. As you read, take notes that help you understand the passage. Then answer Items 1–9 on pages 315–317.

☐ Read the writing prompt in Item 10 on page 317.

☐ Write a narrative on your own paper in response to the prompt.

Part 3: Research Simulation

☐ Carefully read "Superstorms" and *Global Dimming*. Take notes about important ideas and details. Then answer Items 1–9 on pages 318–320.

☐ Read the writing prompt in Item 10 on page 320. Then review "Superstorms" and "Global Dimming" with the prompt in mind. You will use both passages in this task.

☐ Write an essay on your own paper in response to the writing prompt.

Performance Task 1   311

Test-Taking Tips

Selected response items: Remind students to . . .

- read each question closely and follow the directions carefully.
- read every answer choice carefully before deciding on an answer.
- use a pencil so that a wrong answer can be corrected.

Constructed response items: Remind students to . . .

- focus on a clear main idea and point of view.
- organize their ideas before they write, and stay on topic as they write.
- provide textual evidence in the form of facts, details, and quotations from the passage to support their responses.
- use precise language, and include transitions to connect ideas.
- follow rules of formal writing (spelling, punctuation, capitalization, and grammar).

Administration Procedure

STEP 1 Introduce the Performance Task

Tell students that this Performance Task may cover any of the skills they have learned and practiced in Units 1–6 of *Progress English Language Arts.*

Explain that students will read three sets of texts. After each set, they will answer multiple-choice questions and then incorporate what they read into a written response. Familiarize students with the types of items they will see:

- Selected response items have two parts. Part A asks students to answer a question about the reading selection; Part B asks them to identify textual evidence—a quotation, fact, or detail from the selection—that supports the correct answer.

- Constructed response items are writing prompts based on one or more of the reading selections. Students should use textual evidence from the selections to support their responses to these items. They can make notes before writing.

* Repeat Steps 2–4 for each part of the Performance Task.

STEP 2 Reading

Tell students that they will read a set of texts that involves topics about extreme weather. Remind students that they should read the texts closely and that they can take notes about central ideas, key themes, and significant details as they read. Then have students read the text(s) for the Literary Analysis, Narrative Writing, or Research Simulation part of the Performance Task, as appropriate.

STEP 3 Selected Response

Have students complete the selected response items.

STEP 4 Constructed Response

Read the writing prompt, and make sure students understand the directions. Explain: *Your task is to write an essay in response to this prompt. You may use your notes. Also, you should go back to the texts to find ideas and textual evidence to support your response.* Answer any questions. Then have students respond to the writing prompt.

STEP 5 Check the Performance Task

Go over the selected response items so students understand why each answer is correct; help them identify the textual evidence that supports each item. Review the writing prompt, and discuss what an effective response should include.

Part 1: Literary Analysis

Selection (Genre): ONLINE
"River Rising" (Drama)
"A Katrina Story" (Fictional Narrative)

Core Task: Students will read two literary texts and respond to nine selected response items. Then students will write a literary analysis comparing the two texts.

Text Summary: "River Rising" is a brief drama about one family living in the Mississippi River Valley in 1927 and their response to an impending flood. "A Katrina Story" is a fictional narrative set during Hurricane Katrina. The story is told from the third-person limited point of view of a dog who has been left behind in his house and who partners with a cat for his survival.

Score Points: Up to **33 points** total

- Selected response items: Up to 18 points (1 point for each part of nine 2-part items)

- Constructed response item: Up to 15 points for one item

ONLINE Download the reading selections and the Answer Key and Rubric.

Depth of Knowledge Levels:

Item 1:	Item 2:	Item 3:	Item 4:	Item 5:	Item 6:
Level 2	Level 3	Level 2	Level 2	Level 2	Level 3

Item 7:	Item 8:	Item 9:
Level 2	Level 3	Level 3

Selected Response Items: Have students follow the directions on page 311 to read the first text, "River Rising," and answer Items 1–4. Then they will read "A Katrina Story" and answer Items 5–9.

Remind students that every response in Part A must be supported in Part B by evidence from the text. Have students choose from the evidence carefully to make sure that it fulfills the requirement of the question in Part A. For example, one question deals with both texts, and the answer options present evidence from both texts. Tell students to consider which text each piece of evidence in the Part B answer choices is drawn from.

Analyzing Selected Response Items: When students have completed the items, go over the correct answers with them. Help them locate the evidence in the text that supports each answer. Discuss why the correct answer is the strongest choice.

Part 1 Literary Analysis

Read all parts of the question before responding. Circle the correct answer to Items 1–9. Use your own paper to respond to Item 10.

Item 1

Part A How does the setting of "River Rising" shape the drama's conflict?
a. The farm setting creates a conflict between farmers and their neighbors.
b. The flooding river creates a conflict between the farmers and nature.
c. Sam is in conflict with Lois over his desire to move to Chicago.
d. Henry is in conflict with Lois over her demand that he move the mules.

Part B What text does NOT support the answer to Part A?
a. "The river must have overflowed the levee! This whole area is bound to flood!"
b. "Enough to swamp all that low-lying farmland."
c. "Even without another flood, sharecropping will never let us get ahead."
d. "If this flood is as bad as the last one, we won't get our crop in this year."

Item 2

Part A Which of the following sentences best states a key theme of "River Rising"?
a. Natural disasters can bring opportunities as well as suffering.
b. Human ingenuity always finds a way to prevent natural disasters.
c. There is no way to prepare for a natural disaster.
d. Natural disasters bring out the worst in human nature.

Part B What evidence supports the answer to Part A?
a. No one comes to warn Sam and Lois about the break in the levees.
b. Building scaffolding for the chickens and pigs can't save them from the flood.
c. Some parts of the levee may have broken, but Sam and Lois's farm will be protected.
d. The flood makes Sam realize that the family would be better off moving to Chicago.

Item 3

Part A What does the word *rupture* mean in "River Rising"?
a. a disaster
b. a confrontation
c. a crack or breach
d. a weakness

Part B Which context clues in the text support your answer in part A?
a. "the break is relieving pressure"
b. "on our side of the river"
c. "refugees are already swarming over the levee"
d. "It's the only high ground for miles."

Item 4

Part A How does the audience learn about the events as they unfold in "River Rising"?
a. mostly through description in the stage directions
b. by revealing the main characters' inner thoughts
c. almost entirely through dialogue between the characters
d. through language that mimics the rhythmic sound of raindrops

Part B What evidence supports the answer to Part A?
a. The italic text at the beginning of the play sets the scene.
b. Characters share news about events offstage as they appear onstage.
c. Most of the information about the flood comes from a long speech by Sam.
d. The rapid-fire dialogue between Lois and Henry sounds like rain.

Item 5

Part A When the neighbor cat *sidled up to* Isaac in paragraph 5 of "A Katrina Story," how did she move?
a. aggressively
b. secretively
c. curiously
d. clumsily

Part B Which detail from the text best supports the answer to Part A?
a. "he saw the next-door-neighbor sitting on the porch railing"
b. "her stealthy way of moving about the neighborhood"
c. "glistening ripples moved down the street"
d. "she reached out a delicate paw and batted at the door handle"

Item 6

Part A Which of the following best summarizes "A Katrina Story"?
a. A cat and a dog brave the pouring rain and fight a rat.
b. A dog and cat, abandoned in a flood, team up to find food.
c. A dog prevents a rat from stealing food from a starving cat.
d. A cat figures out how to release an abandoned dog from his leash.

Part B What evidence from the text does NOT support your response to Part A?
a. "he never knew where she would turn up"
b. "together they made a thorough survey of the kitchen"
c. "he wearily rose and followed her out the door"
d. "as Isaac once again heaved himself onto the counter, the cat waited"

Item 7

Part A What is the main conflict in "A Katrina Story"?
a. Isaac vs. the cat next door
b. Isaac and the cat vs. the rat
c. Isaac and the cat vs. the flood
d. Isaac and the cat vs. the rain storm

Part B Which evidence from the story best illustrates the answer to Part A?
a. Isaac is irritated by the cat's ability to sneak around undetected.
b. Taking the cat on his back, Isaac paddles through floodwater to find food.
c. Isaac cannot fight the rat because he doesn't have teeth.
d. The rain went on for a long time, preventing the cat from getting to Isaac earlier.

LITERARY ANALYSIS

Item 8

Part A How does the conflict help reveal character in "A Katrina Story"?

a. by highlighting the pet owners' regret

b. by showing Isaac's laziness

c. by demonstrating the cat's ingenuity

d. by bringing out the city's rats

Part B What text supports the answer to part A?

a. Isaac's owner filled the bathtub with water in case the water pipes broke.

b. The cat figures out how to release the dog and finds the sliced meat.

c. Isaac is so tired that he just wants to rest on his comfortable bed.

d. The rat threatens to take the meat before the pets can eat it.

Item 9

Part A Which of the following conclusions can you draw about floods based on evidence in *both* selections?

a. Floods may occur even after the rain has stopped.

b. Cities are worse affected by flooding than rural areas.

c. People who leave their animals behind in a flood don't care about them.

d. Because of technology, today's floods are less destructive than those a century ago.

Part B Choose TWO pieces of evidence that support your answer to Part A.

a. "lead the mules up to the rise in the pasture" ("River Rising")

b. "It ain't going to flood. It ain't even raining out." ("River Rising")

c. "there's never been a safer time to live near the Mississippi" ("River Rising")

d. "during the height of the rainstorm, the water . . . hadn't risen this high" ("A Katrina Story")

e. "the street was deserted and water was up to the windows" ("A Katrina Story")

f. "At that moment, the pointy snout of a rat torpedoed toward them" ("A Katrina Story")

Item 10

In "A Katrina Story," Isaac noted that "the normal order of things was badly askew." Extreme weather has a way of reminding human beings that they can never fully control nature.

Write two or three paragraphs that analyze how the authors of both "River Rising" and "A Katrina Story" use flooding to show that nature, and not humankind, is in control. In your analysis, cite text evidence from both selections. Take care to organize your response logically, and use standard English.

Part 1: Literary Analysis *continued*

Constructed Response Item: The writing prompt deals with both literary selections students read as part of this task. As students read the prompt, they should circle key words that explain what the prompt requires them to do.

Depth of Knowledge Level: 4

Analyzing the Constructed Response: When students have finished writing, present key elements in each of the rubric's four categories: Ideas, Organization, Language, and Conventions. Have volunteers share how they could improve the answer by paying attention to the elements required to achieve a "15" in each of the Performance Task's three categories.

How this task contributes to reading and writing grounded in evidence from literary text: In order to complete the task, students 1. Select and interpret evidence to analyze how texts deal with a universal theme; 2. Analyze how the setting of each selection shapes the characters' actions; 3. Write logically organized supporting paragraphs that develop the topic, including explaining and clarifying supporting evidence and details; 4. Use appropriate transitions, precise language, and a relevant conclusion; 5. Follow conventions and rules of grammar, usage, and mechanics.

Part 2: Narrative Writing

Selection (Genre): **ONLINE**

"The Cyclone" from *The Wonderful Wizard of Oz* (Fantasy Fiction)

Core Task: Students will read a chapter from L. Frank Baum's classic novel and respond to nine selected response items. Then they will write a response in which they place the same characters in conflict with a different type of extreme weather.

Text Summary: Dorothy lives with her aunt and uncle, who are careworn and joyless individuals. Her only friend is her dog Toto. When a tornado threatens their cottage, Dorothy misses her chance to take shelter and is swept up with her cottage and her dog into the tornado. A fantastic sequence follows in which Dorothy calmly contemplates her future in the gently spinning house.

Score Points: Up to **33 points** total

- Selected response items: Up to 18 points (1 point for each part of nine 2-part items)

- Constructed response item: Up to 15 points for one item

ONLINE Download the reading selection and the Answer Key and Rubric.

Depth of Knowledge Levels:

Item 1:	**Item 2:**	**Item 3:**	**Item 4:**	**Item 5:**	**Item 6:**
Level 2	Level 1	Level 2	Level 2	Level 2	Level 3

Item 7:	**Item 8:**	**Item 9:**
Level 3	Level 2	Level 3

Selected Response Items: Remind students that in some cases there is more than one possible piece of supporting evidence in Part B. They should watch for items that specifically direct them to identify two pieces of supporting evidence.

Analyzing Selected Response Items: Emphasize to students the importance of selecting their responses in Part A based on the text, as opposed to prior knowledge they may have about the story based on the famous film, *The Wizard of Oz*. Students will be required to support their responses to Part A strictly based on the correct option in Part B.

Part 2 Narrative Writing

Read all parts of the question before responding. Circle the correct answer to Items 1–9. Use your own paper to respond to Item 10.

Item 1

Part A What does the word *garret* mean in these lines from "The Cyclone"?

"Their house was small. . . . There were four walls, a floor and a roof, which made one room; and this room contained a rusty looking cookstove. . . . There was no garret at all, and no cellar."

- a. attic *(circled)*
- b. basement
- c. floorboards
- d. kitchen area

Part B How do word relationships from the lines of text in Part A help you understand the meaning of *garret*?

- a. "four walls, a floor, and a roof" are examples of *garret*
- b. the words *small* and *one room* imply the meaning of *garret*
- c. *garret* and *cellar* are probably opposites *(circled)*
- d. *cookstove* and *garret* are probably synonyms

Item 2

Part A According to the story, why is the house that Dorothy shares with her aunt and uncle so small?

- a. They are poor.
- b. There is no lumber nearby. *(circled)*
- c. Two-story buildings are not allowed in their neighborhood.
- d. The house was built for a childless couple, not for three people.

Part B Choose the evidence from the list below that supports your response to Part A.

- a. "Dorothy lived . . . with Uncle Henry, who was a farmer, and Aunt Em"
- b. "for the lumber to build it had to be carried by wagon many miles" *(circled)*
- c. "Uncle Henry and Aunt Em had a big bed in one corner"
- d. "Dorothy had a little bed in another corner"

Item 3

Part A Which of the following words best describes the prairie setting of "The Cyclone"?

- a. fertile and productive
- b. dull and harsh *(circled)*
- c. sunny and peaceful
- d. noisy and overcrowded

Part B Which text supports the answer in Part A?

- a. "the house had been painted"
- b. "a small hole dug in the ground, called a cyclone cellar"
- c. "the broad sweep of flat country that reached to the edge of the sky"
- d. "the sun had baked the plowed land into a gray mass" *(circled)*

NARRATIVE WRITING

Item 4

Part A How has life on a prairie homestead affected Aunt Em?

- a. She has risen to the challenge and thrived.
- b. She enjoys the constant sunshine and cool breezes.
- c. The harsh environment has been difficult for her. *(circled)*
- d. She was fine until Dorothy came along.

Part B What evidence in the text supports the answer to Part A?

- a. She runs to the storm cellar ahead of Uncle Henry and Dorothy.
- b. Her eyes and skin are dull, her body is thin, and she never laughs. *(circled)*
- c. When she first arrived on the homestead, she was young, pretty, and lively.
- d. She has made the small cottage cheerful and cozy in spite of the harsh climate.

Item 5

Part A What does the narrator mean in saying that Uncle Henry "did not know what joy was"?

- a. He is uneducated and has a limited vocabulary.
- b. He is an immigrant from a foreign land and never learned that word.
- c. His life is very hard, and he has no time for any kind of enjoyment. *(circled)*
- d. He is happily married to Aunt Em.

Part B What evidence from the story best supports the answer to Part A?

- a. "Uncle Henry . . . worked hard from morning till night" *(circled)*
- b. "from his long beard to his rough boots"
- c. "Uncle Henry sat upon the doorstep and looked anxiously at the sky"
- d. "'There's a cyclone coming, Em'"

Item 6

Part A Which of the following character traits best describe Dorothy?

- a. fearful and solitary
- b. willful and stubborn
- c. sensitive and generous
- d. brave and levelheaded *(circled)*

Part B Select TWO pieces of evidence that support the answer to Part A.

- a. She does not provide good company to her aunt and uncle.
- b. She does not follow her aunt's instructions to head to the cyclone cellar.
- c. She is aware of the danger of the tornado before her aunt and uncle are.
- d. After rescuing Toto, she closes the trap door to prevent future accidents. *(circled)*
- e. She decides to wait calmly and see where the cyclone takes her. *(circled)*

Item 7

Part A Which of the following conclusions can be drawn from this story?

- a. Aunt Em would be happier if Dorothy were not living with her.
- b. Tornados are a foreseeable danger of life on the prairie. *(circled)*
- c. Uncle Henry is less successful at farming than his neighbors.
- d. Dogs often sense dangerous weather events before humans do.

Part B Which evidence from the story supports the answer to Part A?

- a. The family has a cyclone cellar in the event of a tornado. *(circled)*
- b. Aunt Em used to be an attractive and vibrant woman.
- c. Toto jumps out of Dorothy's arms and hides under the bed.
- d. Uncle Henry works constantly.

Item 8

Part A Which of the following shifts occurs in "The Cyclone"?

a. The narration shifts from third person to first person.

b. The setting changes from Kansas to Oz.

c. Uncle Henry, once young and optimistic, becomes old and tired.

d. The realistic narrative details give way to fantasy.

Part B What details support the answer to part A?

a. Although Aunt Em is a frail and elderly woman, a younger version of her is described.

b. Howling winds and a darkening sky signal that a change is about to occur.

c. The description is realistic until the house is picked up, but not destroyed, by the tornado.

d. There is no dialogue until Uncle Henry says, "There's a cyclone coming, Em."

Item 9

Part A Which of the following best summarizes the story excerpt?

a. Aunt Em and Uncle Henry take care of their niece, but they lose her in a tragic storm.

b. Dorothy and her dog Toto enjoy many adventures on the prairie, including chasing storms.

c. Dorothy is a young girl living on a dreary farm until an extraordinary tornado whisks her away.

d. Aunt Em loves Dorothy, but her fear of tornados leads to a suffocating existence for the young girl.

Part B Select TWO pieces of evidence that support the correct summary in Part A.

a. Uncle Henry is stern and untalkative; Aunt Em is cheerless and tired.

b. From Dorothy's house, she can see nothing but gray prairie for miles in every direction.

c. Aunt Em would rather hide in a dark hole than "ride out" the tornado above ground.

d. Uncle Henry risks his life to save the farm animals before taking shelter with Aunt Em.

e. Toto is a small dog with sparkling eyes and silky fur.

f. Dorothy travels for hours in the house atop the tornado, wondering where it will go.

Item 10

As you have seen, weather can play a key role in the plot of a story. Rewrite the story you read in "The Cyclone," but change the setting and the extreme weather event. Show how the new setting and weather event affect the characters and the plot of the story.

To get started, think about extreme weather events you know something about, such as hurricanes, floods, blizzards, or wildfires. Then think about a setting where that kind of weather occurs. How would the new setting shape the characters? What would the extreme weather event bring to their lives? Use narrative elements like dialogue, description, and suspense to bring your story to life.

Performance Task 1   **317**

Part 2: Narrative Writing *continued*

Constructed Response Item: To make sure students understand the writing prompt, have them answer specific questions that you ask about it, such as *What elements of your response will be the same as in the narrative? What elements will be different?*

Depth of Knowledge Level: 4

Analyzing the Constructed Response: Have student volunteers share their responses. Discuss key elements of the scoring rubric, and ask each student to make one significant change to improve his or her response.

How this task contributes to reading and writing grounded in evidence from narrative text: In order to complete the task, students 1. Analyze details about the characters in the source text; 2. Identify an alternate but equally harsh setting that generates a different type of extreme weather; 3. Draw conclusions about the elements of the new setting that would shape the characters' traits and behavior in ways similar to the original setting; 4. Develop a narrative, including character details consistent with the source text and a conflict consistent with the new setting; 5. Employ a coherent narrative structure, appropriate transitions, and a conclusion that follows logically from both the student's text and evidence in the source text; 6. Follow conventions and rules of grammar, usage, and mechanics.

Performance Task 1

Part 3: Research Simulation

Selections (Genre): ONLINE
"Superstorms" (Informational Article)
"Global Dimming" (Informational Article)

Core Task: Students will read two nonfiction texts dealing with climate change and respond to nine selected response items. Have students respond to Items 1–3 after reading "Superstorms." Have students respond to Items 4–9 after reading "Global Dimming." Students will write an essay synthesizing information from the two texts in response to a research question.

Text Summary: "Superstorms" is an article from the National Oceanic and Atmospheric Agency's Web site in which climate researchers discuss the observation that storms have become stronger in recent decades and link this intensification to global warming. "Global Dimming" discusses a less familiar contributor to climate change, the effect of aerosols in the atmosphere on behavior of clouds and the amount of sunlight reaching Earth.

Score Points: Up to **33 points** total

- Selected response items: Up to 18 points (1 point for each part of nine 2-part items)
- Constructed response item: Up to 15 points for one item.

ONLINE Download reading selection and the Answer Key and Rubric.

Depth of Knowledge Levels:

Item 1:	Item 2:	Item 3:	Item 4:	Item 5:	Item 6:
Level 2	Level 1	Level 2	Level 2	Level 2	Level 3

Item 7:	Item 8:	Item 9:
Level 2	Level 3	Level 2

Selected Response Items: Taken out of context, some pieces of supporting evidence in Part B may sound reasonable yet still be incorrect. Encourage students to check their Part B responses by locating their choice in the text and reviewing its original context.

Analyzing Selected Response Items: In Part B of Item 9 in this Performance Task, ask students to consider counterevidence—evidence that argues against a claim—rather than supporting evidence. In these cases, they are choosing evidence from one selection to argue against a claim made in the other selection.

RESEARCH SIMULATION

Part 3 Research Simulation

Read all parts of the question before responding. Circle the correct answer to Items 1–9. Use your own paper to respond to Item 10.

Item 1

Part A What does the word *exacerbated* mean in these lines from "Superstorms"?

"Rising sea levels *exacerbated* Sandy's storm surge, for example. And abnormally high sea surface temperatures in the Atlantic probably intensified the storm."

- a. relocated
- b. uprooted
- c. made worse
- d. decreased

Part B Which word relationship from the text in Part A helps you understand the meaning of *exacerbated*?

- a. *exacerbated* and *intensified* are synonyms
- b. *abnormally* describes *exacerbated*
- c. *exacerbated* and *surge* are antonyms
- d. "rising sea levels" are contrasted with "storm surge"

Item 2

Part A According to the article "Superstorms," what kind of weather disasters caused more than $1 billion in damage in the years 2011 and 2012?

- a. storms, including tornadoes and hurricanes
- b. all kinds, including drought, heat waves, and storms
- c. geological events such as earthquakes and tsunamis
- d. only the smallest thunderstorms

Part B What evidence supports the answer to Part A?

- a. The article says that most, but not all, of these weather events were storms.
- b. The article says that thunderstorms are the smallest type of storm.
- c. When earthquakes and tsunamis combine with storms, the damage is greater.
- d. The article says that all of these weather events were wind and rain storms.

Item 3

Part A According to "Superstorms," why might global warming lead to more intense storms?

- a. Drought-driven wildfires cause high winds.
- b. Carbon dioxide is building up in the atmosphere.
- c. Melting ice caps make storms wetter.
- d. Warmer air and oceans give storms more energy.

Part B What evidence in the text supports your response in Part A?

- a. data about decreased atmospheric water vapor
- b. data about increased global wind speeds and extreme downpours
- c. evidence about global increases in light but steady precipitation
- d. erosion from previous weather events, which increased Sandy's storm surge

---

PERFORMANCE TASK 1

Item 4

Part A What does the word *counterintuitive* mean in this passage from "Global Dimming"?

"Given what we know about global warming, this result may seem *counterintuitive*."

- a. too good to be true
- b. resulting from a simple logical process
- c. the opposite of what one expects
- d. easy to grasp

Part B Which example from the text best illustrates the correct answer to Part A?

- a. Jet exhaust contains carbon dioxide.
- b. Greenhouse gases contribute to global warming.
- c. Global dimming is caused by tiny particles that float in the air.
- d. Temperatures increased when a source of greenhouse gas was removed.

Item 5

Part A Which conclusion is NOT widely accepted by climate scientists?

- a. Global dimming and global warming should not grow unchecked.
- b. Global dimming occurs when aerosols reflect light back into space.
- c. Global dimming is a significant contributor to climate change.
- d. Carbon dioxide is a greenhouse gas.

Part B Which evidence from the text best supports the correct answer to part A?

- a. "Scientists disagree about how much global dimming affects climate change."
- b. "Many scientists believe . . . that global dimming must be addressed."
- c. "Humans shouldn't count on global dimming to 'tone down' . . . warming."
- d. "Most public health experts believe that eventually, Asia will have to come to grips with . . . pollution."

Item 6

Part A Which of these four conclusions that could be drawn from "Global Dimming" is best supported by evidence in the text?

- a. Global dimming is a greater threat to the climate than global warming.
- b. Deserts are mostly to blame for droughts caused by global dimming.
- c. To prevent further environmental damage by global dimming, air traffic should stop.
- d. The root cause of global dimming, aerosols, also causes serious health problems.

Part B What TWO pieces of evidence from "Global Dimming" support the answer to Part A?

- a. "Aerosols . . . come from natural sources, like desert wind storms, and human sources"
- b. "Recent changes in the annual monsoon season have hurt food production in Asia"
- c. "The two animals might neutralize each other, but your personal danger would be high."
- d. "Already the health hazard of aerosols has led the U.S. and other countries to pass clean air legislation."
- e. "The negative health effects of air pollution in countries like China and India are also clear."

Item 7

Part A What is the likely origin of *radiation*, which appears in the sentence below?

"Scientists call the sunlight that reaches earth *surface solar radiation* (SSR)."

- a. Latin *radix*, meaning "root"
- b. Latin *radius*, meaning "ray"
- c. Old French *rangier*, "to put in a line"
- d. Old English *rād*, "riding, road"

RESEARCH SIMULATION

Part B What evidence from "Global Dimming" supports your response to Part A?

a. *Radiation* is related to the rays of sunlight that reach the earth.

b. The causes of increased surface solar *radiation* are rooted in aerosols.

c. The aerosols that cause surface solar *radiation* come from a range of sources.

d. The earth's atmosphere is being warmed by greenhouse gases.

Item 8

Part A What conclusion can be drawn from "Superstorms" and "Global Dimming"?

a. Global dimming plays a larger role in climate change than was thought.

b. Global warming has caused devastating drought in Africa.

c. Changes in the water cycle include less evaporation from the earth's oceans.

d. Changes in the atmosphere have had a strong impact on the earth's climate.

Part B What evidence supports the answer to Part A?

a. Both articles discuss how disruptions in the water cycle relate to drought in Africa.

b. Both articles discuss the relation of increased storminess to pollution.

c. Both articles discuss changes in Earth's atmosphere that affect its climate.

d. Both articles discuss how clouds now produce more rain.

Item 9

Part A According to "Global Dimming," how might global dimming disrupt the water cycle?

a. As less sunlight reaches the ocean's surface, evaporation decreases.

b. As dimming creates a greenhouse effect, evaporation and precipitation increase.

c. As clouds contain more aerosols and rain, cloudiness decreases worldwide.

d. As precipitation increases, monsoons in Asia become more destructive.

Part B Which evidence from "Superstorms" may contradict the correct response in Part A?

a. "Heat waves and droughts have grown more likely and more extreme."

b. "extra water vapor in the atmosphere is making storms wetter"

c. "Concentration of . . . gases in the atmosphere [is] higher . . . ."

d. "Wind speeds have increased by . . . 5% over the past two decades."

Item 10

You have read two texts about different aspects of climate change. Think about how each article discusses climate change through an explanation of causes and effects.

Write an essay that analyzes the causes and effects of climate change. Think about changes that scientists have observed in the atmosphere, changes they have observed in Earth's climate, and their theories about why these changes are connected. Be sure to cite examples from each text to support your essay, and use standard English.

Part 3: Research Simulation *continued*

Constructed Response Item: Remind students that, like much scientific writing, these two selections contain many descriptions of causes and effects. Some of these causes and effects are firmly established, others are still controversial. Tell students to read carefully to understand when a cause or effect is widely accepted by the scientific community and when it is disputed.

Depth of Knowledge Level: 4

Analyzing the Constructed Response: Discuss key elements of the scoring rubric with students. Tie specific criteria to the elements students should include in their essays.

How this task contributes to reading and writing grounded in evidence from informational texts:
In order to complete the task, students 1. Note the changes scientists have observed in the atmosphere; 2. Note changes scientists observe in the earth's climate; 3. Summarize various explanations for the relationship between these atmospheric and climate conditions; 4. Organize ideas in a clear and logical structure; 5. Effectively use transitions and include a logical conclusion; 6. Follow language conventions.

Test-Taking Tips

Selected response items: Remind students to . . .

• pay close attention to words that will help them identify how to answer, such as *in paragraph 2*.

• watch out for signal words such as *not*, *best*, and *except*, that clarify what students should look for in the answer choices.

• be aware of items that ask for more than one correct answer or that include *all of the above* or *none of the above* as answer choices.

• narrow down your answer choices by getting rid of the obviously incorrect choices.

Constructed response items: Remind students to . . .

• plan their responses before they begin writing.

• address all parts of the writing prompt, and use textual evidence in the response.

• review their responses to check for errors and areas that need clarification or elaboration.

• write legibly and make edits neatly.

Performance Task Overview

The Performance Tasks in *Progress English Language Arts* are designed to determine a student's ability to closely read and understand a complex text, locate textual evidence to support analysis of the text, and create an extended response that shows deep comprehension of the text. Writing prompts in each part of the Performance Task address requirements for creating literary analyses, narratives, or research-based texts. Each Performance Task has three main parts: Literary Analysis, Narrative Writing, and Research Simulation.

Each Performance Task requires students to read thematically related texts in a variety of modes and genres and to respond to two types of assessment items:

- **Selected response items** require students to choose the correct answer from a number of options. Selected response items are in two parts: Part A requires students to answer a question related to the content or language of the text; in Part B, students identify textual evidence that supports the answer to Part A.

- **Constructed response items** require students to create a brief written composition—a literary analysis, a narrative, or a research-based text—in response to a prompt.

You can help your students by introducing the overall topic of the Performance Task, orienting students to the requirements of each part of the task, and communicating helpful reminders that will enable students to approach each part successfully. Once students have completed each part, go over the items and correct responses with them, especially focusing on the connection between textual evidence and acceptable responses.

In **Performance Task 2,** students will read and respond to a series of texts relating to the laws society makes to benefit the whole.

- "Battle of the Bike Lane" (realistic fiction); "Film Fest Favorite" (film review); "An Inconvenient Girl" (historical fiction); "Rebel Girl Provokes Massive Strike" (historical account)
- "Meet Jill Schartner—Conservation Warden" (nonfiction narrative)
- "NOHVU Keynote Address" (speech); "NOHVU Keynote Address Hits the Right Notes" (review); "Protecting Federal Lands for 'The Greatest Good'" (magazine article)

Specific information about how these texts are used with each section of **Performance Task 2** is shown in the chart at the right.

ONLINE Digital Resources

Go to **sadlierconnect.com** to download the following resources for **Performance Task 2**:

Texts:
- "Battle of the Bike Lane"; "Film Fest Favorite"; "An Inconvenient Girl"; "Rebel Girl Provokes Massive Strike"
- "Meet Jill Schartner—Conservation Warden"
- "NOHVU Keynote Address"; "NOHVU Keynote Address Hits the Right Notes"; "Protecting Federal Lands for 'The Greatest Good'"

Answer Keys and Rubrics:
- Literary Analysis Task
- Narrative Writing Task
- Research Simulation Task

RECOMMENDED PACING

Administer the entire Performance Task over a three-day period. Students should complete one part per day, accompanied by instructional support and review.

Performance Task 2

PART 1: LITERARY ANALYSIS
(45 minutes)

TASK
Students will respond to questions that require careful analysis of a fictional story paired with a film review and a fictional story paired with an historical account. Then they will write a brief literary analysis text in response to a prompt.

SELECTIONS
"Battle of the Bike Lane" and "Film Fest Favorite"; "An Inconvenient Girl" and "Rebel Girl Provokes Massive Strike"

PART 2: NARRATIVE WRITING
(45 minutes)

TASK
Students will respond to questions that require careful analysis of a narrative text. Then they will respond to a prompt by writing a short narrative.

SELECTION
"Meet Jill Schartner—Conservation Warden"

PART 3: RESEARCH SIMULATION
(45 minutes)

TASK
Students will respond to questions that require careful analysis of a speech, a speech review, and a magazine article. Then students will respond to a writing prompt that requires them to synthesize information from the texts.

SELECTIONS
"NOHVU Keynote Address" and "NOHVU Keynote Address Hits the Right Notes"; "Protecting Federal Lands for 'The Greatest Good'"

Administration Procedure

STEP 1 Introduce the Performance Task

Tell students that this Performance Task may cover any of the skills they have learned and practiced in Units 1–11 of *Progress English Language Arts*.

Explain that students will read three sets of texts. After each set, they will answer multiple-choice questions and then incorporate what they read into a written response. Familiarize students with the types of items they will see:

- Selected response items have two parts. Part A asks students to answer a question about the reading selection; Part B asks them to identify textual evidence—a quotation, fact, or detail from the selection—that supports the correct answer.

- Constructed response items are writing prompts based on one or more of the reading selections. Students should use textual evidence from the selections to support their responses to these items. They can make notes before writing.

* Repeat Steps 2–4 for each part of the Performance Task.

STEP 2 Reading

Tell students that they will read a set of texts that involves topics about laws. Remind students that they should read the texts closely and that they can take notes about central ideas, key themes, and significant details as they read. Then have students read the text(s) for the Literary Analysis, Narrative Writing, or Research Simulation part of the Performance Task, as appropriate.

STEP 3 Selected Response

Have students complete the selected response items.

STEP 4 Constructed Response

Read the writing prompt, and make sure students understand the directions. Explain: *Your task is to write an essay in response to this prompt. You may use your notes. Also, you should go back to the texts to find ideas and textual evidence to support your response.* Answer any questions. Then have students respond to the writing prompt.

STEP 5 Check the Performance Task

Go over the selected response items so students understand why each answer is correct; help them identify the textual evidence that supports each item. Review the writing prompt and discuss what an effective response should include.

There are three parts to this performance task. Your teacher will provide you with copies of one or more reading selections that go with each part.

- *Paired Selection:* "Battle of the Bike Lane"   Genre: Realistic Fiction and "Film Fest Favorite"   Genre: Film Review

- *Paired Selection:* "An Inconvenient Girl"   Genre: Historical Fiction and "Rebel Girl Provokes Massive Strike"   Genre: Historical Account

- "Meet Jill Schartner—Conservation Warden"   Genre: Personal Narrative

- *Paired Selection:* "NOHVU Keynote Address"   Genre: Speech and "NOHVU Keynote Address Hits the Right Notes"   Genre: Review

- "Protecting Federal Lands for 'The Greatest Good'"   Genre: Magazine Article

Part 1: Literary Analysis

- ☐ Carefully read "Battle of the Bike Lane" and "Film Fest Favorite" and take notes about important events, ideas, and details. Then answer Items 1–4 on pages 322–323.
- ☐ Carefully read "An Inconvenient Girl" and "Rebel Girl Provokes Massive Strike" and take notes as you read. Then answer Items 5–9 on pages 323–324.
- ☐ Read the writing prompt in Item 10 on page 324. Review "Battle of the Bike Lane" and "An Inconvenient Girl" with the prompt in mind. You will use both passages in this task.
- ☐ Write an essay on your own paper in response to the prompt.

Part 2: Narrative Writing

- ☐ Carefully read "Meet Jill Schartner—Conservation Warden." As you read, take notes that help you understand the passage. Then answer Items 1–9 on pages 325–327.
- ☐ Read the writing prompt in Item 10 on page 327.
- ☐ Write a narrative on your own paper in response to the prompt.

Part 3: Research Simulation

- ☐ Carefully read "NOHVU Keynote Address," "NOHVU Keynote Address Hits the Right Notes," and "Protecting Federal Lands for 'The Greatest Good.'" Take notes about important ideas and details. Then answer Items 1–9 on pages 328–330.
- ☐ Read the writing prompt in Item 10 on page 330. Then review "NOHVU Keynote Address" and "Protecting Federal Lands for 'The Greatest Good.'"
- ☐ Write an essay on your own paper in response to the prompt.

LITERARY ANALYSIS

Part 1 Literary Analysis

Read all parts of the question before responding. Circle the correct answer to Items 1–9. Use your own paper to respond to Item 10.

Item 1

Part A Which of the following best describes the conflict in the short story "Battle of the Bike Lane"?

a. Lorne vs. Dale

b. Lorne vs. the young cyclist

c. Lorne vs. the city transportation department

d. all the residents of the street vs. the striping crew

Part B What text supports the answer to Part A?

a. "all the new law requires is that you keep Loretta in your driveway"

b. "Dale and his wife were weary of looking at Loretta"

c. "these bicycle lanes are going to be insufferable"

d. "the child snuffled, 'My pants got caught in my chin'"

Item 2

Part A Which of the following sentences best states a key theme of "Battle of the Bike Lane"?

a. The government should do more to encourage physical fitness.

b. Even a positive change can be difficult to accept.

c. Minor disputes between neighbors can turn into bitter feuds.

d. Senior citizens deserve to be exempt from certain rules.

Part B What text from the story supports the answer to Part A?

a. "Dale had resided in the house opposite Lorne's since the neighborhood was constructed in the early 1970s"

b. "they'd filed innumerable covert complaints with the city about the behemoth on the street"

c. "he always seemed to know precisely when to navigate the RV back into his narrow driveway"

d. "I'm talking about custom, I'm taking about tradition!' said Lorne"

Item 3

Part A What does the word *conviviality* mean in these lines from "Battle of the Bike Lane"?

"Lorne Crawford attempted to join in the spirit of conviviality . . . but the meeting . . . had left him feeling prickly and defensive."

a. friendliness

b. rebellion

c. compassion

d. freedom

Part B The word relationship that helped you answer Part A was the relationship between *conviviality* and . . .

a. "attempted to join"

b. "he and his neighbors meandered out"

c. "the meeting with city transportation officials"

d. "prickly and defensive"

PERFORMANCE TASK 2

Item 4

Part A Based on information in "Film Fest Favorite," which of the following is used to focus on the film's conflict?

a. sound

b. costumes

c. makeup

d. contrast

Part B Which detail from the film review best supports the answer to Part A?

a. The film is in black and white.

b. The reviewer praises the film's sound editing.

c. The white bike lane stripe stands out against the black street.

d. The actor who plays Lorne gives a subtle and effective performance.

Item 5

Part A What can you infer about laws governing the workplace at the time "An Inconvenient Girl" is set?

a. There are no laws governing child labor.

b. Some laws govern child labor.

c. There are strict fire safety laws.

d. Employers are required to pay overtime.

Part B What text supports the answer to Part A?

a. "so they lock us in from dawn to dusk"

b. "the only time we get a chance to visit is at lunch"

c. "losing half a day's wages means no dinner for my whole family"

d. "only last week did I turn fourteen, the legal age of factory work"

Item 6

Part A Which of the following claims about the narrator of "An Inconvenient Girl" can be supported by text evidence?

a. The narrator realizes she has to work but would like fairer treatment.

b. The narrator wants the factory bosses and owners to be thrown in jail.

c. The narrator wants the law to require her to stop working.

d. The narrator wants to work more so she can earn more money.

Part B Which evidence from the story does NOT support the answer to Part A?

a. The workers are not allowed to talk while working.

b. The main character works eleven hours a day, six days a week.

c. Fourteen is the legal age for factory work.

d. Workers earn six dollars a week.

Item 7

Part A What connotation does the word *inconvenient* have in the title "An Inconvenient Girl"?

a. ill-timed

b. not handy

c. troublesome

d. uncomfortable

Part B What text supports the answer to Part A?

a. "for my six dollars, I work eleven hours a day, six days a week"

b. "my parents warn me not to cause trouble for the owners, but . . ."

c. "we have exactly one half hour to feel human"

d. "I shrug, trying to look braver than I feel"

Part 1: Literary Analysis

Selection (Genre): ONLINE

"Battle of the Bike Lane" (realistic fiction)

"Film Fest Favorite" (film review)

"An Inconvenient Girl" (historical fiction)

"Rebel Girl Provokes Massive Strike" (historical account)

Core Task: Students will read a literary text and respond to nine selected response items. Then students will write a literary analysis comparing the two fictional texts.

Text Summary: In "Battle of the Bike Lane," Lorne rebels against the appearance of a bike lane on his street. A review of a film based on the story follows. In the next story, "An Inconvenient Girl," a first-person narrator reveals life in a sweatshop in 1909 and anticipates a coming strike. The final text, an historical account, tells of an actual union meeting and the strike that followed it.

Score Points: Up to **33 points** total

- Selected response items: Up to 18 points (1 point for each part of nine 2-part items)

- Constructed response item: Up to 15 points for one item

ONLINE   Download the reading selections and the Answer Key and Rubric.

Depth of Knowledge Levels:

Item 1:	Item 2:	Item 3:	Item 4:	Item 5:	Item 6:
Level 2	Level 2	Level 2	Level 2	Level 2	Level 3

Item 7:	Item 8:	Item 9:
Level 2	Level 2	Level 3

Selected Response Items: Have students follow the directions on page 321 to read the first two texts, "Battle of the Bike Lane" and "Film Fest Favorite," and answer items 1–4. Then they will read the remaining texts and answer items 5–9.

Remind students that every response in Part A must be supported in Part B by evidence from the text. Have students choose from the evidence carefully to make sure that it fulfills the requirement of the prompt in Part A. For example, some questions deal with more than one text, and the answer options may present evidence from both texts. Caution students to correctly identify the text from which the evidence in the Part B answer choices is drawn.

Analyzing Selected Response Items: When students have completed the items, go over the correct answers with them. Help them locate the evidence in the text that supports each answer. Discuss why the correct answer is the strongest choice.

Part 1: Literary Analysis *continued*

Constructed Response Item: The writing prompt deals only with the fictional stories students read as part of Literary Analysis. As students read the prompt, they should circle key words that explain what the prompt requires them to do.

Depth of Knowledge Level: 4

Analyzing the Constructed Response: When students have finished writing, present key elements in each of the rubric's three categories: Content, Organization, and Language. Have volunteers share how they could improve the answer by paying attention to the elements required to achieve a "15" in each of the Performance Task's three parts.

How this part contributes to reading and writing grounded in evidence from literary text: In order to complete Literary Analysis, students: 1. Select and interpret evidence to analyze how texts deal with a central theme; 2. Analyze the reactions and points of view of the main characters; 3. Write logically organized supporting paragraphs that develop the topic, including explaining and clarifying supporting evidence and details; 4. Use appropriate transitions, precise language, and a relevant conclusion; 5. Follow conventions and rules of grammar, usage, and mechanics.

LITERARY ANALYSIS

Item 8

Part A Which aspect of working in a garment factory is dealt with in "An Inconvenient Girl" but NOT in "Rebel Girl Provokes Massive Strike"?

a. the fire hazards present in the garment factory

b. the employment of underage workers

c. the mind-numbing nature of the work

d. the long hours in the workweek

Part B What quote from the text supports the answer to Part A?

a. "The work is so repetitive, I feel I am nothing but an extension of the machine."

b. "If it happens again, I'll send you home for half a day with no work and no wages."

c. "Who but a child would accept $3.00 a week in wages?"

d. "But you could get thrown in jail and beaten!"

Part B Select TWO pieces of evidence (one from each text) that support your response to Part A.

a. "Perhaps it was the fact that this girl has firsthand experience of work in these factories." ("Rebel Girl")

b. "In a recent smaller strike, she was arrested no fewer than seventeen times." ("Rebel Girl")

c. "It is doubtful whether women and girls can stand up to this kind of counterattack." ("Rebel Girl")

d. "I dream we are all streaming into school, a school for girls." ("An Inconvenient Girl")

e. "For my six dollars, I work eleven hours a day, six days a week." ("An Inconvenient Girl")

f. "I've decided to join the union and the next strike." ("An Inconvenient Girl")

Item 9

Part A Which word describes both the narrator from "An Inconvenient Girl" and Clara Lemlich in "Rebel Girl Provokes Massive Strike"?

a. rash

b. dreamy

c. obedient

d. determined

Item 10

Both of the fictional stories you have read deal with society's laws. "Battle of the Bike Lane" is about the law that gives a city government the right to say where bike lanes go. "An Inconvenient Girl" concerns labor laws for factory workers in the early 1900s.

Write an essay that analyzes how the law plays a part in each story and how the main characters react to the law. Cite evidence from each story to support your analysis. Be sure to follow the conventions of standard English.

Test-Taking Tips

Selected Response Items: Remind students to . . .

• read each question closely and follow the directions carefully.

• read every answer choice carefully before deciding on an answer.

• use a pencil so that a wrong answer can be corrected.

Constructed Response Items: Remind students to . . .

• focus on a clear main idea and point of view.

• organize their ideas before they write, and stay on topic as they write.

• provide textual evidence in the form of facts, details, and quotations from the passage to support their responses.

• use precise language, and include transitions to connect ideas.

• follow rules of formal writing (spelling, punctuation, capitalization, and grammar).

Part 2 Narrative Writing

Read all parts of the question before responding. Circle the correct answer to Items 1–9. Use your own paper to respond to Item 10.

Item 1

Part A What does the word *culvert* mean in these lines from "Meet Jill Schartner—Conservation Warden"?

"From this location I can hear the walleyes splashing in the culverts, which run under the roadway."

- a. a natural creek or stream
- b. a ditch running parallel to a road
- c. a footpath passing under a bridge
- d. a sewer or drainpipe that passes beneath a road *(circled)*

Part B Which words from the lines of text in Part A help you understand the meaning of *culvert*?

- a. "from this location"
- b. "I can hear"
- c. "the walleyes"
- d. "which run under the roadway" *(circled)*

Item 2

Part A Choose two words that describe Jill Schartner, based on evidence from the text.

- a. brilliant and determined
- b. bold and dedicated *(circled)*
- c. brave and foolhardy
- d. sneaky and vengeful

Part B Choose TWO pieces of evidence that support your response to Part A.

- a. "Setting up surveillance . . . is one way we're able to do our job"
- b. "Now I need to find a place where I can watch the creek without being seen."
- c. "There is very little brushy area to conceal my location because of the road"
- d. "I decide to give it another hour. I know if I move now, my tracks will be seen." *(circled)*
- e. "I hear the noise of a loud muffler in the distance"
- f. "I move toward the driver and place my hands on his shoulders" *(circled)*

Item 3

Part A Which connotation does the word *discuss* carry in these lines from the narrative?

"Both men paid fines of more than $500.00 each and lost their hunting and fishing privileges for a 3-year period. As for the young boy, he and I were able to sit down and discuss the legal method of catching fish."

- a. argue about
- b. dispute bitterly
- c. debate heatedly
- d. talk over calmly *(circled)*

Part B What text supports the answer to Part A?

- a. "both men paid fines of more than $500.00"
- b. "lost their hunting and fishing privileges"
- c. "he and I were able to sit down" *(circled)*
- d. "the legal method of catching fish"

NARRATIVE WRITING

Item 4

Part A Why does the young boy fail to alert the two men to the presence of a conservation warden?

- a. He is so surprised to see her that he is speechless.
- b. He sees her but is not interested in her. *(circled)*
- c. She signals to him not to make a sound.
- d. He does not see her because he is looking at the men.

Part B Which detail from the text best supports the answer to Part A?

- a. "I decide to try to conceal myself in a small clump of dogwood 20 feet from the water's edge"
- b. "he is more interested in what the men are doing" *(circled)*
- c. "I decide it is time to make my presence known"
- d. "I'm now . . . behind the men, but they are so intent on making the fish look like it has been legally caught . . . "

Item 5

Part A What does Schartner mean when she says, "the game is about to begin" in these lines from the narrative?

"Something in his eyes tells me the game is about to begin, and in one quick movement, the driver bends down, grabs the net and takes one step toward the water's edge."

- a. The driver will try to avoid being caught. *(circled)*
- b. The driver wants to get home quickly to watch a football game.
- c. The driver knows fishing and hunting season is about to start.
- d. The driver will invite the warden to play a friendly game with him.

Part B What text supports the answer to Part A?

- a. "something in his eyes tells me"
- b. "in one quick movement"
- c. "the driver bends down, grabs the net" *(circled)*
- d. "toward the water's edge"

Item 6

Part A At the narrative's climax, which of the following themes emerges?

- a. Female walleyes need protection to lay their eggs.
- b. If you disobey the conservation warden, you'll be sorry. *(circled)*
- c. A landing net or a fishing pole can pose a tripping hazard.
- d. Good role models are found in unexpected places.

Part B Which evidence from the narrative supports the answer to Part A?

- a. "they're busy releasing their eggs among the rocks in the shallow water"
- b. "but he trips on some rocks and falls head first into the icy cold water" *(circled)*
- c. "both men paid fines of more than $500.00 each and lost their hunting and fishing privileges for a 3-year period"
- d. "he and I were able to sit down and discuss the legal method of catching fish"

Part 2: Narrative Writing

Selection (Genre): ONLINE

"Meet Jill Schartner—Conservation Warden"

Core Task: Students will read a narrative text and respond to nine selected response items. Then they will write a response in which they present the events of the narrative from another character's point of view.

Text Summary: Schartner introduces herself as a proud conservation warden and then recounts an experience in which she caught two men illegally fishing. In a dramatic sequence, she and one of the men fall into icy water as she tries to stop him from getting rid of evidence. The narrative ends with Schartner talking about legal fishing methods with a child who accompanied the men.

Score Points: Up to **33 points** total

- Selected response items: Up to 18 points (1 point for each part of nine 2-part items)
- Constructed response item: Up to 15 points for one item

ONLINE   Download the reading selections and the Answer Key and Rubric.

Depth of Knowledge Levels:

Item 1:	Item 2:	Item 3:	Item 4:	Item 5:	Item 6:
Level 2	Level 1	Level 2	Level 1	Level 2	Level 3

Item 7:	Item 8:	Item 9:
Level 2	Level 4	Level 3

Selected Response Items: Remind students that in some cases there is more than one possible piece of supporting evidence in Part B. They should watch for items that specifically direct them to identify two pieces of supporting evidence.

Analyzing Selected Response Items: Emphasize the importance of reading the question stem carefully. For example, some Part A questions may ask students to analyze a particular part of the text. In these cases, students need to be sure that the evidence they select in Part B comes from the same text section.

Part 2: Narrative Writing *continued*

Constructed Response Item: To make sure students understand the writing prompt, have them answer specific questions that you ask about it, such as, *What elements of your response are going to be the same as in the narrative? What elements are going to be different?*

Depth of Knowledge Level: 4

Analyzing the Constructed Response: Have student volunteers share their responses. Discuss key elements of the scoring rubric and ask each student to make one significant change to improve his or her response.

How this part contributes to reading and writing grounded in evidence from narrative text: In order to complete Narrative Writing, students 1. Analyze and select details about a character in the source text; 2. Summarize or describe events or other narrative elements from the source text; 3. Apply evidence-based interpretations of a character's traits in the retelling of the narrative from a different perspective; 4. Develop a narrative, including descriptive details and elaboration consistent with the source text; 5. Employ a coherent narrative structure, appropriate transitions, and a conclusion that follows logically from both the student's text and evidence in the source text; 6. Follow conventions and rules of grammar, usage, and mechanics.

Item 7

Part A Which meaning of the social studies word *conservation* applies in the job title "conservation warden"?

- a. preserving with sugar
- b. the process of using sparingly
- c. relating to the protection of wildlife
- d. maintenance of energy during a phase of changes

Part B What text from the narrative supports the answer to Part A?

- a. "protecting natural resources"
- b. "my job is the best job in the world"
- c. "my thermos is empty"
- d. "'C173, are you ready for a replacement?'"

Item 8

Part A Which of the following is a reasoned judgment, based on experience or logic?

- a. "my job is the best job in the world"
- b. "As I . . . reach into the creek, I am able to touch several of these large fish."
- c. "because of the fresh snow, I decide to give [the surveillance] another hour"
- d. "The young boy asks, 'Can I hold it? Can I get one like that?'"

Part B What text supports the answer to Part A?

- a. "I know if I move now, my tracks will be seen"
- b. "I think I am speaking for all of the wardens here in Wisconsin"
- c. "they all laugh and point into the water as the driver yells excitedly"
- d. "I can see as many as 50 walleyes swimming among the rocks in the shallow water"

Item 9

Part A Below are four claims about "Meet Jill Schartner." Which claim can be supported by evidence from the text?

- a. She regrets that it is necessary to protect wildlife from poachers.
- b. She believes more should be done to protect wildlife.
- c. She enjoys enforcing Wisconsin's conservation laws.
- d. She underwent extensive training to become a conservation warden.

Part B What text supports your response to Part A?

- a. "the . . . cold damp air has been enough to keep me awake"
- b. "at 2:00 A.M. . . . my back is stiff and my thermos is empty"
- c. "I decide it is time to make my presence known"
- d. "he and I were able to sit down and discuss the legal method of catching fish"

Item 10

"Meet Jill Schartner—Conservation Warden" is a narrative told by Jill Schartner, reflecting her point of view and her feelings about the events she describes. Imagine this event from the point of view of one of the other participants—the driver who ends up in the water, his adult passenger, or even the young boy.

Write three or four paragraphs to tell the story of this incident from this other participant's point of view. Include his thoughts and feelings about the incident and his reactions to the events, taking care to show a different perspective than Jill Schartner's. Be sure to use details from "Meet Jill Schartner" in your story. End by having your narrator tell what conclusions he can draw about the incident, such as whether he did or did not learn anything.

RESEARCH SIMULATION

Part 3 Research Simulation

Read all parts of the question before responding. Circle the correct answer to Items 1–9. Use your own paper to respond to Item 10.

Item 1

Part A What does the word *emissions* mean in these lines from "NOHVU Keynote Address"?

"A lot of fuss has been made about the emissions of snowmobiles, ATVs, and dirt bikes. But I'm here to tell you that today's newer engines, whether 2-stroke or 4-stroke, are much less polluting than the old 2-stroke models."

  a. substance released in the air *(circled)*
  b. rapid rise in popularity
  c. bans on public property
  d. fuel efficiency

Part B Which words from the lines of text in Part A best help you understand the meaning of *emissions*?

  a. "a lot of fuss"
  b. "today's newer engines, whether 2-stroke or 4-stroke"
  c. "much less polluting" *(circled)*
  d. "the old 2-stroke models"

Item 2

Part A According to information in Bill Luckenbach's keynote address, which claim about the Wilderness Act is most accurate?

  a. The Wilderness Act is a fundamentally flawed law that should not have been passed.
  b. Through funds provided by the Wilderness Act, OHV users have built new trails.
  c. The Wilderness Act has been used to prevent OHV users from going off trail.
  d. Carrying out the Wilderness Act has led to unforeseen consequences. *(circled)*

Part B What text supports the answer to Part A?

  a. "The Forest Service isn't the only agency threatening OHV use."
  b. "25,000 acres of wilderness were closed under these rules"
  c. "But in effect, three times that acreage is now unavailable to OHV users." *(circled)*
  d. "We want to comply with the trail management rules"

Item 3

Part A According to the reaction to the speech, "NOHVU Keynote Address Hits the Right Notes," what part of the speech marked a dramatic change in the speaker's attitude?

  a. The discussion of the economic impact of OHV retail sales.
  b. The discussion of the effect of OHV tourism on local communities.
  c. The imitation of the sound of a 2-stroke engine starting up.
  d. The discussion of limits on OHV access to federal lands. *(circled)*

Part B What verbal element of Luckenbach's speech showed that his attitude had changed?

  a. "his voice fairly booming" *(circled)*
  b. "he shared good news with enthusiasm"
  c. "he began at an unhurried pace"
  d. "he reported on some of the injustices"

PERFORMANCE TASK 2

Item 4

Part A Based on "NOHVU Keynote Address Hits the Right Notes," which claim about Bill Luckenbach is accurate?

  a. He is a clownish speaker whom the audience does not take seriously.
  b. He is a relaxed speaker who connects with the audience. *(circled)*
  c. He is a serious speaker who intimidates his audience.
  d. He is a hesitant speaker who fails to leave an impression.

Part B Which of Luckenbach's verbal and nonverbal techniques, as reported in "NOHVU Keynote Address Hits the Right Notes," supports the claim from Part A?

  a. He gets nostalgic, makes funny sounds, and pounds the podium.
  b. He speaks in an unhurried tone and makes eye contact. *(circled)*
  c. He stands straighter, pounds the podium, and glares at his audience.
  d. He speaks softly, looks down, and fails to discuss important topics.

Item 5

Part A How does the author of "Protecting Federal Lands" feel about the Forest Service's Travel Management Rules?

  a. She feels they do not go far enough to protect National Forests. *(circled)*
  b. She defends the way the rules have been applied to OHV users.
  c. She feels they are a long overdue response to President Nixon's original Executive Order.
  d. She insists that the original rules should never have been revised.

Part B Which quotation from "Protecting Federal Lands" best counters the claim above?

  a. "the old-style OHV engines account for over half the OHVs in use today" *(circled)*
  b. "the EPA has issued stricter emissions standards for the manufacturers of new OHVs"
  c. "air pollution, of course, is another major problem with OHVs"
  d. "many a bird-watcher knows the frustration that accompanies the ear-shattering blast of an OHV"

Part B Which quotation from the text best supports the answer to Part A?

  a. "this order required the Forest Service to create rules that would accomplish three goals"
  b. "the 2005 revision was an attempt to stem the tide of destruction brought by OHVs"
  c. "the rules still haven't slowed or reversed the damage" *(circled)*
  d. "the growth of OHV use on our public lands has increased steadily"

Item 6

Part A Below are four claims about changes in OHV engine technology. Which claim does Bill Luckenbach make in his keynote address?

  a. The EPA has no right to alter the signature sound of a two-stroke engine.
  b. The engines in newer OHVs are cleaner, quieter, and less polluting. *(circled)*
  c. Changes in OHV technology will not make any difference to our parklands.
  d. OHV users were never fond of the conventional two-stroke engines anyway.

Part 3: Research Simulation

Selection (Genre): ONLINE

"NOHVU Keynote Address" (speech)
"NOHVU Keynote Address Hits the Right Notes" (review)
"Protecting Federal Lands for 'The Greatest Good'" (magazine article)

Core Task: Students will read nonfiction texts and respond to nine selected response items. Then students will write an essay synthesizing information from two of the texts in response to a research question.

Text Summary: The speech to members of an off-highway vehicle association emphasizes the positive impact OHV users have on federal land management and local economies. The speaker also warns about infringement of federal rules upon OHV users' trail use. The reviewer of the speech tells how the speaker used voice and gesture to enhance his speech. The magazine article argues against OHV use in federal lands due to environmental concerns.

Score Points: Up to **33 points** total

- Selected response items: Up to 18 points (1 point for each part of nine 2-part items)
- Constructed response item: Up to 15 points for one item.

ONLINE Download the reading selection and the Answer Key and Rubric.

Depth of Knowledge Levels:

Item 1:	Item 2:	Item 3:	Item 4:	Item 5:	Item 6:
Level 2	Level 3	Level 2	Level 3	Level 2	Level 2

Item 7:	Item 8:	Item 9:
Level 2	Level 3	Level 2

Selected Response Items: Taken out of context, some pieces of supporting evidence in Part B may sound reasonable yet still be incorrect. Encourage students to check their Part B responses by locating their choice in the text and reviewing its original context.

Analyzing Selected Response Items: Several items in Research Simulation ask students to consider both selections. Sometimes students must select counterevidence—evidence that argues against a claim—rather than supporting evidence. In these cases, they are choosing evidence from one of the selections to argue against a claim made in the other selection.

Part 3: Research Simulation *continued*

Constructed Response Item: Remind students that, through reading selections written from opposing viewpoints, they have encountered the key issues around the use of off-highway vehicles in public lands. Though the two authors often use loaded language, students should present these issues objectively in their written responses.

Depth of Knowledge Level: 4

Analyzing the Constructed Response: Discuss key elements of the scoring rubric with students. Tie specific criteria to the elements students should include in their essays.

How this part contributes to reading and writing grounded in evidence from informational texts: In order to complete Research Simulation, students 1. Analyze key elements of two authors' arguments; 2. Write an essay comparing the authors' positions on the key elements; 3. Support the comparison with well-chosen textual evidence; 4. Give their own opinion on the issue and support it with reasoning and evidence; 5. Organize ideas in a clear and logical structure; 6. Effectively use transitions, and include a logical conclusion; 7. Follow language conventions.

RESEARCH SIMULATION

Item 7

Part A Which claim about the economic impact of OHV use does the author of "Protecting Federal Lands" make?

- **a.** OHVs in public lands may discourage "human powered" tourists, which would hurt local economies. *(circled)*
- **b.** OHV users, on a daily basis, spend about as much money on tourism as other users of federal lands.
- **c.** In the future, the government will spend more money enforcing the regulation of OHVs in public lands.
- **d.** OHV users will have to pay a fuel tax and a registration fee for the privilege of using their vehicles on public lands.

Part B What text from "NOHVU Keynote Address" could be used to argue against the correct claim in Part A?

- **a.** "the value of the off-road retail market is $15 billion dollars"
- **b.** "this economic downturn has an upside"
- **c.** "through registration fees, user fees, and the fuel taxes we pay, we've shouldered the cost of using these lands"
- **d.** "OHV users spend more on average than other park users in local economies" *(circled)*

Item 8

Part A In "Protecting Federal Lands," Susan Lund implies that federal land management suffers during economic downturns. How is Luckenbach's view of the economic downturn different from Lund's?

- **a.** He sees it as negative because OHV users cannot afford new vehicles.
- **b.** He sees it as negative because the government can't build new OHV trails.
- **c.** He sees it as positive because OHV users can show their community spirit. *(circled)*
- **d.** He sees it as positive because the government is less likely to enforce rules.

Part B What evidence supports the answer to Part A?

- **a.** a Minnesota study showing the local impact of OHV tourist dollars
- **b.** details about taxes and volunteer work OHV users have contributed *(circled)*
- **c.** an example of how the government has stopped enforcing an OHV ban
- **d.** statistics about a nationwide decline in retail OHV sales

Item 9

Part A Which meaning of *sustainable* best matches its use in these lines?

"This is the best possible kind of economic impact, generated by a sustainable industry that respects the land. What's more, wilderness region economies depend on it."

- **a.** able to be maintained or prolonged
- **b.** able to continue with little environmental damage *(circled)*
- **c.** able to provide the necessities for living
- **d.** able to be propped up from below

Part B Which word or phrase from the text in Part A supports your answer?

- **a.** "economic impact"
- **b.** "generated"
- **c.** "respects the land" *(circled)*
- **d.** "economies depend on it"

Item 10

You have read two texts dealing with the use of ATVs, snowmobiles, dirt bikes, and other off-highway vehicles (OHVs) on federal lands. Write an essay in which you compare what the authors say about the economic and environmental impact of OHV use on federal land. Then tell your opinion on this issue, based on the authors' arguments. Remember to use textual evidence to support your ideas.

Test-Taking Tips

Selected Response Items: Remind students to . . .

- pay close attention to words that will help them identify how to answer, such as *in paragraph 2*.
- watch out for signal words such as *not, best,* and *except,* that clarify what students should look for in the answer choices.
- be aware of items that ask for more than one correct answer or that include *all of the above* or *none of the above* as answer choices.
- narrow down answer choices by getting rid of the obviously incorrect choices.

Constructed Response Items: Remind students to . . .

- plan their response before they begin writing.
- address all parts of the writing prompt, and use textual evidence in the response.
- review their responses to check for errors and areas that need clarification or elaboration.
- write legibly and make edits neatly.

GLOSSARY

A

accompany *(verb)* go with

accoutrement *(noun)* accessories; equipment

acknowledge *(verb)* to admit to be real or true

affected *(verb)* had an effect on; impacted

affinity *(noun)* fondness for; connection to

affirmatively *(adverb)* positively; in a way that expresses agreement

agile *(adjective)* moving and jumping easily; quick and well-coordinated

agitated *(adjective)* upset

allocated *(verb)* assigned when resources are divided up

altered *(verb)* changed

amulet *(noun)* an object that has symbolic meaning; a charm

anecdote *(noun)* brief story describing an event or person

animated *(adjective)* full of life or spirit; lively

apprised *(verb)* informed

aqueous *(adjective)* of water, or containing water; watery

archipelago *(noun)* group or chain of islands

arduous *(adjective)* difficult; hard

armory *(noun)* a place where weapons are kept

artifact *(noun)* an object of historical interest made by humans

aspect *(noun)* characteristic; part or side

assumed *(verb)* took on

atmospheric *(adjective)* of the atmosphere, the layer of air that surrounds Earth

atomic *(adjective)* having to do with atoms, the tiny, basic building blocks of matter

attempt *(verb)* to try; to make an effort at

authority *(noun)* the right to tell others what to do

authorized *(verb)* given permission or authority to do something

aviation *(noun)* the design, production, and use of aircraft

awe *(noun)* a strong feeling of admiration for something grand or powerful

B

bagpipes *(noun)* musical instrument made of a bag and connected pipes, often played in Scotland

beachhead *(noun)* base established on an enemy's shore during an invasion

bemoans *(verb)* complains about

bill *(noun)* a proposed law

biodiversity *(noun)* a great number and variety of plant and animal species in an environment

biofuel *(noun)* fuel created from renewable natural resources

bore *(verb)* carried

brink *(noun)* the edge or critical point after which success or catastrophe occurs

broadside *(noun)* the side of a ship above the water line

buckskin *(adjective)* made from the skin of a deer

buoyancy *(noun)* lightness; cheerfulness

bulb *(noun)* a rounded part, especially at the end of a cylinder

C

carbon footprint *(noun)* the amount of carbon dioxide a person, place, or activity releases into the atmosphere

cargo *(noun)* items transported on a ship, train, truck, etc.

canopy *(noun)* overhanging covering

cellular *(adjective)* relating to the system that uses radio waves to communicate telephone signals

certification *(noun)* official statement of competence or completion

chart *(verb)* to make a map of

chemist *(noun)* a scientist who works with chemicals

circumference *(noun)* the length of the outer boundary of a circle

civil disobedience *(noun)* political action in which participants peacefully break laws as a form of protest

classified *(verb)* placed in a group or category

climate *(noun)* typical weather conditions of an area

colleague *(noun)* coworker; person in a similar position

colony *(noun)* far-off area immigrated into and/or controlled by a country

combatant *(noun)* someone or something that fights against something else

commandeer *(verb)* take control of for military use

commencing *(verb)* beginning

communism *(noun)* form of government in which the leaders control the economy and many aspects of people's lives

compound *(noun)* combination of chemical elements

condensation *(noun)* process in which water collects into clouds or fog

GLOSSARY

confirm *(verb)* to check that something is true

conscientious *(adjective)* careful; exacting

considerable *(adjective)* significant

constellation *(noun)* group of objects in the sky

construction *(verb)* building

contaminant *(noun)* pollutant

contiguous *(adjective)* next to one another; touching

corded *(adjective)* lined with cords or cord-like lines

cosmic *(adjective)* having to do with space or the cosmos

countenance *(noun)* face

coveted *(verb)* became jealous of

crevasse *(noun)* crack in a rock or mountain

crewman *(noun)* a sailor; a worker on a ship

culvert *(noun)* drain crossing under a road

D

dais *(noun)* a raised platform

daunting *(adjective)* difficult and frightening; intimidating

decade *(noun)* a ten-year period

decimation *(noun)* the destruction of a great number of something

deforestation *(noun)* removal of forests and trees

delirium *(noun)* confusion caused by high fever

democracy *(noun)* form of government that recognizes the right of people to rule themselves through elected representatives

demon *(noun)* evil spirit

demonstrating *(verb)* protesting

depleted *(verb)* used up

deposit *(noun)* natural collection of a substance, usually a mineral

desolate *(adjective)* lonely and gloomy

devised *(verb)* thought up; created

diagnosis *(noun)* a medical decision about what illness or condition is affecting a person

diplomatic *(adjective)* involving relationships between countries

dissever *(verb)* to cut apart

disorder *(noun)* disease; disability

dispatched *(verb)* sent

dissipate *(verb)* scatter; spread out and away

diverges *(verb)* to move in a different direction from a common point; to branch off

documented *(adjective)* recorded in documents, as with evidence

duration *(noun)* length of time that something takes or lasts

duty *(noun)* tax

dwindling *(adjective)* becoming smaller or less

E

ecosystem *(noun)* the system of animals, plants, and other organisms that interact in an environment

electromagnetic *(adjective)* associated with the electric and magnetic fields and their interactions with each other

elements *(noun)* weather

eloquent *(adjective)* expressive; meaningful

emblem *(noun)* symbol; sign

emerged *(verb)* came out of

enabled *(verb)* allowed; let happen

encountered *(verb)* came across; met

encrypted *(verb)* placed in code

endurance *(noun)* ability or strength to keep going through difficulties

enterprise *(noun)* project; endeavor

entrepreneur *(noun)* a person who starts his or her own business

entrepreneurship *(noun)* development of a new business

environmental *(adjective)* having to do with nature and the natural world

equilibrium *(noun)* a state of balance

erosion *(verb)* wearing or washing away

estimation *(noun)* approximate calculation; judgment

estuary *(noun)* area where a river meets the sea

evaporation *(noun)* the natural process in which water is drawn up into the air

evidence *(noun)* proof; signs

evoke *(verb)* to cause people to think about; to call up memories or feelings about

exchange *(noun)* discussion

expanse *(noun)* an open, uninterrupted area

exploit *(verb)* take advantage of

exuberance *(noun)* enthusiasm; excitement and eagerness

eye *(noun)* the calm center of a hurricane

F

fateful *(adjective)* connected to the occurrence of something important or terrible

feat *(noun)* extraordinary act; accomplishment

federal *(adjective)* part of or from the national government

fertilizer *(noun)* a substance used to help plants grow, especially a chemical manure

filtration *(noun)* removal of dirt and debris

flight deck *(noun)* area where the astronauts sit to control the space shuttle

frigate *(noun)* a fast, heavily armed ship of the eighteenth century

forest canopy *(noun)* the highest layer of branches and leaves in a forest

forestry *(noun)* care and management of forests and the businesses that use them

forsake *(verb)* forget; abandon

founded *(verb)* began or started a business or other large effort

G

gallantly *(adverb)* bravely

garb *(noun)* clothing; style of clothing

gaudy *(adjective)* tastelessly showy; flashy

generate *(verb)* create; produce

genre *(noun)* style; type

gloss over *(verb)* to give a deceptively good appearance to something; to hide the negative aspects of something

greenhouse gases *(noun)* gases that lead to the warming of the Earth's atmosphere

H

hectare *(noun)* an area of land equal to about 2½ acres

helm *(noun)* place on a ship where the steering controls are located

heritage *(noun)* something one is born to

hide *(noun)* the skin of a large animal

highborn *(adjective)* aristocratic; of noble family

hue *(noun)* color

hurricane *(noun)* a large storm that develops over the ocean but can move inland

hydroelectric dam *(noun)* dam that uses falling water to create electricity

hygrometer *(noun)* instrument that measures humidity

I

immigrant *(noun)* a newcomer to a country or area

impaired *(adjective)* not working correctly

incident *(noun)* event; thing that happened

inclement *(adjective)* stormy; unpleasant

incomparable *(adjective)* better than the others; beyond comparison

indigenous *(adjective)* local; native

infrared *(adjective)* heat-sensing

inherent *(adjective)* existing as a natural or essential part of someone or something

innovation *(noun)* new idea; invention

inspiration *(noun)* something that encourages someone to strive for a goal

intricate *(adjective)* detailed; complex

instrument *(noun)* mechanical or electronic measuring device

intact *(adjective)* whole; in one piece

integral *(adjective)* essential

intense *(adjective)* having or showing great strength or feeling

invaluable *(adjective)* extremely valuable; beyond price

invigorating *(adjective)* energizing

isolated *(adjective)* separated from others; alone

J

joint *(adjective)* united; done by groups working together

jovial *(adjective)* happy and cheerful

K

kinsman *(noun)* relative

L

league *(noun)* a unit of distance equal to about 3 miles

legislator *(noun)* lawmaker

liberation *(noun)* the act of setting a nation or area free

long-standing *(adjective)* in place for a long time

lurches *(verb)* sways or rolls suddenly

luminous *(adjective)* shining

M

mandated *(verb)* stated as a law or rule

manifest *(noun)* list of passengers

manual *(adjective)* done by hand; physical

marshal *(verb)* bring together; gather

marvel *(noun)* an amazing thing

mass *(noun)* substance and weight of an object

meager *(adjective)* small or weak; puny

measure *(noun)* step; procedure

meet *(noun)* a sports competition

merchant *(adjective)* used in sales or trade

meteoroid *(noun)* small rock traveling through space

module *(noun)* small section; unit

momentary *(adjective)* lasting only for a moment; brief

musket *(noun)* an early type of rifle

mutually *(adverb)* done together

N

naïve *(adjective)* having a lack of experience or judgment

nanosecond *(noun)* 1/1,000,000,000 of a second

native *(adjective)* from the area; local

O

occurred *(verb)* happened; took place

onlooker *(noun)* person watching; spectator

oratorical *(adjective)* having to do with speaking and making speeches

orbit *(noun)* path one object takes around another object (such as a planet around the sun)

outfitted *(verb)* supplied; equipped

P

passage *(noun)* arrangements to travel as a passenger

patriot *(noun)* person loyal to a cause or country

peat *(noun)* soil that is thick with vegetable matter

perceived *(verb)* understood

permit *(noun)* official, written permission to do something

perpetuate *(verb)* to keep something going; support

perseveres *(verb)* keeps trying in spite of obstacles

pertinent *(adjective)* relevant; having to do with the matter at hand

philanthropist *(noun)* a person who gives money to do good works

philosophy *(noun)* system of belief

physical *(adjective)* relating to the substances something is made of

plantation *(noun)* a large farm

plummet *(verb)* drop suddenly and quickly

portion *(noun)* segment; piece of the whole

preservation *(noun)* protection; keeping something safe from harm

primary forest *(noun)* a forest in its original condition, mostly unaffected by human activities

processed food *(noun)* food changed from its natural state, usually made in factories

prolific *(adjective)* producing in abundance; fruitful

promontory *(noun)* high point; overlook

propelled *(verb)* pushed in a direction

propulsion *(noun)* a means of pushing something forward

prospect *(noun)* idea; possibility

provocation *(noun)* reason to take offense or be angry

Q

qualifications *(noun)* skills or experience that fits a person for a job, an office, etc.

R

rally *(noun)* public gathering; demonstration

receiver *(noun)* object that receives and processes signals

reconciliation *(noun)* process of becoming friends again

recuperate *(verb)* to recover after an illness

reeling *(verb)* staggering backward unsteadily, such as after being struck

refined *(adjective)* precise or exact

refute *(verb)* argue against; disprove

relapse *(verb)* to fall back into illness

related *(verb)* told; gave an account of

relative humidity *(noun)* a measure of the amount of moisture in the air, based on moisture possible at a given temperature

renewable resource *(noun)* resource of which more can be grown or produced

repose *(noun)* calmness; peacefulness

restraint *(noun)* holding back; control

restricting *(verb)* holding back; containing

routine *(adjective)* dull; ordinary

rude *(adjective)* roughly made; not fancy or refined

S

sabre *(noun)* a type of sword

safeguard *(verb)* protect; guard

sage *(noun)* wise and learned person who gives advice to others

satellite *(noun)* an object that travels around a planet

saturation *(noun)* the state of being as full of liquid as possible

scintillating *(adjective)* dazzling; brilliant

secondary forest *(noun)* a forest that has grown back after a destructive event

sedimentary *(adjective)* made of sand compacted together

seize *(verb)* take hold of something

sentry *(noun)* a soldier posted to stand guard or keep watch

sepulchre *(noun)* tomb

seraph *(noun)* angel

scout *(verb)* search for

sheer *(adjective)* straight and steep

singular *(adjective)* unique or extraordinary

sinew *(noun)* tendon

skirmish *(noun)* a fight between small numbers of opposing troops

smartphone *(noun)* a phone that includes a hand-held computer for Internet access, e-mail, and so on

so-called *(adjective)* known as

solace *(noun)* something that gives comfort or relief

solar array *(noun)* set of solar panels, which store energy from sunlight

soldiery *(noun)* soldiers; members of an army

sophisticated *(adjective)* complex or intricate

sounding *(adjective)* rumbling; booming

sphere *(noun)* a ball or rounded, ball-like form

spike *(noun)* pointed piece of metal like a giant nail

statesman *(noun)* experienced and wise government leader

steed *(noun)* horse

stockpiling *(verb)* storing up supplies

stoicism *(noun)* a lack of concern about pain or difficulty

storm surge *(noun)* flood of ocean water onto land during a hurricane

stowage *(noun)* storage

suborbital *(adjective)* not having the altitude to reach orbit

sultriness *(noun)* damp heat

summit *(noun)* top; peak

subsidizing *(verb)* paying part of the cost for another person or group

sustainable *(adjective)* able to last a long time, especially by using renewable resources and taking care of the environment

sustenance *(noun)* the state of being sustained, or kept going, for a long period

T

tailwind *(noun)* wind coming from behind a ship

talisman *(noun)* an object believed to have magical or protective properties

telescope *(noun)* tool used to magnify objects

temporary *(adjective)* not permanent; of short term

tense *(adjective)* stressed; difficult

theorized *(verb)* made an educated, informed guess or judgment

timber *(noun)* wood; lumber

timely *(adjective)* available at the right moment

tomb *(noun)* grave; place where a person is buried

torrential *(adjective)* falling with great force

toxin *(noun)* poison

trade route *(noun)* road or path used for trade between groups

tragedy *(noun)* terrible event; disaster

transcendentalist *(noun)* a philosopher who believes that true meaning lies beyond ordinary experiences

transform *(verb)* change completely

transmitted *(verb)* sent by signal

treaty *(noun)* an agreement between two groups, especially when they have been in conflict

trek *(noun)* a long walk or journey

tribulation *(noun)* severe trouble or difficulty

trilateration *(noun)* the process of using three data points to figure out a location

tugboat line *(noun)* a business that operates tugboats (small boats that tow or push ships)

tumultuous *(adjective)* wild and disordered; turbulent

tyranny *(noun)* unrestrained abuse of power and authority by a government

U

unassailable *(adjective)* unable to be argued with or attacked

urban sprawl *(noun)* the uncontrolled spread of cities and development into country areas

V

valor *(noun)* boldness in facing danger; bravery

venture *(noun)* an undertaking involving uncertainty as to the outcome

ventured *(verb)* attempted; tried

vessel *(noun)* ship

viable *(adjective)* able to live or grow correctly

vow *(noun)* solemn promise

W

wary *(adjective)* cautious; watchful

water cycle *(noun)* the cycle in which water evaporates from rivers, lakes, and oceans, falls as rain, and then again evaporates

waterfowl *(noun)* birds that live on and near the water

watershed *(noun)* the network of streams and rivers that flow into a lake or ocean

watt *(noun)* unit in which electricity is measured

wholesale *(adjective)* extensive